Curriculum and Instructional Methods for the Elementary and Middle School

SEVENTH EDITION

JOHANNA KASIN LEMLECH
University of Southern California, Emerita

Allyn and Bacon
Boston   New York   San Francisco
Mexico City   Montreal   Toronto   London   Madrid   Munich   Paris
Hong Kong   Singapore   Tokyo   Cape Town   Sydney

Series Editor: *Kelly Villella Canton*
Series Editorial Assistant: *Annalea Manalili*
Marketing Manager: *Darcy Betts*
Production Editor: *Mary Beth Finch*
Editorial Production Service: *Publishers' Design and Production Services, Inc.*
Composition Buyer: *Linda Cox*
Manufacturing Buyer: *Megan Cochran*
Electronic Composition: *Publishers' Design and Production Services, Inc.*
Interior Design: *Publishers' Design and Production Services, Inc.*
Cover Administrator: *Elena Sidorova*

For related titles and support materials, visit our online catalog at www.pearsonhighered.com.

Between the time website information is gathered and then published, it is not unusual for some sites to have closed. Also the transcription of URLs can result in typographical errors. The publisher would appreciate notification where these errors occur so that they may be corrected in subsequent editions.

Library of Congress Cataloging-in-Publication Data

Lemlech, Johanna Kasin.
    Curriculum and instructional methods for the elementary and middle school / Johanna Kasin Lemlech. — 7th ed.
        p. cm.
    Includes bibliographical references and index.
    ISBN 0-13-502005-0 (978-0-13-502005-0) 1. Elementary school teaching—United States—Handbooks, manuals, etc.
2. Middle school teaching—United States—Handbooks, manuals, etc. 3. Classroom management—United States—Handbooks, manuals, etc. 4. Education, Elementary—Curricula—United States—Handbooks, manuals, etc. 5. Middle school education—Curricula—United States—Handbooks, manuals, etc. I. Title.
    LB1555.L434 2010
    372.1102—dc22   2009000319

Printed in the United States of America

Photo credits: Photos on pages 241 and 334 by Johanna Kasin Lemlech. All other photos by Paula Goldman.

10 9 8 7 6 5 4 3   HAM   13 12 11

Allyn and Bacon
is an imprint of

www.pearsonhighered.com

ISBN 10:   0-13-502005-0
ISBN 13: 978-0-13-502005-0

With love and respect,
I dedicate this edition to my husband, Bernard Lemlech,
and to my daughters, Donna Lemlech Stieger and Margery Lemlech Walshaw,
and to the memory of my parents, Mollie and Henry Kasin.

ABOUT THE AUTHOR

Dr. Lemlech is Professor Emerita from the University of Southern California, where she taught in the Departments of Teacher Education and Curriculum and Instruction. She specializes in instructional strategies and curriculum development. She was awarded the Stephen Crocker Professorship for her outstanding work in curriculum. Professor Lemlech was the principal investigator for a professional development school that partnered with the university. Much of her research focused on teacher leadership and the fostering of collegial relationships among teachers.

Prior to her professorship at USC, Dr. Lemlech taught for 15 years in the Los Angeles Unified School District. Her teaching experience enriched her college teaching and provided a realistic perspective for her staff development work and her textbooks, which include *Handbook for Successful Urban Teaching, Classroom Management, The American Teacher, Becoming a Professional Leader, Teaching in Elementary and Secondary Classrooms: Building a Learning Community,* and the six editions of *Curriculum and Instructional Methods for the Elementary and Middle School.*

BRIEF CONTENTS

CONTENTS

PART III
IMPLEMENTING THE CURRICULUM   181

CHAPTER 8
Teaching English Language Arts   183

PREFACE

This book is written for learning professionals, both preservice teachers and experienced teachers, and for administrators. Both school site and consultant staff need substantive references that provide a complete picture of the subject-field disciplines and the pedagogical means to communicate them. I believe that teachers and administrators need reference tools that recognize them as professionals and provide realistic examples of successful teaching and learning.

I have a constructivist/Dewey type of philosophy; however, I believe that instructional strategies need to match the instructional goal and the needs of the students. I was a teacher in the Los Angeles Unified School District for 15 years and a professor at the University of Southern California for 33 years. I am committed to teaching as a profession, and I have great confidence in the ability of teachers as learning professionals.

ORGANIZATION OF THE TEXT

The four parts of the text represent the "commonplaces" of teaching. Part I focuses on the society we live in, with its needs, conflicts, and wants, and the historical development of the curriculum. The learner's development, socially, emotionally, and intellectually, concludes Part I. Readers will find new and updated coverage of school safety, violence, charter schools (Chapter1); bullying, gender equity/gender bias, social class and children's experiences, and cultural values (Chapter 2).

Part II looks at the milieu of the classroom, classroom management, planning and guiding learning experiences, and the important tasks of the teacher. Both individual lessons and long-term unit planning are explained and demonstrated. Two chapters focus on instructional strategies: expository teaching and inquiry/problem solving. This section of the text concludes with authentic assessment and the means to communicate learning progress to students and parents. Explore Chapters 5 and 11 to find new coverage of the 5-E Instructional Model in the seventh edition.

Part III of the text (Chapters 8-13) is devoted to each subject field that is taught in the elementary and middle school. I have tried to make each chapter broad enough to provide substantive information and current happenings in the discipline; each chapter is comprehensive yet brief. The three featured teachers and several of their colleagues contribute teaching scenarios that demonstrate subject fields, instructional strategies, integration of subject fields, and unit planning. Explore Part III of this new edition to find enriched coverage of hints to stimulate language acquisition (Chapter 8) and integration of subject fields (Chapter 10), as well as new coverage of the Singapore Math Bar Model Approach (Chapter 10), the 5-E Instructional Model (Chapter 11), and coverage of creative integration projects (Chapter 12).

Part IV (Chapter 14) concludes with a focus on teacher competence, quality teaching, and the teacher as a learning professional. Suggestions for continuing professional development are offered, and policies affecting the rights and responsibilities of teachers are identified.

Preparing teachers for the realities of teaching in today's schools, Chapter 14 now includes information about school safety and violence, charter schools, and home schooling.

Appendix A provides web site information; however, addresses change frequently so users must beware. New to this edition, Appendix B provides information on planning for a substitute teacher and preparing to be a substitute teacher.

Finally, common features within each chapter provide support for new teachers, including:

- Reader Research, a feature that challenges the reader to immerse him- or herself in action research.
- Research Findings, an updated feature that highlights current research related to chapter content.
- Hints for Teaching English Language Learners, an updated feature that highlights practical teaching tips for working with English Language Learners in today's inclusive classrooms.

THE TEACHERS

The three main teachers of grades 2, 5, and 7 featured throughout the text are fictional, but they represent teachers I know. Through their experiences, teaching contexts, problems, events, and subject matter are exhibited. The teaching examples are not intended to be flawless, but they demonstrate appropriate pedagogy and reflective thinking.

Additional teaching strategies by colleagues of different grade levels and subject field areas provide a realistic and wide spectrum of life in elementary and middle schools. Cited in boxes are research findings, teaching hints, and case studies, the purpose of which is to coach and stimulate successful teaching. At the end of each chapter are questions and application exercises, portfolio activities, technology applications, and a reader research suggestion.

ACKNOWLEDGMENTS

Thanks to all of the teachers and administrators who invited me to visit their classrooms. In those classrooms I observed the kind of learning that encourages students to come to school, to create, to reflect, and to engage in challenging activities. A textbook about teaching and curriculum is not the work of only the author. It is a project that is enriched by many significant others: the teachers whose stories and lessons I've observed and interpreted; the principals who (rightly) bragged about their teachers and classrooms; the students who shared their work and allowed me to sit in on their group work; and colleagues who read and critiqued my efforts. A very special thank-you to all of you.

The following individuals helped to make this seventh edition particularly meaningful: Paula Goldman for outstanding photographic expertise; Amy Cox-Petersen, Professor at California State University-Fullerton, for suggestions, research, and critique of the science and mathematics chapters; Margo Pensavalle, Director of Student Teaching at University of Southern California, for her wisdom about the needs of inexperienced teachers; Michele Zeolla, Physical Therapist extraordinaire, for suggestions in the physical education and health chapter; Kate Thompson for suggestions and critique of the language arts chapter; Janet Levine of the Oak Hills Unified School District, who provided excellent photos of her students at work; Cindy Gonek, who patiently responded to my word processing needs by eliminating those troublesome hidden codes; Samantha Stieger, who created the figures for several chapters and checked the accuracy of Internet addresses; Bryan Starr, who played geek and preserved my sanity; and—last but not least—Bernard Lemlech, who frequently cooked dinners and pried me out of my computer chair.

Additional colleagues across the country painstakingly reviewed the text in its entirety and contributed very relevant and meaningful suggestions. These individuals are Sue Abegglen, Culver-Stockton College; Leigh Chiarelott, Bowling Green State University; Amy Cox-Petersen, California State University-Fullerton; Linda Creel, Troy University-Phoenix City; Duane M. Giannangelo, The University of Memphis; and Margo Pensavalle, University of Southern California.

Readers, I welcome your thoughts after you have had an opportunity to get acquainted with the text. You may e-mail me at jlemlech@verizon.net.

PART I

Exploring Foundational Contexts and Curriculum Challenges

The challenges teachers face in the 21st century relate to the social, political, and economic conditions of the global society. Teachers face many challenges and increasing responsibilities because they influence the lives of students and the quality of future life. Curriculum decisions are based on understanding the developmental needs and interests of children, the learning process, our society, our history, and the possibilities for the future. Chapter 1 of Part I focuses on societal needs, tensions, goals, and traditions. Chapter 2 focuses on the students we teach, how they differ, and how they learn. The two chapters of Part I set the stage for the study of curriculum, instructional methods, and professional responsibilities.

INTRODUCTION: TEACHERS' LEADERSHIP ROLES

Mary Hogan, Greg Thomas, and Karen Adazzio are three fictitious teachers you will encounter from time to time throughout this text. The brief sketches of the teachers that follow highlight their experiences, attitudes, and beliefs about teaching. Each, in his or her

own way, is a teacher-leader. Other teachers also are mentioned throughout the text, but their teaching experiences are not featured in depth.

MARY HOGAN

Mary Hogan is in her second year of teaching. She teaches second grade at a large urban elementary school. There are 1,300 students at the school and 85% of them are native Spanish speakers. Her school district, located in the western United States, enrolls 625,000 students.

Hogan was educated at a private university in a collegial teacher preparation program. In her student teaching experience, she was paired with another student teacher, and together they practiced in the same classroom. The two student teachers planned lessons together and often taught side by side. They were responsible for observing each other teach and for providing each other with feedback. As a consequence of this experience,

Hogan is quite comfortable with having other teachers come into the classroom to observe. She continues to keep in close touch with her student teaching colleague, and they talk frequently about teaching.

Hogan's preparation program emphasized several models of teaching, and she became expert at applying a variety of teaching approaches to accomplish her instructional purposes. She considers the classroom environment extremely important for motivating students, and she frequently uses learning centers to differentiate curriculum content and skill activities. Hogan believes that it is the teacher's responsibility to help students learn how to learn. She works hard to generate the kinds of questions that will provoke students' thinking.

As a second-year teacher, Hogan is not totally comfortable with her own classroom management skills, but she believes that students must learn to become responsible for their own behavior. Her classroom rules were set by the students and are extremely simple. ("We are responsible for our own behavior. We respect others.")

Because Hogan is so skilled in her use of teaching models, she was asked by her principal to demonstrate lessons for other teachers. She gained considerable respect from the other teachers at her school for what they consider innovative approaches and for her willingness to allow others to observe in her classroom.

GREG THOMAS

Greg Thomas teaches fifth grade in a southern rural school. His school district enrolls 3,200 students. The school where he teaches has an enrollment of 475 students. He has been a teacher for 7 years, 5 of which have been at his present teaching assignment.

Thomas likes to use the project method for teaching. He involves students in choosing in-depth investigations, such as the study of ecological problems in their rural community and how these problems differ from or are similar to problems in the past and expectations for the future. His class may study a topic for several days or weeks, with individuals or small groups responsible for different aspects of the study. The project method facilitates both an interdisciplinary conceptual focus and the integration of skills across subject fields. Thomas believes that teachers have opportunities to improve society through their curriculum and instructional decisions.

Students in Thomas's classroom are highly motivated owing to the nature of his projects and their own involvement in curriculum decision making. As a result, parents are always eager to see that their children are placed in Thomas's class.

Thomas is considered a curriculum innovator. Recently his principal suggested to the superintendent that Thomas work with other teachers to develop new curricular approaches. As a consequence, he is relieved from teaching responsibilities two days per month for district curricular planning and for working with other teachers. He also has developed a special parent workshop program to inform parents about the curriculum and to enlist parental assistance in obtaining special funds for resource materials and field trips for students.

Think about your own beliefs about teaching and teachers' responsibilities. What do you want to emphasize as you choose what to teach and how to teach it?

KAREN ADAZZIO

Karen Adazzio teaches seventh grade in a middle school in the northeastern United States. The school district enrolls 32,075 students and has just recently reorganized its schools, changing from the concept of grades K–6, 7–9, and 10–12 to grades K–5 in the elementary schools, 6–8 in the middle schools, and 9–12 in the high schools.

Adazzio is a very unusual teacher. She began her teaching career as an elementary teacher. Then she obtained a secondary credential and taught at the senior high school level. Recently, after 17 years of teaching, she asked to be assigned to one of the new middle schools. Because Adazzio believes that adolescents often feel displaced and unconnected in the departmentalized structure of junior high schools, she was active in convincing other teachers to experiment with her in a new structure, sometimes referred to as a house. In this structure teachers and students are grouped together as a team.

This new approach, popularized by Ted Sizer's Coalition of Essential Schools, has cast Adazzio in the role of the instructional leader for her team. She works with five other teachers, 160 students, and parents. Two periods per day she is released to help improve curriculum, instructional approaches, and student counseling.

Adazzio is eclectic in her educational beliefs. She believes that middle school children need to be involved in problem solving and that teachers need to focus on problem situations to generate students' interests. She also believes that her students must learn to fit in to their community, so her choice of problematic situations tends to emphasize teenage dilemmas and community problems.

CHAPTER 1

Curriculum Today
Influences and Challenges

School is an institution created by society to socialize and democratize the young. But in a diverse society, people differ in their goals, their standards, and what they want taught in the curriculum. This chapter focuses on differing expectations and the ensuing challenges and choices that confront teachers.

Advance Organizer

The following questions are intended to guide your reading and understanding of the content of this chapter.

1. In what ways does society influence the curriculum?
2. What aspects of the curriculum have persisted through the years?
3. In what ways have schools changed yet stayed the same?
4. Should schools be considered factories? Why?
5. How do standards and goals affect the teaching profession?
6. What are some of the challenges that confront teachers?

INTASC

Interstate New Teacher Assessment and Support Consortium (INTASC)

This chapter builds awareness of the development of the curriculum and U.S. schools. As such, it lays the foundation for understanding the INTASC standards deemed important in the preparation of teachers. Standards 1–3, 5–6, and 9–10 undergird the chapter. (See the inside front cover for the standards.)

Professional Lexicon

at-risk students Students who schools can anticipate will have difficulty completing high school education because of associated problems.

common schools Schools established during the nationalist period to teach basic skills to all elementary-age children.

content standards Measures used to judge what is to be taught to students at varied levels of education.

English language learners Students who are nonnative English speakers and are receiving instruction to become fluent in reading, writing, and understanding the English language.

exceptional learners Students who are gifted or talented or have disabilities; individuals whose performance differs from that of the average group of students.

full-service school A school that coordinates health and social services for school community families.

inclusive school and classroom A school and classroom that teaches (includes) students with disabilities.

individualized educational program (IEP) An instructional plan that identifies the needs and capacities of the subject individual.

multicultural education The conscious inclusion in the curriculum of the experiences and culture of all students.

normal school A school for the preparation of elementary school teachers.

performance standards Measures used to judge what has been learned through application.

portfolio A visual record (folder) maintained by the student to display peak experiences (work activities, projects, and the ongoing process of writing) and learning progress.

scientific management An approach that viewed the school as a factory and teachers as workers; the school was to be managed to increase productivity (achievement) and efficiency.

It was recess time and Karen Adazzio's team was having a group meeting to discuss "back to school night." Two of the teachers in the group asked about what they should say to parents/guardians after they introduce themselves.

KAREN: *"You need to talk about your curriculum and your expectations for the semester."*
SELMA: *"Don't we need to tell them how we integrate what we teach among all members of the team?"*
BOB: *"Sure, but parents won't understand about integrating the curriculum—will they?"*
TODD: *"I think we need to start with explaining what is the curriculum."*
MILLIE: *"Why don't we each begin with a definition of curriculum and then explain how we work as a team?"*
KAREN: *"That's a good idea, but let's decide on a single definition so that we are all consistent."*

After a long discussion about content fields, learning experiences, the school club program, and team and school schedules, they finally agreed on a single definition of curriculum. Their definition is the focus of this book:

Curriculum is all the experiences the school provides for students. This encompasses learning experiences and activities, instructional processes, management procedures, and resources planned for students.

WHAT INFLUENCES THE CURRICULUM?

The school curriculum responds to three interwoven components: (1) societal needs and concerns (Chapter 1), (2) beliefs about how children learn (Chapter 2), and (3) significant subject matter (Part III). Figure 1.1 serves as an advance organizer to introduce the concept of curriculum influences.

Schools are social institutions consciously developed by society to control the education of children. Schools can differ markedly by deliberately providing unique environmental experiences. People in the United States expect schools to teach basic fundamentals, transmit selected social customs, develop civility in the young, and foster the development of individual talents. In the United States, schools were first developed during the colonial period (1600–1776) to meet the needs of the early settlers. Table 1.1 identifies the needs, beliefs, and social forces that affected the curriculum during the colonial period.

Although the colonies differed in the ways they educated their children, there were some similarities:

- Religion was a dominating influence and considered a priority in colonial America.
- Except at Benjamin Franklin's academy, subjects were taught separately (not integrated).
- A definite social class structure was evident in the way children were educated.
- The classroom contained children of many ages, and the schoolmasters managed ungraded classrooms.

- Teaching methods were limited to drill, memorization, and recitation.

Agriculture was the colonies' major occupation during the colonial period, and so the schools were open only during the winter so that boys could help during the harvest time. Girls seldom received an education at school; they were educated in the ways their mothers preserved food, baked, and made clothes. Sometimes they were taught simple Bible reading at home.

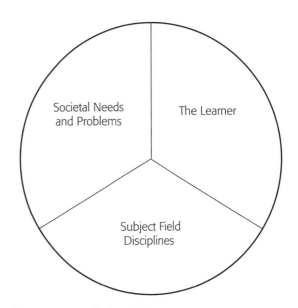

Figure 1.1 Curriculum Influences

Table 1.1   Society and Schools in the Colonial Period

Societal Needs	Societal Beliefs	Social Forces
Field workers for an agrarian society	Children inherently bad, lazy	Economic needs: raw materials for export
For a limited few, a classical education	Strict discipline needed	Sociology: class society, dichotomy rich/poor
Reading the Bible; religion a priority value	Boys should be educated	
	Classical education for some	
	Girls should be homemakers	
	Exercise the mind through drill and memorization	

Table 1.2   Society and Schools in the Nationalist Period

Societal Needs	Societal Beliefs	Social Forces
Loyalty to new nation	Faculty psychology	Economic needs: industry, commerce, agriculture
Patriotism	Mind divided into compartments	Industrial revolution
Practical education	Need to exercise and train the mind through the teaching of science and history	Sociology: equal opportunity
Teaching of the English language		Growth of urban centers
American-produced textbooks	Rote learning, recitation	Westward movement
Universal education		

After the American Revolution, described as the nationalist period of education (1776–1876), societal needs changed. Citizens considered patriotism important, and the curriculum reflected different societal concerns. The young country's new Congress passed the first land grant legislation affecting education when it divided the Northwest Territory into townships 6 miles square and composed of 36 sections. The Land Ordinance of 1785 stipulated that the 16th section of every township was to be used for education. The Tenth Amendment to the U.S. Constitution gave the power and responsibility for education to the states. Education was to be a federal *interest*, but a state *responsibility*.

Proud of its freedom from England, the new nation undertook the development of new textbooks that reflected their patriotism, geography, grammar, spelling, reading, and arithmetic. New schools were opened for girls, many of which were directed by women. The **common school** was established for the education of all students, regardless of social class, and education was considered "the great equalizer."

Horace Mann created the **normal school**, the first school to improve and educate teachers. By 1860, 12 states had preparatory schools for teachers and 15 states required teachers to attend state institutes during their spring recess. The institutes encouraged teachers to discuss common problems and listen to lectures on teaching methods. Table 1.2 identifies the needs and beliefs of American society in the nationalist period.

CHANGES IN THE SCHOOLS DURING THE NATIONALIST PERIOD

As the United States wakened and expanded after the American Revolution, great changes in schools occurred:

- The development of the nation replaced religion as the dominating influence and priority.
- In cities, graded schools replaced the ungraded one-room schoolhouse.
- The curriculum expanded beyond reading, writing, arithmetic, and spelling to include history, geography, physiology, composition, agriculture, music, and drawing. In the academies, a variety of practical courses were offered.
- Kindergartens were established, as were academies for girls.
- Classes to teach English to immigrants were offered.
- Normal schools were established to prepare teachers; female students predominated in these schools.
- Teachers' associations developed.
- Institutes for in-service education were organized.
- Textbooks produced in the United States were used.
- In addition to memorization and drill, the monitor system was developed in which bright students helped teach other students, and group instruction began in some classrooms.
- The ideas of faculty psychologists predominated, but educational theorists also became influential; the child was no longer considered inherently bad.

As the United States expanded (1876–1930s), school districts consolidated and became larger. School boards were no longer representative of the population; instead businesspeople and professionals predominated. School boards wanted schools to be efficient, like factories; values such as punctuality, rigor, attention, and standards were espoused. Graded schools and graded textbooks resulted in standardized instruction.

Creation of School Administration

Scientific management established the role of specialist teachers hired for specific purposes. The separate roles of teachers and administrators were also initiated during this era. In large school districts, many administrative positions were created, but in smaller districts, affected by consolidation, jobs were eliminated. Because of their traditional, subservient roles, women typically did not become administrators. The origin of the efficiency ethic can be traced to this period of history.

Immigrant Education

To escape poverty and persecution in their native lands, more than 35 million people immigrated to the United States between 1815 and 1915 (Tyack, 1967), seeking a higher standard of living, freedom, and tolerance. These immigrants were enormously diverse in their cultural and linguistic backgrounds, and they tended to settle in the large cities, where they sought their own cultural groups, family, and friends. They clung together for economic support and physical security in what became known as ghetto areas.

The schools accepted responsibility to help the immigrants assimilate to life in the United States. Countless tales by immigrants chronicle their experiences in the United States during a period when becoming part of "the melting pot" was considered the only choice. Learning to speak English was as difficult for the immigrants then as it is for new immigrant populations today. Table 1.3 provides an overview of the social forces that influenced the growth of the education system as the United States moved toward the modern era.

APPROACHING THE MODERN ERA

Our fictitious teachers—Greg Thomas, Mary Hogan, and Karen Adazzio—may recognize the emergence of elementary and secondary schools during this period

Table 1.3 Society and Schools in the Expanding United States

Societal Needs	Societal Beliefs	Social Forces
Practical education	Behaviorism	Economics: factory system, efficiency
Focus on real-life problems	Child-centered curriculum beginning	Psychology: behaviorism
Secondary education	Factory-like values	Sociology: rise of middle class
School facilities		Movement from rural to urban centers
Immigrant education		

because such institutions began to resemble the modern schools of today in form, in philosophy, and in focus:

- Educational theorists began to experiment with teaching methods that were more closely matched to the natural development of children.
- John Dewey influenced educators' concepts of the school, the curriculum, and the child. He opened his Laboratory School for the demonstration of teaching methods at the University of Chicago.
- Dewey's reflective thinking process theory affected research and teaching methods.
- The progressive education movement focused attention on real-life problems as appropriate areas of study in the curriculum. The movement influenced methodology by advocating motivation to stimulate students' interests. Education began to focus more on the learner than on the subject.
- The role of the teacher in some schools changed from authoritarian to guide.
- Distinct roles developed for teachers and administrators.
- Advocates of scientific management emphasized factory-like values: efficiency, punctuality, neatness, utilization of resources, and focus on product.

THE MODERN ERA

As the population of the United States increased, more women were attracted to teaching. However, many school districts refused to hire married women for fear they would become pregnant. Not until the 1950s were women treated as equal to men in the teaching profession.

In the years between the end of World War II (1945) and the Soviet launching of *Sputnik* (1957), the elementary curriculum in the United States was consolidated into broad fields of study. Social studies replaced the teaching of history, geography, and civics. Language arts unified the teaching of reading, writing, speaking, and listening. Health education often encompassed physical education and health. Fine arts included music and art education. Science and mathematics continued to be taught separately.

Elementary schools became larger during this period, and the average school enrolled 600 students. Kindergarten enrollments also increased. Most new schools had a single story, instead of the older pattern of two- and three-story buildings. Consideration of the activities of students affected these changes.

Throughout the 1960s, 1970s, and early 1980s, the schools benefitted from federally supported programs, including school lunch programs, funding for special purposes, and funding for students with special needs. The early-childhood program Head Start was begun during President Lyndon Johnson's administration. Table 1.4 lists the goals and beliefs of modern and postmodern society.

Table 1.4   Society and Schools in the Modern and Postmodern Era

Societal Needs	Societal Beliefs	Social Forces
Minority and immigrant education	Isolationism	Economics: criticism of the factory system
Bilingual education	Behaviorism	
Teacher education	Child-centered movement	Depression, consolidation of schools and districts
Life adjustment classes	Attention to the "whole" child	
Attention to health, poverty, and homelessness	Cognitive psychology	Sociology: immigration, crime, poverty, homelessness, racial problems, changes in the family
Equal opportunity	Cooperative learning	
Emergence of middle schools	Civil rights	
Technology	Sexual freedom	
	Accountability	Political: global society and democratic movements
	Standards	

POSTMODERN ERA

The postmodern era, with its focus on school reform, was initiated by the publication of *A Nation at Risk* (1983) published by the National Commission on Excellence in Education. In this publication, the commission challenged local governments and the states to develop goals and set standards for performance of both students and teachers. The report did not mince words, stating that if a foreign power had wanted to impose mediocrity on our school systems, it could not have accomplished more than what we did to ourselves.

The United States had no formally stated national goals until 1989. In 1989, at an education summit, six national goals were proposed, and in 1994 with President Clinton's urging, Congress adopted the goals and created two additional goals. The goals encompassed the following expectations:

1. All children in America will start school ready to learn.
2. At least 90% of high school students will graduate.
3. All students will leave grades 4, 8, and 12 having demonstrated competency in challenging subject matter.
4. The nation's teaching force will have access to programs for the continued improvement of their professional skills.
5. American students will be first in the world in mathematics and science achievement.
6. Every adult American will be literate and will possess the knowledge and skills necessary to compete in a global economy and exercise the rights and responsibilities of citizenship.
7. Every school in the United States will be free of drugs, violence, and the unauthorized presence of firearms and alcohol, and will offer a disciplined environment conducive to learning.
8. Every school will promote partnerships that will increase parental involvement and participation in promoting the social, emotional, and academic growth of children (*National Education Goals Report*, 1994, pp. 13–14).

Congress anticipated that the goals could be accomplished by the year 2000; however, that did not happen. The goals mainly served as a means to stimulate interest in education and provide direction for academic preparation.

CHANGES IN THE SCHOOLS IN THE MODERN AND POSTMODERN ERA

- School districts hired greater numbers of unmarried female teachers.
- Educators criticized the factory system when applied to schools.
- The federal government funded science, math, and early-childhood programs.
- Middle schools were created.
- Behaviorists influenced teaching methodology and the evaluation of teachers.
- The child-centered movement gained attention.
- Cognitive psychology influenced the constructivist perspective of learning.
- Cultural literacy and multicultural education engaged educators in debate.
- Introduction of national standards concerned many people.
- Technology affected the role of teachers, students, and the design of schools.
- The No Child Left Behind Act (NCLB) was enacted in 2001 and reauthorized the Elementary and Secondary Education Act.

NO CHILD LEFT BEHIND (NCLB)

The Elementary and Secondary Education Act (ESEA) of 1965 was passed during the administration of President Lyndon B. Johnson. Its primary purpose was to ensure desegregation by making federal funds available to state and local governments that complied with the desegregation legislation.

The No Child Left Behind Act of 2001 is a reauthorization of ESEA. The act requires all 50 states to submit plans to the federal government detailing how they will ensure that students are at the proficient level on state tests by 2013–2014. If schools fail to make "adequate yearly progress" for two years in a row they are penalized by having their funding from the federal government cut. However, a number of states protest the law because the federal government is not providing the necessary funding to comply with the testing and accountability requirements. Connecticut is the first state to sue the federal government for lack of funding (Archer, 2005). The law also requires that all students be included in the testing program—even English language learners; however, students with lim-

ited fluency and students with disabilities may be given more time or other accommodations when taking the test.

Alternative assessments such as testing in the student's native language is allowed; however, students who have resided in the United States for three years must be tested in English. Because many states have so many diverse populations, it is often impractical to translate state tests into all languages for all students who have resided in the United States less than three years. A further complication is that if the state test is translated for one or more language groups, but not others, then the state may be accused of discrimination.

In addition, the 2001 act required states to ensure that teachers of the core subjects (language arts or English, mathematics, science, foreign languages, social studies, arts) are highly qualified to teach the subject(s) they are assigned by the end of the 2005–2006 school year. However, the act does not require that teachers be certified, yet research indicates that teachers who are certified know *how* to teach and are more likely to stay in teaching because they are prepared to teach *all* students, be they disadvantaged, limited English proficient, or affluent (Darling-Hammond, 2007).

Deborah Meier and Diane Ravitch (2006), two educators who are philosophically at opposite ends of the curriculum spectrum, engaged in a discussion of NCLB. They discovered that, despite their disagreements, they were united in their beliefs about several consequences of this act. Their concerns focused on the following:

1. Due to the time commitment to the basic subjects of reading and math, in many school districts, teachers are not free to make professional

Research Findings

NCLB's focus on testing lowers both teachers' and students' expectations. The curriculum that is taught is geared to the tests, and neither teachers nor students may pursue their own aims or enjoy differentiated curriculum and instruction. This problem affects all students (high performing and low performing) and all teachers (Brooks, Libresio, & Plonczak, 2007).

judgments about what to teach, when to teach it, and how to teach.

2. Curriculum subjects other than math and reading are ignored. Students experience a very lean curriculum diet to produce higher test scores.
3. Both the curriculum and the tests are continually dumbed-down to produce higher test scores.
4. Parent involvement, teachers, unions, and local community organizations are left out of the decision-making process. Corporate leaders have the power to impose what is taught and how it is to be taught.

The Center on Education Policy has studied the effects of NCLB since its inception. On a positive note, they found that schools and districts were more likely to align their curriculum standards and instruction after several years than they did when the law was first implemented. However, their research also confirmed that schools failed to allocate time to teach social studies, music, and art. Schools that were doing poorly were more likely to increase the time spent on the tested subjects rather than expand the curriculum they were teaching (Davis, 2006).

STANDARDS

Since colonial school days, the public has been concerned that standards should accomplish certain goals and benchmarks. The National Council on Education Standards and Testing (NCEST) believed that it was necessary to set performance standards for students in order to improve the curriculum and guide teacher expectations and school decision making. **Content standards** focus on what students should learn in the subject fields. In many of the disciplines, content standards have been identified by professional groups. **Performance standards** are intended to allow students to demonstrate the application of what they know. Some of these standards will be discussed in Part III of this text.

Of greatest importance is to put the issue of standards in proper perspective. If standards mean that the curriculum will have depth and be challenging, and that students' work tasks will stimulate thoughtfulness, then standards will be meaningful. But when standards mean that students will perform 81 homework problems instead of 2 that are relevant and creative, then stan-

dards may be difficult and become meaningless. Too often, schools (states) confuse harder standards with better standards and *require* that every student be successful instead of *expecting* every student to be successful.

STANDARDS FOR TEACHERS

Professional accountability has been an issue since colonial days, when schoolmasters had to sign a contract stating how many children they would teach and for how long (80 days), and that each child would learn as much as he or she was capable. At the end of the period, the schoolmaster was required to identify each student's progress in a written report. The No Child Left Behind Act also affects teaching standards. The law requires not only that highly qualified teachers be assigned to the core subjects, but that parents be informed if their child's teacher does not meet the stated criteria for qualification.

Students' school performance is a national concern and, as a consequence, teachers are expected to be accountable. To accomplish this, three national groups have set standards that affect the teaching profession. The standards begin with the initial preparation of teachers. The National Council for Accreditation of Teacher Education (NCATE) monitors and assesses teacher education courses and fieldwork by sending a team of observers to the college to verify appropriate standards. NCATE certification is valued by teacher education programs.

The second group concerned with standards for teachers is the Interstate New Teacher Assessment and Support Consortium (INTASC). This group is composed of a special task force that was formed by half of the states to set standards for teacher licensing. These standards can be found on the inside front cover of this text. Each chapter in this book integrates some of these standards, which are identified at the beginning of the chapter.

The third group that affects the teaching profession is the National Board for Professional Teaching Standards (NBPTS). This group focuses on experienced teachers who are dedicated to the improvement of teaching and learning. National Board Certification (NBC) is bestowed on teachers who demonstrate, through a teaching **portfolio** and testing, their commitment to the profession and their excellence in teaching.

SOCIAL PROBLEMS AFFECT SCHOOL DECISION MAKING

Poverty and Socioeconomic Integration

In Greg Thomas's rural community, more than one-third of the students live in poverty. Poverty is more prevalent in rural communities than in urban areas. Thomas knows that there is a relationship between socioeconomic status and achievement in school. Sociologists study socioeconomic status by relating information about an individual's occupation, education, and income. Most sociologists also accept that there are identifiable value, attitude, and belief differences related to socioeconomic status. Low socioeconomic status and poverty conditions have been related to poor attendance and failure in schools.

The latest report (2001) from the U.S. Bureau of the Census reveals that the poverty rate and the number of poor have grown to more than 10% of the population, and over 33 million people. The poverty rate is highest in metropolitan areas outside the central city and in the South. The poverty rate increased more in the South than in any other region of the United States.

During periods of economic recession, all classes of people can experience adversities, but for unskilled individuals without an education, the experience of poverty is quite different. Children growing up poor may feel little control over their lives, and they are often frightened and resigned. The poverty rate in the United States is greater than in other industrialized nations—and the United States does not provide tax-supported services, such as health care, prenatal care, child support, and preschools, that other industrialized countries provide.

Poor children lack resource tools in their homes, parental involvement, and support in their schools, and they suffer from hunger and disease. All of these conditions affect achievement. A Los Angeles elementary school principal related the story of a kindergarten boy sent to her office by the teacher because the child was so restless, angry, sour, and mean to others. The teacher's note said, "We need a little rest from Eduardo; please keep him for a while." The principal asked the child to accompany her to the cafeteria so that she could have a late breakfast. The cafeteria manager gave the principal a grilled cheese sandwich and coffee. She and the child sat down, and the principal asked the boy if he would like to help her eat the sandwich. Eduardo

Research Findings

Poverty-ridden schools are too frequently subjected to low-level work assignments and monitored seatwork that stifles students' motivation and interest. Instead J. O. Lee (2003) suggests embedding content standards and process skills into projects with meaningful contexts and interesting activities to teach students that ability is the result of effort.

devoured half of the sandwich, and when the principal offered the other half, he quickly ate that, too. When asked if he wanted more, the child responded affirmatively. Later the child was sent back to class and the teacher asked the principal, "What did you say to Eduardo? He came back to class and for the first time took part in a group activity."

Breakfast and lunch programs in many inner-city schools do help children from low-income families, but sometimes the mechanism for obtaining the help is not in place. Helping children from low-income families requires the collaborative efforts of several social agencies. It is often the responsibility of the school nurse or counselor to recognize children with special needs and contact appropriate help organizations. School personnel clearly recognize the need for more social services for the poor. Studies by the Carnegie Corporation indicate that the United States provides less health care for the children of the poor than most other industrialized nations.

Head Start (initiated in 1965) and other early-childhood programs were created as intervention programs for preschoolers from low-income families to provide health care, nutrition, and nurturing environments and experiences before the children entered school. These programs are intended to equalize opportunity for poor children.

Political leadership rather than the school must resolve the problems of poverty. However, the school is the most accessible institution and has the opportunity to act responsibly toward the people in the community. Teachers' daily contact with children often provides access to the family. Though experienced, veteran teachers often shun poverty-ridden schools, even inexperienced teachers should be able to perceive the needs and suggest supportive services from other specialists and institutions.

Teaching Hints: Sensitivity

- Recognize the problems of the poor and demonstrate sensitivity.
- Recognize that chronic illness often plagues the poor family and that it contributes to absence from school.
- Middle school children may be needed at home to babysit younger children if adult family members are to work.
- Recognize that welfare grants and food stamps do not provide enough support for the poverty family and children may be hungry.
- Recognize that low self-esteem of the adult family members affects their children's self-confidence and self-concept.

Research Findings

Socioeconomic integration has a positive effect on students' achievement. Middle-class students achieve at high levels as long as poverty-level students are less than 50% of the school population (Kahlenberg, 2006).

The Supreme Court's decision in *Brown v. Board of Education* ruled that all children should have equal opportunity to an education to succeed in life. This was interpreted by school districts and the public at large to mean that all schools should have equal resources, facilities, curriculum, and teachers.

In the mid-1960s, the U.S. Office of Education engaged James Coleman and others to assess the equality of public school education. Surprisingly Coleman's research team found that most of the schools that were studied were quite similar. However, White students performed better on standardized tests than did African American students. Coleman attributed these differences in educational achievement to the quality of students' peers (Coleman, Campbell, Hobson, McPartland, & Mood, 1966).

Socioeconomic integration is not a popular plan; middle- and upper-class families are not delighted to have their children travel to low-achieving schools, nor do they want to "mix" economically in their own neighborhood schools. However, much of the research literature advocates socioeconomic integration to close the achievement gap (Kahlenberg, 2006). Clearly there are learning benefits from economic integration of low-income students with middle- or high-income students in contrast to integration that matched low-income students together. Current research literature confirms the Coleman et al. report that students perform better in middle-class schools. Both the learning environment of high-poverty schools and the lack of middle-class peers have a negative effect on learning achievement.

Experiments in several school districts (Wake County, North Carolina; St. Louis, Misouri; Hartford, Connecticut; Cambridge, Massachusetts; San Francisco, California) are attempting to narrow the achievement gap by ensuring that all of their students attend middle-class schools. If the district does not include an appropriate population, interdistrict school choice programs have been implemented (Kahlenberg, 2006).

Full-Service School Programs

The **full-service school** concept is taking root in some urban areas. Child care and family services are coordinated by a school-based social service counselor who has access to social agencies that help the poor. Health agencies and university-based medical and dental care programs are often included in a network of family care providers. The school counselor refers families to the different agencies for care. The counselor may be involved with parent education and screening programs.

Homelessness

The number of homeless children in the United States is growing. For schools, this means that there is a growing transient population that needs to be served. Transferring students' records from school to school and district to district sometimes means that school records never catch up to the child. Homeless children typically lag two to three years behind in reading and mathematics ability. Inner-city schools often lose and gain a full classroom of students each month of the school year.

When working with homeless children, teachers need to be particularly sensitive to their problems and, when possible, facilitate their educational experience by providing the following advantages:

- Provide a means for the students to do homework assignments by giving them the resources they need and finding a place for them to do the work.

- Encourage the school's parent groups to help the homeless by providing clothing and school supplies; and recognize that the homeless child may suffer from malnutrition.
- Encourage another child to act as a buddy and tutor the homeless child to ensure that he or she is aware of school facilities and school rules.

School Safety

We live in a violent society, and schools are not immune to the problems of the community. Both urban and suburban schools lock the gates either to keep the community out or to close the children in. Some schools require students to wear identification badges, limit the size of book bags, and use electronic monitoring; some middle schools and high schools are eliminating hall lockers. But children's daily personal experiences include knowledge of violence—in the home, on television, on the streets, in the movies they watch, and in the games they play.

Studies of violence in the schools reveal that violent behavior occurs most often in the public places in the school that are "unowned" and relatively unsupervised. Astor, Benbenishty, and Estrada (2007) define school violence to ". . . include a wide range of intentional behaviors which aim to physically and emotionally harm students, staff, and property, on or around school grounds" (p. 16). For example, hallways, stairs, the cafeteria, the school library, and areas of the playground are not often considered a teacher's responsibility. Uncertified adults (yard monitors, security guards, cafeteria workers) who often provide the supervision do not appear to have an impact on violent behavior. Young students are more likely to experience violent acts on the playground, in the hallways, and in the cafeteria; older students experience violence in the school parking lot. Within classrooms where teachers are in charge, there are few cases of violent behavior.

Young elementary students who experience bullying, abuse, neglect, and harsh or erratic discipline are more likely to display aggressive and violent behavior. (Bullying is discussed in Chapter 2.) There is some evidence that violent behavior is learned. To help students deal with aggression and violence, schools are implementing curricula that teaches students how to deal with anger and conflict.

Role-playing is an effective teaching strategy with students of all ages. By acting out different roles and perspectives, students gain insight into the causes of conflict. Problem solving culminates the role-playing activity as students discuss how the conflict situation could have been avoided.

Perhaps the greatest contribution schools can make to prevent violent behavior is to focus on communication skills. Learning to express anger and dissatisfaction in ways other than through physical violence has the potential to curb disorderly behavior. Although schools cannot rid society of violence, perceptive and sensitive teachers can be role models and demonstrate

"Unowned" places in schools attract violent behavior.

Research Findings

Chaltrain (2006) recommends strengthening three areas of school life to combat violent behavior and keep schools safe:

1. The culture of the school should have a discipline code that is developed by students, teachers, staff, and parents and is relevant to school life.
2. Student voice ensures that all students may communicate responsibly about problems in the school and community. The act of expression will help students develop self-identity and a sense of community.
3. Accountability of all members of the school ensures the rights of the individual and of groups to engage in free speech and debate and to be treated respectfully.

> ### Teaching Hints:
> ### Diminishing Violent Behavior
>
> - Implement cooperative work groups.
> - Insist that students talk out disagreements by emphasizing communication skills.
> - Role-play conflict situations.
> - Teach conflict resolution through the use of compromise and negotiation skills.
> - Help mediate conflicts among students.
> - Take charge and monitor "unowned" space.

caring behavior to students from all social classes who may lack parental support.

Still another problem that schools and society at large face is recognizing the difference between threats of violence and students' creative expression of their own feelings, identity, and sometimes loneliness. In Texas, a boy was held in juvenile hall for writing a Halloween story about the shooting of a teacher. In California, a boy wrote a poem about his loneliness and it was interpreted as a threat to commit violence. In Massachusetts, a 12-year-old's art picture depicted him shooting the teacher. In all of these cases, the students were enrolled in English or art classes and their creativity was misinterpreted by school authorities.

Child Abuse

Child abuse occurs among all social classes. The Child Abuse Prevention and Treatment Act of 1974 assists states in implementing programs for preventing, identifying, and treating victims of child abuse and neglect.

In Mary Hogan's second-grade classroom, she was introduced to a new female student who appeared shy, withdrawn, and not too alert during instruction. The child's school records were not immediately available, but Hogan kept a watchful eye on the child to see how she interacted with other students. When the records did arrive, Hogan saw that her schoolwork was not remarkable, but what she would describe as average; however, the child's attendance record was poor.

About three weeks after entering the class, the child came to school after a four-day absence with dark circles around her eyes and black-and-blue marks on her upper arms. Hogan decided to request a parent conference. At the conference, the mother said the child had

fallen off her bicycle; she said the child was poorly coordinated and fell frequently. At no time during physical activities at school did Hogan see the child fall or have coordination problems. Hogan suspected maltreatment and reported the case to her principal, who began the process of notification, adhering to school district policy.

Child abuse and neglect is a societal problem and teachers are frequently the first to know. Because teachers see their students every day, they are more likely to note evidence of abuse. Teachers and school nurses are legally responsible for reporting incidents of abuse. (See the discussion regarding instruction about child abuse in Chapter 12.)

Health Education

Karen Adazzio, our seventh-grade teacher, has realized that health education represents a prime example of the societal problems that affect the schools. At her middle school, she sees daily evidence of students using drugs, alcohol, and tobacco. She has counseled pregnant 13-year-old students; she knows of students with acquired immune deficiency syndrome (AIDS).

Adazzio is aware that many critics of the schools do not believe that these problems should be represented in the school curriculum. She would respond with a John Dewey tenet: The school is a social institution and schools are extensions of the community. She believes that the school must educate the community's children; therefore, the school is responsible for adjusting to the needs of the community. Most educators believe that high-risk sexual behavior should be discussed in classrooms beginning in grade 5. School districts need to work with members of the community to develop appropriate curriculum in these sensitive areas. The health education curriculum is discussed in Chapter 12.

CONFRONTING THE CHALLENGES: SCHOOL DECISION MAKING

Equal Opportunity for Education

Equal educational opportunity implies equal access to every facet of education. This includes opportunities to

- interact with the best teachers;
- use the best facilities, including equipment and materials;

- share the wealth of school support;
- interact with other students;
- study all subjects; and
- prepare for all vocations.

All students have not always had equal access to an education in the United States. Students with disabilities were often denied schooling because schools did not accommodate people with special needs. Non-English-speaking students still are often denied appropriate instruction because bilingual specialist teachers are not available. Prior to 1954 (*Brown v. Board of Education*), southern schools were segregated, and students were denied equal access to public schooling.

Despite the fact that all students are compelled to attend school and, in this postmodern era, have free access to the public schools, inequality exists. Rural and inner-city children lack many of the advantages of suburban and middle-class children. For example, the poor child probably has not had the preschool experiences that build readiness for schooling, such as travel, books, problem-solving toys, visits to cultural events, learning-oriented nursery school, in-depth conversations, good nutrition, and medical attention. Equal educational opportunity also is limited by certain school practices. For example, schools may limit access in the way they treat students based on academic performance. If students need a specific grade point average to take part in the school chorus, band, or special community activities, then access is denied to some students. If the math laboratory or the computer is available only to those with special talents or those who finish their math assignment early, then other students are denied these enrichment activities. Tracking and ability grouping may be used to limit access to special subjects and enrichment activities. Frequently, students who are academically below average spend all of their school day in remedial activities in the very subjects they most dislike, rather than in activities that they enjoy and in which they demonstrate success. Crawford (2007) comments that the achievement gap is the focus of the NCLB law, but equal opportunity is not, and as a consequence major teaching time is spent on test preparation and basic skills.

What is the relationship between equal opportunity for education and socioeconomic integration? Which of the needs (opportunities) are ignored and/or curtailed by adherence to the NCLB requirements?

At-Risk Students

Who are **at-risk students**? This category includes students of low socioeconomic status; students who have difficulty participating in school because they are English language learners; students with a high dropout rate in their community; students with special education needs; students who are subject to poverty, homelessness, drugs, violence, life-threatening illness, or teenage pregnancy; and students who have a history of failing school grades and frequent absences. Students at risk are *not* necessarily inner-city children and may be White as well as any other ethnicity (C. D. Lee, 2003).

Schools have a difficult time helping such students because their problems may require the assistance of other social institutions and parental involvement. Many students are at-risk due to a lack of home facilities for studying. If time and facilities can be provided at school, these students will do quite well. Academic assistance can be provided through school-based mentoring and tutoring programs. Through the use of a buddy system, cooperative learning strategies, and cross-age tutoring, some schools have made a difference in the dropout rate. At-risk students often need counseling programs to enhance their self-esteem. The section on differentiation of instruction in Chapter 2 will help you work with at-risk students.

Students who like their teacher and the class and school environment are less likely to drop out. Positive teacher-student interactions are extremely important for creating a satisfying school experience. In one Los Angeles middle school, the performing arts teacher purposefully asked several at-risk students to participate in a forthcoming musical program. The close association with other students and the recognition that they were needed to make the musical production successful served as motivation to encourage their attendance. Participation in the high-visibility program developed the self-esteem of this target group. See Figure 1.2 for suggestions of ways to work with all students in your classroom.

Linking parents to their child's education has the potential to assist at-risk students. For parents who are unaware of their child's problems, communication between teacher and parent may provide the key to attendance and support. However, for some parents, school involvement may be out of the question because of working hours or traditional fear of schools and teachers.

Some success has been achieved by having parent advisory groups communicate with the larger parent

1. Can you name ALL students in your classroom?
2. Are all students encouraged to set personal goals?
3. Do all students have the opportunity to choose some work and leisure activities?
4. In seating students in the classroom, are all students favored?
5. Are all students praised frequently and for the same purposes?
6. Are all students provided with nonverbal behavioral clues such as smiles, eye contact, friendly pats, and understanding looks?
7. Are all students monitored and guided?
8. When asking students questions, are all students provided with content clues if they fail to respond?
9. When misbehavior occurs, are all students subject to the same amount and type of criticism?
10. Is student-to-student interaction encouraged?
11. Is group placement in your classroom changed frequently?
12. Does group placement reflect a variety of teaching purposes?
13. Are different instructional strategies used when a student has failed to learn?
14. In planning instruction, have you considered the needs and interests of all students?
15. During a discussion, are all students called upon?
16. During a discussion, are all students given time to respond?
17. During a discussion, are all students encouraged to initiate a new line of thinking or to ask a question?
18. In small-group work, do all students have an opportunity to be both leader and participant?
19. Are all students allowed to assist each other?

Figure 1.2   Equity Checklist for Working with Students in Your Classroom

population. Involvement in school decision making such as school uniform requirements and after-school program decisions seem to motivate parental interest.

The Inclusive Classroom

Students with disabilities are typically described as **exceptional learners.** Included in this designation are students with a variety of physical or learning disabilities. Special education programs have been designed to meet their needs. These programs attempted to provide a basic education in an environment free from academic competition and the discriminatory behavior of peers.

In the late 1960s, special education teachers and educational researchers began to question the effectiveness of special education placement, and minority parents questioned the validity of IQ tests that labeled their children retarded. Many children whose primary language was not English appeared to have learning problems when placed in a monolingual immersion situation. Teachers who were unable to distinguish non-English-speaking children from those with genuine learning disabilities placed the former in special education classrooms. Mercer (1971) verified that special education classrooms were populated with a disproportionate number of children from minority groups and low economic backgrounds, all of whom were labeled mentally retarded.

Harry and Klingner (2007) question the approach of educators who believe that students with learning needs are disabled. They believe that the disability label destroys students' self-confidence, thereby inhibiting motivation to learn. These researchers recommend a three-tiered approach for students who are having learning difficulties. First, instructional needs should be assessed and then they should receive focused, quality instruction and ongoing monitoring in the regular classroom. If the student(s) does not respond adequately, then the second approach should offer intensive intervention support in the regular classroom. The final approach, if needed, would reevaluate the student's language proficiency and biological or psychological limitations before placing the student in a special education classroom.

Full Educational Opportunities

In 1974, Congress passed the Education Amendments (Pub. L. No. 93–380) to the 1968 Education of the Handicapped Act (Pub. L. No. 90–247), which specified criteria for funding special education programs. The act established a goal to provide full educational opportunities to all children with disabilities. Provisions specified that "to the maximum extent appropriate, handicapped children in public or private institutions or other care facilities are educated with children who are not handicapped and that removal from the regular classroom occurs only when the handicap is of such severity that educational services cannot be achieved satisfactorily" (Education Amendments, 1974).

Teaching Hints: High-Risk Behaviors

- Provide opportunity for students to make decisions that affect their learning experiences.
- Find ways to improve students' self-esteem by focusing on each individual's special talents.
- Integrate social and physical changes into the curriculum so that upper elementary and middle school students recognize their own physical and emotional changes.
- Take advantage of opportunities to interact personally with every student.
- Communicate good news to parents using e-mail or telephone.

Should all students, regardless of disabilities (learning, behavioral, cognitive, or physical), be integrated into the regular classroom?

In addition, Pub. L. No. 93–380 specified that testing and evaluation materials used for the purpose of classifying and placing children with disabilities be "selected and administered so as not to be racially or culturally discriminatory."

Individualized Educational Programs

Pub. L. No. 94–142, the Individuals with Disabilities Education Act of 1975, amended and reauthorized in 1997, has been cited as a bill of rights for children with disabilities. The law (originally the Education for All Handicapped Children Act, amended in 1990 and renamed) has implications for all children, with and without disabilities, because it specifies the use of an **individualized educational program (IEP)** to identify individual needs and capacities. The act guarantees that children with disabilities will receive free and appropriate special education and related services, conforming to the nature of their disability. In accordance with Pub. L. No. 94–142, the IEP must specify the following information:

- The student's present educational achievement level
- Appropriate annual and short-range educational goals
- Special services to achieve or implement the goals
- The extent to which the student can be placed in a regular classroom
- Annual review of instructional goals, progress, and implementation plans

The IEP must be signed by the student's parent or guardian to indicate that the parent or guardian participated in the planning conference and agreed with the proposed program. The IEP conference should be attended by the individuals who have evaluated the student. In practice, the IEP team is made up of the classroom teacher and other specialists, depending on the student's needs (speech therapist, counselor, physical therapist, and teachers from different disciplines for middle school students). It is appropriate also to include the student in the goal-setting conference.

Proponents of the **inclusive school and classroom** believe that all children, regardless of disability, should be educated in a regular classroom (mainstreamed) with their peer group. These educators are concerned that self-contained special education classrooms separate learners and may label them as learning disabled and low achievers, yet offer no special curriculum. However, other special educators are more concerned with how students are to be educated rather than where. Inclusion is sometimes used by school districts as a device to save money by cutting back on special education services.

Do you believe that, in the regular classroom, students can receive appropriate instruction to meet their special needs? Does labeling a student put him or her at a disadvantage? How does inclusion affect all of the students in the classroom?

Diversity and Multicultural Education

U.S. society is diverse in race, ethnicity, religion, social class, culture, and exceptionality. Add to this our regional and geographic differences, and we see a society that must be served by schools that are open to many perspectives and competing viewpoints.

When content and learning experiences are selected for teaching, state, district, and individual perspectives influence choice. This perspective is never neutral. Opinions, criteria, and beliefs about what is appropriate can provide a framework for curriculum choices. When a teacher or school district chooses to teach one thing, something else is omitted. The citizen (or educator) who yearns for the good old days may well be asking for content and learning experiences that in the past were oriented to western civilization, Christians, and White males. Too often curriculum has ignored the experiences of African Americans, Latinos, Asian Americans, and poor Americans.

Multicultural education means that all students are represented in the curriculum; no group is omitted or alienated. Multicultural education does not mean a special social studies unit (for example, a week devoted to African American history). Critics of multicultural education argue that schools are responsible for developing (and socializing students for) a common culture. Proponents of the common culture argue that particular beliefs, ethnic pride, and religious orientations should be taught after school or on weekends; teaching about these ideas is not the job of the public school. However, the question remains: Who decides what the common culture is, and does what is taught reflect all Americans and help us understand who we are?

Bilingualism: Teaching English Language Learners

The role of native language instruction in the public schools has been debated for decades. Educators, as well as society as a whole, appear to be divided between those who view bilingualism as an asset and those who believe it negatively affects a child's academic development. The debate focuses on whether students who are **English language learners** (ELLs) should be taught content in their native language or in English as a second language (ESL).

Landmark Decisions

In 1968, Congress passed the Bilingual Education Act as Title VII of the Elementary and Secondary Education Act. Since that time, more than half a billion dollars has been provided for bilingual education. In *Lau v. Nichols* (1974), the U.S. Supreme Court ruled that the San Francisco Unified School District had to provide equal educational opportunities for all students—in this case, bilingual education to the Chinese-speaking students of the district. The decision required school districts to rectify English language deficiencies that excluded students from effective participation in educational programs.

Later that same year, Congress extended bilingual education to include bicultural education. Congress stated that bilingual education must exhibit an appreciation of the cultural heritage of the target group. The expansion of the Title VII act recognized the intimate relationship of language, culture, and ethnic identity. Teaching Spanish-speaking students in their home (primary) language increases their self-esteem and gives them cultural dignity. When students are taught effectively in their primary language, there is evidence that they will transfer Spanish reading skills to reading English and read English better than students who begin with English-only instruction.

With the advent of NCLB, students with limited proficiency in English are confronted with invalid and unreliable tests of their academic achievement because they are tested in English. Low-scoring students are often encouraged to drop out before test day. Because teachers spend so much of their teaching time preparing students for the tests, most have limited time left to provide instruction in students' native language or devote time to subjects other than reading and math. According to Crawford (2007) instead of the law encouraging ELL students to improve their skills, they are punished, discouraged, and demoralized. Further discussion of teaching ELL students can be found in Chapter 8.

Teaching Gifted and Talented Students

Exceptional-child status is also conferred on gifted and talented students. The Marland Report (Marland, 1972) identified the population of gifted and talented students as children capable of high performance with

Teaching Hints: Helping English Language Learners

- Language skills acquired in the primary language will transfer to the second language.
- Significant concepts should be taught in the primary language; students' stored knowledge can then be used to apply and extend ideas in English.
- It is important to build students' self-esteem by demonstrating respect for their primary language and culture.

demonstrated and/or potential ability in the following six areas:

1. General intellectual ability
2. Specific academic aptitude
3. Creative or productive thinking
4. Leadership ability
5. Visual and performing arts
6. Psychomotor ability

The report served as a federal policy statement assisting in the identification of this target population for the purpose of providing differentiated educational programs and/or services so that gifted and talented students would realize their potential and contribute to society. However, many parents and educators have raised questions about the six categories. For example, most specialists in gifted education recognize that the six categories do not operate independently of each other, yet there is a tendency to use separate identification procedures with each one.

Renzulli (2002) identified gifted and talented individuals as those who are (1) above average, (2) creative, and (3) task committed. He believes that these three components interact with the individual's personality and environment.

Gardner (1995) emphasized that environment and sequential experiences are extremely important for the fruition of native ability. He believes that many talented children go unrecognized because they lack opportunity, developmental practice, and motivation. He raises the question of whether the education of gifted students is a civil rights issue. Minority students are underrepresented in classes for the gifted and talented. Many educators believe this is a consequence of lack of encouragement and opportunity to build the necessary knowledge structure.

Crawford (2007) also believes that minority students who are denied access to club programs, plays, and literature and spend their time on phonics drills and test preparation are cheated out of a full and rich education. Similarly the gifted and talented student wastes away in the classroom for lack of attention because the teacher is focusing on the achievement gap.

Gifted and talented children provide yet another challenge for teachers to develop differentiated programs and services that go beyond the regular school program. These programs should encompass both content acceleration and content enrichment, and will be

Teaching Hints: Gifted and Talented Students

1. Ask open-ended questions to motivate project and study activities.
2. Extend content study through the use of new conceptual ideas.
3. Enrich content study through the introduction of diverse people and places.
4. Stir the imagination by asking students to relate dreams, wishes, and adventures.

discussed in Chapter 2, along with the characteristics of this population.

Public Support and Involvement in the Schools

A great deal of evidence shows that parental support and involvement in schools help children succeed academically. Traditional involvement patterns had parents working as room mothers, chauffeurs, and chaperones and in organizing tasks such as holiday celebrations and bake sales. In this postmodern era, there are many interpretations of the term *parental involvement*. For example, in some regions of the country, parents select their school principal. In some schools, parents serve as special resource instructors and come to school to teach in a club program or serve as guest speakers.

Parental participation in advisory councils is now a common occurrence. Advisory councils can become involved in making decisions about school priorities. In a low-income school in Los Angeles, the parents took part in deciding whether the school should join with other neighborhood schools in a full-service network. In a charter school, the parents decided to donate their time and skills to repair and improve school buildings, plumbing, and property; the money saved was used to upgrade computers in each classroom.

In Greg Thomas's rural community, he contacts each child's family and invites them to visit the classroom. In Mary Hogan's urban school, she recognizes that school visits during the day may be a luxury most parents cannot afford. She greets parents at an open house in the evening and solicits home-based involvement. Karen Adazzio communicates to parents with a newsletter that she and her students compose.

There is no single pattern of parent involvement. Adult education programs for parents can be used to motivate parent interest in the schools. Giving parents some decision-making responsibilities helps generate participation and build a real school community. Burns (1999) studied ways to enhance parent involvement at a middle school. She noted that adolescents typically try to distance their parents from the school and that relationships between the school and parents are more difficult to establish at a two- or three-year middle school than at an elementary school. She recommended the following:

- Provide parents and students with an influential voice within the school decision-making structure.
- Seek an array of connections to establish active involvement for community and families.
- In teacher communication with parents, build on students' strengths, not their deficits.
- Recognize that school problems provide opportunities to develop a problem-solving culture involving the community.
- Communicate with parents concerning the curriculum, teaching strategies, and assessment plans.
- Provide respect for parents' perspectives and opinions by expecting and celebrating parent involvement.

Charter Schools

The charter school movement is still another way in which parents are actively involved. Charter schools are publicly funded and must be approved by the local school district or by county or state boards of education. The charter is granted to a group of people who will participate in running the school. The group is usually composed of parents, teachers, and community members. Charters were originally given to groups of people interested in experimentation and innovation. Though funded with public money, charter schools are not required to have credentialed teachers or adhere to union contracts. As a consequence charter schools teachers' salary may not be equal to their colleagues in traditional settings. In addition, many of the charter schools do not have space of their own and, as a consequence, may have to pay rent for a place to call home (Rubin and Blume, 2007).

Charter schools can be considered to be private entities supposedly focused on poor, inner-city youths.

Some are funded by private organizations with a reform agenda that is not necessarily consistent with current methodologies. For example, the Knowledge Is Power Program (KIPP), by the KIPP Foundation, extols a highly structured program and structured discipline in which students must comply with regimented recitation instead of critical thinking and active participation (Featherstone, 2005). Students in KIPP schools attend from 7:30 A.M. to 5:00 P.M. and are expected to attend school every other Saturday. Robelen (2007) reports that in some of the KIPP schools, attrition rates are high, which leads to questions concerning the validity of test scores.

THE PROFESSIONAL PORTFOLIO ENTERPRISE

Portfolios are created by teachers to demonstrate professional knowledge, insight, skills, and individuality. The concept of a portfolio is not exclusive to teachers. Artists, photographers, public relations specialists, caterers, dentists, and plastic surgeons all use forms of the portfolio to demonstrate their competence, achievements, and skills. Sometimes the professional résumé is used to tell about accomplishments, but the portfolio differs from a résumé because it is a concrete means to display professional growth, creativity, and expertise. Throughout this text, suggestions will be given to facilitate the development of your personal professional portfolio.

WHAT DO TEACHERS' PORTFOLIOS CONTAIN?

Most teachers begin their portfolio with an introduction about their personal beliefs about teaching and learning and their professional goals. Two examples follow.

Karen Adazzio's philosophy and goals began this way:

> I believe teachers can be professional leaders and should be active socially and politically. I try to be a team leader with my colleagues and a counselor/adviser for my students. I feel I have an opportunity to model responsibility and compassionate adult behavior.

Greg Thomas began his introduction with his beliefs about teaching and learning:

> I want students to appreciate their cultural heritage, engage in problem solving, and critically examine our democratic way of life. I consider it important for students to be actively engaged in the study of social problems, and to do this I select projects that motivate in-depth research and concrete activities.

Your portfolio is limited only by your own creativity. You may choose to photograph your classroom and your students' work. You may sketch your room environment. Some teachers include videotapes of lessons. Lesson plans are appropriate. Case studies, annotative reports, journals, letters to and from parents, evidence of the integration of technology, and unit plans are all appropriate. But you should not forget to include explanations of your data, rationales concerning your plans, peer critiques, and personal reflections concerning your professional growth and future aims.

SUMMARY

The curriculum is affected by societal needs and expectations. In the United States, curriculum changed from being dominated by religion to the needs of a new country preparing to support and defend itself. As the country attracted new immigrant populations and territorial boundaries expanded, the schools grew in size, requiring professional teachers, new textbooks, and new requirements.

The work ethic dominated U.S. society and with it came the desire for educational goals and requirements for standards. Schools and teachers were confronted with challenges of poverty, homelessness, school safety, and the special needs of English language learners, students with disabilities, and gifted and talented students.

PORTFOLIO ACTIVITY

Focus on your role as a teacher and as a person. Ask yourself the following questions:

What do I want to accomplish as a teacher?
What is important to me as a teacher?
How does my role as a teacher affect me as a person and as a citizen?

Think about your role as a teacher and write your personal credo.

 DISCUSSION QUESTIONS AND APPLICATION EXERCISES

1. How have historical events affected the curriculum?
2. In what ways are modern school practices similar to those of schools during other historical time periods?
3. Working in small groups, discuss your beliefs and expectations concerning school programs and teachers' responsibilities. Do you agree or disagree with each of the following statements?
   - Teachers should teach children with disabilities in the regular classroom.
   - Teachers should develop a curriculum for sex education.
   - Teachers should be conscious of equity issues in the classroom and consider affected groups.
   - Schools should provide breakfast and lunch programs for low-income children.
   - Teachers need to help students learn conflict management techniques to reduce school and community violence.
   - The school should develop bilingual maintenance and transition programs.
4. How does cultural identity affect school success? Discuss how teachers can integrate multicultural education in all subject fields.
5. In what ways does NCLB affect equal opportunity for education?
6. Why is it important to recognize and provide special curricula for gifted and talented students?
7. Do you believe there should be national goals and standards for curricula and students' performance?
8. Which of the following would be appropriate goals for multicultural education?
   a. Knowledge of diverse cultures and languages
   b. Knowledge of the concept of Manifest Destiny
   c. Knowledge of African American contributions to the United States
   d. The impact of racism
   e. Reverence for American history
   f. Obliteration of cultural differences
   g. Historical and current dissatisfactions of minority groups
   h. Knowledge about dialects in the United States

Answers:

All are relevant goals for multicultural education except b, e, f.

READER RESEARCH

In the early U.S. history of education, who were the most influential educators? What did they contribute to current educational practices?

 TECHNOLOGY APPLICATIONS

Are you acquainted with Internet search tools? Because the Internet does not have standard ways to find resource materials (unlike a library), you need to hone your literacy skills to find information on the Internet for yourself and your students.

The Internet has search directories, search engines, and metasearch engines. A search directory provides general topics with structured categories. A search engine provides a means to ask questions of the database, but there is no categorization. Metasearch engines provide a means for the inquirer to use the search tools of many engines to access information. For practical purposes, search engines and search directories do much the same thing.

Begin to refine your literacy skills by identifying one or more directories, engines, and metasearch engines. Practice search techniques using the following procedures:

1. Ask a question. *(What happened at the Battle of Gettysburg?)*
2. Select keywords for your search. *(Gettysburg)*
3. Select a search directory for your inquiry. *(Google)*
4. If *Gettysburg* brought you too many hits, you may decide to impose some limitations to achieve a better match with your initial question. Join *Gettysburg* with the word *battle* by connecting the two with *and* or a + sign.
5. Refine your search by choosing the most relevant hits. Click on each link of interest and relevance. If you did not find adequate resources, you may need to broaden your search. Think of different ways to expand your inquiry.

CHAPTER 2

How Children Learn

Similarities and Differences

In this chapter, you will examine theories about how children differ in their use of language, moral outlook, and sex role as they develop socially and cognitively. Because theories of development and students' learning styles influence teaching, teachers need to understand the applications of these theories. Social factors controlled by the family also affect students' learning, and these factors are identified. The problem of bullying in the classroom and on school grounds is discussed, along with what teachers can do about it. Studies of brain research are described and applied to classroom teaching. Motivation and its effect on learning is also discussed. The chapter concludes with a discussion of constructivist learning theory. To apply chapter content, a special section on the differentiation of instruction focuses on the means teachers can use to facilitate learning.

Advance Organizer

The following questions are intended to guide your reading and understanding of the content of this chapter.

1. How might a teacher's beliefs about child development affect the teacher's classroom performance?
2. How do the theories of Kohlberg, Piaget, Maslow, and Vygotsky affect the classroom environment and instructional processes?
3. In what ways does the family influence motivation and learning?
4. What are the differences in students' learning perceptions when distinguishing between a mastery and performance goal orientation? How does the student's self-concept affect motivation?
5. How can a teacher learn about students' preferred learning styles, and how can the teacher use that information in the classroom?
6. How do socialization experiences affect learning? Relate your examples to gender experiences.
7. What can teachers do to alleviate bullying?
8. Identify how studies of the brain/mind affect curriculum and instruction.
9. In what ways can teachers apply the theory of multiple intelligences?
10. Why is it important to differentiate instruction? What means can teachers use?

INTASC   **INTASC Standards**

To be successful in the classroom, it is of prime importance to understand the students you are working with. Standards 2–3 and 5–6 are intended to focus attention on the diversity of students in U.S. classrooms and the need to plan learning environments that encourage communication and foster interaction.

Professional Lexicon

attribution Believing that oneself or others are responsible for success or failure; related to the concept of locus of control.

differentiation Individualizing and personalizing the teaching-learning process by distinguishing or modifying content, process, products, and environment.

egocentrism The state of an individual who cannot see others' viewpoints; a characteristic of Piaget's preoperational learner.

extrinsic motivation Using rewards, prizes, and grades to influence the learner to behave or to achieve or complete an assignment.

field-dependent learner An individual who prefers interaction with others and the social context of learning.

field-independent learner An individual who has more success in formal teaching-learning situations that stress rewards and competition.

gender bias Bias related to sex-role stereotyping that leads to different classroom practices for girls and boys.

gender equality The concept that everyone starts out on the same rung of the ladder and has equal access.

gender equity The concept that teachers are aware of traditional biases and act to enhance opportunity for the target group.

intrinsic motivation Striving to achieve for personal satisfaction and pleasure.

learning style The approach to learning that a particular individual favors, for example, a visual learner or an auditory learner.

locus of control The belief about who or what controls events that affect the individual's life.

mastery or learning goal A goal orientation in which the motivation for learning is self-improvement.

performance goal A goal orientation in which the motivation for learning is to outperform others; the student compares his or her performance to the accomplishments of others.

proclivity A predisposition (capacity) related to specific content.

self-actualization Maslow's highest personal goal to enhance potential.

socialization The process by which an individual acquires habits, beliefs, and patterns of behavior.

stereotype An exaggerated belief or fixed idea associated with a group of people for the purpose of justifying personal conduct.

teacher expectations Present and future achievement standards based on the teacher's beliefs about the student's performance.

"I know," said the boy as he stood up and raised his fist; "It's this big." Again he emphasized his fist. Mary Hogan laughed. "Yes, Barry, you're right. Everyone raise your fist. Good, now you all know the size of your heart." Hogan continued the lesson, demonstrating by using a plastic model of the heart. While most of the class was as excited and animated as Barry, several children in the room appeared bored. One youngster was staring out the window. Another student was reading a comic book hidden inside a science textbook.

Individuals differ in a variety of ways. We all have cognitive, affective, and psychomotor abilities. These aptitudes are influenced by **socialization** experiences: social class, cultural group, age, sex, prior experiences, and places of residence. Our interests, motivation and readiness to learn, and efficiency in learning are affected by our characteristics. In the school setting, other factors also influence learning, such as the teacher's characteristics and teaching style, the nature of the learning task, the classroom environment, and the student's peer group. Each of these forces affects the individual in unique ways, and so it is not surprising that, while some of Barry's classmates were enthusiastic and attentive, others found the learning task less interesting and perhaps even dull.

HOW STUDENTS DIFFER: DEVELOPMENTAL PATTERNS

Knowledge of developmental patterns enables the teacher to match subject matter and teaching methods with a child's conceptual level. All the students in a fifth-grade classroom are not at the same conceptual level, and the children's ability to handle different subject fields may depend on the particular subject that is being taught. In the preceding example, Barry may work at a high level in science and health, but he may have a great deal of difficulty with mathematics.

Mary Hogan, Barry's second-grade teacher, must find out whether Barry needs concrete materials to work with or whether he can handle abstract symbols. Greg Thomas, a fifth-grade teacher, needs to know whether his students can understand abstract concepts such as freedom, democracy, and manifest destiny and use them appropriately, or whether these concepts need to be acted out. Does Barry, the second grader, understand the concept of time—immediate, past, and future?

Piaget's Stages

Jean Piaget (1896–1980), a Swiss psychologist, developed a framework for understanding age-level changes or developmental stages as children mature. Because all children pass through these stages, it may seem peculiar that these developmental stages are included in a section about individual differences; because students mature at different rates, however, it is important to recognize that all students in a given classroom are not at the same cognitive developmental stage at the same time.

Piaget studied developmental patterns of intellectual growth and found that each of these patterns identified general behavioral characteristics. The four stages he identified are as follows:

1. Sensorimotor (0–2 years)
2. Preoperational (2–7 years)
3. Concrete operations (7–11 years)
4. Formal operations (11–16 years)

Sensorimotor Stage

The sensorimotor stage is the prelanguage stage, and it is vital to the development of thought. During this stage, the infant and toddler demonstrate intelligence prior to speech. A baby loses interest in any object that is not in sight, but by the end of the first year, the baby will search for a vanished object. Before leaving this stage, the baby learns through experience the rudimentary concepts of space, time, causality, and intentionality.

Preoperational Stage

True language begins during the preoperational stage. In the beginning, all vehicles that move may be cars to a child, who differentiates them by using the words *big* and *little*. All four-legged animals may be dogs, but as the child structures reality and participates in imitation and symbolic play, he or she begins to conceptualize more accurately by breaking down classes into subclasses through the process of categorization. The child in this stage needs concrete objects to manipulate.

The preoperational child has difficulty managing the concept of reversibility. A typical problem in a second-grade classroom may have to do with understanding the concept of conservation. For example, suppose the teacher has two pint containers on the demonstration table: a tall, skinny one and a short, squat one. The teacher asks the children whether the liquid in one of the containers (the tall, skinny one) will fit into the other container (the short, squat one). Invariably the children will respond that the liquid will not fit into the squat container because the tall, skinny container is higher and bigger! The preoperational student has difficulty focusing on several details at the same time, perhaps because of the need for concrete representation, and this accounts for the inattention to the similarity of size of the two containers.

The concept of **egocentrism** is particularly important to understand the preoperational student. During this stage the student is unable to perceive viewpoints other than his or her own, as Flavell (1963) explains:

> Egocentrism . . . denotes a cognitive state in which the cognizer sees the world from a single point of view only—his own—but without knowledge of the existence of viewpoints or perspectives and, a fortiori, without awareness that he is the prisoner of his own. (p. 60)

The student is not role-oriented to others or reflective because of the lack of consciousness and awareness of others' ideas. Because it is so vital that a student be able to perceive his or her own illogical thought to progress beyond egocentrism, the student must encounter others and be forced to accommodate his or her thinking process to that of others. Only through repeated and forced social interaction does the child learn to be reflective and to relinquish egocentric thought.

How might egocentrism affect discipline in the primary classroom?

Concrete Operations Stage

During the concrete operations stage, the child resolves most prior problems with understanding the concept of conservation and can think logically about concrete problems. For example, if the teacher tells the class that the two containers in the conservation problem are of the same size (a pint) and then asks whether the liquid can be transferred from one to the other, a child in this stage will reason logically and reply "Yes," even though he or she may not perceive the two containers as being equal. However, during this stage the student depends on personal experience; therefore, experiences must be appropriately arranged and must be concrete. For instance, an urban child can understand the concept of a rural environment better by seeing a picture depicting farms, tractors, and barns, rather than by hearing a verbal definition only.

Formal Operations Stage

During the formal operations stage, the child is no longer tied to concrete reasoning about objects. The child begins abstract thought; skill in scientific reasoning increases. Data can be organized by classifying, seriating, and corresponding. The results of these operations facilitate logical thinking and allow students to subject thought to inference, implication, identity, conjunction, and disjunction. The student can now reason hypothetically and enjoys "if-then" types of problems.

Applying Piaget's Theories in the Classroom

Developmental models help teachers decide what to teach, when to teach it, the sequence of teaching, and the scope of teaching. Using the Piagetian stages, teachers have an indication of the child's conceptual development and can relate the complexity of subject matter to the appropriate readiness level. For example, for a kindergarten or first-grade child, block play provides a means to acquire information, but for a fifth grader or seventh grader, the teacher expects that the child can learn by listening and observing (although that may not be the best way for the child to learn).

Also, Piaget has contributed to our understanding of children's need for active learning experiences. Through active participation, students discover meaning in their experiences. In Greg Thomas's classroom, the students did not understand that a magnetic field is produced whenever current flows through a wire. Nor did they know how to increase the strength of the magnetic field. Thomas provided the students with iron nails, insulated copper, batteries, and materials for experimentation. Through experimentation, the students discovered that by increasing the windings of the

wire around the nail, they increased the strength of the electromagnet. Thomas was using what is often called constructivist learning.

Vygotsky's Theories

Lev Vygotsky (1897–1934), a Russian psychologist interested in developmental patterns, differed in some ways from Piaget. Piaget believed that egocentric speech in the preoperational child occurs because the child focuses only on self. As children become less egocentric, they tend to talk more to others and less to themselves. Vygotsky (1962) believed that there is a relationship between language development and concept development. Vygotsky viewed egocentric talk in the preoperational child as the way the child learns language. As the child becomes more operational, speech changes and is inwardly directed. Vygotsky proposed that children begin speech by talking to themselves. Their inner speech is in a sense reflective; they are telling themselves how to perform the activities in which they are engaged. Myers (1983) states that this inner speech takes the form of a conversation, lecture, sermon, or graduation speech, depending on the functional activity and context.

Can you contrast Vygotsky's concept of egocentrism with Piaget's interpretation?

For Vygotsky, language development was critical to learning and development. Piaget believed that social development precedes language development, whereas Vygotsky believed that learning precedes development, and that children can often complete tasks with assistance from others prior to independent task completion. This assistance factor helps children internalize learning. Vygotsky called this level of development the *zone of proximal development.*

Vygotsky's theories have implications for the teaching of reading and writing. Practical application of his theory of language and development means that classroom teachers need to encourage social interaction, particularly between older and younger students, parents and children, and more capable and less capable students. The focus of the tutoring process should be on enabling the learner to gain insight and skills so that scaffolding occurs and the learning is internalized.

Research Findings

Theme-focused small schools motivate students and teachers when they have the option to choose both the school and the theme. Small schools organized around a theme inspire faculty to work cooperatively and motivate students' collaborative behaviors and engagement (Raywid 2006). In addition, Meier (2006) recommends a three- to five- year time plan to facilitate the transition from a big school to a small one. Ultimately the school should plan to grow to about 200 students. The plan should provide for smooth transitions from one grade to another.

Constructivist Learning Theory

Piaget and Vygotsky had somewhat similar beliefs about how children learn. Piaget believed that learning occurs as children interact with their environment. Vygotsky believed that children construct knowledge as they are indoctrinated within their community. Both wanted students to be actively involved in learning experiences and to engage in explorations and experimentation, and both believed that new knowledge should be linked with prior learning. Constructivism is discussed later in the chapter.

Kohlberg's Stages

Lawrence Kohlberg (1927–1987), a Harvard psychologist, developed the theory of moral development, a cognitive-developmental theory that, like Piaget's theory of development, proceeds through a series of qualitatively distinct stages. Kohlberg believed that the structure of thought can be separated from the content and that development proceeds in a universal sequence. However, individuals of the same age may differ in their level of development and ultimately in their final level of development. Unlike Piaget's stages of development, Kohlberg's stages extend into the middle or late 20s before the individual achieves full moral maturity. According to Kohlberg, many individuals never reach the highest stages of development.

Kohlberg identified three levels of reasoning about moral issues. Within each level are two stages, for a total of six stages of moral reasoning.

Preconventional Level (Stages 1 and 2)

The individual at the preconventional level typically is a preadolescent. At this level the individual is characterized by a concern for the consequences of rules and behaviors. "Right" behavior serves one's own interest or the interests of someone close. One behaves in the "right" way to avoid punishment, as a deference to power, to serve oneself, or in exchange for a favor. The child is obedient because he or she is afraid of the consequences. Within the preconventional level, the Stage 1 individual is sensitive to obedience and punishment; Stage 2 individuals are instrumental-relativists and may be responsible to others if being so will ultimately affect their own needs. At this level of moral development, loyalty, gratitude, and justice are not considered, and fairness, quality, and reciprocity are considered only when practical.

Conventional Level (Stages 3 and 4)

Chronologically, the individual at the conventional level is an adolescent. At this level, the individual is capable of moral reasoning that considers family or peers. The Stage 3 adolescent at the conventional level aspires to please others to earn their approval. The individual at this stage judges others in terms of whether they are perceived as meaning well. The Stage 4 individual is concerned with upholding societal rules, expectations, and roles. Right behavior is performed because the individual is motivated to act in a manner approved and expected by society, rather than arising from a concern for punishment.

Postconventional, Autonomous, or Principled Level (Stages 5 and 6)

The individual at this level is of adult age; however, less than 20% of adult society acts at the principled level. Universal principles guide the individual's orientation. The Stage 5 individual critically examines laws and acknowledges that they can be changed. Rights are determined by the society of which the individual is a member. The Stage 6 individual considers that he or she has a social contract with society to uphold the rights of others and that the individual should act in accordance with ethical values.

Applying Moral Education in the Classroom

The purpose of moral education is to encourage students to think about issues that involve a social conscience and to act in ethical ways. This can be done through classroom discussions and role-plays of conflict problems, the use of student-identified dilemmas that occur in their daily lives, and current newspaper and magazine articles that discuss community and global problems. The following story is an example of a dilemma that a middle school student identified in a classroom discussion.

The John Adams Middle School's soccer team had won almost all of their games. They were getting ready for the division playoff period. Pedro was their star player. He had been in the United States only two years and he was struggling to learn English. He was worried that he would not be able to continue to play on the team because the school had just adopted a new rule that said all athletes would have to maintain a C average in their core subjects in order to play on a school team. He was afraid he would flunk his history exam. On the day of the test, he decided to make a cheat sheet to use during the test. He placed it on his lap; it was partially hidden by the desktop. During the test, Sylbeth saw him using it.

Classroom discussion focused on the following issues:

1. Should Sylbeth tell the teacher?
2. Should Pedro have cheated on the test?
3. Was the school rule fair for students who were learning English as a second language?

According to Kohlberg's research, individuals at varied levels of development will respond to conflict situations differently. The preconventional individual will respond from an egocentric perspective and be concerned about breaking rules. The conventional individual will think about Pedro's point of view and recognize his problem as a second-language learner. The postconventional or principled individual will recognize that rules can be unfair, and it is important to consider the effect of a rule on different individuals.

BRAIN RESEARCH

In recent years, brain research has focused on brain/mind learning. Advances in technology have helped researchers understand how the brain functions. Wolfe (2001) explains the process of memory by labeling the means by which information is encoded, stored, retrieved, and integrated with prior stored information. She identifies sensory memory, working memory, and long-term memory. Synthesizing what is known about how the brain works, Caine and Caine (1997, pp. 104–108) identified 12 principles of brain/mind learning. I will identify their principles but provide my own interpretation, description, and application.

1. *The brain is a complex adaptive system.* As individuals, we respond to multiple stimuli holistically. We react to what we experience in our environment without separating out elements that affect our bodies, thoughts, and emotions. Mary Hogan motivates her second-grade students through concrete exhibits and demonstrations, then asks them to communicate what they learned. Students benefit from expression of their own thoughts and their classmates' perspectives.

2. *The brain is a social brain.* Brain development is greatest during the first 10 years of life. Associations and interactions are extremely important. Brain research supports Vygotsky's theory of the relationship of social interaction to cognitive development. Greg Thomas emphasizes small heterogeneous work groups in his classroom. Group membership is changed frequently so that students interact with different individuals and form many social relationships.

3. *The search for meaning is innate.* Questioning, curiosity, and imagination are healthy signs of mind learning. Insightful listening to students' questions and thoughts reveals what they know and understand. Karen Adazzio recognizes the adolescent's need to search for personal identity as well as for family and community identity.

4. *The search for meaning occurs through "patterning."* Individuals find meaning encased in their own prior experiences. As the individual seeks meaning, he or she relates new information to past learning. Each individual develops a system or pattern for assimilating meaningful knowledge and rejecting what is irrelevant or meaningless. Greg Thomas notices that when students are engaged in math problem solving, they tend to follow their own means to gain understanding. To encourage individuality and creativity in problem solving, he does not impose a one-system method for solving

problems and he often asks students to share how they went about solving the problem.

5. *Emotions are critical to patterning.* Every individual has a comfort zone. When you visit a classroom, you physically and mentally react to the social and emotional climate of the room. In some classrooms, you want to stay; in others, you can't wait to leave. The climate of the classroom affects how you feel about yourself, what you learn, and how you store your knowledge. In one middle school social studies class, the teacher gave each student a copy of his rules of conduct and told the students they would be tested on the rules the next day. Several of the students asked to have their social studies class changed; the emotional impact of the first-day experience colored their feelings about the class and would probably affect their future learning in that classroom.

6. *Every brain simultaneously perceives and creates parts and wholes.* Although we process information in distinct, individualized ways and may be affected by left-right brain theory, the brain aggregates knowledge and experience. In-depth project engagement provides opportunity for students to utilize their understanding in totality.

7. *Learning involves both focused attention and peripheral perception.* The middle school students who requested transfer to a different classroom reacted to the social structure of that particular classroom. Their focused attention was on classroom rules, and they may not even have been aware of what they were perceiving, yet the classroom management practiced by the teacher was communicated to them and affected their attitudes and beliefs about how life in that classroom would be.

8. *Learning always involves conscious and unconscious processes.* Experiences often have a residual and "sleeper effect." As we reflect concerning a previous learning experience, we gain new meaning; impact may be heightened; new images may be formed. Our three fictitious teachers make it a practice after a lesson to ask students, "What were you thinking about when we talked about _____ and when we read _____?" In this way, they incorporate and feature metacognitive thought into the lesson. In addition, when students are given independent activity at the application level, they are able to reflect on classroom lessons after the fact.

9. *We have at least two ways of organizing memory.* Sprenger (1999) talks about memory and storage systems. She emphasizes that we have five memory pathways that can be used for memory storage: semantic, episodic, procedural, automatic, and emotional. (Emotional memories have the greatest impact on us.) In addition, we have two system processes: short-term memory and working memory. Short-term memory operates for about 15–20 seconds; working memory can function for several hours.

Long-term memory, often stored in classification systems, is available for an indefinite period of time. Some researchers believe we never lose long-term memories, but we may not be able to "find" some of these memories. Memory systems usually focus on ways to associate ideas to trigger what we need to remember. In the classroom, teachers frequently refer to old lessons and experiences to help students find patterns and classification systems to link new, more complex learning to prior knowledge. When learning is significant (powerful), it is stored in multiple "lanes."

When Greg Thomas tested his students on the causes of the American Revolution, one of his students remembered (a) being in the auditorium where the class role-played the English and American settlers (episodic-location memory), (b) the compliment received for portraying Benjamin Franklin (emotional), and (c) the list of causes he wrote and repeatedly tested himself on before class (automatic memory).

10. *Learning is developmental.* Researchers believe we learn more efficiently in our early years. Language is readily learned in the preschool and early elementary years. Although learning is developmental (just like teaching), we can continue to learn throughout our lives as long as we avail ourselves of opportunities.

11. *Complex learning is enhanced by challenge and inhibited by threat.* Learning is negatively affected by admonishments, stress, intimidation, and embarrassment. Discipline systems that focus on behavioral consequences of rule infractions distract students from the real business of classroom learning and are themselves doomed to failure because of negativity. Motivation to learn is enhanced by a classroom environment that encourages risk-taking, creativity, and ingenuity.

Teaching Hints:
Helping Students Learn

1. Actual concrete experience has the greatest impact on students' learning.
2. Symbolic or representational learning built on prior concrete experiences contributes to learning.
3. Abstract learning needs to be tied to students' personal experiences and involves them in real-life meaning-making activities.
4. Problem solving related to school, community, and individual experience motivates thinking processes.
5. Projects that involve students in collaborative work help students construct meaning.
6. Development of a risk-taking environment encourages students' processing and development.

12. *Every brain is uniquely organized.* We learn in unique and diverse ways. As individuals we have preferred means of learning. Some individuals need information in print or concrete form, whereas others prefer listening. Some individuals need group interaction, whereas others prefer quiet and solo activity. Teachers need to provide a variety of opportunities for learning and a reasonable number of choices for students to select from as means for fulfilling requirements. The section in this chapter about differentiating instruction discusses this topic in more detail.

MULTIPLE INTELLIGENCES

The traditional view of intelligence relies on a quantification of human potential based on the individual's score on an IQ test. For example, the SAT (formerly known as the Scholastic Aptitude Test) and the Graduate Record Examination (GRE) are used to measure the individual's verbal and math ability. The scores are used to admit or deny admission to university programs.

Howard Gardner (1993) presents a multifaceted view of intelligence that challenges the traditional model. By looking at different populations, such as children with learning disabilities and adults with brain damage, Gardner identifies eight different intelligences that affect human behavior. He believes that all eight are equal in impact, although the first two have traditionally been more valued in our society.

Linguistic intelligence helps the individual detect sounds, rhythms, and meanings of words. Gardner believes that poets exhibit this intelligence.

Logical-mathematical intelligence is demonstrated by the scientist and the mathematician who have the capacity to detect logical or numerical patterns. Both the SAT and the GRE are based on measuring linguistic and logical-mathematical intelligences.

Spatial intelligence is demonstrated by engineers, surgeons, sculptors, painters, sailors, and others who are able to think about a spatial model and use that model to solve problems. For example, spatial problem solving is used for navigation. Artists demonstrate spatial intelligence in the way they integrate space in artwork.

Musical intelligence is demonstrated by the ability to produce, appreciate, and express rhythm, pitch, and timbre.

Bodily-kinesthetic intelligence is demonstrated by athletes, dancers, craftspeople, and surgeons who use their bodies to express an emotion, participate in an athletic event, or demonstrate skill in handling tools. This intelligence requires coordination, balance, and dexterity.

Interpersonal intelligence is the ability to detect the moods, meanings, intentions, and desires of others. Politicians, teachers, therapists, and parents typically demonstrate this intelligence.

Intrapersonal intelligence is the ability to access one's own personal needs, understandings, strengths, and weaknesses and use them to guide personal behavior.

Naturalistic intelligence is demonstrated by instinctive, intuitive ability to discriminate what is in nature, literature, and art. Professionals such as botanists, biologists, and artists might demonstrate this element of intelligence.

Applying Multiple Intelligences in the Classroom

Teaching strategies that hit the mark with some students may fail dismally with others. We attribute this to individual differences in favored means and proclivities to learn. For example, the button-bar graphic symbols used in computer programs may work well with spatially inclined computer users, but they fail to inform and assist me. Teachers need to use a variety of teaching methods to appeal to natural differences among students.

Each of the intelligences suggests a variety of means that teachers can use to help students learn; however, selecting a learning experience to appeal to one specific intelligence is both time-consuming and inappropriate. It is far better to select experiences that allow students to respond in preferred ways. In Greg Thomas's classroom, when the students worked on science experiments, they had several options for presenting their studies. They could draw the experiment, construct a model of it and demonstrate it, or write or record a story about its use.

Studying a community problem in Karen Adazzio's classroom involved working in a small investigative group. In the group activity, students negotiated with each other to determine how to go about their inquiry tasks. Some students interviewed key people involved in the problem; others took photographs; still others read about the problem or developed a chain of critical events that affected the problem. Each student chose how he or she could contribute to the group study.

Note that in choosing how to take part in an activity, students demonstrate intrapersonal intelligence as well as their inclination. But Gardner (1995, pp. 202–203) emphasizes that learning style is not the same as an intelligence. The decision to engage in reading about a social problem instead of interviewing others affected by the problem may relate to the tasks within the subject field, not the student's **proclivity**. The student might make a different decision if faced with a mathematical problem instead of a social problem.

The concept of style designates a general approach that an individual can apply equally to every conceivable content. In contrast, an intelligence is a capacity, with its component processes, that is geared to a specific content in the world (such as musical sounds or spatial patterns).

Examples of multiple-intelligence activities will be included in Chapter 6.

Differentiating Instruction

Applying brain/mind research and the theory of multiple intelligences requires an understanding of **differentiation**. When teachers individualize or personalize instruction and provide opportunity for students to choose activities and means to complete work

Teaching Hints: Understanding English Language Learners

1. Sometimes students learning English feel ashamed to make progress because they are afraid their family and friends believe they are rejecting their culture.
2. ELL students are frequently embarrassed if they make a mistake during an oral discussion. Provide reassurance to the student and help the rest of the class understand what was said.
3. Because ELL students are literate in their native language, provide ways for them to share their knowledge and culture.

assignments, then they are applying the concept of differentiation. It is possible to differentiate what is taught (content), how it is taught (process), what students are expected to produce (products), and the (environment) that motivates students.

Content is differentiated by modifying the complexity, depth, and pacing (how quickly students accelerate or are exposed to information) of what is taught. Content can be changed by varying the point of departure and the focus.

Process (instructional means) is differentiated through novelty, by changing the purpose and model of instruction and helping students construct meaning in a variety of ways using varied skill options (critical thinking, problem solving, or research skills).

Products are differentiated by providing choices for students to demonstrate learning (writing stories, performing experiments, or creating in the visual arts).

The environment for learning can be differentiated by providing different resources and tools for students to use and by modifying learning centers and workstations.

Teachers use differentiated instruction to provide equal access to developmentally appropriate learning experiences through multiple pathways to a common goal. Students may work individually or in small groups that can be homogeneous or heterogeneous. Differentiation provides a means to challenge all children at appropriate readiness levels, but it requires that teachers also change their expectations of what students will produce. Part II of this text suggests means for differentiating content, process, product, and environment.

When working with ELL students, it is extremely important to think about ways to differentiate both instruction and expectations. Students who are not proficient in English will often benefit from books translated into their native language and from opportunities to keep a journal and write projects instead of talking about their work. Hands-on activities that involve experimenting and creating are additional means to involve the students in significant experiences.

Differences Related to Learning Style

Learning styles emanate from natural, inborn inclinations. The individual's **learning style** manifests itself through preferred senses and personality characteristics. Learning styles have implications for classroom environments and teaching methods. It is important that teachers recognize the value of a teaching repertoire and vary teaching methods and learning options to accommodate students with different styles of learning.

Dunn and Dunn (1987) studied how children and adults learn using educational, industrial, and psychological research. They isolated 18 elements that encompass learning style. Their investigation indicated that learners are affected by their immediate environment, their own emotionality, sociological preferences,

Peer reading allows students to share and learn from each other.

and physical needs. Elements related to each of these preferred ways of learning include the following:

Environment: sound, light, temperature, physical design

Emotionality: motivational need for structure or flexibility, persistence, responsibility

Physical needs: perceptual strengths (sound, sight, touch), mobility (need to move around, ability to sit still), intake (food, drink), time of day (morning, afternoon)

Sociological preferences: works best alone, works best paired with someone else, works best with peers, works best with adults

REFLECTION VERSUS IMPULSIVITY

Consider the following scenario:

Teacher: Boys and girls, why do you think we have laws? Jerry, what do you think?

Jerry: Uh, uh, I don't know.

Mildred: I know, Miss Henry.

Teacher: All right, Mildred, tell us.

Mildred: Because we would get into fights without them.

Ron: Laws don't stop us from getting into fights.

Teacher: Jerry, would you like to tell us now what you were thinking?

Jerry: Well, I think we have laws to help us settle our disputes.

Teacher: Boys and girls, Mildred said we have laws so that we will not fight; Jerry said we have laws to settle disputes. Are they both right?

Yando and Kagan (1968) studied the psychological dimension of reflection versus impulsivity. During classroom discussion and during the reading process, some children tend to respond quickly or impulsively, and others like to reflect and take their time. In the preceding example, Jerry is a reflective responder, whereas Mildred is impulsive. Teachers can help both Jerry and Mildred improve their thinking processes. For example, the teacher should have stayed with Jerry by giving him more time to answer and even cuing him with another question if necessary. A nonverbal look or hand motion may have slowed Mildred down and helped her think a little more about what she wanted to contribute.

Field Dependency

Learning style has been described in yet another way by cognitive researchers, who identify the extent to which individuals respond to relevant elements or are distracted by irrelevant components in a given event or situation.

An individual who has difficulty with distracting factors is considered a **field-dependent learner**. These individuals prefer interaction with others and opportunities for discussion. They enjoy the social context of situations and respond to verbal praise.

An individual described as a **field-independent learner** prefers lectures and more formal teaching-learning situations. These individuals tend to be more competitive and respond to external rewards, such as grades. In the past, schools have been more oriented to the field-independent learner. Many teachers today believe that competition in the classroom affects learning in a negative way.

How does cooperative learning affect field-dependent and field-independent learners?

SOCIAL FACTORS INFLUENCE LEARNING

Family Influences

The family is the primary agency for the socialization of the child. The family transmits religious, cultural, and occupational identity; ethnicity; social class; family name; and nationality.

The early years of family life are crucial for the child because it is believed that 50% of the child's potential intelligence is developed from birth to age 4 and another 30% from ages 4 to 8 (some researchers say age 10). The experiences the child is exposed to during these early years no doubt affect the child's later proclivities. The richness of the family environment (books, pictures, colors, objects, music, games, furniture, and people), rewards, and punishments may influence temperament, personality, and general behavior.

Whether the child is punished physically, by eye contact, by restraint, or by verbal abuse affects social behavior and the child's ability in later years to accept criticism. Status expectations and ultimately educational aspiration are learned in the family group. Experiences with siblings affect the child's expectations. The middle child has a different experience from the oldest child or the youngest. The only child has a significantly different experience from the child who has five siblings. The mother's responsibilities in the home and community (cleaning, fixing the television, working outside the home, socializing with neighbors, or playing tennis) provide status expectations. The father's work and activities (handling the finances, working with tools, dressing the children, playing bridge, cooking or not cooking) provide a role model. The interactions between a child and every other family member influence future behavior.

The stability of the family affects academic achievement. If there is a lack of role models in the home, the child does not learn the social behaviors and attitudes needed to develop self-discipline, training, maturity, and self-control. As a consequence, experience in school is dull and uninteresting. The child may become anxious and frustrated, or even experience cultural shock. However, children of one-parent families who are not economically depressed do not have the same problems as those whose economic status is low. The problems of a low-income family affect how children learn more than differences in family structure.

Race and Cultural Differences

Some behavioral differences in the classroom can be attributed to racial and cultural orientations. For example, teachers in Fresno, California, report that Hmong parents often do not accept the responsibility to visit school and talk to the teachers about their children. Collaborative relationships with the school are not valued. Many Vietnamese parents value education for their sons, but not for their daughters. In addition, some Vietnamese parents resent it if teachers look them in the eye while talking to them.

A Korean middle school student had hurt feelings when his teacher rested his feet on a chair facing the student during a conference. Some Navajo children are taught that a direct look implies anger. Hispanic and African American children often look downcast when

Table 2.1 Social Development—Elementary Students

Social Development	Classroom Application
Dependent on adult approval	Provide positive feedback; reinforce appropriate work habits; communicate child's needs to parents/guardians
Egocentric	Provide curriculum content that encourages students to recognize other viewpoints; provide opportunities to work in small-group situations
Unrealistic performance expectations	Verify students' understanding of work assignments by having them repeat it in their own words
Little attention to detail	Ask students to "tell us about" their work (story, picture, means to solve problem); encourage reflection
Desires help from others who are older or more mature	Allow buddy/partner work
Emotionally volatile	Encourage communication about problems and conflict situations; meet individually and/or with small groups for discipline problems; role-play conflicts

spoken to because they are taught that it is disrespectful for a child to look directly at an adult. Cultural differences between school and home affect relations between teacher and students and between teachers and parents. Consequently, teachers must carefully plan verbal and nonverbal communication.

Applications for Teaching

Implications for teaching go beyond teacher-parent relationships. Methodology for teaching needs to be *culturally responsive*. In multicultured classrooms, cooperative learning patterns may be more effective than a pedagogy that is teacher-dominated. Demonstrations of the teacher's respect and caring for all students through individual personal interaction will help create a positive and friendly classroom environment. Selecting curriculum that is racially and culturally inclusive and relevant for all students promotes interest and motivation for learning. When selecting curriculum materials, it is important to ensure that the White, Eurocentric voice is not the only voice that students see and hear. Tables 2.1 and 2.2 provide means to promote students' social development.

Table 2.2 Social Development—Middle School Students

Social Development	Classroom Application
Peer relationships very important	Encourage/organize group activities; help loners; interact individually with all students
Tries to avoid parental interaction	Teach about family and cultural customs
Tries (desires) to model adult skills; appreciates realism	Avoid criticism that focuses on physical prowess and creative expressions
Attends to details	Provide positive feedback
Feelings easily hurt; sometimes has difficulty controlling emotions	Speak individually to student about discipline or expectations for performance
Self-centered regarding dress, language, behavior	Within reasonable limits, accept student/peer culture
Embarrassed by expressions of affection	Help students understand parents' need for interaction and affection
Recognizes importance of empathy	Design conflict situations to encourage empathetic expression; role-play negotiation and compromise needs

Research Findings

Observing the social environment of the classroom (1) provides insight in how to match students for productive work groups; (2) suggests ways to integrate loners with cooperative, friendly peers; (3) allows you to utilize natural classroom leaders in work groups; and (4) suggests ways to distribute classroom responsibilities and praise students for their participation, thereby bolstering the self-confidence of students (Pearl, Leung, Acker, Farmer, & Rodkin, 2007).

The Gender Gap

In 1992, the American Association of University Women published a report lamenting how schools shortchange girls by failing to advise them to enroll in advanced mathematics and science courses. On college campuses, girls could not enroll in advanced coursework because they lacked the appropriate prerequisites. In fact, girls were in the minority on most college campuses.

But recently the opposite is true; boys are now in the minority on the college campus and the implications are tragic. The root of the problem goes back to the elementary school, the testing requirements, and the ways in which NCLB are interpreted. Let's look at a typical 9-year-old boy in the fourth grade. Lonnie has a winning smile, sparkling eyes, and dimples in his cheeks. When he comes home from school he becomes a nonstop talker, but in school he never opens his mouth. Lonnie reads haltingly. He rarely completes his work in language arts and mathematics. He manages (frequently) to lose his homework or fails to complete it. Watching Lonnie you note that he appears restless and bored. He has difficulty sitting still. At recess he plays enthusiastically with others, but when he returns to class he is solemn and lacking energy. Lonnie's teacher wonders if he has a learning problem and his parents are considering consulting a psychologist.

Lonnie is a victim of "boyology." In the early elementary grades, boys tend not to have fine motor skills and thus have difficulty controlling their manuscript and cursive writing. Boys do not like to (and cannot) sit still for long periods of time, and Lonnie does not like to contribute to class discussions. He is not as fluent with language as the girls in his class. In middle school, Lonnie will probably have difficulty keeping up with assignments because boys tend to have difficulty organizing their workload.

How Can Lonnie's Teacher Help Him?

Teachers need to recognize that boys and girls are different in their physical and mental abilities in the elementary and middle school years. The school day needs to include time for students to be active and participate in peer experiences. It is counterproductive to exclude physical activities from the curriculum and overload reading and math. By providing some activities in which boys can work with boys, and girls with girls, Lonnie and others like him will participate and improve verbal skills. Finally, teachers need to choose learning experiences that engage students in hands-on activities such as using computers, creating objects, writing stories in group situations, and designing and playing games.

Gender Equity

Streitmatter (1994) distinguishes among three concepts: **gender bias**, **gender equality** of opportunity, and **gender equity**. Sex-role bias has been documented in the curriculum, in materials of instruction, and in the ways teachers treat children. A great deal of research demonstrates differences in the ways boys and girls are socialized (for example, toys, responsibilities, career choice opportunities). Socialization practices often have led to assumptions about the sexes (for example, males are more competitive, females are more emotional). Gender bias occurs when these practices persist in school practices and in the workplace.

Equality of opportunity for the sexes means that everyone starts out on the same rung of the ladder and receives the same treatment. Though all students should be subject to the same curriculum, they should not necessarily receive the same instruction. Too often it has been assumed that girls do not like or excel in math and that boys do poorly in the language arts. Consequently, girls and boys have sometimes been counseled and programmed in discriminative ways that limit their opportunities in school and in the workplace.

The concept of equity in education means that teachers are aware of traditional biases and make an effort to provide opportunities for all students. Karen Adazzio attempts to use both the concept of opportu-

Figure 2.1   Equitable Treatment Checklist

	Always	Sometimes	Never
1. Are all students favored in the use of technology and other resources?			
2. Are all students favored when instructional materials are dispensed?			
3. Are all students encouraged to express themselves when they are angry or unhappy?			
4. Are all students encouraged to ask questions when they cannot respond to discussion questions?			
5. Are all students encouraged to ask questions when they are uncertain or puzzled?			
6. Are assignments made differentially to challenge the capabilities of each student?			
7. Are all students in the classroom encouraged to initiate class discussion?			
8. Are the talents and interests of all students considered?			
9. Are the classroom rules predictable and fair for all? (Are they equitably enforced?)			
10. Are all students treated equitably and talked to individually?			

nity and equity. In advising girls, she insists that they take algebra in the middle school; she asks the algebra teacher to be sure that girls receive many opportunities to discuss algebraic theories and to raise questions. Thus, Adazzio is assuring girls of the opportunity to take advanced mathematics and, because some boys have difficulty expressing themselves, she asks that they receive special treatment. For equal opportunity to prevail for both sexes, it is important that teachers are sensitive to both curriculum and instructional means.

Title IX of the Education Amendments of 1972, administered by the Office for Civil Rights, enforces this amendment. Though many programs are included in the Title IX provisions, it has been particularly active in investigating the fair share of funds for women's athletic scholarship, inequitable pay for female teachers, and discrimination against women as a consequence of pregnancy. Affecting elementary and middle schools may be special father-son or mother-daughter programs. The school is responsible for ensuring that both sexes are provided the same opportunity.

But the downside of Title IX is that many higher-education institutions cannot afford to provide equal facilities for both men and women, and as a result some men's programs in lesser sports are eliminated to make room for women's opportunities. If you are already teaching in a classroom, you may want to think about your students and the ways you encourage them. Using Figure 2.1 as a checklist, consider equity issues such as gender, race, social class, and high and low achievers.

Do single-gender classes or schools ensure an equitable education for all students?

Sex Roles and Socialization

Sociologists have consistently observed differences in the ways families socialize boys and girls. In the past, girls were typically socialized to assume domestic chores and child-bearing responsibilities, and boys were socialized to assume job responsibilities. Schools, churches, scouting groups, YMCA/YWCAs, media, and other societal groups have also reinforced sex roles.

Historically, learning a sex role was considered important to emancipate the boy from a dependent relationship with his family, particularly with his mother. Sex-role identity and role behavior were also considered important for girls. Girls typically had a role model in the home, but boys rarely saw their fathers at work. Thus, the socialization of boys was considered more crucial. However, in the modern family, both parents often work, and many children are raised in single-parent families. In addition, due to employment problems and personal family choice, many fathers are now taking over the child care functions traditionally performed by mothers. The wisdom of sex-role socialization is currently questioned. Changing sex-role patterns and an awareness of the limitations of sex-role socialization have led to an understanding of the harmfulness of what in fact was sex-role stereotyping. A

Research Findings

Salomone (2003) is one of many researchers calling for single-sex school programs. The reasons focus on literacy development. Boys often view reading and writing as "sissy stuff." In many middle-class families, boys are not enrolled in school at age 5, but wait an extra year because their development typically lags behind girls. In a coed school, the boys are expected to do as well as the girls in beginning literacy development. Poor children and at-risk students are frequently retained for a year so that the boys will catch up. Salomone believes that single-sex school programs may alleviate this problem.

stereotype is an oversimplified or generalized opinion about a group of people. Sex stereotyping made the following types of uncritical judgments:

- Women are emotional, flighty, and domestic.
- Men are aggressive, strong, and capable of managing any situation.

Past images of the female characterized her in roles of nurse, teacher, secretary, and social worker, whereas the male had a greater range of occupational and professional choices. The school reinforced these stereotypes through differential treatment of boys and girls. It is important that the school provide a non–sex-stereotyped environment, with opportunities for students to engage in a variety of activities and experiences. Curriculum materials should be closely monitored to ensure that they do not reinforce stereotyped expectations of careers, emotions, activities, and relationships.

Applications for Teaching

You can help parents promote nonsexist education in the home by encouraging a variety of group and independent activities for in-class and homework assignments. These assignments can be focused in all the subject fields and relate to Gardner's eight distinct intelligences that all children possess. Thus, as an example, both boys and girls may be assigned to demonstrate visual and spatial intelligence through drawing and painting, creating diagrams, and spreadsheets. Musical intelligence assignments may include creating stories that use songs and developing presentations that include both audio and video components. Note that assignments such as these serve to integrate subject fields.

Social Class and Children's Experiences

Family and community experiences affect a child's interpretation of his or her world and self-concept. Children are conditioned by interactions with peers, siblings, parents, and important others. Children of poverty (lower-lower class) who wait to be fed beyond the time when they feel hunger have a different feeling about food than children who are fed whenever they ask or who know when their meals will be served.

Children who have responsive adults nearby have a different perspective than those who are cared for by an older sibling or no one at all. Children perceive their physical and social environment quite accurately. They know when adults cannot pay the bills, cannot find a job, or cannot face reality.

The family's economic situation affects the child's daily experiences. The amount and quality of food the child eats, the clothes and personal possessions the child has, supervision and role models, single or married heads of household, physical comforts and social enrichment, recreation and hobbies, participation in organized sports activities, health care, and other social services all influence how a child relates to the world. Children who lack social experiences and opportunities to explore and wonder do not accumulate stories to tell about self and others, and are not able to draw on experiences for motivation and school tasks.

The impoverished child's experience may include pessimism and hopelessness as a consequence of observing and listening to the adults in the home. Children learn despair from parents who do not want to transmit optimism or hope that the future will be bet-

Research Findings

Lapkoff and Li (2007) cite five trends affecting schools: (1) enrollment fluctuations, (2) immigration and diversity, (3) family characteristics and stability, (4) an aging population, and (5) obesity.

ter than the present. They may do this to prepare their children for the hard reality of existence.

Changing Demographics

Not only do schools have to deal with enrollment increases, but also the rapid diversification of the school population necessitates that teachers learn new competencies to be successful. It is quite common for teachers to have to deal with half a dozen different language and cultural backgrounds in the classroom. In the 1960s and 1970s, many teachers tried to learn a new language to help them teach in the classroom, but in recent times there are so many different languages and cultures confronting teachers that it is impossible to be educated in all of them.

What Can Teachers Do?

According to Howard (2007), teachers need to reexamine everything they do! Working collaboratively with colleagues, teachers need to recognize that there are differences in cultural backgrounds and the ways in which children are raised. These differences must be openly discussed in a safe, respectful environment. Relationships with parents need to be developed. Instructional strategies need to be examined and probably changed so that students can exercise greater freedom in helping to choose what is studied and how it is to be studied. Howard recommends culturally responsive teaching that includes:

- caring relationships with students
- attention to all students' cultural life experiences
- instructional strategies that appeal to diverse learning needs
- respect for the intellectual growth of all students
- high expectations for all students (p. 20).

Bullying

Bullies resort to three types of physical and emotional behavior: intimidation, domination, and arrogance. Classroom and school ground behaviors may include bumping and pushing others, gesturing, fighting, and making nasty comments to upset classmates. The bully wants to demonstrate his or her power over others and engages in these behaviors to show off and incite riot.

The bully seeks attention and recognition and uses physical and prejudicial means to accomplish his or her purposes. The bully may be a loner or an angry individ-

Teaching Hints: What Can Teachers Do?

1. The bully who seeks attention may respond to an assigned responsibility in the classroom or school environment to satisfy this need. Or perhaps the bully could help mentor another student, thereby feeling recognized and providing a genuine service.
2. The bully who is a loner should be helped to join other classmates in group activities, but it will be important to conference with both the student who needs help and the group to be joined.
3. The angry bully may need professional assistance from a school counselor or psychologist. It is important that you share your concerns with the child's parents. The professional can help guide the student to begin a self-help program.
4. If there are several bullies in the classroom, be sure that you separate them so that they are not seated together. Next, set up an after-school conference for the group. Invite another teacher or a principal to witness the conference. Plan a series of questions to ask the students and insist on their responses. The questions should be focused on learning the purposes and causes of the bullies' behaviors. Be sure that the students understand that their behaviors hurt other students, they disobey school rules and policies, and they are gaining absolutely nothing.
5. When working with bullies try to help them gain empathy for others. Ask the students, "Suppose you had to attend a Japanese language school and none of the other students would listen when you spoke. How would you feel?"

ual who may seek out others to do his or her bidding. Bullies like to perform in unsupervised places on the school grounds. Seldom will the bully bother others in the classroom when the teacher is watching.

Signs of Bullying

Victims of bullying often want to stay home from school. They will exhibit signs of moodiness, depression, sometimes indifference, shyness, and perhaps irritability. Victims can be helped by reminding them of their personal rights. Providing class time to role play what to do when subjected to bullying is another means to assist all students.

The Sea of Pink

Two senior boys at Central Kings Rural High School in Nova Scotia, Canada, demonstrated the power of fighting back and standing up for personal rights. On the first day of school, a freshman boy came to school wearing a pink polo shirt. A bullying group of 6 to 10 older students made fun of him and called him a homophobic. The two seniors overheard the teasing and decided to do something about it. They called the local discount store and purchased pink shirts to wear to school. Also, they e-mailed their friends and asked them to wear something pink to school. They brought a pink basketball and headbands of pink to school. The student body looked like a "sea of pink."

The principal was proud of the solidarity of the student body and the fact that no one would name the bullied young student. The school received a letter of commendation from the Canadian premier and the two senior boys are writing a program to inform elementary students concerning the damages caused by bullying.

MOTIVATION AND ITS EFFECT ON LEARNING

When teachers talk about student motivation, they are usually referring to the way students approach learning tasks and how intently they perform each task. Other ways to describe student motivation include whether the student demonstrates interest and attentiveness in learning tasks and the goals the student sets for him- or herself.

Theories of Motivation

Several theories of motivation influence the way teachers teach. These theories include the *behavioral view, cognitive perspective, personality theory,* and *humanistic perspective.* For many years, behavioral psychologists directed teachers to stimulate appropriate behavior through a system of classroom rewards. This is considered the use of external stimuli to reinforce behavior.

An opposing view of motivation (the cognitive perspective) holds that students achieve satisfaction from learning and from appropriate behavior. This perspective emphasizes intrinsic forces as sources of motivation. The concept of constructivism emanates from cognitive psychology.

Personality theories of motivation suggest that the need for achievement varies among people, perhaps depending on how badly the individual fears failure.

Locus of Control

The social learning theory of Rotter (1966) contributes to the perspective of individual personality differences. Some individuals blame others if they fail an examination, forget their homework, or are late to school. These individuals have what psychologists call an *external locus of control.* Other individuals believe that if they fail an examination, it is their own fault; if they are successful in an endeavor, they credit themselves with working to be successful. These individuals have an *internal locus of control.*

Individuals with an internal **locus of control** view themselves as having control over their environment and fate. They perceive a relationship between personal behavior and consequences. The individual with an external locus of control is just the opposite. This individual believes that he or she has no control over consequences and views others as responsible for and controlling events and circumstances.

Some research indicates that locus of control is influenced by parental behavior. Parents who are continually critical of their children may foster children with an external locus of control, whereas parents who are accepting and approving may develop the internal factor in locus of control. However, teachers also influence students' behavior and locus of control through instructional methods and discipline.

A *humanistic* interpretation explains behavior as motivated by individual needs. For example, Maslow classifies human needs as either deficiency or growth needs. Deficiency needs are dependent on others; growth needs are dependent on the self. Deficiency needs must be satisfied before the individual can enhance personal growth. Visualize a triangle: Maslow describes the top of the triangle as **self-actualization.** After the individual has satisfied all other needs, he or she is motivated to self-actualize.

Another theory concerning motivation focuses on the student's thought processes (a cognitive approach). The essence of this explanation of motivation is that the individual is affected by past experiences with success and failure.

Success and Failure

Weiner and colleagues (1974) developed an **attribution** model of achievement motivation. They identified four causal attributes that affect the individual's perceived reasons for success and failure. They theorized that the individual believes in personal success or failure, and predicts future success or failure, as a consequence of four elements: ability, effort, task difficulty, and luck.

Ability and effort are *internal elements* that the individual can control. Task difficulty and luck are beyond the control of the individual; thus, they are external elements. In addition, ability and task difficulty are stable or invariant dimensions, whereas luck and effort are elements of change and therefore unstable. Using the Weiner model, a student who successfully performs a science experiment could explain the achievement by saying either it was the result of personal ability or it was the result of luck. If the student believes it was ability, his or her confidence will increase; but if the student calls it luck, then success will be less meaningful and the student probably will not gain self-confidence that could enhance future efforts. The self-confident, success-oriented individual believes that future success is positively related to personal effort and ability.

The Goals of Mastery and Performance

In reviewing the research on achievement motivation, Ames (1992) viewed motivation through a cognitive lens and found that positive and negative patterns of response may be elicited by different reasons for task engagement. For example, individuals who view a task as an opportunity to learn new skills, master a skill, or gain a competence based on internalized standards will be more involved and participate for personal satisfaction. These individuals believe that their personal effort will bring them mastery (success) and satisfaction. These individuals develop a pattern of positive achievement motivation. They are also more likely to be risk takers. It is important here to differentiate between mastery learning and a mastery goal. A mastery goal orientation emphasizes learning as a process of self-improvement; the individual is not in competition with others. Mastery learning is a behavioral orientation that uses principles of operant conditioning.

Individuals with a negative achievement motivation pattern focus on ability to perform as compared to others. Interpersonal competition and normative standards guide their behavior; consequently, these individuals are concerned with protecting their self-worth or ego involvement. Because these students are concerned with avoiding failure, risk-taking activities are unlikely.

Ames described these two goal orientations as mastery and performance. Ames ties the **mastery or learning goal** orientation to **intrinsic motivation** and task-related cognitive behavior, such as problem solving. But when individuals are guided by extrinsic rewards, Ames believes their efforts are not focused on the activity itself but are guided by concerns related to the judgments of others.

Student motivation for learning is influenced by a variety of classroom factors, including interaction patterns, rewards, instructional strategies, and even the classroom environment. Researchers have determined that two different types of perception affect students' motivation for performing and completing task assignments. For some students, classroom tasks are perceived as a means to improve, participate, and progress. These students have a mastery goal orientation; they view learning as satisfying, fun, and challenging. They recognize that errors are part of learning and, in fact, a means to learn. They enjoy the process of learning and know that working hard not only provides satisfaction but ensures success.

Another perception of learning has been called a **performance goal** orientation. Students who perceive goals as performance tasks tend to be concerned with how well they perform in comparison with others. As a consequence, they are often anxious about their assignments, overly concerned with grades, and primarily concerned with completing tasks instead of enjoying the process of learning.

Ames concluded that a mastery goal orientation motivates effort and helps students achieve success and personal satisfaction; the students are intrinsically motivated. But with a performance goal orientation, students look for **extrinsic motivation** and are concerned about being judged.

The Power of Effort

Experiments with ways to assist students to learn have focused on memory aids, metacognitive techniques, and a variety of systems to develop logical thinking. Many of these techniques evoked immediate success, but they were not retained by students as a habitual means to help them learn over time.

Cognitive researchers began new studies using strategies that challenged students to create their own means of solving problems, explaining their findings, and making connections to personal experiences and prior knowledge. These studies treated students as intellectual beings, not robots. The researchers found that when students were given demanding curriculum and expected to do well, they learned quickly and developed their own habits for learning (Resnick, 1999). Using this research, Resnick defined intelligence as follows:

> Intelligence is the habit of persistently trying to understand things and make them function better. Intelligence is working to figure things out, varying strategies until a workable solution is found. Intelligence is knowing what one does (and doesn't) know, seeking information and organizing that information so that it makes sense and can be remembered. In short, one's intelligence is the sum of one's *habits of mind* (p. 39).

This concept of intelligence means that the mind can develop and grow and that, through effort, skills expand and intelligence develops incrementally. Incremental thinkers gain confidence about their efforts because they recognize their own errors and treat them as learning devices. Errors and challenges are friends. The challenge for teachers is to provide a thinking curriculum and help students recognize that high effort yields intelligence. The effort expended determines how much is learned and sustained.

Constructivism: Dewey's Pedagogical Theories

The constructivist theory of learning can be traced to Dewey, an American philosopher and educator; Piaget; and Vygotsky. Constructivism is rooted in both a social and cognitive perspective of learning. Dewey contributed the significance of reflective thinking and social interaction; Piaget's concepts of developmental assimilation and accommodation helped explain the process of thinking; and Vygotsky's understanding, similar to Dewey's, focused on the individual's cultural experience and social interaction.

According to Dewey (1859–1952), we learn from our experiences. To facilitate learning, the teacher needs to create an environment that motivates interest and curiosity. The teacher nurtures curiosity by encouraging students to ask questions, thereby promoting students' responsibility for structuring their own problem solving. This in turn leads to experimentation and the testing of new ideas that are linked to prior knowledge and experience.

Dewey's method of education was to cultivate the active side of the child before the passive and to observe and use the student's interests. The student's natural interest was not to be repressed or simply humored. The teacher's task was to penetrate the surface to detect genuine interest and to select worthwhile experiences and appropriate subject matter.

Piaget's concept of the learning process considers that the individual gathers information or data through experiences and takes into account prior knowledge. A state of disequilibrium forces the individual to assimilate and accommodate the new knowledge, which leads to changes in thinking, beliefs, and ways of behaving.

Vygotsky views knowledge construction as dependent on language and social processes. The learner depends on others for sociocultural experience. Vygotsky's concept of the zone of proximal development is related to the individual's interaction with peers and adults. Learning with others is more advantageous than independent exploration; the individual needs social interaction for learning. Examples of constructivism and inquiry models can be found in Chapter 5.

MOTIVATION AND TEACHER EXPECTATIONS

Since Rosenthal and Jacobson's (1968) study of how **teacher expectations** can affect students' motivation and academic growth, educators have been aware that teacher-student interactions are critical to the learning process. If some students are consistently encouraged over time to pursue thinking tasks while others are not, in time students' achievement will closely resemble the teacher's expectations. For this reason, it is recognized that teachers should not behave differentially toward students in their classrooms.

As discussed earlier in this chapter, the teacher's reaction to Mildred, the impulsive responder, and to Jerry, the reflective responder, was an example of how teachers can unconsciously reinforce inappropriate behavior. In responding to the need for differentiation of content, process, product, and environment, teachers must be sure that they are equitable in setting appropriate goals and standards for all students. All students need to be encouraged to achieve to the best of their ability. (Refer again to Figure 2.1, which is a checklist that offers examples of what teachers can do to treat students equitably.)

Individual Differences

There is a wide range of individual differences in every classroom. These differences may be a consequence of developmental patterns; cognitive, affective, and psychomotor differences; socialization experiences; and personality attributes. Teachers need to be sensitive to differences without being overwhelmed by them. Teachers should be able to recognize when students have special needs that require referral to other education consultants (such as a psychologist, speech therapist, or medical doctor). Often students' special problems can be easily identified through careful observation and private conversation with the student. The needs of children with physical disabilities must be met through sensitive academic planning, understanding, and acceptance. Identifying the needs of other exceptional children, including the gifted and talented, is an important professional task.

SUMMARY

Piaget, Vygotsky, Kohlberg, and Maslow's developmental patterns were presented to focus on why teachers need to match instruction to students' conceptual levels. Gardner's multiple intelligences challenge teachers to differentiate instruction using the eight different intelligences that affect human behavior. Students' responses to learning situations differ because of natural inclinations, learning styles, and the social factors that influence their learning, including economic conditions, cultural orientation, and socialization practices. Motivation also affects students' learning; causal attributes discussed included ability, effort, task difficulty, and luck. Also discussed in the chapter are characteristics of bullies, what teachers can do, and the signs of bullying.

PORTFOLIO ACTIVITY

Select a teaching lesson that demonstrates how you considered students' individual differences. In your discussion of the lesson, identify the characteristics of your learning group and focus on the ways you differentiated instruction. Consider learning styles and multiple intelligences.

 DISCUSSION QUESTIONS AND APPLICATION EXERCISES

1. View several TV commercials. Using the information related to social class differences, decide:
   * Which social group is the target audience?
   * Why was this group chosen?
   * What underlying value assumptions are made about the target group?
2. Observe one or more students you consider successful and other students you consider unsuccessful. In what ways are their responses and attitudes different? Report on the following factors:
   * Do they work independently and appear involved in their tasks?
   * Do they ask the teacher questions?
   * Do they appear concerned about others?
3. Identify appropriate experiences for kinesthetic, visual, and auditory learners who happen to be English language learners.
4. Plan a learning experience for preoperational students to help them understand viewpoints other than their own.
5. Explain why you should or should not have the same instructional expectations for all students.
6. Study physical education activities in an elementary and middle school. Do the activities reinforce sex-role differences?
7. Which of the following goals for multicultural education would you choose for implementation? Explain how you would go about it.
   * Knowledge of diverse cultures and languages
   * Knowledge about dialects in the United States
   * Knowledge of African-American contributions to America
   * Options for minority groups
   * The impact of racism
8. Suggest ways teachers could help impulsive students become more reflective and help performance-oriented students become mastery goal–oriented.
9. Observe another classroom teacher. Describe how the teacher:
   * encourages students
   * differentiates teaching and learning
   * disciplines in the classroom
   Assess student motivation in this classroom.
10. Compare the differentiation of instruction to cooking the family dinner when family members have different likes, dislikes, and needs.

READER RESEARCH

Is there an academic gender gap between girls and boys at your school? Using age-related data, study discipline referrals, suspension, specific subject fields, test scores and teachers' opinion. Compare your findings with classmates.

 TECHNOLOGY APPLICATIONS

Use the Internet to develop a constructivist lesson designed to be used by small groups of students working together at the computer. Consider how many subject fields can be integrated into the lesson. Puzzling together helps students clarify, define, and problem-solve.

PART II

Delivery of Instruction: How Teachers Teach

Research that compares effective teachers and struggling teachers indicates that the effective teachers are well prepared with methodology for teaching. Knowing *how* to manage the classroom and selecting appropriate strategies for instruction significantly improve teaching performance. Chapters 3 through 7 are organized to help you understand how teachers manage their classrooms, plan for teaching, and develop a repertoire of teaching techniques.

- Chapter 3 begins with a discussion of classroom management and how it affects planning and organizing for teaching. The chapter focuses on the planning tasks that teachers perform in preparation for the first day of school.
- Chapter 4 examines expository and discussion teaching strategies, research on questioning, and what students' questions mean. The direct instruction model of teaching, cooperative learning, the advance organizer model of teaching, and the comprehension model are featured in this chapter.
- Chapter 5 gives examples of inquiry, constructivist teaching, and problem-solving techniques, and fea-

tures several models of teaching, including the group investigation model and backward problem solving. In addition, this chapter provides a classroom example of students performing research and case study methods for the classroom.
- Chapter 6 explains curriculum development concepts and how to develop a teaching unit. Suggestions and examples for theme teaching and the integration of subject fields are included.
- Chapter 7 completes Part II by focusing on strategies for performance assessment, the use of rubrics, evaluation, and communication of learning progress. The importance of assessment as a critical tool for informing teaching and learning is emphasized.

Before you begin Part II of the text, a general understanding of instructional methods and the author's perspective will facilitate your reading. This introduction to Part II is designed as an advance organizer to prepare you for what is to come.

If you were asked to think about your favorite (and best) teacher, what would you remember? Do you recall a project that you participated in while under the direction of that favorite teacher? Is it the teacher's professional competencies that you remember? Are you thinking about the teacher's personal characteristics? The author asked a group of experienced teachers these questions and was surprised by the number of responses that dealt with the personal dimension. Although we know a great deal about the teaching process and professional competencies, there is obviously little agreement about what is "good teaching." Good teaching is so subjective that it appears to depend on who is doing the describing and who is doing the teaching.

However, we do know that most experienced, "expert" teachers use a variety of teaching methods. They do not rely on a single, multipurpose teaching strategy. Even though we cannot predict with certainty what will always work, we do know that certain methods of teaching, grouping, and classroom environments are associated with specific learning outcomes. Before we examine specific instructional techniques, let us review some of the human and situational variables that affect instruction.

DEFINING INSTRUCTION

Instruction is defined as the activity that occurs in the classroom setting, encompassing the resources or materials used and teacher and student variables. The human variables include the following:

- Student characteristics: age, sex, developmental level, social class, language, academic and achievement motivation, intellectual development, cognitive style, and self-concept
- Teacher characteristics: teaching style, age, sex, social class background, preparatory experiences, warmth, enthusiasm, openness, and management skills

Organizational and content variables also need to be considered for instructional planning. These variables include the following:

- Organizational considerations: size of class, space in classroom, time, class composition
- Content considerations: subject grade level, objectives, sequence, resources, materials

Both human and situational variables affect instruction. The teacher who is cognizant of such variables will use them positively as a guide to planning and implementing instruction. Consider these examples:

- A first-grade teacher who wants to have block work must consider available floor space (which may necessitate moving tables and chairs), the equipment (blocks and accessories), and specific lesson objectives.
- One P.M. on Friday afternoon before Christmas vacation may be a very poor time to have a science experiment. Probably a structured lesson would fit students and teacher better at that particular time.

In other words, the teacher must use common sense in choosing a teaching method. If the amount of time required for a given lesson is not available or other context variables are wrong, then the teacher must make an alternate decision. Human and situational variables should be considered for instructional decisions.

ASSUMPTIONS ABOUT TEACHING

This part of the text makes three basic assumptions about teaching. The first assumption addresses the wide spectrum of instructional approaches:

1. *A variety of approaches to instruction is appropriate.* If an open-ended science experiment is inappropriate on a Friday afternoon before vacation, there is probably another strategy that will be quite effective.

   This text classifies instructional approaches as either expository or inquiry–problem solving. To accomplish expository goals, teachers must typically use lecture and direct instruction with appropriate questioning techniques. The advance organizer teaching model is also considered an expository teaching approach.

   To accomplish inquiry and problem-solving goals, teachers most typically use teaching models in which students must be involved in constructing meaning. These approaches require both inductive and deductive thinking and may involve group investigation, concept attainment, role-playing, and gaming. This leads us to a second assumption about teaching:

2. *The method of instruction affects the learning process.* This means that, although several approaches may be appropriate, each will contribute something quite different to students' learning. The open-ended science experiment contributes toward self-development, problem-solving skills, social participation (if it is a group project), and understanding of science concepts. Reading out of a sci-

ence textbook fosters science concepts, but does not foster discovery learning or affect social participation. The important thing to remember is that students will not become reflective problem solvers without the opportunity to practice problem-solving skills.

When instructional approaches, teaching strategies, or models of teaching are discussed in this text, it is likely that the conditions of the classroom will be discussed as well. To describe classroom conditions or climate, instructional specialists typically use words such as *environment, milieu,* and *structure* of the classroom. This refers to how the teacher controls the classroom, the teacher's behavior toward students, and whether students' behaviors are encouraged or discouraged.

Perhaps it may surprise you, but different teaching strategies require distinct teacher behaviors. Think about what you do during a lecture. Now think about the expectations of the person delivering the lecture. During the lecture, the classroom or hall is quiet, attention is focused on the teacher, and interaction is teacher controlled, usually from teacher to student to teacher. Table II.1 exhibits the relationship between teacher behavior and the conditions in the classroom.

3. *Students react differentially to the instructional process.* The third assumption is based on the interaction of learning environment and teacher behavior. Some students learn more effectively with some approaches than with others. The student who is

Table II.2   Interplay of Strategy Choice and Learning Environment

Strategy	Learning Environment
Lecture, film, direct instruction	Controlled environment, high structure
Guided discussions, questioning, analysis	Controlled environment, moderate to high structure
Role-playing, simulations, gaming, dramatizations	Open environment, moderate structure
Discovery, problem solving, group investigations	Open environment, low structure

visually oriented does not appreciate the teacher who reads test questions orally to the class. This same student tires listening to a lecture. A student's characteristics affect what is learned. Table II.2 depicts the relationship between the choice of teaching strategy and the way the classroom is controlled.

STUDENT BEHAVIOR DURING EXPOSITION AND INQUIRY: PROBLEM-SOLVING STRATEGIES

Visualize a balance scale like the one shown in Figure II.1. Learning experiences that accomplish input goals are on one side of the scale. These experiences are planned so that students consume information and learn specific skills. Experiences may include a museum

Table II.1   Interaction of Learning Environment and Teacher Behavior

Environment	Teacher Behavior
Controlled environment, high structure	Teacher controls the dialogue; teacher sets the stage and controls student responses. Limited instructional materials are needed.
Controlled environment, moderate to high structure	Teacher initiates discussions and programs questions to elicit desired responses; teacher controls student interaction to fit discussion. Some supportive instructional materials are needed.
Open environment, moderate structure	Teacher initiates problem or conflict situation; teacher often guides the problem resolution as it moves from stage to stage. A great deal of student interaction is encouraged; students are expected to accept responsibility for problem solving. A variety of instructional materials are needed.
Open environment, low structure	Teacher facilitates democratic processes; students define problems and initiate methods for solving them. Teacher provides many resources and encourages students to use resources outside the classroom.

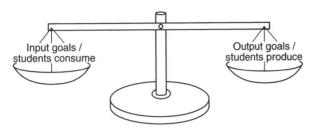

Figure II.1   Balancing Input Goals and Output Goals

visit, a lecture, films and slides, textbooks, television, CDs and DVDs, workbooks, an exhibit, and demonstrations. Student behavior during input includes observation, listening, reading, responding, questioning, and note taking. Students may appear to be passive during input experiences, but in fact, they are using their senses to collect information.

On the other side of the balance scale are learning experiences that accomplish output goals. These experiences are planned so that students produce knowledge. Output strategies require the student to perform in some way. Experiences are extremely diverse and may include some of the following:

- Reports (oral and written)
- Projects, including use of multimedia
- Map making
- Dramatics, performance, singing
- Role-playing, simulations, gaming
- Experiments
- Discussions, debates
- Construction artwork, hands-on activities
- Interviewing
- Committee work

Student behaviors during output experiences may be independent, in pairs, or in groups, and can include some of the following:

- Research skill activity, problem solving, use of the Internet
- Exploration, experimentation
- Speaking, writing, acting out
- Using manipulatives, building
- Questioning, planning, creating
- Valuing, decision making

When students are required to produce something, they process information to develop new meanings. There is a reciprocal relationship between input and output teaching strategies. Think about the teacher's objectives in assigning tasks, and compare the tasks and objectives in Figure II.2

Output strategies depend on prior input; thus, the teacher balances teaching approaches to maximize learning. Portfolio activities at the end of each chapter in Part II will emphasize the use of a variety of teaching methods.

Decide whether the teacher wants the student to consume or produce when tasks are prefaced with the following objectives:

Recite _____   Summarize _____

Imagine _____   Label _____

Measure _____   Contrast _____

Hypothesize _____   Recall _____

Comments: Probably the teacher wants students to consume information or ideas when the following objectives are written: *recite, label, recall, measure*. For students to produce, objectives would probably begin with the following words: *imagine, hypothesize, summarize, contrast*.

Figure II.2   Contrast the Teacher's Objectives

CHAPTER 3

Classroom Management
Planning and Guiding
Learning Experiences

This chapter focuses on two major aspects of successful teaching: classroom management and planning instruction. You will learn about the key components of classroom management, look at examples of each, and compare and contrast classroom management and discipline. Because the use of classroom groups is so important during teaching, both large-group and small-group instruction (the hows, whys, and potential traps) are discussed in depth. The chapter provides both scheduling and lesson plan examples, and concludes with a review of the teacher's daily tasks.

Advance Organizer

The following questions are intended to guide your reading and understanding of the content of this chapter.

1. Can you define classroom management by identifying the key components?
2. How does each of the components of classroom management affect teacher and student success?
3. Can you explain why with-it-ness, overlapping, transition smoothness, and the ripple effect are so important to classroom management?
4. How does recognizing the formal and informal structure of a classroom and school environment inform you about teacher and students' behavior?
5. What are the advantages and disadvantages of small-group and large-group instruction?
6. Why is it important to develop classroom activities that develop a sense of belonging and foster democratic behaviors?
7. Why should teachers anticipate potential problems before using small-group and large-group instruction? What are some of those potential problems and how can you avoid them?
8. Why is it important to allow time for both content and group work evaluation?
9. Why should teachers concern themselves with learning about their school community?
10. Preparing for the first day of school helps to avoid first-day jitters and mishaps. In a subject field or grade level of choice, what should you prepare for the first day of school?
11. Using the headings *management* and *instruction,* what are the daily tasks of the teacher?
12. What makes homework a classroom management problem?

INTASC   **INTASC Standards**

Classroom management requires that teachers understand the students they work with, can create an appropriate classroom environment, plan appropriate instruction, and communicate clearly with the students they teach. Standards 2, 3, and 5–7 emphasize these elements of performance.

Professional Lexicon

academic feedback The process of detecting and responding to students' needs for meaning related to content and task assignments.

assessment Appraisal of what students know and do not know using established procedures.

classroom management Using the key components that affect success in the classroom.

discipline The process of moderating student behavior with others and motivating students to be personally responsible for their own behavior.

formal structure The pattern of actions and human relationships that are expected and can be predicted to exist.

formative evaluation Measurement of achievement during instruction to facilitate future planning.

informal structure Those behaviors that arise as a result of the formal structure.

integration of instruction Using the teachable moment to teach skills as needed; utilizing knowledge and skills from one subject field to reinforce or extend instruction in another subject field.

interdisciplinary instruction Linking subject fields through the use of similar concepts.

monitoring Observing and responding to behavioral and instructional problems.

overlapping Attending to more than one event in the classroom simultaneously.

ripple effect An outbreak of contagious misbehavior often caused by the teacher through public discipline that embarrasses other students.

summative evaluation Measurement of student achievement (performance) at the end of a learning experience or an instructional unit.

task engagement The degree of involvement the student demonstrates while performing a task.

transition smoothness The ability of the teacher to change learning experiences and/or subject fields without causing undue lags of time (and misbehavior).

with-it-ness A teacher's ability to demonstrate to students his or her awareness of and alertness to student behavior and task engagement.

The bus strike caused Harrison to be late for class. He entered the classroom 20 minutes late and saw that his classmates were working in small groups. He was embarrassed and angry. One of his friends called to him; the teacher seemed to be ignoring him. He waved at his friend, dragged his book bag across the floor, and went to talk to his buddy. Harrison's voice carried across the room. His friend was laughing and joking with him. Soon the whole class was trying to listen to them and the teacher was frustrated. She yelled at the class to return to work and ordered Harrison to go sit at his desk.

CLASSROOM MANAGEMENT

Classroom management is the linchpin that makes teaching and learning achievable. In this book **classroom management** is defined using the key components that affect success in the classroom (Lemlech, 1999, p. 3):

> Classroom management is the orchestration of classroom life: planning curriculum, organizing procedures and resources, arranging the environment to maximize efficiency, monitoring student progress, anticipating potential problems.

The key components of classroom management are *planning, organizing, arranging, monitoring,* and *anticipating.* You will learn more about the importance of each of these components in the following sections. Teachers who are successful classroom managers have mastered techniques for planning activities and maintaining high levels of student involvement in those activities, enriching the classroom environment, anticipating organizational and behavioral problems, and monitoring students' progress.

Planning Instructional Activities

Significant insight about classroom management originated with the work of Jacob Kounin (1970). Kounin began his study of classroom management by observing kindergarten children. Because kindergarten children have not been exposed to school and teacher socialization, he learned a great deal about how to keep them involved with classroom activities. Kounin defined successful classroom management as "producing a high rate of work involvement and a low rate of deviancy in academic settings" (p. 63). Kounin studied teacher behaviors that produced high and low work involvement of students. He noted the importance of motivation before teachers change activities and the need for variety and challenge in the tasks demanded of students.

Studies of classroom management among experienced teachers and student teachers reveal that certain classroom conditions, teacher planning before instruction, and teacher behaviors result in a smooth working classroom and high involvement of students. Let's look at a classroom episode to identify some of these significant elements.

GREG THOMAS'S CLASSROOM

It was literature time, and Greg Thomas's students were going to read historical novels. Thomas selected five novels that depict the life and times of pioneers as they traveled westward. Thomas began the lesson by asking the students, "Suppose we are pioneers living in the Midwest during the 1840s. How would you feel if you were told that tomorrow your family would begin an adventure that would take you across the country?"

By evoking student interest and discussion, Thomas motivated the students to read about the lives of early pioneers. Next he gave the students a short synopsis of several novels and urged them to select a book to read. Thomas wrote the names of the books on the chalkboard and each student signed his or her name underneath the selected book. The choice of novel determined each student's literary group.

Before the students joined their groups, Thomas told the students they would have to decide how their group would communicate their pioneer story with the rest of the class. He displayed a chart with the possible choices: skits, simulation games, cartoon strips, dioramas, letters from pioneers to friends.

Thomas told the students they would have all week to read and create during their language arts time. Monitors distributed the books and Thomas gave each group a designated place to work; the students formed small groups to begin their reading and group discussions. Thomas circulated, listening and helping when students needed vocabulary or clarification of concepts.

Analysis of the Teaching Episode

Steps in Planning

1. Selection of historical novels
2. Questions to motivate interest
3. Time for student reaction and discussion
4. Synopsis of novels to stimulate interest
5. Names of novels written on the chalkboard
6. Chart of possible student activities
7. Selection of monitors to distribute books
8. Designation of places for groups to work

---

*See if you can identify each of these steps
in Thomas's lesson.*

These activities represent the teacher's prethinking (antecedent planning) needed to move the lesson along. Some of these same activities could be listed for other classroom management components. Had Thomas not performed these planning tasks, there would be time lags while he gathered the novels, framed a motivating question, decided on how to group students, and distributed the books.

When time lags while a teacher gets organized or thinks out learning activities, deviant student behavior is more likely to occur (Kounin & Doyle, 1975). Classrooms are virulent settings! When Tom talks and gestures to Dan, Mary decides she, too, can engage in play, and before long, the teacher has a whole class to bring to order.

---

*If misbehavior is contagious, consider appropriate
behavior. Can it be contagious in a classroom, too?*

ORGANIZING PROCEDURES

Experienced teachers typically consider the first three weeks of the school year the most important. During this time, elementary teachers socialize their students to conform to the rules and procedures of the classroom, and the teachers develop specific procedures and communicate them to the children. Examples of such procedures are how to obtain assistance, how to line up at the door, how to work in a group, options for free time, correcting homework, standards for seatwork, and where to put seatwork. These procedures are taught just as if they were part of the content.

Researchers who have studied classroom management also note that effective teachers are precise and clear in their directions to students; they communicate well, listen intently, and express feelings to students. Perhaps the most striking difference between effective and ineffective classroom managers is the knack for anticipating potential problems. The effective teacher anticipates resource and material needs, physical space needs, individual and group needs, noise constraints, traffic flow problems, and affective and cognitive student reactions. By anticipating these possible problems, the effective teacher can then plan to avoid pitfalls.

Another characteristic of effective managers is the ability to set clear expectations for behavior, and standards for students' academic work. By reviewing Greg Thomas's literature lesson, we can identify some of his organizing tasks.

Steps in Organizing the Lesson

1. Selecting and gathering historical novels appropriate for his class
2. Deciding how he would distribute the novels
3. Deciding on reading the novels in small groups and the means for organizing the students into groups
4. Planning the work space
5. Making the chart of activities; deciding that students would select their activity in the small group

Monitoring Students' Progress and Behavior

Kounin (1970) described a number of teacher behaviors related to managerial success. Experienced teachers are able to communicate to students that, as teachers, they are aware of what is going on. Sometimes they do this with a special look or a raised eyebrow, or by standing up, or by touching or walking over to a student. In these ways the teacher conveys the message to desist—or else! Kounin called this awareness behavior **with-it-ness**.

Did Harrison's teacher demonstrate with-it-ness in the chapter-opening vignette? What should she have done?

Another behavior that successful teachers manage is paying attention to more than one event at a time, or what Kounin calls **overlapping**. For instance, the teacher may be working with a small reading group; someone walks into the room with a message just as a child raises his hand at his seat for assistance. The teacher leaves the reading group very quietly without disturbing the students, examines the message, whispers a response, helps the child having difficulty, and continues directing the reading lesson without skipping a beat! (What should Harrison's teacher have done that would have demonstrated ability to attend to more than one event?)

Still another characteristic related to managerial success is knowing when an activity needs to be changed and managing the change so smoothly, disregarding any irrelevancies, that students continue in the same manner without the lesson's losing momentum. Kounin called this **transition smoothness**. Arlin (1979) also studied transitions between activities and found that off-task behaviors were reduced if teachers monitored what was happening in the classroom and provided clear directions so that the transition was structured.

Kounin (1970) concluded that a number of consequences related to a teacher's behavior are often not anticipated. When a teacher disciplines a child in front of other children, there is a **ripple effect**. The ripple effect is influenced by the type of desist the teacher uses. An angry response produces emotional conflict—sometimes embarrassment—and does not produce conformity by other members of the class. Kounin's study also found that when teachers clarified their meanings by providing information (feedback) to the deviant child along with the correction, the result was more conformity from other children. Firmness, the "I mean it" factor, also produced more conformity than nonconformity in witnesses.

It is interesting to note that in his research with kindergarten children, Kounin (1970) discovered that by increasing repetition of an activity, the activity changed from being liked to being disliked, and **task engagement** diminished. He concluded that variety and challenge, initiating and maintaining movement, smoothness, and momentum were very important in classrooms.

Studies of effective and less effective teachers have determined that successful teachers maximize their teaching time with students by monitoring individual effort and providing immediate feedback information to the students. These successful teachers appear to accept personal responsibility for their students' achievement.

Thomas's classroom episode does not give us the student dialogue, so we do not know about the teacher-student and student-student interaction, but we do know that Thomas monitored his students' small-group work and engaged in anticipatory thinking about student behavior.

Anticipatory Thinking in the Classroom

- Thomas told students to plan with their group how they would communicate their story to the rest of the class.
- Thomas communicated a time frame for reading their books and completing their group work.

Monitoring Student Needs

- Thomas circulated among groups to assess progress.
- Thomas provided assistance with vocabulary and concepts.

Formal and Informal School Environments

A **formal school structure** may be defined as the expected organizational pattern for actions and human relationships. An **informal school structure** may be defined as the behaviors that often accompany and result from the formal structure. Both the formal and informal structure of school and classroom make up the environment affecting everyone interacting in the school environment. In most schools the day is divided into periods, lunchtime, and recess. Teachers and students are expected to adhere to the formal time pattern. School visitors also need to be cognizant of the time pattern.

The school environment is also affected by the variety of people and jobs in the school community. The typical middle school may consist of a principal, assis-

tant principal(s), perhaps a nurse, school counselor, a welfare and attendance officer, cafeteria workers, custodians, teachers, and teacher specialists. In addition there may be instructional consultants, student teachers, a college coordinator, and sometimes a police officer or two. Coordination of this mass of people is the responsibility of the principal, and it is why the school environment may be formally structured.

However, the informal structure sometimes shocks visitors and inexperienced personnel. The following example illustrates:

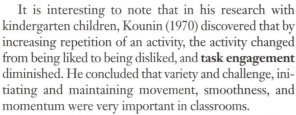

At Manning Middle School the day begins at 7:55 A.M. Students are expected to be in their seats at 8:00 A.M., but in Ms. Randolph's class at 8:10 A.M. the students are still arriving. Ms. Randolph was sitting at her desk in the front of the room and successfully ignoring those students who were seated. The students were just as successfully ignoring Ms. Randolph as they chatted, exchanged insults, and slapped each other. Not until 8:20 A.M. did Ms. Randolph begin class by passing out some duplicated sheets. As she passed the sheets she punctuated the effort with **"Stop the racket: Get in your seat: Where's your homework?"** *As the period progressed, Ms. Randolph would compliment some students and berate others. Although some explanation of the work would be given, students rarely seemed to understand and only a few would ask questions*

Analysis of the case study above indicates that a formal time pattern was ignored, and instead we see the emergence of an informal organization within Ms. Randolph's classroom that governed behavior in that environment. The students had "learned" that punctuality was unnecessary and not valued in that classroom. Ms. Randolph played at the role of teacher as she scolded and dispensed work assignments, but in reality she taught informally, and at times nonverbally, that she did not care about or respect her students.

An example in Mary Hogan's classroom follows:

Fifteen minutes were allotted to languaging, "show and tell", so that the first graders could share their out of school experiences. Although the students were only supposed to talk and take turns, William brought his pet white mouse to class. As he spoke, the mouse jumped out of his pocket; the students seated in a circle on the floor, jumped and then laughed delightedly. Then all eyes turned toward Ms. Hogan; the faces became rigid and quiet as they waited expectantly for Hogan's comment. She smiled, then laughed, and proceeded to fetch a box to hold the mouse. Then Hogan questioned William about the food and habits of his pet and the students relaxed and enjoyed the experience.

Here, a teacher's "formal" role pattern was anticipated by the students, but it did not materialize. Instead, the teacher used the situation to enrich and extend her students' language and science experiences. The teacher as the leader of the classroom changed the formal structure from an interactive expression of conflict to an interactive expression of cooperation.

Each classroom provides a different environmental experience in terms of behavior. The physical setting also affects interactive experiences. Some classrooms are absolutely sterile, nothing but chairs, tables, and printed notices on the bulletin boards. In other rooms, one finds a variety of learning centers to attract students and entice them to learn. Bulletin boards may direct student interest with questions about current events, happenings in the school, or exhibits of student work.

In some classrooms, the tables and chairs are arranged neatly facing forward, curtailing discussion and interactions; in other rooms, the tables and chairs are clustered in small groups to encourage students to look at one another, work together, and talk. In Karen Adazzio's classroom, the chairs are placed in a semicircle so that the students can see each other during a class discussion. The desks are abandoned in the back of the classroom. In some classrooms, observers feel relaxed; in others they feel "edgy." One may only speculate how the student learner feels in these same environments.

A DEMOCRATIC LEARNING ENVIRONMENT

The classroom environment influences students' behavior. This should not be a surprise to any college student who has sat in a lecture hall and automatically whipped out a notebook and pencil. Seating arrangements in rows, in small groups, in a circle, and in the front or back of the room all influence the interaction of students with each other and with the teacher. When students are seated in an auditorium or a library, in a gymnasium or a cooperative group, the environmental setting affects their behavior and the resultant expectations.

The management of the classroom is similarly affected by the environmental setting. Kounin and Sherman (1979) described the fit between preschoolers' behavior and the environmental setting. Preschoolers, who did not have adult structure imposed on them, used a free-play setting and played without dawdling, wandering, crying, or fighting 95% of the time. The author has similarly observed preschoolers in a free-play setting, unconstrained by adult pressure, acting totally involved. Kounin and Sherman concluded that preschoolers exhibit "schoolish" behavior and act appropriately when the setting fits the activities.

When the classroom environment does not support the activities a teacher chooses, management problems arise. For example, in a classroom where the tables are in straight rows, it is difficult to develop student discussion skills. If students do not face each other when they talk, interaction becomes a back-and-forth process from student to teacher. As a consequence, the students are not listening to each other; they are waiting for the teacher to call on them. This type of lesson is really a recitation period rather than a class discussion. The effects of this lesson are student boredom, lags between responses, off-task behavior (horseplay), and teacher frustration. In another example, a science classroom without lab space and equipment curtails learning experiences and defines both teaching and learning. If Thomas had not had space for students to work in

Research Findings

Students in 15 school districts and 108 schools (grades 4–12) were asked by researchers to answer questions about trust, respect, caring, bullying, school safety, racial self-concept, and general school climate. African American students were more likely than other racial groups to believe that their teachers did not respect them. Researchers concluded that (1) school leaders need to monitor their school climate to ensure a positive school environment, and (2) there is a relationship between an "optimal" school environment and "optimal" academic performance (Gewertz, 2006).

small groups to read their novels and create group projects, students would not have been able to select their own groups, and he would have had to impose a rigid learning experience.

Recall the vignette at the beginning of this chapter. All of us have at one time or another entered a classroom late. In most cases we feel embarrassed lest we disturb what is happening by interrupting the flow of a lesson. Harrison was ignored by his teacher, yet his teacher could have acknowledged his presence by smiling at him, suggesting that he join a specific study group, or even getting up and whispering to him. Any of these options would have demonstrated caring.

In a caring environment, teachers are concerned with both the learning and attitudinal needs of each student. Harrison's teacher probably blamed him for disturbing the class and causing the ripple effect. But the teacher was wrong; the teacher caused the ripple effect because Harrison's needs were ignored. In a caring environment, the teacher would have recognized that Harrison needed help and offered it. The consequence would have been that the whole class would have felt more comfortable.

In a democratic learning environment, teacher and students share responsibility for maintaining a comfortable learning community. In a study of elementary, middle, and high school students, the author asked students to characterize a democratic classroom. Though the students were often critical of their teachers, they agreed about teacher and student behaviors in democratic environments. Table 3.1 is a compilation of their characterizations, and Figure 3.1 identifies what you should look for when observing in classrooms.

Classroom Management and Discipline

Classroom management and **discipline** are not synonymous. The definition given previously does not even refer to classroom discipline, yet discipline in the classroom depends on good classroom management. Chaotic classrooms unstructured by group standards restrict the ability of the teacher to teach and students to learn. Dewey (1916/1944) talks about the social environment of the classroom and its influence on the development of attitudes and dispositions:

> The social environment consists of all the activities of fellow beings that are bound up in the carrying on of the activities of any one of its members. It is truly educative in its effect in the degree in which an individual shares or participates in some conjoint activity. (p. 22)

Table 3.1 Characteristics of Democratic Classrooms

Teacher Behavior	Student Behavior
Shares decision making with students	Helps define classroom standards
Emphasizes student responsibility and sense of belonging to classroom community	Recognizes responsibility to classroom community
Requires student discussion if infractions of rules occur	Participates in community decision making
Plans curriculum that attends to cultural diversity	Participates in curriculum decisions that include activities, processes, and products
Plans inclusive curriculum that includes gender studies and attention to immigrant and minority students and second language learners	Is expected to behave respectfully toward peers and teacher
Speaks respectfully and caringly to students	Expresses interests and needs
Demonstrates enthusiasm and listens attentively	Interacts positively with teacher and peer students
Encourages student participation in discussion and small heterogeneous group work	Participates with peers in planning activities and projects
Encourages student problem solving and risk taking	Shares and demonstrates problem-solving skills and insights

1. Which students cluster together? (How many distinct social groups do you recognize?)
2. Which student(s) act as loners?
3. Which students like to work in a small peer group together?
4. Which student(s) are always agreeable and help others when working in a small peer group?
5. Which student(s) is shy and fails to participate with others?
6. Which student(s) fail to coorperate and cannot work peacefully with others?
7. Which student(s) is accepted by others as a leader?

Figure 3.1 Observing the Social Environment of the Classroom

In many classrooms, teachers set the rules, require students (and their parents) to sign classroom rules, provide rewards to students for following the rules (free time, early lunch dismissal, no homework), and punish students who do not abide by them (compositions, detention, extra drill work, no recess, no free time). The problem here is that students in these classrooms take no responsibility for helping set classroom standards and are not motivated to maintain them.

To respond to ongoing classroom discipline problems, teachers often embrace various discipline systems to treat the problem. Bestowing rewards, as in the token economy system, is a means whereby teachers try to reinforce appropriate behavior through tokens. When students misbehave, they have to return the tokens; when students accrue enough tokens, they can exchange them for rewards and privileges. The token

Teaching Hints: Classroom Management

1. Plan a teaching strategy appropriate for students and content needs.
2. Anticipate strategy needs: space, grouping, resources.
3. Monitor students' progress and behavior; demonstrate with-it-ness and ability to attend to ongoing happenings.

economy is a competitive system for reinforcing behaviors that are teacher approved. It promotes teacher authority and control.

Assertive discipline (Canter & Canter, 1992) is another such system that emphasizes teachers' rights to impose classroom rules and establish preset consequences. The system is said to be teacher-friendly and, by definition, student-unfriendly. The teacher establishes a classroom environment to ensure obedience of the teacher's rules. The system fails to promote student responsibility to establish their own classroom rules for working together in a classroom community. The rules are typically sent home for parents to sign. Students are required to learn the rules and are usually tested on them.

I-messages (Gordon, 1974) attempt to define for the teacher who "owns" a classroom discipline problem. According to this system, knowing the "ownership" will improve classroom communication. Thus, if the problem is a student problem, then the teacher presumably can say, "This isn't my problem; you need to deal with it." How knowing this would improve the classroom environment is mind-boggling.

As an experienced classroom teacher, the author believes that these systems—and there are many more—do not attack the root of the problem. Discipline problems are symptomatic of a classroom environment that lacks respect, guidance, and responsibility. In Chapter 2, motivation was discussed and related to the individual's beliefs about who or what controls events affecting the individual's life. Researchers have concluded that success in school depends on the student's recognition that ability and effort are student-controlled and that they are critical elements for school success. Systems that reinforce teacher responsibility, control, and total authority tend to destroy students' self-esteem and do not promote an internal locus of control.

Why Students Need to Set Classroom Standards

Teachers can address discipline problems by insisting on student participation in setting classroom rules and standards, and then monitoring classroom happenings by referring back to those rules and standards when misbehavior occurs. It is time well spent when the teacher stops activities and asks students, "What shall we do? We have some friends who are not . . ." Then the teacher guides students to use their own standards to explain to the abusers that they have not been respectful of others' rights, and that they all have participated in setting the rules.

Clearly it is the teacher's responsibility to establish a democratic classroom community. We must transmit our democratic heritage by communicating appropriate habits, values, and ideals of our social life, and we do this by having students experience democracy in action in the classroom. Both the teacher and the students need to reflect on the reasonableness of a given rule. Why was the rule created? Who is it for? What problem(s) does it address? By asking these questions, teachers and students can decide on the appropriateness and reasonableness of the rule.

Noddings (1999) also raises questions for reflecting and selecting appropriate experiences for students to promote and appreciate democratic citizenship. Her questions address the responsibility of schools, the curriculum, and teachers' pedagogy:

- What experience do students need in order to become engaged participants in democratic life?
- How can education develop the capacity for making well-informed choices?
- If liberal public discussion is a foundation for democracy, how can schools promote such discussion?
- What pedagogical methods are compatible with the aims of democratic education? (p. 579)

Kohn (2003) also notes that teachers sometimes ask the wrong questions, which ultimately impede their efforts to create democratic environments. Questions aimed at making students obey, do what they are told, sit down, be quiet, and so on, do not reflect a caring environment. Instead, he suggests that teachers ask themselves, "What do these kids need—and how can we meet those needs?" (p. 27).

GROUPING FOR INSTRUCTION

Every moment of classroom life is a learning experience. Students work in the whole-class group and in smaller class groups. The grouping experience contributes to each student's understanding of citizenship and inherent responsibility. Whole-group instruction is typically associated with formal, traditional classroom teaching, and small-group instruction is typically associated with flexible, more open teaching approaches. The effective classroom teacher uses both approaches throughout the school day. The skills involved in managing group behavior are basic to classroom management and effective instruction.

Why Group?

Students attending my college classes are often surprised when I (author Johanna Lemlech) group them in clusters of five to seven students on the first or second day of class and present the groups with a problem or an issue for discussion. During the 15 or 20 minutes that the groups meet (out on the lawn, in adjoining rooms, and in our lecture room), I tour the groups to listen to their discussion, to observe them, and to make suggestions if necessary.

The groups have a designated time to come back and meet as a whole class, and I return to the classroom to await their entrance. The change in their behavior is remarkable. They leave the room as individuals; straggling out, wary, and a little apprehensive about doing something that is not typically done in a college classroom. But their return is different. They come in noisily and companionably, and invariably they sit together as comrades.

The debriefing of the activity occurs in two stages. Stage 1 is substantive. Whenever possible, I try to motivate a little bit of conflict among the groups so the reports are not really group reports but, in actuality, a whole-class discussion.

As voices rise and adults forget their discussion manners and begin interrupting each other, I nonchalantly ask, "By the way, is there anyone who did not talk in their small-group discussion?"

They look around and sheepishly acknowledge that everyone contributed. This initiates Stage 2, in which we discuss my behavior as teacher and their behaviors as learners.

I usually end this session by asking the students, "What did you learn from working in a small group that was valuable?" They invariably respond with some of the advantages of grouping:

- They felt less inhibited about talking.
- They learned from their classmates.
- They felt involved.

Every teaching approach has advantages and disadvantages. The effective teacher chooses the teaching strategy that best meets the needs of the teaching situation and accomplishes the desired outcomes. Before reading the discussion of group work, study Tables 3.2

Table 3.2 Large-Group Instruction

Advantages	Disadvantages (Possible)
Efficient means for input: lectures, films, guests, demonstrations	Reduces individual responsibility
	Subordinates individual needs to whole-group needs
Develops sense of belonging	Impedes differentiation of instruction
Facilitates teaching of new skills	Impedes social participation
Promotes teacher-centered authority	Increases physical problems (vision, hearing)
Provides single, continuous signal source	Increases impersonality of teaching and learning
	Reduces task involvement
	Tempts teacher to make an example of disruptive students

and 3.3, which describe specified advantages and disadvantages for small-group and large-group instruction.

Discussion: Large-Group Instruction

Careful study of Tables 3.2 and 3.3 reveals that each strategy has both conflicting and contradictory values. For example, Table 3.2 states that advantages of large-group instruction include teacher-centered authority and a single continuous signal source; this means that control should be facilitated. Yet at the same time, the table states that task involvement may be reduced and that the teacher may be tempted to make an example of disruptive students. What is the explanation of this?

According to Kounin and Sherman (1979), certain environmental settings have more holding power than others. Large-group settings have the potential to decrease socially ineffective behavior; therefore, if the teacher can hold students' attention, the teacher will be the sole and continuing signal source. If the lesson does not lag and the teacher can manage the disparate interests of the group, high involvement can be achieved.

Large-group instruction is potentially efficient because the teacher can introduce a new skill to all students at the same time. The teacher models the skill, and controlled practice occurs under the teacher's watchful eyes. Proper implementation of this approach facilitates keeping the students on task, thereby increasing academically engaged time.

So why are control problems often more difficult during large-group instruction? The discussion in Chapter 2 on the ways in which children differ provided some insight into why this approach is not always successful. Hearing and vision problems or the physical size

of some students may be a factor. When students cannot hear or see, they cause problems. Learning-style differences are not provided for when all students must

Table 3.3 Small-Group Instruction

Advantages	Disadvantages (Possible)
Facilitates communication	Excites students
Promotes interaction	Wastes time if students' group skills are poor
Motivates involvement	Wastes time when introducing new skills
Encourages assisting others, accepting responsibility	Subordinates high- and low-achiever needs to accomplish group goals
Teaches bargaining, negotiation	
Promotes decision making	Subordinates academic content to group process skills
Necessitates listening to others' viewpoints	Extroverted, aggressive students may overrule and subordinate introverted students
Necessitates sharing own values	
Promotes cooperation, group production, and group learning	
Allows differentiation of instruction	
Frees teacher to observe, listen, and diagnose	

Games provide means for students to learn cooperative and respectful behavior.

attend in the same way. As a consequence, some students will be uninterested. (Think back to Barry's classmates studying the anatomy of the human heart at the beginning of Chapter 2.) Large-group instruction assumes that all students need the same lesson, but this may not be true. Because large-group instruction is impersonal, it can decrease involvement. Finally, the spatial arrangement of the students during instruction may cause problems. If students are too far away from the teacher, they can pursue their own interests due to lack of monitoring; if students are seated too close together, the result may be disruptive behavior. A typical mistake of the beginning teacher is to get upset when students begin to fidget. In an uncontrolled burst of temper, the teacher may lash out at the disruptive student—or at the student the teacher thinks is disruptive. This behavior results in embarrassment for others, as well as for the target of the outburst, and is known to decrease students' achievement. Fidgeting is often a sign that students need more active learning experiences, such as student-to-student interaction, movement, and physical activities.

Sense of Belonging

It is very important for students to feel a sense of identity with their classmates and their teacher. A sense of belonging motivates attendance at school, encourages cooperative behavior, and enhances the ability to learn. Classroom management is facilitated when students learn to care about others and about their own role in the group. At the beginning of the school year, the teacher must cultivate this sense of belonging and work to develop pride in group identity. Both schoolwide and classroom activities are used to develop ego-satisfying behavior.

Large-group activities have the potential to develop this important characteristic. Experienced teachers develop it in a variety of ways, as the following example illustrates.

 ## GREG THOMAS'S CLASSROOM

Greg Thomas has his students create a class song at the beginning of each school year. The students select a popular, classic, or folk tune, and then write lyrics to fit the song. Last year his students selected "Puff the Magic Dragon" and wrote a song called "We're the Greatest Students." Using harmonicas, autoharps, and rhythm sticks, they orchestrated the song. This activity helped the students develop a class identity and what human relations specialists call oneness.

Choral speaking and rhythmic and physical activities performed in a group also have the potential to develop strong group feeling. Activities should be chosen based on their potential to develop group cooperation, responsibility, respect, and dependence on classmates. More sophisticated activities of longer duration are also appropriate. For example, an activity that takes students out into the community to perform a service in their own neighborhood has the potential for developing group solidarity and oneness.

Discussion: Small-Group Instruction

It is apparent from the research on teaching strategies that to accomplish creative goals, intuitive thinking, discovery, exploration, and inquiry, small-group instruction with less structure is more suitable. Large-group direct instruction tends to be formal and impersonal; consequently, if it is used exclusively, it can make the classroom a very grim place.

Small groups can take advantage of student diversity as well as homogeneous needs. Teachers can arrange the heterogeneous groups to take advantage of students' special abilities (thereby increasing the likelihood of peer modeling and assistance) or, on some occasions, the students can choose their own group arrangement (affecting student motivation to participate). For teaching and monitoring specific skill development, groups can be arranged homogeneously, but in social studies, science, health, art, music, or physical education, heterogeneous groups are appropriate.

Small-group work facilitates the differentiation of instruction (see Table 3.3). It is more difficult for teachers to manage whole-group behavior and individualize instruction; by utilizing small groups, teachers can match instruction with the precise needs of the individual. Small groups also enable students to learn from each other and to develop respect for classmates.

English language learners benefit when working in a small group because they are less likely to shy away from contributing to the group. In addition, if the group includes a student who is more proficient in the native language of the ELL student, assistance and interpretation can occur.

Sometimes in the modern classroom, we lose sight of the fact that a major purpose of the school is to foster democratic behaviors. If we expect young adults to participate meaningfully in our society, then they need appropriate experiences that teach social participatory skills. Students can learn these skills only when they are confronted by each other and forced to work together. Young children who always get their own way become unsocialized beings. The moment that they are forced to relate to others, they must identify areas of agreement and disagreement with others. This in turn motivates confrontation (see the discussion of the theories of Piaget and Kohlberg in Chapter 2) and the use of persuasion, negotiation, and cooperation. They learn self-control in the process, but it is a developmental process.

Cooperative Learning

Studies of cooperative and competitive efforts in problem solving have revealed that small-group cooperative efforts result in better problem solving than do individual competitive efforts. This occurred particularly when cooperative groups generated problem-solving strategies in mathematical problems and visual-spatial

problems (Qin, Johnson, & Johnson, 1995). Sociologic studies have also looked at students' participation in heterogeneous classrooms when working in cooperative groups. Cohen (1998) reports that teachers need to communicate to students that all can participate and contribute unique abilities. Cooperative assignments can identify some of the skills needed and who in the group can perform the specific tasks. By assigning competent tasks to low-status students, teachers can help all students appreciate diversity and raise expectations of competence for low-status students.

Managing Small-Group and Large-Group Instruction

Preplanning (anticipating potential problems) alleviates most of the difficulties involved in either instructional approach See Tables 3.4 and 3.5.

How to Begin Small-Group Instruction

Regardless of the subject, small-group instruction necessitates specific teacher and learner behaviors. The next classroom episode should provide you with some ideas about how to begin small-group instruction.

 MARY HOGAN'S CLASSROOM

Some of the second graders were seated on the floor in front of Mary Hogan; the rest were seated on chairs behind the group on the floor. On a low table in front of the group, Hogan had a large horseshoe magnet and a number of objects with it, including paper, a pencil, scissors, a crayon, rubber bands, a penny, nails, an eraser, paper clips, a ball, and string.

MOTIVATION

Hogan: Who can tell us what this is? (She holds up the magnet. Many hands go up, and Hogan chooses one student to respond.)
Sue: I bet it's a magnet.
Hogan: What does a magnet do?
Sue: It picks things up.
Hogan: How could we find out?
Bret: See if it will pick those things up that you have on the table.
Hogan: Good idea, Bret. (She uses the magnet to try to pick up the string.)

Table 3.4   Management of Small-Group Instruction

Potential Problems	Means to Avoid the Problem
Need for structure	Appoint or direct students to choose a leader, recorder, and/or reporter.
Need to communicate group problems	Define appropriate behavior; define operating procedures; chart the rules; ensure that students know how to get your assistance.
Need to share problems and accomplishments	Provide evaluation time at the end of each work period.
Content subordinate to process	Evaluate substantive findings, then group process; do not focus on individual behavior.
Group size	Uneven number of students facilitates compromise; the optimal group size is five to seven.
Materials and resource needs	Anticipate, monitor, and provide necessary materials.
Groups fail to "get started"	If it is a continuing activity, begin by asking all of the groups to identify what they intend to accomplish. If it is a one-time or new activity, verify that each group understands what is expected.
Physical space	Provide and designate a working space for each group so groups do not intrude upon each other.
Deviant behavior (individual)	If behavior cannot be corrected with a reminder, decide what you will do: a. Have the disruptive student watch another group and report during the evaluation period on what makes groups function smoothly, and what inhibits effective group work. b. Assign the student an individual project; monitor its completion. c. Share information with and ask for assistance from the parents.
Deviant behavior (group)	Assess whether the problem is a consequence of misunderstanding about the objective. If so, clarify and provide information to refocus group thinking. If there is a nonacademic reason, confer with the group using your best "I mean it" expression; let them know what you expect of them and then monitor their adherence to class rules. Assess whether the combination of students in the group should be changed.

Table 3.5   Management of Large-Group Instruction

Potential Problems	Means to Avoid the Problem
General lack of interest	Choose lesson needed by most students; motivate interest.
High-or low-achievers' lack of interest	Provide special information to interest the high achievers; comfort the low achievers by stating that you will be available to give additional assistance after the lesson.
Deviant behavior due to space problems (crowding)	Direct the less mature students to places where they will not trouble others; arrange the room to accommodate this type of instruction.
Inattention due to space problems (class too spread out)	This happens most frequently when students are at tables or desks and the teacher does not establish eye contact. Have students arrange chairs in a three-sided square to face you, or seat students on floor in front of the chalkboard. Do not start the lesson until all students have directed their eyes on you.
Deviant behavior as a consequence of physical problems	Provide for individual needs; seat students with physical disabilities appropriately.
Impersonality of instruction	Involve students by using short and frequent questions; wait and encourage responses.

Keisha:	Magnets won't pick up string; only certain things.
Hogan:	What do you mean, Keisha?
Keisha:	Well, I know string won't work.
Hogan:	Come show us what will. (Keisha uses the magnet and picks up a pin, a nail, and a paper clip.) All right, we can see that Keisha made the magnet pick up three items. We also know that it did not pick up the string. In what way are these three items alike? (She holds up the magnet with the pin, the nail, and the paper clip.)
William:	I think they must all be made of metal.
Hogan:	What kind of metal will magnets pick up? (Hogan looks around, and students appear to be unsure.)

Assignment

Hogan:	Today I thought you might like to be scientists and explore a problem. I am going to ask you to work in small groups. Each group will have some magnets and a bag of objects. Your job is to find out what the magnet will pull and to make a rule about the objects that magnets will pull. Some in your group will be very good at observing what objects the magnets will pull. Perhaps someone in the group already has experience with magnets and that person can contribute examples. Someone in the group will need to try to write the group rule, and perhaps someone in the group would like to draw a picture to demonstrate what the magnet can do. No one in the group can do everything. You are each responsible for contributing your special ability. If your group makes its rule before the other groups are ready, I will come over and suggest another problem to investigate. When you think your group is ready, or if your group has a problem, have your group leader raise his or her hand, and I will come over and listen to your rule or give you some help.

Organization

Hogan distributed magnets and bags of materials to six different locations in the room. The bags contained a penny, nails, wire, screws, pins, and hair curlers.

Hogan:	We will need to work together cooperatively. I think we had better make some group work rules. What should they be?
Joe:	I think we better have a captain or a leader.
Hogan:	Good idea, Joe; I will write the rules on the board. What else?
Maria:	We need someone to write down our ideas.
Hogan:	Yes, but because writing is a special skill, how about if someone in each group volunteers to be the group reporter for our discussion? (Students nod, and Hogan writes another rule.) How will you decide what to do when you are in your group?
Ben:	I guess we better plan.
Hogan:	Good point, Ben. We need to plan the experiment and decide what each person will do. Suppose I write, "Plan the experiment."
Sam:	Then we need to do the experiment.
Hogan:	OK, so Number 4 should be, "Perform the experiment." What will Number 5 be?
Terry:	We better discuss what we found out.
Hogan:	OK, Number 5 should be, "Talk about the experiment," and Number 6 had better be, "Prepare for class discussion." Is there anything else?
Midge:	Clean up?
Hogan:	Yes, indeed. Let's read our group work rules together.

Group Work Rules

1. Choose a group leader.
2. Choose a group reporter.
3. Plan the experiment and individual tasks.
4. Perform the experiment.
5. Talk about the experiment.
6. Prepare for class discussion.
7. Clean up.

Hogan: Now, boys and girls, when I call your names, please go to the area I designate for your group. Remember to move quietly so that the students who are waiting can hear their names called. If I need your attention, I will flash the lights. (Each group is quietly dismissed to go to work.)

Hogan walked around and observed the progress of the groups while they worked (see Figure 3.2,). Each group had several different types of magnets as well as their bag of materials. As Hogan observed each group, she suggested to them: "Arrange the objects in two groups, those that the magnet will pull and those that the magnet will not pull. Find out if all magnets pull the same things."

When the groups thought they were finished, Hogan listened to their rules. Sometimes the rules indicated a lack of understanding and that would lead to her giving them clues and telling them the names of the metals in the objects that they were testing.

For the groups that demonstrated clear understanding, Hogan had prepared an additional experiment. She asked them to find out if magnets can pull objects through other materials. She suggested that they find out by using books, paper, cardboard, and anything else that was not too thick.

EVALUATION

After about 10 minutes, the students appeared to have concluded their work. Hogan flashed the lights, and all students looked up expectantly. Next she suggested that

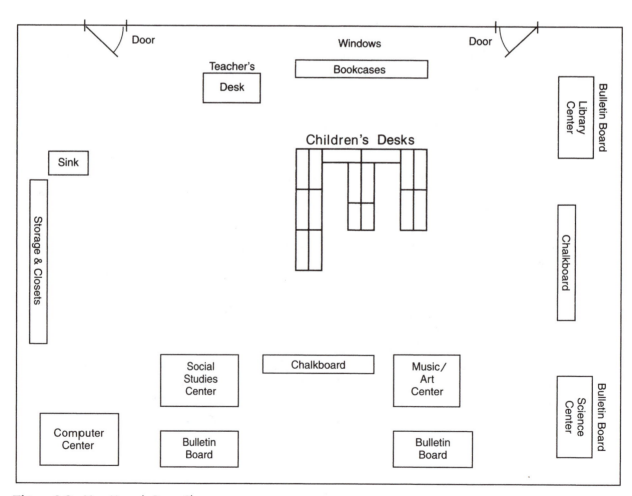

Figure 3.2 Mary Hogan's Room Plan

they leave their magnets and bags on the tables, and she invited each group to bring their work papers to the front of the room to discuss their experiments.

Hogan: Did you test all of your materials and all of your magnets? Sharon, I know you are the reporter for your group; tell us how your group planned its work. (Each group contributes its planning steps.) What did you do next? (Several groups mention her suggestion that they arrange their objects into two groups, those that pulled and those that did not.) Well, what did you find out? Which objects belonged together? (She writes two headings on the board: "Objects Magnet Pulled" and "Objects Magnet Did Not Pull." The students complete the list by classifying the objects they had tested.)

Hogan: Did all the magnets pull the same objects?
Students: Yes!
Hogan: Well, then, it's time to find out what we learned.
Elena: (Tentatively raising her hand) Magnets pull metals.
Hogan: (Writing the names of the metals or metal alloys next to each object in the first list) Will magnets pull all metals?
William: No. Magnets only pull objects that have iron or steel in them.*

GROUP WORK EVALUATION

Hogan smiled and said, "By golly, you have stated a good rule about magnets," and she wrote it on the board. "Now, boys and girls, what did you think about your first experience working in small groups during science? Let's talk about it." Hogan led the discussion so that students responded to the following questions:

- When you do group work, should everyone get to talk? (Yes.)
- Is it possible for all members of the group to agree? (Sometimes yes, sometimes no.)
- How did you decide what to do when you did not agree?

*Content for this lesson was based on information from *Science in Elementary Education* (6th ed., pp. 304–305), by Peter C. Gega, New York: Macmillan, 1990.

- Why was it a good idea to try the experiment in different ways?
- Why is it important to listen to all members of the group?
- What was most difficult about group work?
- What was easiest?
- In what ways was your group successful?
- If you work in groups tomorrow, what will you want to remember?

Reviewing the components of Mary Hogan's lesson using small-group instruction, we note that definite steps were involved in the process:

1. Large-group instruction and motivation
2. Communication of the assignment and differentiation of tasks (attention to multiple intelligences)
3. Organizing for work
   - Standards for group work
   - Providing materials
   - What to do if the group needs help
   - How the teacher can get students' attention, if needed
   - Time constraints (if any)
   - Assigning work settings
4. Small-group instructional process
5. Evaluation
   - Content evaluation
   - Group work evaluation

How Does a Constructivist Teacher Manage the Classroom?

In Mary Hogan's magnet lesson, the students articulated group work standards, and they were made responsible for deciding on individual tasks and choosing a group leader and group reporter. They had to demonstrate the ability to think scientifically. The students knew what was expected of them, and they had the freedom to pursue knowledge in their own way.

In a behaviorist classroom, students come to expect that the teacher will tell them what to do and how to do it; they come to expect rewards through grades, M&Ms, time away, and playtime. Their questions are asked of the teacher—not each other—and they relate primarily to how to perform the task and what is expected of them. In the constructivist classroom, students work to gain understanding because the inquiry tasks are related to their own experiences. Students are more likely to value learning because they are engaged in hands-on activities that are enjoyable and of interest to them. The teacher's planning and well-organized lessons reduce classroom management problems.

WHAT DO CHILDREN LEARN?

This section relates student success to the achievement motivation goals discussed in Chapter 2.

Learning Through Success

Among all the other things that the school teaches, children learn to recognize success and failure. The student who has difficulty learning to read experiences failure. Repeated failures in reading or in other areas of the curriculum affect everything the child does. Lack of success affects motivation and after a period of time, peers and teachers label the student as a loser. If the child perceives this conception by others, he or she learns to play the role of a loser and accepts and anticipates extended failure.

Effective, conscientious teachers can avert the disaster of recurring failure by deemphasizing areas of weakness. This is not to suggest that reading or other skill areas lack importance, but merely that appropriate goals can be set, and legitimate reinforcement bestowed, so all children can earn praise from peers and teacher and experience success. When the teacher provides diverse activities and varied expectations for performance, all students can participate in classroom learning activities.

It is especially important that students rotate leadership roles. Billy should not always be a group leader or a demonstrator of skills. Mabel should not always be the one being tutored. If students are to feel successful, they must perceive that others are aware of their strengths. This will occur only through peer interaction, and it must be programmed by the teacher. Figure 3.1 identified earlier in the chapter, designates matters that affect the social climate of the classroom.

KAREN ADAZZIO'S SEVENTH-GRADE CLASSROOM

Karen Adazzio noted that, although Bert was able to observe every detail in a picture, he read poorly. Bert was often aggressive, and she recognized that he had a very low self-concept. It occurred to her that it might be possible to use Bert's visual strengths to build his self-confidence and ultimately develop his reading skills. She asked Bert if he owned a camera. He said "Yes," and she suggested that the two of them confer about a project. (Before the conference, Adazzio contacted Bert's mother to obtain her permission to initiate a visual literacy program for Bert.) Bert developed a project that involved photographing the community around the school and interviewing homeowners and businesspeople he knew. He presented the project to his classmates. Using a camera and a tape recorder, Bert learned about the community. Other members of the class learned about the community by reading and utilizing resource materials. Bert's activities were developed with Adazzio's assistance. The behaviors she was focusing on and the activities used to achieve the performance components are outlined in Table 3.6.

When Bert and other members of Adazzio's class engaged in small-group work, they had to listen to each other and take turns talking. Group work in the classroom was practiced almost daily. Students rotated the roles of group leader and recorder. Adazzio taught them to participate. As a result of repeated experiences with group work, the students were actively engaged in constructive reasoning.

By changing the typical projects in this classroom, Adazzio manipulated the evaluative feedback that each child received. Bert was perceived by his classmates as a conscientious, creative, rational person, and he began to look at himself as a leader. In time, Adazzio will encourage Bert to talk about his pictures and write stories about them. The stories will be typed, and Bert will develop reading skills by using his own instructional materials.

GROUPING: FROM LARGE TO SMALL

On another occasion, Karen Adazzio's seventh graders were studying world geography and related issues. They had just observed that the area of the Middle East called Israel was in fact about the size of the state of New Jersey.

Hank: How come both the Arabs and the Jews have claimed that they own the same land?

Adazzio: That's a good question, Hank. Let's all consider it. What do you think are the roots of the Arab-Israeli dispute over the land? Mona, what do you think?

Table 3.6 Applying Success-Oriented Behaviors

Activities to Achieve

Ego-satisfying behaviors

Self-confidence	Chooses to take neighborhood pictures with own camera
Self-responsibility	Pursues task and completes pictures
Optimism	Plans and sets goals
Security	Communicates plan to classmates
Status	Demonstrates how to take pictures, use a light meter, focus on center of interest

Learner-assertive behaviors

Questing	Interviews homeowners and businesspeople
Seeking	Tapes interviews
Searching	Edits tapes and pictures
Defining	Prepares tapes and pictures for classroom demonstration
Analyzing	
Conceptualizing	
Evaluating	

Independence-oriented behaviors

Initiating	Mounts pictures on poster board
Decision making	Develops a second tape of background music
Creativity; individuality	Coordinates interviews with background music; sequences pictures
Dependability	Presents project to class and answers questions about it

Group-satisfying behaviors

Cooperation	Works as a small-group leader to discuss community problems and to plan a community service project
Rationality	
Responsibility	
Respectfulness	

Mona: I think Jewish and Arab groups both believe their religious roots are in Jerusalem.

Shelly: Don't both groups call Israel the Promised Land?

John: Those are both related to their religious claims.

Adazzio: Um, interesting point. Are there other issues besides religious concerns that affect this area and their relationships?

Bill: Didn't the United Nations give the land to the Jews after World War II? Who did the land belong to before the Jewish people set up a government?

Angie: Can the United Nations just give away land whenever they want to?

Sal: I think it was important that the Jewish people have a homeland, and Israel is considered the natural home for them.

Adazzio: So far we have considered religious reasons affecting both the Jewish people and Arab people; Bill, Angie, and Sal raised another set of questions. What are they focusing on? Bill, what did you have in mind when you asked the question about the United Nations?

Bill: I guess what is puzzling me are the legal issues. I don't know who the land belonged to, and what right the UN had to make the decision.

Adazzio: OK, and Sal, what did you mean by "natural" home for the Jewish people?

Sal: It was tied to Bill's and Angie's questions about legal rights, but I seem to remember that maybe there is something about historical rights to the land.

Akim: All people need a national homeland. Shouldn't that affect their relationships, and is that connected to historical rights? Arabs live in Palestine; shouldn't they be allowed to set up a separate nation there?

Jean: What about talking about how Israel has had to defend its homeland against Arab attacks, and also the Arab people who have been displaced because of those wars?

Adazzio: You are doing so well, I can barely keep up with you. Let me see if you can help me identify the issues. First, we identified conflicting religious claims, then we raised the issue of legal rights.

Sal: And I said there were historical issues.

Akim: Yeah, and I think you need to consider nationalism as a need or issue.

Adazzio: All right. I have written five categories on the board: religious claims, legal claims, historical claims, nationalist claims, other claims.

Consider what you are most interested in. When I name the category, raise your hand if you want to research that particular question. We will take time today and tomorrow for some group research. We'll have a short discussion today after you have worked for about 25 minutes, and tomorrow you will present your conclusions to the class. Remember, once in your groups, you should decide who will chair the group, how you will take notes, what each person's responsibility will be, and how you will present your conclusions to the class. All right, who wants to study . . . ?

Analysis of Classroom Episode

We do not know what preceded this discussion or much about what the students are studying and the cultural milieu of the classroom, yet certain patterns of behavior are evident:

- The students appear to feel comfortable with initiating questions. (See Hank's first question.)
- It is evident that Karen Adazzio feels no need to have coaction (conversation to and from herself with a single student). The students listen to each other and respond to each other.
- Group research appears to be a regular means of learning in the classroom. (There was a smooth transition in moving from large-group to small-group activity.)
- Adazzio was grouping by student interest and student choice. Again, the students appeared to be accustomed to this.
- Identifying and making decisions about leadership and task responsibilities are left to the students.
- Adazzio communicates task and time constraints so that students can make pacing decisions.

In reviewing the interaction among students in Karen Adazzio's classroom, it is obvious that the students were interested in thinking about the Israeli-Arab issues; they were involved and challenged. As a teacher, Adazzio provided interactive support in the form of her questions. She did not offer her opinion or try to lead the students' exploration of the issues.

TECHNOLOGY AND CLASSROOM MANAGEMENT IN THE REGULAR CLASSROOM

Teachers' Planning

Just as the textbook requires that teachers familiarize themselves with the content and perspective of the text, planning for teaching with technology requires that teachers familiarize themselves with the ideas and concepts presented via computer software, laser disc, or other media. Technology affects the environment of the classroom. The equipment needs to be accommodated with appropriate workstations, which requires advance planning. Lessons also need to be planned for multiple means of information and time must be allotted for work.

Planning Content

What will technology contribute to the content picture? With new sources of information, how will the content differ? What prior experiences will students need in order to use media? How will students' engagement be affected? What will students need to do to produce and verify learning? What content problems and access problems will students confront? Should you plan the sites that students will use? If you do so, how will this affect what they learn about searching the Internet? These questions affect the planning decisions that you will need to consider.

Grouping

Will students work in small cooperative groups? As individuals? In pairs? How will grouping affect the environment of the classroom (noise, space, furniture placement, monitoring)? Student access to computers is limited in most classrooms; thus, it is clear that teachers need to consider grouping in the planning of the curriculum. When students are grouped at the computer, they will need differentiated tasks. Perhaps the group needs to plan their Internet search. Then while one or two students carry out the search, other group members may detail the approach and their hypothesis. Still others may use other sources of information to contribute to the group project. However, you still need to consider how students will rotate access to the computer so that the same students are not always the ones online.

Strategies

The use of multiple sources of information will allow you greater flexibility to select teaching strategies. For example, in planning group work, you can assign one group to computers, another group could use DVDs, and still other groups could search texts and journals or do interviews. Classrooms with telephone access can use interactive technology for video and audio communication.

To take advantage of multiple sources of information, it is important to use teaching strategies like the advance organizer (see Chapter 4) so that students are adequately prepared to gather data and restructure that data for their own use. Most important for students is the ability to work collaboratively. Collaborative skills need to be taught and practiced. Not only do students need to share machines and documents, but what they produce is frequently collaborative. To use databases intelligently, students need imagination for seeking and searching and the ability to learn from each other.

How does computer use foster students' responsibility for their own learning?

Time

Access to the Internet may require more flexible use of time. Teacher planning needs to consider that it may not be possible to define subject fields within strict boundaries. However, because integration of subject fields is greater and easier, time can be accommodated through the planning of content themes that include subject field strands and skills teaching as needed. (Content themes are discussed in Chapter 6.)

Evaluation

Evaluating what students have learned includes not only what students produce, but the changes in student behavior and the process of learning. Before evaluating the product that students have produced, it is important to talk to them about their thinking process. For example, suppose that Greg Thomas's fifth graders used the Internet to search for information on colonial art. How did they travel the Internet? (Or did he program their search?) How many sources did they study? What led them from one source to the next? (This is the rea-

son for one group member to serve as the reporter, to detail the group's thinking and seeking process.)

Because technology encourages cooperative learning, what did students learn from each other? How well did they work together? What task was each student responsible for? How did they make decisions about the use of data?

Finally you need to examine the actual work of the students. How did the students use their data? What did they produce? In what ways do students' applications demonstrate their integration of subject fields? Have students demonstrated writing skills? Research skills? Creativity? Spatial intelligence? (Go back to Chapter 2 and look at Gardner's multiple intelligences.)

Summarizing Teachers' Classroom Management Role Using Technology

Effective use of technology requires that teachers act as guides and facilitators. Now more than ever before, teachers need to know about students' experiences and prior knowledge to select appropriate resources for classroom use. Materials (software, laser discs, DVDs) need to build on students' personal knowledge and serve as a bridge to new understandings. Classroom management tasks include the following:

- Managing the classroom environment to accommodate spatial needs for equipment and grouping
- Managing time to accommodate interactive needs, networking, e-mail, and accessing the Internet
- Managing multiple resources, which requires that teachers be knowledgeable about the quality of information that each resource offers.

Clearly your role in the new millennium requires the blending of many resources with the environment of the classroom and students' needs. Planning the curriculum has become more complex and more interesting.

PLANNING FOR THE BEGINNING OF SCHOOL

School districts often schedule a "pupil-free" day before school starts to provide the staff with an opportunity to plan schedules, agree on committee and whole-faculty meeting times, and most important, give the teachers time to ready their classrooms for students.

Research Findings

Hall and Hall (2003) described the case of an obstinate, aggressive student who was unaccepted by peers and hostile toward the teacher. To deal with the student, the teacher implemented three strategies:

1. The teacher resisted punishing the child for aggressive actions aimed at herself.
2. The teacher devoted extra time to bond with the student by lunching with her and engaging in conversation about the student's interests.
3. The teacher targeted special instruction in an area of need to ensure the student's success.

In Mary Hogan's year-round school, she vacations only three weeks at a time. Greg Thomas still enjoys a summer vacation, and Karen Adazzio has a somewhat modified year-round schedule.

When Mary Hogan was "off track" (using vacation time), her classroom was used by another teacher. In this way, classroom space was never wasted. The school was always open. Arriving in her classroom after a vacation break, Hogan found the tables stacked in the middle of the room. There were four bookcases and two tall display tables. She also found a television, a tape recorder, a computer and printer, and an old record player. On top of one of the cupboards, she found her chart rack, and in the closet area was a chart box on wheels apparently available for her use. Hogan decided to go to the teachers' room and change into work clothes so she could begin the task of moving furniture.

Hogan arranged the furniture first, putting the bookcases under the windows and setting several tables under bulletin boards to serve as interest centers. Using an E formation, she organized the tables to accommodate the 31 children. Figure 3.2 illustrates Hogan's room plan. Her plan encourages some social interaction among the children. She knew that, at times, this might be a disadvantage. (The importance of the physical arrangement of the classroom for class discussion is emphasized in Chapter 4.) Hogan situated her desk so it would not impede the traffic pattern in the classroom, nor would it be a focal point.

With the room somewhat organized, Hogan began the task of reading the students' cumulative records. She wanted to find out which literature books the chil-

dren had used last semester, so she would have a guide in the choice of appropriate books for this semester. The cumulative card in some school districts provides information about students' past experiences in school, such as achievement test scores, textbooks used, and past social studies units. Although Hogan knew that she would do diagnostic testing during the first week of school to pinpoint the children's precise ability levels, she felt it was important that the students begin to read on the first day of school.

Slowly Hogan determined her textbook needs. She conferred with a colleague next door, and then began the laborious task of carrying the different books into the classroom. She reviewed pencil, crayon, and paper needs for the room and brought in chart paper and other supplies for herself. As the room began to take shape, she turned her attention to the bulletin boards.

Room Environment

Mary Hogan recognized the value of a cheerful and thought-provoking environment. She wanted to establish interest centers that would support and encourage students to explore and discover, and she hoped that the centers would provide for individual differences. As she surveyed her classroom, she decided that she needed a science center, an art and music center, a social studies center, and a computer center. Hogan hung a beautiful poster of children reading books on the bulletin board. Then, in the bookcase below, she put out some of her own books. On top of the bookcase, using book stands, she opened several books to display a picture. She put a small round rug and a beanbag cushion on the floor next to the bookcase. She knew that such furnishings would attract the students. Prior to coming to school, Hogan had made a checklist to remind herself of things she needed to do. This checklist is displayed in Table 3.7

Science Center

Hogan perused the science text to see if any of the units corresponded to some of her own interests and to see if she had supportive materials to set up a center. She decided to begin with a unit about rocks and minerals because she had done a similar unit in student teaching, and she knew she could encourage the children to bring in their favorite rocks. She placed several baskets on a table by the bulletin board. In one basket she placed rocks with different textures, and next to it she put a

Table 3.7 Teacher Checklist for Beginning of Semester

Room Environment	Need to Obtain?
Student furniture	
Traffic lanes	
Display tables, cabinets, bookcases	
Bulletin boards	
Storage facilities	
Equipment/Resources	Need to Obtain?
Computer, printer	
Television monitor	
DVD player	
Overhead projector	
Chart rack	
Map rack	
Textbooks	
Maps	
Manipulatives	
Student supplies (pencils, paper)	
Subject field specialty materials	
Procedures: School and Classroom	Plans Completed?
Fire drill, exits, area for class	
Earthquake drill	
Bell schedule	
Physical education schedule	
Recess, lunch, dismissal schedule	
Lavatory facilities (location)	
School-related teacher responsibilities	
Seating chart, name cards	
Class list	
System for checking out texts to students	
How can I reach office personnel, if needed?	
Schoolwide rules	
Availability of nurse	
Monitor/helper chart	
Instructional Planning for First Day of School	Plans Completed?
How shall I introduce myself?	
How shall I have students get acquainted?	
How shall I become acquainted with students?	
How will I motivate students about our semester activities?	
How shall the students and I decide on classroom standards?	
Have I planned adequately for content and activity blocks with appropriate time allotments for the entire school day?	
Do I have extra activities to serve as "sponges" for unplanned time?	

sign asking the students, "How Do These Rocks Feel?" In another basket she placed rocks that were unusual in color, and near this basket she put another sign, "How Many Colors Do You See?" She would plan lessons to encourage the students to categorize the rocks by both texture and shape.

Art and Music Center

On the bulletin board Hogan hung a painting of children dancing. She displayed the second-grade music books and her own autoharp below the picture. She anticipated that she would also display other instruments, but she felt it might be better to develop room standards before she put out too many temptations.

Social Studies Center

Hogan decided that she wanted to display a series of pictures depicting people's basic needs. She had some pictures of her own, and she decided to take a look at the school's resource center to see if there were some pictures that she could borrow. Ultimately she decided on one picture of a shelter in New Guinea, another picture of farmers irrigating a field, and a third picture of a home vegetable garden. Underneath the pictures appeared the caption, "What Do All People Need?" She placed a small picture file near the bulletin board so the students could browse through the file for other pictures that would help them answer the bulletin board question. Social studies books were also displayed.

Computer Center

The computer workstation included two high-resolution monitors, a video-disc player, CD-ROM drive, speakers, keyboard, and mouse for two computers. The hard drives were underneath the tables. A small storage stand held software.

Learning Centers

The learning center is designed to motivate, reinforce, and support students' learning needs. A center approach enables the teacher to differentiate instruction to meet individual ability levels and learning-style needs. The center attempts to lure students, coax them, and appeal to their natural inquisitiveness.

Arranging Seating

Although it was getting late and Hogan was rapidly becoming exhausted, she had to establish a seating chart before she left school that first day. The chart would help her learn to identify the students quickly. Using her class list and her health cards, Hogan began the task of establishing this chart. First she sorted through the health cards to identify students with special problems. She noted that she had one child with a partial hearing loss and another student with a limp. She decided on their placement in the classroom and then she began to cluster the rest of the children. The principal had told her earlier that she had one student who sometimes had difficulty working with others; she seated this student so he had a neighbor only on one side. She did not seat students by ability levels, having decided that this practice often had a negative effect on motivation to learn.

The Daily Schedule

Finally, Hogan tackled the important task of developing her daily schedule. She studied the elementary curriculum and divided the subjects into major time blocks for teaching purposes:

Language arts included reading, speaking skills, written skills, spelling, listening skills, handwriting, and literature.
Social studies/science included geography, history, political science, economics, psychology, anthropology, sociology, the science of living things, the study of matter and energy, the study of the earth, and the study of the universe.
Physical education/health included physical fitness, motor skills, and rhythmic experiences, along with personal and community health.

One of Hogan's main concerns was to mix active and concentrated experiences, so students would not be sitting too long without the opportunity to move around and stretch. First and second graders were at school for five and a half hours; Hogan was aware that this was a little longer than was customary, requiring her to make a special effort to interweave activities carefully. She also intended to use the longer periods of time for integrating subject fields. She knew that there would be occasions when she would want to use the period after recess or lunch for special projects. Hogan developed the following schedule for her second graders:

Lower Elementary Schedule

8:30–8:40 A.M.	Class business/sharing
8:40–9:40 A.M.	Language arts
9:40–10:00 A.M.	Lower grade recess
10:00–10:45 A.M.	Language arts
10:45–11:10 A.M.	Physical education/health
11:10–11:40 A.M.	Mathematics
11:40 A.M.–12:40 P.M.	Lunch
12:40–12:55 P.M.	Literature/music
12:55–1:55 P.M.	Social studies/science/art
1:55–2:00 P.M.	Cleanup/sharing/dismissal

Greg Thomas's schedule provides a contrast. Remember that his students are fifth graders in a southern rural school, and they attend school from 8:30 A.M. to 3:00 P.M. He, too, used broad subject areas to designate his time periods. His daily schedule looked like this:

Upper Elementary Schedule

8:30–8:35 A.M.	Class business
8:35–10:00 A.M.	Language arts
10:00–10:20 A.M.	Upper grade recess
10:20–11:20 A.M.	Social studies
11:20 A.M.–12:00 P.M.	Visual and performing arts
12:00–1:00 P.M.	Lunch
1:00–1:40 P.M.	Mathematics
1:40–2:10 P.M.	Physical education
2:10–3:00 P.M.	Science/health

Karen Adazzio's middle school schedule provides still another variation on how to allocate time during the school day. Adazzio's schedule had to be coordinated with five other teachers who share responsibility for 160 students. Although the whole school was on a block schedule, Adazzio's team worked together to create instructional themes. The following schedule demonstrates how students move through an alternating day schedule. During the first week of the month, the humanities core occurs on Monday, Wednesday, and Friday, and the social studies core on Tuesday and Thursday. During the second week of the month, the schedule is reversed, with social studies three days per week.

Middle School Schedule

8:30–9:50 A.M.	Humanities core, social studies
9:50–10:10 A.M.	Recess
10:15–11:35 A.M.	Math/science/health
11:35 A.M.–12:25 P.M.	Lunch
12:30–1:50 P.M.	Elective modules: practical and fine arts, foreign language
1:55–3:15 P.M.	Physical education/health
3:15 P.M.	Dismissal (three times per week)
3:15–3:30 P.M.	House meetings (twice weekly)

What Are the Advantages of Block Scheduling?

Experiments with block scheduling have discovered improvement in student achievement, teacher morale, and school climate (DiRocco, 1998/1999). For students, the advantages include learning experiences that provide more hands-on activities, greater participation, and greater involvement in the lessons. With fewer scheduling breaks, student engagement is more intense and, as a result, attendance increases and discipline problems decline. Another advantage of this type of scheduling is that less transition time between classes provides fewer opportunities for school problems and violence in the public and unsupervised areas of the school plant.

For teachers, the advantages include the ability to plan more motivating activities that fit a longer class period and increased opportunity for the use of technology. Teachers have more time to work with small groups of students and with individuals who need assistance. The block schedule means that time can be used more productively without interruptions. A decline in discipline problems (because students are more involved) provides more time for teaching. Teacher attendance also improves in schools with block scheduling.

Making Your Classroom Inclusive

Mary Hogan had two children with disabilities in her classroom for part of each school day. As she planned her daily schedule, she thought they would be able to participate during recess, physical education/health,

Research Findings

Smith, Molnar, and Zahorik (2003) reviewed the findings for class-size reduction in the Wisconsin Student Achievement Guarantee in Education program, which mandated 15 students to 1 teacher. They found that attendance was higher and achievement was greater than in normal-sized classrooms, and there was less of a gap between African American students and White students, more time for teachers to communicate with parents, and fewer classroom management problems.

lunch, and the afternoon program, which included literature, music, and social studies. It might even be possible for the special education children to join the second graders for mathematics. Hogan knew that she would have to consult with the special education teacher.

Greg Thomas also had several students with disabilities. He anticipated that these students would join the rest of his group beginning at recess time and probably spend the rest of the day with his class. The more relaxed environment encouraged by block scheduling at Karen Adazzio's school allowed teachers more time to accommodate the needs of students with disabilities and those considered at risk.

THE FIRST DAY OF SCHOOL

Mary Hogan knew that a number of new pupils would likely be enrolling on the first day of the new session. Therefore, she planned academic tasks of a review nature so she could monitor how well students were working and yet be free to give attention to a new student if necessary.

Hogan planned to begin language arts by reading several of Aesop's fables to the class. Then she would group the students heterogeneously and have them read a story about an animal in their literature book. She would ask the students to decide in their groups how the fables differed from the story in their book.

While the students were reading, she would walk around the room, observing the children and offering assistance when needed. She expected that the good readers would help others in their group read the story. The groups would then share their ideas with the whole class.

After the groups discussed the story in their book and how it was different from the fables, Hogan would ask them to draw pictures about either the fables or the story they had read. Then they would be asked to write their own story about their picture. In this way, Hogan would begin the writing process. Both spelling and manuscript writing would be informal activities and part of the editing stage of the writing process.

Hogan planned to talk to the students about the bulletin boards. She would help them read the captions and ask them to identify what interested them. Her intent was to begin the science unit that first day by asking children to name the colors they saw in the rocks. She would also ask the students to describe how the rocks felt, and then introduce the concept of texture. She hoped that they would identify the words *smooth*, *rough*, *slippery*, and *jagged*.

For physical education, Hogan would play the game Around the World, in which the children are organized into two concentric circles. To play the game, the inside circle sits down on the playground, while the outside circle stands behind a seated player. The teacher gives a direction ("Skip") and the outside group follows the direction (skips) around the circle until the teacher blows a whistle. Then each child in the outside circle must scamper to stand behind one of the seated players. Several children stand in the center of the circle, and when the whistle blows they, too, try to find a place behind a seated player. After a few minutes, the two circles change places. Hogan remembered that this was a very active and exciting game for second graders, and she hoped that it would extract some of their wiggles!

Setting Standards

With most of her plans made for the first day of school, Hogan turned her attention to classroom management details. She thought about her room arrangement and pondered the traffic pattern. She would discuss exiting and entering patterns with the students. She was also concerned about the need for classroom monitors, so she prepared a pocket chart for that purpose. She expected the students to be able to handle classroom routines without her direction. The following monitoring jobs would be performed by the students: door, lights, play equipment, office, window, lunch count, library, art, paper, attendance, books, flag, and centers. Some of the jobs would require more than one person.

Because control problems would be less likely if she could name students quickly, she decided to make name cards to place in front of each student.

She anticipated classroom problems that could be alleviated if the students were encouraged to develop class standards or rules. She decided that the following problem areas should be discussed:

- Walking in the classroom (no running)
- Use of quiet voices
- Respecting classmates' right to work
- Putting work aside when the teacher has something important to share
- Maintaining a clean and neat environment
- Pencil sharpening
- Use of the classroom water fountain
- Sharing materials (books, games, equipment)
- Listening to others' viewpoints

She anticipated that she would discuss these problems with her students as the need arose. For example, before recess would be an appropriate time to discuss the traffic pattern for leaving the classroom. Also, sometime during the morning she would talk to the students about fire drill routines.

Hogan would discuss quiet voices and most of the other routines with the students when they began formal classroom instruction. The class rules would be recorded on the chalkboard until the end of the day, at which time Hogan would transfer them to a chart.

Getting Acquainted

Hogan recognized that the cumulative records and the health cards provided her with just a bare outline of information about each child. To personalize her teaching technique for each student, she wanted to become better acquainted with the interests, attitudes, and personality of each of her students. To begin this task she would read a story to her students about hobbies. After motivating the students to talk about their personal interests, she would have each student write and illustrate a book called *All About Me*. This project would initiate an integrated language and art program.

Other Get-Acquainted Techniques

As Hogan observed her students playing at recess and lunchtime, she would learn about their capacity for cooperative play and teamwork. During the first couple of

> ### Teaching Hint:
> ### Classroom Management
>
> One classroom standard says it all: "We respect and care about each other."

weeks, she would test their physical skills through skill-related tasks at physical education time (see Chapter 12).

Hogan planned get-acquainted sessions and would invite small groups of children to eat lunch with her in the classroom. The informality of the small-group lunch session would provide her with new insights about each student.

She would introduce a puppet family to the students and have different students role-play family decisions related to specific problems:

- Maya was not doing her homework.
- Benjy was ill. Who would stay with him if he could not go to school?

They would also role-play family celebrations: Susan's birthday, Dad's commendation from the police department for bravery, Mom's new job. Hogan would use a variety of diagnostic tests to assess students' ability levels, but she was just as concerned with learning about students' self-reliance, social skills, and sense of belonging. For these capacities, she would need to rely on her own observation skills and some sociometric measures (see Chapter 7).

GETTING ACQUAINTED WITH THE COMMUNITY

Karen Adazzio planned to take one of her team members, a new teacher, on a drive around the school community. To understand the students they were to teach, Karen recognized the importance of visiting the community to learn about the problems, interests, services, and cultural priorities of the residents. She had prepared a list of 14 questions they would use to facilitate their observation.

Community Questions
1. Who lives in the community?
2. What is the residential pattern (apartments, single-family homes)?

3. How does the natural and human-made environment contribute to or detract from the community?
4. What businesses appear to flourish in the community? What businesses appear to flounder?
5. Are there social services within the community available to assist residents (hospitals, clinics, police, fire, legal aid)?
6. Do recreational facilities exist within the community (for children, for adults)?
7. Are distinctive culture characteristics apparent (specialty shops, restaurants, cultural sites, unique patterns, or environmental characteristics)?
8. Are there businesses, places of interest, or sites for field trips?
9. Are resource people available in the community to assist in the classroom?
10. What kinds of work opportunities exist in the community?
11. What special problems are apparent in the community?
12. If there are businesses in the community, does any one type predominate?
13. What special interests are obvious in the community? Do these interests relate to cultural priorities?
14. How might your own interests and talents assist the community?

DAILY TASKS OF THE TEACHER

Most of the tasks of the teacher can be subsumed into two major headings of teacher responsibility: instruction and management. (Instruction is the major focus of Chapters 4 and 5.) A third area of responsibility, not yet discussed, is the teacher's leadership role (emphasized in Chapter 14).

Instructional Role Decisions

Lesson Planning

Upon completion of student teaching, most teacher candidates comment, "Hurrah—no more lesson plans!" In reality, the effective (and experienced) teacher continues to use a lesson plan, but one that is less detailed than a student teacher's plan. In this section, we will look at the lesson plan of a student teacher, the lesson plan notes of two experienced teachers, and a teacher's weekly plan. You will learn about long-term planning in Chapter 6.

As teachers become more experienced, they are able to anticipate what students will say and their own responses as well. Therefore, the experienced teacher does not have to write these things into the lesson plan procedures. Provisions for interaction, discussion, and the thinking process for problem solving no longer appear under procedures, as they do in the student teacher's lesson plan in Figure 3.3, because the experienced teacher automatically provides time for these things to happen. Look at the experienced teacher's lesson plan in Figure 3.4 and you will notice how succinct the plan is compared to the student teacher's plan. For discussion to be effective, however, even experienced teachers have to plan their questioning approach prior to instruction and have cue cards ready for use. Figure 3.5 gives examples of some prompts used by an experienced teacher to keep a lesson moving ahead.

Some teachers like to file their lesson plans into a looseleaf notebook or a 4- by 6-inch box. The advan-

Subject: Math
Objectives: Measure, draw, define *rectangle, square, perimeter.* Use formula to find perimeter.
Materials: Guinea pig cage (for motivation), ruler, shapes
Procedure:
1. *Motivation:* Use cage with guinea pig!
2. Introduce L. W. Use cage.
3. Have students draw; observe.
4. Define *rectangle, square.*
5. Have students find P of cage.
6. Explain formula.
7. Have students practice using shapes.
8. Evaluate objectives.

Figure 3.4   An Experienced Teacher's Lesson Plan

tage of doing this is that it is easy to refer to when a student returns from absence or when a parent comes in for a conference.

Figure 3.6 shows Mary Hogan's *weekly planning schedule.* She found this form in a special booklet titled "Weekly Planning Forms" that was given to her by the principal at the first faculty meeting. Hogan still needs lesson planning notes for some subjects, but the weekly plan helps her remember special events and document subject matter preparation through the course of the

Subject:	Mathematics—Fifth Grade
Objectives:	Students will measure the perimeter of a rectangle.
	Students will use a formula to find the perimeter of a rectangle.
	Students will draw a square.
	Students will define *perimeter, rectangle, square.*
Materials:	Ruler, paper, cardboard shapes, guinea pig, and cage

Procedures:
1. *Motivation:* Display a guinea pig in a cage. Comment that cage is too small, but tell the students, "I did not know what size to buy since I didn't know the size of this cage. How can I find out the size of this cage?" (Students will respond, "Measure it.")
2. Allow several students to measure cage.
3. Have students draw size of cage on board.
4. Have students label *length* and *width.*
5. Have all students draw a small cage on their own paper.
6. Observe students' work.
7. Ask, "Do you know the shape of the cage?" (Introduce the word *rectangle* and define it.)
8. Ask, "Do you know another shape in which all four sides are the same?" (Introduce the concept of a square as a rectangle with equal sides.)

Figure 3.3   A Student Teacher's Lesson Plan

1. Display picture of partial environment.
2. Are you familiar with what the picture shows?
3. Does it show everything that is around it?
4. What seems to be missing?
5. What evidence do you have? How do you know something is missing?
6. How do you suppose we could find out what is missing?
7. Do you know what these (resources) are?
8. How do you use these resources?
9. How would a scientist, mathematician, or judge obtain proof?
10. Today you're going to be a research explorer. You are going to collect evidence that will help you decide what is missing in the picture. Let's talk about what you will need.

Source: Adapted with permission from planning notes of Lillian Walker, teacher in the Los Angeles Unified School District.

Figure 3.5   An Experienced Teacher's Lesson Plan: Notes and Question Prompts

	Monday	Tuesday	Wednesday	Thursday	Friday	Special Notes
Reading	Predict endings to stories; Read in literature books	Use science book, Chapter 2	Identify central problem in stories	Read about fossils in science book, pp. 110–114	Free-choice reading; Read orally	Use centers
Writing	Write new endings for stories; Share endings	Choose topic; Begin own story	Revise stories	Edit stories	Share stories	
Spelling and handwriting	Use words from rock center	Teach patterns in words; *slippery, jagged*; Practice writing →	Use words in sentences and stories →	→	Spelling test	
Physical education/ health	Teach side throw →; Play Caboose Dodge Ball	→	Play Circle Relay ↑	Rhythms: Teach Hokey-Pokey*; Practice skipping ↑	Nutrition: Use health book—Chapter 1	*Borrow record from Miss Smith
Math	Use flannel board for story of 5; use sticks; draw story of 5	Practice addition facts through 5	Tell number stories; Use flannel board	Teach hours; use individual clocks; use practice sheets on clocks ↑	↑	
Literature and music	Teach Grey Squirrel ↑; Sing old favorites	↑	Read: *Horton Hatches an Egg*	Teach *America*; Review songs	Read poetry from speech book	
Science, social studies (SS), art	Science: Work in groups to classify rocks; discuss properties of rocks	Science: Use tools to change shape of rocks; discuss	SS: Initiate unit (use arranged environment), "What do all people need?"	SS: Research "Basic Needs"; use picture file, filmstrip, chart, books	Art: Finger painting	
Special Notes	Send note home with Billy M. for parent conference			Remind children to bring aprons for art lesson		

Figure 3.6 Weekly Planning Schedule

semester. It is also a handy guide for the substitute teacher if Hogan is absent.

Integration of Subject Fields and Interdisciplinary Teaching

These two concepts are discussed in depth in Chapter 6, but Mary Hogan needs to consider both concepts as she does her lesson planning. Hogan thinks about **integration of instruction** when she considers the skills students need to read out of the science book and when she uses science and social studies concepts during spelling. Integrating subject fields applies the principle of what Ausubel and Robinson (1969) called integrative reconciliation. Students' prior experiences are utilized as new ideas are integrated with previously learned knowledge. Instead of gaining knowledge in a fragmented or compartmentalized, single-subject approach (as in a textbook), ideas are broadly related across subject fields. This permits the elementary and middle school teacher to develop a balanced curriculum. The daily schedule, defined by broad subject fields, is designed to facilitate integrative and interdisciplinary teaching. The daily schedule should not be interpreted so strictly that it hinders the integration of subject fields or reflects an unbalanced curriculum.

Interdisciplinary instruction helps students make connections between subject fields. For example, one might take the concept of *role* and explore its meaning in different disciplines. Consider playing the role of Peter Pan in a musical production and studying roles in feudal society. Interdisciplinary teaching emphasizes the linkages among disciplines. Teachers must consider both integrative opportunities and interdisciplinary instruction when planning curriculum.

Data Gathering

A student's success in school depends on the teacher's accurate **assessment** of cognitive and affective learner needs. Assessment occurs in a variety of ways. First the teacher must decide what he or she needs to know about students. Specify skills, concepts, attitudes, and values. Once this is done, decide what techniques or procedures to use for the assessment.

Assessment

Use simple checklists to evaluate skill sequences, specific behaviors, or interests and concepts (see Chapter 8

for examples). Record your observations of students' interests, skill performance, and on-task behavior on observation cards. Anecdotal records, conferences, and diaries contribute to the assessment process. Tests you prepare as well as standardized achievement tests provide data for interpretation. Once you have gathered the data, diagnose needs. An accurate diagnosis is essential for appropriate instructional planning.

Diagnosis

The term *diagnosis* is often used in education the same way it is used in medicine. Assessment provides the data, the symptoms, and the signs. You use the data to interpret the condition of learning and the situation most likely to facilitate the learning process. You can record technical descriptions based on the data, although it is not always necessary to do so.

Prescription

Diagnosis is the interpretation of the data, but *prescription* refers to the plan the teacher uses to carry out instruction. Mary Hogan decided that Charlie was continually frustrated trying to complete classroom assignments. She decided to change Charlie's assignments to what she and Charlie thought would be manageable for him. The result was that Charlie expressed delight in his own progress and began to make great strides in several subject fields. Hogan's prescription was obviously accurate and appropriate for Charlie.

Classroom grouping decisions should always be based on a careful analysis of the school and grade-level data. For example, at one school, teachers were told to move five students from an all-fifth-grade classroom to a fourth/fifth-grade combination room and to move five fourth-grade students to a third/fourth-grade combination room. The teachers made their choices without any data about the students.

In both cases, the consequences were atypical; third-grade students were superior in achievement to the fourth-grade students in the third/fourth-grade combination class, and the fourth grade students were superior in achievement to the fifth-grade students in the fourth/fifth-grade combination room. As a result, there were a lot of highly frustrated students whose egos were affected negatively, and there were also control problems for the teachers.

If the teachers had reviewed the evidence before making their decisions, they would have placed average fourth graders with low-to-average third graders and average fifth graders with low-to-average fourth graders. An appropriate prescription provides for a reasonable instructional program corresponding to students' needs. Selection of appropriate learning experiences is also based on the prescription. Instruction is based on the assessment, the diagnosis, and the prescription. These three components make up the planning stage for instruction.

Instructional Planning

Presentation

The term *prescription* was used broadly in the previous section to signify the plan for teaching. That plan should also include methodological decisions about teaching strategy and instructional materials. The presentation can include actual direct instruction by the teacher or indirect instruction through discovery approaches. Teachers base presentation decisions on grouping needs, individual skill levels, the nature of the learning task, and the appropriateness of the instructional materials. In the classroom the teacher mediates instruction using the plan that was conceived before the beginning of the school day. The greater the teacher's skill in the presentation of instruction, the greater will be the engagement rate of students. (In other words, the students will pay attention!) A carefully planned and structured lesson facilitates students' understanding of what they are expected to learn and how they should go about it. Discovery approaches need to be planned and structured just as carefully as a direct instructional lesson in reading or mathematics.

Monitoring

Monitoring is an instructional task component. During instruction the teacher must keep track of student progress. By checking student progress, the teacher knows whether to deviate from the plan or to carry on. Monitoring is closely related to assessment. If the original assessment provided inaccurate data, then the diagnosis and the prescription will be wrong. The teacher monitors instruction by circulating around the room during practice periods or while students are working in small groups. During a direct instructional episode, teachers frequently monitor progress by asking questions.

Reinforcement

As the teacher monitors instruction, he or she gives feedback to the students. Students' engagement rate is higher when teachers let them know whether they are right, wrong, or on the right track. **Academic feedback** has been closely related to students' achievement by researchers.

Teachers reinforce the purpose of instruction and good study habits by providing time to correct seatwork or homework. At learning centers, you can provide reinforcement by developing a system whereby students can correct their own work or find out if their work is on target. Some curriculum materials and programmed textbooks also provide immediate feedback to the student.

Evaluation

Formative (ongoing) **evaluation** need not be distinguished from monitoring and reinforcement because an ongoing type of evaluation helps keep students on task and provides immediate feedback so the students know if they are progressing. **Summative evaluation** is also a progress report to both teacher and student (as well as parents), but it does not monitor instruction in the same interactive way.

Management Decisions

The three components of teacher responsibility—management, instruction, and leadership—should not be separated as if they were distinct entities. The teacher who is not an effective classroom manager will not be an effective instructor, nor will this individual be able to provide leadership. It is only for the purpose of opening up and viewing the varied tasks of the classroom teacher that these three components are isolated as if they were distinct occurrences. The following seven items should provide some insight into teachers' daily management decisions:

1. *Classroom business:* Taking attendance, collecting milk money, handing out notices, collecting parent responses—these are but a few of the daily tasks that teachers perform under the heading of classroom business.
2. *Scheduling:* Coordinating the work of other teachers, such as the music teacher, the special reading teacher, and the special educator, may fall under the heading of arranging the daily schedule.

Facilitating the work of these professionals and coordinating their schedule with your own is an important but sometimes wearing task.

3. *Arranging the environment:* Another management task that must be attended to daily is arranging seating for special instructional strategies. How should children be seated during a classroom discussion? What should you do with the tables for a construction lesson? Should the chairs be stacked during finger painting so students will not touch them? How can you make a learning center more attractive? Should you change the bulletin board display? These and countless other questions are attended to as teachers make environmental decisions.

4. *Anticipating instructional and organizational problems:* One of the most important decisions that teachers make on a daily basis involves grouping students for instructional activities. In physical education, how can you ensure that there will be balanced teams and that less-skilled students will not end up with hurt feelings? For small-group project or planning experiences, students should be grouped heterogeneously. Should you, the teacher, choose the group members who are to work together, or will you allow students to choose? How will you group for the science experiment and the social studies research lesson?

   For example, today is rhythms day, but the auditorium is not available. Should you rearrange the classroom, have rhythms outside, or change the activity? Another example: Yesterday it appeared that the students did not understand the math concepts that you taught. Should you reteach or continue on and hope for the best? Or consider the following: Your students have written a class play and will perform it for the other third-grade classrooms, but Billy, the star performer, has a fever. Should you let him stay and perform, reschedule the play, or attempt it without him?

5. *Providing supplies:* One of the most frustrating but typical problems of the new teacher is failure to anticipate material needs. Paper for writing or math work, pencils, art supplies, colored paper, and tagboard for charts all need to be gathered before instructional time. The teacher who constantly bothers classroom neighbors to borrow materials becomes very unpopular. The need for reference books, such as dictionaries or textbooks, also must

be anticipated before class time. Audiovisual equipment is another common supply item that is forgotten until needed. Successful teachers have the right equipment and supplies on hand at the right time.

6. *Establishing routines:* Many classroom routines can be set on a weekly or monthly basis (monitors, group leaders), but you may need to plan some procedures almost on a daily basis. For example, a learning center for language arts and art experiences provided the opportunity for children to make masks. This activity required the use of colored paper, scissors, and paste. The teacher needed to anticipate where the students would put their wastepaper and how they would clean their hands after using paste. A simple paper bag, tacked to the bulletin board, served as a waste container, and because the classroom had no sink, the teacher brought in a pail of water and placed paper towels next to it.

   Routines concerned with collecting seatwork, self-correcting center work, or handing out paper and other supplies need to be reinforced daily by the classroom teacher.

7. *Monitoring behavior:* Monitoring instruction has been cited as an instructional component; monitoring behavior is specified as a management component. The line is fine between these two classifications. A key task during instruction is to maintain academic interest and involvement of the students. Research indicates that the higher the engagement rate, the higher the achievement. Substantive feedback is important in instructional monitoring, but just as important is the teacher's expression of with-it-ness. The teacher who communicates awareness of what is happening in the classroom knows precisely when to stand by a student and demand attention, when to smile or make eye contact with a student, when to nod approval or disapproval, and when to change activities.

These seven management tasks are daily responsibilities. Each must be carried out in an efficient manner.

Homework: Is It Important?

In some classrooms, homework becomes a classroom management problem because (1) too much time is devoted to verifying that students have completed and brought their homework to class; (2) homework is treated like a "rule"—if you don't have your homework, you've broken the rule and should be punished; (3) homework is ignored by the teacher after it is assigned and students are upset if they do not get closure; and (4) parents are upset if they feel that they are forced to do the homework when, too frequently, the students do not understand the assignment. The monitoring of homework is discussed in Chapter 7.

Why Is Homework Assigned?

Theoretically homework is supposed to improve students' academic performance. Yet there is no evidence that it does so (Kohn, 2007). Even if students' scores on tests directly related to the homework assigned does improve, the test score does not signify actual learning.

A second reason typically identified is that homework is supposed to develop students' study skills and responsibility. However, teachers do not know whether the student completes the homework or siblings or parents do it. Also, how many times parents need to remind the sudent to do the homework is unknown.

Parental Attitude About Homework

Homework is one of those customs that has survived through the ages, and though most parents think students should have some homework to do, they complain about the time it takes and the bedtime that suffers. Second, parents complain because they need to be involved in interpreting the assignment and keeping their child on task. A third complaint is that homework usurps all available time and curtails play/sport activities, which are considered important because physical education time is limited in the schools.

SUMMARY

Classroom management encompasses the teacher's planning, organizing, and monitoring tasks to achieve success in the classroom. Successful classroom management helps students maintain high task involvement. In democratic environments, students accept responsibility for their behavior because they have had the opportunity to define classroom rules and standards. Students should work in both large and small groups throughout the school day. When the teacher fosters a sense of belonging to the classroom group, cooperative behavior is encouraged and learning is enhanced. The environment of school and classroom affects behavioral actions and human relationships.

Teachers' daily tasks include planning short- and long-range instruction, organizing the environment, and attending to supplies. Affecting teachers' planning is the need to diagnose and interpret students' needs, making methodological decisions, monitoring students' work, and reinforcing and evaluating instruction and learning.

PORTFOLIO ACTIVITY

Demonstrate how you treat students equitably. To accomplish this, provide a sample of your classroom standards. Explain how the standards were developed and the rationale for each. Discuss what happens in your classroom when standards are ignored and identify how you reinforce classroom standards. (If you do not have your own classroom, provide an example of what you would like the standards to be, then continue with the rest of the assignment.)

 ## DISCUSSION QUESTIONS AND APPLICATION EXERCISES

1. Students were crowded at lunch tables with about 16 children at each table. They ate their bagged lunches and banged elbows with each other. Some spilled milk; some exchanged sandwiches and desserts. Papers and lunches were flying through

---

Teaching Hints: Homework

- The purpose of homework is to provide opportunity for students to *apply* what they have learned in class. Therefore, do not assign drill, practice, or unfamiliar work for homework.
- Verify that students understand the homework assignment before they leave class.
- Provide class time for students to share their homework assignment and/or determine its accuracy.
- Homework sharing should occur at the beginning of the session or day.

the air. The lunch area was dirty and excessively noisy.

The lunch supervisors blew their whistles. One of the supervisors threatened, "Unless you stop talking and clean up, we will not excuse you to play on the playground." Do you think the supervisors were right to ask the students to be quiet? How would adults act in the same setting? Suggest some alternative ways of handling the lunch problem.

2. Plan a first day of school using your choice of subject field(s) and grade level.
3. Explain how you will integrate several mainstreamed children into your program.
4. Explain why scheduling longer blocks of time facilitates a thinking curriculum.
5. Why are behavioral approaches to classroom discipline considered quick-fix strategies that do not treat the underlying problems? Should students be "paid" for appropriate behavior? Why or why not?
6. Suggest some classroom standards that encourage good citizenship and participation in the classroom.
7. How does small-group work improve students' social skills?
8. Plan a group activity to develop group identity and a sense of belonging.
9. Suppose your ELL students rarely participate in whole-class discussion. What are some ways to encourage their participation?
10. What would you do in the following situation?

Unbeknown to its captor, the small mouse escaped from its cardboard prison and slithered across the room toward the learning center. Charlie, the mouse's owner, had placed the cardboard box on the floor under his seat. Charlie was what his teacher described as "hyper," and he had kicked the lid off the box without being aware that he had done so. Charlie had not bothered to tell his teacher that the mouse was visiting the classroom.

It was 10:10 A.M. and many of the students began to close their books (noisily) in anticipation of recess. The teacher ignored the disturbance, but noted the time and began to give directions to prepare for recess. At the same time, Bonnie saw the mouse and screamed; Erik fell over as he tried to capture it; and Charlie came running. "It's mine," he screamed. The teacher was also screaming. "Everyone stop right now! Don't move."

What can you infer from this incident about the teacher's classroom management skills? Think about some of the key management components you have learned:

- Classroom organization and rules
- Student responsibility and discipline
- Teacher behavior: "with-it-ness," clarity, firmness

If you were this teacher, would you discuss the problem with the whole class or just with Charlie? What would you say to Bonnie and Erik? Would you do anything about the students who noisily anticipated recess? If so, what?

READER RESEARCH

Study the environment of an elementary or middle school. Provide examples of the formal structure and the informal structure of the school that you have selected.

 TECHNOLOGY APPLICATIONS

Why is time such a significant variable when planning a lesson using technology? How will you manage computer activities in your classroom?

During group work it is important that the teacher observe each group and offer guidance when it is needed.

CHAPTER 4

• •

Exposition and Discussion Strategies

In this chapter two modes of instruction are explored: exposition and discussion. The expository mode focuses on the teacher. The teacher's task is to communicate information to students. The teacher may do this through lecturing or sometimes through the use of a combination technique of lecture, question, and short-answer response. Expository teaching is an efficient means to communicate a great deal of information to a large group of students simultaneously. But lecturing and reading are not the only means for expository teaching; direct instruction and comprehension models help to vary the transmission process. Discussion techniques, also discussed in this chapter, provide an opportunity for students to share knowledge and gain information from peers. Good discussions require stimulating questions. Both discussion and question strategies are demonstrated.

Advance Organizer

The following questions are intended to guide your reading and understanding of the content of this chapter.

1. Why is there a specific teaching sequence for the teaching model identified as direct instruction?
2. Why are three distinct types of practices used in direct instruction?
3. In what ways can you provide for multiple intelligences when using direct instruction?
4. In what ways is the comprehension model different from the direct instruction model?
5. Using this chapter, how can you demonstrate the advance organizer model of teaching?
6. What is the purpose of guided discussion during direct instruction?
7. What are the characteristics of oral discussions and how does the classroom environment affect the discussion?
8. How would you identify and define the three types of discussion and corresponding teacher behavior?
9. What are the characteristics of good questions?
10. Why should questions be planned in a cluster sequence?

INTASC

INTASC Standards

Standards 1–8 are all relevant in this chapter. Teachers need a repertoire of teaching strategies *and* must know which strategy is appropriate for the needs of the students and the content and skills that are to be taught.

Professional Lexicon

advance organizer   A framework for organizing and structuring new knowledge to facilitate meaningful acquisition of information via presentations and readings.

coaction   A back-and-forth conversation between two individuals, such as the teacher and a student.

direct instruction   A means to teach specific knowledge or skills efficiently using three major processes: presentation, practice, and feedback.

expository teaching   Communicating knowledge by controlling the input process. The learner's task is to consume the knowledge using visual and auditory means.

guided practice   Engagement of students in acquiring knowledge or skills using practice material while the teacher monitors and provides feedback.

independent practice   Practice sessions in which students work independently to apply what they have learned by using the skill or knowledge in a new way.

interaction   Communication among several individuals involving more than one-way discussion; may be cooperative or combative.
refocusing   Reestablishing purpose by reiterating the assignment and clarifying meanings when students go off in the wrong direction or are off task.

structured practice   Controlled practice sessions in which the teacher uses short-answer questions and elicits responses to verify student understanding of what is to be learned.

Picture a covey of ducklings, all with their mouths open. The mother duck makes the rounds feeding them snails, small insects, and fingerlings. As the ducklings mature, the mother duck teaches them to search and fish for their own food. She observes them and makes them practice until they are skillful enough to feed themselves.

Expository teaching is analogous to the mother duck feeding her young ducklings. The main purpose of expository teaching is to transmit knowledge. There is very little **interaction** among students during expository teaching. The classroom environment is controlled, and there is moderate to high structure. The teacher controls discussion by initiating questions and eliciting short-answer responses.

Direct instruction is a type of expository teaching. Direct instruction usually conforms to the following format:

- Diagnosis
- Prescription
- Modeling (presentation, lecture)
- Practice
- Monitoring
- Feedback

DIRECT INSTRUCTION

Effective Teaching of Concepts and Skills

In the 1970s and early 1980s, a number of researchers confirmed that when teachers maintain a highly structured environment for teaching specific concepts and skills, they are able to maximize student engagement and time spent on task. Teaching in this manner is characterized by large-group instruction, teacher direction, the academic focus, and the preponderance of practice.

Group Instruction

Although direct instruction may occur when the teacher is working with a small group of students, most typically the teacher is directing the class as a whole. Student performance during instruction is closely monitored to verify understanding and academic engagement.

Teacher-Directed Instruction

The most successful teachers (those whose students achieve highest gains) are strong classroom leaders. They plan their teaching objectives, teach to students in a businesslike way, ask meaningful short-answer questions directed to the students, listen to student responses, and give immediate feedback.

Academic Focus

During direct instruction, the teacher relates what is to be learned to what students already know and communicates to students the purpose of the lesson. The new knowledge or skill is introduced using concrete objects or pictures to assist students' learning through both oral and visual means. The teacher models what is to be learned and, through sharply focused questions, verifies student understanding by eliciting responses.

Practice

The most important aspect of direct instruction is the focus on practice. After the presentation and modeling, the teacher directs **structured practice**. During structured practice, it is essential that the teacher ask specific factual questions and elicit student response. It is important to provide immediate feedback, telling students what is correct and what is incorrect. Confident that students are gaining competence and understanding, the teacher assigns a second practice time. During this **guided practice**, the students receive less assistance, but the teacher monitors the practice and continues to provide feedback. The concept or skill is then reinforced through **independent practice** as students *apply* the new knowledge or skill. This may take the form of a homework assignment or an in-class project at a higher cognitive level.

Several studies of low-achieving students verify that convergent questions with single answers should be asked during the structured practice and drill period and that students should be provided with immediate feedback. Research has again confirmed that the frequency of direct, factual teacher questions and the frequency of accurate student responses were positively associated with high achievement.

Success Is Important. A number of studies emphasize that when students work alone and when they work during the controlled practice period, they need to be successful. Correct answers should be possible at least 80% of the time for low socioeconomic students and at least 70% of the time for students of high socioeconomic status.

During skill instruction, students need to experience both fact questions and higher-cognitive questions. Students also need to participate in recitation immediately after reading textbook content. Recitation serves the dual purpose of providing students with practice recalling content and enabling the teacher to provide students with immediate feedback.

Monitoring Independent Practice. The independent practice period usually takes the form of follow-up seatwork during reading instruction or practicing a small number of examples of the skill during mathematics. Because success is so important, the exercises that students do should be relatively easy. As students practice, the teacher monitors the students' work and provides immediate feedback in the form of positive reinforcement or a short explanation when a student needs assistance. The feedback provided to the student should not take more than 30 seconds of the teacher's time; if it takes longer, the teacher can assume that the original explanation was faulty.

Is Direct Instruction Ever Inappropriate?

Yes, indeed! Peterson (1979) compared the effects of open versus traditional approaches on student achievement. She concluded that students who experience direct instruction do slightly better on achievement tests but slightly worse on tests of abstract thinking that validate creativity and problem-solving ability. Open teaching approaches facilitate creative thinking and problem solving. They also improve students' attitudes toward school and the teacher and increase students' independence and curiosity. Student motivation for schooling and self-efficacy increases with opportunity for working with challenging and relevant problems.

The research cited in Chapter 2 tells us that students who feel that they have personal control of their successes and failures do better (achieve more) when the teacher uses an open approach to teaching. The student whose style is self-directed (having an internal locus of control) is frustrated during direct instruction. Students who feel that others control their successes and failures do equally well in either direct or open teaching approaches. However, students who have an external locus of control seem to prefer direct instruction because their learning style matches the controlled setting of direct instruction.

The effectiveness of direct instruction often depends on the ability of the students. High-achieving, task-oriented students appear to do worse in direct instruction. Peterson and Janicki (1979) found that high-ability students did better when the teacher used small-group instruction as opposed to large-group instruction. The low-ability students did better when the teacher used large-group instruction.

It is apparent from the research on direct teaching and open teaching approaches that if the teacher's objective is inquiry teaching/problem solving, analysis, synthesis, evaluation, or judgment, then open approaches are superior. If, on the other hand, the teaching objective is essential skill instruction, learning facts, or simple comprehension of information, then direct instruction should be used. However, the choice of a teaching approach should also be based on students' abilities and strengths. High-ability students may be frustrated with direct instruction, whereas low-ability students may need the structured environment that accompanies direct instruction.

GUIDED DISCUSSION AND DIRECT INSTRUCTION

Direct instruction depends on students' on-task behaviors. To facilitate students' understanding, involvement, and success, teachers question students during skill instruction. The strategy is really a mixture of expository teaching and guided discussion. The questions are oriented to factual and comprehension information. Short-answer responses are required from students. The teacher calls on a student during instruction to verify that he or she understands. If the student makes a mistake, the teacher corrects it, thereby providing instant feedback. Small-group reading instruction may be guided by the following sequence:

• Group question to cue silent reading
• Teacher question to an individual related to the silent reading
• Response
• Teacher question to another student
• Response
• Repeat sequence

During instruction of a new skill, the format is similar. The teacher may present or model the new skill or concept. Next, the teacher questions students about the presentation, providing them with structured practice. The questions are factual and require short answers. To verify that others understand, the teacher may continue the question/answer format. Coaction rather than interaction occurs between teacher and student. When using this format, students must understand the purpose of the lesson so they can concentrate on the essential elements. Then students engage in another practice opportunity with the teacher monitoring their work; this is called guided practice. Finally, students may be

Teaching Hints: Direct Instruction

1. Demonstrate, model, or present new information or the new skill to be learned.
2. Ask students questions to verify understanding of the presentation.
3. Have students practice what was presented and provide immediate feedback (structured practice).
4. Provide additional practice and monitor students' performance (guided instruction).
5. Assign an independent activity for students to apply what they learned in a different or unique way.

During direct instruction, it is important for the teacher to verify students' understanding.

Teaching Hints: Direct Instruction and ELL Students

1. Begin the lesson with concrete examples (manipulatives, pictures, objects).
2. Demonstrate using the concrete examples.
3. Introduce the vocabulary of the lesson slowly, using as many familiar words as possible. (Be dramatic, use expression.)
4. Ask questions using the same vocabulary to verify understanding.
5. Have students practice with each other or with other peers.
6. Monitor students' work and provide immediate feedback.
7. Have students apply the lesson independently with projects, personal stories, or concrete activities using music, art, or experiments.

given an assignment to apply what they have learned in a new way and to see if they have really mastered the skill; this is the independent practice phase.

Independent Practice and Multiple Intelligences

Independent practice provides an outstanding opportunity for student-directed practice with students demonstrating their understandings using multiple intelligences. Time for independent practice may occur in the classroom or as a homework assignment. Students should be encouraged to apply what they have learned using music, art, computers, and other subject fields. For example, consider the following lessons.

Mary Hogan's second graders may illustrate—in sequence—the words of a song using both musical/rhythmic and visual/spatial intelligences.

Greg Thomas's fifth graders could use an outline to construct a timeline of key events, thereby utilizing both verbal/linguistic and logical/mathematical intelligences.

Karen Adazzio is teaching a reading comprehension lesson to her seventh graders. The students are demonstrating verbal/linguistic intelligences, reflection demonstrating intrapersonal intelligence, and discussion demonstrating interpersonal intelligence.

Research Findings

Sternberg and colleagues (2006) studied Alaskan Eskimo children, Kenyan children, and urban children in Baltimore, Maryland. Students were tested on knowledge related to their own environments. The researchers found that students who were taught with an emphasis on analytical and creative thinking outperformed other students on performance assessments.

MARY HOGAN PRESENTS A LESSON USING DIRECT INSTRUCTION

In Mary Hogan's second-grade classroom, she had determined that several of her students did not understand the use of context clues. She planned a lesson using a short story in a literature book, *The Very Hungry Caterpillar* by Eric Carle. First she told the story using only the pictures. (In this way, she modeled the comprehension skill of using context clues.)

Next, she introduced the lesson, announcing, "Boys and girls, today we are going to see if we can play the game of detective. I am going to show some pictures to you, and you try to guess what is happening in the story from these pictures."

Hogan showed the pictures in sequence to the students. Then she asked specific questions about the action in each of the pictures: "Who do we see in this picture? What is Ramon doing? How can you tell? Why do you think Ramon is crying?" (Hogan was providing the students with structured practice.)

She then guided the students through the story using the pictures. Then she said, "Let's find out if we were good detectives."

This time the students read the story in the usual manner with silent reading cued by an appropriate question, but once again the questions related to the sequence of the pictures. When the students recognized their success as detectives, Hogan provided them with another opportunity to practice. She had prepared short, simple stories. The students worked with a partner. One student told the story using the pictures that were provided, and the other student confirmed the story by reading it. Then they exchanged roles with new stories. Hogan watched, listened, and provided feedback. (This time students were engaged semi-independently in guided practice.)

Next, Hogan brought out a number of literature books and asked the students to select what interested them. She told them to see if they could use their detective skills to read the books. In this way, she provided independent practice at the application level. Later she would provide time for the students to tell others their stories.

If you analyze Hogan's lesson, you can clearly see that it had several stages:

1. Planning (diagnosis and prescription)
2. Instruction (presentation/modeling)
3. Practice (structured, guided, and application level)

See if you can identify the stages in the scenario.

 **GREG THOMAS PRESENTS
A LESSON USING DIRECT
INSTRUCTION***

Greg Thomas's fifth-grade class is studying climate in the southeastern part of the United States. Thomas is explaining to the students the difference between weather and climate. He identifies the things that affect temperature and those factors that affect rainfall. As he talks he writes an outline on the chalkboard. His outline looks like Figure 4.1. "The purpose of the outline is to help you take notes when you do your reading about weather and climate."

Thomas purposefully has not completed his outline. He questions the students about each of the items under the heading of *temperature*. Teacher and students talk about how the outline touches on key ideas of their reading and how they can use the outline to help them take notes and remember important information. Then Thomas tells the students, "We need to practice outlining. Let's all read these two paragraphs and see if we can identify the main factors that affect rainfall."

*This lesson is based on content in *Science K–8: An Integrated Approach* (10th ed., pp. 284–285), by E. Victor and R. D. Kellough, 2002, Upper Saddle River, NJ: Prentice Hall/Merrill.

I. Temperature
  A. Latitude
  B. Altitude
  C. Wind
  D. Mountains
  E. Land and water masses
  F. Ocean currents
II. Rainfall

Figure 4.1 Greg Thomas's Outline Chart

He passes out the reading. Students work individually. When Thomas is satisfied that students have had ample time, he asks them to identify what they have learned. He jots down their responses.

Now Thomas asks the students to identify other ideas in the passage. Together they develop a simple outline that Thomas writes on the chalkboard. When it appears that the students are comfortable with their joint work, Thomas directs them to read another passage in their textbook and practice on their own. While they do this, he walks around, assists, and offers suggestions. He reminds them, "If you need help, raise your hand or nod at me as I walk around the room."

After about 10 minutes, Thomas has the students share their efforts. "OK, you seem to have the idea about how to use outlining to help you take notes. Now we will choose our research groups to study how climatologists predict weather. Each group will be responsible for making a weather instrument. When you need to take notes for your investigation, I want you to use the outlining technique we have just studied."

An analysis of Thomas's lesson using direct instruction is as follows:

1. *Orientation:* Thomas introduced the study of weather and climate and integrated the skill of outlining to help students take notes on what they needed to learn.
2. *Presentation:* Thomas demonstrated simple outlining as he discussed with the students the factors that affect weather changes.
3. *Structured practice:* Thomas gave the students a short passage to read and had them contribute to the development of an outline that he wrote on the chalkboard. Questions and discussion contributed to this task.

4. *Guided practice:* Students were given another passage to read out of their texts and asked to develop an outline individually. Thomas monitored and assisted. Students raised hands or caught Thomas's eye if they needed help.
5. *Independent practice:* Students selected groups for research on weather instruments. Groups will apply their understanding of outlining as they read about how to build an instrument to predict weather.

Why is Greg Thomas teaching outlining during the teaching of science? Should he do this?

Classroom Management Notes: Direct Instruction

Planning

Greg Thomas was teaching science and recognized that his students would need to take notes on what they read. He planned to teach them how to use an outline to help them study. He prepared a reading assignment that would communicate science information and could be used for practicing the skill of outlining. In addition, he would have the students use their science textbook as a resource.

Environment

Thomas used the whole class as a group to orient the students about what they were to learn and for structured and guided practice. He used the chalkboard to demonstrate the skill of outlining. Later in the lesson he would have the students move into small groups for studying weather instruments.

Organizing Procedures and Resources

Thomas's decisions involved first large-group teaching, then individual work, and then group work that required organizational skills. His use of a separate reading passage and then texts demonstrated his organization of resources and his consideration of individual needs.

Monitoring

Thomas had to monitor student understanding during the presentation and structured practice. Then he monitored individual work during the guided practice while students worked out of their texts.

Anticipating Problems

By having his materials ready, Thomas had no lag time and no misbehavior occurred. He directed learning throughout the lesson, communicated task instructions clearly, and monitored both whole-group and independent work. Students knew what was expected of them throughout the lesson and how to obtain help.

THE COMPREHENSION MODEL: A VARIATION OF DIRECT INSTRUCTION

Students need to learn and practice comprehension strategies. During reading, comprehension is facilitated when the learner is asked to do the following tasks:

- Summarize what he or she has read
- Identify the main idea of what was read
- Transform the reading into his or her own words by telling others
- Predict future events or applications of the content; extend to other genres and disciplines

As you read about Karen Adazzio's lesson in the next section, pay attention to the students' tasks and the questions she asks them. You may want to classify the tasks and questions into the four categories previously identified.

KAREN ADAZZIO'S COMPREHENSION MODEL LESSON

In Karen Adazzio's seventh-grade classroom, the students are reading Daniel Davis's *Behind Barbed Wire: The Imprisonment of Japanese Americans During World War II.* Adazzio begins the day's reading, asking the students to look at the pictures and captions on certain pages. She asks, "How do you think the little girl feels as she sees all her family's belongings packed in crates and duffel bags?" After several responses, Adazzio asks another question, "What do you think happened to Japanese American stores and businesses that were sealed and padlocked by the government?"

Using the pictures to obtain context information and their own experiences, the students respond. After this initial discussion, Adazzio asks the students to read and identify what actions the U.S. government took against Japanese Americans during World War II. The students read silently and Adazzio observes them carefully. Sometimes a student raises a hand when he or she finds a word that is difficult to read; usually Adazzio can detect when a student has a problem. If Adazzio sees that many students are having a problem with a word or expression, she will stop the reading, explain the word, and have students give examples of the word in different sentences.

When the students appear ready, Adazzio asks, "Who can identify some of the government actions?" Several students respond, and Adazzio makes a list on the board. Next Adazzio asks, "In what ways were civil rights denied to Japanese Americans?" The students return to their books, once again reading about the government's actions.

When the students appear ready, Adazzio engages them in a discussion of civil rights and this period of American history. Then she asks them, "What were the effects of the internment on the lives of Japanese Americans?" This question requires students to once again look at some of the pictures in the book and make some assumptions about what they were reading because the question is not fully answered in the book. Finally, Adazzio asks the students, "Do you think this could happen today? Why or why not?"

Some of the students continue to read; others are reflecting. Adazzio provides considerable time before she begins the discussion and continues to focus on the likelihood of similar actions today.

As you will see in Chapter 5, Adazzio could have easily changed the lesson into a group investigation, with students using a variety of resources to reflect on the consequences of the abridgment of civil rights.

Why is it important for students to tell what happened in their own words?

Reviewing the Steps in the Comprehension Model

1. Direct silent reading with a comprehension question. Help students use context clues. Students read _____ to find out _____.

2. Monitor silent reading and provide vocabulary assistance as needed. If many students have the same or similar problems, then provide whole-group assistance; otherwise, help the individual.

3. Increase the complexity of the questions, but begin with questions that ask students to demonstrate their understanding of the main idea. Next, ask questions that require students to interpret meaning by reading between the lines. Finally, ask questions that require analysis, synthesis, evaluation, and characterization by asking students to use personal experiences and to construct meaning that goes beyond the given information.

THE ADVANCE ORGANIZER MODEL OF TEACHING

GREG THOMAS'S CLASSROOM

Greg Thomas's students are reading about immigrants to the United States. The students are using a variety of textbooks and teacher-prepared material based on their reading abilities. Thomas wants to be sure that his students understand the ideas and information they encounter in their reading. It is important to the lesson that they all search out the same concepts.

Thomas announces to the students, "Today we are going to read about immigrant groups who came to the United States between 1890 and 1920, and compare their experiences with immigrants' experiences today. He tells them that when they have finished reading, they should be able to answer the following questions:

- Why did people leave their native countries and come to the United States?
- Where did many immigrant groups settle in the United States?
- How did the different immigrant groups help the people in the United States?
- How does the immigration between 1890 and 1920 compare to the present immigration surge?

Thomas asks, "Who can tell me what the word *immigrant* means?" (Students respond, and Thomas agrees.)

Thomas then asks, "What does the word *migration* mean?" (Thomas helps the students define the concept.)

Thomas suggests to the class that they may want to take notes from their readings to verify the answers to the questions. He intends to follow up with a class discussion.

During the discussion, Thomas has the students prove their responses by referring to the material they have read. He will evaluate the lesson by asking the class these questions:

- Who came to the United States?
- What was their native land?
- Why did they migrate?
- Where did they settle?
- How did they earn a living in the United States?
- How did they help the United States?

Thomas helps his students integrate the information by having them identify three reasons why groups immigrate and asking them how immigrant groups affect their new country.

Thomas's approach represents the advance organizer model of teaching. The syntax for the **advance organizer** model comes from the work of Joyce and Weil (1996, pp. 265–278). The model is derived from the theories of David Ausubel (1963), an educational psychologist who believes that knowledge can be organized and presented by teachers in an orderly manner to help students process new information. The model is useful in all subject fields.

The advance organizer model has three phases. In Phase 1, students are told the purpose of the lesson and the organizer is presented. In our fictitious fifth-grade classroom, Greg Thomas told the students what they were to read, presented them with organizing questions, and helped them to define key terms they would encounter in their reading.

In Phase 2, the material is presented; the lesson proceeds. In Thomas's lesson, the students do their reading and take notes.

In Phase 3, the lesson is integrated (principle of integrative reconciliation). Thomas used a discussion to elicit the responses to the questions and integrate the lesson. His lesson is an example of integration and interdisciplinary teaching. He is multitasking: teaching reading, oral language, and social studies (history and current events).

An example of the advance organizer model in a lower-grade classroom is a music lesson that Mary Hogan carefully planned.

 MARY HOGAN'S CLASSROOM*

Mary Hogan told her second graders that they were going to learn to read music notation and study rhythm. On the board she wrote the words *rhythm, beat, meter,* and *tempo.* She also drew a staff, a meter signature, and notes of different values.

Next, Hogan told the students that rhythm is composed of different components, which include beat, meter, and tempo. She explained, "We are going to experience these different components today, and at the end of the lesson we will see if you can describe or demonstrate these rhythmic components."

Hogan proceeded to have students feel their own heartbeat. Then she had them tap out the beat of a familiar popular song. Next, she brought out a metronome, and the students clapped to the steady beat.

After the students understood the concept of beat, Hogan played two versions of another familiar song. One version was brisk and the other slow. In this way she taught about tempo. Then she taught about note values and rests and introduced the concept of meter. With each concept, she had the students participate by singing or clapping.

Hogan concluded her lesson by saying, "We have experienced rhythm today. Who thinks they can explain what rhythm is?" The students talked about how rhythm was the overall, ongoing movement of the music. Hogan used each of the components introduced in the lesson to help the students talk about what they had learned about rhythm.[†]

---

*This lesson is based on content in *Music in the Elementary Classroom: Musicianship and Teaching* (pp. 34–35), by M. L. Hoffer and C. R. Hoffer, 1987, New York: Harcourt Brace Jovanovich.
[†]Hogan's lesson had all the elements that would facilitate learning English for ELL students.

The Advance Organizer and Classroom Management

The purpose of the advance organizer model is to clarify and organize meaningful information and ideas to facilitate students' processing skills. For this reason, the teacher plans the lesson and presents the organizer to the students, and then verifies that students understand the structure of the lesson. The teacher controls the presentation and helps students see its relationship to what they are going to learn.

The lesson should be evaluated using the same organizing structure presented at the beginning of the lesson. In this way, the teacher ensures integrative reconciliation of knowledge. Although the advance organizer model is a structured teaching model, the teacher needs to facilitate ample class interaction during the discussion. Throughout the lesson, students are encouraged to ask questions and clarify ideas.

DISCUSSION STRATEGIES

Characteristics of Oral Discussion

A true *discussion* involves the sharing of ideas, thoughts, and feelings. An oral discussion is not a soliloquy; it is a conversation in which two or more individuals participate. During most classroom discussions, it is expected that students will participate equally, and depending on the type of discussion, the teacher may play an equal role, adopt a leadership role, or choose not to participate at all.

Participants in a discussion use background information and experiences or data from recently acquired research or study. Although it is possible to participate silently by listening, the individual who does not express ideas, thoughts, and feelings is probably not involved in the discussion. Participants need to be able to *see* each other so that responses can be directed to the speaker.

Classroom discussions may involve the whole class or a small group of students. The discussion may have a discussion leader, who may or may not be the teacher. The leader may ask questions to focus the discussion and increase participation, or the leader may act as a moderator.

A classroom discussion should have a purpose. Students are assembled in a group to talk in a meaningful way. This underlying purpose differentiates the class-room discussion from an idle conversation. Discussions progress through a series of steps; however, the steps are not necessarily sequentially accomplished. A discussion usually begins with a get-acquainted-with-the-topic stage; it then generally proceeds to a problem definition stage, in which the participants focus on the purpose. The discussion may have a data-gathering stage, and ultimately the discussion terminates with a conclusion or summing up.

What are some of the things teachers can learn about students by observing them during a class discussion?

Discussion Manners

Discussion manners and skills are crucial to the success of the teaching strategy. If participants in a discussion are equal, then the flow of conversation moves around the group and encourages individual responses and contributions. But if the discussion is characterized by a back-and-forth exchange between teacher and student (**coaction**), then group interaction is discouraged, the flow of ideas is limited, the sense of group belonging diminishes, and positive social attitudes are not developed.

Discussion manners are as important for the teacher as they are for the students, and most are a matter of good sense. However, the manners and skills need to be taught, modeled, and practiced. Good discussions do not happen automatically. Taking turns—not monopolizing the conversation—is one of the first things that needs to be taught and modeled. For students to grasp this idea, it is important to call attention to it during the evaluation. Although this is just common sense, it cannot be taken for granted.

Listening to others is another commonsense item, but it entails attending to the discussion. The importance of careful listening is not meaningful to students until they realize that some discussion contributions are repetitious and irrelevant.

The importance of not making conversation asides to a neighbor or to a limited few needs to be constantly reiterated, or the discussion will deteriorate into many small purposeless conversations. That contributions should be meaningful and focus on the topic or purpose hardly needs to be mentioned, except that this is a most difficult task for young students.

The hardest skill to learn is the ability to synthesize the discussion or develop a conclusion based on the discussion. The capacity to do this comes through practice. Even adults tend to allow the discussion leader to assume this responsibility, yet every discussion participant should be developing the conclusion or synthesis and be ready to challenge and contribute to the culmination of the discussion.

Classroom Environment and Discussion Roles

The classroom environment affects the success of the discussion, and the size of the discussion group influences the skills needed by teacher and students. In a small-group discussion, students' faces are close together. They see each other easily; they know when someone is about to speak. If the students are motivated by their discussion, they will not be distracted easily. In small discussion groups, the teacher's role is supportive and facilitative. The teacher walks among the groups, observing and providing assistance when needed.

In large discussion groups, students sometimes cannot see each other. This may occur because the need to see each other was not anticipated in the planning of the discussion formation. "Eyeballing" is crucial in a group discussion. We learn a great deal about each other by watching eyes, hands, posture, and facial expressions. If students cannot see each other, they may not focus on the discussion or become involved. In addition, if you cannot see the speaker, you do not know when you can add a comment and contribute to the discussion.

The teacher's role during the large-group discussion depends both on the purpose of the discussion and on the teacher's own personality needs. If the classroom climate is highly structured and the teacher demands rigid control, the discussion is limited to a select few students. The interaction pattern is from teacher to student and back to teacher. However, if the teacher creates an open, warm, encouraging climate for discussion, the flow of ideas moves among the students and they learn to listen to classmates and take turns. Try to achieve a moderate environment; the teacher who is too rigid or too permissive will have a limited discussion monopolized by aggressive students. Taba (1967a) states that the teacher who is too permissive and abandons the discussion totally to the students will have a limited and chaotic discussion period.

The Leadership Role

All group discussions need a leader. The leadership role may be assumed by either teacher or students. Typically, in a small discussion group, a student is designated as the leader. Ultimately, all students should learn to assume the leadership role.

The basic purpose of a discussion is to encourage students to gather and process information by sharing with others and listening to others. This objective helps define the role of the discussion leader. The leader's attitude influences the discussion. Facilitative behaviors are important for encouraging participation. These behaviors include the following:

- Accepting all responses by assuming a nonjudgmental attitude
- Encouraging spontaneity by not injecting personal statements or evaluative responses
- Soliciting feelings and value responses through questioning and asking for clarification
- Extending thinking through summative statements

These behaviors are thoroughly discussed in the Teaching Tasks and Behaviors section later in this chapter.

Students can learn to assume the leadership role when they are provided with practice situations and given an evaluation of their leadership performance. A checklist for evaluating discussions is included in Chapter 7 as Figure 7.10.

The Participatory Role

This role is assumed by most of the students (and occasionally by the teacher). It needs a great deal of practice. The very young, egocentric child has difficulty sharing and listening to others. Until the child learns group participatory behaviors, discussions are difficult. Acceptance of group responsibility is a developmental process. Behaviors include the following:

- Sensitivity to others' viewpoints
- Listening to and asking questions of others
- Assuming responsibility to contribute ideas, thoughts, and feelings

It is important to remember that these behaviors are learned only if they are practiced, and they can be learned at any grade level.

The Recorder's Role

This role is important in most discussions. The recorder's job is to log the discussion and be ready to recount it during the evaluative period. Group members help the recorder keep an accurate chronicle of the meeting. Verbatim minutes are unnecessary; it is more important to note the trends in the discussion and the decisions made. The recorder may also assist the group leader by recounting the discussion and summarizing it at different times to keep the group on target.

Discussion Problems

Some teachers complain that students never stop talking. However, sometimes these same teachers complain that their students do not participate in class discussions. Why does this apparent incongruity occur? What happens may be related to several factors:

- Students have been successfully inhibited and feel that participation is undesired by the teacher.
- Students feel that they are in a fishbowl during a discussion, and they become shy.
- The teacher or discussion leader or several aggressive students monopolize the discussion, causing others not to participate.
- Students are uninterested in the topic/problem/question posed for discussion.

If the lack of participation is related to the first factor, inhibition, very little can be suggested to remedy the problem. The teacher needs to remember that at school, students are supposed to use language; the teacher's professional expertise should be used to find as many constructive means as possible to develop language use. Students who have been turned off to talking can be helped quickly by eliminating the negative influences and by reinforcing positive speech behaviors.

It is relevant to consider the different types of discussions when dealing with the second factor, shyness. Students of all ages are frequently intimidated by large-class discussion. Shyness can be dealt with through the use of the small-group discussion. In groups of no more than seven students, everyone participates and students' discussion skills can be developed.

If the third problem, aggressiveness, affects participation, the teacher must develop questioning and involvement strategies to guide the discussion and to encourage interaction.

The fourth factor, lack of interest, simply means that the students need to participate in the planning process and help identify meaningful topics or problems.

The Aggressive, Overtalkative Student

If overtalkative students could hear themselves as others do, there would be no problem! The trick is to help these students develop an accurate self-perception. One of the most effective means of accomplishing this is to have the student observe another student who has a similar problem.

For example, when Greg Thomas had this problem in his classroom, he suggested that Ginger, an aggressive talker, observe another group of students during the discussion lesson. Ginger's task was to provide feedback to the group she was observing concerning participation and progress toward the group objective. Thomas cautioned Ginger not to hurt anyone's feelings. Specifically, Ginger was asked to answer the following questions:

- Did everyone contribute and participate?
- Did the group accomplish its purpose?
- Who helped the group most to accomplish its purpose?
- What problems did the group have?
- What suggestions would you make to the group?

Ginger was flattered to be the group observer. When she reported to the group, she observed that one person (Sylvia) had monopolized the conversation on several occasions, with the result that the group did not have time to reach a conclusion.

Thomas talked with Ginger about her findings and asked her if she recalled performing in a similar fashion. Ginger recognized that she, too, had often monopolized the conversation. Although Ginger still needed to be reminded during successive sessions, her awareness of the problem improved her own performance.

If Thomas had not had two aggressive talkers in his classroom, he could have accomplished the same objective by recording a small-group session and asking Ginger to listen and evaluate using the digital recorder.

The Shy Student

A teacher can best help the introverted student by providing opportunities to talk in a small-group situation. The shy student is usually overwhelmed by whole-class participation. Careful group placement with an unselfish group of students will facilitate the shy child's participation. It should be considered extremely unusual if a child does not participate in the small group. If this occurs, the teacher needs to seek assistance from parents and colleagues.

In the large group, it may be possible to encourage participation of the shy child by providing opportunities prefaced with questions directed to the student. "Sally, what do you think about this?" "Rob, do you agree with that statement?" "Helen, how would you handle this problem?" However, this tactic must be done cautiously because direct questions to the shy student may complicate the problem.

Another thing to remember with the shy child is to provide plenty of response time. Sometimes children anticipate that the teacher will not wait for them to respond; thus, the shy child becomes more inhibited because of the expectation of being cut off before a full response has been made.

Types of Discussions

Unstructured or "Free" Discussion

The sharing discussion of kindergarten and first-grade classrooms is an example of an unstructured meeting time in which students simply practice talking, listening, and questioning each other. This type of free discussion has no set purpose other than language usage, the expression of personal feelings, and learning to talk to an audience. The teacher usually refrains from contributing to this discussion in order to encourage spontaneity. The sharing discussion can be made more relevant by suggesting to students that they bring important items to class for the sharing period. These items might include "a book I like," "my hobby," "my collection," "an experiment I performed," or "something I made."

The unstructured discussion is also used to initiate new topics or areas of study, such as a social studies unit. The purpose of the free discussion in this situation is to encourage students to identify interests and problems to find out what students really know about the new topic. The free discussion is typically a large-group activity, although it does not need to be.

Semistructured Discussion

In this type of discussion, students are usually reporting progress toward a specific purpose, exchanging information as a result of a research/problem-solving lesson, or contributing information gained from a field trip or a special experience. The discussion has been structured by the prior activity or by specific instructions. For an example of the semistructured discussion, review Mary Hogan's problem-solving assignment concerning magnets in Chapter 3.

Structured Discussion

This is a guided discussion that has been planned to accomplish specific cognitive functions. The structured discussion depends on a sequenced questioning strategy. The purpose is to facilitate the development of cognitive skills by beginning with a lower-level cognitive skill and moving to the generalization level. The structured discussion can help students develop concepts, make decisions, and learn to solve problems. During the course of the discussion, students contribute information (data) and, as they listen to others and to the questions, they process the data to arrive at the concept, a generalization, a prediction, or a decision.

Teaching Tasks and Behaviors

Keep two basic ideas in mind when using discussion as an instructional approach. The first is that the students need to learn how to discuss, which means that there are skills they need to master in order to discuss well. The second point is that there is a purpose related to academic content to be accomplished through use of the discussion technique. Thus, at the end of a discussion, the evaluation should focus on both the discussion process and on the substantive nature of the subject for discussion. Teacher tasks relate to those two purposes. For example, students learn discussion skills more easily if they practice the skills in a small-group situation. Therefore, the teacher needs to consider the composition of the small group. In Chapter 3, you learned that small groups are more productive if they are composed of five to seven students. Discussion will be facilitated if the group members are different rather than alike. Students' natural differences may be related to dialect, sex, socioeconomic status, verbal ability, and intelligence. Some studies indicate that students' speech develops best when the student has to explain and clarify meanings. So one of the first tasks of the teacher is to consider the size and composition of small groups when assigning students to a discussion activity.

Discussion Rules and Roles

Another teacher task is the presentation, teaching, and follow-up of discussion rules and roles. Conversing in a group is a difficult cognitive activity. The first thing that students need to learn is how to recognize when another speaker has finished talking. Students can be asked, "How do you think you can tell when your friend has concluded speaking?" The basic response is "When they stop." But the next question is the real key, "How can you tell when a friend is ready to speak?" The students' response should be, "I can tell by the eyes or when the person begins to _____." The bottom line in rule making for discussion is that students must learn to take turns without hand raising. Hand raising inhibits the flow of conversation and makes the group leader the recipient of all speech.

The teacher must also decide whether to choose the leader and recorder for the discussion group or have the students do so. In the beginning, it might be better if the teacher exercises that judgment. But the roles should be rotated on successive days. During the course of the discussion, the teacher needs to verify that the discussion leader is encouraging all members of the group to speak. The discussion leader and recorder should be evaluated by the group in an inoffensive manner at the end of the session. During the evaluation session, the teacher solicits ideas from the total group for encouraging all members of the group to contribute. This serves the dual purpose of teaching leadership responsibility to the discussion leaders and participation responsibility to everyone.

Verifying Meanings

Before students are sent off to their discussion group, it is wise to make sure that they understand what they are to discuss or accomplish. Then the teacher should verify that they comprehend the meanings involved in what they are to do. For example, in Chapter 3, Mary Hogan demonstrated what a magnet could do and had the children talk about it before she sent them off to their problem-solving lesson. In this way, she prepared them for the group discovery session. It is also important that students understand the role of using evidence during a discussion. Students should learn the value of backing up their comments with concrete data.

Another aspect of verifying meanings has to do with *establishing the focus.* Children as well as adults tend to digress from the chosen topic. The best way to deal with this tendency is to be sure that a discussion focus

has been set and is understood. You can accomplish this by providing the discussion group(s) with a set of questions. The questions should be open-ended, providing many alternatives in terms of the discussion. There should be enough questions so that when you join the group to observe and listen to the discussion, you are able to ask, "What question are you discussing now?" Of course, certain questions may cultivate enough discussion, making others unnecessary. Questions will be discussed later in this chapter.

Refocusing

When you visit a discussion group, you may find that the discussion disregards the problem focus and needs **refocusing.** Perhaps the students have misunderstood the meanings, or perhaps they have just strayed from the topic. When this occurs, it is the teacher's job to ask a question or make a statement that will bring the students back to the original topic. If Mary Hogan had found that the students were not discussing the rule for magnets when she toured the problem-solving groups, she would have asked, "Did you find out what a magnet can and cannot do?" Or she might have said, "Do you remember that we were to find out what a magnet can and cannot do? After finding out what a magnet can pull, can you tell us how these items are alike?"

Hogan also anticipated that some of the groups might complete the assignment earlier than others. As she visited the groups, she was prepared to change the focus and extend the experiment by suggesting an additional experiment for the students to perform. The same anticipatory act is necessary even if groups are just talking. Some groups get to the heart of the matter quickly, and they may need to consider the topic in greater depth or to move on to a new topic.

Clarifying and Valuing

Many children have been taught that what they say is unimportant and what adults contribute is to be valued. As a result, children tend not to listen well to their peers. They anticipate that the adult will repeat what their peer has said, so why should they bother listening to a classmate? When students reiterate what others have said, it means that they have not been listening. The way to deal with this is to say to the repeater, "Roberto already told us about that. Roberto, will you explain to William what you told us before?"

Another typical problem occurs when students do not understand a classmate's comments. They may just sit there without speaking, or they may ask the teacher, "What did Billy mean?" The trick is to get Billy to explain his meaning rather than have the teacher clarify it. Because students become accustomed to the teacher explaining what has been discussed, they may not focus in and listen to their classmates. To solve this problem, the teacher asks the original speaker, "Billy, will you tell us what you meant by _____?" When the teacher habitually handles the problem in this manner, students begin to ask questions of their peers rather than of the teacher.

Supportive Classroom Climate

We have already discussed the seating arrangement and structural climate of the classroom. There is another type of atmosphere that the teacher must create if the discussion is to be successful. This has to do with the development of an attitude that supports all student contributions, even if they are not terribly helpful at the moment. The teacher must be so objective during a discussion that the students will not be able to discern either approval or disapproval of their comments.

This does not mean, however, that conceptual errors are allowed. When an error in logic or an error involving a specific fact occurs, the teacher should ask the student to clarify the meaning. The teacher should also solicit corrections or additional statements from other students by asking them questions: "Boys and girls, what do you think about that?" "Does everyone agree?" "Who has a different idea?" "Do we have any evidence that this is so?" This process must be handled sensitively so students do not hesitate to make comments because they fear they will make mistakes.

When a student makes an error or irrelevant comment, the teacher must ensure that the child making the comment is not attacked by peers. Once again, the supportive climate and encouragement of the teacher are important.

Extending Thinking

Teachers need to be constantly alert to ways to extend and broaden patterns of thinking. The following points and questions may be useful for this purpose:

- Ask the students to review the major points already discussed, or summarize what has been said yourself.
- After the summary, ask, "What do we still need to consider?"
- If there has been conflict over definitions or values expressed, ask the class if Billy and Susie meant the same things when they discussed communication.

- Remind students that they have already discussed several means of communication. Then ask, "Are there some things we have forgotten?" or "How else might we think about this?" or "Why might individuals misunderstand each other?"

Evaluation

At the end of the discussion, there should be a final summary of what has been discussed and concluded, the main ideas, and the areas of conflict. During the evaluation, help students understand what has been accomplished. Students should learn that a discussion will always be evaluated in two ways: in terms of the content and in terms of the discussion process. They should also learn that no one will dwell on personal behaviors during the evaluation.

If group observers are used, this is when they would give their report. Both group evaluation and self-evaluation may be used at the end of the discussion period.

QUESTIONING TECHNIQUES

Purposes of Questioning

Appropriate use of questioning can be the most effective teaching technique teachers use. Questions can be used for the following purposes:

- Motivate and guide students' study
- Assess what students know and understand
- Orient students to problems and make them aware of values
- Teach students to process information
- Facilitate analysis and evaluation

Questions initiate and guide most class discussions. Research indicates that teachers use questions for both assessment and motivation. In recent years, there has

Research Findings

Villegas and Lucas (2007) urge the use of instructional strategies that motivate immigrant students to share their personal experiences. They suggest giving English language learners access to the curriculum by providing opportunity to talk about and use the resources of their native language.

been a great deal of debate about teachers' classroom questions. Teachers' questions can generally be categorized as either factual or higher-cognitive. Factual questions tend to be used to find out what students know and understand as used in direct instruction. Higher-cognitive questions are typically used to extend knowledge by asking students to apply, analyze, synthesize, and judge or evaluate.

Research on questioning reveals the following:

- Questions should stimulate thinking.
- They should be formulated so that they are precise and concise.
- They should be appropriate to the purpose of the lesson.
- They should accommodate the students who are to answer them.

The following sections explore some of these characteristics of good questions.

Stimulating Thinking

An interesting, thought-provoking question motivates the learner to do the following:

- Pay greater attention
- Reflect on new ideas
- Consider new avenues for thought
- Suggest analysis or synthesis rather than a factual recall of previously learned information

A good question triggers past experiences and knowledge and motivates new thought.

Precision

A good question is clear, precise, and concise. The question should tell students how to frame their response. Too often teachers ask an ambiguous or vague question and then are surprised at the variety of responses. For example, if the teacher wants to know whether the students read an article on the front page of the newspaper that is relevant to what they are studying, the question should not be "Did you see the newspaper this morning?" The class was studying expansionism, so the teacher could have asked, "The front page of the newspaper this morning had an article on expansionism. Who was involved?" or "Why was expansionism in the news this morning?"

Purposeful Focus

Plan questions so they are appropriate to the purpose of the lesson. If the lesson is a problem-solving activity, then the questions must stimulate inquiry. If the pur-

pose is factual recall, then ask mastery questions. Suppose that your students have just returned from a field trip. To focus their thinking about the experience, you might ask the following questions:

- What did you observe?
- What similarities and differences among the incidents did you note?
- Why did these incidents occur?

Because purposeful questioning is often sequenced, the questions are planned rather than off the cuff. However, even though the lesson has been planned to focus on specifics, the teacher should be flexible enough to change the questions if the students' inquiry moves in a purposeful and fruitful direction.

Clustering Questions

Effective teachers use both convergent and divergent questions. Convergent questions involve asking students to recall basic facts and actions; these questions usually call for one best answer. Divergent questions involve students in abstractions, reflections, and beliefs; they usually require analysis, synthesis, evaluation, judgment, and characterization.

Sequencing of questions depends on the teacher's purpose. For example, a common sequence is to begin with the recall of specific facts and then lead to questions that elicit reasoning and hypotheses. Another sequence may begin with an open, divergent question to stimulate student involvement and then narrow to deductive thinking and problem solving. The important point is that questions need to be planned.

In Karen Adazzio's comprehension lesson earlier in this chapter, we saw a sequence develop through the questions. The first two questions she asked *motivated the lesson* and called for divergent responses in order to *elicit student involvement and many responses*:

1. How do you think the little girl feels as she sees all her family's belongings packed in crates and duffel bags?
2. What do you think happened to Japanese American stores and businesses that were sealed and padlocked by the government?

Next Adazzio asked narrow, *factual questions to verify student comprehension*:

3. What actions did the U.S. government take against Japanese Americans during World War II? (Main idea)

4. In what ways were civil rights denied to Japanese Americans? (Summarization)

To elicit higher-level thinking, Adazzio's next question called for *analysis of the facts and evaluation of the outcomes*:

5. What were the effects of the internment on the lives of Japanese Americans? (Transforming reading into students' own words)

Adazzio concluded with a question designed to *evoke both prediction and a value judgment*:

6. Do you think this could happen today? Why or why not?

Note that without the sequence of questions, the last question might be considered a simple convergent thought process, but when clustered with the prior questions, it becomes divergent and thought provoking.

Meeting Students' Needs

Research on questioning and on learning styles indicates that instruction should be differentiated to meet students' needs. Research indicating that disadvantaged students do better with lower-level questions has already been noted. However, some middle-class students who do not tolerate a highly structured environment may do better with open-ended questions. Questions should be adapted to the group of students with whom you are working.

Types of Questions

During the 1960s, Taba (1967b) developed a system for programming cognitive processes through the sequencing of questions. The questions are used to stimulate the students to process information. The strategy is based on the idea that students need input of content in order to be ready to respond to the questions that are asked. Three cognitive tasks are taught to the students: concept formation, interpretation of data, and application of principles. Each cognitive task requires specific questions.

Cognitive Task I

To facilitate concept formation, the teacher stimulates students to list, group, and categorize items using common characteristics. The questions include the following from Taba (1967b, p. 92):

- What did you see? Hear? Note?
- What belongs together? On what criterion?
- How would you call these groups? What belongs under what?

Cognitive Task II

The interpretation of data is taught by asking students the following (Taba, 1967b, p. 101):

- What did you notice? See? Find?
- Why did so-and-so happen?
- What does this mean? What would you conclude?

Cognitive Task III

The application of principles is sequenced through the following questions (Taba, 1967b, p. 109):

- What would happen if _____?
- Why do you think this would happen?
- What would it take for so-and-so to be generally true or probably true?

In Mary Hogan's science unit about rocks, she adapted the Taba strategy to teach her students that rocks differ in shapes, colors, and textures, and that natural forces cause rocks to change. She asked the following questions:

Questions	Responses
Describe these rocks. (What do you see?)	Students described color, shape.
Describe how the rocks feel.	Smooth, rough, slippery, jagged
How could we arrange these rocks in groups?	Color, shape, texture
Why do you think these rocks are not the same?	Rocks break. Different types of rocks feel different and look different. Something happens to the rocks to make them different.
What are some things that might affect the rocks? What else?	Sun, heat, cold, water, wind, plants, snow
What would happen if the rocks were exposed for many years to ice? Sun? Water?	Natural forces (ice, sun, and water) affect the color, shape, and texture of the rocks.

Common Sense About Asking Questions

Reviews of research on types of questions and levels of questions have concluded that learning gains can be correlated with the questions that are asked in the classroom. We know a great deal about the use of questions. The following sections cover some typical questions asked by teachers and some commonsense ideas and advice gleaned from the many research studies.

How Can Teachers Involve Students in Discussion?

Several factors are important. First, ask questions to motivate the discussion in a nonthreatening manner. Questions that are interesting and asked in a conversational voice get the best attention from students. Then after calling on a student, wait for the response; do not scare the student off. After the student responds, let your eyes observe other students; let them know if you want them to contribute. Call on additional students, without repeating the question; encourage other students to respond by asking, "Does anyone else want to comment?" "Who can add to this?" "Well, boys and girls, what else?" Provide feedback through noncommittal, simple responses, such as "OK," "Good," "Interesting thought," "Hmmm."

The process of eliciting additional students to respond to questions is called *redirection*. Only higher-cognitive questions can be redirected because fact questions typically have only one answer.

What Happens When Teachers Call on a Specific Student Before Asking a Question?

By naming the student who is to respond, the teacher encourages all other students to stop listening. Thus, it becomes necessary to regenerate interest through a follow-up elicitation because the class has been effectively inhibited from participation.

However, there are exceptions that merit consideration. If you note that Johnny and Matilda are not paying attention or are misbehaving, it may be profitable to call on one of them and serve notice that you are aware of their inattention and that you will not tolerate it. This lets the inattentive students realize that they had better tune in, and it tells the rest of the class that you are monitoring participation.

Another situation may call for naming the student ahead of time. If there is a very shy student in class who rarely contributes to the discussion, sometimes this student will respond if given extra time to prepare. Decision making, along with an extra measure of common sense, is needed before deciding whether to focus on a specific student or to ask the question of the whole group.

What Types of Questions Should Teachers Ask?

The answer is all types. It is important to provide a variety of thinking experiences. Students' interest in answering questions may depend on learning styles and socioeconomic background factors. The age of the students may also be a factor. Nevertheless, students need practice in answering a variety of question types, not just those we think are better for them. Also remember that reflective questions are dependent on prerequisite knowledge. One of the best ways to determine students' readiness to answer a reflective question is to sequence the questions beginning with a factual one.

What Happens When Teachers Use Leading Questions?

"Isn't it true that _____?" The problem with the leading question is that it is insincere. Students sometimes become hostile because they recognize that they have not been asked a real question. Another problem is that students do not pay attention to the leading question, and so good listening habits are not reinforced. (In addition, leading questions are frequently used in discipline situations, often with a sarcastic tone of voice: "You do want to go to lunch today, don't you?")

What Happens When Teachers Repeat Students' Comments?

If students know that the teacher will repeat every student response, they do not need to listen to their peers—just to the teacher. Recall the discussion about interaction patterns during a class discussion presented earlier in this chapter. Students tend to talk to the teacher rather than to their classmates; repeating students' comments reinforces this behavior.

But sometimes, particularly with young children, a correct response needs to be vigorously emphasized and reinforced immediately. This occurs most frequently during skill instruction. In this circumstance, you may need to repeat the student's comment in a complete sentence. However, it is critical to acknowledge that the student gave the correct answer but that it is so important you are repeating it.

Under What Circumstances Should Teachers Cue Students?

Rowe's research (1974) concerning wait time indicated that teachers should wait about five seconds for a response. Rowe found that student participation, interaction, and involvement increased when the teachers waited three to five seconds before soliciting another response or before providing additional clues. (Teacher silence after calling on a student is an extremely important teaching technique to increase involvement and creativeness.)

Rowe's previous research (1969) also pointed out that teachers are less likely to wait for the low achiever than for the higher achiever. Research also reveals that teachers are more likely to cue students whom they anticipate know the answer, rather than students they anticipate do not know the answer. What this means, in terms of questioning technique, is that teachers must automatically wait an equal amount of time for both low and high achievers to respond, and provide specific content clues to all students who fail to respond after sufficient wait time.

Another device for eliciting greater response and reflective thought is the *probe*. Probing questions are follow-up questions designed to encourage elaboration. A probing question represents a special type of cue. For example, suppose you ask the class, "Why did England send ships to the South Atlantic Ocean when Argentina took over the Falkland Islands?" A student responds that the Falkland Islands belong to England. Now ask the responding student, "Under what circumstances do you believe a country should act aggressively?" This question is intended as a cue to the student to extend his or her thinking in a particular direction. Both the student and the content should be considered before a teacher decides to probe.

Why Should Yes/No Questions Be Avoided?

The yes/no question usually wastes time. Ask the question you really want the student to answer. For example, the questions in this section could have been written as yes/no questions. (Should yes/no questions be asked? Should teachers repeat students' comments?) The problem is that a yes/no response is insufficient,

and the teacher has to ask a follow-up question to get any information out of the student. Another problem is that the yes/no response tells the teacher very little about a student's thinking and thus cannot be used to diagnose needs.

Students' Questions and Classroom Management

The questions students ask provide a great deal of insight about the organization and management of the classroom and the effectiveness of instruction. For example, if students ask many procedural questions, then it becomes obvious that the teacher has not clearly explained classroom procedures to the students. (Or the students have not had the opportunity to provide input into planning classroom procedures.)

When students ask what appear to be very elementary instructional questions, they are telling the teacher they do not understand the instructions or that the lesson is too difficult for them. Students who ask questions to receive assurance from the teacher that they are proceeding correctly probably lack self-confidence, or they have experienced a great deal of teacher wrath in the past and are presently fearful.

It can be a frustrating experience when teachers have to manage many time-consuming and often pointless questions. For this reason, the teacher must analyze why students' needs are not being met and what kinds of questions are legitimate. Teachers receiving many classroom management (procedural) questions should ask:

- Have the students helped to plan and do they understand class standards? Do they know what to do when they need paper, sharpen a pencil, get a drink, or go to the bathroom, and what to do when their work is finished?
- Do they know where to work? Do they know what resources are available to them?
- What should they do if they really need assistance? May they work with a classmate?
- What responsibilities may students assume for their own goal setting?

What kinds of questions should be cultivated in the classroom? Cover questions dealing with the extension of an instructional task, questions that broaden the area of study, and questions that lend depth to the study.

Teaching Hints: Questioning

1. Verify understanding of *all* students, but particularly check on ELL students and students who seldom ask questions.
2. Check whether both boys and girls are comfortable asking questions. (Do both genders tend to ask questions?)
3. Monitor the work of students who rarely ask substantive questions to find out if they need help.

Students will ask these kinds of questions when they are really motivated by instruction and when they feel that their teacher respects them and wants them to take some responsibility for personal learning. In addition, it is important for teachers to model appropriate questioning behavior.

Students' Responses

Language usage is the school's raison d'être, and teachers need to develop students' speech. Listen to what students have to say and reinforce it through respect. This means that nonevaluative comments ("OK," "All right," "Interesting") need to be made along with teacher questioning to elicit clarifying responses from students. Teachers may need to use cues and probing questions to facilitate students' replies.

What are some ways to help students ask better questions?

CULTURALLY RESPONSIVE TEACHING: HELPING ELL STUDENTS

Villegas and Lucas (2007) point out that one in five students speaks a language other than English and the majority of these students are learning English at school. For these students, English is a second language, and to learn it they must apply their own linguistic knowledge. In addition, their cultural experiences are extremely important because they must draw on their own life experiences and integrate them with what they are being taught.

From the teacher's perspective, to understand these children they must be sensitive to students' culture, ethnicity, gender, and social class. Teachers are not born with sociocultural consciousness. It must be developed by studying students' families, ways of life, problems, concerns, and strengths (Villegas & Lucas, 2007). Understanding why immigrant groups come to the United States (economic improvement, religious freedom, political freedom) is vital to gain insight and develop sensitivity.

In some schools, there may be as many as 40 different languages and dissimilar cultural backgrounds, yet students' needs are similar. Because these students depend on their prior experiences and strengths to process English learning and new ways of behaving, they need to be intellectually challenged and reassured that their teacher values their diversity and respects their abilities. Although expository teaching is important to transmit specific information and skills, it does not provide the challenge or the opportunity to integrate students' own cultural experiences, engage in critical problem solving, or communicate with peers. For these reasons, teachers must not depend solely on direct instruction but need to utilize a variety of instructional strategies and develop their own cultural consciousness. Chapter 5 will introduce problem-solving instruction.

SUMMARY

Direct instruction is an expository teaching strategy that is teacher-directed and teacher-controlled. It is used primarily for teaching skills and communicating information needed by a large group of students. Teacher questioning to verify students' understanding and the use of three practices, structured practice, guided practice, and independent practice, are essential in using the model.

The comprehension model is used to verify students' understanding during reading and content instruction; teachers ask students to summarize, identify the main idea, explain in their own words, apply, and predict.

The advance organizer teaching model is used to help students organize and integrate new knowledge.

Authentic discussions are purposeful and involve sharing ideas, thoughts, and feelings. Both discussion skills and discussion manners need to be taught and practiced. To improve group discussions, evaluation must occur after each session. Questioning can be used for assessment and motivation. Questions should be carefully planned and sequenced.

Because most classrooms have students learning English as a second language, it is the responsibility and ethical necessity for teachers to be culturally conscious and utilize a variety of teaching approaches.

PORTFOLIO ACTIVITY

Describe a class discussion. Identify the purpose of the discussion and what you learned about your students' ideas, thoughts, and feelings. Explore what the discussion contributed to your own teaching and students' learning. Sketch the seating arrangement during the discussion. Using arrows and numbers, see if you can diagram the flow of the discussion. Note whether students interacted with each other or directed their comments to you.

 ## DISCUSSION QUESTIONS AND APPLICATION EXERCISES

1. Prepare a skill lesson using the direct instruction model. Identify the factual questions you will ask students during structured practice.
2. Plan a lesson that relies on reading. Use the comprehension model to design your questions.
3. Make a list of classroom atmosphere elements that contribute to a good discussion.
4. Record the questions students ask during either the morning or the afternoon. Categorize the purposes for the questions using the following:
   • To extend thinking
   • To obtain permission
   • To clarify tasks
   • To clarify procedures
   What do the questions tell you about your teaching?

5. For a three- or five-day period, record the time you spend with low-, average-, and high-achieving students in your classroom.
6. Select content for a lesson and plan a series of questions. Think about clustering the questions to achieve content depth and higher-level thinking.
7. Evaluate your students' small-group discussion skills. Look for participation, attentiveness, expression of beliefs, opinions, new ideas, listening to each other, responding directly to each other, and engagement with task and content.
8. Using Mary Hogan's music lesson, identify the three phases of the advance organizer teaching model that she used. Why was her lesson appropriate for ELL students?
9. How would you arrange your classroom for a discussion? Draw a diagram to illustrate your plan.
10. Identify how you will provide for multiple intelligences using the direct instruction model.

READER RESEARCH

Observe students' interactive behavior. (1) Describe an incident you would characterize as cooperative. (2) Describe an incident you would characterize as competitive. (3) Describe an incident you would characterize as conflict. Can you draw any conclusions about what causes students to react in certain ways?

 ## TECHNOLOGY APPLICATIONS

Visit http://www.prenhall.com/lemlech to obtain information on a topic of interest to your students. Write a direct instruction lesson and a comprehension lesson using that information.

Computers can be used in all subject fields, and they encourage virtual field trips.

 **CHAPTER 5**

Inquiry Teaching Strategies

Inquiry teaching has a long, distinguished history. In this chapter, you will examine the historical perspective of inquiry and reflective thinking, along with examples of the process. The twin sister of inquiry, *constructivism,* is also explained. Five inquiry teaching models are demonstrated through classroom teaching episodes: group investigation, the 5-E model, cooperative learning, concept attainment, and backward problem solving. You will learn the importance of the classroom environment for facilitating inquiry and how that environment affects learning, motivation, satisfaction, and student involvement. The chapter concludes with case study methodology and a number of research skills to help students think like researchers.

Advance Organizer

The following questions are intended to guide your reading and understanding of the content of this chapter.

1. How does inquiry learning differ from expository learning?
2. Why is inquiry learning important?
3. What skills are needed for inquiry and problem solving?
4. How do teacher tasks differ when you compare expository and inquiry teaching?
5. In what ways is constructivism similar to inquiry experiences?
6. How can you integrate subject fields using group investigation?
7. How do the six phases of group investigation differ from each other?
8. In what ways does the 5-E model differ from group investigation?
9. How do the phases of the concept attainment teaching model differ and contribute to the teaching strategy?
10. How do group investigation and concept attainment differ from direct instruction?
11. What is the advantage of using backward problem solving?
12. What are some ways to evaluate students' problem-solving skills?
13. Why should students engage in research activities?
14. What are the purposes for using case studies instead of textbooks and other resources?

INTASC   **INTASC Standards**

Standards 1–8 are all significant in this chapter, as they were in Chapter 4. An effective teacher needs a repertoire of teaching strategies that are appropriate to the students' developmental levels, needs, and interests, and the content and skills necessary to learn.

Professional Lexicon

backward problem solving A motivating inquiry strategy that helps the teacher assess students' thinking processes and engages students in divergent thinking.

case study approach An inquiry strategy that provides for thorough investigation of a single event, institution, decision, issue, or individual, and allows the teacher to reduce data to facilitate analysis.

concept attainment An inquiry strategy designed to help students gain specific concepts by comparing and contrasting attributes; this strategy encourages students' use of metacognition.

constructivism An approach to teaching and learning that acknowledges that information can be transmitted but understanding depends on the learner (see Chapter 2).

cooperative learning A learning strategy that promotes positive relationships among students and increases self-esteem and social competency.

group investigation An inquiry-oriented cooperative learning strategy that requires interaction, discussion planning, compromise, negotiation, and research processes.

inquiry The process of examining and checking ideas, beliefs, and knowledge with data to develop meaning and theory.

integration The linking of subject fields and learning processes to facilitate learning by helping the learner see

relationships. (See Chapter 6 for an in-depth discussion of integration.)

interdisciplinary content Concepts from different subject fields (disciplines) used to demonstrate learning through different lenses. (See Chapter 6 for an in-depth discussion of interdisciplinary content.)

reflective thinking The process of using evidence; the active, persistent, and careful consideration of beliefs and knowledge.

structured interview A research situation in which questions are predetermined and never differ during multiple interviews.

I was startled by the sound of the puppy barking. Slowly I opened my eyes. "Was she barking or crying? I wonder what time it is?

"Only ten minutes after 5:00 A.M. Why is she up so early? Is she ill? I wonder if she is developing a new habit—waking up earlier each day. Seems to me she woke up at about 6:00 A.M. yesterday. Maybe that's it. Still, 5:00 is not 6:00; something must be wrong with her.

"Well, I'd better get up and find out. OK, puppy, what's wrong? You look perfectly fine. You don't appear to be sick. Let's go outside. Hurry up, so we can both go back to sleep. Strange, it looks too bright outside for 5:00 A.M. OK, pup, back to sleep.

"Hey, she's still barking. Sounds like her stomach is telling her it's breakfast time. I wonder what the other clocks in the house say? Hmm. They agree with the bedroom clock.

"Ah ha! I hear the rest of the family. Maybe it's later than I thought. If our electricity went out, the clocks would all be wrong. I'd better start breakfast.

"The microwave clock is blinking. That's it! I'll call the time number and verify. Yep. It's 6:20 A.M. Our electricity must have been out for an hour."

WHAT IS INQUIRY?

Marylou, a fifth grader in Greg Thomas's classroom, continually asks to see the nurse. She complains of nausea. Is she really ill? Does she have anxiety syndrome? Is she pretending? Did the recent earthquake bring this on? These are the questions that Greg Thomas is asking himself. He knows he needs to contact Marylou's parents and investigate further. Greg is engaging in reflective inquiry.

Most educational writers define **inquiry** in terms of the processes involved to resolve uncertainty. Although the use of the term is relatively new in educational history, it can be traced to the terms *reflective thinking* and

critical thinking as used by John Dewey. Dewey (1933) defined **reflective thinking** as follows:

> Active, persistent, and careful consideration of any belief or supposed form of knowledge in the light of the grounds that support it and the further conclusions to which it tends. (p. 9)

Dewey analyzed the thinking process and differentiated between thinking and reflective thinking. He stated that thinking begins when the individual is aware of an indeterminate situation or a feeling of perplexity. A common thread runs through reflective thinking. Thought is sequential; there is a chaining effect that aims at a conclusion, and an inquiry into beliefs. The difference between commonplace, everyday thinking ("I'd better wear a raincoat; it looks like rain") and reflective thinking is the ability of the individual to sustain the act while seeking a solution and being critical of the evidence unearthed during the process. The reflective individual subjects the belief and the evidence to reason. The nature of the problem determines the goal to be sought, and the goal determines the process.

Dewey identified five steps in reflective thinking that have served as a basis for all later research into the act of problem solving (1933, p. 107). They also formed the basis for his theory of reflective thinking. Dewey's five steps are as follows:

1. *Considering suggestions*, in which the mind leaps forward to a possible solution.
2. *An intellectualization of the difficulty* or perplexity that has been felt (directly experienced) into a problem to be solved, a question for which the answer must be sought.
3. *The use of one suggestion after another as a leading idea*, or hypothesis, to initiate and guide observation and other operations in collection of factual material.
4. *The mental elaboration of the idea or supposition as an idea* of supposition (reasoning, in the sense in which reasoning is a part, not the whole, of inference).
5. *Testing the hypothesis* by overt or imaginative action.

Guided by Dewey's theoretical work, other authors have studied reflective thinking and distinguished between thinking and reflective activity.[1] The latter is considered purposeful thought, directed and controlled. Thinking consists of three interrelated elements: sentiency, memory, and imagination. An appropriate and controlled balance of these three elements constitutes reflective thinking.

WHAT DOES AN INQUIRER DO?

The chapter-opening vignette can serve as a mini-example of inquiry, providing insight into what an inquirer does during the process of inquiry. Inquiry in the classroom is concerned with more important problems than whether the electricity stopped or a puppy has awakened earlier than usual. But just the same, this little problem-solving episode provides a description of the inquiry process. To analyze it, review what happened:

---

[1]Fendler (2003) traces the genealogy of reflection in teacher education and its meanings and understandings to different researchers.

The puppy barked earlier than usual. Is it really extra early, or is there another reason for the puppy's barking?

Discrepant event/fact	1. The clock is correct; the puppy is developing a new habit. 2. The puppy is ill. 3. The clock is wrong; the electricity stopped.
Evidence/data gathering	a. The puppy looks fine and appears in good health. b. The morning appears extraordinarily bright for 5:00 A.M. c. The puppy continues to bark as if expecting breakfast. d. Others in the family are awakening; it must be time to get up. e. Other electric clocks in the house read the same way. f. The microwave clock is blinking. (It is a digital clock.)
Tentative conclusion	The clocks in the house are wrong. (To verify, the time number is called.)
Conclusion	The electricity stopped. The clocks did not run for an hour during the night.

Because this type of inquiry occurs many times a day, you need to think about why inquiry is important and what value students derive from planned inquiry experiences.

WHY IS INQUIRY IMPORTANT?

When teachers select inquiry problems that are relevant to students and the curriculum, students are motivated to "search" for relatedness. They become engaged in the process of reflective thinking. Sometimes through a process of trial and error, they make discoveries as they problem-solve. Through practice, they become better problem solvers. They also learn to organize and keep track of their thinking process so that they connect their ideas and efforts.

Inquiry is an active process that depends on the learner. It is the learner who must connect what is new to him or her to past experiences and knowledge. The student becomes totally involved in the discovery of concepts, testing ideas, and organizing and structuring new knowledge.

TEACHER TASKS FOR INQUIRY TEACHING

Choosing Appropriate Problems for Study

In planning topics for inquiry, the teacher is confronted with three elements: selecting a problem that provides mileage in terms of content, choosing a problem that is of interest to the students, and formulating a provocative question. Providing mileage in the content means selecting problems that have depth, provide appropriate research skill use, and fit grade-level goals and objectives. The problem you select should be useful in meeting the content needs, provide for the development of inquiry skills, and enable sequential learning of concepts. It is important to remember that the inquiry problem must be significant enough that there is information provided to students as well as questions that motivate skill development.

It is obvious that the topic must be of interest to students. Inquiry problems that do not appeal to students will not be successful. If students do not perceive that a problem exists, it is irrelevant to them, or it is inappropriate to their developmental level, then they will not be motivated to inquire. Not only must the teacher choose carefully, but it is critical to present the problem in a way that creates controversy and real interest. Choose a problem that is closely related to student experiences and concerns instead of a contrived problem that you might select only because of its suitability for inquiry. The teacher must be the judge and consider student involvement, skill needs, content needs, and the transfer of learning potential.

Inquiry questions are problems stated in question form. Formulating an inquiry-oriented question is a very important task. Every question you ask in the classroom should have a purpose. In a sense, there are no bad questions, but the challenge is to ask a question that will facilitate the thinking appropriate for the task. An inquiry-oriented question should motivate inquiry, help the students define the problem, and suggest possible hypotheses.

Consider the following two questions:

1. What is a "mom and pop" grocery store?
2. Why are there more supermarkets than "mom and pop" grocery stores in modern cities?

Question 1 is really a subquestion of Question 2. Obviously, students will need to define the "mom and pop" grocery store; however, this question is not formulated to inspire inquiry, define the problem, or suggest hypotheses. The second graders who were asked Question 2 defined the problem and suggested the following hypotheses for investigation:

Problem

Markets in modern cities tend to be larger today than during past times.

Hypotheses

1. Modern equipment is too expensive for small grocery stores.
2. Small groceries are not profitable.
3. People prefer "one-stop" shopping.

Defining the Problem

KAREN ADAZZIO'S CLASSROOM

Karen Adazzio began a unit on the interdependence of services and work for her seventh graders with the question, "What happens in a large city when the mass transit system is not available?"

Some of the students immediately stated that they would have difficulty getting to school if there were no buses. Other students asked them, "How could you get to school?" The students responded that they would have to walk; others stated that their parents would have to drive them; some said they would have to depend on neighbors.

Adazzio commented, "It sounds like most of you would have to impose on other people to help you; how would this affect them?" To help them decide what the problem was, Adazzio went back to her original question: "Can you suggest hypotheses for investigation about what happens in a large city when the mass transit system is not working?"

The students thought about it and finally came up with the following problems for investigation:

1. Other transit workers would be affected and so would other services.
2. Other people might not be able to go to work.

3. There would be more cars on the road, causing congestion problems.
4. Safety problems might be caused by more cars on the road and people not accustomed to driving.

Whenever students are unable to open up the investigation and specify the problem, the teacher must probe and facilitate problem definition by narrowing the focus. To accomplish this, it may be necessary to ask several follow-up questions.

Developing a Database

Sources for information are so important in inquiry methodology that most teachers consider the adequacy of their materials and resources first before making a decision about an inquiry problem. The second-grade teacher who posed the question about supermarkets had to consider how students would find out why the size of markets had changed in recent years. The teacher's data sources for students may include field-trip observations, social studies textbooks, resource people, pictures, maps, charts, tables, and informational data written by the teacher. Sometimes students generate data sources in the form of interviews, questionnaires, or case studies. Dramatizations or simulations may also be used as data sources.

Students need contrasting content if they are to learn to process information. Practice with such content will teach them to categorize facts, ideas, or events; evaluate information for interpretive purposes; and develop their own generalizations about why something is true or why something usually happens. As students collect data, the teacher asks questions to help them compare and contrast the data and make inferences based on their information.

Creating an Inquiry-Oriented Environment

Both the physical and social environment must encourage students to develop inquiry skills. Students are affected by the physical setting and the context of instruction. Through the arrangement of the classroom, planned strategies, modeling, and choice of materials, the teacher guides students to interact with each other and with the environment and motivates them to engage in discovery learning. Students' needs

and life experiences should be considered both in the choice of inquiry problems and in the materials arranged for use.

An inquiry-oriented classroom is characterized by its ability to sustain reflection. Students and teacher do not hurry to closure, but discussions have a direct focus. In a reflective discussion, the teacher's questions tend to act as a springboard for the discussion rather than focusing on a right answer. The questions probe instead of elicit. The reflective classroom uses hypotheses as its discussion focus and relies on factual material to support the hypotheses. Factual recall is not valued, but facts are used to support or reject a hypothesis.

Time is another aspect of the inquiry-oriented classroom that is used differently than in a more traditional environment. Because the teacher is not rushing to cover specific material in the reflective classroom, the class has time to participate in democratic processes. The act of clarification is important to inquiry. Students need to communicate and search for a consensus of meaning; thus, the reflective teacher does not watch the clock.

In an inquiry-oriented classroom, the teacher assumes a less prominent position and attempts to guide students to resources of knowledge. The teacher's central purpose is to arouse interest and raise questions so students will inquire and learn to draw on their own experiences. In addition, teachers should help students perceive discrepancies in their information. The climate of the classroom allows students to gain self-confidence and to direct their own study and thinking.

What types of behaviors do teachers demonstrate when using inquiry methodology?

Guidance and Objectivity

The teacher's primary role during inquiry revolves around raising questions. Planning a question strategy and preparing materials enable the teacher to direct students' hypothesizing and guide them to appropriate materials to facilitate their thinking. While students are gathering data, the teacher continuously challenges and prods them to explore new alternatives. Student inferences and conjectures are encouraged. Students will need to be reminded of the temporal quality of knowledge and that authority cannot be trusted as omniscient. The teacher needs to be alert to stimulate the students' search for evidence and remind students to challenge an accepted hypothesis.

Taba (1967b) contended that thinking can be taught by identifying cognitive skills and devising strategies to give the learner the opportunity to practice each particular cognitive skill. Taba identified the task of questioning as vital to the teaching of cognitive skills. Questions should be structured by the teacher to accomplish the following:

- Guide the students' search
- Raise the level of thought
- Focus on content
- Program the study as to sequence and transitions

Using Taba's three strategies (discussed in Chapter 4 because they demonstrate strategic sequenced questions) encourages inductive thinking. For this reason, the three strategies taken together are considered to be an inquiry model.

In summary, the teacher's major tasks in using inquiry methodology are to stimulate the use of inquiry processes by students, to guide students' choice of materials, and to arrange an appropriate environment and climate for inquiry. The teacher manages participation, provides cues and feedback, reinforces appropriate behaviors, and directs both formative and summative evaluation of inquiry learning.

Teaching Hints:
Planning Inquiry Learning

An elderly driver has just driven his car into a farmers' market area where many people were shopping. Several shoppers were killed. Though senior citizens have fewer accidents than other age groups, many citizens are clamoring for stricter driver tests for seniors.

1. Write an inquiry question to motivate student interest using this incident.
2. State the problem as you would expect your students to state it.
3. Write a hypothesis that you anticipate your students would propose.
4. Identify sources for gathering data.
5. How will you have students organize their data? (What will the students produce?)
6. How will you evaluate students' inquiry skills?

USING GROUP INVESTIGATION: AN EXAMPLE OF INQUIRY INSTRUCTION

Integrating Different Subject Fields

Although the main components of inquiry instruction are the same, remember that varied purposes will change the way in which it is accomplished. Scientific data gathering usually occurs through experimentation and record keeping. In physical education, discovery may be facilitated through physical movement. In music, discovery learning may focus on the use of instruments or on listening experiences. **Integration** is the linking of subject fields and learning processes to facilitate learning by helping the learner see relationships.

ART AND SOCIAL STUDIES IN GREG THOMAS'S CLASSROOM

Greg Thomas's students are studying U.S. history, and Thomas is integrating art experiences with the social studies unit. He asks his students, "What does the art of the early New England colonists tell us about their cultural beliefs?"

On the edge of the chalkboard, Thomas has displayed photographs of artifacts and paintings from different periods of U.S. and European history. The students begin to react to the pictures and the question. One outspoken student comments that he doesn't think the New England colonists produced much art, and therefore there would be little to study. Others react differently by asking whether they would study only paintings or whether sculpture and architecture can be included, too. Another group of students appears to doubt that it is possible to detect cultural beliefs by studying art or artifacts.

After the students have had sufficient time to react, Thomas calls attention to the different opinions expressed by the group:

- Very little art was produced by the New England colonists.
- The study should be broad and include handicrafts, architecture, and other artwork.
- Students doubt that the study of art can help them determine cultural beliefs.

Thomas asks the students if they can suggest a way to reformulate his original question into a problem for them to study. After several minutes, they agree on the following problem: Using different types of art forms, can we recognize a people's beliefs?

The problem as stated is slightly different than what Greg Thomas had anticipated, but it still enables the students to study much of what he has planned. Next he asks them to decide how to go about the study.

As the students suggest ideas for the investigation, Thomas writes them down on the board. This is their list:

- Look at handcrafted objects from the colonial period.
- Look at artists' pictures.
- Compare artists' pictures in New England with paintings by other artists from other places and other periods.
- Examine tools made during colonial days.
- Look at the architecture of the period.
- Study furniture produced during the colonial period.
- Use the Internet to research information about the New England colonists.
- Study clothing from the colonial period.

The students decide to draw much of what they observe to have a record of their research.

Some of the students begin to express preferences in terms of what they want to do. Not all of the students want to record their information with pictures; some students will take notes instead. The students choose their work groups and plan who will do what in their small groups. The study will take two weeks and will include a visit to the art museum. Several students express an interest in making tools and chairs identical to those produced during the colonial period.

At the beginning of each work period, Thomas tells the students where each group should work in the classroom and how much time they have to work. At the end of each work period, Thomas asks the groups to report their progress. Each group reports how they went about their study during the period, what they accomplished, problems they had or anticipated, and plans for the next work period.

Each day when Thomas evaluates with the students, he asks for a substantive report of progress and a report on how well the group worked together. In this way, he keeps the students on task and improves their cooperative group work skills. On consecutive days, prior to each work session, Thomas recycles the study by asking the students, "What are you going to do today?" and "What materials do you need to use?"

At the end of the first week, Thomas suggests to the students that they might need to make a large chart to record the findings from each group. They decide that at the end of the following week each group will make an oral presentation, and then they will discuss the pertinent information in order to analyze the data.

The students analyzed the following data:

- A list of furniture used in most colonial homes
- A sketchbook of furnishings
- A sketchbook of dress styles
- Notes about the New England work ethic
- Replicated tools and several pieces of furniture (chairs, stools)

The group studying colonial furniture uses a data retrieval chart similar to Figure 5.1, and they continue to fill in the blank spaces as they find more information. To organize data, students make charts and graphs similar to Figures 5.2 and 5.3.

The students can use additional materials, including the following:

- Sketches of household utensils
- Notes about individual artists' pictures
- Pictures of churches
- Notes about colonial recreation in New England
- Notes about religious interests

The class discussion focuses on the data and what they learned. Thomas initiates the discussion by asking, "What do we know about the way of life of the colonists who lived in New England?"

He follows this question by asking the students to compare the art forms and styles of the New England colonists with other periods in American history. During the course of the discussion, the students even compare the furniture of the colonial period with the furniture produced in Europe (Figures 5.1 and 5.2).

	Materials Used	Purpose	Looks	Handmade or Manufactured
CHAIRS				
Colonial	Wood—mahogany	Dining, reading	Straight-backed, simple, hard	Handmade
European	Wood/fabric	Relaxing, dining, reading	Ornate, soft	Manufactured
SOFAS				
Colonial				
European				
TABLES				
Colonial				
European				
CHESTS				
Colonial				
European				

Figure 5.1   Comparison of Colonial and European Furniture

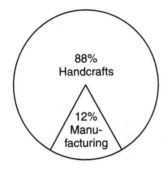

Figure 5.2   Graph Showing Percentages of Handcrafted and Manufactured Products During Colonial Days

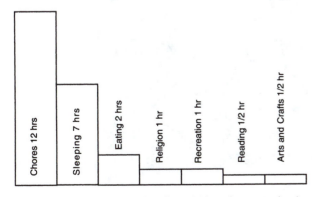

Figure 5.3   Histogram of Daily Activities of New England Colonists

What Did the Students Learn?

Using their data, the students decide that they can say the following about the New England colonists with a fair amount of confidence:

- They appeared to be a grave type of people (Figure 5.3).
- They struggled and worked hard (Table 5.1).
- Their art was practical, functional, and symmetrical.
- The language they used was plain and correct.
- Their household utensils and furniture were plain, simple, and functional.
- The artists sometimes were house painters and performed other needed chores such as painting signs and making decorations for coffins.

Table 5.1   Activities of New England Colonists

Sleeping	7 hours
Chores	12 hours
Recreation	1 hour
Eating	2 hours
Religion	1 hour
Reading	½ hour
Arts and crafts	½ hour

- They used their churches for social gatherings, and the church buildings were designed to accommodate people; they were functional.
- Their clothes were practical, not fancy.

Integration of Learning

Greg Thomas's lesson integrated language arts, fine arts, and social studies. The students engaged in small-group conversation as they planned and made decisions. In the whole-class setting, the students took part in discussion that required them to focus on Thomas's questions and other students' responses. Their reading and note taking required language arts skills.

The arts were integrated as students studied art forms and styles of the colonists, and some of the students recorded their data with their own drawings. Students were able to recognize the relationship between culture and the art that is produced during an historical period of time.

Social studies was the major "vehicle" for integrating knowledge. In the social studies unit, the students studied American history and culture related to New England colonial settlements. Their participation in small-group work helped them practice social skills and cooperative decision making. Students learned important values through their group work by listening to the viewpoints of others, responding, and verifying their own thoughts and beliefs.

It is important to note that significant problems for students' research lead naturally to **interdisciplinary content**. Thomas, through his choice of a motivating situation, deftly integrated content from several social sciences, art, and language arts. (Integration and interdisciplinary content are discussed in depth in Chapter 6.)

Greg Thomas was pleased with what the students had learned. He asked them if they were ready to draw a final conclusion about the question he had asked and their statement about the problem to be investigated. The students responded that they had learned a great deal about the colonists by studying their art, and that in fact they really had discussed the colonists' cultural beliefs (see Table 5.1). The answer to the question posed by the students about whether it was possible to recognize people's beliefs by studying their art forms was affirmative. Students concluded that art provides a visual record of culture.

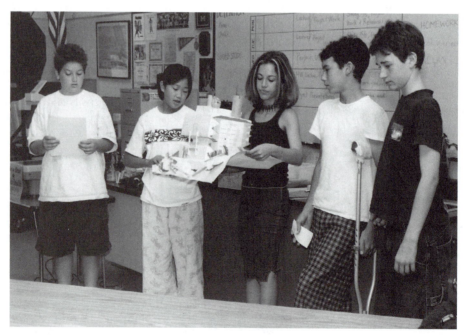

Group work should be observed and guidance should be offered as needed.

The episode that took place in Greg Thomas's classroom conformed to what Joyce and Weil (1996) described as the group investigation model. Thomas's strategy with his students included six phases of inquiry:

Phase 1: Thomas posed the question and encouraged the students to react to the question.

Phase 2: Thomas identified different opinions about the question and asked the students to suggest the problem to investigate.

Phase 3: Thomas asked the students to suggest ideas for the investigation. Students chose what they wanted to do, organized into groups, and decided on tasks.

Phase 4: Students gathered data independently and in their group situation. Thomas asked for formative evaluations after each work period.

Phase 5: Students gave reports and shared data.

Phase 6: Students concluded by reexamining their original question and problem.

Group Investigation and Classroom Management

During group investigation, the teacher's role is to facilitate inquiry and problem solving. The teacher must motivate the students, set the stage for group work, provide the necessary resources, and provide ongoing guidance.

Group students heterogeneously or homogeneously, depending on the nature of the work task. Students are most typically grouped heterogeneously for this strategy.

Verify that students understand what they are to do in their groups before you dismiss them for group work. It is important to plan where each group will work and dismiss each group to its workplace, group by group, so bedlam does not occur as students carry chairs and work materials. Let groups know how much time they have to carry out their work task, and identify a means to get attention during the work period (switch off lights, ring a bell, hold up a hand, and so on).

Monitor group work by walking around and listening in as each group plans, discusses, or carries out the work task. If a group is off task because group members do not understand, help them by refocusing their attention on what they are to accomplish. If their confusion indicates general class uncertainty, stop the whole class and clarify the problem. If the problem is behavioral, you may have to change the group members or stop the whole class and ask, "How can we help this group work together?" Then discuss group work roles and rules.

Students improve group process skills only through repeated opportunities to practice. Therefore, it is essential to evaluate progress (Phase 5). It is often a good idea to assign, or have groups decide on, specific work roles. The roles of group leader and group recorder carry important responsibilities. Specialization of work tasks within the group also creates group responsibility. Each member of the group may have to research something specific to contribute to the group report.

Cooperative Learning and Group Investigation

Cooperative learning strategies are conducted using a small-group structure. Some cooperative learning strategies are useful for teaching skills or specific information. Group members are responsible for helping each other learn a specific skill, and the group is tested as a whole to monitor the group's progress. This type of group learning fits closely with the strategies suggested in Chapter 4.

Another type of cooperative learning is more inquiry-oriented. It is called Jigsaw. Each member of the group is given a number. If the class is divided into five groups, there will be five number ones, twos, threes, fours, and fives. Each number is given an inquiry research question. All of the number ones will meet together (as do all the other numbers) to research their question. After a suitable amount of time the teacher asks students to return to their "home" group. Each member of the "home" group shares his or her information. The home group is now responsible for seeing how the information from each member fits together, and their discussion focuses on what they have learned and what they need to learn. Class discussion at the end of the lesson focuses on how the groups differ in their thinking and what they have learned.

Similarities and Differences Between Cooperative Learning and Group Investigation

In cooperative learning (the Jigsaw strategy), the major focus is on teaching other group members specific information and/or skills. Cooperative practice is emphasized. In **group investigation** the focus is on inquiry, problem solving, sharing diverse viewpoints, and using democratic processes to make decisions.

Both teaching strategies rely on social interaction and group effort. Both conclude with a class discussion that evaluates group processes and substantive progress. In group investigation, students exercise more autonomy in structuring their inquiry, whereas in Jigsaw, the students are often given the research question and more direction as to how to proceed.

Teaching Hints: Group Investigation

Group investigation can be used at all grade levels (Kindergarten through college) and in all subject areas. Student groups need to have space to sit together and talk quietly to each other.

1. Begin with a puzzling problem or situation that motivates your students to reflect and ask questions.
2. Elicit class thoughts and questions. If possible, write them on the board.
3. Either assign students to groups that will focus on specific questions or allow students to select their own group based on their interest in the question or problem.
4. Share time limits for group work. Assign each group a space for meeting together. Before groups leave for their group meeting, verify their understanding of the task.
5. Monitor each group's progress. Warn groups about time limits.
6. Evaluate group processes and group progress in class discussion. (How well did group members work together? What did the group accomplish?) If work has not been completed, tell students when they will be able to work together again. (Recycling stage: Thomas's two-week study of colonial art and social studies provides an example of recycling, an ongoing inquiry problem.)

GREG THOMAS'S CLASSROOM*

Greg Thomas used Jigsaw to teach about the concept of manifest destiny. His students were divided into five groups of five students and each student was given a number. The number one students were English language learners, and all were from Mexico. Thomas wanted these students to work together for the inquiry activity so that they could help each other. The inquiry questions that guided their research included the following:

1. Why did Mexico believe that the Treaty of Guadalupe Hidalgo was unfair?
2. Why did President Polk want the war with Mexico?
3. How did the peace treaty affect citizenship rights?
4. How did the war with Mexico affect other territories?
5. How did the war foster cultural conflicts?

When the students concluded their research, they would return to their "home" group and share the information, and then the group would discuss how the war with Mexico related to the concept of manifest destiny.

Why was it a good idea or a bad one to have the ELL students do their research together?

THE 5-E INSTRUCTIONAL STRATEGY

Developed by the Biological Sciences Curriculum Study in 1989, the intent was to provide teachers with a teaching model that motivated inquiry thinking, group interaction, and active participation. The model is similar to group investigation; the teacher acts as a provocateur to stimulate inquiry thinking and as a consultant to help students refocus their thinking when necessary and to encourage group exploration. Greg Thomas used the teaching model to promote students' thinking about climate change and conservation. As

*Content suggested by Constitutional Rights Foundation, *Bill of Rights in Action,* Winter 2004.

you read through Thomas's lesson, note the five stages of the instructional model.

IN GREG THOMAS'S CLASSROOM

ENGAGEMENT

Teacher

Thomas captures students' interest and attention with pictures of polar bears: (1) a mother and her cub following her in the Beaufort Sea, (2) a bear swimming, and (3) a bear standing on his hind legs with front legs perched on top of a wagon where a man is sitting. Thomas tells the students, "Several things have been happening to the polar bears. Their young cubs have not been surviving. The bears have been losing weight; the population of polar bears is decreasing. Why do you think this is happening?"

Students

"Are they not able to find food?"

"It's odd for the bear to go so close to a person. Why would he do that?"

"Is the Beaufort Sea in Alaska? Is that where this is happening?"

"Maybe the bear knows he needs help."

"Polar bears love the cold weather; maybe it's not cold enough for the bears."

"Our weather is changing from the way it used to be. I think the weather is affecting the bears."

(Students continue to raise questions and to express their opinions and ideas.)

Teacher

"You have expressed very good thoughts about the problems of the polar bears. Let's take a look at the map to see where these things are happening." (Students note the proximity of the Beaufort Sea and Alaska to the Arctic Ocean.) "Some of you seem to feel that the bears cannot find food, and others have expressed the thought that the weather, which we have been studying, may be the problem. Let's work in small groups and see if you can approach the problem by asking: What do polar bears need for survival?" Thomas has the students move into five work groups and he passes out short reading materials, pictures, and science and social studies textbooks. You may seek additional resources available on the bookshelves.

EXPLORATION

The students are accustomed to working in small groups and begin to respond to the question. Thomas walks around the room and listens in to the different groups. He suggests to all of the groups that they begin to make a list of the bears' needs. Some groups note that the bears' needs are not too different from the needs of humans.

Each group is asked to report to the class as a whole. The consensus of thoughts leads to the conclusion that the bears are hurting because of lack of food and temperature change. Students begin to ask: "What can be done to help the polar bears?"

EXPLANATION

Students return to their regular seats and Thomas asks the students: "How do the polar bears differ from other bears?" Students think about their group work list and recognize that the Arctic bears live on the sea, whereas other bears are land-based. Land-based bears can scrounge for food and can eat berries, plants, and other animals if given the opportunity. The polar bears are marine mammals and so most of their food comes from the sea. They eat seals, fish, and plant life that exist in the ocean. But the things they normally hunt and eat are disappearing.

ELABORATION

Teacher

"We have been studying about weather and climate change; what do we know about what is happening in Alaska and the Arctic Ocean?"

Students

"The pack ice is melting and the climate is changing."

"Glaciers are melting and icebergs are breaking off."

"Scientists call this global warming."

"I read that the temperature change is really significant. By the end of the century the seas will be three feet higher."

Teacher

"How do you suppose this affects polar bears?"

Students

"They get stranded on land and cannot hunt the seals and other seafood they are accustomed to eating."

"They go into the villages seeking food."

"Sometimes the females would dig dens on the ice in order to give birth to their babies and now the ice is probably too far away for them to get there."

"Polar bears are threatened by global warming. If the ice goes, the polar bears will go."

Teacher

"Is there anything else that is threatening the polar bears?"

Students

"I've read that oil companies want to dig for oil in the Arctic region. That would really upset things for the bears."

"Human activity affects greenhouse gasses."

"The ice melting disrupts currents and causes hurricanes."

EVALUATION

Teacher

"Let's put our discussion, group work, and readings together—what do the polar bears need for survival?"

Students

"Climate change—global warming—is causing the polar bears to lose their natural places to hunt and build families."

"They don't have food."

"We need to look at the causes of global warming to help the animals survive."

"Mother bears are losing body fat because of lack of food, and so they won't be able to have babies."

Teacher

"You've done a good job identifying the problems that may be too difficult for fifth graders to rectify. But there

are some things you can do. First, you can talk to your parents about the problems of the polar bears so that more people are educated about their needs. Second, we can talk about what students in schools can do to contribute to conservation and consider how people affect global warming. Your job now is to develop a plan outlining what we can do as a class and how we should go about it."

Analysis of the 5-E Inquiry Lesson

The model is composed of five phases: *engage, explore, explain, elaborate,* and *evaluate.* Thomas has integrated three subject fields. (See if you can identify them.)

- In phase one, *engagement,* the students are motivated through the use of pictures of polar bears. The choice of pictures not only creates interest, it also elicits student sensitivity and concern for the bears.
- In phase two, *explore,* students worked in small interactive groups responding to the question, What do polar bears need for survival? The exploration phase is similar to the group work phase of group investigation. At the end of phase two, the group reports lead to the question, What can be done to help the polar bears?
- In phase three, *explain,* Thomas provides additional insight based on what students shared in the prior phase. Past experience/knowledge helped the students differentiate between land-based bears and ice bears. Thomas expects the students to connect the climate change and the lack of food as two events affecting the polar bears. He moves to the next phase.
- In phase four, *elaborate,* Thomas asks the students to integrate what they have learned about the polar bears' problems with what they know about weather and climate change. The students expand their thinking, recognizing that changes in the climate seriously threaten the polar bears.
- In phase five, *evaluate,* Thomas takes the students back to their original question, What do the polar bears need for survival? The students are able to draw some conclusions about the causes of the bears' problems. Thomas goes one step further, moving the lesson to the application level by asking the students

to begin planning how they, as students, can contribute to conservation and consider how people affect the climate.

CONSTRUCTIVISM: WHAT IS IT?

As teachers, we can transmit information to students, but we do not know what students are learning until they do something with the information. According to Lemlech and Hertzog (1995), constructivist learning theory is an approach to teaching and learning that acknowledges that information can be transmitted but understanding must be constructed.

Constructivism and inquiry go hand in hand; they are two sides of the same coin. The teacher assesses what students know, and with this knowledge of the learner, the teacher plans new experiences and knowledge to be gained by the student. Constructivist teaching uses the student's prior knowledge as a building block to integrate new understandings with prior learnings. To accomplish this, the teacher plans active experiences to involve students in explorations, theory building, and experimentation so that students can generate and organize data and communicate with others. As the learner gains new knowledge, previously held beliefs and ideas may change as new interpretations are made.

As in inquiry/problem-solving experiences, the student is challenged to engage in activity that requires higher-level thinking and reflective processes. Ultimately the student must apply the new knowledge to produce a product that demonstrates his or her understanding.

Translated into a teaching model, constructivism has four phases:

Phase 1: A puzzling question or problem is introduced.

Phase 2: The learner explores, talks about the problem, and uses his or her own ideas to create and test understanding.

Phase 3: The learner explains what has happened and what has been learned.

Phase 4: The learner demonstrates the ability to apply new knowledge through social participation, in actions related to the classroom or the community or communicated in projects, discussion, and appreciation.

 ## CONSTRUCTIVISM IN GREG THOMAS'S CLASSROOM

The rain had just ceased and the students were pleased to be released from the classroom for time on the playground. Greg Thomas had assigned team games and he wandered among the four groups of students, observing them as they played. Several students had just noticed a rainbow in the sky, and they were busy showing it to each other. Thomas listened to their talk.

Back in the classroom Thomas questioned the students about the rainbow. "What do you know about rainbows?" Responses included the following:

- Visible after a rain
- Possible to make a rainbow
- Many different colors
- Colors called a spectrum
- Something called white light
- White and black are not considered colors

PHASE 1

Thomas then asked the students what they would like to know. This time they responded with a number of questions:

- What are the colors of the spectrum?
- Are they always the same?
- Why are black and white not colors?
- How do you combine colors of the spectrum?
- What happens when colors are combined?
- How do colors look In the shade? In the sun? In dim light? In bright light?

Thomas complimented the students on their questions and told them that tomorrow he would bring in some materials to let them experiment. In the meantime, he took them outside again and used a garden hose to spray water upward. In this way, he recreated a rainbow for the students to see. Back in the classroom he told them to write down their personal observations for discussion tomorrow.

PHASE 2

The next day Thomas had a variety of equipment for the students to use. The students selected materials and questions and were told to develop new questions that interested them. In small groups, with Thomas providing assistance when asked, the students used prisms, magnifying instruments, mirrors, white cardboard, shoeboxes, and colored papers. Thomas told the students to jot down what question(s) they were investigating, what materials they used, and how they went about their experiment.

PHASE 3

After two activity periods for experimentation, the students recorded their findings and how their findings were meaningful to them. Some of the things the students learned included the following:

- The black paper did not seem to reflect color.
- They saw seven colors in the spectrum. The colors seemed to always be in the same order. (You can make a rainbow using the prism and the sun's rays.)
- The white paper reflected color. (It's better to wear white when it's hot outside.) White is a combination of colors. Black has no color; black absorbs colors.
- You can make the rainbow disappear with a magnifying glass by moving it back and forth.

PHASE 4

Thomas asked the students how they could use what they learned or if they knew of any evidence of its use. They responded:

"It's better to wear white when it's hot outside and black when it is cold!"

"In Florida many of the houses have white rooftops to reflect the heat."

"Light colors look gray when there isn't much light; scenery looks different when it is dim outside."

Once again, as the students talked, Thomas recorded what they seemed to understand so that he could plan his next steps to help them learn more about light and color.

In what ways did Greg Thomas integrate subject fields and provide interdisciplinary content?

THE CONCEPT ATTAINMENT MODEL OF TEACHING

The **concept attainment** model of teaching is an inquiry strategy used to help students gain specific concepts by comparing and contrasting examples that have specific characteristics (attributes) with examples that do not contain the characteristics. Joyce and Weil (1996) developed this teaching model; it is derived from the work of Bruner (1966), who studied the ways in which people categorize, form, and gain concepts. The concept attainment model provides a means for teachers to analyze the ways students form concepts and help them become more efficient.

MARY HOGAN'S CLASSROOM

Mary Hogan writes some words on the board, and as she writes she asks the students to see if they can guess what she is thinking about.

    foot (yes)
    picture (no)
    horse (yes)
    plane (yes)
    dog (no)

"The *yeses* give you clues about what I am thinking," hints Hogan.

The students raise their hands and begin to guess. "Are you thinking about animals?" No, she can't be thinking about animals because the plane is marked yes and the dog is a no. The students continue their questions and responses to each other, and then Hogan offers to make another list to help them.

    car
    train

telephone
books
wagon

"Now," asks Hogan, "which words should be followed by a *yes,* and which should get a *no*?"

The students become excited. Many talk out without raising their hands, and Hogan does not try to restrain them. Finally, Hogan says, "Let's do this together. What should I put next to the word *car*?" The students respond, *"Yes."* "How about *train*?" *"Yes,"* answers James. "What about *telephone*?" "That is a *no* and so is *books.*" "You're doing just fine," says Hogan, "but I wonder if you know what to put after *wagon*?" The students are quiet, and then Bill raises his hand and says, "I think it gets a *yes.*"

Hogan smiles. "You've done very well. Can you tell me what I have been thinking about?" After several minutes, Jed asks, "Does it have something to do with walking and riding?" (Hogan smiles but does not respond.) Jana asks whether she is thinking about ways people travel.

"You are very close, Jana. Suppose everyone thinks about some additional *yes*es and *no*s. Perhaps that would help everyone know what I am thinking about."

The students begin to contribute ideas: *"Raft* is a *yes."* *"Boat* is a *yes."* *"Camel* is a *no."* *"Submarine* is a *yes."* *"Taxi* is a *yes."* *"Radio* is a *no."* *"TV* is a *no."*

"OK, you have done very well. Are you thinking about what Jana said? Could anyone be more specific? Can you think of a big word that has to do with travel?"

"I can, Miss Hogan. Is it transportation?"

"Excellent, Beth. Congratulations, boys and girls. Now can you tell me what you were thinking about while you were guessing the meaning of my *yes*es and *no*s?"

"Well, I looked at all the *yes*es and tried to see how they were alike."

"Gee, I started with the *no*s and compared them to the *yes*es."

"I didn't understand about the word *foot* and that confused me."

"I got stuck on the word *wagon.*"

"Jana, what made you think about travel?" asks Hogan.

"I guess I just put all the *yes*es together and thought about how they all had something to do with traveling. After you said *travel,* I began to think how *foot, horse,* and *wagon* were related. At first I had a hard time because I couldn't understand why *horse* was *yes* and *dog* was *no*!"

"Well, boys and girls, you certainly have done a good job. Now why do you suppose I wanted you to think about transportation?"

Mary Hogan's class is studying cities, and she has used the concept attainment model to introduce the concept of transportation as a characteristic of cities.

At the end of her teaching unit, Hogan again uses this model to help students integrate what they had learned. Let's visit Hogan's classroom four weeks later.

On the board is the following list:

apartments (yes)
farms (no)
subways (yes)
silo (no)
bus (yes)
recreation (yes)

"OK, boys and girls, see if you can guess what I am thinking."

The students begin to talk to each other: transportation (nah), housing (no!); maybe both! Hogan makes another list:

banks
people with many skills
tractors
fields of grain
factories
services

Now the students really begin to buzz:

"Let's do the *yes*es and *no*s."

"What should banks be?" (*"Yes,"* respond the students.)

"How about people with many skills?" (*"Yes."*)

"Tractors?" (A chorus of *no*s greets her.)

"Fields of grain?" (*"Nooo."*)

"Factories?" (*"Yes,* we know it.")

"Services?" (*"No."* "Wait, it's a *yes!"*)

"All right, if you are so positive, give me a list of *yeses* and *nos* before you tell me what I am thinking about."

The students' *"yes"* list includes *museums, opera, tall buildings, doctors, engineers, firefighters, postal workers,* and *shopkeepers.* Their *"no"* list includes *agriculture, farm animals, farmer,* and *farmhouse.*

"What was I thinking about?" asks Hogan.

"Cities?" asks Jamie.

"All about cities," comments Mark.

"The characteristics of cities," says Jana. And the rest of the class nods, content that they have the right concept.

"Tell me what you thought about while you were guessing," says Hogan.

Once again the students describe their thinking processes. Several students comment how listening to the ideas of others had helped them gain the concept. One student comments that services gave the answer away. Another explains that she went back and thought about people with varied skills and that had put her on the right track.

Teaching Hints

The concept attainment model is used to introduce abstract concepts to students by beginning with familiar examples and moving to the less familiar concept. For example, before teaching about the American Revolution, Greg Thomas may need to introduce the concept of revolution and verify that his students understand it.

The model is also useful to help students synthesize material that they have already studied. Mary Hogan's use of the model led to the class identifying the characteristics of cities (people with varied skills, recreation, transportation, services, and commerce) that they had researched in small groups.

The concept attainment model can be used at any grade level (using pictures in kindergarten) to teach selected concepts, initiate units of study, and help students assimilate information. The most important phase of the model occurs when students identify their thinking processes. By doing this, students who are less efficient in hypothesizing learn strategies from the more proficient students. The concept attainment model helps students improve their thinking strategies.

The concept attainment model of teaching helps students think inductively. Instead of starting with an abstract concept and then providing examples of the concept, the teacher begins with the examples and has the students develop meaning using the examples. Cognitive psychologists believe that the best way to learn a concept is through examples. It is just as important to have negative examples as it is to have positive ones because students cannot recognize essential attributes unless they have negative characteristics to compare and contrast.

The concept attainment model has several phases:

Phase 1: The teacher presents positive and negative examples of the concept.

Phase 2: The students compare attributes of positive and negative examples. Students freely discuss their ideas. (They are hypothesizing.)

Phase 3: The teacher neither confirms nor denies hypotheses; he or she writes additional list items on the board but does not label entries either *yes* or *no.*

Phase 4: Students are asked to identify the additional examples as positive or negative based on their prior hypotheses.

Phase 5: Students once again discuss their hypotheses and are asked to state them.

Phase 6: The teacher confirms ideas—or provides help—and names the concept.

Phase 7: Students generate additional examples of positive and negative examples as requested by the teacher.

Phase 8: The teacher asks students to describe their thinking during the hypothesizing stage.

Concept Attainment and Classroom Management

The concept attainment model is effective with the whole class seated together. Of course, it can also be used with small groups. Because the teacher controls the pace of instruction during this strategy, there is moderate structure. A free discussion encourages student ideas and hypothesizing. Students learn to add on to the thinking process of their peers. This makes the strategy fun and improves the thinking process. Shy students should be encouraged to try out their ideas aloud. The teacher should help students analyze their thinking strategies.

The concept attainment model depends on teacher planning. Examples need to be carefully selected and sequenced to cue students' thinking. The teacher is responsible for recording examples, prompting students, and providing additional data.

BACKWARD PROBLEM SOLVING

Backward problem solving is a fun way to capture students' interest and get them involved in an inquiry activity. It also provides an ongoing means to observe students' thinking processes in context. Let's see how it works by visiting Karen Adazzio's classroom. Concern about the violence at Colorado's Columbine High School in the spring of 1999 led to a variety of classroom lessons in both elementary and secondary schools. School districts across the country were urged to provide ways for students to express their feelings about what happened.

KAREN ADAZZIO'S CLASSROOM

Karen Adazzio began the discussion by asking her students, "Could the Columbine incident have occurred here?" The students' response was overwhelmingly "Yes."

"Tell me," said Adazzio, "what you consider to be the most pressing issues that precipitated the shootings."

Adazzio recorded the students' list of items on the chalkboard:

- Prejudice by the teens against minorities and athletes

- Student cliques
- The two teens felt they were outsiders
- Jealousy
- Parents paid no attention to the two teens' activities
- Access to guns
- Internet information on how to build bombs

"That's quite a list," said Adazzio. "Let's focus just on the needs of young people. What would be an ideal situation to prevent teenagers from becoming involved in violent activities?"

Ideally, the students decided, there would be school programs that involved parents and kids, programs relevant to the needs of growing teens, and programs that would make sure kids would be successful and feel good about themselves.

"OK," said Adazzio, "let's assume that is our desired solution; let's just focus on relevant school programs and student success. What would it take to make it happen?"

Adazzio placed the goal inside a large circle (Figure 5.4). "What are the big ideas that are involved in making school programs relevant and ensuring student success?" From this the students identified four components:

1. A caring environment
2. Ending social and racial divisions
3. Vocational and college preparatory program choices for students
4. Opportunity to earn money while attending school

At this point in the lesson, Adazzio divided the students into small groups. Each group selected one of the four components to develop fully. (What would a school program look like if it provided choices for students? What do you consider to be a "caring environment" in the school setting? See Figure 5.4.)

How Does Backward Problem Solving Work?

The strategy assumes that everyone knows the resolution to the problem, but what is not known are the enabling tasks. For example, every teacher wants students to engage in critical thinking (Figure 5.5), but

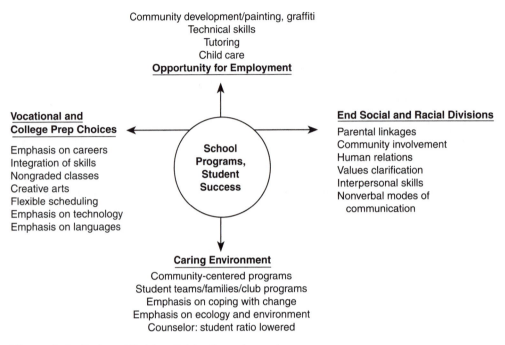

Community development/painting, graffiti
Technical skills
Tutoring
Child care
Opportunity for Employment

**Vocational and
College Prep Choices**

Emphasis on careers
Integration of skills
Nongraded classes
Creative arts
Flexible scheduling
Emphasis on technology
Emphasis on languages

**School
Programs,
Student
Success**

End Social and Racial Divisions

Parental linkages
Community involvement
Human relations
Values clarification
Interpersonal skills
Nonverbal modes of
    communication

Caring Environment
Community-centered programs
Student teams/families/club programs
Emphasis on coping with change
Emphasis on ecology and environment
Counselor: student ratio lowered

Figure 5.4   Backward Problem Solving Example

what is not known is how to align curriculum and instructional process to ensure that students practice critical-thinking skills.

The purpose of backward problem solving is to think about divergent means to accomplish a goal and to recognize that, for most goals, there is not one best

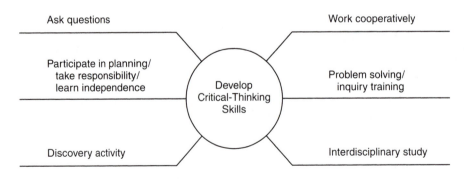

Ask questions

Work cooperatively

Participate in planning/
take responsibility/
learn independence

**Develop
Critical-Thinking
Skills**

Problem solving/
inquiry training

Discovery activity

Interdisciplinary study

Prerequisites:
 • Models of teaching that foster critical thinking
 • Develop risk-taking learning environments
 • Questioning techniques
 • Interdisciplinary unit planning

Figure 5.5   How to Develop Critical-Thinking Skills

way to realize success. The model is open-ended and encourages creative ideas. It is appropriate for whole-class or small-group activity.

The phases of backward problem solving are as follows:

Phase 1: Motivation and recognition of a problem situation.

Phase 2: Identification and acceptance of the desired goal/solution.

Phase 3: Exploration of diverse means to make the solution take place. This phase may be informal brainstorming or actual research.

Phase 4: The model may end at Phase 3 or be recycled to include exploration and in-depth study of the different facets of the enabling mechanisms identified in Phase 3.

DIFFERENTIATION OF INSTRUCTION: HOW CAN ALL STUDENTS ENGAGE IN INQUIRY?

Diverse interests and abilities need to be accommodated in most classroom situations. Much of the time there is a wide range of thinking ability in elementary and middle school classrooms. Inquiry teaching develops intellectual skills by providing opportunities for students to observe, identify, and hypothesize about problems; to gather and classify data; to analyze, compare, and contrast information; to interpret and verify data; and to come to a conclusion concerning the problem. Most students can accomplish these tasks by using a variety of learning experiences and activities. Differentiation occurs when teachers provide opportunity for students to select their own resources or the teacher provides the appropriate resources, when content (problems, questions) matches the student's interests and ability, and when students can choose how to demonstrate what they have learned.

Inquiry encourages active thinking and seeking rather than rote memorization; appropriately chosen problems enable students to work at their own ability level. It is important to remember that students are not discovering new knowledge; they are only discovering what they themselves do not know. This may mean that the low-ability child requires concrete materials and needs to learn by doing, but regardless of ability, the child can engage profitably and successfully in inquiry-related activities.

Teachers can create the desire to think and set the proper conditions for thinking. Teachers can help students develop curiosity, sensitivity, and habits of subjecting ideas to the test of rationality in order to cultivate the method of inquiry. We will now look at a variety of inquiry and research skill activities.

STUDENTS AS RESEARCHERS

USING TECHNOLOGY FOR PROBLEM-BASED LEARNING

Karen Adazzio's students were talking about the supermarket strike in Southern California. The strike affected most of the major markets, leaving very few places for consumers to shop unless they ignored the picket lines. The students' interests and concerns provided Adazzio with a way to motivate historical research into the formation of unions and their significance historically and in present times. She asked the students: "Why do you think so many consumers are loath to cross the picket lines?" Students' responses included the following:

- Probably many of their friends and families work in the markets.
- They probably feel sorry for the picketers.

 Teaching Hints: Problem-Based Learning

Technology serves as a support tool to find relevant and current information about a problem (the market strike). Students' interest in the problem helped the teacher integrate the curriculum so that the research was not an isolated event. The research also enabled the teacher to pull from interdisciplinary areas (economics, mathematics, political science, sociology) to construct a rich, informative learning experience.

- The strike hurts both the workers and the consumers.
- I don't think I understand about how unions control what the workers do.
- Yeah, and I heard that some of the markets "locked" their workers out; what does that mean?

"Since this is such a current topic, why don't we do some research using the Internet to find out more about these questions?" said Adazzio.

With the students' help, Adazzio framed the following questions:

1. When was the first union organized?
2. What happens when strikes affect the public welfare?
3. Do we have laws that forbid or curtail strikes?
4. How does a strike affect workers and consumers?
5. How are strikes settled?

Adazzio then asked students to select the question that interested them, form teams, and use the Internet to problem-solve. After each work period, a class discussion ensued and students shared their information.

Adazzio supported the research with current newspapers about the California market strike, history books, and mini-lectures about economics.

TEACHING OBSERVATION SKILLS IN SARA GARCIA'S THIRD-GRADE CLASS

The students had just concluded a session with the YMCA leader of the Feelin' Good program. The leader challenged them by stating that on her next visit, the class would check their fitness progress by performing some physical fitness tests.

As the students went out to lunch, Sara Garcia heard them discussing whether girls are more flexible than boys and questioning each other about the fitness tests. During the lunch hour, the students got into an argument. Some of the children were performing bent knee sit-ups while others watched. The observers claimed that the children doing the sit-ups were cheating and not

performing the exercise correctly. The teacher on yard duty had to stop the activity because of the heat of the argument. The yard teacher reported the situation to Garcia.

Garcia asked the students to explain the problem during the afternoon class session. The discussion focused on whether the children performing the exercise had performed it correctly. Observers' reports differed. Garcia decided to use the incident to accomplish several purposes: improve understanding of physical fitness, teach research skills, improve playground behavior, and integrate several subject fields.

On the following day Garcia showed a movie in which children were demonstrating exercises. In the discussion that followed, Garcia helped clarify and emphasize the following ideas:

- All individuals need a daily fitness program.
- Children and adults should exercise.
- Playing games will not necessarily keep children fit.
- Both girls and boys have the same physiological capacity to be flexible.
- Children are not necessarily more flexible than adults.

Many of the students were surprised that all age groups need exercise and that girls are not more flexible than boys. The students' interest provided Garcia with the lead-in she was looking for, and she asked the students if they would like to become researchers to find out what others believe about fitness and exercise. The students agreed, and immediately one class member asked if they were going to conduct a survey. Garcia responded that they could do that, but first she wanted to talk about the problem they had on the playground.

Garcia asked the students if they understood why some of the observers disagreed with each other about whether the performers were exercising correctly. The children did not understand why there was disagreement, so Garcia asked several students to demonstrate sit-ups. Then she asked several students to describe what they saw. Once again the reports differed slightly.

Now Garcia said, "All right, suppose that we said that when doing a sit-up you must roll up into a sitting position and keep your elbows extended straight from your ears." She had the students demonstrate the sit-up once again. Then she asked the observers for their report. This time the observers agreed about what they saw. "Why did the observers agree this time?" Garcia asked the students. After some discussion, the students realized that this time the observers were all looking for the same behavior. They were using the same criteria to describe what they saw.

Using this procedure, Garcia helped her students realize why they had been arguing on the playground. Then she said, "Now that you understand why you had a problem, let's trace the sequence of events that led up to the yard teacher disciplining you."

Garcia had the students list the events in the order that they happened. With the list on the chalkboard, Garcia explained to the students that each event was caused by the preceding event: that in fact there was a pattern of causes. Then the class talked about underlying causes of behavior, such as emotions. As a result of the discussion, the students understood that each event was an effect of the prior event and that each had caused the final effect of the discipline.

When Garcia felt comfortable about her students' understanding of their own behavior, she suggested that they begin thinking about their research. She told them, "These are some things we need to know in order to begin our research. We need to know about data and observation." Garcia began a discussion of data and observation with the class, giving them the following explanations:

Data: The word *data* means information; data are evidence. The researcher collects data about a specific problem under investigation. Data can be collected by watching and listening to people; by asking people for information, as in an interview; and by asking people for a written report, as in a questionnaire.

Observation: Although people may supposedly see or hear the same event, observations differ. This occurs because some people are more perceptive than others, people differ about what they have observed, and sometimes people disagree about why something happened.

To improve observation and make observations valid, people must observe specific aspects of behavior. To ensure that observations are reliable, several observers must observe independently, and they must agree about what they are seeing or hearing. For example, because the observers in Garcia's class had disagreed about the playground performance of the students doing the sit-ups, Garcia set a standard for skill performance. The next time the observers watched the sit-ups, they were all looking for the same skill performance using specific criteria. This ensured that the observations would be valid. To ensure reliability, Garcia used several observers. If the independent observers agreed about what they were observing, the observations would be considered reliable.

On successive days, Garcia and her students formalized their research. Using observation skills, interviews, and questionnaires, the third graders gathered and organized data and analyzed the results.

INTERVIEWS AND QUESTIONNAIRES

Advantages and Disadvantages of the Interview Technique

There are advantages and disadvantages to both the interview and the questionnaire. Generally, the interview is a more personal way of obtaining information. Face-to-face contact enables questions to be open-ended and determined by the nature of the interaction. The respondent and the interviewer have greater leeway in answering questions and in asking them. During the interview, the interviewer must make a number of decisions. For example, the interviewer must decide when to probe with a follow-up question and when to change the sequence of questions.

The interviewer also must be careful that the interview situation is objective. Facial expression and voice tone can communicate interviewer bias, thereby affecting the information provided by the respondent. Sometimes the sequence of questions and even the type of question asked can communicate bias. For example, if the interviewer asks a leading question ("Isn't it true that _____?"), the respondent may interpret the question as biased or may consider it presumptuous. Yes/no questions should generally be avoided during an interview situation because they do not exploit the advantage of the personal, face-to-face nature of the interview. Exceptions to this will be discussed.

Another advantage to the interview situation is the opportunity for the interviewer to detect respondent hesitancy, uncertainty, shyness, and bias. To do this, however, the interviewer must be experienced and know what to look for.

It is difficult to organize the interview for analysis. A system must be devised so the interview can be preserved for later analysis. One solution is to record the interview. Recording may be done only with permission from the respondent. Very capable interviewers can write down the respondent's answers, but this technique is difficult for elementary and middle school students.

Special Skills and Problems

Students need to practice two special skills in the classroom before they begin interviewing: (1) the ability to make the respondent feel at ease and willing to be interviewed and (2) the ability to restrain personal comments and expressions so that interviewer bias is not apparent to the respondent.

Courtesy to the person being interviewed is another aspect of the interview situation that teachers should discuss with young students. The interviewer must remember that the respondent is performing a service by permitting the interview. The interviewer should introduce him- or herself, explain the purpose of the interview, and thank the interviewee for taking time to respond. Young students should be made aware of the fact that sometimes adults do not like to be interviewed by youngsters. The result is frequently more positive if students interview in teams.

Interviewing Techniques

Structured Interview

Young researchers may benefit from a **structured interview** format because the questions never differ; they are predetermined and asked exactly as planned, usually in a precise order. Sometimes the respondent is even asked to choose a response from a list of possible answers. Even with preset questions, students should practice with each other in the classroom before the

interview. The practice period ensures that more data will be collected during the actual interview situation.

Questionnaires

The questionnaire is an example of a measuring instrument. It is more objective than the interview and can be mailed to respondents. Questions should be short and precise. Avoid vague words, and take care that each question requires just one response. Inexperienced questioners tend to ask more than one question at a time. It is a good idea to try the questionnaire with a select audience of friends before sending it out. Create a pilot study to determine if the questions ask what the class thinks they are asking. Although it is possible to ask open-ended questions on a questionnaire, they are more difficult to score and interpret. Some questionnaires are designed to provide objective measures with forced-choice answers, and some questions are open-ended so that the respondent may add whatever he or she pleases.

Distribution and Sampling

It is important to decide how to distribute the questionnaire. Because postage can be expensive, this may be a major decision. Typically students decide to hand-deliver their questionnaires to the respondents, mailing only those questionnaires that are going out of town.

Teach the students simple sampling concepts. For example, they can learn that one of the first things the social scientist must do is decide what group of people to study. Then, because it is usually impossible to survey everyone in the group, the scientist chooses a limited number of people, the sample. In choosing the sample, the scientist tries to make sure that the chosen group is representative of the total group so that it will be possible to make statements about the total group after completing the study. Sometimes scientists make mistakes and choose a biased sample that does not represent the group to be studied. When this occurs, scientists cannot generalize accurately about the total population. For example, a second-grade class wanted to find out if children in the second grade liked dogs. Because they could not ask all second graders, they chose a sample to question. After they finished their study, they discovered that almost all of the children in their sample owned dogs. Consequently, they had what is called a biased sample or, in other words, a group that was not representative of the total group of second graders.

Choosing the Format for Questions

There are four possible formats for questions in the questionnaire and interview. Forced-choice questions require the respondent to choose among alternatives, such as yes/no, always/never, many/few, or often/sometimes/rarely.

A second type is the scale question. This asks the respondent to rate an event, trait, or behavior, for example:

I like dogs   (Circle one)

    Very much   Much   A little bit   Not much

A third type is the ranking question. In this type of question, the respondent is asked to arrange events, behaviors, or traits in the order of preference or importance. Ranking items is more difficult for the respondent than answering forced-choice or scale questions, for example:

> Rank the following vegetables in the order that you like them. Number 5 indicates the vegetable that you like the most; number 1 indicates the vegetable that you like least.
>
> _____ Carrots   _____ Celery
> _____ String beans   _____ Broccoli
> _____ Radishes

The fourth question type is the open-ended question, which permits the respondent to say or write anything he or she wants. The open-ended question is the easiest to write but the hardest to score. However, a great deal of information can be gathered when time is taken to use the open-ended question, for example:

> What do you enjoy most about teaching?

Using Information from Interviews and Questionnaires

Before Sara Garcia set her class to work writing questions, she decided that they should have some idea how data are analyzed. She knew that this information might influence their decisions about the kinds of questions to ask.

Organizing the Data

Forced-choice questions can be tabulated and then analyzed in terms of the percentage of individuals responding or the frequency of the response (see Table 5.2). A similar type of worksheet can be designed for scale-type questions (see Table 5.3).

Students can be taught different ways to categorize the information. Questions that ask the respondent to rank the items can be tallied as shown in Table 5.4. Researchers need to decide on criteria to develop

Table 5.2 Tally of Responses to the Statement "All Individuals Need a Daily Fitness Program"

	Third Graders	*Sixth Graders*	*Adults*	*Total*
Yes	20	15	35 (50%)	**70**
No	10	10	20 (21%)	**40**
No response	5	10	15 (21%)	**30**
Total	**35**	**35**	**70 (100%)**	**140**

Table 5.3 Tally of Responses to the Statement "I Like Exercise"

	Boys	*Girls*	*Men*	*Women*	*Total*
Very much	15	10	25	20	**70**
Much	10	5	1	0	**16**
Little bit	2	10	0	5	**17**
Not much	3	3	4	5	**15**
No response	0	2	0	0	**2**
Total	**30**	**30**	**30**	**30**	**120**

Table 5.4 Tally and Ranking of Responses About Vegetables

Points	*Carrots*	*Beans*	*Radishes*	*Celery*	*Broccoli*
5	20	8	1	15	2
4	10	10	4	10	5
3	5	5	5	10	20
2	3	10	5	2	10
1	2	7	25	3	3
Total	163	122	71	152	113
Rank	1	3	5	2	4

Note: The tally was multiplied by the number of points the respondent gave it.

categories for analyzing open-ended questions. For example, if respondents were asked, "What do you like about exercise?" their responses might be as follows:

> "It makes me feel good."
> "I think it is important to do."
> "Nothing."
> "I like sweating."
> No response

To organize this information, the researcher would probably establish positive, negative, neutral, and no-response categories. Then the researcher would need to provide examples of each category to guide the organization of the data. "It makes me feel good" and "I like sweating" would be examples of positive responses. "Nothing" could be interpreted as a negative response. "I think it is important to do" would be a neutral statement. Sara ``Garcia's third graders would have difficulty interpreting open-ended responses; capable fifth- and sixth-grade students could probably manage it quite well.

Analyzing the Data

Sara Garcia assisted the students in developing the following questionnaire that included scale-type responses:

1. Do you think it is important for children to exercise regularly?
2. Do you think it is important for adults to exercise regularly?
3. Do you think aerobic workouts are important?
4. Do you think exercise can make people feel better?
5. Do you think it is important to stretch before you exercise vigorously?

The students were also going to use the same questions in an interview situation, with the interviewer asking one additional question: Do you think exercise is fun?

After the students tabulated their data, Garcia gave them several ways to present the results. She arranged the students into five groups, and each group was told to decide how to communicate the results to others. Each group worked with just one of the questions. Their choices were a bar graph (Figure 5.6), a pie graph (Figure 5.7), a table, or a chart. The students had data for boys, girls, men, and women. They were told that they could sum the data or find ways to present the data

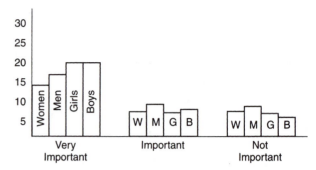

Figure 5.6 Bar Graph: Do You Think Exercise Is Important?

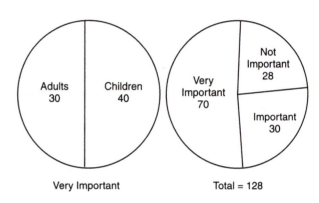

Figure 5.7 Pie Graphs: Do You Think Exercise Is Important?

for each of the four groups. They had to decide how to communicate the importance of the response. The results as communicated by one of Sara Garcia's groups appear in Table 5.5. Her third graders may need help with the concept of *tally* as a mark and a means to count.

Table 5.5 Tally of Responses to the Question "Do You Think Exercise Is Important?"

	Very Important	Important	Not Important
Males	38	18	14
Females	32	12	14
Total	**70**	**30**	**28**

Drawing Conclusions

During the summative evaluation, Garcia's students concluded the following:

- Children have a better understanding of the importance of exercise than do adults.
- Males appreciate the value of exercise more than females.
- Adult females were more willing to be interviewed than adult males.
- Adult males were more willing to fill out a questionnaire.
- Deciding on the questions to ask and their form was the hardest research task.
- Choosing their sample was important.
- They felt shy when doing an interview.
- It was fun!

Integration of Subject Fields and Interdisciplinary Content: What Did the Students Learn?

Sara Garcia used the research study to integrate subject fields, utilizing interdisciplinary concepts. She was also concerned about her students' social behavior on the playground. Subject by subject, here is a summary of what she accomplished:

Language Arts

Reading: The students read questions, charts, graphs, and the questionnaire. They learned to classify data by sex and to use a scale. They arranged information in sequence.

Oral language: Students participated in group and class discussions, practiced interviewing, practiced courtesy during interviewing, listened to others, asked questions, and expressed ideas.

Spelling: Students spelled special words related to the research study, such as *male, female, sample, questionnaire, observations, interview,* and *survey.*

Writing: Students wrote questions using capitals and question marks.

Mathematics

The students learned to tally their data. The students performed addition using two-digit numbers; performed column addition; subtracted two-digit numbers; multiplied two-digit numbers; and collected, organized, and interpreted data using charts, tables, and bar graphs.

Science, Social Studies, Thinking Skills

Students used their senses to collect and process data. They developed and used a classification system. They participated in inquiry, identifying a problem, and forming questions. They planned an investigation; recorded and organized data; prepared and interpreted graphic material; analyzed, evaluated, and interpreted data; and summarized and communicated their investigation to others.

Social Participation

The students demonstrated curiosity, concern about others, willingness to share data and ideas with others, cooperation with others, participation in group tasks, and acceptance of responsibility to distribute and collect data.

Health and Physical Education

Students shared information about physical activities. They considered the relationship of activity to cardiovascular health, recognized the importance of exercise, and shared negative and positive feelings. They performed exercise activities, explained basic ideas about exercise, discussed physical fitness, and participated in fitness testing.

Individualizing Research Problems

Research problems provide means to differentiate instruction. Gifted students, in particular, may need opportunities to learn on their own. Frequently, some students in the classroom will benefit from working independently, and the research project provides a challenging means to structure content, processes, and product to meet individual needs.

Research projects can also be differentiated for small groups of students by providing different problems at varying levels of difficulty and appealing to diverse interests.

CASE STUDIES

What Is a Case Study?

A case study is a thorough investigation of a single event, institution, decision, issue, or individual. Case studies are typically used in business, medicine, law, social work, and therapy. Materials for case studies may include personal records, histories, diaries, graphs, and stories—in fact, a variety of data. Although the data may be varied, they are typically relevant only to the single situation for which they were gathered or prepared. The data should allow systematic analysis. Practice with case study analysis helps students gain insight into similar types of problems or situations. Thinking is usually inductive in nature during the case study.

The **case study approach** enables the teacher to reduce the amount of data to a manageable size to facilitate analysis. For example, suppose a teacher wants students to understand our legal system and the way in which the Supreme Court makes decisions. Instead of asking students to research everything about the Court and the decisions the Court makes, the teacher provides data, or has students gather the data, about a single Supreme Court decision. Once the data are collected and studied, the students may even role-play the case to gain greater insight. The principle illustrated by the case should demonstrate a basic concept that is applicable to similar problems, or in the case of the Supreme Court, it should demonstrate the decision-making process of the Court and how the Court relates to a democratic society.

You can select case studies about real or fictional issues and problems. The studies may be open-ended, involved, or quite simple. Whatever you select should be motivating and provide an adequate database in terms of factual information. The open-ended case requires that students make the final judgment about the outcome, or at least suggest possible alternatives.

EXAMPLES OF THE USE OF CASE STUDIES—KAREN ADAZZIO'S CLASSROOM

LANGUAGE ARTS

Adazzio used the case study method to accomplish both language arts and social studies objectives. She chose the following resources:

- *West from Home: Letters of Laura Ingalls Wilder*
- *A Gathering of Days: A New England Girl's Journal, 1830–32*
- *The Endless Steppe: Growing Up in Siberia*

The Wilder book, composed of letters from Laura Wilder to her husband, provides historical background and information about San Francisco in 1915. *A Gathering of Days,* by Joan Blos, is a fictional work written in the form of a journal about the rigorous life on a New Hampshire farm in 1830. *The Endless Steppe* is a personal account by Esther Hautzig of her experiences as a girl in exile in Siberia during World War II.

Adazzio's goals were as follows:

- To develop an appreciation of authorship
- To differentiate purpose, structure, and style of fiction and nonfiction
- To recognize that personal letters, journals, and diaries are documents—primary resources—and provide a form of autobiography
- To authenticate historical information and background information by reading literature

The students' assignment was to read the selected portion of the book and be prepared to discuss the following questions:

- How does the writer know what really happened?
- What reasons might the writer have for being prejudiced or for exaggerating?
- When did the writer or main character live?
- What event did the writer or main character participate in?
- What decisions did the writer or main character make?
- How would circumstances have been different if the story had been told by a male?
- If you were faced with similar conflicts, what decisions would you make?
- How are you like or different from the author or main character?

Teaching Tasks During Case Studies

Is the Case Study Approach Appropriate?

In choosing a teaching strategy, a teacher must ask: Which approach will facilitate the accomplishment of my objectives? Case studies are appropriate as a teaching strategy when the amount of data about a given problem, situation, or person is so abundant that it would be difficult for students to choose and examine just the pertinent information. When this occurs, the case study approach enables the teacher to reduce the data, thereby limiting the investigation.

Case studies are valuable when the students cannot research the data because of the complexity of the issues or the reading levels of the students. In this instance, the teacher may find it advantageous to write the case study to fit the students' reading levels. Case studies are also suitable when the situation calls for an open-ended role that makes students decide what the decision ought to be.

Once you have decided that the case study is the right approach and fits the purposes of the lesson, it is time to select the appropriate materials or write your own.

Selecting Materials for a Case Study

The first consideration in choosing case study materials is whether the students will be able to read and comprehend the selected data. You must consider both the concept load and the vocabulary level. If students do not have the specialized skills needed to read charts, tables, graphs, or maps, then include a skill lesson first.

Organizational considerations also affect the choice of the materials. How will students be grouped for instruction? If students are to work in small groups during the intake portion of the lesson, have you prepared or obtained enough materials? Can one member of each small group be the reader for the other group members?

A wide variety of commercial publications are available for case study use. In addition, the Internet, newspapers, textbooks, and literature selections provide a wealth of suitable data. Once you become adept at rewriting materials for your own students, you will find that social studies, science, and health textbooks are a fine source of information.

Motivating the Study and Organizing Study Tasks

As in other inquiry activities, if the proposed case study is not of interest to the students, they will not be motivated to perform the necessary analytic tasks. Therefore, it is important that the teacher determine the relevancy of the assignment before sending students off to study. Once again, formulation of the inquiry question is an important teacher task.

Another critical teacher task is deciding how students should organize the data. Suppose the case study involves reading about student misbehavior in the Boston school system. The data include charts on federal aid, maintenance and supply costs, and personnel costs. Facts include information about curriculum, students' difficulties, and class distractions. Because the case study will be evaluated during a whole-class discussion, how should students prepare for the discussion? Consider the case study inquiry sequence in Figure 5.8.

Debriefing Using Discussion Strategy

Guiding the discussion at the end of the case study is the most important teacher task. The teacher or a capable student should record the discussion on the chalkboard. During this stage of the study, the teacher, through questions, facilitates the following:

- A recap of the definition of key terms.
- Clarification of the facts. The teacher asks, "What do we know?" "How do we know that what we know is reliable?"
- Clarification of issues and conflicting values: "What was involved?"
- Whole-class participation in the discussion: "What do you think?" "What else happened?" "Who can add to that?"
- Students' explanation of why the events occurred: "Why did the Boston school system dismiss 710 tenured teachers?" "Why did the students protest?" For the final discussion, this step is where teacher efforts should be maximized.
- Suggestions for solution: "How can the case be resolved?" "What are the alternatives?" Once again, create a list for students to see.
- Consideration of implications or consequences for each of the alternatives: "If such-and-such occurs, what will be the consequences?" "If we were to manipulate this, what would be affected?" "If you were the main character, what decision would you make?" And finally, "How would this solution apply to similar problems?"

Learning Tasks During Case Studies

Unlike other inquiry strategies, students are frequently presented with the problem, the hypothesis, and the data during case studies. This means that student

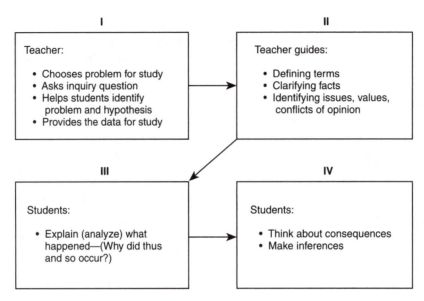

Figure 5.8 Case Study Inquiry Sequence

inquiry begins with data analysis. During case study analysis, students perform the following tasks (Figure 5.8):

- Students read, observe, or consume the given information in some other way. Their task is to evaluate the information by differentiating between facts and opinions. They must evaluate objectivity, reliability, and source of information.
- Students judge the adequacy of their information. If sets of data are available, they must contrast the information, noting similarities and differences.
- They note changes in the data.
- They conclude data analysis with summarization and interpretation.
- Through discussion, students share meanings and interpretations.
- Through auding (listening attentively), students evaluate others' perspectives.
- Through participation, students share inquiry responsibility.
- Students analyze cause-and-effect relationships to reach a conclusion.
- From alternatives, students select the best solution to a problem.
- Students make predictions concerning the outcome of a particular solution or course of action.
- Students make choices based on possible consequences.

Assessing Students' Problem-Solving Skills

It is just as important to evaluate the way in which you, the teacher, accomplish inquiry-oriented teaching as it is to evaluate the students' problem-solving skills. In fact, the two components (teaching and learning) cannot be separated; one is related to the other. The purpose and choice for inquiry, the materials, and the conditions in the classroom all affect what the students do and what they say.

An interesting way to assess students' skills is to give them an inquiry test problem and then ask students to do the following:

- Write a statement of the problem.
- Select appropriate sources for data.
- Suggest ways to gather data.
- Explain how they would organize data for analysis.

Note that this list does not include the final step, concluding. Practically the only way you, the teacher, can evaluate students' ability to form an appropriate conclusion is to provide them with specific data in the form of observed or supposed facts. Then you can ask the students to make an inference about the data in terms of whether it is sufficient for making a conclusion. Or you can give them a number of conclusions and ask them to choose one that is logical and beyond doubt, based on the information given.

Of course, the prime way to evaluate students' skills is to examine the products of inquiry. What students produce while involved in inquiry activities and the discussions that follow the inquiry provide the most meaningful information about their performance.

SUMMARY

The inquiry approach can be traced to John Dewey, who linked inquiry, reflective thinking, and critical thinking. Inquiry processes require the consideration of data, a search for evidence, and inductive thought processes. Inquiry teaching requires choosing appropriate problems for study, consideration of the adequacy of materials and resources, creating an appropriate classroom environment, and providing guidance and objectivity.

The group investigation teaching model uses six phases of inquiry. Evaluation of group investigation requires assessing substantive accomplishment(s) and group process skills. Constructivism is an inquiry learning approach that requires students to be actively involved in integrating new knowledge with prior knowledge. The 5-E model is similar to group investigation in its inquiry focus and use of group interaction and participatory activities. Concept attainment is another inquiry teaching model approach used to help students gain specific concepts by comparing and contrasting attributes. Backward problem solving is an inquiry approach that encourages students' divergent thinking by beginning with desired goals and then reaching backward to discover the process of accomplishment.

Students can be taught to engage in research activity using observation skills, gathering data, interviewing, and developing questionnaires. As researchers, students learn to write appropriate questions, use sampling techniques, and organize and analyze data. Research activities facilitate the integration of skills and content. The case study approach is a means to reduce data to facilitate an intensive study of a single problem, situation, or person.

PORTFOLIO ACTIVITY

Using the four phases of a constructivist lesson, plan an inquiry activity. Ask your students to tell you what they liked best and least about the lesson. Then write a self-evaluation of the lesson in which you evaluate your students' responses.

 DISCUSSION QUESTIONS AND APPLICATION EXERCISES

1. Adazzio's seventh-grade classroom studied the relationship between age and auto safety.
   - Plan an appropriate inquiry question.
   - Suggest sources for data.
   - Pretend that students have obtained data about transportation services and write a sequence of questions to help students interpret and apply their data.
2. Choose an article from the daily newspaper and plan a lesson using group investigation.
3. Think about the example of the fifth-grade students who studied colonial art in order to learn about the New England colonists' cultural beliefs. Plan a concept attainment lesson to teach the concept of culture.
4. In Greg Thomas's Jigsaw lesson, he had the ELL students working together for the inquiry portion of the lesson. What are the pros and cons of having these students work together instead of working with other students?
5. Which of the following statements would make good inquiry lessons in the classroom?
   - There are fewer farms today than 50 years ago, but U.S. farmers grow more food today than they did 50 years ago.
   - Changes in lifestyle affect language usage.
   - Most students dislike mathematics.
   - People do not work hard anymore.
   (If you chose the first two, you are right. The second two statements would be extremely difficult to research; they are too broad and need clarification.) Suggest data for students to analyze to study the first two statements.
6. Use the following inquiry example to design an investigation:
   - Inquiry question/problem—How do the members of your methods class feel about using inquiry methodology?
   - Sources of data
   - Gathering data
   - Organizing data
   - Conclusion

7. Practice backward problem solving. Identify a teaching/learning problem in your own classroom. What would you like to see happen? (Identify the ideal solution.) Now describe enabling tasks to make the ideal a reality.

8. Use the Taba questioning sequence given in this chapter to design an inquiry lesson.

9. Field research should be planned jointly by teacher and students. To practice the skills discussed in this chapter, however, design a questionnaire for your students. Choose one of the following topics to investigate:
   - Number of languages spoken by families at your school
   - Frequency of moving from one community to another
   - Beliefs about sex-role differences (make a list of beliefs such as cleanliness, play differences, and traits)
   - Jobs performed by children
   - Number of hours of television viewing and number of hours of homework

   What question type will you use? How will the data be organized? How will you analyze the data?

10. If you were to use the example about the puppy from the chapter-opening vignette with your students, how would you demonstrate (a) that cause precedes effect in time and (b) multiple causation?

11. In what ways do inquiry-oriented activities make students take responsibility for their own learning?

READER RESEARCH

Using a class of students in any grade between 4 and 8, teach these students a concept using direct instruction and group investigation. Determine how well they have done with both strategies and then question the students to find out which methodology they prefer and why. Critique your two lessons and the students' rationale.

 TECHNOLOGY APPLICATIONS

Select an Internet site with primary source materials and explain how you can use the site to develop a case study for students in grades 5 through 8. How will you use the primary source materials presented at this site? How will you motivate the study? What tasks will students perform? How many days will be needed for your plans?

Hands-on investigations motivate students to gather data, theorize, and reach conclusions.

CHAPTER 6

• •

Curriculum Planning
The Teaching Unit

This chapter begins with a thematic teaching unit developed by Greg Thomas for his fifth graders. Thomas's teaching unit will be used to identify and define key curriculum concepts. Procedures for curriculum development are explained using a step-by-step process. An alternate model for curriculum development is also presented, with suggestions for the reader to try both systems. The chapter emphasizes the importance of a match among the teacher's goals, content, and the learning activities because if students do not actively experience what teachers have in mind in their day-to-day lessons, then the teaching unit does not accurately depict what students are learning.

Advance Organizer

The following questions are intended to guide your reading and understanding of the content of this chapter.

1. What are the characteristics of the three types of units described in this chapter?
2. How do themes and generalizations differ? Write an example of each.
3. Why is the content outline composed of "big ideas"?
4. How do key questions help you demonstrate the teaching-learning process you intend to follow in your teaching unit?
5. Why should the learning experiences fit your content and key questions and demonstrate a variety of instructional processes and activities?
6. How can learning experiences be used to evaluate what students are learning?
7. How can webbing be used as a means to develop a teaching unit?
8. Why is it important to integrate subject fields and skill instruction?
9. What is the purpose of curriculum mapping?

INTASC

INTASC Standards

Standards 1–8 need to be mastered to create effective and appropriate teaching units for the students in your classroom. Standards 9 and 10 focus on your professional concerns to verify that what and how you are teaching match students' needs and interests. These two standards require collegial interaction and personal reflection.

Professional Lexicon

balance Achievement of equity among subject fields and learning processes in a curriculum plan.

concepts The big ideas; the significant content of a subject field.

continuity Reiteration of significant content at different levels to achieve depth in conceptual understanding.

curriculum consonance The balance of elements in the curriculum to ensure that learning experiences are appropriate and support goals.

generalization A concept or idea that demonstrates understanding and provides direction for content and learning experiences to explain the theme of a teaching unit.

integration The linking of subject fields and learning processes to facilitate learning by helping the learner see relationships.

interdisciplinary content Concepts from different subject fields (disciplines) used to demonstrate learning through different lenses.

project-based learning A technology teaching assignment that engages students in producing a product that has depth, is complex, and requires time to complete.

---

resource unit A unit developed by a committee for the purpose of providing direction and assistance to classroom teachers.

scope The breadth of a teaching unit or a curriculum; how much of what is covered in a unit.

sequence The order of content in a teaching unit.

teaching unit The plan that is to be implemented in the classroom and that represents the instructional curriculum.

themes Unit-organizing concepts used to represent the big ideas, overarching concepts, unifying constructs, or underlying assumptions.

webbing A pictorial means to demonstrate the connecting of ideas for a teaching unit (like a spider web).

"Mr. Thomas, what's all this stuff in the room?"
"Yeah, who are the Inuits?"
"Why is there a tea set in the classroom?"
"Are we going to study about these things?"
"I know. We're going to study about Canada and Japan, but how come?"
"Well, Jeb, do you realize that 90% of Canadians live within 100 miles of the United States and that Canada and Japan are our best trading partners?"
"Gee, Mr. Thomas, I don't even know what you mean by a trading partner!"
"OK, let's all sit down and talk about it."

PLANNING A THEMATIC TEACHING UNIT

Greg Thomas wanted to plan a teaching unit that would have the social studies as its major focus, but he wanted to integrate other subject fields (language arts, math, the arts, science) and include interdisciplinary concepts from several of the disciplines. The unit was for his fifth-grade students, who were quite diverse in their capabilities. Before he could choose a theme, he needed to think about his overall goals.

Goals

Thomas decided on the following overall goals:

- Develop students' research skills.
- Develop students' problem-solving capabilities.
- Provide opportunities for applying basic skills.
- Provide opportunities for social participation that include leadership and group member responsibilities.

He intended to plan specific topics in each subject field, relating the topics to an overall theme. The learning experiences (activities) would reflect his teaching objectives because in that way he would develop each subject field systematically. As an experienced teacher, Thomas

was able to meld his knowledge of what his students know (and don't know), his knowledge of subject matter and appropriate content, and his knowledge of instructional processes (see Figure 6.1).

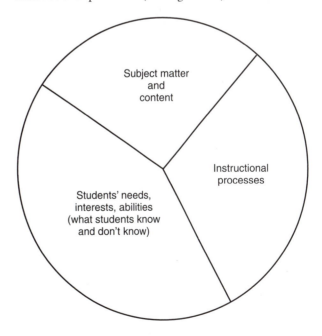

Figure 6.1 Teacher's Knowledge

Theme

Greg Thomas selected *patterns of change* as his theme. **Themes** are typically selected as broad concepts so they can be used in many ways. Next he wrote a **generalization** to give meaning to the theme, patterns of change, as he would be using it: *The interaction of culture and environment results in distinctive patterns of behavior.* (See the "Teaching Hints" box for ideas for generalizations.)

Thomas was thinking about a comparative study of change in the United States, Japan, and Canada. He planned to feature the changing patterns of life for women in these countries as they relate to culture, economics, and geography. As women changed their ways of behaving, he wanted the students to recognize how it affected other members of the family and society in general. To build his own knowledge base, he used the Internet and a variety of textbooks. He began to jot down his ideas about the content of this unit.

The Big Ideas—Content Outline

1. The environment and conditions of living in a region affect human behavior.

Teaching Hint: Choosing a Theme

Before selecting a theme for your teaching unit, it is important to think about the most significant ideas from the discipline(s), then choose a theme that fits.

2. Technology and industrialization affect ways of life.
3. Government, politics, and cultural values affect power and authority, human ideals, and cultural practices.

Key Questions

Next, Thomas framed some key questions to focus his choice of learning experiences. Table 6.1 represents Thomas's teaching unit. Each question generates a

The use of multimedia resources needs to be planned so that they are utilized in the teaching units.

Table 6.1   A Teaching Unit

Key Questions	Learning Experiences (Activities)
In what ways are the topography of Canada, the United States, and Japan similar and different?	• Selecting appropriate maps, students will compare the climate and topography of the three countries. Students will fill in maps, identifying mountains, rivers, and elevations.
How does the topography and climate of a country influence where people live?	• Students will compare the distribution of population in the three countries and hypothesize why people settle in certain areas and not in others. Students will chart climate information, waterways, and resources. • Students will compute time and mileage distances between cities and rural areas. • Using *direct instruction* and an *advance organizer,* students will learn the differences between the natural and human-made environment.

Table 6.1   A Teaching Unit

Key Questions	Learning Experiences (Activities)
How do people earn a living in the cities and rural areas of the three countries?	• Students will participate in a *group investigation* to compare occupations and services in large cities and rural areas. • Using a variety of resources, students will explain the effect of climate, topography, and environment on the way people earn a living and where they live. • Using the computer simulation *SimCity 3000,* students will create their own cities and relate them to the environment of each country. • Students will participate in a *concept attainment* lesson using the concept of *population density.* • Students will visit other classrooms and contrast the population density of their own classroom with that of other classrooms in their school and compare the arrangement of furniture, resources, and computers in the classrooms. Students will tally the data. • During a class *discussion,* students will explain the relationship between the environment of the classroom and students' activities. They will discuss how changes in the classroom environment could affect their behavior. • Students will hypothesize about what influenced size, expansion, and diminution of cities and rural areas. • Students will participate in a class *discussion* of land use after creating their own city. Students will be asked to relate land use to climate, topography, and environment.
How are the economics of the three countries similar and different? What is unique about each country's production?	• Students will participate in a *concept attainment* lesson using the concepts of *import and export.* • Students will practice illustrating similarities and differences with *Venn diagrams.* • Students will illustrate production similarities and differences of the three countries using Venn diagrams. • Students will construct charts to demonstrate trade between and among the three countries. • Using *direct instruction,* students will study the concept of *gross national product* and create graphs illustrating the concept for the three countries.
How has technology and industrialization affected contemporary society in the three countries?	• *Using group investigation and problem solving,* students will explore how technology affects employment of men and women, organization of work, attitudes of business leaders, home life, where people live, and the lives of children. • Using a variety of classroom resources, students will create webs to illustrate manufacturing in the three countries. • Students will create dioramas to illustrate historical changes in agriculture practices in the three countries. • Using menus from Japanese, American, and Canadian restaurants, students will identify differences in foods that are featured and related to cultural tastes. • Students will trace foods and tastes back to the farms and discuss the relationship. Students' dioramas will depict changes in rice production in Japan. • Students will identify and depict changes in the fishing and trapping industry, forestry, and transportation in Canada. • *Group investigation* will focus on the environmental effects of forestry and fishing in Canada, the United States, and Japan. • Students will read about groceries and supermarkets in the three countries and make grocery lists for an average family in Tokyo, Vancouver, and New York City. Students will investigate the "average" size of families. • Students will visit a supermarket in their community and estimate the square footage provided for typical foods (major categories) used in the American home. They will then estimate the layout and space requirements for markets in Tokyo and Vancouver. • Students will compare the currency of the three countries and study the effect of American tourists in Canada and Japan. Students will calculate how far the U.S. dollar will go in Canada and Japan.

(continued)

Table 6.1 A Teaching Unit

Key Questions	Learning Experiences (Activities)
How do housing, purchases, and possessions differ in major cities of the three countries?	• Using pictures and data sources, students will draw the layout of typical apartments and houses in major cities of the three countries. • Students will participate in a *concept attainment* lesson using the concept of *culture.* • Students will read about family life in Japan and Canada and contrast it with that in the United States. • In large-class *discussion,* students will explain the connections among topography, population density, culture, economy, and housing. • Students will explain the connections among living quarters, purchasing, and possessions.
How do the governments of the three countries differ? In what ways are they similar?	• Using classroom resources, students will describe the Canadian parliament structure, the U.S. federal system, and the Japanese system of government. • Students will identify a typical national problem and role-play how the problem would be considered by the government bodies of the three countries.
In what ways do cultural attitudes and beliefs differ in the three countries (traditionally, and in contemporary society)?	• Students will select literature books in which to read about family customs and national differences, and write reports about their books. • Students will listen to the music of Japan and folk music of Canada and the United States. Japanese instruments will be exhibited for students to see. • Students will role-play a Japanese family and the tea ceremony. • Students can investigate favorite sports and recreation activities in the three countries. • Students will consider the role of government in influencing individuality and cultural customs. • Students will investigate differences in schooling in the three countries.
How has the role of women changed in contemporary Japan, Canada, and the United States? (Why is it harder for women to hold jobs than it is for men?)	• Students will study employment charts of the three countries and compare jobs, education, managerial positions, and salaries. • Students will construct graphs using the data. • Students will compare women's roles and responsibilities in rural and urban centers of the three countries. • *Group investigation* will focus on the problems of women in the workplace. • Students will participate in **project-based learning** to compare the economy, family structure, customs, and roles of both men and women in the three countries. Students may use pictures, letters, news articles, Web information, and cartoons in their projects. • Students will participate in the computer simulation Sims to create a family, design a home, and control the activities of the people and neighborhood. They will relate their simulated people to the families they have studied in the three countries.
What are current challenges facing people in the three countries?	• Using newspaper articles, the Internet, and e-mail, students will gather information about current problems confronting youth and families in the three countries. • Students will collect data on the problems of crime, drugs, tobacco, abuse, and suicide. • Students will compare the problems and challenges to determine similarities or differences. Students will discuss citizenship in the three countries and ways that youths can contribute to their community and government.

Teaching Hints:
Ideas for Generalizations
and Themes

- Social groups organize themselves to meet the needs of their members. (Order)
- The interaction of culture and environment results in distinctive patterns of behavior. (Patterns of change)
- Rules represent social values; people make rules to set norms of conduct. (Order)
- Group living necessitates cooperation in and between groups to maintain an orderly, physical, social, and cultural environment. (Interactions, order)
- Living things depend on one another and their environment. (Interdependence)
- Changes in the physical environment affect life in that environment. (Change)
- Our physical and social environments reflect both change and stability. (Change, stability)
- Political and economic systems interact and affect ways of life. (Systems and interactions)
- Culture changes occur as a consequence of time, place, and distance. (Culture, change)
- Learning is essential to human development and is a lifelong experience. (Growth, change)
- People are unique in their cultural adaptations and social organization. (Adaptation, change, culture, systems, order)
- Evolution is evident through patterns, processes, mechanisms, and history. (Patterns of change, evolution)
- Change can be identified; it can be cyclical, be irregular, or exhibit a trend. (Change, patterns)

number of learning experiences. Depending on the students and the depth of activities, the unit could take from six weeks to most of a semester.

Class Organization

Greg Thomas plans to divide his class into six groups. Two groups will focus on the United States, two will focus on Canada, and two will focus on Japan. Students will share their information during class discussions, through their charts, and in exhibits. This will occur each day after a work session. Because the students are grouped in this way, they will not all need the same

resources at the same time. Sharing time will provide opportunity for the groups to question each other and encourage substantiated research to validate the group's presentation. Role-play activities, concept attainment, and advance organizer strategies will involve whole-class participation; group investigation will occur in small groups.

MULTIMEDIA RESOURCES TO FOCUS ON STUDENT LEARNING

Most of Thomas's activities require students to use a variety of resources, including print and picture materials, computer software, laser disc, and hypermedia for combining graphics, sound, and text to construct their projects. Some resources about Canada include the following:[1]

- Canadian parliamentary video obtained from the Canadian Film Distribution Center (http://canada-acsus@plattsburgh.edu).
- http://www.schoolnet.ca. This site has links to information about Canadian law, geography, culture, and history. Another site for cultural information is the Canadian Museum of Civilization, http://www.civilization.ca.

Thomas found a variety of books that were appropriate for his class to read for information and as literature choices about Japan. He will also advise students to use the Internet for information. Sites include the following:

- http://www.bento.com/tokyofood.html
- http://www.altavista.com
- Kid's Web Japan: http://www.japan.org/kidsweb/
- http://kidsyahoo.com/directory/Around the World/Countries
- http://www.countryreports.org/

ASSESSMENT

Thomas will base much of his assessment of students' learning on the quality and completion of work tasks, projects, small-group interaction, and discussions.

---

[1]Web sites change constantly and need to be verified before you give to students.

Charts, graphs, Venn diagrams, literature reports, dioramas, and role-plays will all demonstrate students' progress. Thomas also will ask his students to keep a record of Internet links so that he will know that the Internet is being used productively; it will also give him insight about his students' thinking processes.

Thomas will be evaluating students' work in the different subject fields that are to be integrated. For example, the graphs and Venn diagrams will be part of the students' math assignments. Thomas will be using traditional teacher-made tests to evaluate students' understanding as well as their performance on individual and group projects.

The next section of this chapter will explain basic curriculum planning considerations and curriculum concepts. Thomas's thematic unit will be used to provide examples throughout this section.

Multiple Intelligences

Greg Thomas considered his students' diverse needs when he planned his learning experiences. He used a variety of teaching strategies and activities to engage students in learning. The students had opportunities to work in interactive groups and also autonomously. By integrating subject fields and providing diverse learning experiences, Thomas enabled students to use all eight of the intelligences.

WHAT IS UNIT TEACHING?

A *unit* is a plan that organizes ideas and knowledge into a meaningful structure for teaching purposes. Basic **concepts** within a subject field or across subject fields are selected to achieve specific purposes. Greg Thomas used a number of social science concepts related to each of his big ideas. These included *environment* (both a social and physical science concept), *culture, population density, rural, urban, gross national product, import, export, standards of living, constitutional democracy, parliamentary system, government,* and *politics.*

The content of the unit facilitates communication. Without content, students can communicate about very little for expression and reception purposes. The unit should provide integrative experiences to satisfy students' needs and to develop understandings, values, and skills.

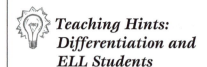

Teaching Hints: Differentiation and ELL Students

All students appreciate variety in their learning experiences. Greg Thomas has identified a number of learning activities to differentiate content, process, and product. These experiences will work well for ELL students who profit from concrete activities, such as dioramas, graphs, Venn diagrams, art, and individual writing.

Research Findings

New construction of schools and renovation projects across the United States feature efforts to accommodate the natural environment by maximizing natural light and conserving water and energy. Within the schools, teachers plan ways for students to study the outdoor environment and energy efficiency within the school. Students gain understanding of the relationship between outdoor temperature and sunlight on energy use (Allen, 2007).

Types of Units

Single-Subject and Broad-Field Units

Units can be developed for most subjects: science (such as biology and astronomy), music, art, health, mathematics, and history. When a unit is intended for a single-subject field only, content is usually structured for the single discipline and is considered discipline-oriented. Relatively little thought is given to meeting the needs of a specific group of students.

But units can be designed to teach content from a broad-field perspective, such as social studies, life sciences, and health education. These units are typically organized around a theme (as Greg Thomas did) and are relatively open-ended so that students can provide input and the teacher can change activities to meet students' interests and needs.

Resource Units

The **resource unit** is often developed at the district level by a committee of teachers or subject-field specialists. The purpose of the resource unit is to provide a great deal of information on possible ways to teach a specific topic. It is not planned with any specific group of students in mind. The resource unit includes learning activities, resource materials, and evaluation methods, as well as lists of objectives and questions.

Thematic Teaching Units

The **teaching unit** differs from the resource unit in degree of specificity: It is focused and planned for a particular group of students and is formulated to teach a limited number of concepts, skills, and values. Before developing a teaching unit, the teacher may make use of a resource unit.

The teaching unit ensures that there is a purpose to the day-to-day lessons. It represents long-range planning for teaching the curriculum. Unit activities should include a broad range of processes and experiences, such as problem solving, research skill activities, language development, and dramatic activities. All of the instructional strategies discussed in Part II of this text can be used in unit teaching.

The teaching unit often is initiated by an inquiry question to stimulate students' thinking and obtain their input about what they would like to know. The inquiry question helps the teacher assess students'

knowledge about the theme and facilitates the planning process.

Single-subject units are often planned long in advance of the time when students will be taught the subject. The thematic unit is typically planned and focused on specific students; therefore, it is ongoing.

CURRICULUM CONCEPTS

When designing a unit, the curriculum developer considers a number of organizing elements that affect the function of the unit, the choice of content, and the length of time the class will focus on the unit.

The **scope** of the unit determines whether the unit will provide broad coverage or in-depth understanding. In a sense, it tells you "how much of what" to teach. Greg Thomas's unit is limited in its scope. He is primarily focusing on four social sciences: geography, economics, political science, and sociology.

The **sequence** of the unit determines the linear organization of content. Some units may be organized chronologically, as from early times to modern times. Some subject matter may be organized from simple to complex; other material may be arranged from whole to parts or parts to whole. Some curriculum developers believe that one should introduce abstract information first to provide an organizing structure, then concrete information to facilitate integration of content. Other criteria for sequence may have to do with beliefs about the need for a logical development of a field or survey coverage before in-depth knowledge. Much depends on how you believe individuals learn best.

Research Findings

Gay's research (2004) revealed that multicultural education too often is taught as an add-on curriculum. Instead it must be taught within all subject fields. She suggests that teachers consider whether multiculturalism is reality-based and relevant. By "reality-based," she means that when a teacher is having students study literature, art, and music, contributions from all ethnic groups should be represented. Second, by "relevant," she means including the experiences of all ethnic groups in the curriculum and providing a variety of instructional strategies appropriate to clusters of students.

Research Readings

Tomlinson (2004) discusses differentiation of instruction and suggests that teachers ask themselves the right questions when planning curriculum. She suggests asking the following questions:

1. What interests and needs do my students have?
2. How can I adapt the curriculum to work for each student?
3. What strengths does each student have?
4. How can I facilitate self-motivation in each student?

Continuity has to do with articulation of content from one level to another. For example, Dewey believed that content should be reintroduced at different times in consideration of the students' maturity. Each time the students experience the content, it should provide them greater depth in conceptual understanding so that they continue to extend and expand meanings. Another common example of this is the social studies curriculum, where students are introduced to U.S. history and political processes in grade 5 and reintroduced to these concepts in grades 8 and 11. Each time the content is extended and expanded further. Thomas introduces his concepts before students begin their research through concept attainment and advance organizer strategies. He then builds on the concepts as he progresses through the big ideas. For example, the concepts of environment and culture introduced at the beginning of the unit are necessary for understanding the content at the end of the unit.

Integration determines whether one focuses on a single-subject discipline or tries to link subject fields and learning processes. Integration helps the learner see relationships in time, space, actions, concepts, problems, and judgments. Integration often makes what is to be learned more relevant for the learner by reaching out into the learner's personal experience and using a societal context for learning. Integration may mean erasing subject-field barriers and teaching both content and skills as they are needed. Instead of the clock controlling when something is taught, the teacher decides, based on students' needs and when and what to teach.

An example of integration can be seen as Thomas uses language arts for reports, projects, content reading, and literature. Mathematics time is used to teach graphing, the Venn diagram, and ways to interpret population density and employment statistics. Science is taught when the students study the natural and human-made environment, topography, and climate. Art and music are integrated as students study folk music, some instruments from Japan, and music from Asia, and construct dioramas and charts. Oral language and dramatics are featured during class discussions and role-plays.

Overarching organizing themes provide another means to structure and integrate the curriculum. By selecting an overarching theme, teachers can help students see the common thread that runs through different subject fields and disciplines. The theme of change may tie changes in historical periods of time into literary fiction from different periods of time. Change may include environmental changes, technological changes, and evolutionary changes. Teaching to a theme is essential for helping students develop a meaningful picture and to connect fields of study.

Interdisciplinary content deals with concepts that are derived from different disciplines. Sometimes the content from more than one subject field is integrated, and sometimes it is studied so that the learner is made aware of how each discipline structures similar knowledge. For example, the concept of *role* in political science may have to do with a function or office assumed by an individual (such as the president); in dramatics, *role* relates to the part one is playing; and in sociology, *role* may determine one's status and degree of power.

It is a good idea to alert students to the different interpretations of concepts that depend on the discipline to be studied. When students go home at the end of the day and parents ask what they have studied that day, they will be able to respond: "We studied sociology today and political science." A number of Greg Thomas's concepts (role, culture, standards of living, population density, environment) relate to more than one discipline.

In curriculum terms, **balance** means the degree to which teachers pay attention to equity among the subject fields and the learning processes. Are social studies and science relegated to 30 minutes at the end of the day twice a week, or are those subjects given the same attention and time as language arts? When we talk about learning processes, balance has to do with whether students are asked to *consume* (listen passively) for most of the school day, or learning processes are balanced so that students *produce* through learning experiences designed to make them construct their own meanings. Examination of the teaching unit demonstrates that almost all of the activities involve students in constructive thinking and acting.

Interdisciplinary Connections

Many of Thomas's activities utilized other subject fields, thereby integrating students' learning; in addition, he made some specific plans for interdisciplinary connections. In brief, these included the following lists of key questions and activities.

Literature Topic

The literary works of a country can reflect people's beliefs, attitudes, culture, and practices.

Key Questions

1. What does literature about Japan and Canada tell us about the everyday lives of families in those countries?
2. How are the work experiences of men and women in those countries similar or different from those of workers in the United States?
3. What character traits were demonstrated? What would you conclude about their culture?
4. How are Americans alike and different from the people in Canada and Japan?

Learning Experiences/Activities

1. Thomas asked his students to select their own books to read, but he intended to introduce several books to the students, including the following: *Japan, Where East Meets West*, by Judith Davidson; *Japanese Fairy Tales*, by Grace James; *Rice Bowl Women*, by Dorothy Blair Shimer; *O Canada*, by George Sherman; and *The Story of Canada*, by Janet Lunn.
2. Through pictures, graphics, and writing, identify the attributes of the characters you have read about and how their lives affected others.
3. Write tall-tale stories typical of life in Japan, the United States, and Canada.
4. Develop a class book of tall tales.
5. Read original stories to younger children at school. Construct popout books for younger children.

Science Topic

Living things share the environment; people affect the ecosystem.

Key Questions

1. What are the meanings of environment?
2. How is our way of life reflective of our environment?
3. In what ways do people affect the natural environment?
4. In what ways do people influence the life cycles of animals?

Learning Experiences/Activities

1. Use group investigation to research endangered species. (How do people upset the balance of nature?) Read about whales, seals, dolphins, salmon, and the fishing industry. Investigate pollution; study forestry, pollution, and urban development.
2. Experiment with plants. (What do all plants need?)
3. Observe and chart the life cycles of specific plants and animals.
4. Explore the Internet for information on the natural environment, national wildlife, and climate change.
5. Use group investigation to research food webs and food chains.
6. Present a concept attainment lesson about environment. Distinguish between the natural and human-made environments.
7. Problem solving: Discuss the relationship among predator-prey cycles, population cycles, and plant succession cycles.

Art Topic

Art is a visual record of culture and history.

Key Questions

1. What can we learn about our ways of life by studying the art of different cultures? What do objects tell us about periods of history?
2. What will future people say about our culture by studying our art and artifacts?
3. If we were to make a visual record of our community, what would it tell future citizens about what we value?

Learning Experiences/Activities

1. Present a concept attainment lesson about images. Describe feelings and characteristics of paintings.
2. Paint images to illustrate *crowded, itchy, scared, angry, cluttered, curious*, and *gleeful*.
3. Explore the Internet using Art Exploration, Art History Information, Art History Server, and Arts Resources (Library of Congress) to read about and see pictures painted during the colonial period of American history.
4. Study light images and construct a pinhole camera.
5. Walk around the community; take pictures; paint pictures. Write captions for the pictures.

6. Mural project: Paint images of city life and the life of agriculture workers.

Review of the Curriculum Development Plan

The planning process begins with the teacher's tacit knowledge of the students' needs, interests, and abilities. In addition, before an actual teaching unit can be developed, the teacher needs to have knowledge of the subject matter (content) and knowledge of instructional processes (refer back to Figure 6.1).

The first real task is the identification of the *theme* and the intended focus of the unit. This can be done by developing a *generalization* to give meaning to the theme. The theme serves as the organizing thread to integrate learning. (Refer again to the "Teaching Hints: Ideas for Generalizations and Themes" box.)

Topics in each subject field can be identified, and this is followed by selecting the *big ideas (content)* for the unit(s) (see Figure 6.2).

To help focus the teaching-learning process, *key questions* provide continuity, scope, and sequence. The questions can be sequenced further by identifying the conceptual focus.

Learning experiences are selected and organized using the key questions, providing significant activities to develop the desired knowledge, skills, and attitudes. Figure 6.3 provides a form to plan teaching units using this process.

Observations About Greg Thomas's Teaching Unit

Historical chronology is not of major importance in the unit in the sense that Thomas does not intend to proceed decade by decade from 1950 to 2010. However, this does not mean that Thomas will not teach time in relation to history, and in fact he will probably go back in history to capture traditional cultural practices and relate current problems to past conditions. Each period of history can be connected through the use of timelines in the classroom and by relating significant events to other events that students recall.

Thomas selected a limited number of concepts to develop in depth. He could have selected others, but his choices do give him mileage and enable him to integrate subject fields. He is wise in not trying to teach "everything you always wanted to know" to fifth graders.

Although the activities are numbered, the numbers do not mean that each experience takes only one day. Some will continue beyond one class period (construction, mural, story writing, science experiments, and group investigations). Some activities may also repeat the following day. The evaluation of an activity like dramatic play might reveal the need for repeated expe-

---

Teachers need to begin with knowledge of students' needs, interests, and abilities; knowledge of subject matter content; and knowledge of instructional processes.

1. Select an overarching theme.
2. Give meaning to the theme through a generalization to describe the theme.
3. Identify topics in each subject field.
4. Establish goals or objectives.
5. Identify the big ideas (content) in each subject field.
6. Write key questions to structure teaching and learning (continuity, scope, sequence).
7. Select learning experiences/activities. Consider integration of knowledge, skills, attitudes, and interdisciplinary connections. Evaluation experiences may be specifically planned or based on the actual experiences. Product and/or performance may be judged.

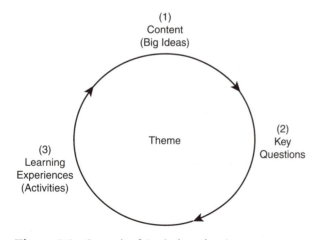

Figure 6.2 Synopsis of Curriculum Planning Process

Figure 6.3 Lemlech Curriculum Development Process

Theme:

Generalization(s):

Subject-field topics:

Goals/objectives:

Big ideas (content):

Focusing questions:

Learning experiences/activities:

1.

2.

3.

4.

5.

6.

7.

Figure 6.4　Unit-Planning Form

rience to clarify concepts. The many research activities may also take more than one class period. This unit will very likely consume about six weeks of the semester.

Integration occurs through a variety of experiences. For example, the students will need graphing skills for their charts and will need to understand the Venn diagram and how to read statistics. Through their studies in science (living things share the environment, people affect the ecosystem) they will learn about modification and adaptation to the environment. Other subjects will be integrated through experiences in dance, music, and art. Literature will contribute to historical chronology and provide insight about the lives of people in other countries. The unit-planning form in Figure 6.4 provides a model for planning an integrated teaching unit.

ANOTHER CURRICULUM DEVELOPMENT PLAN: WEBBING

The **webbing** plan helps the curriculum developer see connections in the process of selecting content and suggests means to integrate subject fields. It is a nonlinear system and graphically depicts patterns and relationships. Mary Hogan used the process to develop a teaching unit using the theme of *order*, as shown in Figure 6.5.

Hogan based the theme of order on the following generalization:

> Group living necessitates cooperation with and between individuals and groups to maintain an orderly physical, social, and cultural environment.

Each of the spokes on the diagram suggested content areas for learning experiences and for the integration of subject fields. For example, from the spoke

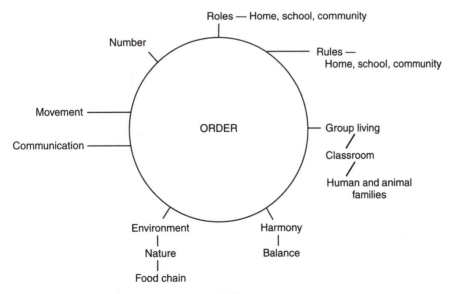

Figure 6.5　Curriculum Development: Webbing

Teaching Hints: Developing a Teaching Unit

- Select significant key ideas for content; develop them in depth. (Balance breadth and depth.)
- Organize content sequentially with powerful learning experiences.
- Provide time for students to use and apply knowledge to make it their own.
- Feature learning experiences that require problem solving or acts of creation.
- Help students relate what they are learning to day-to-day life experiences.
- Make the classroom a democratic learning environment.

labeled Environment, Hogan planned for the study of plant and animal life, balance of nature, natural order, and cyclical patterns.

The idea of *harmony* could be developed in music, art, and nature as well as through interactions in the classroom.

Studying *group living* would be a means to help students develop understandings about basic needs. Both rules and roles would be developed through group membership in the family, school, and classroom. Health and physical education could be tied into the need for social rules and safety for group living.

The webbing plan can be introduced with an inquiry question. Students' ideas are then elicited and incorporated into the webbing plan. By drawing the circle on the chalkboard, students can help identify the spokes. The following ideas for themes can be used to develop a teaching unit:

Ideas for Themes

Change	Conflict	Justice
Energy	Evolution	Structure
Interactions	Interdependence	Systems
Order	Patterns	Conflict
Patterns of change	Stability	resolution
Systems and interactions	Identities	

CURRICULUM CONSONANCE

By observing the work assignments of students and the experiences they are engaging in, the teacher's objectives should be clear. For example, Greg Thomas said that one of his goals was to have students develop research skills; therefore, students should be engaging in activities that enable them to develop those skills. In looking at the proposed learning experiences and activities for Thomas's unit, we note a number of group investigation lessons and lessons specifically labeled "research" that require students to use multiple sources of information.

Curriculum consonance means that teaching objectives (goals) and instructional processes are mutually supportive. Another way of describing it is to say that goals and processes match or are in alignment. It is quite useless to expect students to develop skills that are not supported in the classroom through appropriate practice opportunities.

Assessment procedures also need to be consonant with instructional goals and processes. If the goal is the development of research skills, then students should achieve a product based on the use of those skills. If students are to be tested on their understanding of a particular set of events, then the facts related to those events must be specifically taught. You cannot assume that students will remember and apply information and ideas or skills unless they have had the opportunity to practice them in a variety of situations.

Consonance depends on appropriate materials and resources, as well as on the instructional processes. If the practice/application materials are not suitable to the learning experience or task, then consonance will not be achieved.

Curriculum Mapping

What is curriculum mapping and what purpose does it serve?

Curriculum mapping is a means for teachers to share what they are teaching in their classroom with other teachers and interested persons. The underlying purpose is to develop a dialogue among colleagues "to identify gaps, redundancies, and misalignments in the curriculum and instructional program" (Erickson, 2004, p. vi).

The "map" is composed of several questions that will enable teachers to identify by calendar months the content they are teaching in specific subject fields, the skills they are focusing on, and the means they will use to assess students' progress. According to Jacobs (2004, p. 1), "curriculum mapping is a procedure for collecting data about the operational curriculum" directly related to the calendar.

To obtain the data, teachers respond to specific questions decided by the school planning committee. For example, Figure 6.4 could be used by all teachers at a specified school. The unit planning form, with the addition of the months of the school calendar inserted across the top of the form, would be appropriate for collecting the data. Curriculum mapping will be discussed in Chapter 14 as a means for staff development and school/district improvement.

SUMMARY

A teaching unit is a way to organize ideas and knowledge into a meaningful structure. In planning the unit, teachers must determine goals, select an organizing theme, identify content, and select learning experiences. Learning experiences should focus on student learning and provide multiple perspectives of content information. A variety of means can be used to assess students' progress, including projects, classroom discussion, interaction with peers, choice of links on the Internet, and performance on written tests. Curriculum consonance is achieved when teaching objectives (goals) and instructional processes are planned so that they are mutually supportive. Curriculum mapping provides a means to collect data about the curriculum and instructional program in all subject fields, using the calendar as the basis for information.

PORTFOLIO ACTIVITY

Using your plan for a thematic unit, identify the integrative and interdisciplinary links you have included. Explain how you have connected your students' prior knowledge, life experiences, and interests in your choice of learning activities.

 DISCUSSION QUESTIONS AND APPLICATION EXERCISES

1. Select a resource unit from a school district professional library or a university library and develop a teaching unit for your students. Choose learning experiences to integrate subject fields. Search the Internet for resource information for your students.
2. Visit an elementary or middle school classroom and interview the teacher. Ask about the goals of the teaching unit and compare the goals with students' activities to determine consonance.
3. Select a science, literature, or social science concept and define it using different perspectives.
4. It is important for students of all ages and grade levels to have opportunities to engage in problem solving and research. What materials might be used for primary-grade children (grades K–2) so that they can do research?
5. How does a teacher decide what to teach?
6. Identify a goal you consider important for students to attain. What will you teach and what experience will students have to achieve the goal?
7. Select a theme and write a generalization to give meaning and direction for the development of a teaching unit.
8. Develop your own system to plan a teaching unit.
9. Plan a talk for parents in which you will explain the significance of thematic teaching.
10. Review your own teaching unit and explain how your choice of learning activities responds to students' diverse needs. (Did you consider multiple intelligences and multiculturalism?)
11. Review your own teaching unit and explain how your learning experiences engage students in problem solving and critical thinking.
12. Using Greg Thomas's teaching unit, match the eight intelligences with Thomas's learning experiences. Explain which of the experiences would be particularly valuable for ELL students.

READER RESEARCH

Select a group of students in any grade from 3 to 8. Find out in what ways parents are involved in their child's schooling. Describe parents' involvement and find out if students appreciate their parents' interest. Do you think teachers should encourage parent involvement?

TECHNOLOGY APPLICATIONS

1. Using Greg Thomas's teaching unit, identify appropriate websites for students to use.
2. Use your own teaching unit to trace some of the links that students might follow to research content.
3. Use a computer simulation (such as Sims) to plan activities for groups of students, ensuring that all students will have an opportunity to work at the computer.

CHAPTER 7

Monitoring and Assessing Students' Progress

In this chapter, you will learn about several ways to monitor, assess, and communicate students' learning progress. The chapter emphasizes the improvement of the teaching-learning process through monitoring students' work and conducting continuous assessment related to ongoing purposes and long-range goals. Assessment data can be obtained in a variety of forms, including work samples, exhibits, hands-on experiments, observation and interviews, checklists and rating scales, tests, and projects. Whenever possible, the learner should take part in designing rubrics to be used as criteria for critiquing performance.

Feedback is necessary for the improvement of performance. Grades and test scores provide no feedback and can lead to misinterpretation. Teacher-student conferences provide a means to share mutual goals, provide information, explore thinking, and teach self-evaluation. Both the one-on-one parent-teacher conference and the three-way student-parent-teacher conference are explained in the chapter as ways to communicate progress and help students develop responsibility for their own learning progress.

Advance Organizer

The following questions are intended to guide your reading and understanding of the content of this chapter.

1. How do teachers differentiate between means for assessing progress and the products of performance?
2. What can teachers learn from observing the process of learning?
3. Why should teachers monitor students' learning processes?
4. What problems affect successful test taking?
5. What are the typical types of tests used in the classroom, and what is the purpose of each?
6. How does an essay examination differ from other types of tests? (Write examples of several types of tests.)
7. Why do rubrics help students critique their own work?
8. How do you go about using authentic performance assessments?
9. What are the purposes for using portfolios?
10. How can an exhibition be used in the classroom?
11. Why might a teacher want to construct a social matrix or sociogram?
12. Why should a teacher keep an anecdotal record of student behavior?
13. What are some ways that a teacher can communicate learning progress to students and parents?

INTASC

INTASC Standards

All of the standards are evident in this chapter. One cannot assess performance without knowledge of subject matter, students' needs and diversity, instructional means, and the classroom environment. A teacher needs to plan appropriate instruction to meet the needs and interests of students and have the understanding to communicate objectives and processes to students and parents. Professional judgment is also an important ingredient when you consider monitoring and assessment.

Professional Lexicon

anecdotal record An informal record maintained by the teacher to study specific behavior exhibited by a student.

assessment The process and procedures used to gather data, utilizing a variety of factors, about student performance.

authentic assessment The process of using everyday student work projects to make decisions that inform teaching and provide information about students' progress.

content validity The idea that test items must be true to the actual content taught and the learning activity experienced by the students.

criterion-referenced evaluation Evaluation of student performance based on a specific criterion for performance.

evaluation The judgment made from the process and procedures of assessment.

monitoring Purposeful observation of students as they work independently and in groups to detect problems related to teaching and learning.

performance assessment Student assessment based on a demonstration of knowledge and skills in a variety of activities and contexts.

portfolio A visual record (folder) maintained by the student to display peak experiences (work activities, projects, and the ongoing process of writing) and learning progress.

rubrics Criteria statements, designed by the teacher and/or students, used to evaluate performance.

sociogram A graphic technique for organizing data that depicts social relationships in the classroom.

Dear Mr. Thomas:

Yesterday my son William told me he was getting a C in science. William's father works for the Jet Propulsion Lab; he specializes in astrothermodynamics. Mr. Chan spends a great deal of time with William teaching him important scientific facts. It is obvious that William takes after his father, and we know that he is gifted in science. My husband and I would like you to explain how it's possible for a gifted science student like William to receive a C. Please call us and set an appointment for a conference.

Sincerely yours,

Mrs. Theodore Chan

Dear Mrs. Chan:

I will be pleased to meet with you and Mr. Chan regarding William's progress this semester. I would like to take the opportunity to share his learning progress in several subject fields during the conference. Will Thursday, May 28, at 3:30 P.M. be satisfactory?

Yours sincerely,

Greg Thomas

Mrs. Chan does not sound irate, but the tone of her letter certainly indicates that she is displeased with William's grade in science. Greg Thomas will need to explain the following:

- *That scientific giftedness probably is not hereditary*
- *How students are graded in his class*
- *How teachers find out what students have learned*
- *How William is progressing in other subject fields*

Before Thomas has his conference with the Chans, he may want to think about his assessment process so that he is prepared to answer questions about how he arrives at specific grades for students. Thomas uses assessment to inform teaching, to improve learning, and to provide feedback for curriculum design.

MONITORING

Monitoring is the act of attentive observation. It occurs as teachers walk around their classroom listening to their students, noting the room environment, and observing students' on-task (or off-task) behavior, student involvement in independent work or group work, participation in classroom discussion, and interaction with peers.

Sometimes teachers monitor instruction unconsciously, taking note when students are restless or not paying attention. Often this means that students are not motivated or do not understand. When this occurs, experienced teachers know to change their plans, increase or decrease their pace, and ask students questions to find out what is wrong.

Monitoring Independent Work

After direct instruction, students are asked to practice a skill. This is when the teacher provides guided practice. To accomplish this, the teacher visits each student to verify understanding and provide assistance, if needed. Sometimes all that is needed is encouragement. Obviously, monitoring independent work is time-consuming, so it is wise to work a system whereby students can raise their hand or in some way signal you if help is needed.

Monitoring Group Work

When students are working in small groups, it does not mean that this is a time-out for the teacher! It is very important that you visit each group and sit down with them for a few minutes. Listen to their planning and discussion. Determine whether they understand their work task and are headed in the right direction. If not, guide them by refocusing on their task. See whether all of the students in the group participate. One way to do this is to ask questions of both individuals and the group as a whole. Encourage all students to be involved. Take notes on who is in the group and how each student is participating. Check to see that if the students were assigned roles to perform, they are really taking the roles seriously.

Monitoring English Language Learners

Guided practice time is ideal for providing individual help to English language learners. One-on-one assistance builds a special relationship with the student and provides opportunity to encourage the student's performance. It also will ensure that the student is comfortable asking you questions.

In particular it is important to check understanding of content and instructional processes. If you speak the

Teaching Hints: Monitoring Group Work

- Listen to the group discussion to determine if the group is on task and proceeding realistically.
- Ask questions of the group to see what each student is doing.
- Provide guidance if it is needed.
- Take notes to use during whole-class discussion.

Teaching Hints: Monitoring Independent Work

- Observe not only students' actual work, but students' demeanor.
- Plan a visual signal whereby students can let you know when they need help.
- When providing individual help, encourage students to find a variety of ways to demonstrate understanding.
- Encourage students' questions.
- Ask students to explain their work.
- If several students have misunderstood their work task, then reteach it to them or to the whole class, if necessary.
- Take notes on individual needs.

Teaching Hints: Monitoring English Language Learners

- Does the student participate in whole-class planning and discussion?
- Does the student participate in small-group work?
- Does the student need a buddy for assistance?
- Does the student understand when content and instructional tasks are presented in English?
- Can the student tell you in English what he or she needs to do or is doing?

student's native language, you can provide an overview of both content and instruction in the student's primary language. Be sure to ask the student to tell you what he or she is doing and understands. If you do not speak the student's native language, you may need to find a buddy for the student to provide some language assistance.

Monitoring Homework

It is very discouraging to students if their homework assignments are never discussed and there is no feedback concerning them. Homework should not be assigned to keep students busy. The purpose should be for students to apply what they have been taught in class in an independent and creative way. Parents should not be expected to be teachers, so it is important to verify that students understand their work before they are given a homework assignment.

Lack of feedback on homework assignments has been found to cause more student dissatisfaction than any other classroom situation. Monitoring students' homework provides a great deal of information for teachers. For example, teachers will recognize whether students really understood the content and were able to apply it constructively. Homework also tells the teacher whether the student has appropriate tools at home to perform the assignment. Practice assignments only tell the teacher that the student can repeat what was performed in class.

Homework can be used at the beginning of class to motivate students by encouraging them to talk about what they did with an assignment. This provides an opportunity for students to share unique ideas and teach their peers, and also to see what they have in common with others. Homework assignments can introduce the next lesson so that students can link past experiences with new content.

ASSESSMENT

Most of us are more comfortable with an idea when we can define it. **Assessment** is not a single element but rather a process for gathering data and utilizing a variety of factors to gain information about student performance. The information that is gained might be called the evidence. Using all of the evidence, the teacher can then make a judgment or evaluation.

Assessment is considered a naturalistic means to gather data—natural because it occurs in the classroom using the real experiences (and activities) of students as they go about performing tasks and, as Dewey would

Research Findings

Popham (2003) discusses the importance of data to inform teaching and learning. He advocates teacher-designed classroom assessments based on significant content and worthwhile skills that the teacher taught. The assessment should provide information on what students learned and whether instruction was effective.

say, constructing meaning. The monitoring process, just described, provides the evidence teachers need for natural assessment. **Authentic assessment** is another means to express the focus on real-world activities using the experiential base of students.

The assessment process examines students' performance matched to instructional goals. Students' knowledge is often assessed before teaching a unit of study or a cluster of skills to determine individual and group needs. During teaching, the assessment process is used to determine how well students and teacher are proceeding toward instructional goals. Assessment at the conclusion of an instructional unit helps the teacher evaluate overall performance.

To judge students' learning progress, it is necessary to identify what students are expected to learn and then measure how well students perform what is expected. The teacher knows the purpose of instruction and uses assessment to find out if the purpose was accomplished.

When teachers write behavioral objectives for instruction, they are translating teaching purpose into a standard for performance. The following is an example of a teaching objective: *Students will compare and contrast the lifestyle of people living in Arctic areas with that of people living in temperate zones.*

During instruction, the learning activity should be designed to accomplish the objective. For example, perhaps students will view a film that depicts both Arctic and temperate climatic regions. After the film, the students will discuss similarities and differences in lifestyle related to the social and physical environment. Ultimately, these students could be expected to respond to a test question that asks them to explain how living in an Arctic area affects people's lifestyle and contrast that lifestyle with the lifestyle of people living in a temperate zone.

A teacher who wants to test students at the conclusion of a unit of study must be careful to write valid items. The test questions must be a representative measure of what was actually taught. If the students' learning activity was an inquiry activity in which they observed, researched, and discussed the ways in which the physical and social environment affects people, then their evaluative activity should also be inquiry-oriented. It is important that objectives, learning experiences, and assessment activity match. One cannot expect students to learn through an inquiry strategy and perform in an objective manner. Both teaching strategy and the process of assessment should match. Let us look at some of the ways teachers gather evidence about what students are learning.

Informal Strategies for Assessment

Testing may not be the best way to determine what students are learning. Teachers can use a variety of means to assess students' learning progress. The constructivist teacher will ask students to create, produce, demonstrate hands-on comprehension, or perhaps perform in a certain way. Using these strategies, teachers can determine the student's problem-solving ability and higher-level thinking.

In Mary Hogan's classroom, students were asked to build magnets. As Hogan monitored students' activity, she observed whether students understood how to use the dry battery. Did they strip the coating off the wire before connecting to the battery? Did they know how to make their magnets more powerful? Could they conceptualize the real-world value of a magnet? Could they generalize about what magnets attract?

In Karen Adazzio's classroom, the students helped create a rubric for evaluating their essays. Then they used the rubric as a tool to write and edit their compositions before giving them to Adazzio. Adazzio discovered that students' writing skills improved as a result of the self-evaluation that students engaged in while writing and perfecting their work.

How to Use Informal Assessment

The process of building an assessment system in your classroom is not really different from using a formal testing system; the process is much the same. The following steps will illustrate:

1. Decide what you need to know. (Skills: performance abilities, interactive abilities, specific concepts, higher-level thinking)
2. Decide what tasks students can do to demonstrate their abilities.
3. Identify how you will judge performance of the task(s). (Will you set specific criteria and standards of performance?)
4. Test your process to determine whether you are learning what you anticipated. (Were your tasks appropriate? Are the criteria specific enough? Are they fair? Have you shared the criteria with students? What are you learning from the assessment?)
5. Refine your process, if needed, and share your results with students and parents.

As you refine the process you should ask yourself whether the tasks students perform are really meaningful. Do they represent the content/concepts you want students to learn? Can students transfer what they have learned to several subject fields?

Checklists and Rating Scales

Informal strategies can be used by students and teachers for evaluating skills, specific behaviors, interests, and concepts. The checklist or rating scale utilizes descriptive statements such as "Listens attentively to story," "Recognizes and uses antonyms," and "Seeks appropriate assistance or guidance." The evaluator checks or rates the item, either numerically or descriptively. By utilizing the checklist at regular intervals throughout the semester, the teacher and the students have a record of learning progress. Monitoring students' performance will usually provide the data for responding to a checklist or rating scale.

This chapter provides examples of different types of checklists or rating systems. The statements included are not necessarily more appropriate for assessment than other descriptive lists; they are intended for illustration purposes only.

Let us suppose that Mary Hogan wants to create a checklist to verify that her second graders are learning the enabling skills for sentence processing; Figure 7.1 lists the items of concern.

Greg Thomas was concerned about his students' dictionary and reference skills. He decided to construct a checklist to verify students' progress (see Figure 7.2).

Skills	Students' Names			
	Gene	Betty	Sam	Rachel
Demonstrates under-standing of word order	+	✓	✓	✓
Identifies a simple sentence	+	✓	✓	✓
Uses modifiers to expand a simple sentence	+	✓	✓	✓
Uses transformation to manipulate sentences	✓	✓	–	✓
Unscrambles simple sentences	+	+	✓	✓
Retells a story in sequence	+	+	+	–

Code: + ✓ -
+ = consistent mastery of skill
✓ = accurate use of skill
– = inconsistent use of skill

Figure 7.1   Sentence Processing

Skills	Students' Names			
	William	Everett	Tina	Jen
Alphabetizes letters and words by first letter	+			
Second letter	+			
Third letter	✓			
Uses guide words to locate information	✓			
Uses dictionary keys	✓			
Demonstrates use of phonemic respellings	+			
Uses and interprets diacritical markings	+			
Selects appropriate meaning of a word	✓			
Uses stressed and unstressed syllables	✓			
Uses tables of contents	✓			
Uses index	✓			
Locates, identifies, and uses reference sources	✓			

Code: + ✓ –
+ = consistent mastery of skill
✓ = accurate use of skill
– = inconsistent use of skill

Figure 7.2   Dictionary and Reference Skills

Hundreds of items could be included on a critical-thinking checklist. These skill items would relate to reading as well as thinking. The checklist in Figure 7.3 illustrates typical skills considered to demonstrate critical thinking. Figure 7.3 could be used diagnostically to determine group teaching needs. For example, it would be possible to total the scores of the children on each skill; the skills in which most of the class had low scores would identify areas to teach. Suppose that in a class of 30 children, the total group score for "Uses chronology" was 58 out of an anticipated average of 90 points; obviously the class needs help with this skill.

When using an individualized reading approach, individual student records are extremely important to identify the mastery of reading skills. As the teacher confers with the child about his or her reading performance, the teacher may want to note specific comprehension skills (Figure 7.4).

The mastery of skill items is often more important than how well the skill is performed. For example, at the fifth-grade level, it is important to find out how many students can read and interpret different types of maps. Either students can do it or they cannot; thus, it is the mastery of the skill that the teacher is concerned about. Figure 7.5 provides a checklist example for map reading.

A kindergarten teacher was concerned about the performance of locomotor movements. To keep track of the students, the teacher used a checklist and recorded either *Yes* or *No* beside the movement (Figure 7.6). It is important to remember to date the records so progress can be verified.

This same teacher noted that many of the students had difficulty remembering the songs that were taught. The teacher decided to record information about each student and the student's singing skills. Figure 7.7 is a checklist that the teacher used.

Knowledge components can also be identified on a checklist for recording students' progress. Figures 7.8 and 7.9 identify illustrative art and music concepts, respectively.

Skills	Students' Names	Total
Identifies ideas from different resources		
Classifies information by fact and opinion		
Sequences ideas/events		
Uses chronology		
Defines concepts		
Locates relevant data		
Uses evidence to state generalizations		
Applies generalizations to new situations		
Makes inferences based on data		
Identifies cause-and effect relationships		
Judges reliability of information		
Makes judgment based on consequences		

Code: 1 = Poor, 3 = Average, 5 = Superior

Figure 7.3   Critical Thinking

Skills	Students' Names
Identifies main idea	
Identifies cause and effect	
Explains emotional reactions	
Predicts story outcome	
Uses pictures/written material to make inferences	
Identifies pact, make-believe, opinion	
Distinguishes between relevant and irrelevant information	
Discusses story in personal terms	

Code: Awareness = A, Mastery = M

Figure 7.4   Comprehension—Individualized Reading Program

Reads and Interprets the Following Maps:	Students' Names
Climate	
Demographic	
Historical	
Physical	
Political	
Product	
Relief	
Transportation	
Vegetation	

Code: Awareness = A, Mastery = M

Figure 7.5   Map Reading

Movements	Students' Names
Walk	
Run	
Jump	
Skip	
Hop	
Gallop	

Code: Yes or No

Figure 7.6   Locomotor Skills

Skill	Students' Names
Sings rhythmic patterns	
Sings short song	
Sings song with syncopated rhythm	
Sings in minor mode	
Sings songs changing meters	
Sings with variety of tone qualities	
Sings expressively	

Code: Accurately/Appropriately = A, Inaccurately/Inappropriately = I

Figure 7.7   Singing

Concepts	Students' Names
Identifies several American painters, sculptors, and architects	
Relates the purposes of art to different historical time periods	
Recognizes similarities and differences among art objects	
Uses art resource materials to obtain information	
Discusses field trips to galleries and museums	
Identifies the various uses of art	
Identifies career options for artists	

Code: 1 = Poor; 3 = Average; 5 = Superior

Figure 7.8   Art Heritage Concepts

Concepts	Students' Names
Identifies: Staff notation Scale patterns Rhythmic notation Math relationship Familiar song from notation Chord pattern Sharps and flats Natural symbol Names of tones Repeat signs	

Code: 1 = Poor; 3 = Average; 5 = Superior

Figure 7.9   Music Concepts

Group Work Assessment

To improve both teaching and learning, teachers find that class discussions need to be evaluated for participation, interaction, listening, relevance, and synthesis.

The checklist in Figure 7.10 can be used at the conclusion of (or during) a whole-class discussion. Greg Thomas decided to record a discussion session and play it back for his students. The students then critiqued their own discussion using the checklist shown in Figure 7.10. They realized that one of their main problems was that they did not listen to the contributions of other speakers, resulting in unnecessary repetition. With the teacher's help, they came to realize that they needed to prepare for a discussion with notes and evidence so they could challenge each other's facts. They decided to take turns at the end of a discussion to practice making summative statements.

How many . . . Participate Utilize facts Utilize relevant ideas Listen to others Use evidence to present ideas Use ideas of others to present own information Challenge ideas of others Refute ideas using evidence State main point in summation	

Code: Few; Many

Figure 7.10   Whole-Class Discussion Skills

	Good/Poor
Our planning/discussion was . . . We made the following agreements/plans . . . We accomplished . . . Our plans were spoiled by . . . We need to . . . We anticipate the following material needs . . . We need assistance to . . . We do not need assistance because . . .	

Figure 7.11   Formative Evaluation of Small-Group Process Skills

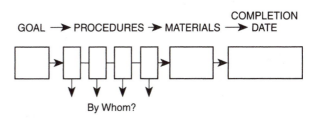

Figure 7.12   Small-Group Planning Form

To improve small-group work, students can be asked to evaluate their work sessions together. The open-style checklist shown in Figure 7.11 suggests that students write in their comments. Sometimes a planning form such as the one in Figure 7.12 facilitates group work. When students participate in group work or simulations and gaming, their social participation skills should be evaluated (Figure 7.13).

Participates and cooperates with others
Observes and shares observation
Listens to others
Expresses own viewpoint
Plans with others
Assists others
Accepts personal responsibility
Carries out group tasks, plans, and actions
Shares efforts
Concludes tasks
Identifies agreements or disagreements
Interprets agreements or disagreements
Facilitates cooperation
Bargains and negotiates

Figure 7.13   Social Participation Skills

Self-Assessment

Just as good teachers evaluate themselves, students should be encouraged to appraise the development of work skills, social skills, and academic skills. Self-actualization depends on accurate self-appraisal. Teachers must carefully guide students in their self-evaluation because sometimes students are extremely hard on themselves. Students should be taught that some skill development is individualistic and dependent on growth characteristics; however, social skills and work study skills may depend on personal effort.

Student Accountability

Students can be held accountable for their performance when:

- They know what their assignment is.
- They know how to accomplish it.
- They have the necessary work materials.

Classroom problems typically result when students are unclear about the purpose of the assignment, how to use the resources, or when the assignment is due. A number of records can be designed to help students keep track of their responsibilities and to self-evaluate. Figure 7.14 shows an example of a contract a student can use to keep track of accomplishments.

After group work or learning center participation, the "I Learned" record (Figure 7.15) is useful. Figures 7.16 and 7.17 are examples of evaluations students can complete after participating in a specific learning activity.

To evaluate work habits, Figure 7.18 can be used with a yes/no response, or it can be made open-ended so students write in their responses. Figure 7.19 is an example of a form students can use to give their own impression of the day's activities.

Name _____

1. I learned . . .
2. I am excited about . . .
3. I am disinterested in . . .
4. I feel good about . . .
5. I was surprised . . .

Figure 7.15   I Learned . . .

Mathematics

I really learned a lot today. _____

I learned a little bit today. _____

I did not learn much today. _____

This happened because _____

Figure 7.16   Learning Activity Evaluation

Mathematics

I really needed help today. _____

I needed a little bit of help today. _____

I did not need help today. _____

This happened because _____

Figure 7.17   Learning Activity Evaluation

Did I . . .	Yes	No
1. Plan my work?		
2. Understand my assignments?		
3. Begin to work immediately?		
4. Need help?		
5. Help others?		
6. Enjoy my task?		
7. Work quietly?		
8. Feel satisfied with what I accomplished?		
9. Complete my assignment?		
10. Clean up?		

Figure 7.18   Work-Study Skills—Self-Evaluation

Today is _____   Name: _____

I will do this: I accomplished this:

1.
2.
3.
4.

Figure 7.14   Student Contract

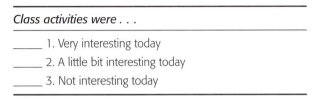

Class activities were . . .

_____ 1. Very interesting today

_____ 2. A little bit interesting today

_____ 3. Not interesting today

Figure 7.19   Class Activities

Scheduling Group Work

When there are many work groups in the classroom, it is often difficult for both students and teacher to remember who is to work where—and when. Different types of assignment charts can be devised to keep students on target. Figure 7.20 is illustrative of a work assignment chart. In a pocket chart such as the one shown in Figure 7.21, students' names are on cards that are placed in a pocket designating the appropriate center and work period.

Sometimes teachers use sign-in sheets at each center. Thus, the teachers can verify who worked at the center at a given time and day. In addition, one box for finished work and another one for unfinished work should be available at each work center.

Centers	M	T	W	T	F
Science	Green				
Music		Green			
Research			Green		
Media				Green	
Skill					Green

Figure 7.20   Work Assignments (Centers and Groups)

	Work Periods		
	I	*II*	*III*
Library			
Media			
Art			

Figure 7.21   Work Assignments—Pocket Chart

OBTAINING INFORMATION ABOUT THE CLASSROOM ENVIRONMENT

Finding out how students feel about others in the classroom, about their relationships with others, and about their studies provides the teacher with information that assists in planning learning experiences. Frequent assessment of the learning environment communicates to students that a teacher cares how students feel and respects them.

For very young children, it is possible to obtain an accurate measure of their feelings by asking them a question and having them respond by checking the appropriate facial expression. Use five faces, with the face on the far left reflecting a positive, happy, smiling person. The face on the extreme right would reflect a negative, unhappy person, and the faces in between would exhibit varied stages of emotional reaction, from positive to negative.

Students with a positive self-concept typically have several friendships in the classroom and enjoy their classroom and school work. Good academic work appears to be related to a healthy mental attitude about the self and one's relationship to others. When teachers can help students relate to several others in the classroom, the school situation is perceived more favorably. For this reason, it is valuable to measure social relations in the classroom. Simple questionnaires can be devised to obtain the information. With very young children, it is possible to interview each child and obtain the information orally. Another system is to provide each child with a list of classmates. Each class member will have a number in front of his or her name, and in responding to the questions, the child can refer to the classmate's number rather than write the whole name. The following types of questions can be used to generate information about social relationships:

• Which students in this class are always willing to help others?

There is no magic number of suggested names that students should write, but three seems to be indicative of students' feelings about others. Figure 7.22 shows a sample questionnaire.

• Which students in this class do you like to work with most often?

Which students in this class are always willing to help others?

1.

2.

3.

Figure 7.22 Questionnaire to Evaluate Social Relations in the Classroom

When students are responding to these questions, it is important to assure them that there are no right or wrong answers.

- Which students in this class do you not want to work with?
- Who can always be counted on to help in class?
- Who always gets their work done?

It is natural for students to have negative feelings about some of their classmates, and it certainly is valuable for the teacher to know which students cannot work together; however, good judgment is advised before using too many questions that ask for negative judgments about peers. Information derived from questions ("Which student do you like to work with?" "Who would you most like to sit next to?") can be used to develop a matrix or sociogram of social relationships. Armed with this information, teachers can try to improve relationships among students by helping the isolated and rejected students develop patterns of behavior that can be respected by peers.

School Climate

School climate has to do with the relationships of people who work in the school environment. It is an intangible element that one senses. Cohen and Pickeral (2007) refer to it as "—the quality and character of school life."

Observing in a positive school climate, one notes a helping and caring philosophy among staff and faculty. People in this mileu share their concerns and goals that affect school life. Children in this environment feel the warmth and the passion of their teachers and recognize that they can bring up problems concerning school life and anticipate not only interest but a forum for discussion.

Cohen and Pickeral have assessed school climates and found that a healthy, positive school climate shapes learning and student development. In this mileu, students learn how to be a friend, lifelong learner, and contributing member of society.

Developing a Social Matrix

Let us pretend that in a classroom of 25 students, the teacher asked the question, "Which students do you like to work with?" A matrix like the one shown in Table 7.1 is constructed in the following way:

- Each student has a number from 1 to 25.
- The top and the side of the matrix are numbered.
- Each time a student is named positively, the student receives a + in the square under his or her number in the row of the person doing the choosing. The left column indicates the choosers, and the top row indicates the chosen.

Analysis of the data in Table 7.1 reveals that students 4 and 24 are isolates and student 19 was chosen by only one person. However, there are several mutual choices in the class: students 1 and 3, 6 and 7, 5 and 10, 6 and 13, 20 and 2. These students appear to have mutual good feelings about each other. The matrix also reveals that students chose widely among their classmates. In some classrooms, you will find several stars and many students who are not recognized at all by others. In this classroom, that does not appear to be the case. The teacher should be able to use the established friendship choices to help students 4, 19, and 24. Note that this matrix does not reflect differences among first, second, and third choices; however, a matrix could be designed to do so.

Developing a Sociogram

A **sociogram** is another way to organize data to detect social relationships. A sociogram is dramatic because it represents pictorially the social relations or social distances in the classroom. When making a sociogram, it is often interesting to depict boys and girls in different ways so one can see instantly whether there is a split between the boys and girls or in the structure of interaction.

Figure 7.23 exhibits a sociogram for a group of 15 students. It is easy to see that Bill is popular with both boys and girls. Fara, Evelyn, and Dick are isolates. The sociogram is usually used to designate one or two choices, whereas the matrix can represent as many as desired. Colored ink or different types of lines can be

Table 7.1   Matrix of Social Relations

		Chosen																							
		1	2	3	4	5	6	7	8	9	10	11	12	13	14	15	16	17	18	19	20	21	22	23	24	25
Choosers	1		+	+				+				+														
	2																+					+				+
	3	+					+						+													
	4		+				+												+							
	5										+					+						+				
	6					+		+						+												
	7						+						+					+								
	8					+											+		+							
	9			+									+									+				
	10					+																	+			+
	11		+														+					+				
	12	+																+						+		
	13					+				+			+													
	14														+						+			+		
	15	+		+		+																				
	16	+								+					+											
	17							+											+							
	18	+				+				+																
	19																				+	+				+
	20		+				+	+																		
	21						+		+			+														
	22					+																				
	23	+				+	+															+				+
	24		+				+							+												
	25																					+	+	+		
Total		6	4	3	0	8	5	4	2	2	3	2	3	3	2	2	2	2	2	1	3	5	3	3	0	4

used in the sociogram to differentiate among the choices.

In evaluating the relationships in the classroom, it may be worthwhile to determine whether choices would be different if the questions were phrased to make students differentiate between work partners and friendship partners. Would students choose the same individuals to work with as they would to play with? Or they might also be asked, "Who would you most want to be tutored by?"

Sociometric devices should be used periodically to determine whether there are changes in students' attitudes and values about others in the classroom. Information is incomplete if the teacher does not follow up several weeks or months later to determine whether changes have occurred.

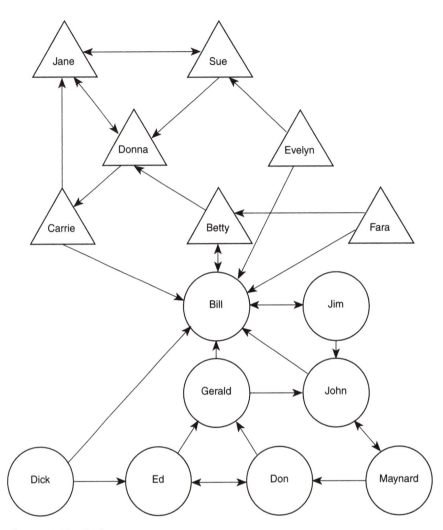

Figure 7.23 Sociogram

ANECDOTAL RECORDS

The **anecdotal record** is an informal technique used to study specific behavior exhibited by a student when that behavior appears to be discrepant or problem-causing. The anecdote describes the specific event and behavior as objectively as possible. If the anecdote contains an interpretation or evaluation by the observer, it is separated from the description. The purpose of the anecdote is to preserve information about the discrepant behavior so it can be analyzed by the parent, teacher, or another professional. Sometimes the anecdote also contains the observer's suggestions or pre-scription for treatment. Figure 7.24 demonstrates the technique.

The usefulness of the anecdotal record depends on the teacher's observation skills. Any interpretation of an observation record must be based on the observed facts. General observations of students' work skills or of teachers' performing instructional techniques should be purpose-oriented. The observer should be looking for specific behavior and have criteria for recognizing the behavior. A review of the checklists in this chapter will reveal that each was designed to gather data about specific behaviors, skills, or attitudes. Teacher observation is a valid assessment technique.

	Observation (What Happened?)	Interpretation (Why Did It Happen?)	Prescription (Planned Action!)
Mon., Mar. 10	Complained of a headache during math; did not finish work; was excused to see nurse.		
Tues., Mar. 11	Same time; same complaint; same effect	Hm-m-m-m. I will talk to nurse.	
Tues., 3 P.M.	No temperature; vivacious; fine after rest (nurse's report).		Conference with student.
Wed., Mar. 12	Same time; same complaint plus stomachache. (Suggested she rest in classroom.)	Must be having problems with math; no apparent inter-action problems with peers.	Conference: Helped her with math, but she did not need the assistance.
Thurs., Mar. 13	Same problem: different time!	Nothing to do with math. Home problems?	Call mother. Set up conference.

Figure 7.24 Anecdotal Record: Shirley Barry

PERFORMANCE ASSESSMENT

Performance assessment is not a new concept. In *My Pedagogic Creed* (1929; pp. 11–12), John Dewey advocated observing the child's "expressive or constructive activities" to assess what the student is learning and as a way to develop meaning.

William Kilpatrick (1951) advocated the use of projects for students as an exhibit of what the student has learned. In fact, schools of the 19th century typically used the student's work output as a measure of his or her success.

Performance Assessment and Differentiated Instruction

Traditional testing methods fail to indicate the breadth and scope of students' learning and tend to limit opportunities to learn for lower socioeconomic groups. Using performance for assessing students' learning promotes student choice of process and product to demonstrate their knowledge, understanding, and past experience. The use of **performance assessment** helps teachers gain insight that informs curricular and pedagogical decisions.

Selecting Appropriate Strategies for Performance Assessment

Review Greg Thomas's teaching unit in Chapter 6. Note the following activities: small-group work, independent and small-group problem-solving and research activity, oral discussions, dioramas, role-plays, and listening to folk music. Each of these experiences provides the opportunity for Thomas to assess how his students are performing. Thomas gathers data using the following means:

- Observation of students' independent and group work
- Projects produced by the students (reports, experiments)
- Artifacts (artwork, simulated creations on the computer, graphs, displays, science inventions/demonstrations)
- Individual teacher-student conferences
- Oral participation in discussions
- Teacher-made tests

Note that many of the activities (experiments, reports) occur over a fairly long period of time. These tasks require not only content knowledge and the ability to sustain the activity, but transformation through application and interpretation. In conjunction with the planned learning experiences that will yield data for Thomas, he will also rely on students' portfolios and exhibitions.

Some data, such as projects, artifacts, and tests, are easy to accumulate and preserve over the course of a semester. Other evidence, such as observation data, needs to be consciously gathered, recorded, and preserved. The data include many of the informal strategies suggested in this chapter: checklists, anecdotal records, sociograms, students' own evaluations, and journal writings.

What is really important in assessing students' performance is the variety, scope, and breadth of evidence that is used to judge how students are progressing. Although it may be perfectly obvious, data need to be collected in all subject fields and in all settings. This means that teachers in departmentalized schools must share data in order to help each other understand the needs of students. This was one of the prime reasons why middle school restructuring was initiated. In Karen Adazzio's school, the teachers meet in house meetings to share information about the students that will facilitate planning the curriculum.

As another example, if students were asked to find out how to increase the strength of an electromagnet, the teacher might observe the alternatives they try, the care or inconsistency of their tests, and the accuracy of their results and conclusions. In addition, the students could be asked to document their experiments so that others can learn from them. The documentation should then be studied for clarity and accuracy.

Portfolios and Exhibitions

Portfolios and exhibitions provide visual records of progress. In the classroom, a student's **portfolio** should represent a choice of peak experiences. Not everything should be put in the portfolio. Students should be asked to consider what the portfolio says about their performance. (What story does it tell?) In addition, students need to consider how the portfolio should be arranged. Portfolios may be kept in several subject fields or integrated, like the curriculum.

What Should Portfolios Contain?

Portfolios can contain the following types of items:

- Creative representations (stories, poems, artwork)
- Process development (writing process: drafts, revisions, and final edited version, all dated)
- Experiments and problems that are self-evaluated and teacher-evaluated
- Reports (individual and group-based)
- Journals, logs, and records of investigations

There should be a table of contents for the portfolio and a preface by the author describing the items. Assessments by the author, teacher, or classmates may appear with the different displays. Some students may

Teaching Hints: Assessing Students' Work

If possible, review students' work papers with another teacher. Eliminate the students' names from the work and review work objectively.

1. What was the purpose of the work? (Share the purpose with colleague.)
2. Does the work demonstrate that the student understood the purpose?
3. Does the work demonstrate that instructions were clear to the student?
4. Does the work demonstrate that the student had use of appropriate resources?
5. Did the student apply what you think you taught?
6. What help does the student need as evidenced by the work?
7. What does the work tell you about your teaching?

prefer to make a recording that describes and assesses the various items.

How Should Portfolios Be Evaluated?

Adams and Hamm (1992) and Lemlech (1995) suggest the following means to evaluate the content of portfolios:

- Evidence of critical and creative thinking
- Appropriateness of selected display items, variety of items
- Organization of displayed data
- Patterns in processes and in the way assignments were completed
- Evidence of understanding
- Use of intellectual tools (inquiry) and subject-field skills
- Use of technology (computers, calculators, video, audio)
- Understanding of democratic values, social responsibility for the social studies
- Research skills (location skills, note taking, use of the Internet, applications, final report)
- Logical developmental processes, such as in the writing process and the search process for research
- Integrative self-assessment

Teachers need to use a variety of techniques to obtain information about students' learning progress. Effective planning and instruction depend on mean-

Teaching Hints:
Assessing Hands-On Experiences

Mary Hogan was teaching mathematics and gave the students ice cream sticks to manipulate. Hogan observed the students moving the sticks on their desktops as she directed them to work problems. She noted that several students, when asked to create the problem of 5 + 4, counted out the sticks one by one. When asked to reverse the problem so that it was 4 + 5, they put all the sticks together and began counting one by one all over again. It was clear to her that these students lacked the concept of reversibility.

ingful evaluation. So far in this chapter, a variety of techniques, both formal and informal, have been presented. The assessment process depends on students' ages and capabilities as well as the interest and philosophy of the teacher. It is up to the classroom teacher to choose performance measures that fit teaching style and students' needs. Performance assessment tells us what students can do, *not* what they cannot do. The teacher's job is to link learning to assessment.

TESTING PROBLEMS

Reading

Both formal and teacher-made tests provide important information for teachers to help guide instruction, but sometimes students have problems associated with test taking. Teachers frequently have a number of concerns about testing elementary and middle school students. In the academic subject fields, when students do poorly on a test, it is difficult to know whether their performance is a consequence of not knowing the subject matter or not being able to read the test. Teachers need to exercise care that they are not testing reading skills when they want to evaluate academic content.

"School Stomach"

Another problem encountered by teachers occurs when young students appear to be sick during a test. These students may be afflicted with what school nurses frequently call "school stomach." This affliction is a response to the pressure that testing exerts on students

and sometimes results in a fear of peer competition. In extreme circumstances students have been known to fear school attendance.

Test-Taking Skill

A third related problem has to do with students' inexperience in test taking. Unaccustomed to performing when required to do so, some students do poorly on a test just because they lack experience or do not recognize the importance of personal effort during the testing situation.

Limitation of Objective Tests

Formal paper-and-pencil tests place still another constraint on teachers. Because students' ability to write involved responses is limited, most elementary school tests need to be objective. Although essay examinations can be designed to be open-ended and more appropriate for elementary students, the students' lack of verbal capabilities limits their use.

Test Bias

Test bias is also a concern of teachers. Bias occurs when the content of the test penalizes students for lack of experiences that may be a consequence of race, gender, or social class or when the test items use language that is blatantly stereotypic. If a test problem given to a group of U.S. students required knowledge of the sport of rugby, the students might feel that the test was biased against them because they were unfamiliar with this sport. If boys in the class were exposed to rugby, but the girls were not, then the item could be construed as gender-biased.

If collaborative problem solving were to be tested by a researcher who was interested in comparing the performance of individuals with group problem solving, but the group tested had no experience working collaboratively, then the test item would be both invalid and biased.

High-Stakes Testing

Berliner and Nichols (2007), like many educators, believe that high-stakes testing is putting our nation at risk. The No Child Left Behind law relies on standardized test results. All students do not reach high levels of proficiency on these tests, and they certainly do not learn during the same amount of time. As a consequence students, teachers, principals, schools, and districts are punished for low scores. Students may be forced to repeat a grade level; teachers and administrators may lose their jobs or be forced to transfer to another school; the publicity embarrasses everyone involved. As students enter middle school, many who have failed decide to leave school to avoid the humiliation.

Educators recognize individual differences and that *all* students cannot be expected to be proficient in all subject fields; students learn at different rates and in different ways. Because these scores are used for social purposes instead of educational reasons, Berliner and Nichols believe that the validity of the tests are compromised. These authors conclude that "high stakes testing corrupts American education."

A well-known adage in education is, "Let me write your test and I will have designed your curriculum."

TYPES OF TESTS

Achievement Tests

Achievement tests are used to find out what students have learned and what they need to learn. Many school systems use standardized achievement tests so they can compare how well their students do against the performance of other students across the nation. Standardized achievement tests are norm-referenced; the performance of students in California can be compared with that of students in Maine. Suppose William in Greg Thomas's classroom scored 75 on a science achievement test. Greg Thomas could compare William's performance as a fifth grader with other fifth graders. Norm-referenced evaluation is always used to compare the results with an established norm. However, norm-referenced evaluation is sometimes deceiving. In subject fields such as social studies or science, the test depends on the student's reading skills; thus, conceptual attainment may not be measured. If the established norms do not represent minority populations—as many do not—then the test may be related to sociocultural factors and not fair to or indicative of the ability of a minority student. Another problem with standardized achievement tests is that they tend to measure low-level objectives because these objectives are easier to prepare on a test instrument.

Criterion-Referenced Evaluation

It is often desirable to know how well a student can perform a specific skill or deal with specific concepts. When teachers need this information, they focus the test on individual performance of a designated task or a specific behavior. The criterion for performance is the desired behavior (or task). **Criterion-referenced evaluation** is used for diagnostic purposes and, as such, is appropriate for use before instruction, during instruction (formative evaluation), or after instruction (summative evaluation). If the criterion for performance is used to determine whether students should be taught the next successive skill, then it can be said that students do not proceed until they have mastered a specific task. This is characteristic of mastery learning.

Teacher-Made Tests

The vast majority of tests given in classrooms are pencil-and-paper examinations designed by teachers to meet specific instructional purposes. As mentioned earlier, the teachers' main task in developing test items is to ensure the **content validity** of each item. Valid test questions correspond with what has been taught and the way in which it was taught. Teachers must also exercise care that questions are clearly stated. If students do not understand the question or if there are several interpretations of the question, then clarity of purpose has not been achieved. Test items must be appropriate for the students taking the test. Sometimes good test

Research Findings

Guskey, Smith, Smith, Crooks, & Flockton (2006) admire the New Zealand literacy assessment, which thrives on formative information instead of high stakes' threats. Literature assessment occurs both individually and in team work. Instead of work sheets, students perform authentic learning tasks that include reading, writing, speaking, listening, viewing, and presenting. Teachers use one-to-one interviews; stations where four students work independently; teams in which four students work collaboratively; and independent, physical, videotaped performance tasks.

questions are not appropriate to the age group or sensible in terms of what the responder must do. For example, asking students to name the presidents of the United States in order of their presidency is an inappropriate question because the objective is inappropriate.

Essay and Objective Tests

Teachers typically write two types of tests: essay and objective. Each has advantages and disadvantages. Essay tests take less time to prepare, but they take more time to read and evaluate. The essay examination is also more difficult to grade because the teacher must decide on criteria for evaluation. Essay responses tend to be open-ended, with each response differing; this is why essay responses are considered subjective. Rubin (1980, p. 446) suggests the use of essay examination under the following circumstances:

- The class is small and the test will not be reused.
- Written expression is being encouraged.
- Attitudes are being explored.
- The teacher is more adept as a critical reader than as a writer of objective test items.
- The teacher has more time to read the exam than to write it.

Essay tests enable students to respond in depth, whereas objective exams tend to be more comprehensive. An essay examination requires that the student spend time planning what to write and thinking about ways to express the response. The planning and the writing time use up the bulk of the test time. The objective test requires that the student spend time reading and thinking. When writing essay questions, provide opportunity for students to expand their thoughts and respond in depth. The questions should be clearly written and focused on significant ideas. Before asking students to begin writing, it is a good idea to verify that students understand the question. Then caution students to take time to outline their ideas. The following question provides an example of an essay question that requires higher-level thinking.

Sample essay question: Make a list of safety rules to be used when experimenting with chemicals. Explain why each rule is important.
Discussion: This question is specific in delineating what kinds of rules students are to write. It is open-ended

because it does not tell students how many to write; the only constraint is that the rules be important. The question should let the teacher assess how much students know about chemicals because if the rules are inappropriate, the teacher will be able to judge learning.

Sample essay question: Identify the two emotions described in Robert Frost's poem "Fire and Ice." Which emotion does he consider more significant? Do you agree with Frost? Why or why not?
Discussion: The question is specific in directing students' thinking to the purpose of the poem. Students' comprehension can be quickly assessed. By allowing students to respond with a personal opinion, the teacher has added the open-ended dimension.

True/False Tests

True/false tests are easy to grade, and it is possible to include many questions on a test, thereby increasing the comprehensiveness of the examination. Because many elementary students lack the ability to write essay responses, an objective test gives these students the opportunity to demonstrate their understanding of what was taught. However, a disadvantage associated with the objective test is the tendency to write low-level questions. Also the test may not match the teaching strategy if inquiry or problem solving was used.

Sample true/false question: Rocks are moved from place to place by water and ice.
Discussion: This is a good question because it is clear rather than ambiguous, it expresses only one idea, and the question is totally true. (It is not half true and half false.)

Similar to the true/false test, yes/no statements are ideal for lower-grade students. In the following examples, students would be instructed to circle the right answer.

- Members of the family depend on each other.
  Yes   No

- In some families, fathers work at home and mothers work away from home.
  Yes   No

- Boys and girls should always perform different types of jobs in the family.
  Yes   No

- Some families depend on children to work.

  Yes   No

Multiple-Choice Tests

Multiple-choice tests are difficult to write because the choices must be reasonable and similarly written. Students are instructed to choose the best answer in multiple-choice questions, such as in the following examples:

1. If you were ill, who would you talk to? (for primary students)
   a. Someone who had the same illness.
   b. A friend who understands health problems.
   c. A doctor in the community.
2. Division of labor means that each person performs (for middle/upper grades)
   a. as many jobs as possible.
   b. a specific task to produce a specific commodity.
   c. a job as a skilled or non-skilled laborer.
3. Which of these should you consult to find out how to make enchiladas? (middle grades)
   a. A recipe written by someone who speaks Spanish.
   b. A recipe written by a nutrition specialist.
   c. A recipe written by someone who has lived in Mexico.
   d. A recipe written by the author of a Mexican cookbook.
4. Reading books is (middle grades)
   a. a lot of fun.
   b. sometimes interesting.
   c. sometimes dull.
   d. very dull.

Please note that these four questions would never appear on the same test together! Question 4 could be used, along with additional questions, to diagnose students' interest in school and school-related tasks.

COMMUNICATING LEARNING PROGRESS TO STUDENTS

Feedback is necessary for the improvement of performance. However, low and high achievers often react differently to teacher feedback. The feedback may confuse the low achiever because he or she may need more information than the feedback provides or additional clarification. The high achiever may experience an "aha!" moment from the feedback and be able to use it to extend his or her thinking. Teachers need to understand their students' responses to success and failure, and perhaps their own motivational patterns as well. Teachers who are discouraged by students' failure will react differently from teachers who perceive failure as a challenge to improve performance. Review Chapter 2 for information on motivation and the effects of success and failure.

The communication of learning progress is an extremely important and difficult professional responsibility. Teachers perform this task in as many different ways as they obtain information about achievement. Students need to feel successful, and sometimes the best way to promote success is to sequence learning activities to gradually increase successful performance. While doing this, teachers need to emphasize to students that effort is critical to success. It is also important that learning tasks be challenging, relevant, and interesting to the students. Practice that offers no challenge has questionable value.

Retention

The No Child Left Behind Act suggests retention as a means of ensuring that students leave schools with the necessary skills. Retention punishes the student for not obtaining the high priority score. There has never been evidence that retaining a child at the same level improves achievement. In fact, there is considerable evidence that the more a student is retained, the less likely that the student will continue in school. It appears that the testing movement is encouraging students to drop out of school.

Research Findings

The No Child Left Behind Act has pressured many schools to almost totally eliminate physical education classes and recess. However, a number of recent studies confirm that exercise has been correlated with improved scores on state reading and math exams. Regardless of gender or socioeconomic differences, students who do well in organized physical fitness activities score higher on standardized academic tests (Viadero, 2008).

The Teacher-Student Interview or Conference

Teacher-student interviews or conferences should be carefully planned to accomplish specific purposes. The conference can be used to gather information about the student's progress and to communicate information to the student concerning achievement. During the interview, the teacher should assess the student's performance in terms of the child's own ability and personal growth and in terms of a criterion considered appropriate for the student. The conference enables the teacher to recognize the student's accomplishments privately; thus, the student does not derive satisfaction at the expense of others, nor does the student feel that he or she suffers by comparison to others. The teacher needs to exercise judgment concerning what is to be communicated to the student. Consider the long-range effects of positive versus negative criticism.

The conference provides an opportunity to help the student reflect and self-evaluate. A checklist may be used at this time. During the conference, the teacher can help students select portfolio items and edit their work. The teacher can also determine whether students expressed themselves clearly in writing by listening to them describe their thoughts.

The conference provides a marvelous opportunity for a one-on-one discussion and a means to respond to the specific and differentiated needs of all learners. All subject fields can benefit from the conference as a means to learn about students' needs and communicate performance accomplishments by providing appropriate feedback.

Rubrics

Rubrics are criteria statements. When the rubric is well designed, both students and teacher know what the expectations for performance should be. The rubric is a means to focus on performance. It helps students design their projects, writing, or general work papers to measure up to the desired standards. The rubric helps teachers be precise in using criteria for evaluating students' work. Table 7.2 provides an example of a rubric to help students design a group project.

The rubric may be as simple as a checklist, or it may be complex and provide a number of different elements of performance. For example, in a research project, the rubric may identify the following criteria: number of research sources, alternative ideas, organization, writing composition, and bibliography. The rubric may specify a scale (1–5) for evaluating each dimension.

Designing the rubric helps both teachers and students. It can be used for professional education to facilitate the examination of the curriculum. Students, too, can develop classroom rubrics. For example, a research rubric like the one just described can be designed by the students to evaluate their own research projects.

During the teacher-student conference, the rubric can be used to help students improve their work because it provides a means to talk about the student's performance in very concrete language.

Table 7.2 Using a Rubric for Project Work

	Excellent	*Satisfactory*	*Needs Improvement*
Content	Detailed, in depth, clearly expressed ideas	Some depth, somewhat clear	Lacks depth, unclear
Organization	Clear: introduction, development, conclusions	Somewhat organized, conclusions need to follow from content	Lack of organization; beginning, middle, and end confused
Creative use of resources	Variety of texts and technology; well documented, interesting	Some variety of resources, better documentation needed	Few resources, lack of documentation
Group interaction	Good communication among members, cooperative work, all accept responsibility, good use of time, motivated	Some group problems with participation, adequate use of time	Limited participation, group problems, unmotivated, poor use of time
Mechanics of writing	Carefully edited for spelling and grammar, well written	Some errors in written expression	Lacks clarity and editing for errors

Diaries and Logs

Students can be asked to keep a diary or a log of their personal activities, accomplishments, tasks, and behavior. The written record can be examined in terms of accomplishments and goals. The diary or log is a fine assessment instrument to facilitate self-evaluation. It can be shared with others if the student so desires, or it can be used in the teacher-student conference. Allow primary-grade children to dictate their logs and illustrate their activities.

Graphic Techniques

Another way to encourage students to self-evaluate their progress is to teach them how to record their accomplishments using a broken-line graph (Figure 7.25) or bar graph (Figure 7.26). These records are particularly appropriate to help students keep track of their spelling achievement, math achievement, completed

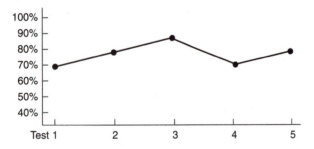

Figure 7.25 Shirley Barry's Math Test Scores

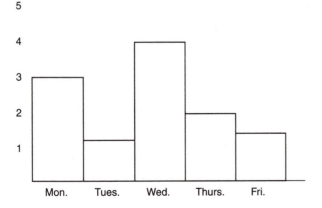

Figure 7.26 Teacher "Reminders" (Shirley Barry)

homework assignments, or decreasing frequency of teacher admonishments. Once again, these graph techniques can be discussed during the teacher-student conference or shared with parents.

Grading

Grading students' work and reporting grades to parents did not occur in the public schools until the mid-19th century. It was not until the late 1800s that teachers were required to report students' progress. Early reports of student progress would identify the specific skills that the student had attained. Increases in the number of children attending schools as well as compulsory attendance led to the use of percentage scores to document students' learning.

Percentage scoring tended to have wide ranges of scores, making interpretation difficult. Divergence among teachers for scoring practices led to the ultimate use of letter grades. Grading establishes labels for specific categories (A, B, C, D, F); each category has specific characteristics. In determining grades, the teacher must decide whether the student fits the characteristics of a particular category. If C is the average or satisfactory category, then the teacher must decide on the criteria to be considered average or satisfactory in each subject or skill being graded. Whereas feedback provides information for the student to use for improving performance, grading actually provides no useful information. Knowing that you received a C in science does not tell you how to improve your performance. Nor does it tell you, or anyone else, what you really have learned. Depending on the criteria that were used, or the group to whom you are being compared, the grade tells you only that the teacher considers your work "satisfactory."

A typical problem during grading has to do with the composition of the class population. Suppose that Greg Thomas believes that school grades should reflect the normal bell curve, but his fifth graders happen to be unusually bright. Their math tests reflect a narrow range of scores from 85 to 100. Using the normal curve would mean that a student with a score of 85 could conceivably receive a D or F on the math test. If, on the other hand, the class composition was primarily low-ability students, then a score of 85 might be an A if the range turned out to be 60 to 85. Thus, it is important to remember that the normal curve should not be used to grade groups of students who do not represent the norm.

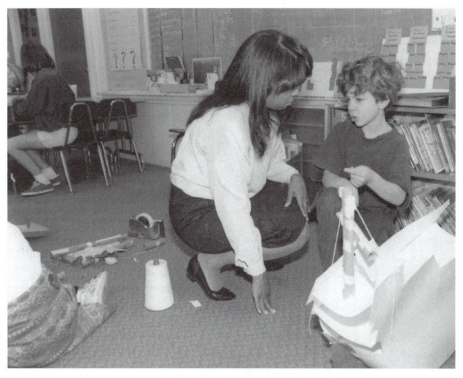

Students' progress needs to be monitored and assessed in all subject areas.

Although teachers try to be objective about grading, there are many subjective elements. Teachers usually tell students that homework assignments, class participation, neatness of work, and effort are all considered when assigning a grade. But these elements allow for a great deal of subjectivity, and students and parents are well aware of the selective nature of some of the evidence. Grading can never be totally fair; as a consequence, many schools prefer parent-teacher conferences or the use of descriptive, criterion-referenced evaluation instead of the traditional report card.

When criterion-referenced evaluation is used, parents receive a list of competencies with information about how their child is performing relative to the list of specific skills or competencies. For example, the sixth grade may have a list of 20 reading skills that have been identified as essential by the school or school district. Perhaps 15 of the 20 skills have been verified in terms of the child's progress; the remaining skills are still beyond the competence of the student. In this way the parents know precisely what skills the child is capable of performing.

PARENT-TEACHER CONFERENCES

The conference is a time to gather information and to share information. This means that teacher and parent are talking with (not at) each other and listening to each other. As the teacher attempts to establish rapport with the parent at the beginning of the conference, it is important to let the parent know that the teacher is the child's advocate. (Remember that the parent ought to be the child's advocate.) Sometimes parents have preconceived ideas about the conference based on their own childhood memories. For this reason, it is a good idea to be sure that the parent is at ease before focusing on the purpose of the conference.

Guidelines

Conferences, whether planned or unplanned, involve the expression of personal feelings, ideas, and judgments. It is as essential for the teacher, as it is for the parent, to listen. Suggested guidelines for conferences are as follows:

1. Greet parent(s) and establish rapport through a sharing of interest. Try to put the parent at ease. Sit next to or across from each other. Do not put the teacher's desk between you.
2. Establish the purpose for the conference. If you requested the conference, tell the parent about the problem or the reason for the request. If the parent requested the conference, ask the parent to "tell me about your concern." (If the conference was called to solve a behavior problem, focus on the problem, but be sure to avoid judgmental comments such as "Cecil is a weasel!" or "Howard is a coward!" Remember, you are an advocate for the child!)
3. Bring evidence of the student's work to the conference, and share the data with the parent. Interpret test scores and progress for the parent. Remember that you are the expert.
4. Answer the parent's questions; listen to the parent's observations.
5. Discuss your instructional approach. Present ways to help the student and discuss anticipated progress.
6. Ask for parental suggestions; remember that the parent knows the child better than you do.
7. Establish joint goals for the future. Set a time for a follow-up conference, if necessary.
8. Summarize the conference. Ask the parent, "Do you have any questions you want to ask?" Then state your concept of the conference's accomplishments. For example:

   "We have both agreed that we are concerned about Jed's progress in math."

   "I intend to _____."

   "It is my understanding that you and Mr. E. will monitor Jed's homework."

   "Our plan is to _____."

   "We will keep in touch about _____."
9. Thank the parent for attending.

Student-Parent-Teacher Conference

Perhaps one of the most effective means to communicate with parents about students' progress is to make students responsible for the conference. The portfolio provides the ideal mechanism. Early in the semester, students should be made aware of their responsibility for selecting exhibits of their work for documentation. When rubrics have been used, students can call attention to how their papers and projects complied with the rubric.

At the conference the student talks to the parent, explaining each item in the portfolio. The student needs to explain to the parent the rubrics involved in the various exhibits:

> "The criteria (or the rubric) for this assignment was _____."

The student should be encouraged to discuss why she or he selected particular items for the portfolio:

> "I am proud of this because _____."

> "If I were to do this assignment again, I think I would fix _____."

> "To begin with, I didn't understand, but now _____."

> "This isn't perfect, but I did learn _____."

The three-way conference provides interesting insights into how students and parents communicate, and it allows students to take charge of their own learning.

Data for the Conference

It is essential to accumulate evidence of the student's work for the parent to examine. This may be done through portfolios or other, more traditional means. When Greg Thomas has a conference with the Chans, he will need to show them their son's work. The following evidence can be assembled for the conference:

- Results of daily activities: work papers (follow-up materials in reading and math), independent projects, work accomplished at learning centers (social studies, science, art projects, experiments)
- Checklists of skills and social participation (the critical-thinking checklist)
- Observational data by teacher or others
- Test results from both teacher-made tests and achievement tests
- Data generated by the student in the form of self-evaluative evidence (exhibit or portfolio)
- Rubrics for the different work tasks

After the Conference

Record information about agreements and decisions. Note any follow-up plans. If there is a need for other professional assistance, arrange for the appropriate personnel to consult on the case. Record the data and note the evidence that was shared with the parent(s). Many teachers find it advantageous to keep a journal that is dated and can be used to refresh the memory about the conference or other events. It is very important to assess accomplishments derived through the conference and to carry out professional commitments.

SUMMARY

Monitoring students' work provides an informal means to gather data on student learning and teacher performance. To judge students' progress, it is necessary to identify what students were expected to learn and to measure how well students performed what was expected. However, learning activities need to be selected to match the instructional objective. Teachers can use a variety of ways to assess learning progress, including hands-on tasks, rubrics, checklists, and portfolios. Many of these informal assessments can be used to encourage student self-evaluation.

Parent-teacher conferences and student-parent-teacher conferences were discussed in the chapter. The conference is a means for parents and teachers to share information and demonstrate that both are advocates for the student. When students are old enough to be included in the conference, they should play a major role by exhibiting work and explaining it to the parent.

PORTFOLIO ACTIVITY

Guide your students in the development of writing rubrics to self-evaluate (a) creative writing, (b) informational writing, and (c) a social studies projects. Survey your students on their use of the rubrics. Find out how they used the rubrics (for planning, writing, and/or editing) and whether the rubrics helped them.

 ### DISCUSSION QUESTIONS AND APPLICATION EXERCISES

1. Make a list of activities that demonstrate integration of subject fields and can be exhibited to show how much students have learned.

2. Develop an objective test using a content field of your choice at any grade level.
3. Choose a specific skill and design a criterion-referenced test to find out if students can perform the skill.
4. Formative evaluation means that a teacher checks on how things are progressing during an instructional episode. What are some ways that you can informally assess whether students are learning what you want them to learn?
5. What are some ways to determine what students have learned at the end of an instructional period?
6. Select a subject field and create an authentic problem-solving activity for performance assessment. Identify the rubrics that will be used.
7. With one or more others, role-play a parent conference for the following purposes: to communicate learning progress, to respond to a concern or complaint, and to communicate behavioral problems.
8. Plan a presentation for parents to explain the purpose of performance assessment, the use of rubrics, and portfolio assessment.

READER RESEARCH

Several studies indicate that elementary students spend over five hours a day on academic work that is stressful and requires sitting and paying attention. Many of these students do not engage in any aerobic activities. Select one or more classes of students and survey how much time they spend on academic work (including homework), TV and computer games, physical aerobic activities, and sleep. Describe the school you have chosen and the implications of your research.

 ### TECHNOLOGY APPLICATION

Replace your grade book with a spreadsheet to track the progress of your students in several subject fields.

Students can help each other with suggestions and evaluation of performance.

PART III

Implementing the Curriculum

GOALS FOR PART III

1. Introduce the disciplines taught in elementary and middle schools.
2. Demonstrate the integration of content and instruction.
3. Identify classroom management and inclusion targets in each subject field.
4. Suggest ideas for multiple intelligences and learning centers in the different subject fields.
5. Propose teaching hints for working with ELL students.

Curriculum is the "what" (content) and instruction is the "how" (delivery system). The two components represent two sides of the same coin. Teachers are constantly challenged by the question of "how much of what to teach." Teachers often wonder whether they are responsible for dispensing as much information as possible. (This is the conflict of coverage.) Should teachers focus on specific "facts" that are then memorized by children in each of the subject fields? Should content considered significant in 1870 or 1950 constitute the curriculum of the 21st century? The issue of depth or breadth is a continuing problem for teachers—as is where to begin and where to end.

In the implementation of the curriculum, teachers need to rely on what they know about their students, what they know about the subject matter, and what they know about strategies for teaching (Figure 6.1). In the professional lexicon, knowledge of students means that teachers must consider whether the content (curriculum) and means for teaching the content (instruction) are developmentally appropriate.

Still another concern when planning your curriculum is whether it is "lopsided." It is easy to fall into the testing trap. Because reading and math are state-tested, the temptation is to spend too much time on these two areas of the curriculum. Think about a balance scale and decide whether the output of teaching energy is fairly proportioned.

The six chapters in Part III focus on major content experiences provided by elementary and middle schools. But the content areas by themselves are not the curriculum. The curriculum can be defined as all the experiences the school provides for students. This encompasses learning experiences and activities, instructional processes, management procedures, and resources planned for students. The selection and sequence of experiences, activities, resources, and processes are what must be appropriate for the specific students in the classroom.

Each chapter focuses on a specific subject field and identifies goals, concepts, programs, teaching approaches, ways to evaluate growth, and relevant issues, such as performance assessment. Examples of the integration of curriculum and instruction will ask you to refer to the teaching units discussed in Chapter 6. Integration of the content area with other content fields is discussed in each of the chapters. Suggestions for inclusion and classroom management are included, with specific applications for the content field in most of the chapters of Part III. Ideas for the application of multiple intelligences and the use of learning centers in each subject field are provided.

Many states have curriculum frameworks that provide teachers with a basic structure for the scope and sequence of instruction. Such frameworks help teachers select appropriate instructional experiences and instructional materials. National curriculum standards have been developed in some of the disciplines. When appropriate, these standards are referred to in the relevant chapter; however, they have not been universally accepted by all educators or by every state. When reading standards, you should consider how each standard affects the overall curriculum design and student performance expectations. For example, does the standard allow teachers to be flexible and creative in providing a rich curriculum that is appropriate (there is that word again!) for the specific students to be taught? Or does the standard narrow the curriculum and dictate what is to be taught and how students are to be assessed?

CHAPTER 8

- -

Teaching English Language Arts

This chapter emphasizes the interrelationship of the language arts (reading, listening, writing, and talking). Reading and writing are considered parallel processes, one focusing on comprehension and the other on composing. Both are enhanced by prior knowledge and experience. This chapter emphasizes a constructivist approach to teaching language arts and provides several teaching episodes to demonstrate language arts lessons and activities, in addition to referring to teaching units and examples in Parts I and II. Spelling, handwriting, punctuation, and capitalization are considered the writer's tools, and they are discussed from that perspective.

Included in this chapter are suggestions for helping students who are learning English and related research, sheltered English strategies, and helping the nonstandard-English speaker. The chapter concludes with a section on students' portfolio assessment and ideas for learning centers.

Advance Organizer

The following questions are intended to guide your reading and understanding of the content of this chapter.

1. Language arts is a broad subject field; what are the language arts components?
2. How are the language arts related?
3. What is the importance of language and why does language constantly change?
4. What factors affect language development and what are the stages of literacy development?
5. How do traditional language arts programs and a constructivist language approach differ?
6. Why are reading and writing considered parallel processes?
7. In what ways are reading and writing taught?
8. Why are cooperative heterogeneous groups used for teaching language arts, and when and how are homogeneous groups used?
9. How can teachers facilitate inclusion during language arts?
10. How can teachers assist English language learners and nonstandard-English speakers?
11. What are some options for creating language arts learning centers/stations to accommodate varied needs and multiple intelligences?
12. In what ways can you use performance assessment in language arts?

INTASC
INTASC Standards

All of the INTASC standards are necessary to be proficient in teaching the language arts. Language arts is considered the most important subject field for students' literacy development. It requires knowledge of the four components that make up the language arts, understanding of how students learn, consideration of the vast diversity of students' experiences, ability to plan appropriately, and use of a variety of instructional strategies, as well as application of Standards 5–10.

Professional Lexicon

emergent literacy The preschool child's progress in reading without formal teaching.

graphemes Letter combinations.

hypermedia Media involving both hardware and software that provide access to audio, text, and visual information; the composition of the data is nonsequential. Hypermedia systems can be used to link documents into webs.

media Message systems that communicate information to the user.

morpheme A word unit that combines phonemes into a pattern.

multimedia Media involving a variety of communication systems that may be used sequentially or simultaneously.

nonstandard English Any dialect of English governed by its own rules and language complexities.

phonemes Sound symbols.

primary language Native language; the first language of an individual.

sheltered English instruction A strategy to help a student who is learning English understand content in the second language.

software Computer program information stored on disks or tapes; also may refer to audiovisual materials.

transactive process The process by which the reader interacts with reading material to negotiate meaning.

The first graders talked eagerly about where they would go if they had their very own flying machines. The oral language lesson had been motivated by the reading of the children's book Me and My Flying Machine *by Mercer Mayer. As the teacher read, pictures were held up for the students to view. After sufficient time had been devoted to the oral lesson, the teacher directed the students' attention to the collage-type materials set up on several tables in the classroom.*

The oral lesson was to be followed by an art experience in which the students would make their own flying machines. The teacher explained that each student was to make a flying machine on a piece of colored paper, which would then be used as the cover to his or her very own creative writing book. Collage materials for the lesson included Popsicle sticks, colored pieces of plastic, propellers, string, straws, rubber bands, and small blocks of wood. Over the course of several weeks, the students would be reading about flight, performing experiments, drawing pictures, and writing stories about where they would go and what they would do in their flying machines.

In reviewing this teaching vignette, we can identify some distinct phases of the lesson plan. By reading the book to the children, the teacher motivated students' interest and prepared them for reading and listening. The story was enhanced by showing the students pictures in the book. This was followed by oral discussion and helped the teacher assess students' listening and viewing skills, oral skills, and interest. The teacher recognized that the children needed to be active after listening and discussing, so she had the students demonstrate their comprehension of the book by participating in a creative art experience. (In this way the teacher integrated art content.) The third phase of the lesson would involve the children in composing their own stories. The teaching episode demonstrated the interrelatedness of the various language arts and the way in which language arts can be integrated with other subject fields.

WHAT ARE THE LANGUAGE ARTS?

The purpose of language is communication. Language is a tool we use to express ourselves. Through speaking and writing (and artwork) we convey ideas and feelings. Listening and reading require focused participation of the listener and reader in order to attain meaning. The children in the vignette about the flying machine listened to a story first; then they had the opportunity to speak and practice oral language skills. Next, they will have the opportunity to demonstrate understanding and creativity by making their own flying machine. Finally, they will write about their ideas. When their stories are completed, they will read (and present) their own thoughts and listen to the thoughts of others.

Communication between individuals means that those individuals are sharing ideas, feelings, and information. It is an active process. They are talking about their experiences and knowledge and demonstrating their ability to hear and listen to each other. The language arts curriculum can be defined as activities that occur throughout the school day in which communication happens through the learner's active participation while listening, viewing, reading, speaking, and writing.

The Language Arts Are Interrelated

The receptive and expressive language arts are interrelated. Success in reading and writing depends on an adequate oral foundation. For this reason, most early-childhood classrooms and primary classrooms stress oral language skills. Teachers who hurry to start children reading books are often frustrated because they fail to recognize the importance of speaking and listening skills. Helping children interpret picture clues (viewing) provides context information, which in turn increases vocabulary and comprehension.

During infancy and early childhood, children spend most of their time listening. Because speaking skills are modeled during this period, the quality of the child's models is critical to development. When the model makes funny sounds and talks to the infant, the infant smiles and maintains eye contact with the speaker; in doing this, the baby is demonstrating the beginning of literacy. Clay (1991) calls this *emergent literacy* and believes that it begins at birth.

Competence in listening involves decoding speech meanings; the process of speaking involves encoding sounds so they are meaningful. In writing, the individual must encode sounds into graphic symbols; reading involves decoding those graphic symbols to attain meaning.

The children in the chapter-opening oral language lesson were sharing ideas. Their teacher recognized the value of motivational reading to stimulate children's natural curiosity. Because they all had the same experience (listening to the story, viewing pictures), their thoughts were meaningful to each other. Communication is the sharing of common meanings for the words that are spoken or written.

WHY IS LANGUAGE IMPORTANT?

Speaking is a natural act of humans. We communicate meanings through language. Every society shares meanings through some form of language. Our meanings are based on our perceptions of reality. When a young child goes home from school and tells his mother that the teacher is "mean," the child is probably basing his perception on the behavior of the teacher toward the child. We use language to express our conception of, or ideas about, reality, but by the same token we are imprisoned by the language that we use. Language is symbolic; it represents sounds and symbols that are mutually agreed on as representations of objects and concepts by the society that uses it.

Language is also related to personality. Through language, the child expresses emotions and thoughts, and as facility is gained, so is self-confidence in the ability to put one's own ideas into words. Social competence is aided by the individual's use of appropriate language. Language also gives us away. The words we choose, the things we say, the way in which we say them (pro′cess versus pro cess′), and the things that we do not reveal contribute to the picture we transmit and that others receive.

Language helps relieve tension. Psychologists have confirmed that the use of occasional swear words relieves personal stress. When you drop the open pitcher of orange juice on the floor, using an expletive may help!

Another purpose of language is the sharing of culture. The literature of our own society and of other societies is available to us and serves to convey information about the human experience. Without language, we would have no means to transmit our experience or to profit from the experience of others.

Nonverbal Communication

All individuals communicate nonverbally, and some nonverbal communication is culturally related. Nervousness is often conveyed by hand and body mannerisms, excessive movement, fidgeting, or drumming with the fingertips. Anger may be expressed by showing a clenched fist, shaking the index finger, drawing a finger across the throat, pounding on the table, glaring with the eyes, or exhibiting rigid body posture. Rocco Mediate, the golfer, moves his head and his hands to emphasize his speech. From his movements, it is clear that he is an emotional person.

Studies of classroom life by researchers reveal specific expectations by teachers. For example, when providing information or introducing a new concept to students, most teachers expect students to respond by looking attentively at them. If this response does not occur, the teacher may believe that the inattentive students are uncooperative or, at the least, not listening. Misunderstanding occurs when teachers are unable to read nonverbal signs. But Hispanic, Native American, and African American children rarely direct their eyes at an adult because in these cultures it is considered impolite to look directly at another person. However, in these same cultures, when an individual is angry, he or she will look directly into the eyes of the person causing the anger. If teachers are unaware of these cultural characteristics, management problems in the classroom can occur.

Body language is very expressive. During a role-play situation, the author observed a student's disdain for a statement made by the person next to her. This individual turned completely around in her seat so her back was to the person she wished to isolate.

Certain physical movements are culturally related. Some Japanese people still bow as a form of greeting. In a recent visit to Portofino, Italy, I experienced a traditional good-bye with a cheek-to-cheek *arrivederci*. The touchdown dance of football players provides another example of expressive body language related to male culture. Teenagers often perform a special handshake to indicate group membership. Barak Obama touches fists with his wife when something good has happened. Nonlinguistic body movements (kinesics) while speaking are also expressive and typical of many European peoples.

Teachers frequently rely on nonverbal communication to control behavior in the classroom. A raised eyebrow or a finger to the lips can be a very effective means to forestall misbehavior, and a commiserating look or a smile of encouragement may be successful in motivating students to continue work or to try harder.

Factors Affecting Language Development

Individual differences in age and background experiences need to be considered in the development of the language arts program. Language development is affected by the individual's cognitive and affective development, experience, intellectual ability, attitude, motivation, and culture. Readiness for the language arts may also be affected by sex differences, although many of these differences have been culturally induced. Readiness for reading is affected by maturity; research indicates that girls mature earlier than boys. The child

who can sit still longer can usually listen more efficiently, and listening skills are positively related to success in learning to read. Verbal ability favors girls at young ages; young females are more skillful at expressing themselves than young males.

Language or dialect differences also affect success in the language arts. School English or standard English may cause communication problems for children accustomed to speaking a dialect that is different from the standard structure. Dialect differences are often a result of geography; where a person has lived affects speech sound, expressions, and usage. Researchers are often able to trace where an individual has lived by listening to his or her dialect.

When the **primary language**, or the home language, is different from English, children may have a great deal of difficulty—even if they are working in a bilingual program. The sounds of English are different from the sounds of other languages, and the ear needs to be trained to hear the appropriate sounds. Aural development in a language needs to precede the development of reading and writing skills. This is another reason why it may be important that children begin formal instruction in their primary language. Teachers must remember that in adulthood, social competence—the ability to speak standard English—and economic success are closely related.

The child's first language models are in the home. Socioeconomic class, cultural priorities, and the number of siblings in the family affect the encouragement and reinforcement the child receives. Parents encourage the development of language by modeling language and by listening attentively to the child's speech. Children who do not have language models will be at a disadvantage in school. Differences in child rearing related to socioeconomic status should be reviewed; these differences will affect success in the language arts.

LITERACY DEVELOPMENT

Preschool and Primary Student Development

Emergent literacy is the term currently used to describe the preschool child's progress in reading without formal teaching. The preschool child is typically more interested in the illustrations in stories than the story itself, but the child will recognize that the illustrations tell a story. Through scribbling and attempts at drawing, the child tries to express ideas and recognizes that print and pictures are used for expression. The preschooler recognizes environmental signs and responds to them. Traffic lights and the McDonald's arches convey meaning to the preschooler. Preschoolers typically do not connect letters with sounds and, when trying to write, will often mix letters and numerals. According to Smith (2003) the alphabet was not designed to help people read but rather to facilitate consistent written communication.

The young child's achievements are greatly influenced by an enriched environment that displays materials of interest to the child. Adults and older children who read to the youngster motivate interest in reading. To encourage oral language development, the child needs opportunities to ask questions and to interact with adults. Asking for the young child's opinions and interests helps develop the preschooler's speech.

Beginning Literacy

Children entering kindergarten should have a sense of understanding about books. The children quickly learn to recognize traditional beginnings ("Once upon a time") and traditional endings. They soon learn to appreciate books with rhyming patterns and repetitive structures. In the author's recent visit to a kindergarten classroom, the teacher was reading *Five Little Monkeys Jumping on the Bed*, by Eileen Christelow. As the teacher got to the appropriate place, the whole class would bellow, "No more monkeys jumping on the bed!" Allowing the class to participate in the story enhanced their enjoyment of the book. The singing and reading of *Old MacDonald Had a Farm* is another example of repetitive sentences that encourage students to participate and follow the sequence of the story.

Learning to recognize story patterns is important for the development of comprehension skills for primary children. The Laura Numeroff books *If You Give a Mouse a Cookie* and *If You Give a Moose a Muffin* provide examples of sequential patterns that require the primary child to listen, identify the pattern of the story, and anticipate what will happen next. In these books, the child begins to recognize that each time the mouse or moose is given something, they will want something in addition. The ability to recognize what the next object will be is a test of the child's comprehension skills.

The Dr. Seuss books help primary-age children recognize rhyme and rhythm. In *Green Eggs and Ham*, the cat in the hat is asked whether he likes green eggs and ham. He responds repeatedly, "I do not like them, Sam-I-am. I do not like green eggs and ham." (I have never yet seen a class of first and second graders who could resist chiming in and repeating the structure.)

Folktales have special appeal to young children and are particularly appropriate for children with diverse backgrounds and cultures. A popular Ukrainian folktale, *The Mitten*, translated by Jan Brett, demonstrates a sequential repetitive sentence structure. In this tale, the main character (Nicki) asks his grandmother (Baba) for snow-white mittens. Although he is warned that snow-white mittens could be lost in the white snow, Baba makes them and Nicki loses one. As the story progresses, the children need to recognize and anticipate that the mitten becomes a haven for a variety of animals.

It is fun to type or duplicate the script of one of the students' favorite books on separate sheets of paper. Then you hand the sheets out to a reading group. Each sheet identifies a passage in the book that the student should read aloud. Mary Hogan began a lesson urging students to read with expression and listen closely to their classmates' reading so that they will know when it is their turn to read. Hogan was careful to hand out the scripts so that students could not figure out when it was their turn other than by listening. In this way she emphasized listening skills, reading skills, and reading with expression (oral language). It was a very successful lesson.

When reading aloud, the primary child often lacks expression. This, again, is a problem of fixating on single words and not anticipating meaning. By previewing stories with the children, motivating interest, and talking about probable happenings, you will facilitate their comprehension and help them develop the confidence to read aloud.

Interest in writing can be motivated in the primary classroom by naming and posting signs on frequently used items. The students can help label classroom tools and identify classroom supplies kept in cupboards. The primary child can help write experience stories, draw posters about books, help construct classroom rules that are then displayed on charts, and exchange messages with other classrooms.

First and second graders may point at words, and as a consequence sometimes fixate on single words instead of allowing the eye to move along the line of print. By closely observing the child during silent reading, you can detect eye patterns and reading difficulty. It is important at this stage to encourage the child to anticipate meaning from the context of the sentence. A little bit of guessing and risk-taking will help the child figure out words.

The primary student begins to value spelling and develops some spelling strategies. Writing and spelling can be encouraged by providing opportunity for students to dictate stories and compose their own stories to describe their pictures. In Mary Hogan's classroom, each child has a notebook that is used as a dictionary book. During writing time, when a child asks for assistance in spelling, Hogan writes the word in the child's notebook. This practice encourages the child to look up words and learn the skill of alphabetizing.

Intermediate Grade Development

This is usually a transition period for literacy development. Most children gain independence as readers. They develop expression when reading aloud because they have learned to think about the meaning of what they read. Their reading is more fluent, and they enjoy reading silently to themselves. Their sight vocabulary has increased, and they are more accurate in guessing about new words. To increase the student's confidence when he or she is asked to read aloud, the student should be given opportunity to *preread* the selection.

The intermediate reader has developed personal taste in choosing what to read. The child likes to select his or her own books. At this level, children also enjoy sharing preferences with others and relating the book to their personal experiences. Book reports in which children share what was most exciting or what surprised them is an effective way to develop both oral speech and independent reading.

During this period of development, students begin to edit their own work. They recognize many of their own spelling errors and the length of their stories increases. Their writing becomes more purposeful as they try to communicate a special message to the reader. Students at this level can begin to plan written reports as projects in content fields. They are able to take notes from texts and make simple charts and tables. They enjoy writing for different purposes.

Advanced Level of Development

Most students in Grades 5 through 8 can read and write quite proficiently. They recognize that print sources provide knowledge, and they have learned to read to acquire knowledge. When they read in textbooks, their fluency is dependent on experience and familiarity with the content. With appropriate assistance and guidance, they are able to use the Internet to access information. Although these students acquire the special vocabulary typical of a subject field, their progress will be facilitated by the teacher's introduction and preparation of abstract concepts. (Refer to Greg Thomas's concept attainment lessons in Chapter 7.)

Students at this level are capable of thinking deeply and reflectively about the stories they read as well as current events. This is a good age to encourage newspaper and magazine reading. Students can take notes for research purposes and write meaningful reports. They enjoy writing for their classmates but tend to "play" with words to express their unique meanings.

Students usually enjoy presenting their book reports to their classmates. They have fun acting out the emotional features and segments of their fiction books. Presentation skills are an important component in the language arts program; it is often subsumed in the speaking/oral part of the subject field.

LITERACY PROGRAMS

Literacy-Rich Classrooms

An enriched classroom environment often contains learning centers for math, science, language, writing, and art. There is usually a library center with a variety of literature books and bulletin boards that reflect the different subject fields, including students' work products. Classrooms that lack such an environment feature classroom standards such as the alphabet and phonics and handwriting (manuscript) charts.

In the enriched environment, students engage in a wide variety of activities that link oral development, listening, reading, and writing. Students are encouraged to engage in small-group conversations to enhance oral vocabulary and practice conversation skills. Much reading occurs in subject fields, and students draw pictures and write stories about what they read. Both reading and writing skills are taught in context of the content.

For example, when studying at a science center, the students write poems about ants and spiders. At the social studies center, the students learn to read a map and then discuss current events.

Play centers encourage young students to engage in literacy activities. For example, students can play-act and engage in conversations at a market center, a post office, a doctor's office, a local restaurant, a pet store, and a department store. Each center can be set up with appropriate materials to encourage students' role-play. Researchers have found that students in enriched environments have higher reading achievement, which is associated with reading and writing in the content fields.

The Center for the Improvement of Early Reading Achievement (CIERA) studied effective reading instruction that maximized cognitive engagement in literacy learning. The researchers (Taylor, Pearson, Peterson, & Rodriguez, 2003), found that growth in reading and writing was related to teachers' questioning ability and student participation activities.

The teaching practices that contributed to greater growth included questions and activities focused on the following:

Story theme
Story characters
Relationship to students' life experiences
Events in the story
Asking students to retell the story in their own words
Predicting what will happen
Taking students on a picture walk through the story prior to reading
Having students discuss the story in small groups or in pairs

The researchers concluded that higher-level questions and small-group discussions contributed to reading growth in high-poverty classrooms.

The Reading and Writing Workshop

The purpose of a workshop environment is to allow students time to read books of choice and write stories and articles of choice. This requires setting a schedule for workshop time, a monitoring system to see what students are accomplishing on a daily basis, opportunity for individual and group work, and teacher instruction and conferences.

The first task in setting up the workshop is to gather a variety of books and magazines for different interests and purposes. Thematic reading may occur during workshop time. Next, students must be given instruction in how to choose appropriate books for their reading level. Procedures need to be communicated concerning what to do when they finish a book (such as writing about the book, planning for a class presentation, or having a conference with the teacher). Materials also must be prepared for the writing activities. These may include different colored pencils for editing, bookmaking supplies, and a variety of paper—both lined and unlined.

Teaching Hints:
Studying Multicultural Literacy
in Your Classroom*

1. How many different languages are spoken by your students?
2. What impact do diverse cultures and languages have on students' social relationships?
3. Are all students equal members and participants in the classroom community?
4. How can you establish small-group or partner interactions to encourage English language learning?
5. What teaching strategies seem to work best to capture students' interest and motivation to learn?
6. Do some of your students have unique strengths? How do they use these strengths?
7. Could students' strengths be used to help classmates gain access to learning?
8. How does home language and culture affect customs and interaction in the classroom?
9. Do community beliefs and values affect classroom practices?
10. How can native English speakers help second-language learners?
11. What efforts do you make to encourage families to come to school and learn about the school program?
12. Do you have a means of communication, such as e-mail or notes in primary languages, to share ideas and school happenings with families?

*Content suggested by Hawkins (2004) to learn more about your students and their needs.

Free choice of reading books motivates students to read and share their interests.

Portfolios and journals can be constructed as part of the workshop procedures. Students maintain a writing portfolio and a journal documenting their reading selections. Portfolios and journals can be shared during conference time; presentations and writing selections can be shared during a read-aloud time for the whole class.

Teacher observation is the real key to making the workshop environment effective. The monitoring system forms the basis for direct instruction. As you observe students' vocabulary and comprehension problems, mini-lessons need to be delivered. This means that you anticipate students' needs and deliver instruction at the appropriate time. Sometimes the mini-lesson is delivered to the whole class and sometimes to small groups of children who are experiencing similar difficulties.

Monitoring students' writing is as important as monitoring their reading. Students need to learn to write first drafts and not to expect the draft to be perfect. Self-editing needs to be taught. Writing processes need to be taught to the students, and these will be discussed later in the chapter. Writing rubrics can be developed to assist students in the editing process. Students should be urged to date their work and keep all drafts so that both they and the teacher can follow their thinking process. Students should be taught the value of reading their own work out loud as a first step in the self-editing process. Because this can be disruptive in the classroom, it is a good idea to have a special corner of the classroom where students can sit and read aloud.

Technology and Language Arts

Computers are now used at every grade level for reading, writing, and research activities. Computers with modems have taken the place of film projectors, filmstrips, and record players. Viewing skills need to be taught along with the traditional components of language arts. Not only can students read material on the computer, but they can create their own **multimedia** projects that include their own commentary.

Hypermedia describes hardware and software used to access nonsequential programs that are interactive and can combine text, graphics, video, and audio. The purpose of using hypermedia is to create an environment in which the student can seek out information without a required or systematic predetermined structure or sequence. This characteristic makes the **software** particularly meaningful and attractive to students

Research Findings

Popham (2008b) warns that when attempting to appraise the success of a program or project, do not be fooled by numerical scores. Determine who are the learners and how the program or project meets their needs. Searching for the effect of the project on the group of learners should be the focus of evaluation. Gather affective assessment evidence by using self-report inventories with the involved group of students.

because they build their own relationships and content becomes represented in multiple ways.

Authentic Performance

Instead of one-dimensional term papers and reports, students may create **media** projects using hypermedia systems. They may hand in to the teacher computer disks that combine graphics, sound, and text. By harnessing technology to prove their own understandings, students can integrate their skills and approach problems from an interdisciplinary perspective.

The computer offers an endless array of opportunities for student learning. Students working in small groups may participate in simulations that require them to make choices and decisions. Also, students may develop their own simulations for others to use.

One caution is evident. Though students profit from cooperative relationships as they work, the work groups must be monitored carefully to verify each student's responsibilities and ability to access and contribute to group thinking.

Technology has the potential to adapt to students' instructional needs. Accurate assessments of students' knowledge and their prior experiences allow the teacher to choose relevant and appropriate experiences in the technological environment.

Other Literacy Components

Reading to Students

By listening to good readers, students develop their own interest in reading. When a teacher reads an adventure story to students and needs to continue the story over several days, it is not uncommon for students to ask if they may borrow the book and read it on their own. By modeling oral reading techniques, teachers teach pronunciation, intonation, punctuation, enthusiasm, and the fun of reading.

Storytelling

Telling a story without a book is a marvelous art that captures the imagination and stimulates interest in stories. After telling the story it is important to ask students: What did you like? What was the plot? How did the story begin? How did it end? Which character did you like best? Why? Telling the story using a flannel board or puppets or other objects increases the interest in the story.

Readers' Theater

Readers' theater is a technique for having students assume the part of a character in a story. The students read the story precisely as it is, creating the mood and characterization through their voices and expressions. The narrator's part may be read by the teacher or a student. Readers' theater is appropriate at all grade levels.

Tompkins (2006) suggests procedures for readers' theater presentations:

1. Select a script with an interesting story and plot and believable characters. Make sure that stage directions and character roles are clearly discernible so that students are not confused.
2. Choose parts. Students should volunteer to read specific roles and practice how they will portray the role.
3. Rehearse the production. Students practice their parts concentrating on pronunciation, projection, and interpretation.
4. Stage the production. Students may sit or stand for the presentation, either standing when they read their part or stepping forward to read if they are already standing. If props are available, they may be used to motivate interest and enthusiasm.

Listening Centers

A listening library in the classroom provides for the individualization needed by students and allows the teacher to create diverse listening experiences. For example, tapes may be purchased in a variety of dialects and styles to enrich students' listening experiences. Audiotapes can also be used in conjunction with library books. Students often enjoy reading a story as they listen to it. By listening to a well-read story, students learn expressive techniques to improve their own oral reading.

CHARACTERISTICS OF A CONSTRUCTIVIST APPROACH TO LANGUAGE ARTS

Because humans learn language without formal instruction, many language experts believe that the best approach to language development is through natural social processes in the classroom. Advocates of a constructivist approach to language development suggest that language processes (speaking, listening, reading, and writing) be integrated so that a full range of processes is used in all subject fields. Skills are to be taught as they are needed in relationship to the content. Both teaching and learning become more real and natural. Relevance and involvement characterize the curriculum. Experiences and activities are selected based on their degree of interest and usefulness to students. Students are involved because experiences are participatory. Whenever possible, students should make real choices concerning the language processes they use.

HOW ARE THE LANGUAGE ARTS TAUGHT?

Language itself has no natural content. Thus, when teachers provide language arts instruction, they must use content from subject fields, such as science and social studies, or contextualized elements, such as those experienced in a field trip to a museum or a retail store. Skills must be taught as they are needed. For this reason, constructivist language programs urge the exploration of reading and writing in a natural way. In most school districts, teachers rely on the following to facilitate the teaching of language arts:

- Core literary works identified by a school or district to provide common cultural experience
- Use of language arts to interrelate curriculum fields; skill instruction applied to all curricula
- Informal use of language in all subject fields
- District-developed goals for each language arts component
- District or state recommendations for the allocation of time devoted to language arts instruction

- Magazines, newspapers, schedules, and game and model directions
- Content field textbooks

Integration of Experience and Curriculum

To integrate the child's experiences and facilitate language learning, teachers need to draw upon the child's cultural life. If a child has no one to relate to—in the textbooks, peer group, or teacher model—interest in learning will be nil. The teacher's task is to find ways to enable each child to contribute information, stories, and interests and build these elements into the language arts program.

Integration of experience also has another meaning. In the elementary school, subject fields are melded, even though we still talk about teaching science, math, and history. Students learn more efficiently if experiences fit and build on each other rather than if the experiences are compartmentalized. Because language is used in all subject fields, language is taught throughout the school day. Students need to learn the special language of math (*subtrahend, minuend, difference*) and the special language of social studies (*interdependence, migration, democracy.*) Although we may schedule a time for creative writing, we teach writing skills in every subject. Reading can be taught while using the social studies textbook, reading cartoons in a magazine, playing games, or watching filmstrips.

Examples of Integration

In Chapter 5, Greg Thomas's fifth graders were investigating the cultural beliefs of the New England colonists. The students observed colonial artwork to determine the colonists' cultural beliefs. To perform their tasks, they had to share and communicate information, read texts, and write a report. Thomas was integrating instruction in language arts, social studies, and art education.

Another example (in Chapter 5) occured in Sara Garcia's classroom, where the students were studying the importance of exercising regularly. Review what the students learned, and you will find the integration of language arts, mathematics, science, social studies, health, and physical education.

Integration is achieved through the use of unit teaching, with the unit related to the overall curriculum theme. Units allow content fields to be integrated in meaningful ways. The integrated unit of study is characteristic of constructivist teaching.

Additional Characteristics of the Constructivist Classroom

Relevance and *involvement* characterize the curriculum. Experiences and activities are selected based on their relevance to students' past experiences and present interests and their usefulness.

Learning centers are focused primarily on conceptional learning. Language processes are featured and integrated. Rarely are skills isolated in the centers. The centers fit the ongoing units of the whole program.

Materials for instruction include a wide range of resources. Both fiction and nonfiction books are used. Materials need to be appropriate to the unit and to the students. Materials should be interesting and challenging.

Heterogeneous grouping is used most of the time. As demonstrated in Greg Thomas's classroom (see Chapter 5), students may be grouped because of interest in a topic, task, or problem. Students may also be placed in a cooperative work group, as Sara Garcia did for writing personal letters (see Chapter 5). Although heterogeneous grouping is typical of the constructivist teacher, students may also be grouped as special needs arise. The important point is that grouping is purposeful and changes as the purpose changes. The case study about Mary Hogan's classroom illustrates this.

Differentiation of instruction means to recognize individual needs and to provide instruction based on those needs or variations. Individualization does not necessarily mean that teaching becomes a one-to-one situation in the classroom. In practical terms, it usually means that students are grouped in small clusters to improve instruction.

 MARY HOGAN'S CLASSROOM

Mary Hogan detected from individual conferences that some of her students were having difficulty sequencing events in the stories they were reading. She decided to have 10 of her students read a story out of a reader. Then Hogan suggested that they play the Sequence Game. She asked the child at one end of the semicircle to begin to retell the story orally. Each child, in turn, was to add the next event in the story. As the story progressed around the semicircle, it was apparent that three

of the students were unable to recall events in the order in which they had occurred in the story.

When the game and story were concluded, Hogan told the students to continue reading in their own self-selected story books. The three children who had difficulty with the activity were asked to remain in the reading circle. Hogan told another story to these three students. This time she used flannel board pictures of the story, asked the three children to take turns arranging the pictures on the flannel board in the order in which they had occurred in the story, and used words that expressed the sequence of time *(before, then, next, after)*. Using the tangible pictures and understanding the language concepts, the three children were now successful. Because they now understood what was expected of them, Hogan had the students return to their own reading.

Features of Effective Language Arts Programs

The use of language in the classroom must be the primary concern of teachers. Through language, we express our feelings and ideas and discover what others have expressed. Language facilitates access to knowledge and helps students prepare for a fulfilling life. Effective language arts programs emphasize an oral language program using activities to help students develop fluency in language. The program should encourage all students to express themselves. The oral language program should be integrated with reading and writing.

There should be an emphasis on the enjoyment of *literature*: historical fiction, biographies, poetry, current fiction, folktales, and subject-field content books. Literacy should go beyond mechanical ability. Students can gain important societal values by being exposed to significant literary works as they read about value conflicts and dilemmas faced by others.

There also needs to be an emphasis on *thinking processes* versus a narrow skills-based program. Reading for information and inquiry in the content fields facilitates meaningful thought. But skills should not be forgotten. It is important to teach word study skills, phonemic awareness, and phonics at the appropriate point of need.

A *writing program* should help students create, revise, edit, and share their ideas and feelings. Just as students should gain fluency in speaking, they should also be fluent in the use of language to express themselves through writing. Plan for the use of computers for word processing and use of the Internet for inquiry.

Thematic teaching helps integrate the language arts with all of the content fields. Selecting literature and information books, articles, and selected chapters is one of the first tasks in planning a unit of study. Consideration should be given to multicultural stories, different genres, and a variety of authors and opinions. Identify appropriate multimedia materials, including CD-ROMs, audiotapes, and videotapes, and teach students to read and use different types of graphs, maps, and globes.

The total school program should develop students' *pride* in their correct use of the conventions: spelling, punctuation, capitalization, and handwriting.

Personalizing Instruction

In the case study about her classroom, Mary Hogan let her students know that she cared about them. By personalizing the lesson, Hogan communicated that three of the students needed "teacher" time. Students in Hogan's classroom learned to be unselfish because they were accustomed to receiving the teacher's attention when they had special needs.

Decision Making

Another element that is important to the differentiation of instruction is the idea of personal choice. There should be occasions during the school day when students may choose how to learn. Mary Hogan accomplished this with the design of optional learning centers and workshop time. Because objectives can be accomplished in a variety of ways, Hogan arranged an array of learning experiences, all related to the same objective. Students had to make decisions about how they would meet the objective.

Hogan was not an indulgent teacher, and she did not believe that learning experiences should be unstructured. She recognized the advantage of student decision making, however, and whenever possible she provided opportunities for student choice.

Interactive Instruction

Communication involves more than one person. We talk with others and we write for others. Although reading and writing may be solo activities, we pursue them so others may take advantage of what we know, so we may learn from others, and so we may enjoy literature and dramatics. Although sometimes teachers rue the fact that students can talk, in actuality speech improves only through practice with others. Speech practice must be planned just as reading skill development is planned.

Because students do not view peers as authority figures, they often learn more from peers than they do from teachers. Picture second graders stretched out on the floor as an example of the contagious nature of reading in groups. At first, one student will curl up on the rug with a library book; soon other readers will arrive, arranging themselves in comfortable positions on the floor!

Planning for Interaction

Interactive language experiences need to be planned. By grouping students or allowing them to work in a partner situation, students stimulate each other to accomplish routine chores, homework, or projects they would never accomplish working alone. Because language activities are basically skill activities, they need to be practiced. The teacher's role is to choose activities that are worthwhile and to provide appropriate practice opportunities. For example, if students need practice in oral communication, the teacher needs to choose activities that will allow students to do the following:

- Hold conversations and discussions
- Give informal and formal talks or reports
- Participate in dramatic activities
- Participate in choral recitations

If students need practice in written communication, the teacher can choose from among activities that encourage them to write

- Notes, reports, outlines
- Letters
- Stories and plays
- Summaries
- Advertisements and publicity
- Diaries, descriptions, or histories

The rationale for interactive instruction is that more student participation and effort leads to more active learning behavior. Oral communication has two components: listening and speaking. Both need to be practiced, so group work is essential. Active learning behavior can be translated into active engaged time in academic tasks.

Reading with a Buddy

Reading with a buddy satisfies two purposes: First, it's fun! Second, with a buddy students can help each other and can often read books that they would not dare tackle alone. However, buddy reading needs to be taught (modeled) and practiced. When this strategy is used, it is important that students realize that each must take turns reading to the other.

Buddy reading can be helpful for students who are English language learners. However, the buddy needs to speak and understand the friend's native language and be proficient enough to correct pronunciation and recognize language misunderstandings.

READING INSTRUCTION IN GREG THOMAS'S CLASSROOM

Greg Thomas began the reading period by picking up the book *Old Yeller,* by Fred Gipson. The students instantly became quiet. Thomas had begun the book several days earlier, and the students were thoroughly engrossed with the story about the big, ugly yellow dog who came to live with Travis and his mother and brother.

After about 10 minutes of reading aloud to the students, Thomas wrote the following on the chalkboard:

- Determination (yes)
- Pluck (yes)
- Cowardice (no)
- Guts (yes)
- Fainthearted (no)

Next, Thomas turned to the students and asked, "What do you think I'm thinking about?"

Several students asked if he was thinking about Old Yeller. Thomas smiled and began to write another list on the board.

- Bravery ( )
- Fearfulness ( )
- Valor ( )
- Timidity ( )

"How should I label these words? Yes or no?" The students responded appropriately. "Can you tell me what I'm thinking about?" asked Thomas.

The students immediately began to talk about the dog, Old Yeller, and how he had demonstrated courage and bravery in the story in so many different ways. Thomas confirmed that he was thinking about the concept of courage.

Next, Thomas asked the students about their feelings and emotions as they listened to the story. He asked them how they thought Travis felt about his dog. He encouraged the children to talk about their own pets and ways that animals demonstrate courage. ("What are some examples of courageous acts?" "What do you consider cowardly acts?") In this way he made the students consider positive and negative examples of the concept courage.

"What were you thinking about when I put the first list on the board?" asked Thomas.

The students responded: "I thought about my own dog." "I knew you were thinking about Old Yeller." "I wasn't sure what *pluck* meant, but then when I saw the word guts I got the idea." "The second list really helped me."

Next Thomas asked, "What makes a person act bravely? Do you think all people are brave?"

The students expressed different opinions. Then Thomas said that he had two very special books in the classroom for them to read over the next several days: *Snow Treasure,* by Marie McSwigan, and *Three Without Fear,* by Robert C. Du Soe. Both books, he told them, were about children. "How do these children feel, and how do they act? See if you can find sentences that describe the character of the children in the story. Try to decide if these stories could really have happened. Compare the characters in these stories with the characters in *Old Yeller.*" (Thomas turned and wrote the assignment on the chalkboard.)

The students selected their books, and Thomas then divided them into small groups of four. The students sat together and helped each other, if needed. Thomas also encouraged the students to stop now and then to discuss different passages that revealed the emotions and characters of the people in the stories.

As the students read, Thomas observed them. Sometimes he would discuss a particular passage with a student. After about 30 minutes, Thomas stopped the class and began a discussion. He asked them if their stories were real. The class then talked about realistic fiction. Thomas had several children select and read aloud short passages from their books to demonstrate emotions and characters. He told them that the story about the Norwegian children in *Snow Treasure* actually did happen. He explained that the book was an example of historical fiction. He helped them recall other historical fiction books they had read or listened to, such as a book about Abe Lincoln. He asked the students to compare realistic fiction and historical fiction.

Then the class discussed characterization. Finally, Thomas asked the students to once again think about synonyms and antonyms for courage.

The next day, Thomas would have the students continue their reading, and in their small groups he would ask them to do the following:

- Write a short paragraph to tell others the plot of the story.
- Describe the locale of the story.

He would also sit with different groups and have them read aloud so he could see if they were reading meaningfully and understanding what they were reading.

Now let's look at the components of Thomas's reading lesson.

- Whole-group listening (Thomas reading aloud)
- Whole-group concept attainment lesson (courage)
- Whole-class discussion of *Old Yeller*, using concept of courage
- Small-group reading using a class assignment to focus the reading on character and mood, feeling, and tone
- Teacher monitoring—diagnosing, providing assistance as needed
- Whole-class discussion about the books, focused on assignment—some oral reading to prove understanding

The time block used by Thomas was about 70 minutes. Very likely he would follow up the reading period with spelling, using words from the literature period.

What Literary Elements Should You Emphasize?

In Greg Thomas's lesson, he focused on one literary element—*characterization*—but in addition, it is important that students perceive the following elements:

1. Where is the story taking place? *(setting)*
2. What is the story about? *(plot, underlying theme)*
3. Do the characters confront a problem? Is there a struggle? *(problem)*
4. Are the characters convincing? *(characterization)*
5. How does the author keep you interested? *(literary style)*

Don't forget to review the elements identified earlier in the chapter by the Center for the Improvement of Early Reading Achievement (CIERA).

Reading assignments should require students to provide examples from their literature that convinces them of these literary elements. Students should also be asked whether any of these elements change as the story progresses. For example, does characterization differ at the introduction or beginning of the story from that in the middle or the conclusion of the story?

READING INSTRUCTION

Reading is a comprehension activity. It has been considered a receptive form of communication; however, reading requires that the individual interprets meaning. Listening, which has also been considered a passive or receptive form of communication, requires active thinking in order to comprehend. The listener must translate speech into thought. In reading, the reader must decode print into speech and decode speech into thought. Thus, the reader must perform two different activities simultaneously. Reading is difficult because it depends on visual processing as well as comprehension. Researchers do not know how the reader joins the two functions, but they now recognize that this is a **transactive process** (Tompkins, 2002).

In the teaching of reading, teachers are teaching the communication process. Reading instruction depends on oral language proficiency and experiential background, and on the self-confidence and motivation of the beginning reader. To understand reading as a communication process, the beginning reader must take an active role in the learning process and be willing to take risks.

To learn to read, the beginner must discriminate between letters that often look alike. Therefore, it is important that the reader discover the critical attributes that discriminate between these letters. It is almost impossible for a teacher to tell students what to look for in order to discriminate between various letters, such as *b* and *d* and *p* and *q*. The student must be sophisticated enough to know what distinctive features to look for.

Teachers need to differentiate between learning to read and fluent reading. The beginning reader must first learn to discriminate the critical features and translate them into an identification system of letters and then into a given word name. The fluent reader discriminates the critical features and moves immediately to the word name or word category. Because the beginning reader must learn to identify words and store them in memory to make sense of what is being read, the process of making sense is often tedious. For this reason, the beginning reader must be motivated to learn to read and have the necessary self-confidence to proceed with a difficult task. Reading materials for the beginning reader should use short, predictable sentences so the memory system is not burdened unnecessarily. Beginning reading is more difficult than fluent reading because, in learning to read, one must identify words before attaining meaning; the fluent reader obtains meaning directly from the visual features.

However, reading experts such as Smith and Krashen disagree with the idea that one must identify words before meaning is attained. They believe that reading is a natural act and that students learn to read quite easily when they are not forced to identify individual words. Instead meaning is attained through the context of a sentence or groups of sentences. Smith (2003) comments that written words do not have to be translated into spoken language before understanding is achieved:

> We have no more need to identify and classify individual letters to understand written words than we need to identify and classify individual eyes, noses, and mouths before we can recognize faces. (p. 28)

Approaches to Reading Instruction

Silent Reading

Silent reading is an individual activity and has a variety of purposes. It is usually performed during the teaching of reading when students are asked to read to accomplish a very specific objective. The silent reading time is usually preceded by a short discussion to prepare the reader. New vocabulary words are presented during an oral discussion, and then the teacher asks the students to read in order to clarify, predict, understand, or determine sequence.

Oral Reading

After a passage has been read silently, the teacher may ask students to read the same passage orally. During oral reading, the teacher verifies understanding by the way the passage is read. Expression, intonation, and rhythm are practiced during oral reading. Sometimes the oral reading is used as evidence to prove or verify what the students were looking for in their silent reading. Listening to others read and following the text as others read are also objectives for the oral reading session. When students are to read orally, it is important that they cannot anticipate when it is their turn to contribute. Students need to listen to their classmates read in order to keep the place. In this way, the teacher can check both listening and oral reading skills.

Work/Study

One of the most advantageous ways to teach reading skills occurs when reading is the tool for obtaining information, such as reading maps, charts, and graphs, and for problem solving. As students progress through school, work/study reading becomes more important and more closely tied to school success. The ability to read within different subject fields and for a variety of purposes needs to be taught and practiced throughout the school day. During work/study reading time, students should be taught to do the following:

- Adjust the speed of reading to the purpose and subject
- Locate information using a variety of source materials

 Teaching Hints:
Oral Shared Reading

1. Do oral shared reading in small groups (not in the whole class because students get bored).
2. To encourage critical listening and reading, call on students in random order so that they do not count paragraphs and figure out when it is their turn to read aloud.
3. Emphasize appropriate intonation, characterization, rhythm, and expression.
4. Discuss the accuracy of the characterization without discussing the readers.

- Extract and interpret information from a variety of sources (charts, maps, cartoons)
- Compile and organize information using a variety of sources

Recreational Reading

Reading for recreational purposes should be like frosting on a cake. If students are to develop lifelong interests in reading, their enthusiasm must be cultivated by providing a variety of reading materials to satisfy diverse interests. Students need to have the opportunity to share with others something that they have particularly enjoyed.

How Is Reading Taught?

Reading Readiness

Before charts or books are used to teach reading, the teacher's first task is to determine whether the child is ready for formal reading instruction. Readiness has different meanings to different people. Some believe that readiness is indicated when the child expresses the interest or desire to read. However, interest and motivation are not the prime determiners of readiness.

Physical factors, such as the ability to discriminate visual differences and the ability to hear likenesses and differences, affect learning to read. Eye-hand coordination affects reading. Understanding directions and differentiation of right from left are important because print is directional; the child who has difficulty with directions will have similar problems in learning to read.

Children who are unable to follow instructions or who have poor memory retention or unusually short attention spans will not have the mental maturity needed for reading. Social and emotional factors also affect learning to read. The child who cannot sit still, lacks self-confidence, or cannot work cooperatively with others may have difficulty during reading. Experiential factors may affect success in reading. Awareness of environmental signs and limited interactions with others are examples of the background experience needed by children learning to read.

The assessment of readiness for language arts is an important teacher task. If the teacher judges that the student lacks readiness for instruction, then it is the teacher's responsibility to create learning experiences to develop readiness systematically in those areas in which the student lacks the prerequisite capacities.

The teacher's prime responsibility is for the environment of the classroom. To encourage literacy, use pictures, open-ended questions, objects to manipulate and talk about, book jackets, or popup books. Literally everything you can think of to encourage talk and interest in reading and writing is appropriate for creating a literate environment.

What are some activities a teacher can use to determine if a child is ready to read?

Phonemic Awareness

The 26 letters of the alphabet represent about 44 phonemes. Children need to learn to identify (name) the letters (**graphemes**) in order to learn to write. By the time children enter kindergarten, most can recognize the letters in their own names. However, if the child does not associate the letters with appropriate reading and writing experiences, then the letter names will not facilitate learning to read.

Because the phonemes represent more than 500 spellings, phonetic analysis facilitates the reading process only about half the time. As a consequence, the complicated rules concerning phonetic analysis often confuse more than they enhance learning to read. The word *cat* is often used as an example to help children develop phonemic awareness. Yet the letter *c* represents three different sounds: *k* as in *cat*; *s* as in *circus*; and when paired with an *h*, it has a *ch* sound as in *church*. Primary teachers cannot depend on phonics as a means for teaching reading, yet many people believe that it is one of the important strategies for teaching reading.

Phonemic awareness can be facilitated through singing songs with specific sounds (*tra-la-la*), rhyming, calling attention to animal sounds (*moo, moo*), and playing with nonsense sounds and words (*Peter Piper picked a peck of pickled peppers*). Many of the *predictable* books assist the beginning reader to recognize sounds. Teachers can also prepare picture charts with a specific letter at the top and ask students to select the pictures on the chart that begin with that sound. For example, a chart with the letter *d* might have pictures of a *duck, door, deer, diamond,* and *dollar* and pictures of nonexamples. Students can also be asked to match sounds when listening to rhymes (*net, pet*).

Another discrimination skill deals with the blending of sounds. It is important to provide experiences in which students are asked to identify words that begin with blended sounds (*th*, *ch*, *sh*). Attention should also be directed to medial (*mail*, *tame*, *blame*) and ending sounds (*finding*, *running*, *teaching*).

Phonics

Phonics teaching emphasizes the relationship between sounds (phonology) and spelling (orthography). Phonics and phonemic awareness are not the same. For children to understand phonics, they need to have phonemic awareness. Educators do not agree on how much emphasis phonics should have in the reading program. The complicated rules that many teachers ask students to memorize are one of the reasons for the conflict.

When two vowels go walking, the first one does the talking.
When *y* appears at the end of a word, it is pronounced as a long *i* or a long *e*.

However, certain word study patterns, such as the consonant-vowel-consonant (CVC) pattern, are valuable to both the beginning reader and the reader who is having difficulty; this includes middle school students.

Most students learn to use phonics naturally as they learn to read and write. Phonics can be taught when students encounter difficult words in the context of a story. Examples should be provided at that time. For teachers, the critical point is that if students do not hear sounds, then they cannot use phonics generalizations. (Does the student hear the *s* sound in *sat?* Does the student hear the *at* sound?) This is why phonics skills depend on phonemic awareness (Lyon, 1998).

 EXPERIENCE CHARTS

Ricardo, a first grader, brought his hamster to school in a cage. The teacher asked all of the children to sit on the rug in the front of the room so Ricardo could tell about his hamster. But Ricardo was too shy, so the teacher said to the class, "Boys and girls, why don't you ask Ricardo questions about his hamster?"

The children asked questions and learned that the hamster's name was Pepe, that he was gentle and clean, and that he ate lettuce, carrots, cabbage, and peanuts. The teacher added to the information by explaining to the students that hamsters need to be kept in metal cages because they can gnaw their way out of a wooden cage. After talking and watching Pepe for several minutes, the teacher suggested that the class compose a story about him. The students readily agreed, and the story was written on the chalkboard.

> *Teacher:* Who came to school today?
> *Student:* Pepe came to school today.
> *Teacher:* Who is Pepe?
> *Student:* Pepe is a hamster.
> *Teacher:* What do hamsters eat?
> *Student:* Hamsters eat lettuce, carrots, cabbage, and peanuts.
> *Teacher:* What else do we know about hamsters?
> *Student:* Hamsters are gentle and clean.

The story written on the board was ready for the students to read:

> Pepe came to school today.
> Pepe is a hamster.
> Hamsters eat lettuce, carrots, cabbage, and peanuts.
> Hamsters are gentle and clean.

The children took turns reading the story. If they had difficulty, the teacher would prompt them with the original questions that motivated the story. ("What else do we know about hamsters?") Because the children had just experienced the story, they were able to read it easily.

The teacher rewrote the story on a piece of tagboard and hung it on a chart rack for use during reading and science throughout the semester. The teacher also placed a picture drawn by the students (she could have used a picture from a magazine) on the experience chart to help the students recall "Pepe the Hamster."

Literature-Based Approach

Simply stated, the purpose of a literature approach to the teaching of reading is to develop students' appreciation and enjoyment of a variety of literature. Through literature, students learn about cultures and societal values. Thus, it is important that students experience the literature of all cultural groups. Literature can be the basis for and integrating core of the total language arts program. Greg Thomas's lesson on *Old Yeller* is an example of how all the components are taught through the use of literature. Literature can be taught in special literature-focused units of study or related to an overall theme that integrates all the subject fields (see Chapter 6).

Whether teaching to an overall unit theme or a specific literature theme, teaching time is divided between actual reading and specific skill lessons. The significant point of the literature approach is that skills are related to students' needs as they are reading. They are not taught out of context. The literature approach is appropriate for all grade levels, but time allotments for skill lessons will vary. The following lists provide some examples:

Beginning Literacy Students: Grades K–3

Preparation for reading (discussion, reading aloud to students, motivation): 10–15 minutes
Reading and discussion of literature: 30–40 minutes
Skill lessons (decoding and comprehension): 15–20 minutes
Writing: 20–30 minutes
Sharing: 10 minutes

Intermediate Students: Grades 3–5

Preparation for reading (motivation, discussion): 5–10 minutes
Reading and discussion of literature: 30–40 minutes
Skill lessons (decoding, comprehension, writing rubrics): 20–25 minutes
Writing: 30 minutes
Sharing: 20 minutes

Advanced Reading Level: Grades 5–8

Preparation for reading (motivation, discussion): 5–10 minutes
Reading and writing: 30–35 minutes
Skills: 10–15 minutes
Discussion/sharing: 10–15 minutes

In departmentalized classrooms with 55-minute periods, the time allotments will need to be adjusted.

Building Vocabulary

The purpose of increasing students' vocabulary is to improve their comprehension of spoken and written language. Teachers go about vocabulary development in a number of different ways. For example, some teachers waste no time with motivational tricks or morphemic analysis (focusing on meaningful parts of words). Instead they list the words on the chalkboard and help students define them. They then expect the students to recognize the words in their reading selection.

Teaching Hints: Guided Reading

Grouping Versus Whole-Class Reading

Advantages of Grouping	Disadvantages of Whole-Class Reading
Books may be appropriately selected for individual needs and interests.	The whole class needs to read the same selection.
Mini-lessons on vocabulary, recognizing characterization, themes, and conflicts can be emphasized.	The whole class may not need the same emphasis; lesson time is wasted.
Students can be given an opportunity to decide on reading choice.	No opportunity for individual choice and decision making.
Small-group guided reading provides an opportunity for the teacher to diagnose students' comprehension.	Reading aloud becomes burdensome and boring.

Other teachers spend time on teaching prefixes, suffixes, and phonetic rules, asking students to "sound out" the word. However, because letters have so many conflicting sounds, the student is often lost in saying the word correctly and understanding the meaning.

Contextual analysis seems to yield the greatest success (Baumann, Edwards, Boland, Olejnik, & Kame'enui, 2003). Primary teachers often help students preread a book by showing them the pictures. They ask questions about the pictures and in this way get the students to guess the story before they actually read it. As new words emerge, the teacher writes them on the board for the students to see.

Another method is to introduce the words in sentence form so that students immediately latch on to the meaning. Most students can guess the meaning of a word from the context in which it is used.

MARY HOGAN'S CLASSROOM

Mary Hogan held up a banana with brown spots all over it. Then she called attention to the following sentence in the students' reading book: "Todd did not like the banana because it was too ripe." She asked the students to find the word *banana*, which they did immediately. Then she asked, "Why didn't Todd like the banana?" The students spoke in chorus, "Because it was too ripe." "Show me the word *ripe*," Mary said, and the students pointed to the word.

Smith (2003) demonstrates the same concept using a nonsense word: "*I left my glerp at home this morning and got soaked by rain later in the day*" (p. 55). Students in this example could guess the probable meaning of *glerp* as either an umbrella or a raincoat. With either word, the meaning of the sentence is clear.

Meaning precedes speech. I encountered the word *facet* in a diagnostic MRI report. I told my husband that I needed an injection in the *fas'-et* joint area. But when I repeated this to a nurse, she corrected me: "No, you need the injection in the faa-set'." I knew the meaning, but not how to pronounce the word correctly.

Content-Field Instruction

Because the language of content-field textbooks often poses a problem for elementary and middle school students, these textbooks have a great deal of value for reading instruction. The main purpose of the content-field text is to convey information, but because the vocabulary may represent conceptual understanding in an academic discipline, students may have difficulty obtaining meaning. Therefore, it is essential that the teacher introduce the specialized vocabulary and verify conceptual understanding before students attempt to read.

 MARY HOGAN'S CLASSROOM

Mary Hogan's students had explored the texture of rocks and had talked about how rocks felt and about their varied colors. Now she wanted them to learn how rocks are made and how they change. Hogan had a science text for each student that had a chapter about rocks that she considered useful. She had her students find the correct page and look at the illustration of the Grand Canyon. She asked them if they knew how rocks were formed. During the discussion, Hogan asked the stu-

dents what they would like to know about rocks. She wrote their questions on the board. Then she introduced the key vocabulary used in the chapter. She used the rock samples in the classroom as concrete examples. Her teaching strategy was direct instruction (review Chapter 5). After reading the textbook material, the students worked in cooperative heterogeneous groups to answer their own questions from the reading. The lesson ended with the groups sharing their responses.

Intermediate- and advanced-level students should be taught the skills of scanning and note taking when using content-field texts. It is often advantageous to have students scan the material and provide time for them to ask questions about words and concepts they do not understand.

 KAREN ADAZZIO'S CLASSROOM

Karen Adazzio had several teaching goals in mind. She wanted to introduce the genre of historical literature and wanted her students to be enthusiastic about it. Also, she wanted to improve reading comprehension and increase students' vocabulary related to both history and literature. To accomplish these goals she brought out five books for the students to see and introduced each of them with a short synopsis. All five books related to the South before and during the Civil War.

Students were to select the book they preferred to read. Groups were to be formed based on the selected novel. Groups would be seated together so that they could help each other or signal for Adazzio's assistance. Her plan included (1) individual and group reading, (2)individual note taking, and (3) group discussions at the end of each chapter. Because the books were all focused on a specific period of history, Adazzio introduced some of the vocabulary words the students would encounter as she introduced the books and provided the synopsis.

Students were expected to respond to the following questions in individual writing compositions:

1. Why do you think the author wrote this book?
2. What motivated the main character of the book? Describe the character traits of the person.
3. What dilemmas confronted the main character?
4. If you had lived during this period of history, would you have chosen the same or a different course of action?

Language Experience Approach

The language experience approach to reading instruction is based on the idea that what you can think and say, you can read. For example, the students who wrote the experience story about the hamster will be able to read that story because they just composed it. The story can be used for reading instruction with a group of students or with an individual child. The students in that first-grade classroom can be asked to draw pictures about Pepe the hamster and then write personal stories about him.

The students' stories can be taped or dictated to an aide. The aide (or teacher) will type the story for the student, who will then practice reading it aloud. Teachers need to exercise care that, in the typing process, they do not change a student's story to make it perfect. The major advantage of the language experience approach is that it integrates all of the language arts components.

Individualized Approach

Another particularly motivating approach to reading instruction is an individualized reading strategy. By providing for a wide range of choices and interests and having many books on hand, the teacher enables the students to select what they want to read. This approach assumes that students will naturally select what they are *able* to read.

In using this approach, the teacher meets with students individually to check comprehension and skill needs. Skill instruction is usually taught in a small group as the teacher identifies common learning needs. Students progress at their own rate; they do not have to cover any specific number of books. Because they choose their own books, interest is usually high. Students read individually two or three days per week, confer with the teacher at least once during the week, and

have a skill lesson at least once a week. Basal readers are sometimes used in conjunction with this approach.

Record keeping is the most important aspect of the individualized approach. Each child keeps a personal record of what he or she has read, plus comments about what he liked or didn't like about the books. The teacher keeps notes of their conferences. The child's reading folder could be turned into a reading/writing portfolio, with the student creating his or her own stories.

Which Approach Is Best?

The research you believe is the research that is best. In the constructivist, whole-language classroom, you will see evidence of students selecting books to read, spending a great deal of time writing responses, working on projects, analyzing literature, working on skills in learning centers, and reading and writing both individually and in small heterogeneous groups. The teacher will provide mini-lessons on skills as they are needed, sometimes to the whole class and sometimes to small homogeneous groups. The teacher recognizes that students' prior and present experiences are relevant and should affect instruction.

The conservative classroom will look quite different. The whole class may be reading the same book, usually a literature anthology. The literature anthology has replaced the basal reader but in fact is much the same. The anthology uses abridged versions of real literature with a controlled vocabulary. Students take turns reading aloud. The classroom is quiet; students are in their proper seats, and the teacher is up front monitoring the oral reading. Direct instruction is the teaching strategy favored by the teacher to impart phonetic "rules," and worksheets are used for students to practice what has been taught. There is an underlying assumption that the teacher knows what students need to learn and will provide it. Instruction follows a planned lockstep sequence.

Rarely, however, does a classroom teacher use a pure form of one specific approach. Most teachers want a balanced approach for reading instruction and thus use aspects of several approaches or a combination of approaches in the course of a week. In many classrooms, literature is the basis for instruction at least two days per week, content-field instruction occurs one or two days per week, and literature anthologies are used one or two days per week.

ORGANIZING THE READING PROGRAM

Classroom Environment and Classroom Management

The learning environment of the classroom affects students' ability to attend to instruction. A classroom that is too warm may make students lethargic. A classroom that is noisy may affect concentration. A classroom that is cluttered with distracting displays may make it difficult for students to settle down and study. Space, temperature, ventilation, aromas, orderliness, and light may influence learning and students' adjustment to instruction.

Furniture arrangement and the placement of materials (flannel board, charts, chalkboard) are important considerations. For example, the teacher must decide where in the classroom instruction will take place. Will the students move their chairs to a designated place for instruction? Will the teacher move from group to group? If the teacher moves, will students always be seated with their designated reading group? The arrangement of learning centers and computers must be considered in the overall planning of the reading program.

Appropriate use of time is a major consideration in the reading program. The minutes used for organizational or procedural purposes as students change places for group instruction can detract measurably from the achievement of reading goals. For this reason, movement patterns and classroom rules should be jointly decided and agreed on by teacher and students.

Grouping Patterns

Cooperative Groups

Group investigation is an example of cooperative group work. There is a great deal of evidence that students' self-esteem increases when they work in small cooperative groups based on special interests, problems, or tasks. Students working in such groups also achieve higher academic performance and develop a positive attitude about school. Cooperative grouping improves intergroup relations and facilitates ethnic and cultural understanding. When students are grouped heterogeneously, they learn to use language with their peers and take responsibility for helping their peers learn. Cooperative groups are particularly effective for teaching out-of-content textbooks and for teaching literature. A variety of methods exist for using cooperative groups. (Research on grouping was cited in Chapter 2.) Group investigation is one strategy (see Chapter 5).

Skill Grouping

Grouping students for skill instruction is a means to individualize the reading program to meet special needs as they arise. Typically, students are flexibly grouped for a limited period of time when a skill need arises. An effective reading lesson can be provided to several students at the same time if student needs and skills are matched.

Teacher observation, informal assessment, and student questions can be used to facilitate the grouping of students for skill instruction. The advantage of doing this on occasion is that direct instruction can be provided in an area of need, and students who are proficient in the skill are not bored with unnecessary instruction.

WRITING INSTRUCTION

Writing may be the most difficult language arts component to develop. Students typically have a large listening vocabulary but a much smaller speaking vocabulary. The child depends on the speaking vocabulary for written expression. For this reason, the speaking component should be emphasized. Students who do not use correct sentence patterns or expanded sentences in speech will have difficulty in writing.

Writing involves both composition and transcription. Composition represents selecting and ordering words into a logical pattern for self-expression. To compose effectively, students need to understand the relationship of words to thoughts. Composition is not dependent on transcription; one can compose a story by orally recording it. When the kindergarten child tells the story of his or her picture, oral composition is occurring. When the story is transcribed on paper, the student is transforming speech into graphic symbols. The transcription process is sometimes difficult for the student because it involves muscle control while using a pencil or crayon and writing legibly. However, when writing down a composition, the individual can revise thoughts, whereas oral composition requires recalling and retelling.

For some time now, both educators and the public have been concerned that we are producing nonwriters as a consequence of assignments that require multiple-choice selections, short answers, and worksheet responses. Also, if students are required to produce "perfect" compositions without spelling or grammatical errors and the opportunity to revise and edit, they lose confidence in their ability to write.

Students should be helped to use their background knowledge and experiences, as well as contextual cues, to communicate meaning. Proficient readers and writers are aware that meanings are structured in a coherent way. Whereas the less proficient reader-writer focuses on individual words and spelling, the skillful reader-writer perceives how things fit together.

What Should Students Write? How Is Writing Taught?

The purposes of the writing program are:

1. To develop functional writing to communicate ideas
2. To develop creative writing to express thoughts
3. To develop skill in the mechanics of writing

These three purposes are developed through student activities such as journal writing, letter writing, creative writing, informational writing, record keeping, note taking, outlining, research, and proofreading. Reading and writing should be taught together; what you write, you read. (The processes are separated in this text for presentation purposes only.) The language experience lesson related earlier in this chapter is an example of interactive writing (Pinnell & Fountas, 1998). The teacher and the students are composing a story using their experience. The students are doing the composing and the teacher is demonstrating the relationship of written words to expression. The students can see how their ideas are transposed into a written product and because they composed it, they can read it. The children are able to see how:

- Composing a story is transcribed into print
- Letters are formed into words
- Words are spaced
- Words are spelled
- Sentences are punctuated
- Writing is connected to reading

Writing personal stories is often used to help students who are having difficulty with reading. The student is asked to write a story about some experience he or she has experienced. With the teacher's help the story is transcribed. Because the student composed the story, he is familiar with the words. The student then uses the story to practice reading.

Six phases of the writing process are taught to students: prewriting, drafting, responding, revising, editing, and sharing.

Prewriting

During this phase, the classroom should provide an environment that stimulates ideas and provides opportunities for students to interact and talk informally with each other about their ideas. Sometimes a motivating story, film, picture, or activity may provide the seed to stimulate creativity and composition.

Drafting

This is the first phase of composing on paper. The writer is confronted with the task of deciding, "What do I want to say?" The writing program should help students develop fluency, the ability to use appropriate language with relative ease. The writer should be concerned with writing down what Kucer and Rhodes (1986) called "chunks" of meaning. Concerns should not be focused on form, grammar, handwriting, or spelling.

Responding

This is an optional phase that may be done in conjunction with the revision stage. In this phase the young writer may share or confer about what is written with one or more others (including the teacher) to gain perspective and additional ideas.

Revising

In this phase, the writer uses the suggestions gained in the conference or from sharing with others. It is time to rethink, rearrange, change, and refine the composition. From the sharing phase, the writer learned whether he or she had communicated meaning. Now the writer attempts to achieve greater clarity, emphasis, and wholeness.

Editing

The editing phase of the writing process includes the appreciation of form and the writing conventions. Here the writer examines spelling, punctuation, grammar, accuracy of information, syntax, and precision of word usage. It is often helpful for young writers to have a checklist to go over during the editing stage.

Sharing

This final phase is the icing on the cake. Classroom activities may include sharing the final product by reading it aloud with an audience, publishing the writing as a book, creating class books, and creating magazines with collections of stories from several students.

Writing Activities

Writing is taught in an integrated fashion throughout the school day using a variety of activities, including descriptive, creative, factual/informative, and expository writing.

Letter Writing

To enable students to recognize the importance of letter writing, personal letters and business letters should be an integral part of the writing program. Many occasions can be used to generate a letter-writing session. For example, if there is to be a school open house, students can write personal invitations to their families and friends.

The purpose of the letter, the form, punctuation, and capitalization—even the way a letter is folded—should be taught at the moment of need rather than as a special language lesson. Students need to learn sensitivity to the timing of letters, appropriate greetings and closings, and the amount of detail a letter should contain.

Creative Writing

Creative writing may involve writing about personal experiences, feelings, or make-believe. Poems, rhymes, and stories are all appropriate. All writing that is individually derived is creative. During creative writing, teachers should allow students to attend to the content of their work; they should not spoil the creative effort by insisting on correct form. When creating, students should use any words they desire, without concern for correct spelling. If students ask for assistance, the teacher can provide it by writing the desired word on a slip of paper for the student's dictionary word box or by writing the word directly in a dictionary notebook maintained by each student.

Motivation is extremely important to initiate creative writing; as a consequence, teachers need to remotivate each time the students are to write. Part of the time, the teacher will have individual children read their stories to the class; the students will serve to motivate each other. The writing workshop, discussed earlier, is another way to encourage creative writing.

Note Taking

Note taking begins at the personal level to meet the needs of the individual. The notes may be used for studying purposes or eventually to write a report or to communicate orally to others. Young students rarely know how to take notes. The skills involved in note taking have much to do with the act of studying. For example, the note taker needs to know the following:

- Purpose/importance of the assignment or task
- Background knowledge
- Organization of the materials to be used

The significance of note taking for preserving information for future reference, for evaluating print or nonprint information, or as a basis for future outlining needs to be communicated to students. If students are to take notes to study for an examination, then the students also need to know whether the examination will be essay, multiple-choice, or true/false. If students are to use the notes for an oral report, the notes will be different than if they are to be used as evidence citations during a discussion. The purpose and the importance of the assignment must be communicated to students.

Note-taking skill may depend on prior knowledge and information about the topic to be researched. When Greg Thomas's students researched architecture and furniture produced during the colonial period (see Chapter 6), they had to have some background experience recognizing early American furniture and architecture. The students in the furniture group also had to know that their notes would be used to develop a retrieval chart about colonial and European furniture. This knowledge would influence their research and the type of notes they would preserve.

Note taking is influenced by the nature of the materials to be used. An art history book may be organized differently from a science or health textbook. Students need to be alerted to the author's use of headings or questions as an organizing structure. If students are to take notes about slides they have viewed or during an interview situation, they will need to have a way to judge what is important to record.

In helping students develop note-taking skills, it is important to communicate that note taking is a personal aid to learning and, as such, requires each person to develop an individual notation style.

Outlining

Students need to learn the purpose and structure of an outline. Kindergarten students learn to group items that belong together, such as scissors, doll clothes, paints, and puzzles. At the first-grade level, students may be able to separate items, discriminating between real and make-believe, foods to be cooked and foods that can be eaten raw, or warm-weather clothing and cold-weather clothing. At the second-grade level, students continue grouping activities but are able to make finer discriminations among items. For example, the second grader may be able to identify different compositions of rocks or classifications of plants. Third graders become even more sophisticated and learn to classify ideas in a more organized fashion. The third grader may categorize using several different headings and become fairly adept at developing a table of contents for stories and pictures.

Formal structural rules for outlining can be introduced in the fourth grade, and middle school students should be able to use outlining to develop research reports and projects. However, once again, the outline should be related to the area of study and should be taught when outlining will be useful to the students. In addition, students can be exposed to the relationship of the outline to an advance organizer that helps structure a report or project.

Informational Writing

Informational writing includes writing reports, personal experiences, and news articles. This type of writing may communicate information or personal feelings. Students need to learn how to organize a report to make it interesting, and they need to adhere to a specific form. The development of the form may be decided by the teacher, or guidelines for the report may be developed by the class. Unlike creative writing, informational writing demands that spelling and punctuation receive prominent attention. A class or school newspaper is a particularly motivating way to teach informational writing. Because a newspaper has so many different types of stories, students have the opportunity to choose special interests and styles.

Writing Descriptions and Observations

Students need a great deal of practice communicating information about events that have happened. Remembering and reporting objectively (who was involved, what was involved, where an incident occurred, and the length of time of the event) are difficult tasks. Yet every time there is a problem in the schoolroom or out on the playground, teachers ask students: "What happened?" "Who did what to whom and why?"

Strategies for teaching objective writing can be practiced by assigning students to be reporters, historians, judges, or scientists. School or classroom newspapers or magazines are popular ruses to develop observational skills. Other useful activities for practicing these skills include writing science and health experiments, making a procedural accounting of how to make something, or giving a report of what happened in Room 28 yesterday, with students asked to stress accuracy and objectivity.

Record Keeping

A variety of activities throughout the school day provide opportunities to learn this type of writing. A small-group planning session requires a group recorder, who takes the minutes of the meeting by recording the plans. Individual, group, or class science experiments require a different type of record keeping. In some classrooms, students take turns writing the daily news on the chalkboard. Writing individual or class diaries provides another type of experience in record keeping. First graders may just begin to record facts or experiences, whereas fourth graders may be expected to record information in outlines. Through record keeping, students learn the value of accuracy, a sense of time, continuity, cause and effect, and the need for attention to detail. Records should always be written in the students' own words rather than in adult language.

Research

The style of writing used in research papers is similar to the writing of informational papers. The main difference involves the skills that are taught. First graders may begin to learn research skills by filing words in a dictionary box. Third graders may be expected to use picture dictionaries, a table of contents, and an index to locate information. Fifth graders can be taught to make and use bibliographies, utilize several sources of information, write questions about what they want to research, and take notes to answer the questions they have developed. Middle school students should be expected to structure research reports using all of the components discussed. These students should also be able to achieve a balance between their own ideas and what they have learned through research.

Proofreading

Proofreading skills need to be modeled as well as taught. Few adults know how to edit their own work, so it is not surprising that students seldom reread their own reports or compositions for the purpose of self-editing. Teachers can model proofreading by acknowledging to students, "Just a minute, let me reread this," or the teacher may say to students, after recording something on the chalkboard, "Does this say what we wanted it to say? Do the sentences fit together?" Often the best way to proofread is to read aloud what you have written. The combination of reading and listening helps you discover your mistakes.

Mechanics of Writing

Composition skills include capitalization and punctuation, sentence processing and paragraphing, spelling, and handwriting. These skills are best taught in a meaningful situation rather than as isolated lessons. In the primary grades, the teacher provides independent help while circulating and observing the students at work. By the middle grades, students can edit their own work.

Punctuation and Capitalization

As a general rule, young children tend to overpunctuate and overcapitalize. The relationship between punctuation and speech needs to be demonstrated to the students. By the end of second grade, most students recognize the need to end sentences with a punctuation mark, begin sentences with a capital letter, and capitalize the personal pronoun *I*. By the end of the middle grades, most students have mastered the use of capitalization in abbreviations, in the first word of greetings, in topics in an outline, and in the first word of a direct quotation. Commas used in a series, in writing the date, and between city and state have typically been mastered by the end of fourth grade.

Sentence-Processing Skills

In the primary grades, sentence-processing skills begin with students demonstrating understanding of word order in a sentence by unscrambling simple sentences.

Sentence transformations begin in the second grade, and the ability to expand a simple sentence is typically mastered by the end of the primary grades. Independent writing of simple sentences is usually mastered by the third grade. Simple paragraph writing occurs during the middle grades.

Word Usage

Selecting and using nouns, pronouns, verbs, and adjectives are typically mastered by the end of the third grade. Students can recognize the use of synonyms, antonyms, and homonyms during the middle grades. Students can be taught not to repeat the same word in consecutive sentences and to choose a synonym instead.

Style

It is extremely difficult for an elementary student to develop writing style until composition skills have been mastered. Sentence structure, logic, and clarity come first; however, teachers need to exercise care that, in their editing and assisting zeal, they do not discourage students from expressing themselves in unique ways.

SPELLING INSTRUCTION

Students have the opportunity to learn and to use spelling words whenever they are expressing themselves in written form. The spelling program should be integrated with the language arts program and taught along with reading and writing. Spelling is considered a writer's tool. A planned spelling period is usually provided by the time students are in the second grade.

The classroom environment can be used to facilitate good spelling habits. When spelling becomes a natural part of the writing program and is viewed as a courtesy to readers, children are more apt to develop the dictionary habit to perfect their own writing.

Research Findings

Perkins-Gough (2007) cites the need for special programs for adolescent English learners. Middle school English language learners are extremely diverse in their prior educational backgrounds. They need special programs, assistance, and time to develop speaking, reading, and writing skills in English.

During the spelling period, teachers typically use methods and techniques that include observing the word to be studied, hearing it, saying it, defining it in the student's own words, and practicing it by using it in writing. Students should not be given a list of rules and exceptions to memorize, asked to spell unknown words, or given meaningless dictionary exercises. Games such as Scrabble for Juniors, anagrams, and spelling lotto are popular with elementary and middle school students. Many games (crossword puzzles, word wheels) can be created by the teacher to encourage students to use the dictionary and to study spelling words.

HANDWRITING INSTRUCTION

Like spelling, handwriting is viewed as a writer's tool and is best practiced during actual writing activities. The purposes for teaching handwriting include the following:

- Development of legible and fluent manuscript and cursive writing
- Development of pride in neatness and correctness of writing

Manuscript writing is taught beginning in the first grade, but its mastery depends on the maturity of the individual student. The transition from manuscript to cursive writing is customarily accomplished in the third grade.

Readiness for handwriting is determined by eye-hand coordination and the ability to differentiate the forms of letters. The use of manipulative materials facilitates readiness for handwriting. These experiences may include the use of clay, tempera, finger paint, and physical activities involving motor skills.

LISTENING INSTRUCTION

Students are requested to listen more than 50% of the school day. A listener has no control over the tempo of speech. If school language is different from home language, listening problems are compounded. Listening is considered the basis for the other language arts components. The child who hears *bus* for *boss* obviously is not going to understand what has been said. Similarly, the student who hears *git* for *get* may not be able to read or write the word *get*. Discrimination of sounds is critical to learning language and to communication in general.

Listening requires decoding what is heard. We hear sound symbols. These sound symbols are called **phonemes.** When phonemes are combined into a pattern, they become a word unit, or **morpheme.** Morphemes are combined to form a sentence. If the individual does not discriminate among phonemes, then it will be impossible for that individual to interpret what has been said. We know that students differ in their auditory discrimination and that auditory discrimination is subject to the maturation process. Frequently, students do not mature in the development of this skill until they are about eight years old. There is a positive relationship between poor auditory discrimination and poor reading. The student who does not hear well will not learn to read well.

Activities to Develop Listening Skills

The following list of activities can be used effectively in the classroom to develop students' listening skills:

- Oral games (such as Simon Says)
- Musical instruments (repetition of rhythm patterns)
- Reciting nonsense sentences
- Pantomiming
- Recitation of rhymes and poems
- Listening to a story and sequencing pictures and events of the story
- Listening to a story and then role-playing it

Additional suggestions for using and relating listening skills will be found in the other approaches to the language arts components.

ORAL LANGUAGE DEVELOPMENT

Oral language is really the result of learning by doing. Speech is generated from the experience of listening. Although speech is a natural development, it is affected by the substance of the child's environment. An only child can be expected to have advanced language development. The language development pattern is qualitatively affected by the child's enriched experiences. Oral language also reflects the child's emotional and social adjustment. Children who lack adult contact and love fail to extend the quality of their language.

Studies of school-age children indicate that in most cases children's oral language growth increases at around age 5 to 6 and once again when the child reaches age 10 to 12. During the years in between (grades 2–5), growth appears to be much slower.

Although the developmental sequence of syntactic structures appears consistent among children, the ages during which it occurs are inconsistent. To encourage speaking and listening, the following activities are suggested:

- *Dramatics.* Students make up plays and participate in role-plays.
- *Art experiences.* Students participate in art activities and describe them.
- *Small-group interaction.* Students plan a project or resolve a conflict.
- *Interviewing.* Students interview peers or others.
- *Storytelling.* Students listen to a story, read it, and retell it to others.
- *Puppetry.* Students make hand puppets for dramatics.
- *Singing.* Students sing current favorites and rewrite the words.
- *Choral verse.* Students participate in group speech activities.
- *Touch and tell.* Students describe what they feel: *hot, cold, soft, rough, smooth, sandy.*
- *Listen and tell.* Students listen to strange sounds and describe them.

Why is oral language development a concern for middle school teachers?

ENGLISH LANGUAGE LEARNERS

Children learn language naturally and unconsciously through imitation; experience in the family, peer group, and environment; and practice. When students come to school knowing a language other than English, they need to (1) *acquire* English and they need to (2) *learn* English. Krashen and Terrell (1983) distinguish between acquisition and learning.

According to the authors, *acquisition* happens naturally, in a manner similar to first-language acquisition. Students gain language through informal means by communicating with peers or playing games. Subconsciously the individual breathes in the second language and begins to use it, often without thinking about it. However, the individual acquires language only and when it is comprehensible. That is why pictures and realia are so important to the process of acquisition (Krashen, 1985).

Language *learning* is a formal process. Students learn about language explicitly. They receive direct instruction in language. To help English language

learners, the teacher needs to provide a language-rich environment with many opportunities to engage in communicative activities. The second-language learner often finds that the primary language and second language collide, causing interference with oral language learning and with reading in the second language. For this reason many teachers believe it is wise to delay reading instruction until the English language learner has acquired a substantial speaking vocabulary.

KAREN ADAZZIO'S CLASSROOM

In Karen Adazzio's classroom, she has eight students from three different sociocultural backgrounds. She treats the students as one group, but she needs to recognize that the students are not alike and often require individualized attention. On this particular day, she is anxious to introduce some concepts and vocabulary words to the ELL students so that they can participate in group and class discussion. She displays a large piece of tagboard with a graphic organizer that exhibits a bunch of light bulbs, many cars lined up on a freeway, ice melting off a glacier and an iceberg breaking off, and finally a polar bear hunting a seal. Then she shows an arrow pointing at water rising and endangering a residential community.

With the ELL students participating, she initiates a discussion of the causes of climate change. When she is comfortable that the English-learning students understand the vocabulary, she transfers her attention to the whole class. Again she displays the chart, and the students quickly recognize the relationship of the different pictures to the concluding picture. Adazzio divides the class into small groups and tells them to discuss the following questions:

1. What do you think is the problem depicted by these pictures?
2. What do you think causes the problem?
3. What are some possible solutions?

The ELL students are included within the different groups and, because of their advance assistance, they are able to contribute.

English-learning students suffer when teachers stress phonics approaches because they are unable to link what they are hearing with the English vocabulary they have acquired. When English language learners try to sound out words, they may be trying to relate the sounds to their primary language because that is what is familiar to them (Quezada, Wiley, & Ramirez, 2000). Quezada, Wiley, and Ramirez (2000) believe that it takes four to six years for English language learners to become proficient in English.

The language experience approach to reading instruction helps ELL students make the transition from reading in the primary language to reading English.

SHELTERED ENGLISH

Sheltered English instruction, also called *content-based second-language instruction*, is one means of helping students understand and acquire language. In using this technique, the teacher speaks slowly and uses simple, predictable sentence forms. Concrete objects and visuals are used to clearly relate the subject to everyday life experiences. Facial and body expressions and gestures enhance the delivery. Explanations or instructions should be repeated and summarized.

Repetition of key concepts that reinforce vocabulary helps students acquire language. Verification of students' understanding can be done by asking students to repeat instructions and to practice by telling others.

ELL students need opportunities to talk about their own experiences and should be encouraged to use props similar to what the teacher uses. This will assist students who are having difficulty understanding the English language learner as well as the teacher. It also provides a means for ELL students to express themselves when some of the words are unknown. Cooperative work groups with group membership adjustment so that language-proficient students are working with ELL students are a means to provide support.

SPECIALLY DESIGNED ACADEMIC INSTRUCTION IN ENGLISH (SDAIE)

MARY HOGAN'S CLASSROOM

There are a number of English language learners in Mary Hogan's second-grade class. Hogan uses a variety of concrete materials to foster student understanding. While reading a book about Curious George, Hogan uses puppets and miniature toys to illustrate the action as she slowly reads the story. She uses techniques that are described as SDAIE.

When asking questions, Hogan allows plenty of time for her ELL students to respond. She makes it a point to accept the student's response without making a correction, but she may repeat the response in her own words. When explaining concepts to her students, she uses simple language and provides many examples to help students comprehend. She tends to use a lot of body language to convey her messages. She exaggerates emotions and tries to provide sensory activities for the children. Whenever possible, she encourages her students to explain what she has taught in their own words. At the end of the school day, she asks her students, "Tell me what you learned today." In this way, she prepares them to tell their parents about school.

Mary Hogan's students receive some of their instruction in their native language, and she believes that this has a positive effect on their self-esteem. Whenever possible, Hogan uses the students' own language and culture in her lessons. (This is described as an "additive" approach to language instruction.) However, in some classrooms, students speak so many different languages that primary-language instruction is impossible. Consequently, teachers need to use SDAIE techniques and provide many opportunities for students to work in small groups with native English speakers to learn English from their peers. (Review the "Teaching Hints" box about helping English language learners in Chapter 1.)

NONSTANDARD ENGLISH

It is especially important in the teaching of language arts that teachers demonstrate to students their acceptance of all languages and language differences. There is no conclusive evidence that speaking **nonstandard English** has any effect on learning to read or learning to spell. Cultural gaps between school and community appear to be responsible for most learning problems. Speakers of nonstandard pronunciation automatically adjust for dialectical differences in pronunciation, grammar, and vocabulary. When reading a text aloud, the student may automatically read standard English in dialect format. (*I am going to the circus* may be read as "I be goin' to the circus.") Older students should be asked to read as they see it printed.

Research indicates that both nonstandard dialects and standard English have language rules and complexities. Nonstandard-English speakers are able to

Teaching Hints: Questions to Stimulate Language Acquisition

Students hesitate to respond in English

   Ask students to find a picture and name it
              help a friend
              draw a response

Students appear to understand but make errors in grammar

   Ask students to write short/simple sentences
              identify characters in a story

Students appear to have mastered comprehension

   Ask students open-ended inquiry questions
              What would happen if . . . ?
              If you were (a character), what
              would you do?

communicate just as well as the standard English speaker. The dialect speaker is not language deficient—just different (McCormick, 1995).

The nonstandard-English speaker understands standard English, enjoys television, and understands print. During reading instruction, it is important to differentiate between reading errors due to miscues and reading errors due to the student's expression of the nonstandard dialect that does not affect meaning. Reading problems are not caused by speaking a nonstandard dialect. Teachers need to help nonstandard-English speakers develop awareness of nonstandard speech and sensitively demonstrate alternate ways to express themselves.

ASSESSING PROGRESS THROUGH PERFORMANCE USING PORTFOLIOS

Standardized tests and informal teacher-made tests can be used to evaluate student progress, but performance assessment is the most effective means to determine what students have learned. Although it is not possible to know how well students are listening or how much students comprehend when they are reading, it is possible to evaluate growth when students produce a product. Receptive growth can be measured by expressive acts. When students discuss, dramatize, or use written materials to produce something, comprehension can be evaluated.

The teacher's task is to diagnose any learning problems and design instruction to facilitate the learning process; students will profit from involvement in the evaluative process. It is important for students to be aware of their own strengths and weaknesses. However, it is also important that they not be overwhelmed by failures. Particularly in the area of reading, it is significant to confer with students and develop goals jointly for future progress.

Students' portfolios provide an ideal way to assess the progress students make in their writing. Beginning with the prewriting ideas, followed by the written draft, revision process, and final edited version, students can self-evaluate and discuss their progress with others. The portfolio can be used to exhibit the many types of writing students perform: creative, informational, report, or diary.

Students' writing can also be evaluated in terms of content (relevancy, clarity, originality, interest) and form (organization, style, punctuation, capitalization, word usage, legibility, appropriateness). Specific writing skills, such as the ability to write a business or personal letter, a journal, and a research report, can be evaluated. When possible, encourage students to develop their own rubrics to self-evaluate growth. Students' book reports can be used to judge their ability to analyze plot and characterization.

THE INCLUSIVE CLASSROOM

Typically, elementary and middle school classrooms have students with a wide range of ability levels, from gifted to slow. The addition of students with physical or learning disabilities can also be expected in most classrooms. Mainstreamed children customarily are provided with individualized instruction in language arts; however, appropriate instruction can occur in the regular classroom provided that the individualized educational program has been developed with instructional materials and supportive services available to the student and teacher.

An advantage to regular classroom placement is the availability of peer tutors. Working with a partner, mainstreamed children can practice reading and oral language skills. Proper reinforcement with peer tutors can have a positive effect on motivation and interest.

Research on direct instruction is applicable to the teaching of academic skills to students with disabilities. Review the following sections in the text:

- Chapter 1: "The Inclusive Classroom" and "Individualized Educational Programs"
- Chapter 4: "Direct Instruction"

INTEGRATING TECHNOLOGY IN LANGUAGE ARTS

Word-processing software programs designed for students of all ages provide motivating means to teach both reading and writing skills. Beginning literacy students can use programs that have drawing features and simple graphs, enabling them to produce drawings for their stories and to learn to write their stories on the computer. Young students can produce signs for the classroom and greeting cards for family and friends. Print Shop and Print Master can be used by young elementary students.

Intermediate and advanced literacy students can use the spell-check feature and the thesaurus to improve their writing and vocabulary. Middle school students enjoy desktop publishing programs. The PageMaker program allows students to produce a class or school newspaper. They can also create handouts for their oral reports. Microsoft's Word and Corel's WordPerfect have desktop publishing capabilities. Review the discussion on hypermedia that appears earlier in the chapter.

Authentic Performance

Instead of one-dimensional term papers and reports, students may create multimedia projects using hypermedia systems. Computer disks that combine graphics, sound, and text may replace hard-copy reports. By harnessing technology to prove their own understandings, students integrate skills and approach problems from an interdisciplinary perspective.

LEARNING CENTERS/STATIONS

Learning centers can be an integral part of the instructional program. The centers facilitate reinforcement of skill development, offer opportunities to explore creative aspects of subject matter, and individualize and expand instruction to meet students' needs while accommodating multiple intelligences. The centers presented in this section should be used as points of departure. Let your own creativity be your guide.

Research Findings

National Association Educational Progress data show that when ELLs are assessed, they perform at lower levels on reading and math tests at all grade levels. According to NAEP, they tend to perform somewhat better on math and science items than they do on English reading (Duran, 2008).

Figurative Language Center

Language Arts, Social Studies—
Advanced Literacy Students

Objectives. To improve comprehension of word meanings, appreciation of language, use of figurative language, and development of cooperative work skills.

Materials. An envelope or box to contain the figurative expressions; a direction card.

Assessment. Observation and discussion.

Procedures

1. The direction card explains that students are to take turns choosing an expression from the box or envelope. Each student pantomimes an expression while the other members of the group try to guess the expression.
2. Expressions may include the following:
   - *long arm of the law*
   - *on the face of it*
   - *put on the dog*
   - *eye of the storm*
   - *cat got your tongue*
   - *out of the woods*
   - *horsing around*
   - *leg of the journey*
   - *paint the town red*
   - *jump on the high horse*
   - *bounce a check*
   - *into the frying pan*

To Simplify. Students may work with a partner to pantomime the expression.

To Extend. Students may write their own expressions and hand them out for others to act out.

Technology Center—Book Reviews

Language Arts—All Levels

Objectives. To encourage students to use the computer for writing and reading book reviews; to develop a class Web site for book reviews.

Materials. Literature books, information card suggesting ideas for book reviews (theme, setting, characters, author's style, what you enjoyed and why, what you disliked and why).

Procedures
1. Students may work individually, in pairs, or in groups sharing ideas for the review.
2. Students may go to a class Web site to read reviews written by classmates.

To Extend
1. Ask students to write more complex reviews that include some of the problems that confronted characters in the book.
2. Have students relate characters' situations with their own experiences.

To Simplify
1. Ensure that students use books at the appropriate level for their reading ability and interests.
2. Simplify the review suggestions.

Assessment
1. Have students take turns editing the reviews.
2. Have students present varying viewpoints about the characterization and relate to their own experiences.

Listening Center

Language Arts—Beginning Literacy

Objectives. To improve listening skills; to sequence pictures related to a specific story.

Materials. Story record, flannel board pictures.

Procedures
1. Students listen to a familiar story.
2. Students take turns retelling the story using the flannel board pictures.
3. Students self-evaluate by turning pictures over and checking the number sequence.

To Extend. Familiar routines are identified on the tape. Students take turns sequentially dramatizing these routines.

Examples. Making breakfast, getting ready for school, bike riding, painting a picture, making ice cream, making tortillas.

Category Center

Language Arts, Art—Beginning Literacy

Objective. To categorize objects in order to improve comprehension.

Materials. Picture file, scissors, paste, paper.

Assessment. Students share pictures and identify categories and objects.

Procedures
1. Students sort pictures by categories such as pets, fruits, animals, toys, transportation, vegetables, clothing, and shelter.
2. Students cut out pictures and make a collage to demonstrate one selected category.

Comic Strip Center

Language Arts—Intermediate and Advanced Literacy

Objective. To improve creative writing and expand writing skills.

Materials. Variety of comic strips with the dialogue eliminated, pencils.

Assessment. Students share composed comic strips.

Procedures
1. Students choose a comic strip and compose and insert the conversation in the appropriate spaces.

To Extend. Students may draw and write their own comic strips.

To Simplify. Students may work with a partner to compose the dialogue.

Information Center

Language Arts, Science, Social Studies, or Health—Intermediate and Advanced Literacy

Objective. To improve listening, note-taking, and informational writing skills.

Materials. Taped stories, paper and pencils.

Assessment. Students share information about the stories with others.

Procedures
1. Students listen to an incident and take notes.
2. Students write a news report of the story, identifying the following:
   - Who is involved?
   - What happened?
   - How did it happen?
   - What were the results/consequences?

To Extend. More than one incident can be used; students may dramatize the story; students may take the roles of reporter and interviewees.

To Simplify. Students write stories with a partner. Less complicated, taped incidents may be used.

Critical Reading

Reading—Advanced Literacy

Objective. To improve critical reading skills identifying adjectives, facts, and opinions.

Materials. Commercial product boxes or advertising pages from newspapers and magazines.

Assessment. Group evaluation, class discussion.

Procedures
1. Products or advertisements are displayed at the center.
2. Students write out the descriptive advertising slogans, adjectives, and gimmicks used by the advertiser.
3. Students compare their answers with each other.

To Extend
1. Students write their own advertising slogans for products.
2. Students identify the target audience for the product and the advertising.

To Simplify
1. Limit the quantity of products.
2. Simplify the advertising to be read (write your own).

SUMMARY

Language arts is a broad field of study encompassing reading, writing, listening, and speaking. Viewing and presenting are subsets of reading and speaking. With the use of technology in the classroom, appropriate viewing skills also need to be taught. The major purpose of teaching language arts is to improve communication skills. Language development is affected by students' experiences and culture, cognitive and affective development, attitudes, and motivation.

Classrooms that provide a literacy-rich environment help stimulate language development, as does technology in the classroom, which can be used to integrate several subject fields. Reading and writing workshops provide means to give students choices in accomplishing their work.

Constructivist classrooms differ from traditional classrooms by involving students in learning centers, choosing books to read, and utilizing heterogeneous grouping. Primary language or dialect is a factor in language development and school success. The constructivist classroom tends to integrate students' experiences and cultural life to facilitate language learning.

Reading instruction usually encompasses silent reading, oral reading, work/study reading, and recreational reading. Content-field texts are valuable as sources of reading material. Students are encouraged to read through story reading, storytelling, readers' theater, listening centers, and recreational reading. Grouping patterns affect students' self-esteem and achievement.

Writing involves composition and transcription. Three purposes govern the writing program: functional writing, creative writing, and skill development in the mechanics of writing. Writing should be integrated throughout the school day and encompasses letter writing, creative writing, note taking, outlining, informational writing, writing observations and descriptions, record keeping, research, and proofreading. Mechanics of writing are best taught in meaningful situations rather than as isolated skills.

Language development is qualitatively affected by the child's experiences. Oral language activities include dramatics, art experiences, small-group interaction, interviewing, storytelling, puppetry, singing, listening, telling (presenting). A language-rich environment facilitates acquiring English language skills and provides opportunities for communicative activities. The teacher's use of SDAIE and sheltered English helps students understand content in the second language.

Nonstandard English is a dialect governed by language rules and language complexities. Nonstandard-English speakers are not language deficient. The nonstandard English speaker needs to appreciate the value of speaking standard English and recognize the differences between standard and nonstandard forms of English.

Students' language progress can be assessed in a variety of ways through performance, standard tests, informal teacher tests, expressive acts, portfolios, and ability to converse with others.

In the inclusive classroom, students can work advantageously with a peer tutor. Most often, the mainstreamed student is provided with an individualized educational program.

Word-processing software programs for students of all ages help to motivate learning reading and writing skills. Hypermedia help students access and link information to fit their own thinking style. Students can create multimedia projects using hypermedia systems.

PORTFOLIO ACTIVITY

Using a subject-field textbook, plan and implement a lesson that integrates language arts with the content area. Discuss the lesson and explain how you introduced specialized vocabulary and involved students in language arts activities. Ask a colleague to critique the lesson.

 ### DISCUSSION QUESTIONS AND APPLICATION EXERCISES

1. Select a reading text that you would use for guided reading.
   - Identify words that your students will not recognize and plan how you will introduce them.
   - Make a list of words that are not phonetically spelled (neighbor, broad).
   - Make a list of words that are spelled differently, sound alike, but have different meanings (oh, owe; see, sea; to, two, too).
2. Plan a field trip for a group of elementary students. Identify the new words that the experience could provide.
3. Design a learning center that integrates several subject fields. Use the learning centers in this chapter as a guide.
4. Observe a group of students participating in block work or dramatic play. Describe your observation and explain what value the experience had for the participating children.
5. In what ways are language and culture related? (What does a teacher need to know?)
6. Identify classroom activities that you can use to expand language uses.
7. Why is it important for teachers to be language sensitive?
8. One of your students has had a great deal of difficulty learning to read. You have just discovered that the student owns a camera and has taken a number of pictures of the neighborhood. How could you use this information to teach reading?
9. Suggest activities to improve middle school students' skills in writing reports and motivating ideas for creative writing.
10. Write questions to be used as an advance organizer to help students in grades 5–8 develop critical reading skills.

READER RESEARCH

Research nonverbal communication and use your own observations. See if you can identify characteristics of a variety of cultural groups, including teens, seniors, romantic language groups, and sport groups. Relate what you have learned to specific emotions, such as nervousness, anger, fear, joy, celebration.

 ### TECHNOLOGY APPLICATIONS

1. For advanced literacy students, use a novel to plan a virtual field trip that takes students to the setting and historical time period of the novel. (Hint: Go to http://dmoz.org, select "Regional," and then select the correct geographical region.)
2. Design a trip to an author's home environment to develop an understanding of the author's experiences and perspective.
3. Locate information for young children using the Children's Literature Web Guide located on the Educational Resources Page of the Teachers Helping Teachers Web site.
4. For beginning and intermediate literacy students, find Web sites to help students explore the natural habitat of animals using Metacrawler.
5. For students interested in J. K. Rowling's books about Harry Potter, find Web sites that students can use to contrast Potter's magical experiences with personal experiences. Ask students: Would Harry be able to navigate the Web? Would Harry be comfortable using technology? Have students explore their own reactions when using the Internet.

CHAPTER 9

Social Experiences
The Nature of the Social Studies

The purpose of the social studies curriculum is to provide essential knowledge, skills, and values for citizenship participation in our democratic society. Beginning in the primary years, students learn about the history and culture of the United States and the world; they study geography, government, economic theories, social institutions, global relationships, and inter-group and interpersonal relationships. Beliefs in our democratic society are developed through an understanding of due process, equal protection, and civic participation. Skill competencies depend on systematic practice. Study skills, critical thinking, and social participation are essential and contribute to the major purposes of education in the United States.

This chapter presents a wide range of content and teaching approaches applicable for social studies teaching. The overriding concern is that teachers prepare students for participation in the democratic system and for problem solving in an increasingly diverse, interdependent, and complex world.

Advance Organizer

The following questions are intended to guide your reading and understanding of the content of this chapter.

1. Why is the field of social studies considered a basic subject?
2. What should students learn in the social studies?
3. How can a teacher integrate thematic strands and local and/or state sequences of content?
4. What are the social science disciplines that constitute the social studies?
5. In the grade level you teach, what are several performance expectations that you would plan as a focus?
6. Using this chapter as a guide, can you identify and describe several strategies for teaching social studies?
7. What resources would you choose for teaching social studies?
8. Plan several classroom activities that require three categories of social studies skills. What would you name the categories?
9. How can you use authentic assessment in the social studies?
10. Why are learning centers and stations and learning packets important for use in the social studies?
11. What are some ways to use technology and other resources for inquiry teaching of social studies?
12. Where would you plan to take students on a virtual field trip to extend their knowledge of people, places, and environments?

INTASC   **INTASC Standards**

Social studies are about people, their culture, their diversity, their environments, and the ways in which they get along with others in their communities and in the global society. To teach the social studies, teachers need knowledge of the seven social science disciplines, the diversity and learning abilities of the students they teach, and how best to foster social relationships and productive communication among learners. Standards 1–10 contribute to these keys to professional behaviors.

Professional Lexicon

arranged environment A classroom environment that uses realia, pictures, and print materials to motivate students' interest in a teaching unit.

culmination Activity at the end of a teaching unit to finalize the unit and determine what students have learned.

development activities The activities that make up the body of the teaching unit; the learning experiences between the initiation and the culmination.

initiation An experience at the beginning of the teaching unit to stimulate student interest and enthusiasm.

semantic maps A webbing technique to help students construct and link categories of information.

social sciences History, geography, political science, economics, psychology, anthropology, and sociology.

social studies The umbrella term used to describe teaching the social sciences integrated for pedagogical purposes; the integration of experience and knowledge concerning human experience.

virtual field trip A curricular field trip using the Internet.

The study of war is without doubt the most controversial issue students can be asked to consider. Karen Adazzio asked her students to discuss the U.S./Iraq conflict: "Why do many people want a war, and do males and females have a difference of opinion about waging war?

JESSIE: *Wars are supposed to solve problems. We believed that Iraq was responsible for 9/11.*

MARIA: *I don't think wars solve problems, and I don't think Iraq was responsible for 9/11; I think wars create problems, and we didn't have any evidence that Iraq had weapons of mass destruction.*

ADAZZIO: *Let's get some clarification here. Who would like to explain how wars solve problems? OK, Fredric.*

FREDRIC: *When nations differ over important issues or attack each other, the winner can impose its view of how life should be. So the war solves some problems, but not all.*

SALLY: *A lot of people gain from a war, and a lot of people get killed, maimed, and lose their way of life. I don't see how wars solve anything, and yes, I believe that women and men do differ in perspective about wars.*

ADAZZIO: *Interesting points. Let's think about who gains from a war.*

CARLOS: *Well, guys that don't know what to do with their lives after high school go into the military and learn a whole new way to behave. Sometimes they even become heroes during a war. So in a way they gain from the war.*

MAY: *Wars create jobs. Planes, tanks, ships, guns, and food and clothing for the military all are stimulated by a war.*

MARIA: *Yeah, and after the war is over these same people lose their jobs and many of the youth lose their lives.*

JERRY: *True, but after the war is over, some industries still profit and help the defeated nation rebuild—like in Iraq. But sometimes these companies profit unfairly.*

TERRI: *I don't understand why the United Nations doesn't help rebuild Iraq. Why do we need to have so many soldiers there? Every time there is a terrorist attack, other nations seem to blame the United States.*

MARIA: *We started the war. It was a preemptive strike! Most of the world didn't think we should invade Iraq.*

ADAZZIO: *We seem to have many diverse questions and beliefs about the value of war, and even our right to go to war. I'm going to write some of your questions and mine on the board. Then you may choose a question to research. If there are others who select the same question, you may form a group to discuss the question and write a group response. We will have another whole-class discussion tomorrow using what you have learned.*

This scenario will be discussed later in the chapter.

WHY DO WE TEACH SOCIAL STUDIES?

Social studies can be the most exciting and challenging subject field in the curriculum. It is also one of the most important subjects taught to students. Teaching the social studies prepares young people to participate fully in American society. The emphasis of social studies is citizenship responsibility. Before children come to school, their group experiences are often limited to the family, the preschool (if the child attended), or the neighborhood. Learning how to work with a partner or in a group and use group process skills are developmental processes. The interaction that occurs when working in a peer group is different from that which occurs in the family group. The assumption of a group role cannot be learned unless one experiences social organization. Interaction in groups requires understanding and adhering to group norms, roles, and social control.

Children come to school knowing very little about people in their own society or elsewhere. They typically are ignorant of U.S. social institutions, customs, and values. Our school population is extremely diverse, but the intention of our country is for all of the people of the United States to share a common mainstream culture. This culture has to do with our economic system, our political and judicial systems, and our heritage. U.S. citizens should be able to speak English and should be educated to participate in the social, economic, and political life of our country. Participation in the mainstream culture can be considered a basic need if one is to live in the United States. Social studies is the subject field responsible for the achievement of this goal.

Parents teach certain behaviors that they value in family life—the family always gathers together for Sunday night dinner, or celebrates birthdays together, or plans vacations or holiday observances together. Society also has values that are shared. Loyalty, unity, respect for others' rights, responsibility to vote, innocence until proven guilty—these are but a few of the general values that are shared in our society.

Teachers are responsible for teaching our country's values. If teachers do not teach about our culture and our values, our country will not have a future. Students are taught about the Bill of Rights and about our branches of government so they understand and appreciate U.S. democracy. We use the symbol of the flag and the "Star Spangled Banner" to promote group unity; we

Teaching Hints: Working in Small Groups

Refer to Chapter 3 for help with group work. For students who have not had experience working in small groups, it is often a good idea to assign group roles. The following are examples:

1. Suggest that the group select a group leader.
2. Suggest that a member of the group be responsible for selecting and gathering resources.
3. Make the group aware of areas in which certain members excel, such as drawing, generating creative ideas, reasoning, using language, applying knowledge of different cultures and environments, and taking notes.

enjoy a school holiday on Presidents' Day; but before we do, we teach students about our country's accomplishments. Students learn about rights and responsibilities in their daily participation in classroom life.

Why do we teach social studies? Through the teaching of social studies, we prepare students to participate in a democratic society. We facilitate the development of humane, rational, and understanding individuals who will preserve and continue our society. We recognize that to be effective citizens, there are specific skills, knowledge, values, and attitudes necessary for social participation. It is the role of the school to foster civic virtue and a sense of citizenship. These goals direct the social studies program.

However, of great concern to many teachers (and parents) is the marginalization of social studies content to the NCLB curriculum. In many classrooms social studies is taught only two to three days per week for less than two hours per week. Like the arts, social studies is shortchanged by NCLB and is often eliminated from the elementary curriculum.

Because our classrooms are so diverse, teachers can take advantage of the multicultural background of the students with the teaching of social studies. Using a world map, teachers may ask students to locate their native country. ELL students can be asked to talk about similarities and differences between their native land and the United States. Ask students to discuss schooling, sports, and cultural ways of life. Encourage classmates to ask questions of these students so that you can take full advantage of the "experts" in your classroom. All of this is possible when you teach social studies.

WHAT ARE STUDENTS EXPECTED TO LEARN?

The National Council for the Social Studies (NCSS)—the professional organization of teachers and university faculty who care about social studies teaching—adopted the following definition of social studies:

> Social studies is the integrated study of the **social sciences** and humanities to promote civic competence. Within the school program, social studies provides coordinated, systematic study drawing upon such disciplines as anthropology, archaeology, economics, geography, history, law, philosophy, political science, psychology, religion, and sociology, as well as appropriate content from the humanities, mathematics, and natural sciences. The primary purpose of social studies is to help young people develop the ability to make informed and reasoned decisions for the public good as citizens of a culturally diverse, democratic society in an interdependent world. (National Council for the Social Studies, 1994, p. 3)

In the same document, the NCSS specified four purposes for social studies programs:

1. Social studies programs have as a major purpose the promotion of civic competence—the knowledge, skills, and attitudes required of students to be able to assume "the office of citizen" in our democratic republic.
2. K–12 social studies programs integrate knowledge, skills, and attitudes within and across disciplines.
3. Social studies programs help students construct a knowledge base and attitudes drawn from academic disciplines as specialized ways of viewing reality.
4. Social studies programs reflect the changing nature of knowledge, fostering entirely new and highly integrated approaches to resolving issues of significance to humanity. (pp. 3–5)

SELECTING AND ORGANIZING CONTENT

Whenever curriculum experts discuss what makes up the curriculum, they are discussing the *scope* of the curriculum pattern; when experts discuss the order or grade level of the pattern, they are referring to the *sequence*. Surprisingly, there is very little variation in the United States from school to school as to what is taught in the social studies.

Expanding communities, designed by Hanna (1965), is the name given to the most typical pattern found in elementary and middle schools. The pattern developed as a response to the developmental needs and interests of young children. Curriculum content focused on the widening perspective of students as they progressed through the grades and moved away from their own egocentric world to study human behavior in far-off places. The young kindergarten and first-grade student studied about self, family, and the school community; the study of state history was typical for fourth graders; the study of U.S. history, culture, and geography dominated study for fifth, eighth, and eleventh graders.

But the expanding-horizons design often was interpreted too narrowly by teachers and social scientists. Students today have far more experience with people in remote areas of the world, travels in space, and diverse cultures. Consequently, teachers need to incorporate conceptual content and skills related to controversial problems, societal issues, or student concerns.

Many states adopt their own guidelines to provide a basis for determining the scope and sequence of the social studies program. For example, the California State Board of Education adopted the *History–Social Science Framework for California Public Schools* (California Department of Education, 1997) to provide guidelines and recommendations for teachers and publishers of materials and curriculum developers. The framework is intended as both a policy statement and a guide for designing curricula and courses of study. It also serves as a base from which criteria for instructional materials can be developed. Each grade level in

Research Findings

Martin (2007) observed and interviewed twenty eighth-grade middle school students to find out how they studied for class tests and discussions. The students used a variety of learning strategies taught by self, parents, peers, and teacher. The students' favored choices of learning strategies included verbal rehearsing, multiple reviewing of class notes, rereading their textbook, rephrasing information in their own words, and making flashcards. Students decided on their own when and under what circumstances to use the strategies for improving learning.

the framework has specific recommendations for a major setting or topic, and then a number of subtopics are recommended. The major topics in the California *History–Social Science Framework* are presented here as an example of scope and sequence of curriculum content:

- Kindergarten—Learning and Working Now and Long Ago
- Grade 1—A Child's Place in Time and Space
- Grade 2—People Who Make a Difference
- Grade 3—Continuity and Change
- Grade 4—California: A Changing State
- Grade 5—United States History and Geography: Making a New Nation
- Grade 6—World History and Geography: Ancient Civilization
- Grade 7—World History and Geography: Medieval and Early Modern Times
- Grade 8—United States History and Geography: Growth and Conflict

---

Compare the scope and sequence suggested in your state with the California framework.

The Spiral Curriculum, conceived by Taba (1967b), is another approach to the selection and organization of content in the social studies. Basic concepts are structured so that they are used at different levels of abstraction, depending on the age and ability of the students. For example, the concept of diversity could be taught at increasing levels of complexity by first introducing the concept in kindergarten, when students study working together, and continuing to eighth grade when students study the content about regional development in the West, Northeast, and South.

Standards for teaching social studies were developed by the NCSS in 1994. (Standards have also been developed in the different social science disciplines. These other standards are not presented here.) The purposes of the NCSS standards (1994, p. 13) are as follows:

- To serve as a framework for the K–12 program
- To serve as a guide for curriculum decisions
- To provide examples of classroom practice to guide teachers in designing instruction

The NCSS identified 10 themes to serve as organizing strands for the social studies curriculum:

1. Culture
2. Time, continuity, and change
3. People, places, and environments
4. Individual development and identity
5. Individuals, groups, and institutions
6. Power, authority, and governance
7. Production, distribution, and consumption
8. Science, technology, and society
9. Global connections
10. Civic ideals and practices

GREG THOMAS'S FIFTH-GRADE CLASSROOM

The NCSS topics are intended to be interrelated. For example, Greg Thomas had been concerned about how to make the study of the industrial revolution relevant to his students. He received a phone call from a teacher friend who complained that she needed wood boxes to hold crayons for her first-grade students.

Suddenly, Thomas got the idea that if he created a factory environment with his students producing wood crayon boxes, the students would gain the perception of factory life. He told his students about the need for the boxes and asked them if they would be willing to undertake the job. The students thought it would be a lark and a great means to avoid studying history!

Materials were obtained and student groups formed to propose how to go about the task. At first, the students proposed individual construction but then decided on partner work. Thomas allowed them to start work with a partner, but after about 20 minutes he stopped them for discussion. The students complained that:

- There were not enough saws and hammers.
- It would be difficult to find a place in the room to nail the pieces together.
- People were cutting the wood different sizes.
- The wood should be sanded.

Thomas guided the discussion and then asked the students to think about the following questions: How can we (1) make the boxes a standard size? (2) share the tools? (3) speed up the operation? The students slowly formulated a plan. They needed a template for standardization and specific areas of the room devoted to each task. After more discussion, a student proposed a "factory" system with groups responsible for the different operations. Thomas was ready to cheer and began to plan how he would integrate several of the social studies topics.

Which topics did Thomas choose? Review the NCSS topics; then compare your list with the one at the end of this chapter.

CONTENT STANDARDS

The NCSS also identified content standards for each of the topics. To get the flavor of the standards, the topic of culture and several of the examples given for curriculum development are presented next.

Performance expectations for elementary *grades* include the following:

- Explore and describe similarities and differences in the ways groups, societies, and cultures address similar human needs and concerns.
- Describe ways in which language, stories, folktales, music, and artistic creations serve as expressions of culture and influence behavior of people living in a particular culture.
- Give examples and describe the importance of cultural unity and diversity within and across groups.

Using the same topic, the *performance expectations for* middle school *grades* include the following:

- Compare similarities and differences in the ways groups, societies, and cultures meet human needs and concerns.
- Explain and give examples of how language, literature, the arts, architecture, artifacts, traditions, beliefs, values, and behaviors contribute to the development and transmission of culture.
- Articulate the implications of cultural diversity, as well as cohesion, within and across groups.

DIVERSITY OF TOPICS AND PROGRAMS

As you have probably realized by now, the social studies curriculum encompasses almost everything that society is concerned about—multicultural education, environmental education, career education, technology, consumer education, global education, law education, and moral education. The teacher is continually faced with making choices about what to include in the relatively short period of time devoted to social studies.

Let us take a brief look at several of the modest proposals for some of these topics.

Law Education

Elementary and middle school students need to understand the nature and function of law. The purpose of a law-related unit is to help students understand how laws affect all citizens. Law-focused teaching units have great potential to teach students how to participate in a society governed by laws. Critical-thinking skills and problem solving are taught through law-related education.

MARY HOGAN'S SECOND-GRADE CLASSROOM

To clarify the purpose of laws, students should engage in research, debates, role-plays, mock trials, or simulations. Field trips and neighborhood walks make it possible for students to observe the use of laws in their daily lives. For example, Mary Hogan took her second graders on a walk around the school community so that they could observe the following:

- The use of street signs to ensure orderliness
- The observance of traffic regulations by pedestrians and motor vehicles
- Rules that affect traffic entering and leaving the school parking lot
- Rules that regulate school visitors
- Rules that affect playground conduct

When the students returned to the classroom, they were asked to judge the purpose of the rules and whether they thought there was a real need for the rule. Then they examined some of their classroom rules to see if they were really needed. Hogan helped the students see that rules can be viewed as laws that govern behavior.

More mature students touring the neighborhood could be asked to identify:

- Rules that protect the environment
- Rules that regulate businesses
- Rules that regulate residential and commercial land use

Controversial topics can be introduced to students in law-focused lessons to stimulate critical thinking, improve interpersonal communication skills, and help students resolve conflicts. In a mock trial, students can play the roles of plaintiff, defendant, and judge. If the mock trial is performed several times, the judges can compare their decisions. The role players can share how they felt as plaintiff and defendant.

The Constitutional Rights Foundation publishes a quarterly newsletter titled *The Bill of Rights in Action*, which presents issues about the law, U.S. history and government, and suggestions for classroom use. Most of the activities are appropriate for both elementary and secondary students. A recent issue dealt with the history of how welfare began in the United States and then presented conflicting positions concerning the responsibility for welfare.

Should welfare be the responsibility of the federal or state government? Should welfare be the responsibility of charities and church groups? Should it be a family responsibility?

Suggested activities include small-group discussion and reports, debate, and writing individual editorials.

Students are well acquainted with controversy in their homes, on the street, and in school with their peers, but they lack experience in resolving conflict situations. Confronting controversy and making it part of the contemporary social studies curriculum helps make school relevant, meaningful, and motivating. Later in the chapter, strategies for conflict resolution will be discussed.

 Teaching Hints

Middle school students can be asked to view some of the law-based TV programs and take notes on the behaviors of lawyers, judges, and defendants. Discussion in class can focus on the legal system and the fairness of the decisions by juries and judges.

Career Education

Career education programs in elementary and middle schools focus on the world of work. Their purpose is to acquaint young students with the diverse occupations that are available as career choices. The program's primary aim is to develop awareness of occupations that may be beyond the child's immediate experiences. The special skills and training required by different occupations make up the substance of the unit. Teachers who choose to develop career education programs must take particular care to avoid sex-role stereotyping.

Multicultural and Multiethnic Education and Gender Issues

Investigation of multicultural and multiethnic education reveals great divergence in program implementation. Some teachers design a program about our multicultural heritage; others tend to focus on specific ethnic groups. Certainly the goal of multicultural education is to help students appreciate the contributions of all the people who are part of our cultural life. This goal can be achieved most effectively in a total, integrated social studies program rather than in a fragmented program called "multicultural."

The infusion of multicultural content is both an equity issue and an issue of integrity. When teachers present only the mainstream perspective of academic knowledge, students fail to learn about their own culture and others; they fail to recognize that knowledge reflects human interests and social relationships. For example, most social studies textbooks fail to mention African American and female pioneers. The westward movement has been described primarily through the eyes of white men, usually described as rugged individualists. (Review the discussion of gender issues in Chapter 2.)

Paxton (1999) reviewed and analyzed history books written for adults and for K–12 students. He comments that many texts used by students can be faulted for errors of both commission and omission and criticized for their "Eurocentric male dominated account of the past."

It is interesting and valuable to have students compare historical interpretations using old history books and newly written ones. Suppose that students used social studies texts written in the late 1950s and early 1960s to learn about the Montgomery bus boycott and compared them to Rosa Parks's statements about the boycott. Classroom discussion must be focused on historical interpretation and author perspective. Still another means to gain an understanding of historical interpretation would be to ask the students to write their own perspective of "How would you feel if you were Rosa Parks and you were expected to give up your bus seat?" Other means for historical interpretation will be discussed later.

Moral Education

The work of developmental psychologist Lawrence Kohlberg has been influential in motivating interest in moral education programs. (Review the discussion on stages of moral development in Chapter 2.) Kohlberg believed that children need to be confronted with moral dilemmas to improve their moral reasoning. Teaching strategies designed to help students perceive that there is not necessarily one best answer to moral dilemmas generally follow this pattern:

1. Presentation of the dilemma (whole class listens to or reads the dilemma)
2. Opportunity for students to think aloud; consideration of the question, "What's the problem?" (whole-class discussion)
3. Reasoning: Why did it happen? What should be the response to this dilemma? What will happen now as a consequence of the dilemma? (small-group discussions)

The teacher's role during moral education strategies is that of a facilitator, encouraging discussion and helping students learn to reason. It is not the teacher's job to preach. Selecting appropriate situations for elementary and middle school students may focus on values that young students are concerned about, such as the following:

Honesty	Helping
Friendship	Courage
Caring	Respect
Loyalty	Compassion
Justice	

Strategies for handling anger and conflict should also be included in moral education.

HOW IS SOCIAL STUDIES ORGANIZED FOR INSTRUCTION?

The organization of related and sequenced segments of work is described as a *unit of study*. Teaching units in the social studies may be as short as a week or as long as a semester. The selection of a unit of work is related to an overall theme. It should conform to school district or state framework guidelines or NCSS standards, and should be designed to meet the needs and interests of a specific group of students. The social studies unit should be planned to integrate subject fields. The content for the unit focuses on social science concepts. Through the concepts, interdisciplinary ideas are interrelated. The theme provides the overarching structure to integrate the curriculum. Illustrative themes and topics were identified earlier in this chapter. The actual unit-planning process was outlined in Chapter 6. The following is a list of concepts typically taught in elementary and middle school classrooms:

acculturation	interdependence
adaptation	justice
artifacts	land use
assimilation	law
behavior	migration
change	motivation
citizenship	multiple causation
communication	needs and wants
community	norms
competition	power and authority
conflict	privacy
cooperation	property
culture	resources
diversity	roles
emigrant	rules
enculturation	scarcity
environment	social control
family	socialization
freedom	space
government	supply and demand
groups	technology
immigrant	time
interaction	

HOW IS SOCIAL STUDIES TAUGHT?

Strategies for teaching are diverse and numerous. They range from reading and discussion to construction, dramatics, projects, and role-playing. Critical-thinking and analytic skills are emphasized; reading and research are featured. Values and human relations skills are often taught through games and simulations. Interviewing and case studies are used. Arts and crafts, music, and dancing are all integrated in the social studies. Many of the aforementioned techniques were described in Part II of this text.

Social studies teaching uses all of the teaching models described in Chapters 5 and 6. The special cooperative learning strategies used by Greg Thomas (see Chapter 8) are appropriate for teaching social studies. A combination of teaching models is often needed during the social studies lesson. For example, a teacher might begin a lesson with concept attainment to ensure that students understand a key concept and then utilize group investigation. Or the teacher might begin a lesson using direct instruction while reading out of a social studies textbook, proceed to role-playing, and then culminate with concept attainment to verify that students understand a specific concept.

The teaching unit is vital to good social studies teaching. Not only are the key concepts and big ideas identified in the unit, but planning ways to integrate other subject fields in social studies is critical to effective instruction. Greg Thomas's use of historical literature (Chapter 8) was relevant to his social studies teaching unit. Using trade books to teach social studies is another very successful strategy, particularly for middle school students.

The classroom environment is very important to the teaching of social studies. The latitude of social studies activities and experiences is so great that an **arranged environment** needs to be considered. The environment for social studies is not only for motivation but to provoke inquiry or serve as a resource for learning.

In a social studies teaching unit, strategies are planned to initiate, develop, and culminate the unit. An **initiation** may be simple or complex. Greg Thomas initiated his unit that included the historic industrial revolution by setting up a factory environment (see the case study on page 222). This beginning was provocative and motivated students' interest.

Development activities are all the experiences that move the unit from beginning to end. If students' inter-est lags during the course of the unit, the teacher may have to find a way to initiate new interest.

The **culmination** serves as a means to evaluate what has been learned and to end the unit. Greg Thomas ended his unit with the production of a class mural. Sometimes dramatic play is an appropriate means to culminate a social studies unit. The production of a play, a mural, or project provides a fine way to let parents know what their children are learning in the social studies. These activities serve as authentic assessment techniques. In addition, they provide means to integrate a number of subject fields.

Reading in Social Studies

During social studies, teachers have the opportunity to develop a variety of reading skills: location skills, reading for details and specific facts, skimming, note taking, proofreading reports and projects, choosing reading selections to fit specific historical time periods, and reading historical fiction. These skills can be taught more efficiently using subject-field textbooks and materials instead of basal readers. However, the reading of subject-field materials presents special problems.

1. *Organizing questions and subheads.* Frequently the organization pattern of social studies, science, and other subject-field texts uses too few questions and

Research Findings

Terence Beck (2008) studied himself as he coped with living as a foreigner during a six-month sabbatical in France. What he learned provided him with greater understanding of how to help ELL students. His suggestions follow.

1. Treat ELL students as intelligent human beings.
2. ELL students try to hide their misunderstandings. Provide suggestions and require high standards for them.
3. Use ELL errors as feedback to your instruction.
4. Encourage peer collaboration.
5. Teach basic concepts that help students understand other concepts.
6. Select a broad range of examples and nonexamples of concepts.
7. Provide visual clues that relate to concepts being taught.

subheads. Major and minor content focuses cannot be differentiated by immature readers. As a consequence, young readers cannot make sense of what they are reading, and they quickly lose interest.

Planning by the teacher can counteract this problem. Using the advance organizer teaching model to introduce and prepare students for the reading assignment will alleviate the problem. (Don't forget to evaluate the lesson, utilizing the organizer, so students integrate what they have learned.) When you provide task instructions to facilitate structuring of the material and help students frame questions about what they are to read, a content outline will emerge, and students will then have the necessary insight and motivation to read.

2. *Concept load.* Another problem has to do with the concept load. Students cannot easily define words like *interdependence*, *culture*, and *change*, and as a result they do not understand what they are reading. The remedy is the same as that in reading instruction. By prescanning the selection to be read and noting the concepts that students will not understand, the teacher can give examples to the students and then allow them to generate their own examples of the concept. The use of the concept attainment teaching model will be useful for this purpose.

3. *Out-of-date texts.* Old textbooks can be updated with new pictures (maps, graphs, cartoons, charts, and photos) and with new information. However, sometimes it is valuable to use old and new information and pictures side by side; by doing this, teachers can help students make comparisons and develop interpretive skills.

Use of Pictures

In primary-grade classrooms, many teachers develop picture files related to their teaching unit. These files are not for bulletin board use, but rather for students' research activities. Pictures can be used to facilitate the development of the following social studies skills:

- Gathering data
- Grouping data
- Comparing and contrasting
- Forming generalizations
- Making inferences
- Making predictions

However, it would be a mistake to believe that students can use pictures without guidance. Young primary-age children will certainly need help. Even older students may have difficulty developing categories. To group data, it is necessary to develop classifications for sorting. As students get better at classifying data, they will learn to develop their own categories.

Sometimes pictures disagree with each other. Paintings of early Revolutionary War battles that appeared in English and U.S. history textbooks are remarkably different. These pictures, now available, can be used for students to form generalizations or to make inferences based on the data. This lesson is more interesting if the students are not told the source of the data.

Older students enjoy cartoons and can be introduced to the political cartoon. Students can be asked to interpret the picture and the words (if there are words). The cartoon can be used to trigger historical research. (See Reader Research at the end of the chapter.) For example:

- What motivated the cartoonist?
- What event is the cartoonist telling us about?
- What is the cartoonist's message?
- Why did this happen?

 ## MARY HOGAN'S CLASSROOM

Small-group research is a very effective teaching strategy in the social studies classroom. Students should be grouped heterogeneously. Let us suppose that in Mary Hogan's second-grade classroom the children are studying cities. Hogan has arranged the students heterogeneously into five groups, and each group is to study a different city in order to answer the question, Why do people live in cities?

The students are using the following types of materials:

- Group A is using a social studies textbook about Japan to learn about Tokyo.
- Group B is viewing pictures about London on the Internet.
- Group C is using teacher-written information about New York City.
- Group D is using a picture file developed by the teacher after her visit to Honolulu.
- Group E is using some chart material, with the teacher assisting them as they read about Atlanta.

Hogan knows that it is important for all students to contribute to a class discussion. For this to happen, the students need unique information. If all groups used the same material, there would be limited contributions during the discussion, and these contributions would be made by a chosen few.

Hogan chose to study five cities because she wanted the students to be able to generalize about the following:

> In what ways are all cities similar?
> In what ways are cities different?

Small-Group Research

This was a personal teaching decision, not a decision that was absolutely necessary.

Teaching Hints: Reading Subject-Field Books

1. Scan the page(s) students are to read.
2. Provide students with headings, questions, subheads—in other words, an advance organizer.
3. Verify that students understand the concepts in the passage. Introduce the concepts through a concept attainment lesson or provide examples and ask students to give examples of the concepts.
4. Use the pictures in the books and ask students to tell you what the pictures are communicating.

Group Investigation

Suppose Mary Hogan had asked the students to plan a city. This lesson would probably follow the preceding lesson. She would group the students heterogeneously, remind them to choose a group leader and a recorder, and then designate places for the groups to work.

The students would begin their task by reviewing what each student knew about the characteristics of cities. If they needed to verify their information, they would be responsible for finding the resources in the classroom. Their work would be enriched because they had been in different groups and used different resources for the previous lesson; their work would also be enriched by their own diversity. Because at least one student in each group could read well, the children would not have a reading problem.

Data Retrieval

For Mary Hogan's students to get to the point where they can make generalizations about the nature of cities, there had to be a system to amass the data that each group brought to the class discussion about the question, "Why do people live in cities?" Hogan's system was to write the pertinent information on the chalkboard and then to guide the students to develop categories and accumulate the data for later use. With her students, she developed a data retrieval chart (Table 9.1).

Table 9.1   Data Retrieval Chart

	Tokyo	*London*	*Honolulu*	*New York*	*Atlanta*
Types of housing	Apartments Houses			Apartments Townhouses Houses	
Types of work Types of services		Police Health Fire Schools			
Types of recreation Types of transportation				Subways Bus Taxi Auto	

Semantic Maps

Semantic maps (Figure 9.1) allow students to visualize information and see how things fit together. They are another way for students to learn to conceptualize and to compile information for application and integration.

In Mary Hogan's group investigation lesson on why people live in cities, the groups could have been asked to develop a semantic map depicting the characteristics of cities. The semantic map could have the question, "What are the characteristics of cities?" in the middle of a sheet of paper. From this focal point, the students would draw arrows illustrating the characteristics. Each set of characteristics would be captioned with a concept about the characteristics of cities. For example, the captions might be "Workers," "Manufacturing," "Commerce," "Services," and "Transportation."

Oral History

Children tend to be fascinated by the experiences of the adults in their lives. Interviewing parents, grand-parents, and other older relatives provides insight into what life was like at earlier times in history. Historical memory reveals cultural stories. By listening to these stories of the past, students learn about symbols, ceremonies, values, and dreams. Learning that Grandma rode in the rumble seat of an automobile made in the 1930s—without a seat belt—and that Grandpa had to crank the car to get it started can motivate study of the early modern historical period.

Oral history projects can be initiated by inviting guests into the classroom to tell about the important happenings in their lives. Asking guests where they live and when they moved into their neighborhood can initiate a study of the community. Students are often surprised to find out how a community has changed as a consequence of the residents and cultural identity. Students can map their community and highlight the areas that have changed: Did a park disappear or is it a new addition to the neighborhood? Were there hiking trails and empty lots? Were those apartments always there? Who built the houses with the neat picket fences? Who were the students who first attended our school?

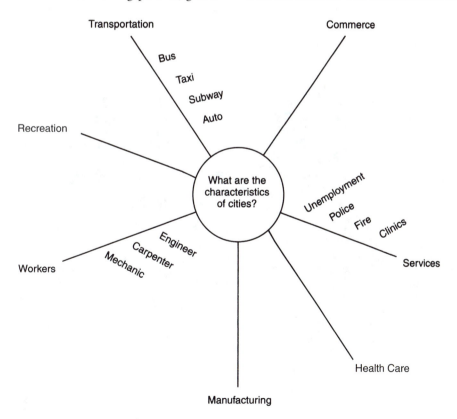

Figure 9.1 An Example of a Semantic Map

Students can study the architecture of the neighborhood, the shrubbery, the rings on trees, recreation sites, water and sewer lines, and fast-food locations, and even visit the local museum's historical archives. All of these ideas for project sites can be initiated through oral reconstruction of the past.

Projects

Project-based learning stimulates students' interest and thinking. Projects should focus on real problems and worthwhile questions and should require meaningful tasks (David, 2008). Projects may be used to unify and integrate a curriculum unit, or a project can be used as a single activity within a unit. Projects may be conceived for students to work on individually or in groups. An individual project may involve a report about an individual or a particular event. Group projects usually require many different skills and involve several individuals or the whole class. (Review Sara Garcia's class research project in Chapter 5.)

Projects can focus on historical problems that require extensive research. For example, suppose students are studying the Civil War period. They might be asked to investigate what the slaves did during the war period: Where did they live? How did they get along? Did they join the Union army? Or they might investigate the Underground Railroad: Who escaped? Who helped the slaves? What risks did people take in order to help? (This question provides a good topic for a moral dilemma: Would you have been willing to take the risk of helping the slaves?) In Greg Thomas's classroom, the students' projects included the study of child labor laws, inventions related to the textile industries (spinning machines, weaving machines, power loom, cotton gin), the steam engine, iron and steel, transportation, and trade.

Projects such as these may require that students use the Internet; read a variety of books, including historical fiction and science texts; create maps of the period; dramatize events; write and produce plays; and construct dioramas and murals. These activities provide an interesting and highly motivating means to involve students in interdisciplinary studies.

SERVICE LEARNING

Service learning gives students the opportunity to contribute to society as citizens. They do not have to wait until they are 18 years old. Service learning is appropri-

Working together on a project requires the practice of social participation skills.

ate for all grade levels. Its roots can be traced to the philosophic beliefs of Dewey and Piaget, who advocated active involvement in learning. The Corporation for National Service defines service learning as follows:

> The term "service-learning" means a method under which students or participants learn and develop through active participation in thoughtfully organized service that:
>
> - is conducted in and meets the needs of a community;
> - is coordinated with an elementary school, secondary school, or community-service program and with the community;
> - helps foster civic responsibility;
> - is integrated into and enhances the core academic curriculum;
> - provides structured time for the students to reflect on the service experience. (Billig, 2000, p. 659)

Teaching Social Studies Skills

Study skills, critical-thinking skills, and social participation skills are taught in the social studies. Many subskills can be identified for each of these skill areas.

Study skills have to do with acquiring information: locating the information, organizing it, interpreting it, and communicating what has been learned. Such skills are best taught at the proper moment. For example, when students encounter a graph that they cannot read, the teacher might say, "Just a moment, boys and girls, some of us may have a difficult time reading this graph. Let's all put our pencils down and look up here while I explain how to read a graph."

Study skill needs in the social studies should also be anticipated. If students will be required to gather information from a variety of sources, then they will need research competencies to locate information in textbooks, encyclopedias, and other reference materials. Because these competencies are critical to many subject fields, they may be taught during social studies or during reading.

Critical-thinking skills, like all other skills, need to be practiced. Such skills include both convergent and divergent thinking. The development of critical-thinking skills in social studies includes the following abilities:

- Compare and contrast ideas, happenings, objects, or periods of time
- Set criteria to group data
- Formulate appropriate questions
- Use evidence to make inferences

Teaching Hints: Service Learning

What kinds of action projects should engage students?

Teaching other students in subject fields
Assisting students with language learning
Serving as docents in libraries and museums and at school sites
Assisting at local animal shelters and clinics
Performing cleanup services at parks, beaches, and local community sites
Repairing graffiti on ruined public street signs, fences, and walls
Providing services for the elderly
Making cookies and bread for the homeless and senior centers
Wrapping Christmas gifts for seniors
Delivering valentines to children and seniors confined in institutions
Helping in local offices of city leaders and congressional representatives
Reading for audiobooks
Participating in stage plays for children and adults in hospitals and senior centers
Raising funds for buying books, software, and computers for schools and libraries
Collecting canned foods for the homeless

- Formulate hypotheses
- Detect bias, stereotyping, ethnocentricity
- Make decisions and judgments

Social participation is another important skill area in the social studies and is considered a major social studies goal. Literature on social participation indicates that students should be involved in group decision-making activities that necessitate the following:

- Cooperation with others
- Observing and sharing observations with others
- Listening to others' viewpoints
- Planning individual and group research or projects in school and the community
- Voluntarily assisting others; accepting assistance from others
- Accepting responsibility and recognizing the need to act
- Identifying and interpreting group agreements and disagreements

- Using persuasion to influence others
- Negotiating and bargaining to influence intergroup action (Lemlech & Marks, 1976, p. 45)

Activities that emphasize social participation help the elementary and middle school student become aware of how people participate in rational decision making, how social change occurred in the past, and how social change will occur in the future.

Social participation strategies are action-oriented; they utilize both small-group and large-group participation. Content typically springs from students' personal experiences in the neighborhood and at school. The newspaper, the student council, and the playground are good sources of information for choosing relevant problems for student investigation.

Conflict Resolution Skills

Personal controversy arises out of real, petty, or imagined disagreements. Gender differences are apparent in the way males and females deal with personal problems or controversy. Chapter 1 discusses some of the reactions that lead to violent behavior. Behavioral responses can lead to bullying and violence at school or out of school. Let's look at a personal conflict between two sixth-grade girls, Jeri and Marcy.

The two girls had been best friends for several years. Suddenly Jeri went out of her way to avoid talking to Marcy. She joined a very popular clique of girls who were interested in social activities more than school academics.

Marcy couldn't understand the transition from friend to foe. Her mother recognized that the two girls did not talk on the telephone any more. One evening Marcy's mother saw her at the computer crying. She looked over her shoulder and read an e-mail that made fun of Marcy. It was addressed to several other girls, but sent to Marcy by mistake.

When reason and empathy failed to sustain her daughter, she decided to consult the homeroom teacher of both girls. The teacher had noticed the gap in the girls' relationship. She commented that (1) Marcy was superior academically to Jeri, and Jeri probably was resentful of Marcy's success; and (2) Marcy was very competitive academically, and as a consequence her classmates felt that Marcy ignored their feelings.

The teacher decided to talk to the two girls and provide them with a hypothetical case study. After consid-

---

erable time the girls shared their feelings about the story and recognized the similarity to their own behavior. Jeri apologized to Marcy for the e-mail to other students, and Marcy explained that she wasn't trying to show off or compete with Jeri or other students. The teacher helped the two students clarify and reflect on their own behavior and suggested that each girl write the other a letter explaining how each felt about their friendship.

Controversial Issues

The chapter-opening vignette about war is an example of a controversial issue that involves students in a current event that they are experiencing in their daily lives via television, newspapers, the Internet, and their own family relationships. There is much that they do not understand, and they probably express opinions that they have heard from others. Controversy in the classroom is used to motivate thinking about citizenship responsibilities, stimulate critical thinking, and involve the students in productive research. It is often a good practice to have students role-play the institutions, businesses, leaders, and common people involved in decision making.

Now let's suppose that the teacher, Karen Adazzio, has already had students gather information about wars in which the United States has been involved. The conflict that was primarily between the United States and Iraq caused students to express several different opinions.

Before students can be involved in role-playing or discussing and writing about an issue, they must first gather "facts" about the issue. In the chapter-opening vignette, the teacher uses some of the students' comments and questions (and some of her own) to write questions on the board. Then the students are involved in research to clarify what is known and what is not known. Their research should reveal not only factual issues, but the values of many of those involved in the conflict.

"The government doesn't pay the soldiers enough. My brother-in-law was in the National Guard and his children and my sister had to move in with us."

"Certain industries, like Halliburton, make a lot of money when there is a war."

"France and Germany disagreed with the war and refused to help out. The United Nations did not agree with the invasion of Iraq. Most of the world did not agree that Iraq had weapons of mass destruction."

"Iraq was responsible for terror attacks on the United States and other nations."

"We needed to go to war to stop the production of weapons of mass destruction, and we needed to break the power of Saddam."

"I think males and females think differently about wars."

"Wars create more problems than they solve."

"It is important to establish a democracy in Iraq, and the Iraqi people want a democracy."

Adazzio: You have certainly identified many of the problems our country has faced. Let's see if we can role-play the different groups involved in these problems. The groups should include a gender group, industry, those who feel the war was necessary, those who feel we should not have invaded Iraq, and the United Nations.

Adazzio divided the students into five groups, each group decided on the perspective of the group they represented. Each group chose one person to represent them, and then all of the representatives engaged in the role-play.

Abraham: People lose their jobs when they are drafted, and their families suffer because there isn't enough income.

Carrina: Well that's not necessarily true; many employers hold the job and some even make up the pay loss.

Rona: War is harder on females than males. Women often have to go to work to support the family and still take care of the children or move in with their families.

Sam: This may all be true, but the government must take care of its citizens and so it was necessary to call up the National Guard because there weren't enough volunteers. Don't forget, this was a war against terrorism.

Anna: A lot of people like war; it's exciting. I think men particularly like to show off their manliness by going to war.

Sam: I don't think you are right, Anna, but men don't have the privilege of refusing to serve.

Andy: Other countries did not want to participate in this war. They felt it was unnecessary and premature. We wanted to invade Iraq just to get rid of Saddam.

Sam: We had good reasons for invading Iraq. They probably were responsible for 9/11.

Andy: (responding in an angry fashion) I don't think that's true, and yeah, many of our corporations made a lot of money from the war and probably still are.

Adazzio: I think you have expressed the opinions of the groups you represent. Who can summarize for us?

Ginny: It was clear that none of the groups were really pleased about the war, though Sam's group seemed to support it; however, I think we need more information from the representative of the United Nations. Also, we need to talk about how the war affects our economy. And Sam and Andy really were angry with each other!

Adazzio: Well done, Ginny. Let's have another enactment by different representatives. Each group needs to coach its player so that you get all the facts out in the open. Let's try to keep our cool when we role-play. After the enactment we will do a summation about the consequences of this war.

A new enactment was presented and the students did a conscientious job of representing the beliefs of their group. Then the whole class had a discussion focused on the consequences of increased terrorism; how the nation needs new tools, machines, and war equipment during a war; the need for the United Nations to take charge when nation building is necessary; and the problems of families when they lose the mother or father and their income.

 Teaching Hints:
Personal Conflict Situations

1. Encourage students to share feelings and emotions.
2. Elicit personal perspectives about the problem.
3. Help students focus on the cause(s) of the problem.
4. Help students project probable consequences of the conflict.
5. Help students consider how to resolve the conflict.
6. Decide on future action to prevent misunderstandings.

This role-play is called a *caucus group* because the whole class is involved in framing what the representatives will say during the enactment. Instead of just observing the role-play, groups are engaged in critical thinking about whether they coached their representative correctly and what else needs to be said. When there is whole-class involvement, role-players tend to be more assertive and less self-conscious.

Resources for Teaching Social Studies

Resources for teaching social studies are almost too numerous to mention. Nonprint materials include pictures, films, tapes, television, realia, records, resource people, and places. Print materials include textbooks, trade books, newspapers, and the Internet. The Appendix contains suggestions of appropriate Web sites.

Obtaining and utilizing resources require anticipation of classroom needs. This is an important management prerequisite for successful social studies teaching. Because it is fairly easy to anticipate what your social studies unit will be, advance planning of resources is not as difficult as it might seem. For example, the teaching of a unit on the community can include photos or a video taken by the teacher of the immediate neighborhood. Magazine pictures can be collected. Software programs may be borrowed from the library. Travel agencies and large corporations often are willing to supply teachers with pictures. Groups like the National Dairy Council or meat industry organizations welcome teachers' requests. Many teachers take advantage of their vacation travels to photograph places that will be useful in teaching social studies.

Field trips (and virtual field trips) also should be planned. The teacher should know what students will see and what they will do on a field trip. The best way to assess this is to take the trip yourself before you take the students. Before the field trip, students should be programmed with questions about what to observe. A walking trip through the neighborhood can be a valuable experience, but only if students are directed to observe some specifics.

Realia can be collected bit by bit and purchased when funds allow. Quite often friends have special objects such as tapestries, knickknacks, or items from personal travel experiences that they are willing to share. Realia can often be borrowed from teacher resource centers.

Videotapes and films can usually be ordered from the school district or county school offices. Many large libraries allow teachers to borrow media, but orders have to be placed well in advance of need.

Print materials include books, maps, graphs, charts, newspapers, and printouts of information from the Internet. (Reading during social studies is discussed in the section titled "How Is Social Studies Taught?") When considering the use of textbooks in the social studies, it is important to remember that grade-level designations are not necessarily pertinent. It is possible to do a community study at almost any grade level, and it is possible to study other societies at many grade levels. Social studies books should be shared rather than designated for a particular classroom and stored on a closet shelf. For preparation purposes, the teacher needs to survey what is available at the school and what is useful for teacher resource purposes and for students' resource needs.

Teaching Hints: Caucus Group Role-Play

1. Motivation for the problem is set by the teacher.
2. The class discusses the problem.
3. Groups are formed to represent varied perspectives.
4. Groups discuss the problem and select a role-player to represent their perspective.
5. The representatives present the role-play.
6. The whole class discusses the enactment.
7. New representatives are selected and a new enactment occurs.
8. A final class discussion summarizes and projects consequences based on the two enactments.

Teaching Hints: Controversial Issues

1. Present a motivating issue for students to discuss.
2. Elicit what students know about the issue.
3. Involve students in research to differentiate facts, opinions, and values.
4. Decide how students will share what they have learned (role-play, writing, class discussion).
5. Culminate by having students synthesize what they have learned and by differentiating among facts and values.
6. Have students project the probable consequences of the current controversy.

ASSESSMENT: FINDING OUT WHAT STUDENTS KNOW— AND DON'T KNOW

Teachers need to diagnose what a child knows (knowledge) and what a child can do (skills), as well as the student's learning characteristics, attitudes about learning and working with others, and ability to work cooperatively with others.

Greg Thomas needs to know whether his students understand the concept of adaptation. One of the easiest ways for Thomas to find out is to ask his students the meaning of *adaptation*. If his students can define it and provide examples both of what the concept is and what it is not, then Thomas may feel relatively confident that the concept of adaptation can be used by the students as a tool to study human behavior. Although it is fairly simple to write a paper-and-pencil test to find out what students know, it may not be necessary for diagnostic purposes.

The ability to use study skills is easily diagnosed. If students are able to extract and interpret information from charts, tables, pictures, or cartoons, then the teacher can be confident that students have mastered a certain level of competence. On the other hand, if students are unable to utilize reference materials to locate information, then the teacher knows that reference skills need to be taught.

Critical-thinking skills can be similarly diagnosed. Given evidence about certain events, students are asked to suggest probable conclusions. If they cannot do so, then they have not mastered that skill. Skill diagnosis should be systematically performed by the teacher. This can best be done with the use of checklists. Chapter 7 provides examples for use in the social studies.

Interpersonal and social participation skills, such as listening to and respecting other's opinions or recognizing one's own and others' biases, can be diagnosed by observing students. During a whole-class or small-group discussion, the teacher can observe how students work with their peers. Observation of students at lunch or on the playground also reveals a great deal about social participation skills.

Growth can be measured by teacher-made tests. These tests are often more reliable than standardized tests because the test can be designed to measure what was actually taught. The NCSS Advisory Committee on Testing and Evaluation recommends that evaluation instruments focus on curriculum goals and objectives, measure content and process, and be selected for instructional, diagnostic, and prescriptive purposes. The main purpose for evaluation should be to improve teaching and learning.

AUTHENTIC ASSESSMENT

Authentic assessment focuses on using what students actually produce to learn what students know. Suppose that Karen Adazzio wants to test her students' social science skills and whether they understand that all social groups have a purpose and a means to make decisions, and that these decisions affect group interaction and the overall structure of the group. She could ask her students to give an oral report or write a written report according to the following instructions:

- Investigate two social groups (at school or out of school) and identify the purpose of each group.
- Interview at least three members of each group.
- Ask each person the same questions. (Include the questions in your report and use follow-up questions, if needed.)
- Describe how the group is organized.
- Describe the decision-making process for the group.
- Identify ways in which group members support each other.
- Discuss what happens if members do not agree with each other.
- Make a note of differences in opinion.
- Decide whether the group serves its purpose and provide evidence to support your conclusion.

Note that this type of assessment crosses subject matter lines because students need to use a variety of skills. In addition, the test is related to precisely what the students are studying—it is context bound.

Assessment should provide information to enlighten curriculum and instruction. If what students produce does not make sense, then you know they did not derive meaning from content and instruction. There should be a relationship among the content that is taught, the instructional process (the delivery system), and the activities students are asked to perform. They should all add up to accomplish the goals that were set. In using authentic assessment to inform curriculum and instruction, it is extremely important that what students are asked to do corresponds to the social science goals. Also, what students are asked to do should promote student learning and reflection.

RUBRICS

Rubrics provide a means to assist students develop and self-evaluate their social studies projects. Karen Adazzio's students, who were asked to write a group report about their research and discussion, may want to work with a rubric. Table 9.2 provides an example of what her students might create for their controversial war project. (Review rubrics in Chapter 7.)

CLASSROOM MANAGEMENT

Classroom management during social studies is no different than during reading or math, in the sense that the teacher still needs to perform planning, organizing, anticipating, arranging, and monitoring tasks. However, certain aspects of classroom management may be more significant when teaching a subject field like social studies. For example, if students are to use a variety of instructional materials (books, media, pictures, computers, and so on) and use them in different places in the classroom because of grouping arrangements, then all of the classroom management components assume greater importance. The teacher needs to anticipate what learning materials students will need, where these materials will be used, how students will be grouped, and how evaluation will be handled. Monitoring behavior and learning needs become crucial to the success of the lesson.

Suppose that you are going to teach a unit that will ask students to compare traditional Japanese culture with contemporary urban culture. In the classroom, you will have a number of Japanese artifacts for students to see and touch. These may include a traditional tea service, robes, musical instruments, women's shoes, and a diary of a young girl.

Before attempting this strategy (an arranged environment), you will need to consider the following:

- How many students should visit the items on display at one time?
- While waiting for a turn to see the items, what will the rest of the class be doing?
- How much time will be needed for the activity?
- Because you want to find out what students know (and don't know), how will you listen in and take notes?
- How will you debrief students after they have seen the exhibits? (Whole-class discussion?)

The trick to social studies classroom management is the anticipation component. The teacher needs to think about and plan for the following:

- Where students will work
- What resource tools will be needed
- How the lesson will be motivated
- How much time will be needed
- What problems might be anticipated
- How evaluation will be accomplished

THE VIRTUAL FIELD TRIP

Although field trips are enjoyable learning experiences at any time during a unit, they are particularly valuable as a motivating, initiating experience and as a culmi-

Table 9.2 Controversial Issue Group Project

	Excellent	Satisfactory	Needs Improvement
Organization	Clear, has an introduction, controversial issues explained, conclusions and consequences identified.	Organized, issues explained, consequences need to stem from content	Lacks organization, issues unexplained, conclusions and consequences unclear
Content	In-depth discussion of beliefs and data from resources	Some discussion of beliefs, resource data limited	Discussion of data limited, few resources utilized
Use of resources	Utilizes class discussion, Internet, newspapers, and journals; well documented	Some variety of resources and group discussion used, documentation needed	Few documents used, class discussion ignored
Group interaction	Opinions of group members well documented, cooperative work in writing report, good use of time	Some disagreements in what should be included in report, adequate use of time	Group unmotivated, time not considered, poor coordination
Writing mechanics	Well written and edited	Spelling and grammar errors, more editing needed	Clarity and editing needed

nating experience. The **virtual field trip** using the Internet is similar to its real-life counterpart because it is a semicontrolled, structured experience limited to sites that the teacher has designated. Suggestions for planning the virtual field trip include the following:

1. Preview the sites you will have students visit.
2. Prepare students for the trip. Explain the purpose and create an advance organizer that tells students what they are to look for and what they are to do. This may be in the form of an outline or questions that integrate the experience. Divide students into small groups for their Internet work.
3. Begin with a specific URL for students to search. Then insist that students keep a list of the linking sites and addresses they explore.
4. When students have completed their simulated field trip, they should work in their small groups to discuss the assignment.
5. The field trip may be a significant component in students' projects.

MULTITEXT READING, DIFFERENTIATING INSTRUCTION, AND USING THE INTERNET

The use of more than one textbook to study the content of social studies is characteristic of most classrooms. Perhaps the custom originated because many school districts failed to buy enough textbooks for each child to have a copy. However, when studying historical events, it is much more valuable to read what different authors have to say to detect bias and to compare the authors' interest in the event. Another good reason for using more than one social studies textbook is that most students cannot read at the same level. By utilizing more than one textbook, it is much easier to find print material appropriate to students' ability levels. Because the social studies book is a resource, each text is a little bit different; by utilizing more than one textbook, the students learn research methods. Multitext reading is a fine approach to adapt textbook reading to ability levels and to teach research skills, but it does not respond to learning-style differences.

The Internet provides still another means to diversify and enrich the input for students. Newspapers can be read using the Internet. Internet Yellow Pages can be used by students to find the addresses they need for their research studies. However, the students may need a skill lesson to learn how to use the Yellow Pages for

Teaching Hints: Using Primary Resources

1. Call attention to who wrote the document and its purpose. (Ask students "who" and "why.")
2. When was the document written?
3. Why is the document valuable?
4. What does the document tell us about our social/cultural history (time, events, problems, people, culture, beliefs)?

finding information. Although using the computer is appealing to many students, its use needs to be supervised and carefully guided.

Students should be taught the difference between *primary* and *secondary* resources. If students were to visit the museum and view archival records, they would experience observing and using primary resources. When they read a personal account, such as a diary of personal experiences or an oral history by someone involved in an experience, they are obtaining primary data. But when they use the classroom texts and most information on the Internet, they are using secondary resources, which may not be as reliable as primary data. An example is the crime scene highlighted on television programs where individuals are considered reliable only if they were actual witnesses at the scene.

LEARNING CENTERS/STATIONS IN SOCIAL STUDIES

The learning center provides a means to enrich and expand social studies teaching. The learning center technique can be used to reinforce skills, teach concepts, and differentiate instruction to accommodate learning-style needs. The learning center may be planned for use by an individual or for small-group work.

The Direction Game

Social Studies, Mathematics—Lower Grades

Objective. To reinforce spatial directions (north, south, east, west)

Materials. Game board constructed of tagboard, 20 pictures, spinner, playing pieces

Assessment. Cooperative play, recognition of directions

Procedures

1. Construct a square game board of tagboard with 120 squares.
2. Collect 20 small pictures of places in the neighborhood (gas station, stores, fire station, homes) to place on 20 squares.
3. In the center of the game board, designate a START square.
4. Write a rules card.
   - Place the pictures on the game board. Space them around the board.
   - Take turns spinning the spinner. Tell the other players the direction you will move your playing piece.
   - If you land on a picture, you may take it.
   - The person who has the most pictures wins the game.

New Business

Social Studies, Language Arts—Upper Grades

Objectives. To reinforce reference skills, decision making, social participation

Materials. Task card, fictional Yellow Pages, want ads, map of a city, books about how to study a community, pictures of businesses in a fictional city

Assessment. Group evaluation of social participation skills (see Chapter 10). Provide time for group sharing of decisions after all groups have used the center. Provide an evaluation card with a list of possible choices, if desired.

Procedure

1. Write task card instructions:
   - If you were to start a new business in the fictional city of Abercrombie, what would it be? List the steps your group will follow to make the decisions.
   - Choose a recorder and a group leader.
   - Decide what each person will do to gather data.

To Simplify. Use easier materials; control the data.

To Extend. Increase the data to be used.

Choose a Role

Social Studies, Language Arts—All Grade Levels

Objectives. To reinforce communication skills, data-gathering skills, comprehension skills

Assessment. Class discussion, after the learning center has been used, about the importance of insightful questions and the authenticity of role-playing

Procedures

1. Write role card instructions:
   - Choose a role.
   - Study the role using pictures, books, information sheets, and audiotapes.
   - Play the role when you are interviewed.
2. Write interviewer card instructions:
   - Write questions for an interview.
   - Play the role of an interviewer.
   - Guess the role of the person you are interviewing.
3. Develop roles related to a historic time period (pioneer in colonial America, surveyor, shipbuilder, mill owner, pirate) or to careers in contemporary society, such as community helpers for primary children.
4. After students play the role of the interviewer and the interviewee, they should exchange task cards, with a new role chosen and with the new interviewer writing new questions to ask.

Beliefs

Social Studies, Science, Health, Language Arts— Grades 5–8

Objectives. To categorize concept attributes and develop problem-solving, decision-making, and research skills

Materials. Text materials, pictures, media

Assessment. Use of evidence to prove or disprove hypotheses

Procedures

1. Students are given text and pictures related to patterns of behaviors, customs, and beliefs of specific groups of people or beliefs/practices of society, for example, beliefs about AIDS. These beliefs may be associated with cultural ideas or scientific or environmental beliefs.
2. Included in the learning packet is a retrieval chart.
3. Students are to write several hypotheses about the beliefs and practices.
4. Hypotheses are to be supported with evidence from the written material or the pictures.

Road Maps

Geography, Mathematics, Language Arts— Grades 4–8

Objectives. To learn to use a map scale, calculate distance, and write an itinerary

Materials. Maps, paper, pencils, rulers

Assessment. Students may check each other; answer sheets may be created for specific distances.

Procedures
1. Using a road map, students decide (a) where they want to go and (b) where they are starting from. (Or the teacher may choose designated points.)
2. Students need to decide on the route they will take, traveling by automobile, and identify the route on paper (for example, Highway 101 to Route 33 to Route 1). Students must identify the directions in which they will be traveling.
3. Students must use the map scale and numbers identified on the road map to calculate distances between the starting point and the ending point. Rulers will be needed to measure distances.

To Simplify. Designate set points of travel (such as Los Angeles to San Francisco) and keep distances reasonably close together.

To Extend. Use a variety of maps (vegetation, topographic, population) and ask students to read the legend and identify natural vegetation, sites they will visit, mountains, lakes, deserts, and elevations.

Characteristics of Learning Centers in Social Studies

- Learning centers in social studies integrate fields of study. The Direction Game uses social studies and counting skills in mathematics.
- The learning centers are social. While it is true that a learning center can be used to individualize instruction and it is possible to design a learning contract for a student using a center, the purposes of the centers proposed here involve goals related to social studies. These centers are for two or more students and promote interaction, communication, and decision making.
- The learning center provides an element of fun and satisfaction. The use of the center should be different from typical classroom activities.

- The center is arranged to attract and motivate students. Materials do not have to be elaborate, but they can be colorful and appealing. The center can utilize bulletin board space, or a special area can be designed to create the illusion of privacy.
- The center is purposeful and meaningful. Gimmicks are not needed. The activities should be designed to accomplish specific learning objectives.

Learning Packets

Learning packets are sometimes called *learning modules* or *instructional modules.* They are most typically used in upper elementary and middle school grades. Their primary purpose is to individualize instruction. Similar to the learning center, they often integrate fields of study. The author believes they should provide both fun and satisfaction. Learning packets in the social studies are not intended as a programmed, behavioral approach to teaching; instead, they provide a means to differentiate content and processes, and what students produce. Although packets are often used by a single student, they can be used in pairs or for small groups of students. Most of the learning center examples can be organized into learning packets.

SUMMARY

The purpose of social studies is to cultivate social behaviors through the teaching of group process skills. Social studies should prepare students for citizenship responsibilities. In the social studies, students learn skills, values, and beliefs, and how to participate in a democratic society.

The National Council for the Social Studies recommends that content be selected using 10 organizing topics. Social studies encompasses diverse topics and programs such as global education, law education, environmental education, moral education, and the integration of multicultural education.

The planning of a teaching unit helps organize the concepts and learning experiences for teaching social studies. Small- or large-scale projects, including service learning, may be used as learning experiences for the body of the unit. Learning experiences are diverse and include constructivist activities, print and nonprint experiences, oral history, and service learning. Study skills, critical-thinking skills, and participation skills are taught in the social studies.

Student knowledge can be determined through both formal means (tests) and informal projects. Observation of group work provides information on social participation skills and critical thinking. Authentic assessment is valuable and crosses subject field lines as students develop reports and projects.

Resources provide means to differentiate content and process for students. Students should use both primary and secondary resources. Planning is critical in the social studies. Classroom management needs to focus on organizational, resource, spatial, and time needs.

PORTFOLIO ACTIVITY

Demonstrate through lesson planning that you provide students with multiple paths to knowledge. Identify a problem you will pose to students and then discuss the different activity formats that will allow students to (a) connect the problem to prior knowledge, (b) identify their own ideas or opinions, and (c) plan their own investigation.

 ## DISCUSSION QUESTIONS AND APPLICATION EXERCISES

1. Design a social studies learning center or a learning packet to differentiate instruction for gifted students in your classroom.
2. You are to deliver a talk to parents about the social studies at Back to School night. What will you tell parents about how the social studies curriculum facilitates the transfer of what is learned in school to the outside-school lives of students?
3. Your students are studying the concept of culture. Develop a data retrieval chart using the components of culture.
4. Privacy is a basic value in a democratic society. Develop a rule-making activity focused on privacy needs. Decide how to divide the class into groups so that each group will develop its own rule. Decide how to motivate the activity and how to evaluate the rules generated by the groups.

5. Develop a list of ideas on how primary and middle school students can participate in their community through service learning and how upper-grade and middle school students can participate in school, city, or state affairs.
6. Identify a motivating activity to initiate a study of global problems; identify a culminating activity for the same unit that can be used for authentic assessment.
7. Design a research lesson that requires a group of students to use the Internet and integrates subject fields.

READER RESEARCH

Political cartoonists have influenced campaigns, issues, and elections. Who were some of the great ones? What elections were influenced? What favored statements did the cartoons make? How would you use the cartoons in the classroom? Should cartoons be considered historical documents? Why?

 ## TECHNOLOGY APPLICATION

Plan a virtual field trip for your students. Prepare by visiting the site(s). Provide a URL to begin the assignment. Divide the class into groups, and assign specific topics for each group. Decide how you will monitor students' work on the Internet and what other resources students will use.

Answers to Greg Thomas's Use of Social Studies Topics

> Time, continuity, and change
> Culture
> People, places, and environments
> Power, authority, and governance
> Production, distribution, and consumption
> Science, technology, and society

Internet sites of interest in teaching social studies appear in Appendix A.

Small-group work projects teach cooperative work habits and improve students' research skills.

CHAPTER 10

Mathematics Education

This chapter examines how children learn mathematics concepts and links that process to the Piagetian stages of development and Vygotskian thinking about social interaction. Five content strands and five process strands are identified, along with six principles that govern the teaching of the mathematics program. The *Principles and Standards for School Mathematics* was produced by the National Council of Teachers of Mathematics (NCTM) in April 2000.

Current directions in math education will be highlighted in this chapter, with appropriate teaching episodes to demonstrate processes. Inquiry and constructivist learning are contrasted with a traditional orientation to teaching mathematics. Both small-group cooperative learning and whole-class discussion during mathematics are examined, along with research studies concerning cooperative learning during mathematics.

The importance of concrete instructional materials is emphasized, including the use of the calculator and computer. The special issues that receive attention in this chapter include gender, race, class, and culture; integration of subject fields; inclusion suggestions; performance assessment; reporting to parents; and mathematics learning centers.

Advance Organizer

The following questions are intended to guide your reading and understanding of the content of this chapter.

1. What are several significant purposes of the mathematics program?
2. Why is the use of concrete materials important to the development of mathematical ideas?
3. How do the Piagetian concepts of reversibility and transitivity relate to mathematics education?
4. How do Vygotskian theories about social interaction affect math education?
5. What are several content and process strands in mathematics and how do they differ?
6. Can you identify several objectives for each content strand and describe the process to be used?
7. Can you distinguish between lower-grade and upper-grade mathematics and describe the sequence of mathematics instruction in a lower-grade classroom?
8. Why do mathematics specialists advocate inquiry learning?
9. In what ways is there a conflict between behavioral and developmental psychologists related to math content and method?
10. What instructional materials should be available for use in the math program?
11. In what ways can calculators and computers be used in the classroom?
12. How do gender, race, class, and culture affect mathematics achievement for some students?
13. What planning considerations should be anticipated for teaching mainstreamed students in math?
14. How can you assess progress in mathematics?
15. How can a learning center that you create be used to reinforce a math concept?

INTASC

INTASC Standards

In mathematics, students need to be able to ask themselves, "What is the problem? What do I need to do to solve the problem? How is this problem like others that I have learned to solve?" The teacher needs to know how to trigger these thoughts from their students and assess their ability to do so. This requires professional competence in Standards 1–10.

Professional Lexicon

automatize To perform mathematics skills (procedures) effortlessly.

cardinal numbers Numbers such as 1 and 2 that indicate quantity but not order.

conceptual knowledge The understanding of concepts, relations, and patterns to make sense of mathematics.

functions Relationships among quantities and how they can be made explicit without dependence on symbolic example.

ordinal numbers Numbers that indicate order or position in a series, such as *first, second,* and *third.*

procedural knowledge Knowing how to use symbols and rules to do mathematics.

relations The associations that are made as objects are counted or compared or related in some way with other objects or pairs.

reversibility A Piagetian concept applicable to the preoperational-level student who may not realize that a number is not affected by the ordering process.

transitivity A Piagetian concept applicable to the individual who can or cannot coordinate a series of relations using physical objects ("This stick is longer than . . .").

Jana was walking along the beach when she saw a gigantic footprint in the sand. "Look at the size of that footprint," she said to her friend Enriqué.

Enriqué was stunned. "My goodness," he said, "How tall do you think that person was?"

"Whoever it was must be a giant," said Jana. "How can we figure out the height of the person who made this footprint?"

HOW DO CHILDREN LEARN MATHEMATICS CONCEPTS?

Problems like the one in the chapter-opening vignette typify the changing curriculum in mathematics. The standards shift the emphasis of mathematics programs from rote memorization of formulas and algorithms to reasoning processes and constructivist learning in order to understand algorithms.

A sound mathematics program emphasizes specific content and the means for acquiring the content. Through the study of mathematics, students learn to work with and communicate quantitative relationships. Mathematics can help students solve real-life problems by providing them with an abstract model for analysis. The study of geometrical and numerical ideas should encourage the solution of practical problems and contribute to students' personal satisfaction.

The mathematics curriculum focuses on significant mathematical concepts that are taught in a coherent plan and articulated through the grades. The curriculum should not be just fun activities but instead should require logical reasoning and independence of thought rather than the production of correct answers. Learning experiences need to progress from the concrete to the abstract, with an emphasis on real-world problems to generate students' interest and utilize their prior knowledge. The mathematics program should provide an understanding and appreciation for mathematics concepts, structure, and terminology.

The students' ability to use proportional reasoning is tested by the chapter-opening problem, and the students could be asked to prepare a report describing their thinking process. The teacher could draw a footprint on the chalkboard or display one on the bulletin board. The students' ability to communicate effectively through the presentation, explaining the thinking process, ideas, graphs, formulas, and calculations, would all be considered in the assessment of students' mathematical thinking.

The ability to think logically affects the learning of mathematics concepts. Copeland (1982) linked Piagetian stages of development with mathematics learning. At the preoperational level, the student uses sensory impressions when confronted with the question, "Are there more objects in one set than in the other, or are the sets the same?" See Figure 10.1.

At this level of development, the student would respond that there are more objects in the first set than in the second. The critical element is the spacing of the two rows. Only by making the two rows of equal length will the student believe that the two sets are equal. Not until the concrete operational stage will the child recognize that the number is conserved or invariant and that the arrangement of the set does not affect the number of objects. Primary teachers need to know that even though the primary student counts the number of objects in each set, the student may believe that the spaced row of objects has more objects than the set that is not spread out.

Students are ready for formal abstract-level mathematics at approximately age 11, when they can think at the formal operational level. However, Copeland cautioned that most 11- and 12-year-old children still need experiences using concrete materials to understand many mathematical ideas.

The concepts of **reversibility** and **transitivity** are useful to understand how children learn mathematics concepts. At the preoperational level, students do not realize that number is not affected by the ordering process. Students will count objects from left to right and right to left before discovering that the set is the same from both directions. Not until students are 6 or 7 years old, at the concrete operational level of thought, will they understand the logic of reversibility.

Transitivity refers to the ability of the individual to coordinate a series of **relations** using physical objects. For example, if students have several sticks of varying lengths, they can indicate which stick is longest, shortest, longer than another, and shorter than another. They are aware that there is a relationship among the sticks, making one stick longer than the preceding stick but shorter than the successive stick.

According to Piaget (1969), physical and logical-mathematical experiences with objects are significant foundations for the development of deductive thought. Concrete activities with objects should begin during the nursery school years. The use of **cardinal numbers** (1, 2, *how many*) and **ordinal numbers** (*first, second*) begins during the preschool years. Activities during both the preschool and primary school years should focus on matching objects using one-to-one correspondence to determine which group has more, fewer, or as many objects. Number names (*one, two*) can be associated with the matching activity along with practice in reading and writing numerals.

Experiences with logical thinking should begin with concrete activities. Children will not learn seriation through observation; they must have the opportunity to order objects from large to small or tall to short. Varied experiences are necessary for logical thought development.

Experiences with geometry should focus on exploring shapes, developing spatial sense, and recognizing geometry in the classroom and home. Students should be encouraged to construct their own objects and figures using a variety of materials.

Measurement ideas should be developed through activities of sorting and comparing length, mass, volume, area, and time. Children should be encouraged to verbalize about what they perceive ("This stick is shorter than or longer than _____"). Opportunities need to be provided for students to develop the concepts of conservation and transitivity of length.

Mathematical ideas depend on discovering and creating patterns and classifying and comparing physical objects. Students lacking these experiences during the preschool years will need direct experiences during the primary school program. The primary program should be characterized by informal and exploratory experiences (Figure 10.2). Observation of students as they work with physical objects should reveal whether they can compare and classify objects and whether they understand symmetry and balance. The primary child should be encouraged to verbalize about experiences involving numbers and to ask questions about activities. Many primary teachers find that cooking experiences develop vocabulary and natural interest in mathematics; for this reason it is a favored primary activity.

Vygotsky's theories also provide understanding about ways to assist students in mathematics. Working

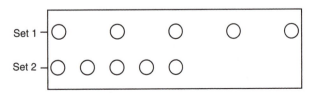

Figure 10.1 Set Size

At the concrete operational level of thought, the student will recognize that if two glasses contain an equal amount of water, the amount of water will not change when water from one glass is poured into a tall, skinny glass.

Figure 10.2 Comparing Volume

in small heterogeneous groups provides interaction experiences that allow students to learn from each other. When students work with older and more capable peers, they are able to profit from assistance and gain insight on how to approach new problems. (This would be a good time to review the work of Piaget and Vygotsky in Chapter 2.)

THE MATHEMATICS CURRICULUM

What Content Should Be Taught?

The mathematics program has typically been organized into major content strands. The NCTM committee identified five content strands and five process strands that should be taught. The content strands are:

1. Number and operations
2. Algebra
3. Geometry
4. Measurement
5. Data analysis and probability

The five process strands are the means for acquiring content knowledge:

1. Problem solving
2. Reasoning and proof
3. Communication
4. Connections
5. Representation

The strands represent the curriculum from pre-kindergarten through grade 12; however, there are different emphases and expectations at different grade levels. For example, number and operations are emphasized from pre-kindergarten to grade 2, but there is less emphasis on this strand in the middle school. Algebra receives greater emphasis in grades 6 through 8 than in the primary grades.

The new document *Principles and Standards for School Mathematics* (NCTM, 2000) lists six principles as the basic underlying philosophic foundation for the curriculum. These principles are as follows:

The equity principle: This refers to the need for high expectations, assistance, and support for all students.

The curriculum principle: This principle emphasizes that the focus of content should be on significant mathematics concepts, not just an aggregation of activities.

The teaching principle: In Chapter 6 (Figure 6.1), I emphasized the need for teachers' pre-knowledge—not only of subject matter, but of what students know and don't know. The intent of this principle is that teachers assess students' knowledge and then provide them with challenging and appropriate content.

The learning principle: This principle focuses on instructional processes. Using students' prior knowledge and experience, instruction must help students link new knowledge with old by involving students in active, constructivist experiences.

The assessment principle: Assessment should match instruction and content; it should inform the teacher and the student by providing useful information.

The technology principle: Technology must be integrated with the teaching process. This means that students need to receive instruction using a variety of electronic tools to extend comprehension, reasoning, and problem-solving skills.

The strands are intended to provide a means to balance content of the mathematics program. It is not intended that a strand be designated at a particular grade level. The strands are to be integrated with each other and run throughout the program. Some strands need to be used in conjunction with other strands.

Number and Operations

This strand emphasizes number systems and how they are used. Techniques for computing are taught. Experiences include counting and comparison activities using concrete sets of objects. Basic addition and multiplication facts are presented. Manipulative materials are used to motivate the development of computational algorithms. To develop students' abilities to work with abstract symbols, informal experiences are provided with physical models. Suggested activities include building with blocks, sorting objects of different shapes and sizes, sorting and classifying objects, fitting objects into each other, arranging objects by size and shape, experimenting with balance, recognizing positional relationships and symmetry, and discovering patterns. The standards specifically state that students should be able to do the following:

- Understand numbers, ways of representing numbers, relationships among numbers, and number systems
- Understand meaning of operations and how they relate to one another
- Compute fluently and make reasonable estimates (NCTM, 2000, p. 32)

Algebra

This strand is used in the context of students' experiences and problem situations. Algebra represents the language of variables, operations, **functions,** and symbol manipulation. Algebra can be taught in a variety of ways to children at almost any grade level. Number sentences and patterns can be used to illustrate algebraic thinking for even young elementary children. Algebraic expressions (symbols) can be taught to students in grades 3–5. For example, they will need to learn that the symbol x does not mean multiplication; "5 times x" may be written $5x$. The standards state that students should be able to do the following:

- Understand patterns, relations, and functions
- Represent and analyze mathematical situations and structures using algebraic symbols
- Use mathematical models to represent and understand quantitative relationships
- Analyze change in various contexts (NCTM, 2000, p. 37)

Geometry

Through geometry, students link mathematics to space and form. The geometric concepts of line, point, plane, and three-dimensional space are developed. Once again manipulative objects are used for investigation, exploration, and discovery. Awareness of geometry in the environment is encouraged by utilizing art forms from business and industry, from nature, and from cultural experiences. Major topics include geometric figures, reasoning/logical thinking, coordinate geometry, and measuring geometric figures. The standards state that students should be able to do the following:

- Analyze the characteristics and properties of two- and three-dimensional geometric shapes and develop mathematical arguments about geometric relationships
- Specify locations and describe spatial relationships using coordinate geometry and other representational systems
- Apply transformations and use symmetry to analyze mathematical situations
- Use visualization, spatial reasoning, and geometric modeling to solve problems (NCTM, 2000, p. 41)

Measurement

Measurement is considered a key strand because understanding of measurement permeates our daily life. Simple measurement tools are used to develop concepts of measuring distance, capacity, and the passage of time. Topics include arbitrary units of measure, standard units of measure, the approximate nature of measurement, and estimation in measurement.

The purpose of arbitrary units of measure as instructional content is to encourage students to measure using differing units in order to discover the need to compare objects using common properties and accepted units of measure. Techniques of measurement used during the arbitrary units are utilized when students recognize the need for standard units. As students use measuring tools, the concepts of approximation and estimation are taught. The development of the educated-guess skill needs to be expounded as students practice measurement using measurement tools and observation skills. The standards state that students should be able to do the following:

- Understand measurable attributes of objects and the units, systems, and processes of measurement

Measuring concepts include distance, capacity, and the passage of time.

- Apply appropriate techniques, tools, and formulas to determine measurements (NCTM, 2000, p. 44)

Data Analysis and Probability

Appreciation of human achievement and a healthy skepticism of capital T–type truths necessitate understanding, interpreting, and analyzing data that affect our everyday lives. Statistics involves collecting, organizing, and interpreting data, as well as making inferences from data. Experiences beginning in kindergarten should involve gathering, organizing, and analyzing data. (Examples are provided in Chapter 6.) Topics include collection, organization, and representation of data; interpretation of data; counting techniques; and probability. Problems in science, health, physical education, and social studies provide good content experiences for students to use in the collection, organization, and representation of data. The standards state that students should be able to do the following:

- Formulate questions that can be addressed with data and collect, organize, and display relevant data to answer them

- Select and use appropriate statistical methods to analyze data
- Develop and evaluate inferences and predictions that are based on data
- Understand and apply basic concepts of probability (NCTM, 2000, p. 48)

Problem Solving

Problem solving is viewed as an important goal of the mathematics program and requires that the student draw on prior experience. Our society values good problem-solvers. Problem solving requires curiosity, concentration, persistence, risk taking, and self-confidence. Learning math content depends on the ability to solve problems. Specific standards state that the student should be able to do the following:

- Build new mathematical knowledge through problem solving
- Solve problems that arise in mathematics and in other contexts
- Apply and adapt a variety of appropriate strategies to solve problems
- Monitor and reflect on the process of mathematical problem solving (NCTM, 2000, p. 52)

Reasoning and Proof

Reasoning and proof are the means for verifying understanding. They allow the individual to evaluate and judge. Although reasoning and proof are significant processes in mathematics, they are critical in all aspects of life and all subject fields. Specific standards state that students should be able to do the following:

- Recognize reasoning and proof as fundamental aspects of mathematics
- Make and investigate mathematical conjectures
- Develop and evaluate mathematical arguments and proofs
- Select and use various types of reasoning and methods of proof (NCTM, 2000, p. 56)

Communication

When students are required to explain their reasoning process to others, they not only share their own perceptions, but they gain insight into their own thinking process because sharing requires the organization of thought. Communication helps the individual reflect on his or her own thinking. Because communication is vital to learning mathematics, it is important that students work on interesting and relevant problems that open the door to class discussion. Specific standards state that students should be able to do the following:

- Organize and consolidate their mathematical thinking through communication
- Communicate their mathematical thinking coherently and clearly to peers, teachers, and others
- Analyze and evaluate the mathematical thinking and strategies of others
- Use the language of mathematics to express mathematical ideas precisely (NCTM, 2000, p. 60)

Connections

To enhance students' understanding of mathematical concepts, it is important to link mathematical ideas and topics to other subject fields and to a variety of contextual problems. Although the NCTM has identified five content strands, they are not independent ideas; each is connected to the others and students must learn to build on each strand and recognize the interconnections. Specific standards state that students should be able to do the following:

- Recognize and use connections among mathematical ideas

- Understand how mathematical ideas interconnect and build on one another to produce a coherent whole
- Recognize and apply mathematics in contexts outside mathematics (NCTM, 2000, p. 64)

Representation

When young children learn to write their name using letters, they learn that the collection of letters represents the name. The same is true in mathematics; students must learn different ways to express ideas, and so representation is both the idea itself and the process. For example, a graph is a means of expressing relationships and communicating the product of specific information. Specific standards state that students should be able to do the following:

- Create and use representations to organize, record, and communicate ideas
- Select, apply, and translate among mathematical representations to solve problems
- Use representations to model and interpret physical, social, and mathematical phenomena (NCTM, 2000, p. 67)

HOW IS MATHEMATICS TAUGHT?

JED BENSON'S FIRST-GRADE CLASSROOM

The students were seated in a group in front of the flannel board. Their teacher, Jed Benson, was telling them a story using five flannel airplanes. He explained, "These airplanes belong to the daring Navy pilots known as the Blue Angels. These pilots often fly their planes in formation like this." (Benson demonstrated on the flannel board.)

"Let's count the airplanes together. (One, two, ...) Now let's see if we can tell some stories about the numeral 5 using the airplanes."

Benson arranged the airplanes to tell the story of the numerals 2 and 3. He called on the students to verbalize about what they were seeing. Then he called on different students to arrange the airplanes into the various subsets of five. When the students seemed confident with this activity, Benson passed out counting sticks to each student and sent them to their tables. He told them to arrange the sticks in a straight line in front of them and to count them. ("How many do you have?") After verifying that the students recognized that they had five sticks, he said: "Let's see if you can group your sticks to tell the story of 5 with subsets of 3 + 2. Now do 2 + 3."

As the students worked, Benson observed their manipulation of the sticks. In making the transition from 3 + 2 to 2 + 3, Benson watched to see if the students reversed the arrangement of the sticks or had to count each stick individually. If a student had to count the sticks to make the transition, Benson knew immediately that the student did not understand the relationship of subsets to the original set of five and probably lacked the concept of reversibility.

After the manipulative experience, Benson went to the chalkboard and again presented the information visually, this time using dots. Then he presented it using numerals (1, 2, 3, 4, 5) and symbols (1, 5). Following the visual representation, he passed out practice sheets for the students to use. Students were encouraged to use their counting sticks to help them as they worked with the abstract numerals on the practice sheet.

Benson's lesson had the following components:

- Motivating visual story of the numeral 5; verbalization
- Concrete manipulative experience using counting sticks
- Visual presentation using numerals
- Reinforcement of the manipulative and visual experiences with abstract numerals

During each stage of work, Benson monitored the students' performance and provided both positive and negative feedback.

Analysis of Jed Benson's Lesson

Clearly Jed Benson was focusing on the number and operations content strand and the representation process strand. He was very conscious of the need to use concrete materials (planes) for visual representation and then counting sticks for manipulation before he introduced the abstract symbols. Benson's knowledge of developmental patterns led him to verify the students' ability to use the concept of reversibility.

Instruction in mathematics is enhanced by the use of objects or pictures. Elementary students learn best when they work with real objects and realistic problems. It is more effective to introduce new concepts and skills with a concrete referent than with paper-and-pencil exercises. Benson's teaching sequence was appropriate; he began with a concrete experience that appealed to the students' senses. He provided objects for manipulation. He then moved to the visualization stage and concluded with the abstract symbol stage of representative mathematical ideas. In addition, he provided appropriate dialogue to connect each stage. He was explicit in his directions, and the teaching strategy was basically direct instruction. In the following case study, a teacher introduces fractions using a physical object.

GREG THOMAS'S FIFTH-GRADE CLASSROOM

The students were asked to bring egg cartons to school. Greg Thomas provided the students with dry beans. He asked the students to fill one half of the carton with beans and leave the other half empty. Then he had the students compare the different ways in which their classmates arranged the beans in order to fill one half of the carton. The lesson continued with directions for the students to represent one third, one fourth, two thirds, and three fourths.

Throughout the lesson, Thomas had the students compare their arrangements and talk about the number of ways that each fraction could be depicted. As the students improved, Thomas had students go to the chalkboard and use symbols to represent the part-to-whole relationship as fractions.

On successive days, to extend ideas, Thomas had the students use Cuisenaire rods and sets of tangram

Teaching Hints: Problem Solving

Cathcart, Pothier, Vance, and Bezuk (2006) recommend a variety of strategies for teaching problem solving: dramatization and modeling, drawing pictures or diagrams, constructing tables and charts, searching for patterns, and solving similar but simpler problems.

pieces. Finally the students were asked to bring in some simple cooking recipes to help reinforce the applications of fractions. These activities precede formal abstract work with fractional numbers. Thomas was aware that not until about age 10 can students use an operation approach to study fractional numbers.

Analysis of Greg Thomas's Lesson

Greg Thomas connected content and process strands in his lesson. Number and operation were obviously important as the students worked with their beans to fill parts of the carton, but as the students shared their configurations, they were developing understanding of geometric patterns and relations taught in the algebra content strand. Process strands included representation and communication. Because the students had opportunity to arrange their configurations in different ways and were encouraged to talk about what they were doing, we can see some evidence of constructivism in Thomas's lesson.

Discovery and Constructivist Learning

Mathematics specialists advocate learning by discovery with a constructivist perspective. The story by Funk is an example of constructivist teaching. Traditional teaching of mathematics required a **procedural knowledge** orientation, in which students learned "how to." They learned to plug in a formula and perform an operation based on certain learned rules. For example, the young student learned to add 18 + 3 without understanding the concept of place value or a base 10 numeration system.

In contrast, discovery and constructivist learning requires **conceptual knowledge** of a physical action or a mind picture that can be talked about, written about, reflected on, and ultimately translated to the abstract level. Logical-mathematical knowledge is internal to the student rather than external.

Discovering patterns is much more difficult for students than writing answers. The former involves the process of thinking and requires that the student discover which particular pattern will apply to a specific situation. Discovery learning is enhanced by peer interaction. Communication between student and teacher and among students encourages students to share a variety of ways to solve problems, express inventive

Research Findings

Popham (2008a) objects to timed tests in mathematics used for the purpose of preparing students for the standardized tests they will be taking months later. Tests should be used to make inferences about students' math skills, needs, and attitudes about math. The tests should be used for teachers' planning purposes. The timed math test fails to nurture positive feelings about math.

thinking, make connections to prior learning and other subject fields, and obtain creative results.

Motivation is an important element in mathematics teaching. Problems should be selected by the teacher to foster discovery learning. Students need to feel that the problem is relevant and interesting as well as challenging.

The process of discovery may involve the use of unsophisticated (rudimentary) procedures. As students direct their own learning, they will apply familiar procedures until they are ready to speculate about or guess a new pattern or a new way to approach the problem. Discovery occurs in the form of applying the discovered generalization.

Active learning is another way of describing constructivist learning. It may involve working with and transforming physical objects in order to learn through real experience what happens when, for example, you transfer a liquid from one vessel to another or manipulate clay from one shape to another.

Active learning also means involvement in group discussions and verbal clashes with classmates over which solution is right. The group discussion should focus on the thinking process so students are forced to clarify why they believe their solution is correct. An encounter about mathematical ideas can be as important as a discussion carried out in science or social studies.

The teacher's role during discovery and constructivist teaching is to ask questions, encourage students to make guesses, focus the search when needed, and select appropriate situations and experiences to apply the new ideas.

Singapore Math

On international math tests, Singapore fourth- and eighth-grade students consistently beat the rest of the world (including the United States). Using a bar model approach (Figure 10.3) Singapore textbooks demonstrate simple and complex math problems, which help students to think symbolically (Hoven & Garelick, 2007). English language learners using a Singapore textbook would not have a comprehension problem as they do using the U.S. math text. Using the bar model, students are able to figure out what math processes are needed to solve the problem. Problems typically require multisteps to solve and as a consequence help students develop a range of skills. The Singapore texts demonstrate the problem to be solved and include a little cartoon figure who offers advice. Students in the program achieve mastery and teachers do not have to reteach concepts.

Leinwand & Ginsburg (2007) do not believe that the United States has a shared common vision for teaching mathematics, unlike the Singapore math program. The Singapore program framework has five main elements: attitudes, process, concepts, metacognition, and skills. These components are connected by a focus on mathematical problem solving. These authors believe that the U.S. program is disconnected and ineffective as a consequence.

The Third International Mathematics and Science Study

The Third International Mathematics and Science Study (TIMSS) found that U.S. students in elementary grades scored above their counterparts in other countries in these subjects, but in middle and high schools, U.S. students' scores dropped below those of students in other comparable nations. Studies that examined mathematics teaching in Japan and Germany (two nations that scored above the United States) noted interesting differences between U.S. teachers and teachers in these nations. According to Hoff (2000), U.S. teachers begin class with a short-answer question, check students' homework, assign a worksheet, monitor students' work, and explain the work if students get stuck. Class ends with the assignment of homework.

In Japan, teachers begin by reviewing the previous day's work and then assign the students a problem for the day that is based on a mathematical principle. The students go to work, often in small groups, and talk about the problem. If students are having difficulty, the teacher coaches them by asking questions to motivate further study. At the end of the work period, students go to the chalkboard to write their processes and explain their thinking.

The TIMSS Video Mathematics Research Group (2003) performed a video study follow-up of the original study. They noted that Japanese students often spent 15 minutes on one problem, performing a variety of learning activities focused on the problem. U.S. students, in contrast, averaged 5 minutes on one problem. The Japanese students were involved in proving and verifying mathematical statements and analyzing alternative solutions, versus performing repetitions of similar problems.

Still another difference between top-ranking Japan and other countries was that teachers in Japan spend more time making connections to other subjects, real-life problems, and what students have already learned. The problems are conceptual in nature, not procedural.

William Jackson Changed the Way He Taught Mathematics

In Paterson, New Jersey, at one of the worst schools in the district (School #2, K–8), teacher William Jackson took the TIMSS study seriously and, after 16 years of teaching, changed the way he taught mathematics. He begins class with a challenging problem. Using a cartoon of a male and female rabbit, he explains that the rabbits will mate after one month and will produce another pair of rabbits after another month. He asks his students to assume that the pattern of reproduction will continue and to figure out how many rabbits will be in the warren at the end of one year. The students work in small groups. He coaches his students with

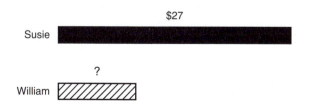

Susie has $27. She has three times as much money as William. How much money does William have?

Figure 10.3 Singapore Math Bar Model

Teaching Hint

Check your students' motivation in mathematics.

1. I like to invent ways to solve problems.
2. I like to know a specific way to solve a problem.
3. I like to know why a problem is correct or incorrect.
4. I like to study problems related to things outside school.
5. When I work hard, I do better in math.
6. I like easy problems to solve so I can get done faster than my classmates. (See answers below.)

Answers:

1. Constructivist orientation
2. Procedural orientation
3. Conceptual orientation
4. Constructivist orientation
5. Effort orientation
6. External motivation/performance motivation

leading questions. Students talk, question, draw pictures to discover the pattern. When students think they have discovered the pattern, they write their processes on the board. Nineteen minutes after the beginning of the period, one of the students is ready to present his findings, and students debate whether this student has discovered the best way to solve the problem.

KAREN ADAZZIO'S SEVENTH-GRADE CLASSROOM

Now let's take another look at the giant's footstep in the sand.[1] Suppose Jana and Enriqué want to solve this problem, and they bring it to the attention of their teacher, Karen Adazzio. She proceeds to draw several giant footprints on butcher paper and asks Jana and Enriqué to present the problem to the class. Adazzio then divides the class into five teams and gives each team a drawing. She writes the following questions on the board:

1. How can you find out the height of the giant?
2. What ideas does your group have to solve the problem? (Describe each idea.)

---

[1]Problem and suggestions contributed by Judith Hillen of Fresno Pacific College, Fresno, California.

3. Was each idea based on an underlying assumption? Explain the assumption for each of the possible solutions.
4. Did you test each idea? Describe your procedures for each idea that was tested. What math processes were used?
5. What worked? What did not work? Why?
6. Draw a picture of how you solved the problem.
7. Is the group satisfied with its solution? Explain why the group thinks its solution is accurate. If some members of the group are unsure of the accuracy, explain why.

Adazzio gives each group several sheets of paper with key headings on them:

1. Idea # _____; Assumption: _____; Description of Idea:
2. Testing Procedures for Idea # _____; Math Processes:
3. We solved the problem using these procedures and processes:
4. We are satisfied with our solution because:
5. We are dissatisfied with our solution because:

Using the content and process strands, analyze Karen Adazzio's lesson. Decide whether it was a good lesson and explain why you think so. Compare your responses with another teacher or classmate.

Repetition, Reinforcement, and Application

In the general population and within the math community, there has been a great deal of controversy concerning traditional methods of teaching math and the curricular reform policies for teaching math. Teachers need to be cognizant of the dialogue and research in mathematics education concerning these practices and make and communicate decisions related to the following questions:

• Does drill and practice teach procedural knowledge or facilitate conceptual understanding? (What purpose should be served?)
• To what extent should drill and practice be used for the correction of errors?
• In what ways does drill and practice affect motivation?

- To what extent does drill and practice facilitate the application of concepts to new and varied situations?
- Should students be challenged to discover mathematical concepts or should teachers lecture and have students practice using the concept(s)?

GROUPING AND WHOLE-CLASS MATH DISCUSSION

Cooperative Groups

A number of math learning activities can be best performed in small heterogeneous groups. Small groups enable students to express themselves easily and share problem-solving approaches. It also facilitates the exploration phase of problem solving. Students who are more able can explain problems in "kid language," thereby facilitating understanding for the student who is less able. More positive attitudes about mathematics appear to develop when students interact with each other and with instructional materials in the small group.

Whole-Class Discussion

Class discussion during problem solving helps students become better and more efficient problem-solvers. By asking students how they solved or approached the solution of a problem, students learn to verbalize the problem-solving phase. Because students do this in different ways, less efficient students learn problem-solving strategies by hearing the step-by-step approach of problem-solvers who are more able.

Teachers' questions during the class discussion can stimulate student thinking and reasoning. Too often students attempt to implement a procedure for prob-

lem solving without understanding the concepts involved. It is important to give students time to respond and think through the solution of a problem, to determine why an approach did or did not work, and to develop alternative approaches and methods for solving a problem.

Discussion format in mathematics may be an unfamiliar method of instruction for many students. As a consequence, the shy and less confident child may be fearful of participation.

INSTRUCTIONAL MATERIALS FOR TEACHING CONCRETELY

A variety of instructional materials are available for use in the mathematics program. These learning aids enrich the climate of the classroom, pique students' interest, and encourage experimentation.

Types of Materials

Materials are needed for counting, sorting, comparing relations, measuring, and practice purposes. Most of the materials are relatively inexpensive or can be made by the teacher.

Size Relations

Objects such as wooden blocks, buttons, nails, wooden rods (Cuisenaire), string and ribbons, and rulers can be used to help students observe size relations. Students may be asked to determine the following: Which is longer? Which is shorter? Which is wider? Which is smaller than _____? Which is taller?

Research Findings

Futrell and Gomez (2008) urge the elimination of tracking to close the achievement gap. They suggest the use of cooperative learning groups with an emphasis on interdisciplinary, interactive learning using block scheduling to teach English, science, and technology.

Teaching Hints: English Language Learners

Because there is less reading in mathematics, ELL students often do better in math than in language arts. But the ELL student needs to participate in group discussions; as a consequence, small-group discussions assist these students more than whole-class discussion. Using some of the following ideas will help build vocabulary for the ELL student.

Characteristics

Students (especially ELL students) need help in defining the characteristics of objects. Identify some math concepts students should learn. Make a graphic organizer to represent math concepts such as exactly alike, similar, different. Select means to compare objects such as fruit, vegetables, house plans.

Tessellations

Tessellations can be made with a variety of materials, such as tiles, pattern blocks, and a variety of paper shapes. A tessellation is a covering or tiling of a surface with one or more shapes. It can be done on a tabletop, the bulletin board, or the floor. Students can get ideas by looking at traditional quilt designs or parquet floors. Tessellating helps students sort and arrange shapes. It is a visual activity that helps students learn geometry.

Mass Relations

Students estimate and measure ounces, pounds, grams, and kilograms. The measurements can be performed using a balance scale. Suggested materials for measuring mass include beans, marbles, stones, coins, buttons, and sand.

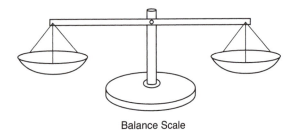

Balance Scale

Volume Relations

Containers of various shapes and sizes need to be available in the classroom so students can experiment with volume relations. Students should measure capacity using cups, pints, and quarts, as well as milliliters and liters.

Time Relations

To explore time relations, students will need to use model clocks, a sundial, and a calendar. Many teachers like to make clocks from paper plates; the hands can be made of chipboard and attached with a brass brad. Teacher-made sundials for use outside are usually adequate for demonstration purposes.

Temperature

Both Fahrenheit and Celsius thermometers should be provided for students to learn to measure temperature.

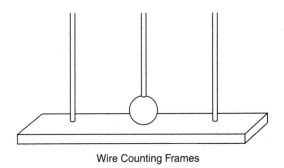

Wire Counting Frames

Counting

For counting and learning place value, the following materials are recommended: ice cream sticks, beans, straws, counting frames, an abacus or *soroban*, small wooden blocks, coins, a place-value chart, and a number chart. An abacus can be made using a coat-hanger wire, a wooden frame, and counting beads. First used by the ancient Romans, Chinese, and Japanese, and still used in banks and businesses in Asia, the abacus or *soroban* is used to teach place value. In Japan, contests between individuals skilled in the use of the *soroban* and other individuals using calculators have demonstrated that the *soroban* can be used more rapidly than a calculator.

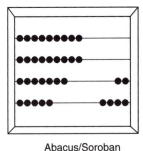

Abacus/Soroban

Other Concrete Instructional Materials

The number chart (0–100) is displayed in most primary classrooms. It is used to help students identify numerals, learn to write number symbols, discover patterns in the base-10 system of numeration, and perform addition and subtraction.

0	1	2	3	4	5	6	7	8	9
10	11	12	13	14	15	16	17	18	19
20	21	22	23	24	25	26	27	28	29
30	31	32	33	34	35	36	37	38	39
40	41	42	43	44	45	46	47	48	49
50	51	52	53	54	55	56	57	58	59
60	61	62	63	64	65	66	67	68	69
70	71	72	73	74	75	76	77	78	79
80	81	82	83	84	85	86	87	88	89
90	91	92	93	94	95	96	97	98	99
100									

Number Chart

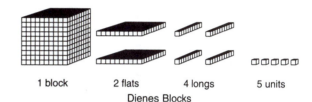

Pocket Chart

Dienes Blocks

1 block   2 flats   4 longs   5 units

The number continuum is a useful semiconcrete tool in the classroom. All that is needed is heavy tagboard or chipboard on which is drawn a straight line with points and arrows pointed in both directions to convey the number continuum. It is a good idea not to write the numerals on the number line. When the number line is displayed on the chalk ledge, numerals can be written in at designated points. The number line can also be used on the classroom floor.

Commercially made rods of varied lengths and colors are functional in the primary-grade classroom. Students learn quickly that if they want to make 6, the 6-rod will be as long as two 3-rods or the 2-rod plus the 4-rod.

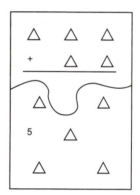

Puzzle Card

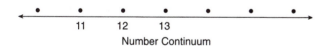

11   12   13

Number Continuum

The pocket chart that is used so frequently in reading is also useful in mathematics. The pocket chart is labeled for place-value use in mathematics.

Dienes blocks or place-value blocks help students perform subtraction. The blocks allow students to visualize the exchanging of hundreds, tens, and ones.

Students enjoy using puzzle cards to practice their basic facts. These can be made out of chipboard or wood for long-term use. The cards should have pictures or dots for counting, along with the abstract numerals.

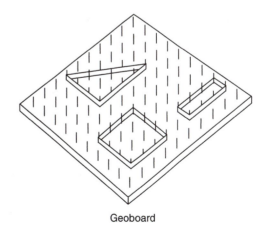

Geoboard

Geoboards, used to explore geometric figures, shapes, and relations, can be made or purchased. A square piece of wood is used, with nails spaced one inch apart, vertically and horizontally. By stretching rubber bands around some of the nails, students study geometric concepts, relations, and measurement.

Dominoes can be used for sorting and learning number facts.

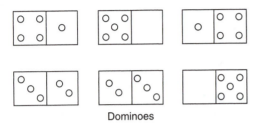

Dominoes

Rummy-type games are popular in the lower grades, and the cards are easy to make from tagboard. More challenging rummy-type games using tiles require students to process numbers in a variety of ways. (The Rummikub tile game for ages 8 to adult is an example.) These games can be used for middle school students. Games and puzzles are ideal for helping students automatize procedures. (To **automatize** means to perform mathematics skills [procedures] effortlessly.)

Rummy-Type Cards

Game materials for practice-and-drill purposes can be bought or made. Useful items include number cards, lotto- or bingo-style games, dominoes, and Old Maid or Go Fish card games. The game Battleship has been popular in middle-grade classrooms to help students

	1	2	3	4	5	6	7	8	9	10
A										
B										
C										
D										
E										
F										
G										
H										
I										
J										

Battleship Grid

use a number grid. The ocean grid in Battleship teaches coordinate graphing and location skills as students graph and plot the opponent's ships through a series of hits and misses.

CALCULATORS AND COMPUTERS IN THE CLASSROOM

Calculators and computers affect not only how mathematics is taught in classrooms, but what is taught. Handheld calculators can be used in a variety of ways; the calculator allows students of all ages to experiment with mathematical ideas. The calculator motivates exploration of place value. It is also useful for the investigation of concepts and problems that would be too difficult for students if they had to do it on their own with pencil and paper.

The calculator allows students to extend their thinking in creative ways and makes computation less tedious. Students can use calculators to study real-world problems, such as budgeting, marketing, and balancing a checkbook.

The calculator can also be used during the trial-and-error stage of problem solving to enable students to project and estimate a possible problem solution. Students will gain insight into the problem-solving process that would not be possible without the calculator.

Copeland (1982) cautioned that students should be introduced to the basic operations using physical objects before learning to use a calculator; however, the calculator can be used as a recorder of what the students have experienced. Calculators can be used in primary-grade classrooms, but their use is more typical in grades 4–8.

To use the calculator productively, the student needs to know what operations are necessary to perform in a given problem. The calculator only helps the student speed up the computation step. Because the student needs to plug in the operation(s), it is important that teachers require students to think through the correct operation or sequence of operations.

The computer has been used successfully to assist in instruction (computer-assisted instruction [CAI]) and to manage instruction (computer-managed instruction [CMI]). CAI has been used for drill-and-practice programs and computer programming. Although most math experts agree that drill and practice on the computer may help automatize procedural learning, it will not help students learn to think conceptually about mathematics. Most math specialists recommend that automatization should be an objective of the mathematics teacher *after* the students have the conceptual knowledge that underlies a procedure.

USING THE INTERNET FOR MATHEMATICS

The Internet can be used for communication among classrooms through the use of e-mail (Ameis, 2000). For example, in Chapter 5, Sara Garcia's class was surveying other children's feelings about exercise. Data collection could have been done using e-mail between classrooms. Computer programs can be obtained for graphing and other means to communicate math data. Ameis recommends the Kids Did This in Math! site, with its links to different projects. This site is appropriate for a variety of grade levels (http://sln.fi.edu/tfi/hotlists/kid-math.html).

Another site of interest for both teachers and K–12 students is the Swarthmore College site A Tour of Fractions, which can be accessed through the http://www.prenhall.com site provided in the Introduction, or directly at http://forum.swarthmore.edu/paths/fractions/. This site provides answers to students' questions by Dr. Math.

A wide variety of games, simulations, and skill reinforcement activities are available for computer use. *Mathematics on the Internet* (Ameis, 2000) provides examples.

Also of interest is use of the Internet to study the work of great mathematicians. For example the site Fibonacci Numbers and Nature would be appropriate for older middle school students, as would Pascal's Triangle. For elementary students, Gertrude's Secrets and Puzzles and the Moptown Parade will be of interest.

MULTIMEDIA PROJECTS FOR PROBLEM SOLVING

The Adventures of Jasper Woodbury is a video series developed at Vanderbilt University for upper elementary and middle school students. Jasper Woodbury, a fictional character, and his teenage friends are involved in real-life complicated mathematical problems. Each problem is equivalent to a 15-step story problem. Students perform math problems involving meaningful situations, such as computing how many residents of a town would take part in a recycling project and what pickup service would cost.

There are several advantages to the video productions:

- They are more motivating than the flat textbook.
- They can present more information than a textbook can.
- A video can be repeated so that students can search for more clues and additional information.

The *Jasper* series keeps the students actively engaged. Not only must they collect data while watching the video, but when it is over, they must use that data to solve minor problems that lead to their major inquiry problem.

Another problem-solving multimedia project is *The Voyage of the Mimi*, developed by the Bank Street College of Education. The package contains videos, print materials, and computer materials for studying science and mathematics. The video is typically used to present the context of the problem. It is the story of a fictional crew aboard the *Mimi* who are engaged in a scientific study of humpback whales. The viewers see the scientists at work solving actual problems. The computer materials involve students in interactive situations through games and simulations. The print materials provide a text version of the video story and worksheets for students to use. The advantage of the *Mimi* package is that the teacher can choose the entry point for students based on their needs and classroom time. The materials are particularly valuable for enrichment purposes and can be used by individuals or groups of students.

The Activities Integrating Mathematics and Science Program

Activities Integrating Mathematics and Science (AIMS) is a program for effective instructional integration of mathematics and science in grades K–9. AIMS activities provide students with experiences in four learning environments:

1. Interaction with the real world through hands-on activities
2. Design, construction, and use of appropriate data records
3. Utilization of graphic/pictorial representations to display data

4. Engagement in the higher-order thinking processes of hypothesizing, inferring, and generalizing

Information about the program, mathematics resources, and teacher workshops can be found at http://www.aimsedu.org/.

SPECIAL CONSIDERATIONS: GENDER, RACE, CLASS, AND CULTURE

Careers in the 21st century require greater numerate capabilities. Yet current practices in classrooms often discourage female students, minority students, and low-income male students from higher-level studies in mathematics. Teachers still tend to give majority male students more time and attention than female students, minority students, and low-income students receive during mathematics.

Sometimes this teacher behavior is unconscious, yet it persists. Although girls' participation in math and science course work in high school has increased, few girls are in advanced-placement classes in science and mathematics course work. Fourth- and twelfth-grade boys are more proficient than girls in math; girls are at the "basic" level (Campbell & Clewell, 1999).

Campbell and Clewell also confirm that the gap between majority male students and students belonging to racial and ethnic minority groups (other than Asian Americans) is even greater than between majority boys and girls. The concern of these researchers is that, as a nation, we are losing the benefit of different perspectives by not taking advantage of the human potential of all of our citizens. They claim that genetics is often used as an excuse by schools that are providing unequal opportunities. There is no math "gene," and all students need to be nurtured and encouraged.

From the review of research concerned with gender-related differences in mathematics education, it is apparent that fewer females enroll in higher-level mathematics courses that are prerequisite to, or will prepare them for, advanced careers in technology and the professions, and fewer female and minority students are encouraged by their teachers to enroll in higher-level mathematics courses. Gender, race, class, and cultural differences must be eliminated, and can be if teachers make a conscious effort to encourage the tar-

get groups to engage in problem-solving activities, demonstrate the usefulness of mathematics, and verify that all students receive quality support.

O'Brien and Barnett (2003) played inference games with sixth-grade students grouped in "friendship" groups of both low- and high-achievement students. They found that the low-achieving students were just as apt as the high-achieving students at coming up with solutions to the problems. The researchers concluded that all of the students did well in the games because they were not "labeled" or asked to "spout memorized facts and there was no pressure on them."

INCLUSION

Although skill instruction for exceptional children frequently occurs in special education classrooms, students with special learning problems and disabilities can benefit from mathematics instruction in the regular classroom. Instructional planning for the mainstreamed student should focus on the following considerations.

Learning Style

- For the kinesthetic learner, provide more manipulative aids than is typically done. Be sure that students have counting sticks and other aids for computation tasks.
- For the auditory learner, record math facts on a CD; record skill activities.
- For the visual learner, utilize individual chalkboards for students to write and draw on; suggest that stu-

Research Findings

Konstantopoulos (2008) studied whether small classes would reduce the achievement gap between low and high achievers. The researcher found that all students benefited from small classes, however high-achieving students benefited more than low-achieving students. Included in the sample were 11,000 students in grades K–3 studying math and reading.

dents draw problems; use the Language Master for math facts.

Motivation

- Choose situations that are relevant to the mainstreamed child to motivate skill development.
- Explain the practical use of the skill (calculating gasoline consumption, identifying health risks).
- Vary activities to increase interest.
- Reinforce strengths; do not dwell on deficiencies.
- Program instruction in short segments so that the student does not sit too long.
- Allow the child to work with a friend who will be of assistance.
- Reinforce positive accomplishments with realistic praise.

Instruction

- Diagnose needs carefully. Identify the precise need or error to be corrected.
- Determine the missing link in the chain of understanding. Reteach using concrete materials.
- Verify understanding verbally. Provide appropriate practice.
- Group students heterogeneously; mainstreamed students profit from group experiences. (They need opportunities to listen to others solve problems.)
- Utilize math learning centers for reinforcement activities.

Instructional Materials

- Clarify instructions and verify that students understand instructional tasks.
- Be certain that materials are clear and understandable. Some students may need large-print materials.
- Verify that students can read the instructional materials and understand the math operations and processes.
- Avoid burdening students with too many problems or assignments at one time.

Time

- Monitor the amount of time the child is working to ensure that activities are varied; movement needs are provided for; and the length of the assignment is reasonable, individualized, and motivating.

ASSESSMENT OF LEARNING

Progress in mathematics learning can be evaluated by teacher observation, performance assessment, teacher-made tests, standardized tests, and student-teacher conferences. As Jed Benson observed his students manipulating the ice cream sticks, he was able to detect which students had not attained the concept of reversibility. Students' interest and enthusiasm for working with math concepts usually can be detected through observation. Observation of students as they work is usually the first step in evaluation of growth. For example, if a student appears confused, the teacher can then engage the student in a discussion: "Show me how you found the answer." "How do you know that you should multiply first?" "Explain the pattern to me."

Most important is student discussion of their reasoning process and ways of proving that they have gained the mathematical concept and algorithm. Students should not have to follow a single-formula procedural system. They need to be free to think through their problems and demonstrate their own way of solving a problem.

Teacher-made tests can focus on math vocabulary, identifying processes, estimation, explaining problems, or performing computation. The tests can be completion, multiple choice, or matching. It is important that the mathematics test is not a test of reading skills. Teacher-made tests in math have greater content validity than formal standardized tests because teachers know what they have taught. The tests can be designed to gather information about the concepts and skills taught and practiced during the mathematics program.

The test can be a creative endeavor, with students asked to represent their problems and solutions with different types of pictures, graphs, and patterns for communication. Students should be asked to make connections to other subject fields and relevant problem situations.

Performance Assessment Using Rubrics

Performance assessment can use rubrics (standards). The rubric must be commonly shared by teacher and student. Some rubrics may prescribe exactly what needs to be present; others may be more open-ended and state what needs to be accomplished.

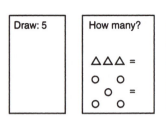

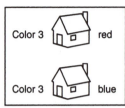

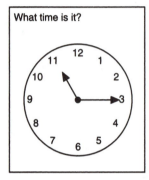

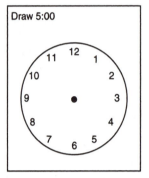

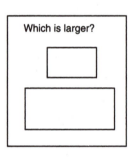

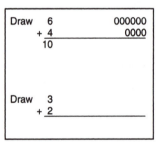

Review the giant footstep problem. Karen Adazzio provided specific tasks to engage her students in thinking processes and mathematical ideas, the need to use math tools, and the opportunity to communicate both in the group and in what was expected of the group in terms of output. These tasks could have been accompanied by a rubric, jointly agreed on by teacher and students, that would define expectations of the task by specifying for students what would be conceived as "really well done" or "acceptable" performance, and suggestions for improvement.

The goal of performance assessment is to examine what students produce, rather than to focus on the students themselves. Teachers can use portfolios of student work, direct observation, conference talks between student and teacher, and group work. It is important that students participate in the assessment process and learn to explain their thinking.

Reporting to Parents

In reporting progress to parents, it is important to remember that the isolated mathematics test is meaningless unless it is accompanied by an explanation of the concept that was taught. If all the parent sees is a test sheet that informs him or her of a score (5 out of 12), the parent will focus on the number of correct answers instead of gaining a perspective on what the child understands. Communication about a student's progress in mathematics is best achieved through a parent-teacher conference rather than through test papers.

Performance assessment provides a more meaningful way to let parents know how their child is doing. When students become accustomed to describing their thinking process, they can talk about their work and explain to parents what they were trying to accomplish. The three-way conference enables students to participate in communicating to parents about their mathematical power.

LEARNING CENTERS

Learning centers in mathematics are used to reinforce math concepts, individualize instruction, and provide for special needs. Learning center use can be an integral part of the instructional program.

Estimation

Mathematics—Lower Grades

Objectives. To practice estimation by predicting and comparing mass

Materials. Two-pan balance scale, small objects (rocks, erasers, blocks). *Note:* To the scientist, a balance scale measures mass and a spring scale measures weight.

 Teaching Hints

1. Teach more about less. Introduce fewer concepts in a lesson and provide opportunity for students to use the concepts in a variety of learning experiences.
2. Insist that students explain concepts in their own words and provide concrete examples of the concept.
3. Assign application projects using concepts taught in class for homework assignments.

Assessment. Observation of mass, small-group discussion, self-evaluation

Procedures

1. Students arrange objects from light to heavy, or heavy to light, on the tabletop.
2. Items are measured and compared with original guesses.
3. Objects are rearranged on the tabletop to see if original estimation was correct.

Which Container Holds a Cup? Pint? Quart? Liter?

Mathematics—Lower and Middle Grades

Objectives. To compare containers of different sizes and shapes; to use standard and metric units; to estimate volume

Materials. Plastic containers of different sizes and shapes, sand, plastic dropcloth or newspapers, large spoon or scoop, measuring units

Assessment. Observation, discussion, self-evaluation

Procedures

1. Table and surrounding floor area are protected with the dropcloth or newspapers.
2. Students are encouraged to guess and record how much each container will hold before measuring.
3. Students use standard measuring units to fill plastic containers with sand in order to determine how much each container holds.
4. Containers are compared and estimation is validated.

Congruent Figures

Mathematics—Upper Grades

Objectives. To identify and draw congruent figures and line segments

Materials. Rulers, paper, pencils, task cards, examples for self-evaluation

Assessment. Self-evaluation with peers

Procedures

1. Set of task cards explains what students are to do. Example: Draw two congruent geometric figures.

Draw two geometric figures that are not congruent. Draw the radius and diameter of a circle. Label each. Draw and label: angle, ray, line segment, isosceles triangle, parallelogram, trapezoid.

2. Compare your drawings with examples at the learning center.

Mathematics—Lower Grades

Objectives. To identify and draw geometric figures

Materials. Crayons, paper, examples of different sizes and shapes, ruler

Assessment. Teacher observation, self-evaluation

Procedures

1. Find three objects (in the center) that are rectangles. Draw them.
2. Find three objects that are circles and draw them.
3. Find three objects that are triangles and draw them.
4. Draw two squares that are different sizes.

Tessellations

Mathematics—All Grades

Objectives. To cover a region with pieces of the same or different shapes; to discover characteristics of geometric shapes and designs

Materials. Large paper or the floor for tessellating; tiles, pattern blocks, or paper shapes

Assessment. Self-assessment, teacher and/or group observation and discussion

Procedures

1. Provide tabletop, floor, or large sheets of paper on which to work.
2. Provide shapes (paper shapes, cardboard shapes, tiles, pattern blocks) for students to use.
3. Students may work individually, in pairs, or in small groups.

Problem Solving

Mathematics—Middle and Upper Grades

Objectives. To identify problem components; practice problem solving; develop the ability to generate data;

participate in peer discussion of problem components and processes

Materials. Problems, box, paper and pencil, guide card

Assessment. Answer sheet; discussion of processes, patterns, and probability

Procedures

1. Prepare a guide card to remind students how to solve problems. The guide card should ask:

   What do you need to find out?

   What facts are given?

   What ideas do you have?

   What processes do you need to use?

2. Students may choose the problems from a special shoebox or "fish" for the problems.
3. Students should first identify the information, draw the problem, or use manipulative materials.
4. Explain the problem and how you would solve it.

Illustrative Problems for a Problem-Solving Learning Center

1. Pretend that you have $300 for a vacation. Travel will cost you one-fourth of your total; food will cost you one-fifth of the total; accommodations will cost one-third of the total. How much will you have left for entertainment and gifts?
2. Make a chart of class absences for the month of October. See how many ways you can illustrate the information. (Table 10.1 shows a sample chart.) Were more boys or girls absent during October?

Table 10.1   Class Absences for the Month of October

	Week 1		Week 2		Week 3		Week 4	
	Girls	*Boys*	*Girls*	*Boys*	*Girls*	*Boys*	*Girls*	*Boys*
Monday	2	3	3	4	3	4	3	5
Tuesday	2	2	1	2	3	4	3	4
Wednesday	2	1	0	0	0	1	2	2
Thursday	3	2	1	2	2	3	3	1
Friday	3	3	1	2	3	3	4	2

Did absences increase or decrease during October? What reasons might account for this? Which day of the week had the most absences? The least? What reasons might account for this? Is this pattern typical of other classrooms at school?

3. In a fourth-grade classroom, seven children had birthdays in December; fourteen children had birthdays in January, February, and March; five children had birthdays in April; four children had birthdays in May; and two children had birthdays in June. None of the children had birthdays during the summer or fall months. Was this distribution of birthdays unusual? How could you find out? In solving this problem, students should be encouraged to organize the data, suggest ways to detect a pattern, and interpret the solution. Is this pattern of birthdays typical of other fourth-grade classrooms? Fifth-grade? Sixth-grade?

Money

Mathematics—Lower Grades

Objectives. To identify the value of coins; to find equivalent sets of coins

Materials. Charts, paper and pencil, manipulative coins, task cards

Assessment. Self-check with charts at the center

Procedures

1. Task cards should identify a set amount of money that is to be illustrated. Examples: Draw all the ways you can make 42¢, 53¢, $1.00.
2. Students use the coins to help them find the answers.
3. Students draw their answers.
4. Students check their answers with prepared charts at the center.

SUMMARY

Well-implemented math programs emphasize conceptual understanding, problem solving, logical structuring of math ideas, and functional application of content. In addition, it is important that students learn to communicate their rationale for problem solving.

Developmental levels affect the learning of math concepts, and concrete and life experiences help students comprehend concepts. The math program is structured using content strands and processes identified by the NCTM.

Constructivist and discovery learning are advocated to facilitate conceptual understanding. Small heterogeneous groups and whole-class discussion contribute to math learning. A wide range of materials, including manipulatives, motivate student interest and encourage experimentation.

Gender, race, class, and culture should not be an issue in teaching mathematics as long as all students are engaged in problem-solving activities. Instructional planning that attends to students' learning styles and special needs should be considered.

Performance assessment should examine what the student produces, and students' products should be shared with parents instead of isolated math tests. Students need to be asked to share with their parents what they have produced and their thinking process.

PORTFOLIO ACTIVITY

Provide evidence, through descriptive information, that you are aware of differences in mathematical understandings among the students in your classroom. Write a lesson plan that incorporates both content strands and process strands and that demonstrates innovative instructional formats, such as discovery learning, conceptual mapping, brainstorming, and working with computers.

 ### DISCUSSION QUESTIONS AND APPLICATION EXERCISES

1. Perform conservation tests with children of different ages and describe the stages of development.
2. Prepare a speech for a parent-teacher association meeting on the value of using concrete materials in mathematics. For example, explain the use of Cuisenaire rods.
3. Prepare a lesson to teach subtraction that requires renaming tens to ones. Use concrete materials.

4. Plan a mathematics learning center to reinforce the understanding of fractional parts.
5. A student's response is totally irrelevant to the given problem; how will you discover what the student knows and what he or she does not understand?
6. Using one of the teachers in this chapter as a model, develop a math lesson plan. Identify the content strands and process strands. Share your plan with a peer and critique each other's plans.
7. What subject fields could be integrated with the study of the giant's footprint? Explain how you would do it.
8. Write a problem to engage students in math thinking, math ideas, use of tools and techniques, and communication. Write a scoring rubric for the investigation.
9. Suggest several ways to assess students' problem-solving abilities.

READER RESEARCH

There are gender inequities in the salaries paid to professional athletes. Examine the following sports in which both men and women play: golf, tennis, basketball, soccer, volleyball. Describe the percentage of men's earnings that women earn. Explain why you think inequities occur.

 ### TECHNOLOGY APPLICATIONS

1. Blaise Pascal was born in France. Some believe that he launched the computer age because he developed the first adding machine. Using the Internet as a reference tool, find out what he contributed to the study of geometry. Write a lesson plan based on an application of Pascal's discoveries.
2. Go to http://www.nctm.org and find the NCTM principles and standards. Read the technology principle. Use the principle and appropriate content strands and process standards to write a lesson plan, including how you will assess what students have learned.

CHAPTER 11

Science Education

The development of science as a way of thinking is of primary importance in the teaching of elementary and middle school students. Greater emphasis on experimentation and inquiry-oriented teaching has made the process of teaching science as important as the content of science.

Science enlarges the student's perspective of the world and its environment. Science experiences are varied and appealing to the natural interests and curiosity of most students.

There are innumerable possibilities for science units; the choice can be based on the interests and maturation level of a specific class of students. Science teaching units typically reflect an interdisciplinary approach, are based on a curriculum theme, and integrate subject fields.

We can help students appreciate scientific principles and the processes of science by modeling a scientific attitude and demonstrating methods of inquiry.

Advance Organizer

The following questions are intended to guide your reading and understanding of the content of this chapter.

1. What are the purposes for teaching elementary and middle school science?
2. What content is appropriate for elementary and middle school science programs?
3. How is science taught (describe several ways)?
4. National science programs have contributed content and processes to the teaching of science. What do these programs emphasize?
5. If you were gathering science materials and equipment for classroom use, what would you choose?
6. How can you assess science learning?
7. If you were to create a science learning center emphasizing inquiry learning, what would you choose to do?
8. Why should mainstreamed students have a hands-on approach to help them learn science concepts?
9. When planning a science lesson, what classroom management considerations should you think about?
10. What are some ways to integrate science and technology?

INTASC   **INTASC Standards**

Science is one of the most controversial subjects that teachers are responsible for teaching. As a consequence, it is very important that teachers are competent in the subject field and recognize students' level of understanding. Hands-on experiences help students learn science concepts, so it is important that teachers have appropriate materials and are competent in methodology. All of the INTASC standards are required for teaching in this subject field.

Professional Lexicon

constancy and change The state of something that does not change; other aspects of constancy may be described as stability, steady state, and conservation.

models Physical (concrete), mathematical, or conceptual objects, patterns, or descriptions that demonstrate the ways things are alike.

open-ended science teaching An approach that provides opportunities for students' own questions and opportunities for students to expand their inquiry by asking, "What would happen if . . . ?"

scale Differences in magnitudes; the ratio between upper and lower limits of variables. Scale affects the way things work.

systems Groups made of parts that relate to each other and to the whole. The study of systems involves attention to the connections and interactions among the components and how parts *affect* the whole.

The Wump world was a small world, very much smaller than our world. There were no great oceans, lofty mountains, giant forests, or broad, sandy deserts. The Wump world was mostly grassy meadows and clumps of leafy green trees, with a few winding rivers and lakes. But it was perfect for the Wumps, who were the only creatures living there.

Mary Hogan continued reading The Wump World, *by Bill Peet, to her students. When she finished, she showed her students several globes displaying only water and land masses. She asked the students, "What covers most of the earth's surface?" In this way, Hogan introduced a unit of study on the earth and the environment.*

Mary Hogan enjoys teaching science; she feels competent and secure in her science teaching. However, many elementary and middle school teachers feel insecure about their science knowledge and their understanding of science concepts. For these teachers, it is critical that they study their science books and other materials and learn to use science supplies and equipment. Curriculum guides and professional books on science are also helpful in planning the science program.

Scientific, mathematical, and technological literacy are central in our changing society. If knowledge in these three areas is not the cause of change, it certainly is helping to shape the character of society. Science taught in elementary and middle schools does not ensure that young people will be budding scientists, mathematicians, or sophisticated technicians; however, by building literacy in these fields, young students will recognize and appreciate how scientific knowledge influences and changes their lives. Two publications by the American Association for the Advancement of Science (AAAS) have led the charge for reform of the curriculum in science, mathematics, and technology

education: *Science for All Americans* (1990) and *Benchmarks for Science Literacy* (1993). In 1996, the National Committee on Science Education Standards and Assessment published the *National Science Education Standards*, which identify what it means to be a scientifically literate person.

The *National Science Education Standards* provide teachers with eight science categories for content:

Science as inquiry
Physical science
Life science
Earth and space science
Science and technology
Science in personal and social perspectives
History and nature of science
Unifying concepts and processes

Standards are specified for grades 1–4, 5–8, and 9–12. However, it is important to realize that standards do not represent the curriculum. Curriculum is composed of both content and instruction, including the integration of other subject fields and the activities that engage students. The content standards do provide significant scientific ideas that should be explored by students through meaningful investigations. The standards are considered by experts to be critical for the development of scientific literacy.

WHAT ARE THE PURPOSES OF SCIENCE IN THE ELEMENTARY AND MIDDLE SCHOOL?

Science is an essential and fundamental subject within the curriculum. Science provides students with opportunities to do the following:

- Think critically and practice methods of inquiry
- Develop science concepts that facilitate understanding of the biological and physical environment
- Develop appropriate attitudes and skills essential for democratic citizenship

It is important to note that elementary and middle school students do not really discover new knowledge in science (though it may be new to them), but they can inquire, and so the term *inquiry* is used in this chapter rather than *discovery*. In the same vein, we should not expect that students are really hypothesizing, but they are engaging in the process of predicting.

Science offers unique opportunities to interrelate curriculum areas. Language development is facilitated when students have an experiential base to practice reading, writing, listening, and speaking. Science provides relevant situations for the integration of other subject fields, such as social studies, language arts, and mathematics. The problem-solving skills learned in science and social studies facilitate the development of decision-making capacities that enable students to accept citizenship responsibilities. Science teaching is concerned with content (facts, concepts, theories, generalizations) and with process (observation, measurement, classification, comparison, inference, generalization, theory building).

CONTENT OF SCIENCE PROGRAMS

Both content and process are intertwined in the science program, using the content as the subject of the inquiry. The emphasis of the science program is on inquiry to develop problem-solving skills and scientific attitudes.

Content for science units should focus on the eight categories that make up the *National Science Education Standards*:

1. Living things
2. The earth and the universe
3. Matter and energy

Topics related to these scientific fields of study include the following:

Living things

Organisms
Life cycles
Plants and animals
Human body
Health and disease
Our senses
Fossils
Dinosaurs
Ecology
Environmental issues
Conservation
Recycling
Natural resources
Pollution
Food chains

The Earth and the Universe

Rocks and minerals
Earthquakes and volcanoes
Erosion
The changing earth
The sun and planets
Stars and the universe
Air and weather
Wind
Sun, air, water

Matter and energy

Molecules and atoms
Physical and chemical properties
Temperature and heat
Solar energy
Machines
Magnetism and electricity
Sound
Light
Space travel

These topics are taught through the use of integrative themes. According to the AAAS project 2061, these themes should be areas of major emphasis in the science curricula. The themes provide the overarching structure and major ideas for science inquiry and teaching. *Benchmarks for Science Literacy* (AAAS, 1993) states that the themes are ways of thinking rather than theories or discoveries. Benchmarks suggests four common themes (described below) that pervade the teaching of science: **systems, models, constancy and change,** and **scale.**

Themes for Science Instruction

Systems

The purpose of teaching about systems is to help students consider the interaction of all of the parts of a system—how each component may affect or influence the function and processes of other things. The airplane may be considered a system that is affected by the human mechanics that service the plane, the parts of the plane, the fuel needed to fly, the National Aeronautics and Space Administration, pilot knowledge, the weather, and local airfields. However, systems do not necessarily have purposes. *Benchmarks* gives the example of the ecosystem or the solar system.

Models

Models may be physical, mathematical, or conceptual and are a means for learning about things that are similar. The model represents what it resembles. A model airplane represents the real thing. A model school is supposed to represent the way most schools should operate. Young children recognize concrete objects with physical likenesses, but they learn that the model differs in some ways from the real thing. The middle school student learns that different models may be used to represent the same thing and that complexity of the model changes depending on its purpose.

Constancy and Change

Students understand that change occurs in nature, technology, and social patterns. That there is constancy in the midst of change may be more difficult for young children to comprehend. Aspects of constancy that need to be taught include stability, conservation, equilibrium, steady state, and symmetry. The young elementary school student learns that, although things

change, some aspects stay the same, and sometimes change is so slow that it is hard to recognize. The intermediate elementary school student learns that features of things may change, but other aspects stay the same. The middle school student understands that some cycles of change may be frequent or vary in length of time, and some feedback systems maintain constancy or keep change within specified limits.

Scale

Scale has to do with proportion, such as size, distance, weight, temperature, speed, color, and so on. The young elementary school student can grasp that objects and people vary in size, in age, and in other ways. Intermediate elementary school students understand the value of knowing what is typical or atypical of an object, the weather, or the size of something. Middle school students need to learn how to summarize data, figure averages and ranges, and describe typical examples.

HOW IS SCIENCE TAUGHT?

How students learn science is just as important as what they learn. In the teaching of science, a major objective is to develop students' problem-solving capacities. To do this, teachers must structure learning experiences to provide students with opportunities to participate in inquiry processes.

For example, in Chapter 3 there was an episode about second-grade students studying magnets. First, the children observed the teacher using a horseshoe magnet, then they themselves used the magnet. Their inquiry problem was to find out what magnets will pull.

As the children experimented with different objects that magnets attract, they discussed their observations in their small groups. They predicted that there were different explanations for what they were observing. They continued to experiment until they were satisfied with their explanations. The students classified their data by grouping their objects into those that were attracted to the magnet and those that were not. With the teacher's assistance, they formed a generalization about their experiment.

Students' Attitudes

One of the purposes for science is to develop appropriate attitudes and skills essential for a democratic soci-

Students create a model for experimentation.

ety. A scientific attitude is considered essential in our society. Students will learn to accept the tentativeness of certain evidence; they will be willing to subject their ideas to testing; they will understand that it is okay to change their mind and that predictions often need revision.

Research Findings

Cavanagh (2008) describes how an elementary teacher in Kansas grouped her fourth graders to build miniature bridges. Using plastic straws, tape, and scissors the groups competed with each other to see which group could build the strongest bridge spanning the distance between lab tables. (Strength was tested using golf balls.) The hands-on lab is conducted in an empty classroom, though a regular classroom works just as well. The use of labs encourages students to enjoy science and boosts their enthusiasm for the subject.

Gega and Peters (1998) comment that when we talk about scientific attitudes, we really mean the development of critical thinking. These authors identify four attitudes considered to be part of scientific literacy: curiosity, inventiveness, critical thinking, and ability to accept uncertainty. These four areas are certainly relevant not only for science but for other curriculum fields as well. In science teaching, teachers may have opportunities to encourage curiosity and to confront students with interesting problems to stimulate an investigation.

In a sixth-grade classroom, the students were disdainful about washing their hands before lunch. Jim's attitude was typical of many of the students: "Phooey, all we've been doing is sitting and writing. Why do we need to wash our hands?"

Teacher: All right. How could we find out if dirty hands make a difference?

Rhoda: What happens to food or to us if our hands are dirty?

Teacher: Why don't we design an experiment to find out?

Jim: Well, most of us eat sandwiches; maybe we should preserve one touched by us unclean ones and another one by the cowards who wash up!

Teacher: Well, Jim, I'm not impressed with your terminology, but I think you are on the right track.

Sean: If we preserve a whole sandwich, how will we know whether what happens is a result of dirty hands or natural food spoilage?

Tina: Maybe we should just use bread without anything in between that would spoil.

Rod: Yeah, Tina, that's a good idea. But there's another problem.

Tina: What's that?

Rod: Even the air can contaminate; we still won't know if it's dirt or bacteria in the air.

Bart: We could enclose the bread in some airtight jars.

Jan: Ah, good. Why don't we get two jars with lids and put the bread inside?

Susan: Wouldn't we need to sterilize the jars?

Rod: That's a good idea.

Teacher: Boys and girls, you are doing great. It sounds to me like you have developed a good test to see if dirty hands really make a difference.

The next day the teacher brought bread and jars to class. The students talked about sterilization, and several students were appointed to take the jars to the school cafeteria for sterilization. The students refined their procedures and decided that each slice of bread would be handled by several students. One jar was labeled Dirty, and the other Clean. Three students were assigned the task of washing with soap, and three were chosen at random to touch the piece of bread to be labeled Dirty.

As the week progressed, the students were rewarded by being able to record how the presence of mold changed the bread in the jar labeled Dirty, while the other piece of bread showed no noticeable change.

Let's review the teaching format in the preceding activity.

1. The teacher took advantage of students' feelings, attitudes, and interest about washing up before lunch and encouraged them to think about it.

2. The teacher encouraged whole-class discussion to enable students to express themselves concerning the question of whether to wash.

3. The teacher encouraged the students to design an experiment to test their beliefs.

4. Students expressed ideas and planned means to investigate the question.

5. The teacher brought in necessary materials for the investigation.

6. The teacher conveyed information about sterilization and students talked about it.

7. Students refined procedures for the investigation.

8. Students observed and recorded what happened.

9. Students developed generalizations about mold and bacteria.

10. Students were encouraged to study more about mold and bacteria.

This teacher demonstrated confidence in her students. She gave them enough time to think about how the experiment could be designed. She herself modeled a scientific attitude by allowing the students to reflect instead of telling them or having them read to find out the answer. As the experiment progressed, the students observed, questioned, and developed generalizations. Ultimately, the students' curiosity led them to their textbooks to study mold and bacteria.

Open-Ended Teaching and Constructivism

The teaching of science provides a marvelous opportunity for teachers to release their own and students' creativity. Constructivism in science encourages hands-on activities. By asking questions like "What would happen if both pieces of bread developed mold simultaneously (heaven forbid) or if someone sneezed on the bread as they touched it?" new ideas for experimentation are explored. If the sixth-grade students had not thought about the possibility of bacteria in the air contaminating their experiment, the teacher might have said, "How can we make sure that the only variable affecting the bread is dirt?"

The 5-E Model of Instruction

Open-ended science teaching is similar to inquiry teaching, which is discussed in Part II of this text. It is important to identify the ways in which science can be taught most successfully. For this reason, examples of open-ended science teaching will be cited. The 5-E model is similar to the group investigation model discussed in Chapter 5. This model was developed by the Biological Sciences Curriculum Study (1989). You will note that there are five components to the model.

ENGAGEMENT

Seven fifth-grade students had been working on a timeline of great inventions through the ages. They were asked to share their work with their classmates. Listening to the students' discussion and questions, the teacher realized the children had little conception of how magnetism was converted to electricity, even though they were discussing the inventions of Faraday, Henry, and Oersted. The teacher brought out a display of several items that she had constructed: an electromagnet, a motor, a telegraph, and a radio. She demonstrated how each worked. The students were excited by the possibilities and asked if they could construct their own motors, telegraphs, and radios. The teacher tentatively agreed but said that they had to prove that they know how an electromagnet works.

EXPLORATION

The next day in class, the teacher provided the following materials: dry cells, insulated copper wire, sandpaper, large nails, and paper clips. The students were divided into small groups. Each group had the following problems to solve:

- How do you make an electromagnet?
- What ideas did your group have? Describe how you went about solving the problem.
- How do you know the electromagnet works? Describe your testing process.
- How do you change the strength of the electromagnet?
- What ideas did your group have? Describe your experiments.

Through experimentation, the students learned that an electromagnet is made by winding the wire tightly around the nail and connecting the ends of the wire (which have been stripped of insulation using the sandpaper) to the dry cell. Further experimentation led to the discovery that the strength of the electromagnet was affected by the number of turns of wire on the nail. (More coils of wire increased the strength of the magnet.)

EXPLANATION

Although this procedure is relatively uncomplicated, many of the students did not realize that the wire had to be stripped at the ends before attaching it to the dry cell, nor did they realize that the amount of wire would affect the outcome. Many had no idea that the dry cell had both negative and positive poles and that both would be required to make the electromagnet. By comparing the electromagnets made by different groups of children, students were encouraged to find out who made the strongest magnet. (A simple way to find this out is to see which magnet picked up the most paper clips.)

ELABORATION

The homework assignment for this class was to make a list of ways that electromagnets are used at home. Students were so enthused with their experiments that the teacher presented them with a list of projects they could make to continue their study of electricity. The list included a telegraph system, a lifting crane, a motor, and a crystal radio. The students chose their projects and were divided into project teams for the planning stage. Each student was required to draw a plan and list the specifications for the intended project. The students had a variety of pictures of telegraphs, motors, cranes, and radios. They were able to choose which model they wanted to make.

To make the models, the teacher provided wood for the bases, tin from tin cans, nails, copper wire, sandpaper, coat hangers for the station finder on the radio, empty spools of thread, thin sticks, corks, masking tape, different types of clips, tubes from aluminum foil for winding coils, and diodes for the radios.

The projects motivated students to read about electricity and experiment with their projects. For example, students asked the following questions:

- Does it make any difference if you use more than one dry cell? If two are used, how do you go about it? (A connecting wire is needed.)
- Will radio waves pass through different materials? Which ones?
- How can we make our radio louder or softer?
- How do you send messages using Morse code?
- How does an electromagnet differ from a regular magnet? Do they both pick up the same things?

- How can we make the motors faster? Slower?
- How much weight will our crane pick up?

The students' own questions, rather than the teacher's, became the focus of individual experimentation. Their questions served to expand their interests and open up the study of electricity, and their teacher was able to raise questions about ethical behavior and the relationships of science, technology, and changes in society.

CONSTRUCTION

On the first day of construction, the teacher demonstrated correct tool safety procedures. Construction is considered a creative and socializing experience. During construction, students attempt to create a likeness to the original model. Projects are evaluated for authenticity even though some of the materials may be somewhat different. Projects to be constructed required the following processes:

- Group planning
- Selection of materials
- Manipulative skills
- Sharing of materials and ideas
- Cooperative problem solving
- Measurement skills
- Experimental attitude
- Continuous evaluation
- Appropriate use of tools and materials
- Research related to use and function

As an activity, construction satisfies students' natural urge to produce something of their own and provides a means to motivate research about the real thing or product. Social and scientific concepts are learned when construction is carried out in a purposeful manner.

Analysis of 5-E Model of Instruction

Engagement

Students reveal their lack of knowledge about magnetism and electricity.

To generate students' interest, the teacher displays and demonstrates several electromagnetic models that could be constructed by students.

Students ask if they can make the models.

Exploration

The teacher provides materials to make electromagnets.

The teacher divides the students into work groups.

Each group solves problems related to how an electromagnet works.

The teacher observes the students at work and questions students as they work.

The students offer their ideas and a description of the experiments, which reveal what they know or think they know about what is an electromagnet and how it works.

Explanation

Students' experimentation provides experience with how to make an electromagnet and how to increase the strength of the magnet.

Students discover that dry cells have positive and negative poles and that both are needed to make an electromagnet.

Teacher listens to students' discussion and encourages them to draw conclusions for their experiments.

Elaboration

Homework assignment asks students to apply what they learned based on their class experiences and discussions.

Teaching Hints: Making Science Teaching Interesting

1. Determine students' prior knowledge and connect the new lesson to students' knowledge and interest.
2. Ask students questions and elicit their ideas.
3. Encourage students to plan their own investigations and projects.
4. Group students for investigations; encourage the exchange of ideas.
5. Evaluate progress and encourage reflection on hypotheses.
6. Encourage testing of hypotheses.
7. Connect the lesson to future plans and generate new questions.

Students asked to choose what they want to construct and to draw a plan with specifications of their proposed model.

Evaluation

Students' construction and experimentation with their designed model leads them to think deeply about electricity and to raise questions that focus their own further experimentation.

The teacher elicits students' questions and thoughts.

Students engage in cooperative problem solving, demonstrate an experimental attitude, and perform research related to use and function.

INTEGRATION AND INTERDISCIPLINARY TEACHING

Language Arts Integrated with Science

Reading is used as a way of teaching science when students need to find out something (research), as a way to extend information and experience, and as a substitute for original investigation and experimentation. Reading is a particularly natural means to learn about science. Because of the benefit in terms of scientific attitudes, it is considered important for students to inquire on their own; however, reading materials provide classroom resources that are not available in any other way.

GREG THOMAS'S CLASSROOM

It was after lunch and the students needed to settle down. Greg Thomas picked up the book *Mr. Popper's Penguins*, by Richard and Florence Atwater, which he had been reading to the class. After several chapters, he put the book down (much to the disappointment of the class) and asked, "Who can find the South Pole on the globe?" Tom raised his hand and said, "I would like to find it." Thomas nodded and waited. After showing the location to the class, Tom asked, "Is the South Pole and Antarctica in the same place?"

> *Thomas:* Antarctica is the continent that surrounds the South Pole. Who else has a question?
> *Jill:* What is the temperature at the South Pole?
> *Famie:* How can Mr. Popper keep his penguin healthy when the climate must be so different?

> *Sonia:* Is the weather the same at the two poles? What makes it different from our climate?
> *Thomas:* Wow, you're asking great questions. Suppose we spend some time studying climate and see if we can figure out what Mr. Popper will have to do to keep his penguin healthy.

Thomas wrote some questions on the board to serve as an advance organizer for the students:

1. How does knowing the latitude of a region provide us with information about the climate?
2. What factors affect an environment's climate?
3. How are climates classified?
4. If we wanted to travel to Antarctica, how would we get there?

Thomas encouraged students to go on a virtual tour of the McMurdo Station in Antarctica using the Internet. They studied sun, wind, and temperatures at the pole. Using their interest in the climate conditions at the South Pole, Thomas then had students study about tropical and middle-latitude climates. Reading *Mr. Popper's Penguins* motivated the students to continue asking questions.

Students' questions led to the effect of altitude, ocean currents, and land and water masses on climate. Finally the students read about the greenhouse effect and the concern of many nations that the earth's atmosphere is warming and affecting worldwide weather conditions.

Thomas integrated three subject fields by reading to the students and having them research weather conditions and climates (language arts, science, and social studies). Sometimes the students worked in small groups to share information and sometimes individually. Each session was followed by a class discussion. Thomas included social studies through information about the greenhouse effect and the discussion of worldwide concern and differing perspectives about what to do.

MARY HOGAN'S CLASSROOM

When the students in Mary Hogan's classroom began to discuss the environment, one of the students asked,

"What is a desert like?" Hogan, in her best teacherly fashion, responded, "How can we find out?" When the students asked if there were any books in the classroom about deserts, Hogan suggested a number of different resources. She identified the characteristics of the different resources:

- This book shows the author's interest in plants and animals of the desert.
- This book has many pictures of deserts.
- Our own classroom picture file will provide some information about desert sands and rocks.
- This resource may provide some information about the temperature of deserts.

Hogan then directed the students to choose their own resource for research about deserts and plan to have a classroom discussion about deserts after about 10 minutes. To facilitate the students' reading, she wrote several questions on the board.

1. What is a desert?
2. Why can some plants live in deserts?
3. What are some desert plants?
4. What animals can live in deserts?
5. What is the name of a place in the desert where water can be found?
6. Why is a camel suited to desert travel?

More advanced students can use the questions in the case study as advance organizers to assist them in their note taking.

Reading and writing during science (or during any other academic subject) should be purposefully directed. Unfamiliar words or concepts should be introduced and explained as needed, using the context of the material. Science reading should not be a session where the teacher directs students to "Take out your science book and read Chapter 5."

Utilization of different resources develops students' research and location skills and provides opportunities to gain different viewpoints and perspectives on what is to be investigated. It also provides means for individual differences in reading ability and in reading interests.

Demonstrations

Should teachers ever demonstrate an experiment? Certainly they should. There are occasions when it is more

Teaching Hints: Integrating Science and Literature

Mr. Popper's Penguins, by Richard and Florence Atwater (climatology)

The Grouchy Ladybug, by Eric Carle (protective adaptation, food chain, time, sequencing)

Millions of Cats, by Wanda Gag (overpopulation, depleting of resources)

Strega Nona, by Tomie DePaola (chemical change, physical change)

The Relatives Came, by Cynthia Rylant (fruit, seeds, inclined plane, seasons)

The Very Hungry Caterpillar, by Eric Carle (time, metamorphosis, counting, sequence)

The *Eyewitness* Series, published by Dorling Kindersley (fossils, seashore, pond, river, ecology)

Tyrannosaurus Was a Beast, by Jack Prelutsky (poetry about dinosaurs)

Just a Dream, by Chris Van Allsburg (conservation, environmental education)

appropriate for the teacher to demonstrate a science concept or perform an experiment than to have students do so. Some experiences are beyond the manipulative skills of students and may, in fact, be unsafe for students to perform. Under these circumstances, it may be wise for the teacher to perform the experiment and have students observe. Sometimes the purpose of a teacher experiment is to motivate new areas of interest or to evaluate students' observation skills, attitudinal growth, and conceptual understanding. Here again, a demonstration may be the most efficient means to accomplish the purpose.

Gathering Data and Record Keeping

If students are to improve their ability to use scientific processes, they need to learn how to gather data and describe their observations so they can ultimately decide why something happened. All kinds of records for writing experiments can be devised. Examples of the kinds of questions teachers can use to motivate thinking processes and communication during inquiry can be found in Chapter 10 (the "giant footstep" questions) and in this chapter (the episode involving electromagnetism).

Figure 11.1 Third-Grade Experiment Record

Problem: Miss Garcia's plant looks sick.	*Results (observations):*
Predictions: 1. She did not water enough. (Plants need a lot of water.) 2. She watered too much. (Plants need a little bit of water.) 3. There was not enough sunshine. (Plants need sunlight.)	
Materials: New plants	
Procedures:	
1. Plant #1 will be watered daily and placed on the windowsill.	
2. Plant #2 will be watered twice a week and placed on the windowsill.	
3. Plant #3 will be watered daily and kept on Miss Garcia's desk.	
4. Plant #4 will be watered twice a week and kept on Miss Garcia's desk.	

Results (observations):

	Plant #1	Plant #2	Plant #3	Plant #4
Third day				
Sixth day				
Ninth day				
Twelfth day				
Fifteenth day				

Conclusions:

Figure 11.1 is another example. Students should be encouraged to devise their own records for writing experiments. For young children, it is often a good idea to create a large chart to record class observations. Sometimes the data can be recorded using smiles or frowns or other pictorial means to reflect the observation. The emphasis should be on describing what is, not what ought to be. If an experiment does not come out as the teacher and students anticipated, then the discussion should focus on why. Sometimes an experiment should be duplicated for verification purposes. This, too, can be explained to students.

Field Trips

As discussed in preceding chapters, field trips must be planned by both the teacher and the students and be an integral part of an ongoing science program. Students should be prepared for the trip with information about what they will see and what they may do. If they are to take notes, this too must be communicated. If specific students or groups of students are to be responsible for particular information, then those tasks should be assigned and agreed to before the trip commences.

The field trip should be evaluated in terms of "What did we learn that we didn't know before?" "What surprised us?" "What did we verify?" and "What did we enjoy?" It is important to discuss the field trip and accurately record essential information, but it is not necessarily important that the field trip be written about by students individually.

Summary of How to Teach Science

Science teaching utilizes scientific concepts and focuses on the processes used by scientists. Inquiry learning is featured because it motivates students' curiosity and interest in scientific subject matter and provides opportunities to practice the skills of observing, measuring, classifying, comparing, generalizing, and theorizing (see Table 11.1).

Table 11.1 Science Activities for Data Collection and Data Evaluation

Discussing	Planning, reporting, sharing
Recording	Record keeping, listing, describing
Writing	Reports, information
Constructing	Making gadgets, science equipment, projects
Expressing	Talking, singing, drawing, painting
Reading	Science information, reports
Experimenting	Soil, magnets, sound, light, etc.
Observing	Animals, plants, events, experiments, etc.
Dramatizing	Role-plays, plays
Collecting	Pictures, plants, rocks, etc.

The teacher's role as a resource person and facilitator is featured in science teaching, in contrast to the teacher as an authority figure. Science teaching attempts to develop students' skills in other subject fields such as mathematics, social studies, and language arts. There is an effort to integrate cognitive, affective, and psychomotor behaviors. Learning how to learn science is as important as learning the content of science.

SPECIALIST SCIENCE TEACHERS

In several states, science specialists augment the science program by introducing new concepts to students, demonstrating lab experiments, and helping students participate in hands-on activities (Jacobson, 2004b). Some specialist teachers roll a mobile science cart into the classroom with all of their laboratory equipment. In other situations, the specialist teacher works out of a science lab and the students go to the lab accompanied by their classroom teacher. The classroom teacher is expected to reinforce the new concepts taught by the science teacher. States that have hired special science teachers have done so because of the concern that science is not being taught if it is not part of the NCLB testing program.

SCIENCE CENTERS

Some schools set up one classroom as a science center. The center is scheduled for use by the teachers, and each teacher is responsible for keeping the center equipped and ready for the next class's use. The center may also be used by a science club or students with special interest in science activities. The major advantage of a science center is that equipment and materials can be shared by many teachers, instead of each teacher being responsible for obtaining personal resources.

RESOURCE PEOPLE

The science program, whether it is taught in the self-contained classroom or in a science classroom, should utilize resource people at the school and in the community; however, it is important for teachers to verify that the expert knows how to talk to students. Before turning the classroom over to a resource person, the teacher should verify what is to be communicated and how it is to be communicated. Young students may not react positively to the parent photographer who wants to lecture about the use of light meters; however, these same children may be very interested in how to build their own camera.

HOW IS SCIENCE ORGANIZED FOR TEACHING?

Using a Theme and Planning a Teaching Unit

On a rainy day in Seattle, Washington, some first graders entered their classroom and asked their teacher if she had seen the rainbow. She responded, "Yes. Do you know how to make a rainbow?"

The students were perplexed. It had not occurred to them that it was possible to make rainbows. Their teacher took them outside to observe the rainbow once more. This time she asked them to name the colors they observed and the sequence of the colors (violet, indigo, blue, green, yellow, orange, red). She asked them to observe the way the colors merged. Once more the teacher asked the students. "How can we make a rainbow? What do we need?"

Observing the rainbow across the sky, the students realized that they needed sunlight and water. The next day, the teacher provided jars and suggested that the students take them outside to see if they could make rainbows. With the teacher's assistance, the students soon learned that they would also need mirrors to reflect the sunlight through the water-filled jars. The students' interest in and curiosity about light and colors led the teacher to develop a teaching unit that integrated science, art, and mathematics. Some of the science generalizations included the following:

- The earth is warmed by heat from the sun.
- Sunlight is a mixture of many colors.
- Most of the earth is covered by water.
- The sun heats the water.
- Rainbows are made because water changes the direction of the light.

- Some colors change direction more than other colors do.
- Color depends on the light that is reflected.
- Light that is not absorbed is reflected.
- White light is composed of the colors of the rainbow.
- A sundial can be used to tell time.

Science discovery lessons included the following:

- Using magnifying glasses and mirrors
- Making, mixing, and matching colors
- Learning how shadows help us tell time

Using the theme *patterns of change*, the unit developed by the teacher in this case study effectively integrated science, mathematics, and art, but as the unit progressed, the teacher realized that health could also be integrated by having the students study the care and use of their eyes. The development of a teaching unit in science is similar to the development of a unit in social studies. Just as a social studies unit can be planned to fit an all-encompassing theme, so can the science teaching unit.

The unit plan discussed in Chapter 6 is appropriate for planning the science unit. It is advantageous to use a unit plan in science because it ensures that important concepts, rather than trivia, are taught and it provides the teacher with a format to ensure continuity in the lessons planned. It is customary in science teaching to have a series of short units to present throughout the semester.

Science Textbooks

The teacher should be the one to decide what is to be taught during the semester. Science books are not organized to be followed in sequence necessarily. Although the content of the book is organized in unit form, it is up to the teacher to choose the sequence of the units. Most textbooks emphasize inquiry learning and suggest appropriate experiments to help children understand the science concepts.

Bradley (1999) studied middle school science textbooks. She and Project 2061 evaluators believe the texts are inadequate for middle school students. The reviewers concluded that the texts covered too much information with too little depth, that key ideas were not

well developed, and that suggested activities did not lead students to significant scientific concepts.

NATIONAL SCIENCE PROGRAMS

Curriculum improvement projects have been developed by scientists and science educators for use in the schools. These projects emphasize the following:

- Inquiry learning
- Sequenced experimentation by students to learn science concepts
- Understanding the underlying science disciplines
- Understanding the environment
- Development of mathematics skills
- Use of technology

Some of the major national projects will be discussed in the following sections.

Windows on Science

Windows on Science was one of the first videodisc science programs developed. The laser disc K–8 curriculum program, now available on DVD, integrates reading and writing in the science curriculum with interdisciplinary and cross-disciplinary instruction. Each of the 15 laser discs contains hundreds of photographs, diagrams, movie clips, and animations. The visuals are motivating to students and support the suggested lesson plans. Research studies questioned the effectiveness of the program and concluded that *Windows on Science* evoked greater interest in science topics and was equally effective with male and female students and English language learners (ELLs).

Research Findings

Peters and Stout (2006) studied the constructionist approach to teaching. They concluded that the teacher's role is to select activities for students that guide them into "developing meaningful scientific concepts" and that teachers need to use open-ended questions to stimulate discussions. Students are influenced by past experiences, their knowledge base, and their classroom environment (p. 36).

The Voyage of the Mimi and *The Second Voyage of the Mimi*

These interdisciplinary programs, developed by Bank Street College of Education, are examples of a micro-computer-based laboratory system available for class-room use. The programs require students in grades 4–8 to analyze, hypothesize, and evaluate as they gather data, explore, and discover. *The Voyage of the Mimi* programs have several learning modules: maps and navigation, whales and their environment, introduction to computing, and ecosystem. The programs are inquiry-based and engage students in a simulated experience. The students must use the information they are gaining to solve ecological problems and live for a year on an island without upsetting the ecosystem.

Project Learning Tree (PLT)

Focusing on environmental education, this project is intended to build students' awareness, appreciation, understanding, skills, and commitment to environmental issues. The project is appropriate for pre-kindergarten through grade 12. PLT is interdisciplinary and can be infused in all of the subject fields. Content encompasses the total environment: land, air, and water. Students are engaged in simulations that involve them in a decision-making activity that affects their communities. Major themes include diversity, interrelationships, systems, structure and scale, and patterns of change. The project is used in all 50 states and Canada, Japan, Mexico, Sweden, Finland, and Brazil. An activity guide provides teacher assistance. Information can be obtained from Professor Lou Iozzi, environmental education at Rutgers University.

Project Wild

This project is sponsored by the Council for Environmental Education and the Western Association of Fish and Wildlife Agencies. It is an interdisciplinary, supplementary conservation and environmental education program for teachers of kindergarten through high school. Information can be obtained on the Internet at www.projectwild.org.

National Audubon Society Program for Grades 3–6 and Middle School

This project is aimed at helping teachers develop instructional units using discovery-oriented learning, hands-on experimentation, group projects, decision making, and technology. The Audubon program orients teachers to the latest issues in environmental science and suggests innovative uses of video and computer resources. Information can be obtained on the Internet.

Carolina Science and Technology for Children (STC)

Planned for students in grades 1–6, this comprehensive curriculum contains 24 units of study that explore life, earth, physical sciences, and technology. The curriculum is aligned with the science content standards and is developed so that students can follow a four-step, research-based learning cycle:

1. Focus: Students examine a topic and discuss what they want to explore.
2. Explore: Using hands-on equipment, students investigate concepts and record their observations.
3. Reflect: Students analyze their findings, draw conclusions, and discuss results with classmates.
4. Apply: Students apply what they learned in other contexts.

The program is quite flexible and does not need to be used at the identified grade level.

Lawrence Hall of Science Projects

The Lawrence Hall of Science at the University of California at Berkeley has produced a number of science projects for classroom use since the 1960s. The programs are targeted to elementary and middle school students. The programs are quite diverse and ongoing, and they come complete with kits and teacher guides. GEMS and FOSS are two of the programs sponsored by the Lawrence Hall of Science. They will be briefly described next.

GEMS

The Great Explorations in Math and Science (GEMS) units are based on the *National Science Education Standards and Benchmarks*. The GEMS guides feature skills, concepts, themes, mathematics strands, and nature of science categories. The themes traverse all disciplines and are considered unifying concepts and processes. Data sheets for students can be obtained in Spanish. More than 50 guides can be obtained from the Lawrence Hall of Science #5200, Berkeley, CA 94720-

5200. Examples of the guides include "Buzzing a Hive," "Bubbleology," "Fingerprinting," "Moons of Jupiter," "Mystery Festival," and "Shapes, Loops & Images."

FOSS

The Full Option Science System (FOSS) focuses on the natural world and is based on the proposition that students learn science by doing science. The program provides hands-on equipment kits, science background information, lesson plans, student information sheets, interdisciplinary activities, embedded assessments, suggestions for extended reading, videos, and a Foss web site. The program is developmentally constructed. Second graders learn to observe, compare, and organize information; fifth graders consider cause and effect and delve into relationships among variables. Assessment variables include content knowledge, ability to conduct investigations, and students' ability to build explanations based on their investigations. Information can be obtained from the Lawrence Hall of Science at www.lhs.edu. (Information about both FOSS and GEMS can be found on the Internet.)

MATERIALS AND EQUIPMENT FOR TEACHING SCIENCE

Science materials and equipment should not be a problem for the imaginative teacher. Common, everyday materials and equipment from the immediate environment can be used to enrich the science program. Students should be urged to use materials typically found around the house, school, or street. Students and their parents can usually be counted on to help equip the science program.

Iron filings, used frequently when students are studying magnets, can be obtained by sending students to the school sandbox with a magnet and an envelope to collect the filings. The teacher's main problem is to develop science kits for the different investigations or science units. Apple boxes, obtained at the produce department of large markets, make marvelous storage containers for the science materials and equipment.

ASSESSING SCIENCE LEARNING

Three purposes for science education were presented at the beginning of this chapter:

1. To provide students with opportunities to think critically and practice methods of inquiry

2. To develop science concepts that facilitate understanding of the biological and physical environment

3. To develop appropriate attitudes and skills essential for democratic citizenship

These purposes should be used to guide the assessment of science learning.

Assessing Critical Thinking and Use of Inquiry

Observation of Students' Performances

Observations of students as they engage in group discussions, experimentation, group work, and individual projects provides information about how well students are progressing in using methods of inquiry. For example, a checklist (like the one shown in Figure 11.2) provides a format for observation of inquiry skills.

Communication

Listening to students as they talk with each other, respond to questions, and participate in discussions provides evidence of what they know, how they have reasoned, and the testing to which they submit their inner thoughts.

Written Reports and Record Keeping

Earlier in this chapter and in Chapter 10, classroom lessons illustrated the types of reports students can be asked to make while involved in problem solving and experimentation. These reports represent a fine assessment tool to verify students' understanding of scientific processes, critical-thinking power, and ability to describe the thinking process. The observation record (refer again to Figure 11.1) for the third-grade experiment is another means to verify students' methods of inquiry.

Drawings and Graphing

Students can be asked to draw or make graphs to communicate their understanding of processes, ideas, progress, or solutions. Students may sketch or diagram inventions and understandings. The drawings, along with the written records and reports, can be used for portfolio assessment.

Cox-Petersen and Olson (2007) used drawings and interviews to assess the conceptual understandings of third-, fourth-, and fifth-grade English language learners with limited English proficiency. They had the

Figure 11.2 Critical-Thinking and Inquiry Skills Checklist

	Names of Students			
	Malcolm	*Jean*	*Maria*	*Rick*
1. When presented with a problem situation, does the student attempt to identify and define the problem?				
2. Does the student identify relevant information?				
3. Does the student suggest possible solutions or raise questions about cause and effect?				
4. Does the student suggest means to test or find ways to explain the data?				
5. Does the student attempt to gather data, observe, or collect evidence in a variety of ways?				
6. Does the student accurately report about and observe the evidence?				
7. Does the student interpret the data accurately?				
8. Does the student recognize the need to validate the experiment and the research?				
9. Does the student attempt to generalize, make inferences, or theorize based on the interpretation?				

students draw pictures of the ocean using as much detail as possible. They did this four times during the year so that they could use the drawings to assess each student's progress from September to June. Drawings were assessed using a rubric that the students helped to design. "Draw Talk" interviews were conducted by the teachers *after* the students had the opportunity to talk with other students.

Products

Students can construct what they have been studying. Examples in this chapter have included electromagnets, crystal radios, and motors. Students can build pinhole cameras, kaleidoscopes, and inventions. Products can be used as part of a science fair or other type of exhibition.

Suppose that some upper-grade students were studying sound. Their teacher brought a megaphone to class. To determine whether the students could think scientifically, the teacher asked them the following questions on a test:

1. How can we make a megaphone?
2. How is a megaphone used?
3. How can a megaphone help us hear?

The students in this class were expected to identify the materials needed to make a megaphone and to identify how they would go about discovering its use. They were also expected to suggest ways to find out

how the megaphone would improve their ability to hear sound. This type of test measures the application and use of methods of inquiry. It does not focus on facts or scientific concepts.

Evaluation of Scientific Concepts

If those same upper-grade students had made megaphones, discovered their use, and determined how a megaphone could be used to help them hear better, their teacher could then develop a test to determine whether the students understood the concepts associated with sound energy. The test could be short answer, essay, or multiple choice. In this test, the teacher might ask the following questions:

1. Why does a megaphone conserve sound energy? (A megaphone reflects sound in a specific direction.)
2. Explain how a megaphone works. (A megaphone concentrates the sound waves instead of allowing the sound waves to spread out equally in all directions.)
3. Does it make any difference which end of the megaphone you use? Explain. (The large end gathers the sound; the small end magnifies the sound.)

Students can also demonstrate knowledge of scientific concepts by what they say during an evaluative discussion or by what they write when they interpret an experiment. After studying organisms, students should know that living things are interdependent and that organisms may be classified by similarities and differences in characteristics. Concepts such as these should be generated by the students after performing experiments or reading about the adaptation of organisms.

Assessing Students' Attitudes and Skills for a Democratic Society

A scientific attitude describes the individual's skill development and willingness to do the following:

- Be open-minded (unbiased)
- Use reliable sources of information
- Validate information from a variety of sources
- Be curious
- Examine evidence and deliberate
- Interpret data on the basis of evidence
- Understand the significance of multiple causation
- Reject superstitions

These behaviors can be evaluated by critically observing students' performance on work tasks, in group participation, and by the kinds of things that students choose to do or to share. For example, the student who chooses to participate in a science fair, pursues science hobbies, or suggests a class experiment certainly is expressing personal choice and a scientific attitude. A scientific attitude is vital in a democratic society because the individual is more likely to believe in and practice the following:

- Question results
- Search for causal relationships
- Use several resources
- Accept responsibility
- Critically evaluate his or her own and others' work
- Contribute thoughts and opinions
- Apply scientific methods to a variety of situations

Review Chapter 7 on assessment procedures.

INCLUSION

Science teaching, as described in this chapter, emphasizes student participation in inquiry learning. All children need a hands-on approach to learning, and differentiation of instruction is always appropriate. Sci-

Research Findings

Cox-Petersen and Olson (2002) suggest the following guidelines for assessing students:

1. Find out what students know about a topic and use that information for planning instruction.
2. Use formative assessment to guide teaching, not just for grading.
3. Use multidimensional assessment practices to determine students' understanding and performance.

ence is ideal for facilitating the acceptance of students with disabilities. Teachers must make accommodations for students with physical impairments so that they can access needed equipment.

Because most science activities are group-oriented, the mainstreamed student can work in a carefully selected small group or be instructed to work individually. The experiences themselves should be of high interest to the student because most students enjoy the study of animals, plants, magnetism, and the solar system. Manipulative experiences tend to be therapeutic, thus increasing the significance and attraction of science. Experimentation is particularly appealing, and the use of the senses in science enhances the study experience.

For students with learning disabilities, it is important to build in appropriate background information and perhaps a concept map to guide these students before they begin to experiment. The organization of content, though always important, is particularly necessary for students with learning disabilities. During instruction, monitor these students to help them stay engaged and on track. When the activity is concluded, verify that the student can explain the concept and apply it in a purposeful manner.

CLASSROOM MANAGEMENT

Classroom management considerations in science are similar to the concerns expressed about social studies. Anticipatory planning is of greater significance when students are to perform experiments in small groups that are not under the immediate supervision of an adult. The teacher needs to consider student safety, work space, and need for material resources. The modeling aspect of experimentation should also be considered. Suggestions follow:

Safety: Before students use science equipment or tools, they should be given specific instruction in their care and use.

Work space: Before students work, the work space should be designated, and consideration should be given to providing sufficient work space for each group.

Resources: Equipment, materials, and textbooks should be inventoried to ensure that they are of sufficient quantity to meet the study or experiment needs of students.

Modeling: Modeling by the teacher of open-ended, inquiry-oriented learning is important so that students recognize that it is okay if an experiment fails, and that most experiments need validation.

LEARNING CENTERS

Science learning centers may be part of the ongoing science unit or an added dimension used to reinforce skills during reading or mathematics. The centers may be used by a group of students working together or by an individual working alone. Following are five experiments that can be used in science learning centers.

Soil Testing

Science, Language Arts—Upper Grades

Objectives. To observe and participate in a simple investigation to determine the composition of soil; to explain how the composition of soil affects the growing of crops

---

Teaching Hints: English Language Learners

ELL students benefit from active learning experiences in science. To assist students:

1. Build background knowledge and vocabulary using concrete materials.
2. Team students with others who have greater proficiency.
3. Help students feel more secure in working with their classmates while doing science experiments.
4. Structure science content around a theme, thereby reinforcing vocabulary and concepts.
5. Provide nonverbal means for students to demonstrate their understanding.

Materials. Blue and red litmus paper, soil samples from different places, paper cups, bottle of water, bottle of limewater, teacher information sheets or science books about soils and farming

Assessment. Discussion of the following question: How does the composition of soil affect the growing of crops? Self-evaluation of experiment using teacher-prepared exhibit of acid, alkaline, neutral litmus paper

Procedures. Task card
1. Place a soil sample in a paper cup. Prepare at least four samples.
2. Add a small amount of water to each sample to dampen the soil.
3. Test samples with the litmus paper.
4. After 5 minutes, remove the litmus papers and observe their color. (Blue litmus paper turns red or pink in an acid soil; red litmus paper turns blue in an alkaline soil. If the paper colors do not change, then the soil is neutral.)
5. How do your soil samples differ?
6. If one of the soil samples is acid, change it to a neutral condition using the limewater.
7. What difference does the composition of the soil make to a farmer? Read and find out.

Making Magnets

Science, Mathematics—Middle Grades

Objectives. To compare the strength of temporary magnets; to generalize about temporary magnets

Materials. Iron nails, steel pins, steel screwdriver, head of a hammer, iron bolt

Assessment. Discussion and self-evaluation using teacher-prepared answer sheet

Procedures. Task card
1. Brush the nail with a magnet.
2. Use the nail to pick up the steel pins.
3. How can you make the nail a stronger magnet? (Brush the nail longer.)
4. How do you know when it is stronger? (It will pick up more pins.)
5. Does it matter how you brush the nail with the magnet? (Brushing the nail in one direction makes the nail's magnetism stronger.)
6. Try the experiment with other objects. Record your results. (It will be more difficult to magnetize steel than iron; however, the students should also

discover that once magnetized, the steel will retain magnetized longer.)

Life Cycles

Science, Social Studies, Language Arts, Mathematics—Lower Grades

Objectives. Observation of life cycle; sequencing the life cycle in appropriate order

Materials. Tank of tadpoles in different stages of development; garden exhibit in different stages, from seed to mature plant; duplicated pictures of the two exhibits; scissors; paste; paper

Assessment. Students may compare their life-cycle sequence with a teacher-prepared exhibit.

Procedures. Students are to observe the two exhibits. Students cut out pictures and paste them in sequential order to illustrate the life cycle of the frog and of a plant.

Visual Arts

Science, Art, Language Arts—All Grade Levels

Objectives. To observe and describe accurately; to improve art skills; to enjoy an aesthetic experience

Materials. Weeds, flowers, leaves, and branches, or fish, insects, and pets; drawing or painting materials

Assessment. Self-evaluation and group sharing

Procedures
1. Observe the exhibit.
2. Describe the exhibit.
3. Draw or paint what was observed.

Create an Environment

Science, Language Arts, Social Studies, Art—Upper Grades

Objectives. To select an environment and identify latitude and factors affecting climate and ways of life

Materials. Science and social studies texts, globe, maps, Internet, magazine pictures, scrapbook-making materials

Assessment. Scrapbook product, individual presentations, class discussion

Procedures. Task cards
1. Using the globe, texts, or pictures, select a place (an environment) to study.
2. Locate the place and identify its latitude, continent, country.
3. Determine how its location affects the climate of the region.
4. How does the environment affect ways of life, such as work, housing, food, and play?
5. Create a scrapbook that illustrates your research. Draw or cut out pictures that demonstrate the way of life of people in your selected environment.
6. Write short descriptions of the pictures.

SUMMARY

The purposes for teaching science are threefold: development of critical thinking and inquiry methods, development of science vocabulary and concepts, and development of appropriate attitudes and skills. Content of science intertwines content and process. Programs focus on living things, the earth, the universe, and matter and energy. Use of themes helps integrate topics.

Good teaching of science features student observation, discussion hypothesizing, and explanation. Students learn to accept the tentativeness of their findings until subjected to testing. Students' own questions often lead to content study. Hands-on experimentation is encouraged. Inquiry learning through use of many resources is featured. Teaching units developed through themes serve to integrate several subject fields. Common, everyday materials and equipment are used to enrich the science program.

In some schools, science specialist teachers may be responsible for the science program and help introduce new concepts, which are then reinforced by the classroom teacher. Resource people in the community are often called upon to assist with the science program.

Assessment focuses on students' critical-thinking ability and use of inquiry. A variety of student products are used for assessment, including observation, communication, drawings, projects, graphs, written reports, journals, and computer links. Attitudes and skills can be assessed through observation, note of students' open-mindedness, deliberation, and testing of findings.

All students, regardless of personal, physical, or language learning problems, should be engaged in science activities and included in the regular classroom. Peer assistance and interaction are valuable.

Classroom management needs to focus on students' safety, work space, use of equipment, consideration of others, and the use of modeling experiences.

PORTFOLIO ACTIVITY

Describe how your science program matches the interests, experiences, and developmental level of your students. Identify the time you have planned for science, available resources, opportunities for science inquiry, content strand, and performance assessments, and include samples of students' work.

DISCUSSION QUESTIONS AND APPLICATION EXERCISES

1. Identify scientific concepts and processes to be taught to a specified group of students. Describe three inquiry learning experiences to teach the concepts and processes.
2. Develop several science kits for use in science experiments. List the equipment and materials to be found in each of the kits.
3. Your upper-grade students have discovered how to light a bulb using wire and a dry-cell battery. What additional open-ended experimentation can they perform?
4. Your lower-grade students are studying plants. Suggest some experiments they can perform to learn about seeds, plant growth, and plant propagation.
5. You have been asked to explain to parents why inquiry teaching is important in the teaching of science. What will you say?
6. Describe an investigation that students will perform and the way in which you will require them to communicate their processes and solutions.
7. Draw a webbing concept map with a theme in the center; identify the science content and interdisciplinary connections.
8. Outline a thematic unit that focuses on the interrelationship of science, technology, and society. What science concepts will you use?

READER RESEARCH

1. What are the roots of the group investigation model of inquiry and the 5–E instructional model? In what ways do the two models differ? Under what circumstances would you choose one model over the other?

2. Read about the Cox-Petersen and Olson study in *Science and Children*, 44(6), 46–49. Replicate the study using ELL students you teach or observe.

TECHNOLOGY APPLICATIONS

1. Create a timeline that depicts significant changes of time and changes in our patterns of life. Begin with the industrial revolution. Use the Internet to research historical and scientific events that affected our concept of time. Use the information to plan several lessons for your students that will integrate social studies, science, and mathematics. (If students are to use the Internet, remember to provide several sites to help them begin their study.)
2. Consider the interrelationship of science, technology, and society. Describe a problem that affects people and the environment. How will you involve students in the study of the problem? What information will students need? What Internet sites will students use? What other resources will they use to seek information? What public policy implications need to be considered?

Some example problems follow:

- Water pours down the driveway of a house in the neighborhood. The water floods neighbors' yards, and the runoff is filling the street drainage system. How does this problem affect others and society in general?
- Developers apply to the city to build a tract of homes on the local hillside. Much of the hillside will need to be cut and leveled to accommodate the houses. Predict and research the environmental implications if permission to build is granted. Consider human and animal consequences.
- Plan a virtual field trip for small groups of students that will require them to study weather and climate conditions in the different continents. Assign each group a different continent to study and have them identify their web sites, take notes, and share the information with the class.

Students' Own Investigations Motivate Interest and Questions.

CHAPTER 12

· ·

Health and Physical Education

Physical fitness experts are concerned that children's fitness is frequently ignored in the school curriculum. Clearly this is due to the attention given to the teaching of subjects that are required to be tested. However, appropriately designed physical education programs are needed to ensure that students develop and maintain good health in their young years and in adulthood, and gain the knowledge and skills needed to balance academic learning. Only 11 states require physical education in the elementary school, and only 2 states require a minimum weekly number of minutes (Graber et al, 2008).

The wellness concept has been suggested to integrate the teaching of health and physical education. This concept encompasses nutrition, physical fitness, stress management, and personal responsibility for a healthy lifestyle.

In this chapter, goals, content, and teaching strategies are discussed for both subject fields. Key ideas presented in the chapter include the following:

- Physical conditioning activities and good sportsmanship
- Exercise and nutrition
- The development of healthful ways of living
- Self-awareness and self-esteem
- Thematic teaching and the integration of health and physical education with other subjects

Advance Organizer

The following questions are intended to guide your reading and understanding of the content of this chapter.

1. In planning the physical and health education program, what content areas should be emphasized?
2. How would you personally define physical fitness, and what are the purposes of physical and health education?
3. How should stabilizing, locomotor, and manipulative movements be described?
4. How can classroom activities be used to foster a positive self-image? Can you explain how play activities foster appropriate social behavior?
5. What are some learning experiences that can be used to develop health education goals?
6. What is the instructional sequence for teaching both a directed and indirect lesson in physical education?
7. Why is it important to plan movements appropriate for warm-up and cool-down exercises?
8. How can growth in physical and health education be assessed?
9. In what ways would you integrate the teaching of health education with other subjects?
10. What classroom management plans should be considered when teaching physical education?

INTASC   **INTASC Standards**

Most states have identified curriculum time allotments for teaching physical and health education, yet those time allotments are frequently overlooked. In elementary schools, teachers are sometimes not prepared to plan and teach the two subject fields, and in the middle school, teacher specialists are often required to teach a variety of subjects that may interfere with their required specialization. However, all of the INTASC standards apply to the teaching of physical and health education and are often of greater significance to the well-being of students.

Professional Lexicon

adapted physical education Individualized ideas and suggestions provided by a physical education specialist to service students with special needs.

biomechanics The science that studies the effects of both internal and external forces on human body movements.

locomotor movements Progressive movements that involve changing body position, as in running and walking.

manipulative movements Activities that involve giving or receiving force to and from objects, as in kicking, striking, and throwing.

stabilizing movements The most basic human movements that affect balance, posture, and axial movements.

Jimmy, who is just 6 years old, participated in a soccer game over the weekend. When he entered his classroom on Monday, it was obvious to his teacher that he was limping. The teacher asked him what had happened to him, and he said that his father wanted him to play soccer and while playing, someone had tripped him. "I don't like to play soccer, but my dad says it's good for me. I don't see how it can be good for me when everybody gets hurt and the adults are all yelling." "You need to tell me a little more about how this happened," replied his teacher, "but for today, you'd better not participate in physical education."

PHYSICAL FITNESS AND WELLNESS

Physical fitness experts believe that children's fitness has declined through the years. Reasons for this decline may include the following:

- Less emphasis is placed on physical education in the schools.
- Funding for after-school playground activities is almost nonexistent.
- The attractiveness of television and computer games has distracted children from outdoor activity.

It appears that in the information age, our technological society has decreasing demands for physical exertion but increasing opportunities for spectator and nonphysical recreation, such as computer games and television sports. In the urban United States, children rarely climb trees, play sandlot or street ball, or even walk to school.

Dargan and Zeitlin (2000) studied the play patterns of children in urban environments. They believe that children's play activities on the city streets provide a sense of neighborhood. "Play is one way that a city street becomes 'our block'" (p. 73). Older generations used the pavement, dirt lots, hydrants, curbs, and lampposts for hide-and-seek, red rover, ring-a-levio, double

Dutch, and kick the can; they imitated the knights of the round table, Xena, and Anakin Skywalker. Children made up their own rules and boundaries, and they played until it was too dark to play outside. Through these creative games, they developed a sense of community that is rarely present today. Both Piaget and Vygotsky noted that spontaneous play facilitates intellectual growth.

Dargan and Zeitlin point out that today's play activities are more frequently indoor activities: watching television, using computers, and listening to CDs. As a consequence, the sense of community is lost. Many of the outdoor activities are antagonistic to adult culture (graffiti, gang activity, rapping). Their conclusion is that adults must help make the streets safe for children to play: "streets that are safe for children, are safe for adults" (p. 75). Teachers can contribute by encouraging creative games on school playgrounds. These games need not have rigid rules and should provide students with the freedom to improvise.

Rasmussen (2000) corroborated the Dargan and Zeitlin findings. She states that approximately 2 million children age 5 to 17 years participated in agency-sponsored sports activities. Major sponsors included the American Youth Soccer Organization and Little League baseball. Although these sponsored activities

Research Findings

Peter Gray (2008) a research psychologist, has studied age-mixed play and has found that children benefit from Vygotsky's zone of proximal development. Older children benefit by exercising their nurturing instincts and sense of responsibility. Younger children are rewarded by being taught game rules, strategies, and concepts. The value of age-mixed play capitalizes on children's natural ways of learning.

provide organized activities, all of the decisions that affect rule enforcement and the play itself are made by adults. Children do not learn to resolve disputes. Still another problem with these organized activities is parent interest in winning. Winning may be important, but it should not be the major focus. But for many youngsters, these organized play activities may be the only physical play available for their participation.

The World Health Organization emphasizes that good health is closely related to physical, social, and mental well-being. The concept of wellness emerged from this idea of the integration of physical fitness, nutrition, and stress management. The wellness concept assumes that individuals are responsible for their personal healthy lifestyle. The significance of physical fitness is often ignored in the school curriculum; however, the Council of Chief State School Officers and the Association of State and Territorial Health Officials cite "research evidence that students' health significantly affects their school achievement" (Pateman, 2004, p. 70).

HEALTH AND PHYSICAL EDUCATION PROGRAMS

Health and physical education are interrelated and need to be coordinated in order to attain a complete school and community health program. Foundation disciplines for both subjects come from the life sciences, medical sciences, physical sciences, and social sciences. Content for both subjects includes the following:

Physical Education

Rhythm and dance
Aquatics
Outdoor education
Gymnastics, tumbling
Team sports and individual sports
Movement patterns and skills

Health Education

Personal health
Nutrition
Family health
Consumer and community health
Communicable and chronic diseases
Alcohol, tobacco, and drug education
Environmental health
Safety and accident prevention

Physical and health education programs emphasize the development and maintenance of total body fitness. To medical specialists, fitness means freedom from disease. To social scientists, particularly psychologists, fitness has to do with mental health; physical educators describe fitness in terms of the individual's physical performance. The physical educator determines fitness by testing muscular strength and endurance, flexibility, circulorespiratory endurance, and body weight and composition.

Physical and health education are taught as separate lessons and as integrated lessons within other subjects, such as language arts, science, and social studies. Incidental learning, unrelated to a particular health or physical education unit, can be provided advantageously. For example, when the first graders were studying about light and color (described in Chapter 11), health instruction focused on care of the eyes. Health and physical education lessons may come about as a consequence of safety needs, class discussions, and school or community concerns.

GOALS OF PHYSICAL AND HEALTH EDUCATION

Physical Education

While the basic purpose of physical education is to provide students with movement experiences, the underlying goal is optimal growth and development consistent with each individual's characteristics, interests, and abilities. Physical education experiences should be of a developmental nature so that students progress competently. Physical education goals focus on movement skills and personal and social development. However, Kretchmar (2008) suggests that the *fun* aspect of exercise and activity should be emphasized and receive priority attention. Skills to be emphasized include the following:

- Sensorimotor and perceptual motor skills
- Locomotor skills
- Nonlocomotor skills
- Balance
- Eye-hand coordination
- Eye-foot coordination
- General coordination
- Creative movement

Health Education

The purpose of health education is to prepare students to accept responsibility for applying health principles in their daily lives and to promote family and community health. Health education should develop positive habits, motivation, and patterns that enhance healthful ways of living. The curriculum emphasizes personal responsibility; understanding the process of growth and development; and using health-related information, products, and services.

HOW ARE PHYSICAL EDUCATION GOALS DEVELOPED?

The National Association for Sport and Physical Education (NASPE) advocates a daily minimum of 30 minutes of physical education (excluding recess and lunch activities) at the elementary school level and increasing time at the middle school level. However, those time allotments are rarely adhered to, and block scheduling in middle schools usually means that students have physical education every other day. In many elementary schools, children have physical education just once per week.

Movement Skills and Movement Knowledge

Movement abilities advance in a sequential manner. Gallahue, Werner, and Luedke (1975, p. 6) identified six stages, from simple to complex movements:

1. Reflexive behavior—infancy to 1 year
2. Rudimentary movement abilities—0 to 2 years
3. Fundamental movement patterns—preschool age to 7 years
4. General movement skills—8 to 10 years

5. Specific movement skills—11 to 13 years
6. Specialized movement skills—14 years to adulthood

Children's movement abilities are progressive. Although each phase is distinct, the child may advance through more than one phase at a time. Motor skills may be categorized within three sets of movement activities: stabilizing, locomotor, and manipulative. Students improve in these categories of movement through practice. At school, this practice is mediated through the content of physical education (self-testing activities, games and sports, rhythms, and aquatics). As in other subjects of the curriculum, the teacher's task is to sequence learning experiences appropriate to the students' developmental levels. Primary students (K–2) need basic movement experiences for each of the categories of movement; middle-grade and upper-grade students need both general and specific movement skills within each category of movement. The physical education program should help students not only enjoy movement for movement's sake but appreciate the aesthetics of creative movement.

Stabilizing Activities

Maintenance of stability is considered the most basic of all human movements. Although we may place our body in a variety of positions that may include axial movements and varied postures, the trick is to control equilibrium. Both locomotion and manipulative activities depend on stability.

Stabilizing movements are those in which the body maintains balance, changes posture, or engages in axial movements. Stability includes axial movements and postures. Axial movements are those involving the trunk or limbs. Postures are concerned with the maintenance of balance. Examples of axial movements include bending, turning, stretching, and swinging.

Research Findings

Mckenzie and Kahan (2008) researched the relationship between academic achievement and physical fitness. They concluded that physical fitness scores are related to classroom achievement; physical activities improve classroom performances.

Examples of postures include standing, rolling, stooping, and dodging.

Biomechanics

Body movement is affected by internal and external forces, such as friction, gravity, and the laws of motion, i.e., **biomechanics**. Newton's laws of motion, center of gravity, buoyancy, spin, and force vectors apply. Science can be integrated with physical education through inquiry activities that allow students to experiment with body movements. Understanding of these laws can help improve students' skills and performance.

Locomotor Activities

Locomotor movements are progressive and involve changing body position relative to fixed points on the ground. Locomotor activities include running, walking, hopping, skipping, jumping, climbing, leaping, galloping, and sliding.

Teachers need to be alert to the following typical locomotor movement problems:

- Students need to be able to alter their performance based on circumstances peculiar to the movement situation. For example, a faster or slower pace by others means that the student must be flexible in order to change the original movement.
- Locomotor activities are often combined with stabilizing or manipulative movements, and this combination may cause difficulty.
- Some students have difficulty alternating feet and using both sides of the body; it is difficult for some students to begin a movement with both feet.
- When running, some students tend to land on heels first; some students tend to run on toes only.

Manipulative Activities

Manipulative movements involve giving or receiving force to and from objects. Activities include kicking, striking, throwing, catching, bouncing, rolling, trapping, and volleying. These activities depend on locomotor and stabilizing movements. Manipulative activities combine one or more movements (locomotor and/or stabilizing) and use those movements together with other movements. For example, in throwing an underhand toss, the performer must assume a stable position with one foot ahead of the other, bend slightly, project the ball forward and upward, release the ball, and follow through with arms in the direction of the propelled ball. Manipulative movements are more difficult than stabilizing or locomotor movements and depend on the performer's understanding and integration of space, time, force, and flow.

In the chapter-opening vignette, Jimmy no doubt had difficulty kicking the soccer ball and continuing to run. Combining the two movements required slowing his pace to kick the ball and then speeding up. It is more likely that he lost his balance and tripped himself, than that someone else interfered with his performance. Because Jimmy is just 6 years old, he probably is lacking coordination and balance.

In teaching manipulative movements, the teacher needs to be aware of and anticipate the following problems:

- Some students do not develop proper follow-through in movements.
- Some students position their feet improperly, tending to place feet together instead of one ahead of the other when throwing or kicking.
- Some students have difficulty shifting their weight as they kick, trap, or throw.
- Failure to maintain balance when throwing or kicking is a typical problem.
- Maintenance of eye contact with the target when catching, trapping, or kicking is a common problem.

Appreciation of physical fitness can be enhanced through the study of biomechanics. Students can experiment with how body movements are influenced by gravity, friction, and the laws of motion.

Self-Image

The goal of a positive self-concept can be fostered by providing students with opportunities to learn about self and about others, to learn to face adversity, and to overcome problems. Self-image is enhanced through planned experiences and opportunities such as the following:

- Learning about the body and its parts and functions
- Exploring movements
- Expressing ideas and emotions through body movement and physical exercise
- Choosing, demonstrating, and satisfying personal skills and recreational interests

Certain customs in elementary classrooms and middle school physical education classes can have a negative effect on the self-concept. Frequently, older students are allowed to elect captains and choose teams. The student who is not coordinated will be the last one to be selected, with the natural psychological consequence to the child's ego. The following case study describes an incident in a fourth-grade classroom where the teacher anticipated the problem and found a way to develop a student's self-concept and promote social behavior.

Drew was considered the best athlete in the fourth grade. The children in his classroom consistently chose him for captain. After the election process, Drew and the other three captains would go through the formality of selecting their teams. If asked, Emma Wellesly, the fourth-grade teacher, could have listed the order in which each child would be chosen, and that was precisely what was troubling her. She knew that Ben would be the last to be selected because out on the playground he was uncoordinated. Ben seemed to be going through a trying period; he did quite well in the classroom, but his ego seemed destroyed when he came in from recess or lunch.

Ms. Wellesly decided to delay the selection process until later in the day so she could think about the situation. Sometimes she had the captains use the attendance cards and select their teams outside, away from the class, to spare hurt feelings; yet as soon as the teams were written on the board, the students would know instinctively who had been chosen first and who had been chosen last.

As she watched the children work on their spelling, she observed that Ben was quizzing Drew. She saw Ben shake his head as Drew made a mistake; she went closer and heard Ben tell Drew a trick for remembering the word. Drew nodded and said, "Hmm, i think that will help. Thanks, Ben."

It occurred to Ms. Wellesly that the two boys worked well together and seemed to have a genuine friendship, yet they were rarely together on the playground because of Drew's physical prowess. Ms. Wellesly decided to talk to Drew. She asked him if he had ever wanted to do something and had tried very hard but had failed because he lacked the necessary skills. Drew recalled that he had wanted to ski with his older brother but had been unable to do so. Ms. Wellesly then explained how much Ben wanted to do well in sports and that he needed someone to have confidence in him and to assist him.

Drew confided that he really liked Ben and felt sorry for him when he wasn't selected for a team. "Ben helps me a lot in class. Do you think he would really like me to try to help him on the field?" The teacher assured Drew that Ben would be pleased.

Just before lunch Ms. Wellesly settled the class, called the captains to the front, and said "Now is the time to choose your teams." When it was Drew's turn to make his first selection, he said, "I want Ben to be on my team." Ben was shocked, but he walked to the front to stand next to Drew, as was the custom. Drew put his arm around Ben's shoulders and whispered, "Who shall I choose next, Ben?"

Physical education offers rare opportunities to develop both self-image and social behavior. Emma Wellesly modeled both humanistic and respectful behavior. Students imitate teacher behavior; in the preceding case study, Drew modeled compassion.

Instead of allowing students to choose their teammates, many problems would be alleviated if teachers grouped students randomly for physical education just as they do for other subject fields. Team assignments should ensure equity and should be changed frequently so that teams are evenly composed and students' self-concepts are safeguarded.

Social Behavior

Play activities help the child move from egocentric behavior to social behavior. During the primary-grade

Success on playground apparatus requires the use of stabilizing movements.

years, students play most cooperatively with a single partner or in a small group. As physical skills improve, students can play in small groups and in teams. Students enjoy competitive play during the middle-grade years; however, students should compete with others of similar ability rather than with older students or adults. Successful group behavior occurs when students have opportunities to be both a group leader and a group participant.

Social behavior can be developed by providing opportunities for students to assume leadership responsibility. Students can be scorekeepers, umpires, referees, and play leaders for younger children. They can play the role of statistician and tally the performance of teammates. They can be in charge of equipment; they can demonstrate and teach specific skills to a friend or a small group of students; they can be team leaders.

As group members, they can demonstrate cooperative behavior and good sportsmanship. They can offer encouragement to others by their own participation and by praising others. They can accept responsibility for their own behavior.

Recreational Interest

It is quite natural to develop interest in activities where there is some proficiency and in activities that are particularly enjoyable. Physical education activities can be extremely satisfying to students when a relaxed atmosphere is created for participation. Activities that are paced so students experience a warm-up period, a period of vigorous exercise, and a cool-down period will usually result in relieving classroom stress and providing students with a feeling of ease and good health.

Teachers can help students identify play areas for after-school participation (parks, playgrounds, community facilities) and encourage students to suggest appropriate games and sports for after-school recreation.

HOW ARE HEALTH EDUCATION GOALS DEVELOPED?

School health programs encompass health guidance, health instruction, and the development of a healthful school environment. Health guidance begins with obtaining a health history when the child first enters school. During preschool admission programs, parents should also be given information about immunization rules, vision and hearing screening tests, and school health rules that affect attendance. Health guidance continues throughout the elementary school years.

Teacher observation of students should be performed daily. Teachers are often the first to detect signs of illness or child abuse. Teachers as well as other members of the school staff (doctors, nurses, principal) should prepare reports and solicit cooperative assistance from other social agencies to ensure the health of the child.

A healthful school environment includes teaching about sanitation; the use of school facilities such as the drinking fountains, the lavatories, and the cafeteria; and the maintenance of a healthful classroom environment. Students are asked to accept responsibility for the following:

- Opening windows to provide appropriate ventilation
- Controlling lights and window shades to provide for visual health
- Emptying trash
- Placing clothing and lunches in the proper place
- Washing hands before meals and after using the bathroom
- Maintaining the classroom so it is orderly and attractive

Health instruction goals are accomplished by expanding the students' awareness from self to family to others. Development of awareness begins as the student shares his or her own feelings of wellness. The primary-grade student is helped to differentiate between health and illness. Knowledge about individual needs for rest, sleep, and relaxation are introduced during the primary grades.

Nutrition and dental care are emphasized throughout the grades, and teaching strategies focus on providing students with food choices and consumer information about food nutrients appropriate to their grade level. At an early age, children should learn about correct procedures for brushing, not only their teeth but also their gums, and the importance of flossing.

Food choices influenced by culture and ethnicity are featured in the health program so that students learn to accept and understand other students' likes and dislikes.

Students in grades 5–8 need guidance concerning what to eat before and after athletic events. Energy needs and hydration concepts need to be taught so that students will avoid high-fat and high-sugar items and instead eat complex carbohydrates for efficient energy, and drink adequate water before physical activity.

Fitness and cardiovascular health are developed by teaching about the body and how it works, and how physical activity is related to the increase of pulse and breathing rates. The school nurse, along with the classroom teacher, may provide fitness counseling and guidance to develop positive attitudes about fitness and

Research Findings

The goal of the physical education curriculum is to motivate children to adopt a physically active lifestyle. The authors believe that an effective curriculum will develop motor skills, encourage and value participation in active sports activities, and create a positive and stimulating learning environment (Rink & Hall, 2008).

exercise. The relationship of healthy gums and flossing to cardiovascular health needs to be emphasized.

Family and community health problems focus on student responsibility for maintaining personal good health. The value of regular health and dental care is advocated, and the utilization of community health resources is encouraged. Laws affecting health practices are studied, and the responsibilities of health agencies are identified.

Heredity and genetic disorders are studied in the upper grades. Students learn to differentiate between the effects of environment and heredity on human organisms, and inherited traits are studied and contrasted with acquired traits.

Mental and emotional health goals are developed by providing opportunities for students to make decisions and learn to cope with stress and anxiety. The health program is responsible for providing instruction about alcohol, drugs, narcotics, and tobacco and for relating the use and misuse of these substances to family and community health. Responsibility of individuals in the prevention of the misuse of these substances is the focus of instruction.

Disease prevention and control are studied during health education. Often community resource people are invited to the school for special programming. The school shares responsibility with the community for providing information about communicable diseases and ways to control such diseases.

Environmental studies are integrated with both social studies and science. Students learn about ecological conditions that affect the environment and how a healthful environment affects the quality of life. Water, soil, air, and noise pollution are appropriate areas of study to develop understanding that living things are interdependent with others and the environment. The

Teaching Hints

1. Provide students with real-life health problems and have them problem-solve and discuss the implications for themselves and the community.
2. Ask students to role-play how they would refuse to indulge in the use of tobacco, drugs, or alcohol offered by an acquaintance.
3. Have students research typical mental and physical changes that occur as a consequence of puberty.

conservation of human resources along with natural resources may be integrated into a health/science unit to learn that people can control, change, and improve the environment for the benefit of all.

HOW IS PHYSICAL EDUCATION TAUGHT?

Planning

Planning physical education instruction should be based on the purposes to be accomplished and the students' characteristics, interests, and abilities. Unit planning for instruction is appropriate in physical education just as it is in other subject fields. Themes selected for use in social studies and science are appropriate for inclusion of physical and health education.

GREG THOMAS'S CLASSROOM

Greg Thomas developed weekly plans for physical education (Table 12.1) and, whenever possible, he correlated his physical education activities with other subject fields. For example, using his theme of change, his students studied the importance of water in land use and human adaptation. He taught his students the Israeli song "Mayim" (which means "water") and also taught them the dance "Mayim," which required learning the grapevine, running step, and hop (Hall, Sweeny, & Esser, 1980, p. 157). He integrated health education by emphasizing how much water the body needs, particularly before participation in competitive sports. Thomas

made it a habit to encourage his students to get a drink of water before beginning play activity.

Thomas's students were learning to play softball. The students were organized into four teams. The students knew the rules and were in the second week of a three-week unit on softball. (Mondays and Tuesdays the students were engaged in team sports.) On Monday, Thomas worked with teams A and B to practice batting, catching, throwing, and running skills. Team A was in the field. Four students played first and second bases, shortstop, and catcher; the other students positioned themselves in the outfield. Team B was lined up at the batting tee at home base. The students in the field rotated positions, practicing throwing and catching, and the students at home plate each had three turns batting and running to first or second base. To teach more effective base running, Thomas had placed cones on first and second base so the students would try to increase their rate and their efficiency. Thomas stood near first base, coaching the catching, throwing, and batting. He also timed the batter's run to first base. He could have had students use a stopwatch and do the timing. This would increase student participation and motivation.

On Tuesday, Thomas provided the same instruction for teams C and D, while teams A and B played an actual game of softball.

On Wednesday, the whole class participated in the mechanics of body movement through engagement in exercise relays. Thomas drew three lines on the playground 15, 30, and 45 feet in front of the start/finish line. The teams were in four lines. Each team member performed three exercises: one on the 15-foot mark, another on the 30-foot mark, and the third on the 45-foot mark. The player then ran back to the starting line and tagged the next person on the team. The exercises chosen by Thomas were sit-ups, jumping jacks, and half-knee bends.

On Thursday, the students participated in gymnastics and tumbling. Thomas taught individual and partner stunts. He borrowed resting mats from the kindergarten rooms for use in this activity. He chose the V-Seat exercise, the Russian Dance, the Rooster Fight, and the Double Bear.

On Friday, the students used the auditorium, where Thomas taught rhythm and dance. The selected dances

Table 12.1 Weekly Schedule for Fifth-Grade Physical Education

Monday	Tuesday	Wednesday	Thursday	Friday
Teams A & B	A & B Softball	Exercise Relays		
Skills workup:			Individual and Partner Stunts:	Square Dancing:
Batting			1. Russian Dance	1. All-Amer, Promenade
Catching		(Whole Class)	2. Turnover	2. Mayim
Throwing			3. Rooster Fight	3. Virginia Reel
Running				
Teams C & D	C & D	Exercise Relays		
Softball	Skills Workup			

correlated with the social studies and the science units. Each week Thomas taught one new dance and practiced two familiar routines. He allowed the students to select another dance when time allowed.

Thomas's physical education lesson had four components:

1. A warm-up period
2. An instructional phase
3. An activity phase
4. Discussion of the day's activity

For the warm-up, he worked with the whole class doing simple stretching exercises. During the instructional phase, he often grouped the students in teams (see Monday's and Tuesday's lessons). The activity

phase received the bulk of time (usually 20 minutes). Discussion occurred when the students were back in the classroom and concerned personal and group problems, good sportsmanship, what students had learned, and relationships to other subject fields.

MARY HOGAN'S CLASSROOM

Mary Hogan's students enjoyed playing sockball and kickball, but Hogan observed that they needed to improve their skills in catching, pitching, and kicking. She planned a skills workup session for half the class on Monday and the other half on Tuesday (see Table 12.2). Before going out to the playground, Hogan explained to

Table 12.2 *Weekly* Schedule For Third-Grade Physical Education

Monday	Tuesday	Wednesday	Thursday	Friday
One-half class		One-half class		
Apparatus		Teach catching, throwing, and kicking skills		
Teach skip ring				
Travel on horizontal ladder				
One-half class	(Teams reverse Monday's activities)	One-half class	(Teams reverse Wednesday's activities)	Rhythm
Small group		Play kickball		Whole class
Skill games				
Ishigetigoko				
Jumping Fancy				
Duck on the Rock				

Teaching Hints: Integrating Physical Education with Other Subject Fields

Students can use the Internet to study the following:

- The origin of the Olympic Games and how world events and new sport interests have affected the games
- Newton's laws that affect body movements
- Archimedes' discovery of the laws of buoyancy and why he was called "the Greek Streaker"
- The ways in which games and play activities have changed (make a timeline to reflect both the years and the changes)
- Paintings and sculpture of the human figure by artists through the ages

---

the students where she wanted them to stand while she demonstrated the skills; she wanted to make sure that they would be able to see and hear her. Half the students were assigned to play a game of sockball; the other half would receive the skill instruction. Once out on the playground, Hogan demonstrated correct catching, pitching, and kicking. She emphasized how to hold the hands for catching, how to focus on the ball as it approached, the position of the feet for pitching, and the correct follow-through for kicking. Then she set the students up in groups of four and helped each group establish a drill formation to practice the skills. As the students practiced, Hogan observed them and assisted students who were having difficulty. Throughout the drill session, she encouraged the children to proceed quickly. She praised them and gave them instructions: "Watch the ball." "Look at the target." "Extend your fingers." "Follow through."

Hogan's directed lesson had the following six components:

1. *Warm-up*. The whole class did stretching exercises.
2. *Instruction*. Hogan gave the students organization instructions and instructions about skills to be taught.
3. *Demonstration*. Hogan demonstrated the skills to be practiced.
4. *Practice period*. The students had the opportunity to practice the skills that were demonstrated.

5. *Reinforcement (assessment)*. As the students practiced, Hogan encouraged them and offered suggestions for the improvement of their performance.
6. *Discussion*. Students were given time to talk about the activity and relate it to other subject fields, cooperative behaviors, good sportsmanship, and what they learned as a consequence of the activity.

During the reinforcement phase, Hogan was careful to offer only positive feedback. If she had not been satisfied with the students' performance, then she would have repeated Steps 2 through 4. At the end of the lesson, during the discussion, she might go back over the skill components to offer additional guidance.

Student Exploration

Greg Thomas asked his students, "How many boys and girls know how to play hopscotch?" (They responded both positively and negatively.) "Good, let's all get up and show each other movements for playing hopscotch."

Greg Thomas observed the students as they jumped on two feet and did some hopping. He noted that many of the students had difficulty landing on two feet simultaneously, and very few could move from the two-footed jump to a one-footed hop.

Thomas chose several students to demonstrate the jump and the hop; then he suggested that all the students try once again. This time he suggested that they

Teaching Hints: Warm-Up Exercises

Physical therapist Michele Zeolla emphasizes the need for appropriate warm-up exercises (personal communication, May 14, 2008). The following are her suggestions:

Neck: Side bend head to right and left, several times
Shoulders: Shrugging, forward and backward
Back: Touch toes; perform a backward bend
Arms: Controlled circles in both directions
Hips, legs, ankles: Running in place; jumping

Warm-up exercises also may be used when students are fidgety and need to get out of their chairs, as well as before physical education. The same exercises work well for the cool-down.

jump and then hop on the left foot. Next he had them practice jumping and hopping on the right foot.

After the students had practiced, he asked them which had been easier, the right- or the left-footed hop. The students discussed the movements and decided that much depended on whether they were right- or left-handed. Thomas followed up with a lesson on dominance in their health books.

Children (and adults) learn more effectively when there is an opportunity to experiment (explore) with the movements involved. After experimenting with the movement, the students begin to watch others to see if they can correct their own performance. Thomas observed his students to detect when it would be appropriate to demonstrate the desired skill. He was careful to allow the students to move through the exploration stage and be motivated for a demonstration. His sequence of instruction was as follows:

1. Experimentation (exploration)
2. Observation of others
3. Demonstration by others
4. Practice
5. Assessment

The advantage of the indirect approach used by Thomas is that it allows students to match their own developmental levels, and satisfy their curiosity and creativity. The approach also allows the children to decide on their own actions. It is less structured than the directed instruction lesson, even though Thomas suggested the movements for exploration.

Small-Group Activities

Dividing students into small groups, squads, or teams in physical education allows greater participation and lessens waiting time for turns. Because a variety of activities can be planned, all of the groups do not need equipment for play. For example, primary-grade students may be grouped so that one group is playing on the apparatus, another group is involved in a circle game that requires a ball, and a third group is participating in stunts and skills. The activities can be rotated during the class period or on successive days. The tennis ball/beanbag activity lends itself to this arrangement. The small-group strategy allows the teacher to provide individualized instruction to a small group of students who are able to see and hear and respond to the teacher. Instruction to a large group on the play-

ground sometimes involves management problems. Mary Hogan chose small-group skill games when she was teaching half her class an apparatus skill.

Skill Instruction

Students do not necessarily learn a skill just because they play a game that requires the skill. Skills need to be taught, and they need to be practiced. The movement skills described earlier in this chapter are developmental; the student must learn to maintain balance, change direction, and adjust to environmental problems. The student's safety may depend on the movement skills learned at school. Skill instruction can begin as an exploration lesson or as a direct instructional lesson. (Jimmy in the chapter-opening vignette needed skill development requiring kicking, changing directions, and balance.)

Middle School Experiences

Additional experiences for middle school students should include the following:

- Exploration of and preparation for careers in health and physical education
- Social dancing
- Camping
- First aid and cardiopulmonary resuscitation (CPR)
- Outdoor education
- Bowling
- Field hockey
- Lacrosse
- Racquetball
- Golf
- Tennis

PHYSICAL EDUCATION INSTRUCTION IN THE CLASSROOM

On many occasions, it is more propitious to teach physical education inside the classroom. This may be necessary because of inclement weather or students' need for physical activity. Typically, physical education in the classroom has meant low-involvement activities that provide teacher and students with a change from the normal routine, but nothing lively enough to elevate the pulse rate. There is nothing wrong with choosing low-intensity activities for the classroom; however, when students sit for several hours during the school day, they will feel more alert and more joyful if they are involved in activities that require muscular strength, endurance, and aerobic exercise.

Many movements can be taught inside the classroom to help students relieve tension by stretching, exercising actively, and then relaxing to prepare them for academic study. The following suggestions for music, props, space, exercises, and clothing will assist in motivating students for classroom exercises.

Suggestions for Classroom Exercise

Music

Themes from movies and popular songs are motivating. Have students suggest movements appropriate to the music. Be sure that the music has a good beat. Change the music for the cool-down period to help quiet and relax the students.

Props

The purpose of props is for motivation. The use of chairs or other props enhances the exercise period. Dowels or short ropes can be used to keep the arms straight for bending exercises. Ropes or dowels can be used with a partner for resistance movements.

Space

Obviously an empty classroom or auditorium would be optimal for indoor exercising. However, in the normal classroom, students can be arranged in staggered formations around the room. Make sure that they are able to see you model the exercises and that they will not touch another student as they exercise.

Exercises

Students will always complain that they are tired. Use good judgment as to the number of repetitions for each exercise. Always model the movement to be performed. Encourage smooth movements using full range of motion. Physical fitness periods should have three distinct stages: warm-up, active exercise, and cool-down.

ASSESSING GROWTH IN PHYSICAL EDUCATION

Assessment in physical education should be based on individual growth and development. Students should be apprised of their personal progress so they can relate

Research Findings

K. T. Thomas and J. R. Thomas (2008) studied the long-range research on motor development, and categorized their findings:

1. Children's bodies are different from adults' bodies. Therefore, both their activities and their equipment must be consistent with their developmental level.
2. Prior to puberty both boys and girls are similar in their physical performance. Therefore they can be randomly grouped for learning and practice activities. However, for some activities, grouping by similarity of skills, size, and experience may be more effective.
3. Physical growth is partially a result of diet and weight-bearing activity. Boys and girls differ in the amount of body fat during and after puberty; therefore, it is important for teachers to select appropriate activities to produce desired results.
4. Bodies are not perfect. Motor performance for healthy bodies are the result of the integration of a healthy diet and appropriate physical activity, practice, and feedback.

progress to practice and personal goals. Because both the potentials and the abilities of students differ, students should not be compared with each other.

It is important to identify the individual needs and abilities of each student. This may be accomplished through observation, interviews, and physical fitness tests. The following procedures may be used:

1. Observe the student as he or she relates to other students to determine basic needs and interests.
2. Review and analyze the student's health record; review vision and hearing records.
3. Evaluate growth (weight and height) using standard growth charts.
4. Observe the student performing movement activities:
   - Can the student exercise actively and recover quickly, or does the student continue to look fatigued?
   - Can the student control body movements?
   - Does the student's performance improve after practice and feedback?
   - Is the student enthusiastic about activity?

- Does the primary-age child support his or her weight when using the horizontal bar?
- Can the primary-age child climb the jungle gym?
- Does the student share equipment and take turns?
- Does the student help others or interfere with others?

Self-Assessment

Students should be encouraged to self-assess and keep records of their own performance. For example, students could check their heart rate before, during, and after intense exercise. Students should establish personal goals and evaluate their progress toward each goal. Self-assessment helps students accept responsibility for their own wellness. Middle school students can perform peer assessment by establishing rubrics and then evaluating progress using the criteria.

HOW IS HEALTH EDUCATION TAUGHT?

Inquiry Experiences

Many aspects of health education can be taught via the scientific method. The students who developed the experiment for testing the effect of dirt on their hands when handling bread were studying health as well as science. Personal health care studies are often motivated and initiated through science experiments. Upper-grade students studying light can construct cameras and microscopes and then go on to the study of the eye. Experiments with food decay, contamination, and growth of bacteria are typical of the studies appropriate for health instruction. Students should be encouraged to guess and predict the outcome of these experiments.

Research

The use of relevant problems for study has a positive effect on health attitudes and habits. In a sixth-grade classroom, the teacher initiated a safety unit by asking the students to research every day safety problems at school. The students analyzed the safety records in the school office and then investigated the areas where accidents were occurring. They observed other students at the bicycle rack area, on the playground, on the stairways, and on the sidewalk in front of the

school. They watched before school, during recess and lunch, and after school. They studied the frequency of accidents, the location, and the activity. Then they recorded their findings and wrote their conclusions (see Figure 12.1). They compared their own study with the school district's study at other schools. Finally, the students wrote plays to dramatize the safety problems. Using their own dramatizations, they taught other students at their school about safety. The students also wrote reports about their study and sent their findings and conclusions to other schools in the school district and the board of education.

Resource People

Community resource people are valuable assets to the school health program. Health department professionals and fire and police personnel are usually willing to come to a school and perform demonstrations or lecture. Hospitals frequently have a list of speakers to assist in health education. The American Heart Association has developed two kits for teaching about the heart and exercise. The kits contain filmstrips, cassette tapes, and an instructional booklet for the teacher. The

Figure 12.1 School Safety Record

	Frequency			
	K–3		4–6	
Location and Activity	*Boys*	*Girls*	*Boys*	*Girls*
Bicycle rack area				
• Fighting				
• Falls				
• Skidding				
Playground				
• Unorganized activities				
• Fighting				
• Running				
• Apparatus mishaps				
Stairway				
• Skipping steps				
• Pushing				
• Running				
Sidewalk				
• Carrying too many objects				
• Watching others				
• Running				

materials are in both Spanish and English. One kit is appropriate for lower grades, the other for upper grades.

Health Guidance and Examinations

Students are usually examined several times during their elementary and middle school years by a school nurse. The examination can be a learning experience if the students know in advance how it will be performed and what will be learned from the examination. Students can study growth charts from health textbooks. They can study problems of being underweight and overweight. Nutrition and food habits can be the focus of a unit. Dental hygiene can be studied in conjunction with the dental examination. However, due to the shortage of school nurses and health care professionals, in most school districts, students are screened only for eyesight and hearing.

Demonstrations, Discussions, Textbooks, and Special Projects

Media resources, exhibits, and models are useful for demonstrating health concepts. Many materials can be borrowed from community resources, but student-made models and exhibits are most meaningful. Pictures and posters are readily available from health organizations and the national safety council.

It is extremely important in health education that the teaching approach be positive, calmly presented, and as objective as possible. Issues in health education may elicit emotional reactions from different segments of the community; thus, it is essential that the teacher help students discuss problems in a nonthreatening classroom climate.

Textbooks are available for grades 3–8, and most textbooks integrate science and health concepts. Textbooks should be used for resource purposes. Many new texts encourage students to assess their fitness habits and evaluate what they eat and drink. Childhood obesity is a growing problem and because students spend so many hours at school, teachers can make a real contribution by stressing good eating habits, including teaching about appropriate food choices.

The Health Activities Project (HAP), developed by the Lawrence Hall of Science at the University of California at Berkeley, is an activity-focused health curriculum for grades 5–8. The program is organized into four modules: breathing and fitness, sight and sound, heart fitness, and action. The overall goal of the project is to help students understand their own bodies and develop a sense of control through their ability to effect physical improvement, fitness, and decision making.

Sleep and the Middle School Adolescent

Studies by a Stanford University summer sleep camp researched the needs of 10- to 12-year-old boys and girls during 72-hour assessments for 5 or 6 years. Researchers found that regardless of age or the child's developmental stage, all of the children needed $9\frac{1}{2}$ to 10 hours of sleep per night. Surprisingly the researchers found that more physically mature youngsters are sleepier at midday than less mature youngsters.

Children's sleep is affected by a number of societal demands, peer group interaction, and social factors in the home (McDevitt & Ormrod, 2004). During middle school years, parents lessen their restrictions and supervision. Instead of a specified bedtime, the child sets his or her own bedtime depending on homework and social desires. Instead of awakening the child to get ready for school and breakfast, parents expect the child to take responsibility. As a consequence, children tend to go to bed late and use an alarm clock to waken.

Overzealous parents expect homework for students, and schools and teachers comply with parental pressure and assign too much drill (and too little application) of schoolwork. Parents often have to teach youngsters to help them complete assignments, and students are spending a great deal of time on the telephone with friends to do the homework. Television programs attract the child who needs relief from school and homework demands. Both TV and homework combine to rob children of their natural sleep time.

The Center for Applied Research and Educational Improvement (CAREI) at the University of Minnesota assessed the attitudes of parents, teachers, students, and community concerning changing the starting times of schools (Wahlstrom, 1999). The researchers found that changing the starting time of a school resulted in emotional reactions from all of the stakeholders. However, although the researchers were warned that the transportation department, school coaches, and food-service employees would protest later starting times, none of these stakeholders refused to cooperate with an experiment to test the results of a later start time (from 7:15 A.M. to 8:40 A.M.). Although the experiment focused on adolescent needs and the start time for the high schools in Minneapolis and Edina, Minnesota, start times at the middle schools and elementary schools would be affected as well.

Clearly the research on adolescent sleep needs suggested that a later school start time would be beneficial for the children. However, teachers were divided: some felt the later start time helped their planning; others were concerned that it made a later and longer work day for them. Some parents found the later time burdensome for transportation needs and were concerned about children walking home later in the day. Differences in attitudes were apparent in both urban and suburban areas. The research continues with a long-term look at how the change affects students' achievement and the community. The question of a later start time for middle school students continues to be an ongoing concern because the evidence indicates that students would profit from it.

ASSESSING HEALTH EDUCATION

Health education should be evaluated in the same ways that growth is assessed in other subject fields. Paper-and-pencil tests may be designed to test health concepts. If students produce projects, models, or dramatizations, these may be used for evaluation. Attitudes and habits may be observed to see if there is continuous and consistent growth. Because much of the learning in health education should be organized so that students engage in inquiry and discover for themselves, the use of scientific methods and attitudes should be evaluated.

Assessment should focus on health literacy:

- Does the student accept responsibility for his or her own health?
- Does the student demonstrate respect for the health of others?
- Does the student understand the process of growth and development?
- Does the student use health-related information to guide the use of products and services?

Whenever possible, students should be encouraged to assess their own health and physical fitness. They should be encouraged to set goals for physical, emo-

Teaching Hints: Gender Bias

Gender interpretations are often made as a consequence of the speaker's choice of words, tone, and directions.

"Boys, don't forget to clean up around your lockers." (Interpretation: Boys, not girls, are messy.)

"Girls, let's see if you can get dressed and ready for play quickly today." (Interpretation: Girls are always late and slow.)

tional, and social behavior and then evaluate their own progress toward those goals.

INTEGRATION OF HEALTH AND PHYSICAL EDUCATION WITH OTHER SUBJECTS

Thematic teaching should predominate. Themes identified earlier in the text should be extended to health and physical education. In addition, physical education experiences can be used to enhance other curriculum fields. For example, the teacher can give auditory directions that require students to remember a sequence of directions and rhythmically produce it. The rhythm can be orchestrated by the teacher. Students might be asked to clap hands overhead, snap fingers, shake fingers, and roll arms. The students can even be asked to remember a set number of repetitions.

Mathematics can be enhanced by having students learn to time their skill performances or measure their running distances. Students can research and graph the long-term effects and costs of smoking on the individual and society.

For science, Newton's laws of motion can be taught:

- Bodies in motion tend to stay in motion, and bodies at rest tend to stay at rest, unless acted upon by some outside force.
- The change in speed when acted upon by an outside force is proportional to the force applied and occurs in the direction of the force; the greater the force, the greater the acceleration.
- For every action there is an equal and opposite reaction. (This can be illustrated by bouncing a ball against a wall or dribbling the ball.)

For social studies integration, teach regional and cultural games and dances. Study the effect of the environment (overpopulation and pollution) on people's health.

Music and art integration are discussed in Chapter 13.

INCLUSION AND ADAPTED PHYSICAL EDUCATION

Whenever possible, students with disabilities should participate in a physical education program. However, participation should be guided and modified when necessary. Some physical problems require temporary accommodations; others need long-range planning and special services. Neither the disabled student or the class is physically and socially comfortable if the student cannot achieve normal physical activity.

Temporary Services

When students have accidents and occasional muscular or orthopedic problems, special accommodations need to be arranged. Depending on the seriousness of the problem, students can often participate in a modified physical education program. For example, they may be able to play Ping-Pong, board games, caroms, and shuffleboard (see the section below titled "Specially Designed Programs"). (Jimmy, who was limping due to his soccer accident in the chapter-opening vignette, would need to participate in an activity that did not require leg movements.)

Specially Designed Programs

Students with cardiovascular disorders, nutritional problems, postural deviations, temporary physical problems, and hyperactivity may be able to participate in the general physical education program with physician approval. In some cases, however, the physician may prescribe a modified program or individualized program. Modifications may be specified, such as no running, no contact sports, and use of crutches permitted.

All students need relief from classroom learning activities, so it is important that they are able to participate in fun activities during lunch, recess, and physical education time. Even checkers and chess, Monopoly, and Candyland offer a change of scenery and opportunity to relax.

Mainstreaming

In cases of learning and emotional disorders, in general, these students can participate in a regular physical education program with their classmates.

Adapted Physical Education

For students with permanent physical disabilities, sensory problems, or cerebral palsy, direct designated physical education by a physical education specialist is necessary. The **adapted physical education** program may include assistance from parents and other faculty members and aides.

Students' readiness to participate in physical activities is determined by their developmental level. Students with special problems, whether because of developmental disability or other disabilities, may not be ready to participate in group activities. Because students with disabilities are often overprotected by parents, peers, and teachers, many do not have the necessary motor skills to participate with others. Before these students can be integrated with peers in group activities, they should be allowed to progress using self-testing individual sports activities.

CLASSROOM MANAGEMENT IN PHYSICAL EDUCATION

Classroom management problems occur during physical education because sometimes there is a tendency to let physical education be a game or free-time period for students. As a consequence, teachers do not perform the planning, organizing, monitoring, and anticipatory tasks that they engage in for other subject fields.

This idea of physical education and playtime being one and the same is most evident when teachers tell students, "We are not going to have P.E. today because you have been too noisy," or "You didn't finish your mathematics on time, so . . . ," or "We have had so many interruptions today that we need to skip P.E." All of these comments should be seen as evidence that physical education is important every day. If students are noisy, less alert than they should be, or feeling pressured, then the need for vigorous exercise is all the more evident.

Typical classroom management problems in physical education relate to decision-making concerns: class organization and grouping, equipment, and instructional approach.

Class Organization

Whenever teachers need to change the place where an activity occurs, management considerations will occur. Unless a teacher wants the whole class to surge forward to the door at the same time, he or she should not direct students with the comment, "Let's go out to P.E. now." Directions to students should include the following information: Who is to leave the classroom? When are they to leave the classroom? Where are the students to go to participate in the activity? What equipment will they need? Should they walk, run, or skip to the destination? These directions should be stated clearly and concisely.

Consideration should also be given to how to get the students back to the classroom. The following decisions need to be made: Should students line up before returning to the classroom? Should they move by groups, games, or all together? Will they go to the bathroom or obtain drinks? (If they do not obtain drinks on the playground, will they want to do so in the classroom?)

Instructional Arrangements

Another organizational problem has to do with instructional arrangements. If skill or game instructions are needed, will they be provided in the classroom, out on the playground, or in the gymnasium? Game or rule-type instructions are best handled while students are sitting at their desks. Sometimes a "chalk talk" before an activity is helpful. But if students are to observe a demonstration, then it is important to plan how they will stand or sit in order to see and hear. Several arrangements are advocated by physical education specialists for facilitating skill demonstrations. For example:

- *Semicircle.* Students can sit or stand in a half-circle formation, and the teacher can demonstrate the skill. This arrangement works particularly well if only half the class is involved in the demonstration.
- *Circle.* The teacher or a model can demonstrate from the center of the circle. However, if the teacher/model is to give instructions orally, the semicircle is better for talking/listening.

- *Squad/small group.* Students stand in short lines by group. This is a good arrangement if students are to practice or give evidence of having attained a skill. The teacher can walk between the groups or stand in a central location to observe performance.
- *Scatter.* If the teacher/model has a megaphone or is standing on a stage, this formation minimizes students' "messing around" tactics. Teachers who use this formation for demonstrations usually assign students to a special spot on the floor. Whenever the teacher calls for a scatter formation, the student moves to the special spot. The scatter formation facilitates students' exploration of movement.

The decision about how to arrange students for demonstrations should also be based on the type of learning situation. Are students to learn by way of direct instruction, or is the instructional planning based on student exploration? This decision will need to be made prior to the decision about the type of formation.

Grouping for Play Activities

A third decision that frequently causes management problems is grouping students for play activities. Should students be grouped randomly, or by friendship patterns, size, ability, or interest? Tradeoffs are involved in each of the choices. Whichever pattern is chosen, the decision, along with the objective of the lesson, should be shared with the students.

Physical Education Equipment

In some schools, activities must be chosen on the basis of the available equipment. Sometimes there is not enough equipment for an entire class of children to participate in the same game activity. The trick is to plan ahead, be knowledgeable about your resources, and present the game plan to the students confidently. Most management problems in physical education can be avoided with unit planning and anticipatory thinking about instructional arrangements, grouping, and equipment needs.

ADOLESCENT PROBLEMS

Health and physical education may provide unique opportunities in the presentation of subject matter for teachers to help students confront very typical problems of early adolescence, such as the problems of grooming and personal hygiene. Helping students use common sense in their attire, cleanliness, and healthfulness can be achieved through subject-field content. Teachers also need to serve as role models for students. In addition, it is important for students to recognize others' unique qualities and learn to appreciate classmates who are different.

Adolescents also have problems with self-confidence. Young boys (age 10–14) believe that they should be as competent as the adult male and may be sadly disappointed if competition proves otherwise. Girls are overly concerned with their appearance and tend to feel that everyone is looking at them. As a consequence, they are extremely sensitive and critical of themselves.

Teachers need to offer cheerful comments to protect the self-esteem of the middle school student. Working with students in small groups instead of whole classes to provide guidance with skills and health can help students adjust to changes in their relationships and physical appearance.

CONTROVERSIAL ISSUES

Child Abuse and Neglect

Teachers learn to recognize when their students do not look quite right. You note symptoms of illness, you can tell when a student is hyperactive, and you can tell when a student is depressed. You are also likely to be the first person to recognize when a child has been mistreated. Telltale physical signs and emotional reactions will cue the alert teacher to child abuse or neglect.

It is the teacher's legal responsibility to report instances of child abuse and neglect. The teacher should make this report to the school nurse or the school principal if the nurse is not present. However, it is the school nurse's responsibility to report cases of child abuse. The nurse's training, knowledge, and responsibilities for reporting are manifest in their role (Honish, 2000). The National Center for the Prevention of Child Abuse (1995) reports that if comprehensive reporting occurred in all 50 states, there would be 4 million substantiated cases of child abuse annually in the United States. Most schools have report forms to be filled out for this purpose.

Child abuse and neglect have been defined as follows (section 3 of the Child Abuse Prevention and Treatment Act, Pub. L. No. 93–247):

The physical or mental injury, sexual abuse, negligent treatment, or maltreatment of a child under the age of eighteen by a person who is responsible for the child's welfare under circumstances which indicate that the child's health or welfare is harmed or threatened thereby.

Instruction in the classroom about child abuse and sexual exploitation can occur after parents are notified of the forthcoming lesson(s). Students should be provided with information on sexual abuse and rape. They should learn to identify ways to seek assistance if abused or threatened. They need to learn how to avoid high-risk situations and practice through role-plays how to avoid negative social influences and pressures.

Teachers need also to recognize that they too can be accused of child abuse. Should this occur, one should immediately obtain legal assistance. Emans (1987) points out that both the laws to protect children and the enforcement procedures often deny constitutional rights to the child and the person accused of the crime. For as long as I can remember, teachers have been counseled never to work alone with a student, particularly a student of the opposite sex. This is good advice for all ages.

Teaching About Drugs

It is now recognized that elementary school teachers need to begin during the primary grades to develop students' knowledge and understanding about the use and abuse of drugs, narcotics, alcohol, and tobacco. Health and physical education provide great opportunities to accomplish this. There have been a variety of approaches to teaching students about substance abuse, but most have failed. These approaches have included programs that communicated information only, programs based on affective education, and scare-tactic programs using the testimony of former addicts.

What works? The Southwest Regional Laboratory has found that students need to be aware of the immediate consequences of drug use (how drugs affect your breath, your eyes, your ability to concentrate, your mood) versus the long-term effects. Many students wrongly believe that their peers condone the use of drugs; they need to learn that most students their own age do not use drugs and do not condone drug use.

Students often experiment with drugs because they are under stress. The curriculum should teach students positive ways to relieve stress: recreation with friends, exercise, sharing and communicating, developing friend-ships. Students need to be taught conflict-resolution skills and the process of decision making. They may also need to learn how to develop positive friendships. Finally, they should be given information on the ways peers, family, and the media influence their use of drugs, narcotics, and alcohol.

Elementary and middle school students react posi-tively to role-playing activities, Socratic-type question-ing, and small-group discussion strategies. These approaches seem to work best to teach about substance abuse. Lecturing, preaching, and moralizing are doomed to failure.

The first strategy for teachers is to verify that an alcohol or drug problem exists. Keeping a log to docu-ment student behavior may be the first step. The next step is to share the log with other knowledgeable peo-ple and to determine if the behavior occurs in other classes or other settings. When possible, involve the student's family and try to determine why the student is using drugs. (However, if a parent conference is called, it is wise to have another teacher, principal, or assistant principal sit in on the conference.) The most common reason for alcohol and drug abuse among young stu-dents is to gain peer acceptance. For this reason, stu-dents need to learn ways to resist peer pressure. To respond to drug and alcohol problems, it helps to com-municate with the student's family.

Blood-Transmitted Diseases

Information about communicable diseases such as sex-ually transmitted diseases (STDs), including HIV/ AIDS and hepatitis B, needs to be discussed in the health curriculum. Students need to understand that many health-related choices are theirs to make. Many communicable and chronic diseases are the conse-quences of ignorance and shortsightedness.

Because teaching about communicable and chronic blood-transmitted diseases can have cultural, socioeco-nomic, genetic, and religious implications, teachers need to be sensitive in the development of curriculum. Before initiating teaching lessons, parents should be notified so that they may withdraw their children from this segment of the health curriculum, if they wish.

Both students and teachers should exercise care in helping an injured person. A wounded individual should be guided to the health office, but other stu-dents and the teacher should not come in direct contact with an injured person who is bleeding. In some school districts, teachers are advised to wear latex gloves when supervising on the playground, and students should be cautioned about touching other students' wounds.

Most educators agree that STD education needs to be part of the school curriculum beginning in the ele-mentary grades. Middle school students should be given specific information on ways to eliminate or reduce the risk of HIV infection. Parents and commu-nity members can be invited to work with teachers in preparing the curriculum.

SUMMARY

Good health is related to physical, social, and mental well-being. Health and physical education need to be interrelated and coordinated. Foundation disciplines include life, medical, physical, and social sciences. Both subjects are taught separately and integrated within other subject fields.

Physical education goals include movement skills and knowledge, self-image development, and social development. The goal of health education is to develop health literacy. Movement abilities develop sequentially and are progressive. Motor skills are cate-gorized as stabilizing, locomotor, and manipulative. Positive self-image is fostered through opportunities to learn about self and others and to understand one's own capabilities and limitations.

Health education programs should expand the stu-dents' awareness from self to family to others. Nutri-tion and dental care are emphasized through teaching strategies and consumer information. Cultural beliefs and preferences about food are discussed to build appreciation and understanding. Fitness and cardiovas-cular health are taught in the classroom and on the playground.

Physical education is taught through direct instruc-tion in skills, exploration strategies, teams, and small-group and large-group activities. Growth is assessed by relating practice to individual goals and the individual's health record. It is important that students self-assess by keeping records of their personal performance and taking personal responsibility for their health.

Health education is taught by engaging students in research studies, safety studies, and nutrition studies. Demonstrations, texts, projects, models, and the Inter-net are available teaching materials.

Health education is assessed in the same ways that other subject fields are evaluated. Health education can easily be integrated with science, social studies, mathematics, art, and language arts.

When possible, students with disabilities should participate in the general physical education program. Individually designed programs may be necessary for some students with, for example, cardiovascular disorders. Adapted physical education is designed for students with permanent disabilities.

When physical education is treated as a free period rather than an instructional period, classroom management problems can occur. Typical problems in classroom management relate to grouping, use of equipment, use of space, or the instructional approach.

Classroom teachers need to be alert to signs of child abuse and neglect. Classroom instruction should discuss abuse, exploitation, and bullying. Teachers are responsible for teaching about the potential harm of tobacco, alcohol, and drugs.

PORTFOLIO ACTIVITY

Both physical and health education are related to students' self-concept, motivation, peer relationships, and the development of character. Describe how you are considering these elements in your lesson in physical or health education, or how you integrate these elements in other subject fields. Provide a lesson plan and a sample of students' work or a description of their activity.

DISCUSSION QUESTIONS AND APPLICATION EXERCISES

1. Identify people, animals, objects, and emotions that students can dramatize to music.
2. Compare the motor skills of a physically disabled primary-age student and a normal primary-age student. How were the performances similar? How were they different?
3. Develop a lesson plan for students that allows them to explore movements.
4. Visit a YMCA or sports club and observe an aerobic exercise workout. Create an aerobic rhythmical sequence for students in grades 5–8.

5. Evaluate the nutritional value of food in the school cafeteria and at fast-food restaurants; plan a lesson for grades 5–8 based on your findings.
6. Prepare a presentation for parents to explain the relationship among coronary heart disease, diabetes, and obesity. Emphasize the need for exercise and emphasize that children, too, can be subject to these problems.
7. Develop a checklist for evaluating students' track and field skills.
8. Investigate which social agencies in your community provide health services to elementary and middle school students. Find out how a teacher can obtain help for a student.
9. Survey the boys and girls in your classroom or in one of your classes to find out what kinds of physical activity they like (both in and outside school), how often they participate, and how important they consider physical activities. See if there is a difference between boys and girls.

READER RESEARCH

Interpersonal behaviors tend to change during the middle school years. Research those behaviors that relate to cultural differences and gender. Then make suggestions about how teachers can help the adolescent acquire effective interpersonal behaviors.

TECHNOLOGY APPLICATIONS

1. Use the Internet to locate national and state policies affecting students' health and learning, such as time requirements. Consider policies that affect enrollment and policies that affect nutrition and health services. Identify web sites that are appropriate for your students to study about health issues. (Middle school students can help you locate web sites.)
2. Develop a plan to integrate literature and health education. Visit the Children's Literature Web Guide at http://www.ucalgary.ca for assistance. This site provides short background information on a variety of children's books.

CHAPTER 13

· ·

Arts Education

The creative arts emphasize the development of aesthetic sensitivity as well as personal and creative expression. Child development concepts are used in the planning of curriculum experiences. Instructional programs should develop competence in a wide variety of knowledge and skills, including creation, performance, production, history, culture, perception, analysis, criticism, aesthetics, technology, and appreciation. The integration of subject fields is encouraged, not only so that students experience a total, balanced school program, but because the arts represent the history of humankind. "No one can claim to be truly educated who lacks basic knowledge and skills in the arts" (National Arts Education Association [NAEA], 1994, p. 5). But sadly, more than any other subject in the elementary school, the arts are ignored and rarely included in the total school curriculum.

Advance Organizer

The following questions are intended to guide your reading and understanding of the content of this chapter.

1. Why is it important to teach the arts?
2. What are the fundamental purposes of teaching music, dance, theatre, and visual arts?
3. Can you identify and discuss content standards of the various arts programs?
4. What are some classroom activities appropriate for teaching the arts to students in your classroom?
5. In what ways are activities in the arts related to the child's developmental level?
6. How does the current testing regimen affect the teaching of the arts?
7. What are current trends in the teaching of the arts?
8. How should you evaluate growth in the creative arts?
9. What resources and equipment would you like for teaching the creative arts?
10. How do national programs and projects in the arts improve classroom teaching and what is the emphasis of each?
11. In what ways can you integrate the arts with other subjects?
12. Why are the arts an effective means for implementing mainstreaming?
13. Why are the arts a significant means to work with English language learners?

INTASC

INTASC Standards

The arts are a reflection of the human experience throughout the ages. The arts engage students in exploring their personal creative skills and thinking processes and help students appreciate different perspectives and abilities. The array of arts activities encourages students to refine their skills, identify unique talents, and relate the arts to other subject fields. As a consequence, teachers need to reflect on all of the INTASC standards in the planning and implementing of arts experiences for their students.

Professional Lexicon

aesthetic judgment The expression of preferences and appreciation based on understanding of form, content, technique, and purpose.

arts disciplines Refers to dance, music, theatre, and the visual arts. Also known as *art form*.

constituent elements The rhythm, melody, harmony, and form of music.

eurhythmics The art of interpreting music by involving the whole body in rhythmic movements.

expressive elements Music tone qualities, tempo, and dynamics.

the arts The totality of all of the arts disciplines and their activities.

Meesha just couldn't dip her fingers in the paint. She looked around and saw the other children making streaks and designs on their paper with their fingers covered with paint. The girl next to her was humming and smiling; the boy across the way was intently designing a park. She felt like running away. Finally her teacher spotted her and came over to encourage her to try it. Instead the tears rolled down her face and the teacher put her hands around the girl's shoulders and encouraged her to go get a drink of water and choose something else to do.

IMPORTANCE OF THE CREATIVE ARTS

The arts encompass both the visual and the performing arts: art, music, dance, and drama. Each of the arts is a discipline with aesthetic, perceptual, creative, and intellectual components. Together they contribute to the total development of the individual and increase an individual's ability to communicate with others. The creative arts contribute to the goal of self-realization by helping students express themselves, enjoy creative experiences, and make qualitative judgments.

The visual, aural, and performing arts encourage students to explore their own personal responses to creative experiences. The arts enable students to utilize creative imagination, to see and hear clearly, and to express essential feelings. The emphasis on the senses in the arts motivates consciousness and exploration of aesthetic experiences.

The arts benefit society. More than other curriculum areas, the aesthetic arts help students appreciate different cultures and the challenges of a pluralistic society. Through the arts, students become receptive to unfamiliar sounds, customs, styles, languages, and preferences. The arts of every culture are valued: None is superior to another; each is distinctive. Arts instruction acts as a means to acquire cultural literacy and study cultural diversity.

The visual and performing arts contribute to and clarify concepts and skills in other subject fields, but it is important also to teach them as essential discipline-based subject fields. There needs to be systematic and sequential teaching of the arts as well as an effort to integrate other subject fields with the arts. The arts allow the individual to make a personal statement. Each provides a continuing and lasting record of a people and is a reflection of a society's way of life. Each provides a means to analyze society and culture. Universal communication is facilitated through the arts. Aesthetic experiences in the arts involve the mind and the feelings.

Constructivism in the Arts

Perhaps more than any other subject area, the arts invite students to create, improvise, communicate, and express their own emotions and thinking. The arts provide means to express grief, violence, love, and other emotions. They stimulate creative ideas and problem solving and encourage teamwork and the development of social skills. The arts help students make meaningful connections with their own life experiences.

Research Findings

Mulder-Slater (2001) identifies several reasons why teaching the arts "is a good idea":

1. The brain is stimulated by exposure to the arts.
2. The arts facilitate understanding of other subject fields.
3. Self-esteem, self-discipline, cooperation, and self-motivation are stimulated when students participate in arts projects.
4. The arts help students gain tools to express themselves in a variety of ways and respect the perspective and work of others.

WHAT STUDENTS SHOULD KNOW AND BE ABLE TO DO

The *National Standards for Arts Education* (NAEA, 1994) were developed by the consortium of National Arts Education Associations and funded by the U.S. Department of Education, the National Endowment for the Arts, and the National Endowment for the Humanities. Several examples of the standards for K–12 follow:

- Students should be able to communicate at a basic level in the four **arts disciplines**—dance, music, theatre, and the visual arts.
- Students should be able to develop and present basic analyses of works of art from structural, historical,

and cultural perspectives, and from combinations of those perspectives.
* Students should have an informed acquaintance with exemplary works of art from a variety of cultures and historical periods and a basic understanding of historical development in the arts disciplines, across the arts as a whole, and within cultures (NAEA, 1994, pp. 18–19).

Examples of Content Standards for Music

* Singing, alone and with others, a varied repertoire of music
* Reading and notating music
* Understanding music in relation to history and culture (NAEA, 1994, pp. 26–29)

Music educators are concerned that music instruction not be viewed as a field for the entertainment of students or that it be viewed for only serious and talented students. All students need music education. However, there have been questions about the emphasis on music performance. Former education secretary William Bennett advocated study of the historical and cultural roots of music, but many music educators believe that music history courses make students resent music as a field of study. These educators believe that cultural literacy can best be accomplished through study of the music students perform.

Examples of Content Standards for the Visual Arts

* Understanding and applying media, techniques, and processes
* Understanding the visual arts in relation to history and cultures
* Reflecting on and assessing the characteristics and merits of their own work and the work of others (NAEA, 1994, pp. 33–35).

The basic purposes of the visual arts are to enable students to see clearly, to express feelings, to demonstrate and communicate individuality, and to understand and apply art knowledge.

Art education frequently aims to expose students to art production and art appreciation. Students are to enjoy discovery and be discoverers. The art curriculum

should increase sensitivity and heighten perceptual and creative awareness. Art educators want students to integrate thinking, feelings, imagination, and senses in the application of art knowledge to personal experience. Art instruction should help students perceive visual relationships, produce art, understand the art of others, and judge artistic products.

Examples of Content Standards for Dance

* Identifying and demonstrating movement elements and skills in performing dance
* Understanding dance as a way to create and communicate meaning
* Demonstrating and understanding dance in various cultures and historical periods
* Making connections between dance and healthful living (NAEA, 1994, pp. 23–25).

Dance has been an integral part of the socialization process of many cultures. It is considered the oldest component of the arts. Dance communicates nonverbally through body language; it is considered an alternative to oral language. Dance links movement with feeling and provides for multisensory integration and creative expression; it contributes to historical and cultural heritage, and aesthetic valuing.

Examples of Content Standards for Theatre

* Script writing by planning and recording improvisations based on personal experience and heritage, imagination, literature, and history
* Acting by assuming roles and interacting in improvisations
* Researching by finding information to support classroom dramatizations
* Comparing and connecting art forms by describing theatre, dramatic media (film, television, electronic media), and other art forms (NAEA, 1994, pp. 30–32).

Theatre experiences should capture the student's world of pretend play by acting out roles and interactions with life experiences, situations, customs, and beliefs. The standards suggest that there be "a seamless transition from the natural skills of pretend play to the study of theatre" (NAEA, 1994, p. 30). The emphasis in theatre is improvisation.

ART EXPERIENCES AND STUDENT DEVELOPMENT

The 1947 research of Viktor Lowenfeld, reported in Lowenfeld and Brittain (1987), has been influential in the organization of art experiences for children. Lowenfeld found a progressive pattern to the development of children's drawings. Like Piaget, Lowenfeld noted the egocentric behavior of the young child and observed the changes in children's drawings from representations of the self in early childhood to objective realism in the later elementary school years. Although levels of development should not be rigidly interpreted, the stages provide a guide to the choice of art activities. Growth is continuous for each child; objectives for art lessons will overlap at the skill levels.

Lowenfeld's stages were described by Brittain (Lowenfeld & Brittain, 1987):

- *Scribbling stage:* This stage generally lasts until about age 4. During scribbling, the young child makes random marks on paper.
- *Preschematic stage:* Children make their first representational pictures during this stage. Generally this stage lasts from ages 4 through 7.
- *Schematic stage:* From ages 7 to 9, children's drawings symbolize their environment. Typically the drawings are arranged at the bottom of the paper in series fashion: house, tree, flower, person, dog.
- *Dawning realism:* This stage lasts from ages 9 to 12. Drawings symbolize rather than represent objects. During this stage, children rarely want to display their work.
- *Pseudonaturalistic:* This stage begins around age 11 or 12. The students are highly critical of their own work. The work is often kept hidden. Human figures are drawn in great detail with awareness of sexual characteristics. Students are interested in cartooning during this stage.

The primary-age child (K–2) emerging from the scribble stage is spontaneous, usually nonreflective, and unconcerned with reality. The young child loves to express drawings and paintings in vivid terms using bright colors. The child works best with large pencils or brushes on extra large paper. Content for the primary-grade child typically relates to the child's self and family.

The middle-grade student is sociocentric rather than egocentric and is able to work both independently and cooperatively with others. The student is more oriented to reality and wants to produce art objects that are more truly representative—details are important. The student will describe similarities and differences in shapes and patterns. Color is used more realistically and with more restraint. The concept of space becomes important to the child of this age, and he or she will attempt to express it in landscapes, figures, and total composition.

Because the upper-grade student's motor skills are more controlled, he or she can create more mature art productions. The student can work for longer periods and more intently and is able to work independently. If the student has been exposed to art experiences, the vocabulary will be more developed and art appreciation will be more sophisticated. The student should be able to compare artists and artworks in relation to sensory qualities, style, and materials. Students at this age are more analytical about what they see and more evaluative about what they like. However, it is important to remember that middle school students are extremely sensitive about physical development and appearance. They want to conform to their peer group rather than express personal style, and they are extremely restless. While the arts help middle school students express themselves, they are sensitive to criticism.

WHAT DO TEACHERS EMPHASIZE IN THE ARTS?

Music Education

Music instruction is typically organized to teach concepts, process skills, music skills, and attitudes and values through the activities of listening, singing, moving, playing, and reading and writing notation. Concepts are related to **expressive elements** (tone qualities, tempo, and dynamics), to **constituent elements** (rhythm, melody, harmony, and form), and to the structure of music. The process skills interact with the concepts as the teacher asks students to organize data, generalize and make inferences, and apply knowledge. Students develop music skills as they pursue the aforementioned activities. Attitudes and values are developed through the total music experience and are encouraged by motivating students to choose musical experiences and by providing opportunities for decision making. Musical activities are planned to correspond to the developmental characteristics of K–8 students just as the art activities are.

Students participating in musical training improve their fluency in both speaking and reading.

Dance

In grades K–4, students develop an awareness of body movements and begin to relate choreographic skills in **eurhythmic** contexts. Young children learn to perform basic locomotor movements, such as walking, running, hopping, skipping, jumping, galloping, sliding, and leaping. They learn to respond with these movements to music. They enjoy improvising and inventing movements and "showing off" their talents. Typically they are not self-conscious about learning folk dances and enjoy relating the dances to various cultures. They will try to connect their knowledge of dance and movement in their paintings—and not be critical of their lack of realism!

Students in grades 5–8 are much more versatile in their ability to perform movement skills. They are interested in balance, shifting of weight, and body alignment. They can imitate rhythmic patterns and reproduce movement sequences; however, they tend to be quite self-conscious when demonstrating body movements. Consequently, students work better in small groups or with partners to demonstrate choreographic processes.

Middle school students understand how to communicate through gesture and dance. They can create, improvise, and critique what they see. They understand how dance reflects culture and historical time period. They make connections between concepts of dance and concepts in other subject fields.

Theatre

Students in grades K–4 enjoy acting out and assuming roles and characterizations from the stories they listen to and read. To a limited degree, they can improvise dialogue. They like to visualize and then create environments for their plays, and they enjoy wearing costumes and makeup. They willingly perform for other students and their parents. They are able to compare roles and characterizations from other cultures, and identify similarities and differences by comparing and contrasting with themselves. With guidance, they can construct meaning from presentations on film, on television, and in classroom dramatizations.

Students in grades 5–8 enjoy writing scripts for plays. They will invent characters, environments, and actions. They like constructing scenery and costumes for their plays and want to direct all aspects of the production. They are able to research the information needed for historical and cultural productions. They critique (all too willingly) all aspects of their productions (dance, music, visual elements, characterization). They are able to analyze the impact and role of drama portrayed in different media on their own lives, their community, and other cultures. Once again, students in grades 5–8 prefer working in small cooperative, collaborative groups.

Visual Arts

The visual arts provide a means for students to convey visual expressions; consider their ideas, feelings, and emotions; and judge the value of their efforts. The visual arts include drawing, painting, sculpture, design, architecture, film, videos, and folk arts, and each of these arts requires specific knowledge, skills, tools, techniques, and processes.

In the K–4 classroom, students learn to apply different media, techniques, and processes. They learn to select the appropriate tool or technique based on the media and what they are trying to express. They learn to judge their work (and others) based on the characteristics, media, and merits of the work. Students learn to relate works of art to culture and historical time periods.

Students in grades 5–8 become more sophisticated and realistic in their use of subject matter, symbols, images, and visual expressions. They can reflect on their own and the artist's feelings and emotions. They select appropriate media to communicate their ideas. They are able to integrate the visual, spatial, and temporal aspects of visual images with subject-field content to communicate meaning in their productions. Students understand the relationship of the visual arts to historical periods and cultural identity. They can compare works of art from different periods and cultures and express the characteristics and meanings of the artworks.

HOW SHOULD THE ARTS BE TAUGHT?

Two lesson plans (provided in two case studies in this section) demonstrate teaching approaches in the arts. In both examples, the arts are integrated. However, there is a wide range of appropriate techniques for teaching the four disciplines, and there should be specific teaching in each of the arts. As in other subject fields, both exploration and direct instruction are appropriate.

 MARY HOGAN'S CLASSROOM

Mary Hogan's major objective was to teach the concept of rhythmic pattern duration. In addition, she wanted to incorporate movement and build appreciation of folk music typical of the Caribbean, South America, and West Africa. She planned to demonstrate to her students that rhythm patterns have long and short sounds and that, when a melody uses a rhythm pattern, the words are sung in a long and short rhythmic sound pattern. She chose the calypso song "Tinga Layo."

HOGAN'S OBJECTIVES

1. To recognize and identify rhythmic changes
2. To sing and move to the rhythmic pattern accurately
3. To clap and produce the rhythmic pattern using coconut shells
4. To recognize the rhythmic pattern written in blank notation on the board

MATERIALS

Recorder and CD
Four sets of coconut shells

 Teaching Hints: Starting Arts Programs in Schools

Fineberg (2004) advises:

1. Survey art courses (middle school) and art units (elementary school) to find out what is being offered.
2. Survey teachers' talents at your school.
3. Survey local art groups and artists in your community to see who can assist the school. Promote partnerships.
4. Begin small; do not overreach your capabilities. Limit the menu when you first begin.

PROCEDURE

Hogan: Yesterday Benny brought in a calypso record for us to listen to. Who remembers what impressed us about the calypso music? (The students respond that it was the rhythm that was unusual and that they had enjoyed it.)

Hogan: Good, I thought you'd remember, and because you enjoyed it so much, I brought another calypso record for you to hear. (Hogan plays "Tinga Layo" and students listen. Some students nod and seem to know the words.)

Hogan: This time, boys and girls, see if you can clap the rhythm of the song when I give you the signal. (Hogan provides the cue for the rhythm pattern that occurs six times during the song. Then she brings out some coconut shells and claps them together.)

Hogan: What does this sound like? (The students respond that is sounds like a pony's hoofbeats.)

Hogan: Yes, who would like to play them when we hear the rhythm pattern? (She chooses four students to participate.)

Hogan: While our friends play the shells, let's have everyone else count the number of times we hear the same pattern. (After the song, Hogan has the students respond, and several had counted correctly; the pattern was repeated six times.)

Hogan: I'm going to write the notes on the board; see if you can recognize which are short sounds and which are long sounds. (She writes the notes on the chalkboard.) Let's see if we can sing the pattern. (She leads them by pointing to the notation on the board. Next she teaches the entire song and asks them to match the words to the rhythm pattern written on the board. She asks them to identify the words that represent the short sounds and those that represent the long sounds.)

Hogan: All right, let's give some other people a chance to perform using the shells. (The children pass them to friends.)

Hogan: While some of us are using the shells, who would like to pretend they are a pony and move to the rhythm of the music? Good. (Hogan chooses several children.) Now, lets have the rest of us cup our hands this way and clap to make the sound of hoofs. (The lesson continues in this way until all of the children have had a turn to use the shells or create movements to the music.)

Hogan: Well, boys and girls, we have done such a good job with "Tinga Layo," let's talk about what the music tells us.

Analysis of Mary Hogan's Music Lesson

Hogan chose the lesson for three reasons:

1. She needed to teach the concept of rhythmic patterns.
2. She wanted to introduce folk music to the children.
3. The lesson fit neatly with the students' prior experience of listening to Benny's record.

She motivated the lesson by having the students recall the previous day's listening experience. To develop the concept, she had the students participate in the following activities: listening, singing, movement (clapping), performing (using the coconut shells), body movement, and reading notation. Hogan verified the students' understanding of the concept by having them clap the rhythm, count the number of times the pattern was used, identify the words to fit the pattern, and move in rhythm.

She would follow the lesson on a successive day by having the students use different instruments (bongos, maracas, claves) to accompany the rhythmic pattern and to compose patterns of their own. She intended to have the students gain some understanding of folk music by learning other folk songs and comparing them with "Tinga Layo."

Teaching strategies for music should be varied. They may begin with singing, listening, creative movements, or performing. Music may even begin with an inquiry lesson. The important point is to sequence lessons so that they relate to each other and fit the developmental needs of the students. Children should have the opportunity to learn music concepts, to enjoy, to feel successful, and to release emotion.

Harmonic Vision's **Music Ace** *(a computer program) allows students to practice and compose music as they learn.*

GREG THOMAS'S CLASSROOM

Greg Thomas's fifth-grade students were excited about Halloween. He decided to use that stimulation advantageously, so he planned an art lesson in which the students would make papier-mâché masks.

THOMAS'S OBJECTIVES

1. To make three-dimensional masks using the medium of papier-mâché appropriately
2. To work imaginatively to express and communicate personal feelings
3. To work individually and explore the fanciful and the strange
4. To create movements to characterize the masks.

MATERIALS

Strips of newspaper
Paste
Balloons
Tempera paint and brushes
Scissors, plastic spray

PROCEDURE

Thomas: I've been listening to several of you talk about your Halloween plans. How many of you like to wear a mask on Halloween? (Many of the students respond affirmatively.) How does it feel to wear a mask?

Linda: I can't breathe when I wear a mask.

Jerry: I like it because it lets me hide and surprise people.

Cora: I like to scare my friends.

Jeff: It makes me feel different—kinda strong.

Thomas: Does wearing a mask change how you see or hear?

Linda: Well, I feel like the character I'm pretending to be.

Thomas: What do you mean?

Linda: If my mask is of a pirate, then I feel like a pirate.

Cora: This year I'm going to be the Greatest American Hero.

Thomas: I thought I would wear this mask when I answer my door this year.

Jeff: Wow! Did you make that mask?

Thomas: Yes, and I thought that perhaps you would like to make masks today. (Students respond very positively.) All right. Listen carefully: This is what we are going to do. This is a papier-mâché mask. It is made by pasting strips of paper over a balloon. Then it is decorated to suit the character you want to be. When it is dry, it is sprayed to protect the finish. The last step is to pop the balloon and cut openings for the eyes and other features. It is even possible to add other materials like yarn or paper, as I did on my mask, to obtain special effects and features.

To plan your masks, you must first think about the medium that you are going to use. How can you use it to convey the mood that you want your character to portray? Remember that you must design your mask to fit your face. Visualize your own face. Do you have a large forehead? Do you need a big space between your hair and your nose or a smaller space? Make a sketch of the way you want your mask to look. When you are satisfied with your plan, begin work with the paper and the balloon.

I'm going to ask our art monitors to set the materials out on each table, but before you begin to work, I want each table to be covered with newspaper so that you don't spill paste on the table-top. Now—everyone look over here at the chart rack. If you have a question about the procedures for working with papier-mâché, you may look at this chart. If you have a question that you need to ask of me, raise your hand and I will come over to your table.

Thomas's art lesson took three consecutive days to complete. On the second day, the students cut, painted, and decorated their masks. On the third day, they sprayed them to protect the finish. At the end of the week, Thomas suggested that all the students put on their masks and walk to the auditorium. Thomas carried his own mask with him and asked the students, "How do you think I should act when I wear this mask?"

After students responded, Thomas turned on a special tape of recorded music. He told the students to take their scatter positions on the floor and assume a body posture that would be appropriate for the mask that each student was wearing.

Next, the students were asked to create movements that would indicate how each character feels, thinks, and acts. Thomas also brought a number of props for the students to use to help them create their movements and characterizations.

Thomas will also ask the students to write about their characters as a special creative writing lesson.

Analysis of Greg Thomas's Art Lesson

Greg Thomas was interested primarily in developing creative expression. He motivated this by providing an opportunity for the students to talk about how it feels to wear masks. He asked the students to use their imagination, but he also suggested that they plan the design of the mask. He called attention to the spatial organization of the face.

Because every medium poses special problems, Thomas was probably wise in allowing the students to explore the medium instead of giving too much direction about its use. He carefully provided for individual needs by telling the students to raise their hands if they needed assistance, and he also provided a step-by-step procedural chart for using papier-mâché.

Thomas culminated the mask making in an interesting way. Instead of just talking about and sharing their masks with each other, Thomas had them assume the characterization of and portray with movements the mask each was wearing; in this way, he incorporated dance and provided opportunity for students to express feelings, images, and thoughts. We can assume that Thomas developed aesthetic judgment, as well as creative expression, through the art, oral language, and physical movement lessons.

Art is taught through direct instruction to develop art concepts and art skills; art is also taught using discovery approaches that allow students to explore a medium and express feelings and individual perceptions. Strategies should be varied depending on the medium to be used and the concepts to be developed. A great deal of planning is necessary for art activities so when the actual lesson is implemented, the teacher is free to observe and express encouragement to children. Although in most subjects the teacher acts as a model for students to observe, during art it is better if students are free to express their own creative nature instead of trying to imitate the teacher.

In the chapter-opening vignette, we have a young student who is probably terrified at the idea of getting her hands "dirty" with paint. This may be a consequence of parental discipline, culture, or extreme shyness. Clearly the student needs opportunities to express herself using some elements of art, but finger painting may not be an appropriate medium for her at this time. The point of the vignette is that the teacher must make use of professional skills, knowledge of growth and development, subject field, and understanding of this particular child.

CONFLICTS AND CONTROVERSIES IN THE ARTS

Since the late 1990s, instruction in the arts has deteriorated. Too frequently the arts are left out of the curriculum. Whether it is because school districts believe that the arts must be taught by specialists and budget shortfalls have eliminated specialist teachers, or because the current climate focuses only on accountability and assessment, the arts are forgotten (Manzo, 2004). It is an example of the adage, "Let me design your tests, and I will have developed your curriculum."

In 1997, the National Assessment of Educational Progress Arts Report Card "verifie[d] that most American children are infrequently or never given serious instruction or performance opportunities in music, the arts, or theater" (Manzo, 1998). The majority of schools that participated in the assessment (81%) revealed that students received instruction in music only once per week. Eighth-grade students could not identify half-notes; most could not identify errors in songs or play any instrument. Clearly the curriculum shortchanges the arts.

Many school districts have restricted the teaching of the arts to reduce their budgets. Specialist teachers are given the option to teach other subjects (not in their specialization) or be fired. Many believe that the influence of mass media makes it critically important for students to learn to critique visual and aural messages. However, many individuals in leadership positions who set policy do not consider the arts as basic to an education in our society, and as a consequence budgets for teaching the arts are cut or eliminated.

Because the teaching of art is often considered unimportant, it is frequently reserved for holiday teaching, Friday afternoons, and rainy days when students are restless. As a consequence, students perceive the "hidden" message: Art is a frill, not a hardcore subject; there is nothing to be learned.

Still another controversy that affects the arts is the perceived effect of avant-garde music, books, and paintings (McBride, 1999). Jazz music, at its inception, was banned because it featured rhythms of the Black American experience; moralists tried to suppress it. Edouard Manet's *Olympia*, when first displayed in Paris in 1865, was considered too sexually provocative because it featured a painting of a prostitute who stared at the viewer. *The Adventures of Huckleberry Finn* is currently banned in many schools because it epitomizes the attitudes about Black Americans in the 1880s; as a consequence students are deprived of judging the book and learning about how prejudice affected our society.

In Chapter 1, you read about the problem of children expressing themselves in poetry and art and having their creative expression interpreted by adults as dangerous. The consequence was probation of a 12-year-old boy who was considered violent.

ASSESSING STUDENTS' GROWTH IN THE ARTS

As in physical education, assessment in the creative arts must be measured in terms of the student's own progress and performance. The student's contribution to discussions and enjoyment of the arts provide an index of the student's competencies in art and music.

Musical skills, such as listening to, reading, and writing music; creative skills; and performance skills (playing instruments, moving, singing, and conducting) are best evaluated through sensitive observation by the teacher. Students' behavior as they participate in rhythmic activities, singing, or expressing ideas about music are primarily evaluated by direct observation. A music checklist can be constructed to record information about the student. Listening competencies can be evaluated during a discussion that focuses on identifying the mood of a melody, the instruments, rhythmic patterns, or phrasing. Observing children writing notation provides another observational method to evaluate whether the student can read and write music.

Dance activities can be evaluated by students' enjoyment in movement, their observation of form and interpretation, and their discussion and comments about participation.

Judging drama activities is similar to judging dance experiences. The teacher needs to observe students' ability to imagine, to recall experiences and utilize them, to express characterization, and to communicate through verbal and nonverbal means. Drama also provides a variety of related language arts experiences that can be part of the assessment: writing plays, retelling stories, and improvising story lines.

Both acting and taking part in theatre production can be evaluated. In theatre production, students can learn about and perform directing, stage management, publicity, set design, use of special effects, lighting arrangement, and costume design. Students' appreciation of drama and theater can be assessed, as well as their recognition of cultural forms and historical periods and major themes in theater.

Art products should be self-evaluated by the child. The teacher's task is to guide the self-evaluation so students are not too harsh on themselves. One of the best ways to stimulate the student to talk about an art project is to say: "Tell me/us about your picture/project." The teacher should help the child focus on what is good about the picture or art object by calling attention

Research Findings

Three years of studies by neuroscientists and cognitive psychologists at seven universities have provided insight into the relationships of the arts and thinking skills related to the study of math and science (Viadero, 2008b).

1. At Stanford, students age 7–12 who had musical training made faster gains in reading fluency than students without the musical background.
2. Middle and high school students enrolled in art classes were better in basic geometric skills than students without the study of the arts.
3. Long-term and working memory demonstrated a link for students between music and manipulating information.
4. A link between music learning and speaking fluency was demonstrated in second language learning.
5. Researchers noted a link between dance training and the ability to learn by observing movement.
6. Spatial skills and nonverbal IQ skills improved for students studying music.

to the use of the medium, color, spatial organization, design, or whatever else will encourage the student. With success recognized, the teacher can then help the child set some realistic goals for the next project.

Group discussions of artwork should be handled in a similar manner. Each child should be praised in some way—for creativity, ideas, expression of feelings, discoveries about the use of the media, or solutions to problems. Pictures should not be evaluated to choose the best picture. Classroom exhibitions should represent all students' work, not just those appreciated by the teacher.

RESOURCES FOR TEACHING THE ARTS

Resources for teaching music and dance experiences include textbooks, computers, tape recorders, record players, CDs, DVDs, films, slides, and videotapes. Audiovisual aids can enhance the music program, but as in all other subjects, good teaching is the most important element for a good program.

Using computers in arts classes helps students link visual art and music.

Instruments have great appeal to students. Simple instruments can be made by the teacher and students, or they can be purchased. Students enjoy rhythm instruments, percussion instruments, and melody and harmony instruments. Typical rhythm instruments are sticks, triangles, tambourines, castanets, cymbals, bongo and conga drums, claves, maracas, autoharps, and flutelike instruments. Students enjoy making unusual instruments out of boxes, bottles, metal containers, and cardboard.

Art and materials for theatre productions appear to be limited only by a lack of imagination. A vast number of choices are available to teachers and students. Materials are needed for modeling, lettering, picture making, painting, crafts, set production, props, and design activities.

Art materials should be well organized for accessibility and for ease in use. Materials may be stored in boxes, shelves, or drawers. Tin cans, five-gallon ice cream containers, plastic pans, and foil pie plates are all useful for holding art tools and materials.

Work areas for art activities include the floor, tabletops, easels, and outside patio areas. Newspapers or plastic or oilcloth dropcloths should be available to cover any area that is to be used for work or storage. Large work areas available for groups of students are optimal because students can share tools and materials.

Museums, libraries, galleries, and music and art centers provide marvelous field-trip experiences for students. These community resources usually have docents or artists available to discuss what students will see or hear. Local artists and musicians are frequently interested in visiting schools and providing some leadership to young people interested in the arts. Don't forget to use the Internet to study artists and take virtual field trips to foreign museums.

PROGRAMS AND PROJECTS IN THE ARTS

Performing History Programs

Dramatic play has a long history of use in primary classrooms, where students act out social problems, conflict situations, and current events. But the use of historical narrative is relatively new in upper-grade and middle school classrooms. One such program is described by Otten, Stigler, Woodward, and Staley (2004). Fifth-grade students at Marquez Elementary School in Los Angeles worked with a jazz musician and composer to dramatize three musicals that depicted (1) the writing of the U.S. Constitution, (2) the Louisiana Purchase, and (3) the industrial revolution.

Marquez Elementary School, along with 7 other elementary schools, feeds into Paul Revere Middle School. Combined, the new sixth graders make up a school population of 440 students. The researchers tested the sixth-grade students using a 38-item multiple-choice history test. All of the students, including the Marquez students, had participated in a traditional textbook history program in fifth grade. (The performing arts program was an add-on for the Marquez students.)

The study demonstrated that the performing arts program had lasting effects. The Marquez students outperformed the other students and, most important, they reported their enjoyment of the study of history. The authors report, "The results of the study are consistent with theoretical evidence suggesting that dramatic art can be instrumental in learning" (p. 202). The study demonstrated a connection between achievement and enjoyment.

Image Making

Image Making Within the Writing Process is an arts-based literacy program that integrates children's visual imagery and the writing process. The project has been in operation since 1990 and is used in grades K–12 to inspire illustrating and authoring. Image making is used in a variety of genres and integrates other subject fields. Some students begin with the writing process first, and then illustrate; others begin with visual modes of expression and then create stories to fit the pictures. Often students cut and paste their ideas to rehearse, draft, and revise their stories. Students' writing is improved through the combination of visual and kinesthetic modes of thinking at each phase of the writing process.

The Laboratory for Interactive Learning at the University of New Hampshire has studied the image-making program. Researchers compared the writing abilities of project students with a control group and found the following about project students (Olshansky, 1995, pp. 44–47):

- Writing topics were more varied and imaginative.
- Story plots were more fully developed.
- Stories had a beginning, middle, and end.
- Stories were better crafted.
- The authors used more descriptive language.

Teaching Hints: English Language Learners

1. The arts provide opportunity for English language learners to express themselves without the pressure of processing language.
2. Art production allows the English language learner to create and explore media and record observations.
3. Art history encourages the English language learner to share his or her culture using artifacts and writing and talking about native-language artists.

Learning Through an Expanded Arts Program (LEAP)

Art and music are used in this program to teach basic skills, including English to second-language learners. This arts-oriented program, begun in New York City for gifted and talented students, has been extended successfully nationwide to all students through the college level. It is presently used in 450 schools, museums, and community organizations.

Professional artists, musicians, and education consultants work with students in grades K–8 (and help train their teachers) using innovative approaches to teach a variety of ideas in diverse fields, such as architecture, archaeology, robotics, opera composition, and African storytelling. The LEAP approach uses materials and projects that are interesting to students. The students gain a sense of accomplishment and self-confidence through the completion of creative tasks.

Dean and Gross (1992) described one of the many LEAP programs, Promoting Success. Students in this program make puppets, paint murals, and create their own songs, plays, and dances while learning reading and writing. The project leader uses a storyboard to help students learn sequencing and recall details of a story. After reading a story, the students draw simple figures for their storyboards. The consultant then rereads the story, and students recognize each scene in the story. Students then use their storyboards to retell the story in their own words. If students' sequencing is incorrect, the consultant goes back and rereads that section of the story so that students understand the impact of each idea. In this way, students learn to recognize both the main ideas of stories and the consequence of sequencing. Subsequent sessions focus on making puppets and their characterization using the story elements, students' rereading of the story, and visualizing the scenes through murals.

Other LEAP projects focus on developing math abilities. Musical math appears to reduce students' anxieties and provides a sense of self-confidence. As in the reading and writing program, the math program uses storyboards, murals, puppets, plays, and dances.

Getty Institute for Educators on the Visual Arts

Prairie Visions is a weeklong professional development institute used by 97 school districts for teachers in

Nebraska. Funding comes from the Getty Education Institute and the Annenberg Foundation. The purpose of the institute is to provide continuing education for teachers in the theory and practice of discipline-based arts education. The program focuses on art making, art history, art criticism, and aesthetics. The institute is led by a team of professors from the University of Nebraska at Omaha. The teachers experience lectures, tours of the Joslyn Museum, workshops, and group discussions. The discussions focus on stylistic analysis, periods of art history, and ideas for teaching (Hill, 1999).

The Getty Institute program, in existence since 1983, was designed to help teachers develop discipline-based art education for the classroom. Its program is similar to many state frameworks and to the standards advocated by the National Art Education Association. The institute provides summer workshops for teachers to study art curricula and resource materials. Teachers also observe art demonstration lessons. The institute provides continuing support to the teachers during the school year through regular activities and an information bulletin. Participating teachers become district leaders responsible for in-service activities in their school district. To date, more than 12,000 teachers, representing all grade levels and all subject fields, have participated in the institutes.

At the conclusion of the institutes, teachers return to their school districts and participate in rewriting their art curriculum, developing thematic teaching units, and sponsoring student art shows. One teacher commented that she "knew her students were learning when a boy said he'd 'buy an O'Keeffe. It would be a really good investment,' he pronounced."

The Getty Institute program has been implemented in many school districts across the country. The discipline-based approach is given a variety of names. For example, in Ohio it is called the Balanced Comprehensive Art Curriculum; it is described as "balanced" because equitable instructional time and resources are provided in grades K–12. The Ohio program emphasizes art production, art history, art criticism, and art in society.

Arts in Education

Arts in Education is a concept that was developed in the Humanities Division of the U.S. Office of Education. The concept has been used to encourage school systems, curriculum developers, arts organizations, and teacher preparatory programs to develop sequential, integrated arts programs in the schools. Professional artists participate in the school programs. Programs have been cooperatively funded by private foundations and the National Endowment for the Arts, the National Institute of Education, the National Endowment for the Humanities, and the Office of Education.

The programs are diverse in nature, with different states setting different priorities for the arts in education. Magnet programs have been established in several states to attract majority students to inner-city schools with strong arts-related curricula. Other states have assigned state personnel to develop strategies for school improvement with a focus on the arts. Another strategy has been the use of networking. Network members are partners and peers committed to Arts in Education. Professional educators service the network, facilitate program development, and secure community resource personnel to assist in the schools' programs.

Comprehensive Arts Program

The purpose of this program is to offer an integrated, comprehensive, discipline-based approach to art education. Four content areas are featured: art production, art criticism, art history, and aesthetic inquiry. The art program is designed to develop students' awareness and appreciation of the role of artist, the art critic, and the art historian (Phillips, 1998).

Art Production

Students use a variety of art media to create their own work. Examples provided in the program's scope and sequence include crayon drawing, tempera paint technique, sponge painting, cutting paper on a line, and pulling forms from clay. Students learn craftsmanship, patience, and self-criticism.

Art Criticism

For this component, the students observe and discuss the works of artists and begin to analyze and evaluate artworks. The students analyze American, European, and Asian landscape paintings; Japanese screens in the twentieth century; and sculpture. Questions about artworks focus on the content of the piece, its meaning, and its value. The program includes a program guide, a critical analysis guide, filmstrips, and assessment materials.

Art History

Students begin to see art in historical and cultural context. They compare and contrast pieces of art, looking for recurring themes and techniques. They compare cultures and technical links among people. (Greg Thomas used art history in his study of the Pilgrims, in Chapter 5.)

Aesthetic Inquiry

Students are asked to exercise **aesthetic judgment** as they study works of art. "What meaning and value does this art convey?" "How does this piece represent the culture of the early pioneers?" "Why do you like/dislike this design?" "Why do you think the work of Chagall is valuable today?"

The music program component is organized around six basic music concepts: rhythm, melody, harmony, form, tone color, and dynamic level. Awareness, appreciation, and performance tasks enable the students to understand music in terms of its expressive properties. Program components are performance proficiency, criticism proficiency, and composition proficiency:

Performance proficiency encompasses singing, playing instruments, reading standard music notation, and moving to music.
Criticism proficiency includes labeling and describing, analyzing, and evaluating.
Composition proficiency focuses on writing music notation, elaborating existing music, and composing original music.

The program is organized into 16 blocks of instruction. Each unit of the block is organized around one of the six basic music concepts. For example, during the second block, concentrating on rhythm, the students learn double and triple meter; for notation, they learn bar line, sets of two quarter notes, and sets of three quarter notes.

The music program includes a program guide, assessment materials, song tapes, unit tapes, instrument posters, and notation performance cards for the tone bells and the autoharp, along with aids for teaching standard music notation.

INTEGRATION OF SUBJECT FIELDS

Although integration has been emphasized throughout Part III of this text, nowhere should there be greater emphasis than in the arts. Carpenter (1999) describes the work of artist and author Faith Ringgold, who produces story quilts. In 1991, she created *Tar Beach*, which is the story of a family that picnics on their rooftop and the dreams of daughter Cassie, who wants to end discriminatory practices that have affected Native Americans and Black Americans. The book has inspired both elementary- and secondary-grade students' artwork, reading, and social studies. Interpreting the book and the artwork, students are able to gain greater understanding of a historical time period, and the context and events that influenced the author to create the story quilt.

In another example, Carpenter calls attention to the work of Joseph Stella, an immigrant from Italy who painted pictures of the Brooklyn Bridge. His paintings have stimulated classrooms of children to study immigration, technology, science, and the arts. There is considerable evidence that the integration of arts motivates students and improves their performance in the core subjects as well as the arts.

Heidi Hayes Jacobs, in discussing the curriculum of the future, notes that "the arts are central to what it means to be human" (Perkins-Gough, 2004, p. 15). Both Jacobs (2004) and Eisner (2004) comment that meaningful literacy must include the ability to experience and gain meaning from music, the visual arts, and dance. The arts facilitate and motivate learning from a variety of subject fields. In arts-integrated schools, interdisciplinary learning is enhanced.

Listed by subject fields, fusion ideas are identified next. The ideas should also serve as concepts for developing learning centers.

Social Studies and the Arts

- Use the arts as a visual record of cultural development. Study history through paintings, architecture, sculpture, dance, drama, occupations, fashion, and furniture.
- Study and reproduce artifacts; observe statues of famous historical figures; create statues and write a dialogue between historical figures.
- Draw historical events. Create a courtroom and role-play a famous trial, re-creating the events as they occurred. Then re-create the trial with new information.

- Dramatize historical events and plays from different historical periods.
- Contrast handicrafts and manufactured products.
- Draw murals.
- Research occupations, furnishings, fashion, and the like, and keep notes through the use of a sketchbook.
- Study the cultural use of silhouettes in different historical periods.
- Draw maps.

Social Studies, Music, and Dance

- Use music and dance as records of cultural diversity and development.
- Interpret social, political, and economic change by listening to and singing songs from different historical periods and different cultural groups.
- Study customs, beliefs, and values by listening to and singing folk songs, work songs, religious music, sea chanteys, recreational music, and lullabies.
- Study ethnic and cultural differences by listening to lullabies.
- Trace technological development through music. (How many steamboat and choo-choo songs are written today?)
- Use environmental materials to reproduce early instruments.
- Identify a specific culture or society by studying the instruments used in a musical selection.
- Study cultural groups through their dance customs.
- Perform folk and square dances depicting cultures and historical periods.

Science and Art

- Study and draw the natural and humanmade environment.
- Use a sketchbook to record observations of experiments.
- Draw Darwin's theory of evolution.
- Study and draw landscapes, rainbows, plants, animals, and human anatomy.
- Experiment with, study, and draw light and color, and warm and cool colors.
- Use natural materials to make colors.
- Use natural materials to make instruments.
- Record (sketch) observations while looking through a magnifying glass, prism, or microscope.
- Record the development of inventions.
- Study the human eye and compare it with a camera.

Science and Music

- Find answers to the following questions:
  What causes sound?
  How does temperature affect sound?
  How does the thickness of bars and strings affect tone?
  How does the frequency of vibrations affect pitch?
  How are vibrations made?
  How do sounds differ?
  How does distance affect sound?
  What happens when you use a megaphone or other devices?
  Through what substances will sound travel?
- Study the human ear; compare it with animals' ears.
- Make instruments out of different materials and compare sounds.

Language Arts, Art, and Drama

- Use artworks, literature, and theatre to stimulate creative writing.
- Create murals or cartoons with talking people.
- Create the stage design for a play or musical.
- Draw posters and write slogans.
- Make puppets for dramatics or puppet shows.
- Convey moods and feelings of pictures, stories, and plays.
- Draw or act out a book report.
- Use visual images to communicate.

Language Arts and Music

- Use music as a stimulus for creative writing.
- Interpret moods and feelings from music.
- Interpret lyrics of songs.
- Compose new lyrics for popular or old familiar songs.
- Describe the style of musical selections (happy, proud, militant).
- Read a play and identify stage sounds that will help the audience interpret the plot or understand the characterization.

Mathematics and Art

- Illustrate math problems involving weight, balance, measurement, or geometry.
- Illustrate the time of day using the sun and appropriate shadows.
- Draw designs; divide using the concept of positive and negative space.
- Draw patterns.

- Use symmetry in design work.
- Plan a board game; divide spaces.

Mathematics and Music
- Identify the pulse or beat of songs.
- Study the speed of sound.
- Measure how sounds differ in decibels.
- Working in groups, use different numbers of beats to get a set distance.

Physical Education, Health, and the Arts
- Study space and form in movement activities.
- Study and draw the human body.
- Study health factors related to appearance. Draw posters depicting good health practices.
- Use a sketchbook to record observations of experiments.
- Draw action figures; depict through dance.
- Study artists who specialize in sports pictures.
- Paint a sports picture. Use pantomime to demonstrate a sports event.
- Perform folk games and dances.
- Enjoy creative and interpretive dance movements.
- Perform exercises and stretching to music.
- Working in small groups, develop rhythm movement patterns; each group should perform for the other groups.

CREATIVE INTEGRATION

"Bulldog Beat" was developed by a music teacher and a school counselor (Feller, Jr., & Gibbs-Griffith , 2007). The program has three goals: to engage students, improve achievement and morale, and teach life skills. It is used in a middle school in North Carolina and taught for 45 minutes a day for one semester. The program combines drum circles, team building, counseling, and community service. The students learn songs and study the cultural aspects of the songs. Students sit in a circle for both the practice and the performance. A leader plays a drum pattern and the group then echoes the pattern. As the group echoes the pattern, the leader simultaneously plays a new pattern. The students must not only play the pattern correctly, but they must focus on the next pattern so that they are ready to imitate the new pattern. The process forces students to focus on their skills and behaviors, which they discuss as character *traits*. Community service is accomplished by performing for pediatric patients at a local hospital.

"Kids as Curators" was developed by D'Acquisto (2007) for sixth graders at an elementary school in Wisconsin. The students learned how to create a school museum that focused on environmental issues, which they shared with the community. The process motivated their interest and developed communication skills, problem solving, and interpersonal skills. Similar to planning a curriculum unit, the students and teacher(s) decided on a big idea: *Humans can hurt or help the environment.* Next they decided on topics and focus questions. Students were divided into exhibit teams who worked with an adult facilitator. With their facilitator, they developed research questions (What will happen to Lake Michigan if it isn't kept clean?) The students consulted with specialists like a library media person, museum professionals, and community organizations. They interviewed community members and specialists in environmental problems. When their research was concluded, they wrote their research findings and determined what museum visitors would see and interact with. Their displays included artifacts; interactive objects; time lines; video presentations; and a variety of maps, charts, and diagrams.

Bowers and Croley (2007) decided on a project in which students would become art detectives. Their teacher (Croley) developed a teaching unit she called Stolen Art. It was planned for fifth graders in language arts classes. The unit integrated language arts, social studies, and art. The students learned the concept of *provenance*, which means "the written documentation of ownership of an art work." Provenance of a work of art traces the work from point of origin to ensure that it is not a forgery or illegally obtained. The teaching unit also focused on moral ownership, in which a painting's provenance was disputed when it had been seized by the Nazis. Students produced paintings using magazine photos and wallpaper samples to imitate the artist's style. They debated the concept of moral ownership and based their judgments on the research they had engaged in.

INCLUSION AND THE ARTS

The arts can be the great classroom equalizer. Students who do poorly in other subject fields may be talented in the arts. Children with physical disabilities frequently perform exceptionally well in music and art. Students with physical or psychological problems may find personal satisfaction in the expression of the arts. The arts program can focus on students' abilities rather than their limitations. Most students enjoy using color, space, line, and textures in art, as well as rhythm instruments in music. These experiences allow students to do different and special things and, at the same time, keep in contact with their environment.

Although music and art activities can be individualized, in most situations, students enjoy participating in group activities. Small work groups for music or art can accommodate individual differences, special abilities, and varied interests. In music, group work can consist of practicing and learning songs using recordings, planning accompaniments, or composing music. In art work, students may be grouped to use different media; some groups may be experimenting, other groups may be extending an art project, or they may be grouped for special instruction.

When grouping is used as an organizational technique during instruction in the arts, it is very important for the teacher to move from group to group to observe students' progress and to provide the guidance needed to encourage skill development. The mainstreamed student probably will need more guidance and feedback than other students. Motivation and involvement enhance learning in the arts; for this reason, students need both small-group work and whole-class involvement.

SUMMARY

The arts encompass both the visual and the performing arts (music, dance, drama, and art), and invite students to create, improvise, communicate, and express thinking and emotions. The *National Standards for Arts Education* (NAEA, 1994) has identified major standards as competencies affecting dance, music, theatre, and the visual arts for K–12 students.

The use of art materials should be based on students' motor skills, perception of space, and manipulative abilities. Each of the arts is organized to teach concepts, skills, attitudes, and values. Both direct instruction and discovery approaches are used in teaching the arts; however, coping with budget cuts, assessment, and accountability in most school districts often means that the arts curriculum is taught infrequently.

Evaluation in the creative arts should be measured by the student's personal progress and performance.

Sensitive observation by the teacher as students participate in the arts can be used to assess progress.

Programs and projects in the arts are varied; many use professional artists and musicians. Some projects are intended to develop teachers' knowledge, and teachers are expected to translate what they have learned into appropriate pedagogy for the classroom.

The arts are enjoyed by all students and provide ideal means to work with special populations. Interdisciplinary learning is enhanced by using the arts as unifying strands. Integration of the arts motivates students and improves their performance in academic areas. The arts offer ELL students opportunity to express their cultural ties and frees them from processing language. Education through the arts enhances thinking skills, imagination, and oral and written expression.

PORTFOLIO ACTIVITY

Review your thematic unit planned for Chapter 7. Assess whether you have provided for interdisciplinary learning and the integration of subject fields. Identify the topics where you can integrate arts education. Be specific about what you will include and how you will include the arts in your unit.

 ## DISCUSSION QUESTIONS AND APPLICATION EXERCISES

1. Consider music, dance, theatre, and the visual arts, and develop a lesson that will integrate the four components of the arts.
2. Develop lessons for integrating the arts with other subject fields.
3. Identify basic supplies for an art center.
4. Explain why arts lessons may be particularly appropriate for students who are considered discipline problems.
5. How can arts programs open the classroom climate and make it more challenging and exciting?
6. What music and art competencies do you believe students should develop in grades K–8?
7. Observe a preadolescent group of students on the playground or in an after-school activity. Attend specifically to gestures, fashion, movements, and

verbal expressions. Record your observations by categories. Judge how school programs in the arts contribute to what you have observed and how the arts program could relate more meaningfully to these students.

8. Study the drawings of students in grades 1–3. Describe the differences and relate differences to developmental stages as described in this chapter.

9. Select a historical event and create a series of lessons that involve students in literature, theatre, art, and music or dance.

10. How can the arts be used to assess the progress of English language learners?

READER RESEARCH

Using one of the three creative integration ideas, develop a project for students of your choice. Identify the goals, procedures, and activities. Demonstrate how the project utilizes national content standards for the arts.

 TECHNOLOGY APPLICATIONS

Karen Adazzio's students were studying the industrial revolution. She planned to integrate the arts. See if you can carry out her planning ideas. She would have students view impressionist paintings and select an artist that interests them. With the use of the Internet or other resources, she would have students read about the artist's life experiences.

Her next task was to plan a virtual field trip to a museum for students to view more of the artist's work. Then she would ask students to interpret the artist's paintings using the perspective of the artist's life experiences. Major impressionist artists include Monet, Renoir, Pissarro, Sisley, Van Gogh, and Degas.

See the Web site at www.prenhall.com for links. Review the site for the Louvre. See Appendix A for site locations.

Art instruction should expose students to both the production and the appreciation of art.

PART IV

· ·

Professional Growth

Both student achievement and societal goals depend on the quality of the teaching profession. The challenge for teachers in a technological world, with an extremely diverse student population, is to create appropriate and relevant curriculum and adapt instruction to students' developmental needs, experiences (including cultural differences), and cognitive understandings. Student learning is inextricably linked to teacher expertise in subject matter and pedagogy.

As a professional, it is your responsibility to judge not only what your students need to learn, but what you yourself need to learn so that you can improve your practice. You need to know a variety of teaching strategies and how to adapt them to your teaching needs. You need to know how to use current technologies in the classroom and curriculum resources to enhance your teaching and students' learning. Most of all, you need to reflect on your own professional practice. Are you

motivating students? If lessons fail, do you ask yourself why and then reflect on your planning and actions? Do you provide an enriched curriculum? Are you facilitating the learning of significant subject-field concepts? Do you interact professionally with other teachers? Do you and your colleagues consult with each other, and do you assist others?

Reform in public education depends on the insight and sagacity of teachers. Expert teachers must accept leadership responsibilities, not only for self-growth but as a source of advice for colleagues. You and your colleagues need to be courageous risk-takers in the professional domain; otherwise, there will be no experimentation, and problems of practice will not be critiqued, challenged, or scrutinized. You cannot rely on public policy and tests alone to define the curriculum. Teachers are professionally accountable and must accept responsibility for what and how they teach.

CHAPTER 14

Professional Development and Teacher Leadership

Personal Responsibilities

Requirements for teacher credentialing as well as the roles and responsibilities of teachers have changed dramatically during the last several years. In this chapter, performance expectations and some of the ways that teachers are performing leadership roles are discussed. The hierarchical, bureaucratic governance structure of schools has also changed. Although reform strategies in schools do not cause teachers to be leaders, participation beyond the doors of the classroom certainly is related to teachers' shared decision making in schools.

New professional roles require that teachers concern themselves with their own professional development and the development of their colleagues. This chapter explains the ways that teachers can reflect on their practice, self-assess, and grow professionally. Teacher portfolios are a means for authentic assessment, and many teachers are preparing them to exhibit their professional prowess and excellence.

Teachers' legal rights and responsibilities and students' rights conclude the chapter. Teachers are affected by tenure laws, malpractice and negligence, and copyright laws. These legal issues are discussed, along with teacher benefits and salary issues.

Advance Organizer

The following questions are intended to guide your reading and understanding of the content of this chapter.

1. What are some ways to continue your own professional education?
2. In what ways have teachers' responsibilities been expanded in some schools?
3. Why is it important to develop collegiality for professional development?
4. How can clinical supervision assist the beginning teacher?
5. What are some purposes of staff development programs?
6. How will you collect data for self-evaluation, and can you set a timeline for improvement?
7. Which professional association would you like to join?
8. How does copyright law affect teachers in the classroom?
9. In what ways do tenure and dismissal procedures affect teachers?
10. Under what circumstances are teachers liable?
11. What instructional, supervisory, and assessment responsibilities should teachers assume?

INTASC

INTASC Standards

This chapter focuses on teachers' professional responsibilities. Standards 9 and 10 speak to those issues; however, to demonstrate those two standards, teachers need to be proficient in Standards 1–8. To accomplish Standards 9 and 10, a competency checklist of teaching performance is included in the chapter to help you assess your own capabilities.

Professional Lexicon

collegiality The establishment of a professional relationship for the purpose of service and accommodation through the mutual exchange of perceptions and expertise.

comparative negligence Negligence in which the teacher is held responsible commensurate to the extent of negligence when both teacher and student are liable for an injury.

continuing contract A type of employment contract that protects nontenured teachers from "summer dismissal"; notification of dismissal must occur by a certain date, usually May 1.

contributory negligence Negligence in which the injured person fails to exercise reasonable self-care.

indefinite contract A type of employment contract for tenured teachers that is renewed automatically each year without mutual action.

in loco parentis Literally "in place of the parent"; the ability of teachers to act in a parent's place in school situations.

negligence Failure to exercise reasonable care and judgment to protect students from injury.

participation rights The rights of children to participate in decisions that affect their lives and futures.

restructuring Reorganizing schools to improve student achievement and develop a professional environment for teachers.

right of protection The right of children to protection from abuse.

rights of provision The rights of children to have physical, social, economic, and cultural well-being.

TEACHERS AS PROFESSIONALS AND LEADERS

Three fictional teachers have been introduced in this text; in his or her own way, each is considered an expert teacher. Mary Hogan, Greg Thomas, and Karen Adazzio have demonstrated that they care about their students. They have demonstrated their skills in planning and implementing lessons and their ability to assess students' needs, interests, and accomplishments. We will now explore how they demonstrate leadership skills, how they work with colleagues, and how they feel about teaching as a profession.

MARY HOGAN

"Sometimes I get really tired of teaching. Particularly after what feels like a bad day—when there's too much noise and commotion, nobody is listening to me, and time gets away from me. But then after school I talk to a friend who is also a teacher, and she helps me think back about the day and figure out what went wrong. I know I do like teaching; I like being able to think about what to teach and how to teach it, and anticipating stu-

dents' reactions. I really like it when I see that special look in students' eyes that says, 'Hey, that's neat!' and 'I got it!' and then they begin to talk about their own experiences that make it all fit together.

"Because so much of the day is spent talking to children, I really was excited when I was asked to demonstrate teaching models for other teachers. It's fun talking to colleagues about the decisions involved in choosing one model over another. We are going to set up a peer coaching plan, and I look forward to the opportunity to work with other teachers at my school."

GREG THOMAS

"What I like best about teaching is thinking about what will involve the students in real problem solving. I like arranging stuff to create a situation or event for students to explore—and then listening to them wonder. I've never had to worry about students getting out of hand. I like listening to students talk about their ideas together. I don't think you need to set up artificial means so that every student participates; all you need to do is plan challenging experiences. I guess one of the first things I learned as a beginning teacher was to throw out the teacher's manual, look at and listen to the kids, and then reflect on my goals and how to achieve them.

"Two days per month I work with new teachers, helping them with classroom management and instructional problems. I am involved in developing a new resource guide for the district for teaching social studies. These activities are very rewarding professionally. I think these activities with other teachers help me, personally, to be a better teacher."

 ## KAREN ADAZZIO

"The other day I was teaching a lesson within a lesson—using Roger Green's story of *King Arthur and the Knights of the Round Table*. The class had recently read the book, so it was perfect to use as an advance organizer for a historical timeline to study the Middle Ages, the High Middle Ages, and the Renaissance Reformation. I really had fun with it, but it took a little bit before the kids caught on that the story was a means to study feudalism, help us connect the historical time period, and study geography. I told my teacher friend Jan about it, and she shared a similar experience where she was 'nesting' lessons together and integrating several subject fields. When Jan and I start talking about teaching, we tend to lose track of time. I really learn so much from her during these sessions, and it always makes me realize how fortunate I am to be a teacher. No two days are ever the same. Teaching is constantly challenging.

"When I began talking with several other teachers about teaming and grouping our students, I really felt like I was on a high. Pretty soon we realized that we needed to figure our block scheduling to lock in our students so that the teaming would work. The other teachers asked me to serve as the group leader; I think that really made me feel good—that they would choose me—and I work hard to keep the team on track. We are really committed to improving the instructional program for students, and it's great sharing decisions and designing a new program."

ACCOUNTABILITY AND ASSESSMENT

Most teachers recognize that teaching is not just about focusing on state testing systems and state standards. It is about teaching significant concepts in subject fields, meeting students' needs, and preparing students for successful lives. Plitt (2004) shares his perspective of the teaching challenge by asking himself three questions:

1. Who are my students and what are their needs and strengths?
2. What is it that I believe my students need to know and be able to do?
3. How will I know that my students are different as a result of the learning experience? (p. 746)

Teaching to the tests may be attractive if one considers the consequences for teachers, schools, and districts. Teachers' performance is measured by students' achievement schoolwide. In schools where test scores do not improve, the school is subjected to publicity and ultimately may be closed. The teachers are branded as inadequate and will have difficulty obtaining another position. But as Posner (2004) points out, students whose curriculum is limited to the ability to answer standardized test problems also will be limited to solving simplistic and routine questions that will not prepare them for dealing with complex situations and analysis of real-life problems.

For teachers the dilemma causes many professional questions. For example, how do you deal with reading programs or social studies programs that your school district has bought where the format is structured with precise questions and, as Posner notes, exact material, timing, and wording for instruction? Would Plitt be able to address his three questions? Would you really need a teaching credential to mimic and follow the directions in the teaching manual? What should teachers do? The balance of the chapter will provide suggestions for improving practice.

TEACHER DECISION MAKING

Many Hogan, Greg Thomas, and Karen Adazzio demonstrated that they are constantly engaged in making judgments because what they do in their classrooms cannot be routinized. They need to be involved in problem solving about teaching. Through advance planning and throughout the school day, teachers need to decide what to teach, how best to teach it, how to accommodate diverse learners, how to utilize both theory and pedagogy, and how to meld subject-field academic concepts into concepts appropriate for teaching. All three of the teachers called attention to *time* as a critical constraint on their professional activities.

TIME AND TEACHING

One of the biggest constraints on improving teaching, student achievement, and reforming schools is the lack of time for teachers to plan, reflect on teaching with colleagues, and interact with students, parents, and other professionals (Lemlech, Hertzog, & Hackl, 1994). The U.S. Department of Education's report titled "Trying to Beat the Clock" (1998) verifies that teachers have very little time to plan lessons and very few opportunities to interact with colleagues. Stevenson (1998) compares U.S. teachers with German and Japanese teachers and notes that only in our country are teachers expected to provide instruction for almost the entire day. In Germany, teachers provide instruction until noon and have the rest of the day for planning and professional activity. In Japan, teachers provide instruction for only half of their day.

Still another problem for teachers in the United States is that they are paid for only 9 months of teaching. As a consequence, many teachers need to find employment for the remaining 3 months. In other countries, teachers are paid a 12-month salary and are provided time for professional and curriculum development. Clearly, we need to invest in our teachers and

---

Teaching Hints: Professional Development

Paez (2003) teaches in a school committed to professional development: (1) Teachers are expected to make time for teacher collaboration. This occurs in a weekly meeting. (2) School time is used for teacher demonstrations to observe each other teach. (3) Literacy training focuses on what students need to learn to be successful readers and writers. (They do not use scripted lessons.) (4) Professional-development consultants work collaboratively with teachers, sharing ideas, information, and opinions.

---

provide time for professional learning. Some teacher responsibilities beyond the classroom are listed next.

Teachers' Professional Responsibilities (Outside the Classroom)
- Consideration of school organizational structures (Adazzio's block scheduling)
- Teacher teaming for instruction
- Collaboration to develop new curricula
- Uses for technology
- Self-assessment and peer coaching
- Responsibility for continuing education for self and with colleagues

IMPROVING TEACHING AND REFORMING SCHOOLS

A great deal of research points to several strategies for improving teaching and reforming schools. Some of what has been learned includes the following:

- *Teachers talking together about teaching:* providing ideas for what works (and what doesn't), sharing problems, reflecting on lessons
- *Participation in professional communities:* may be within the school or participation in a professional association; the important aspect is that teachers are sharing learning and expertise, engaging in collaborative teacher research, and supporting each other with knowledge and assistance
- *Sharing in school governance:* involvement in decision making that affects the school culture and the school community (an example follows in the next section)

School Organization

At Karen Adazzio's school, students are now grouped in clusters that are assigned to several teachers for teaching and guidance. In addition, class periods have been changed to provide larger blocks of time so that teachers can implement thematic units and interdisciplinary instruction. To accomplish this, the teachers began to work together planning instruction and at times teaming during instruction. The teachers also assumed responsibility for counseling the students. The process of restructuring affected teacher relationships, content of instruction, how students are grouped, the way time is structured, and schoolwide decision making.

The small-school concept is being shared at many middle and high schools throughout the nation. In

Planning together, these teachers are sharing ideas for a thematic unit to be taught in their three classrooms.

New York City, 15 small schools serve grades 6–12, with 41 more serving grades 9–12. The small schools reside within the walls of huge comprehensive high schools. The major purpose of the small school is to keep the dropout rate low and achievement high. Help for these fledgling schools comes from community partners (museums, cultural organizations, higher-education institutions, social agencies). Aside from space problems encountered by most of these small schools, teachers need to work harder to implement collegial projects, new curriculum, sharing materials, and taking responsibility for teams of students.

In Houston, a 3,100-student school was changed into 10 small learning communities. Each community is semiautonomous and is designed around a particular theme (performing arts, health sciences, law-related careers). In these small communities, students recognize that teachers "know them." But teachers need to work harder at communicating and collaborating with other teachers, engaging in social work, and preparing to teach a variety of subject fields instead of specializing in one subject.

Teaching Processes

Restructuring should affect the ways in which students are taught. Thematic teaching emphasizes the relationships of the different disciplines. Factual information is deemphasized; instead, deeper meanings are sought. Use of students' prior knowledge becomes integral to the process because the focus of teaching is on student engagement and participation.

The Teachers

The "egg-crate" structure of the classroom and the isolation of teachers disappears in the small-school setting. Teachers have access to each other for planning, collaboration, consultation, and coaching (Lemlech, 1995). Teachers are actively engaged in developing curriculum, selecting resources, and defining assessment processes. Teachers "teach" differently. They encourage self-directed learning. They guide and facilitate through creating appropriate environments for learning. They question instead of telling.

The Students

Students are engaged in active learning, which means that students interact frequently in small groups—not just in skill activities—for the purpose of raising questions, experimenting, sharing knowledge, discussing, and using technological resources. Students manipulate objects and data to construct their own understanding. They are expected to explain and demonstrate what they are learning through the products they create (stories, reports, pictures, programs, and projects).

Schoolwide Decision Making

The involvement of teachers in decision-making and problem-solving teams, teacher networks, learning communities, and school-to-school networks affects the structural organization of the school. Traditional hierarchical relations fade and the school's organizational structure becomes flat. Faculty dialogue and support for risk taking affect policy decisions and professional development.

Teacher Reflection

All three of the teachers featured in this text think about teaching. They are active learners and they attempt to understand the following:

- What their students know and are learning
- What worked and why, and what didn't work and why

The reflective teacher constantly wonders: "If I had tried this or that, would it be better?" "What else would work?" "How could I have . . . ?" "What would have happened if . . . ?" "This reminds me of the time when . . . ."

Researchers have long been aware of the value of reflection on practice. Changes in practice depend on thinking about tradition (routines you are accustomed to enacting) and consideration of alternatives. Interaction with others and collaboration stimulate the process of reflection. The process of reflection requires that the reflector detach self from the situation or event and reconsider it for the purpose of perceiving alternative actions and interpretations. Talking to others about actual teaching happenings stimulates the reflective process. Making reflection a habit of professional practice has the potential to improve our thinking about teaching and improve our instructional practices.

Assessment Informs Instruction

Many researchers have concluded that professional development must focus on using student achievement data to guide instructional decisions. Too often, students' tests are forgotten after scores are recorded. Instead teachers need to (1) analyze their teaching goal, (2) verify that students were tested on what was taught, (3) check what students achieved, and (4) target what they failed to learn. The gap between what students know and what they failed to learn needs to guide immediate instructional lessons.

Teaching Hints: *Meeting the Needs of English Language Learners*

Miller and Endo (2004) describe the language shock experienced by new students who enter an English-speaking environment and suffer anxiety and stress because they do not understand anything that is said. As a consequence, their motivation to learn is nil and self-esteem is destroyed. What should teachers do?

1. Know your students' schooling history so that lessons can be planned that fit prior knowledge, interests, and needs.
2. Select learning activities that allow the ELL student a variety of ways to respond (verbal, written, project).
3. Do not be afraid to meet with parents to learn about the student and discuss the needs of the child. Team up with the parents.
4. Demonstrate respect for the culture of each ELL student. Include pieces of the child's culture in the lesson and the environment of the classroom. Treat the student as an "expert" about his or her culture.
5. Reduce concept load when teaching by using simpler sentences and words to convey meaning.
6. Encourage second-language learners to keep their native language intact through either home and community or in school at appropriate times.

Research Findings

Cox-Petersen (2001) asked 44 science teachers partici-pating in an advanced science methods class to perform action research in their own classrooms. Teachers were to report the problem, rationale, literature review, method for collecting data, findings, and instructional decisions made as a result of their research.

Findings indicated that, as a consequence of the study, teachers planned changes in their practice, and critically reflected on tactics that impeded or enhanced science learning and teaching. The teachers found that their own action research was more effective for their personal development than reading and applying the research findings of others.

TEACHERS AS RESEARCHERS

Action research is another way in which teachers work individually and collaboratively to solve school-based problems. Action research is the name given to research conducted by teachers in their own classrooms or on school grounds. Research planned and carried out by teachers tends to be *authentic*—meaning it is genuinely needed to improve instruction and provide professional learning.

In a collaborative mode, teachers jointly identify a problem that they feel can be solved by school-based research. They develop the research process together and then conduct the research in their own classrooms. They report their results to each other and modify instructional procedures as needed or design an inter-vention strategy.

Although many teachers involve themselves in short action research projects in their own classrooms, oth-ers seek peer collaboration on an action research agenda. An example of action research that began as an individual project and ultimately became a collabora-tive project was told to me by an inner-city fifth-grade teacher. She was curious about the effect on school attendance if she initiated active learning experiences that would be introduced on Monday and concluded on Friday, so that students would recognize that if they were absent, they would miss out on constructing and

experimenting. She found that her students' attendance improved as a consequence. Teachers need to be active researchers and reflect on practices in their schools and classrooms. Many such studies have been extremely valuable and have contributed to knowledge about teaching and to the dialogue about teaching.

PREPARATION FOR LEADERSHIP: COLLEGIAL RELATIONSHIPS

Preservice Preparation

Beginning in 1987, the University of Southern Cali-fornia experimented with a collegial teacher prepara-tion program for student teaching. Student teachers were paired for their classroom practice experience. The purpose of the program was to create a bond between partner student teachers to enhance their abil-ity to become professionals and teacher-leaders. The authors defined **collegiality** as "the establishment of a professional relationship for the purpose of service and accommodation through the mutual exchange of per-ceptions and expertise" (Lemlech & Kaplan, 1990).

Lemlech and Kaplan (1990, 1991) studied the devel-opmental pattern and sequence of collegial relation-ships among the student teachers (Figure 14.1). They found that collegial relationships progress from a friendly and helping relationship to the exchange of ideas and to dialogue about beliefs and knowledge, appreciation of each other's strengths, and ultimately to trust and commitment to each other based on a feel-ing of proficiency and equality.

As colleagues, the partner student teachers estab-lished their own identity, recognized each other's expertise, and accepted responsibility to provide each other with consultant services. In essence, colleagues become co-problem-solvers. The collegial relationship generates reflective thinking about teaching processes, enhances the individual's own learning, and promotes problem solving and insight. Lemlech and Kaplan (1991) theorized that the professionalization of teach-ing depends on the development of expertise in the knowledge base of teaching, teacher empowerment, teacher leadership, and collegial relationships.

Just as the collegial teacher preparation program changed the student teaching program from an appren-ticeship model to a collegial model, the program also

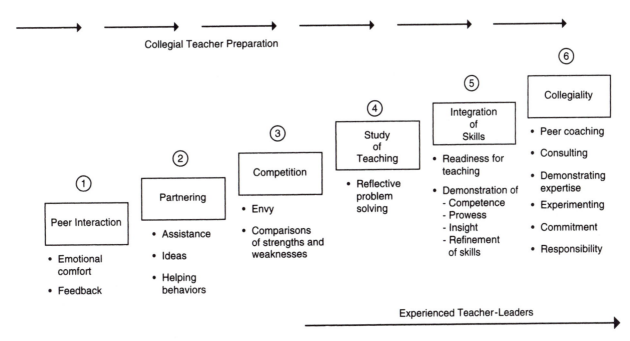

Figure 14.1 Figure Collegial Development Stages and Characteristics

Source: From *Collegial Preparation, Reflective Practice, and Social Studies Teaching*, by J. K. Lemlech and S. N Kaplan, 1991.

necessitated changes in the roles and responsibilities of the public school supervising teachers. Hertzog-Foliart and Lemlech (1993) compared traditional supervision with collegial supervision of preservice teachers. They found role changes in three teaching components: planning, lesson enactment, and feedback. Traditionally, the supervising teacher directs what the preservice teacher should teach, and then during the lesson, watches to see that it is enacted; for feedback, the supervising teacher traditionally "tells and critiques." But in collegial supervision, the supervising teacher becomes part of the planning team as the partners and the supervisor engage in the process of planning. During the lesson, the supervising teacher guides partner observation. During feedback time, the supervising teacher guides the reflective thinking of the colleagues, models professional dialogue, and facilitates the collegial relationship of the preservice teachers.

CONTINUING EDUCATION— PERSONAL DEVELOPMENT

All professionals need to be concerned about keeping abreast of current knowledge and skills in their field of endeavor. For many years, medical and dental professionals have been required by state law to attend professional-development classes. Accountants and attorneys are also required to obtain continuing education credits each year. Thus, it is not surprising that the public expects public school teachers to attend continuing-education classes in their school districts or on college campuses.

Personal/independent continuing education can be accomplished in a variety of ways. For example, with membership in one or more professional organizations, you receive monthly professional journals. Articles in these journals help you keep abreast of new ideas, research, and current problems affecting public education.

Another form of continuing education is attendance at state and national conferences sponsored by professional organizations. Membership is not required to attend these conferences, where you will hear leaders in the field discuss current happenings in the field. You will also be invited to join subcommittees focused on specific areas of interest.

Listening to audiotapes from the conferences provides another means of tuning in on significant issues that were recorded at national conferences. These can be purchased soon after the conferences and can be listened to in your car on the way to work.

Accepting Personal Responsibility for Professional Development

National Board Certification

The National Board for Professional Teaching Standards (NBPTS), created in 1987, developed a set of national standards to certify highly accomplished teachers. National Board Certification requires that teachers demonstrate specific knowledge and skills appropriate to the level they are teaching (early childhood, middle childhood, and so on) and appropriate to what they teach (generalist, social studies/history, art, mathematics, and so on).

Research Findings

Lemlech and Hertzog (1999) studied the reciprocal relationship between student teacher partners and their master teachers. They questioned: What do master teachers and student teachers learn from each other? They learned that the value of pairing student teachers to develop collegial relationships affected the professional relations of prospective teachers and their master teacher because the master teachers assumed the roles of coaches, mentors, and team leaders. Dialogue among partners and master teachers encouraged professional reflection and motivated risk taking by master teachers with new teaching approaches. Similar benefits are possible between beginning teachers and mentors if collegial relationships are developed.

Research Findings

A four-year study of test scores in Florida and North Carolina questioned whether nationally certified teachers actually raised students' test scores. The answer was yes. The study confirmed that teachers who have earned National Board certification "are more effectively producing learning goals and raising test scores" (Viadero & Honawar, 2008).

Quality Teaching

School districts, schools of education, and the public all want and expect a connection between teacher competence (quality of teaching) and student achievement. In every chapter of this text, attention has been directed to the Interstate New Teacher Assessment and Support Consortium (INTASC) standards. The certification process in most states requires that teachers pass an examination in which beginning teachers' performance is assessed by their responses to aspects of teaching. Performance expectations relate to teachers' knowledge of students' development and what students know and do not know, content/subject matter knowledge, and instructional processes (review Figure 6.1). In addition, teachers are expected to know how to develop and maintain an appropriate environment for learning, and understand personal legal and ethical responsibilities as an educator. Table 14.1 uses the INTASC standards as a performance checklist to assist your planning for professional growth.

Set Personal Goals

To improve personal performance, it is important to set goals that focus on your own planning and teaching behavior, rather than on students' behavior or on the improvement of the school's educational program. The following goals are recognized as important to instructional improvement:

- Base learning experiences on significant conceptual content rather than on "fun" activities.
- Select learning experiences that are consonant with personal goals. (If critical thinking is a goal, then the activity should engage students in practicing critical-thinking skills.)

- Increase student-to-student interaction versus student-to-teacher-to-student interaction.
- Encourage constructivist thinking.
- Differentiate instruction based on students' needs, interests, and learning styles.
- Improve organizational skills to decrease nonteaching time.
- Integrate subject fields to unify learning.
- Utilize academic fields to teach reading comprehension skills.
- Increase teacher feedback to students during direct instruction.
- Increase flexible grouping of students throughout the school day.
- Increase output activities for students.
- Increase professional reading.
- Apply research findings in the classroom.

Analyze Your Own Performance

It is possible to analyze your own performance to verify what you need to improve. Using a recorder in the classroom, small episodes of instruction can be recorded for later analysis, or you may want to ask a student or another teacher to videotape a teaching episode. Before listening to or viewing the episode, decide on the purpose of your evaluation:

- Do you want to listen to the questions you asked?
- Are you listening for the number of responses and degree of interaction?
- Are you concerned about management skills?
- Is enthusiasm or clarity of instructions what interests you?

Research Findings

Viadero (2004) reports that research studies of kindergarten, elementary, and middle school students from a national sample and in Texas confirmed that math scores were higher when students were taught by qualified teachers. Studies were controlled for students' differences in socioeconomic status, previous achievement, and teachers' experience. Qualified teachers were those who were credentialed and state certified and had had pedagogical instruction in teacher preparation. The studies also revealed that poor students were less likely to have qualified teachers.

Table 14.1 Teaching Competencies

Rate yourself using a scale from 1 to 5, with 5 as the highest level.

1. I am comfortable with my conceptual knowledge of the subject matter I am required to teach.	1 2 3 4 5
2. I am able to translate subject-matter concepts into meaningful experiences for students.	1 2 3 4 5
3. I am able to use my knowledge of child/adolescent growth and development to create appropriate intellectual, social, and personal learning experiences.	1 2 3 4 5
4. I am able to identify ways in which my students differ in learning preferences and adapt learning activities to address their needs to achieve content standards.	1 2 3 4 5
5. I am able to implement teaching strategies to assist English language learners' progress in achieving content standards.	1 2 3 4 5
6. I am able to implement a variety of teaching strategies to encourage students' skill development, critical thinking, and problem solving.	1 2 3 4 5
7. I can create a motivating learning environment that encourages students' interactions and active engagement in learning experiences.	1 2 3 4 5
8. I am able to communicate effectively with the whole class and with individuals to stimulate inquiry and collaborative endeavors.	1 2 3 4 5
9. I am able to engage in both short- and long-range planning in the subjects I teach to meet the needs of my students.	1 2 3 4 5
10. I am able to use a variety of assessment techniques to inform teaching and determine what students learned and what they need to know.	1 2 3 4 5
11. I engage in reflective inquiry to determine what works and what doesn't and to evaluate my decisions' effects on others in the learning community.	1 2 3 4 5
12. I have developed relationships with other teachers, collaborate with them, and recognize the significance of collegial interactions to support the learning of students.	1 2 3 4 5
13. I interact with parents and community representatives to foster the well-being of students.	1 2 3 4 5

- When students work in groups, do you encourage them to ask for and give each other help?

Do not attempt to critique everything. Focus on one or two elements of your teaching style and develop a checklist that will enable you to listen in a purposeful manner.

Another way to help you analyze your performance is to invite a trusted colleague to observe. You and your colleague should develop an observation chart to enable your friend to observe specific elements of instruction.

Design a Self-Help Program

After analyzing your performance, decide on your goal and arrange a timeline to accomplish your objectives. Use Table 14.1 to help you in your analysis. Consider what you have learned about successful staff development programs and, using that information, model your personal program. For example, to increase your awareness and knowledge about your goal, you could decide to do the following:

- Read professional literature.
- Attend a professional class.
- Talk to a knowledgeable expert.

Your next task may be to find another teacher who is an expert in the technique you want to master. Ask your colleague if you may visit his or her classroom during a particular session so you will have an appropriate model. You may need to share your goal and your plan with your principal so provisions can be made to allow you to visit other teachers.

Your third task is to develop a plan for practicing the skill. You will probably have to arrange to have someone observe your performance so you can receive feedback.

Finally, after appropriate practice and feedback, work out a system whereby you utilize the technique consistently in your teaching. Once again, you may want the assistance of a colleague to help you plan instruction implementing the new skill.

COOPERATIVE/COLLEGIAL DEVELOPMENT

Many teachers, including me, find it rewarding to work with one or more colleagues for the purpose of professional growth. Speaking with others about what works and what doesn't helps to clarify teaching theory, per-

Research Findings

Strahan (2003) described a three-year study of three elementary schools in North Carolina engaged in promoting a collaborative culture among teachers and administrators and improving low-income and minority student achievement. Each school began the process of change in slightly different ways, but all accomplished reform. The process at each school followed a general framework:

1. Faculty members identified priorities for professionalism.
2. Teachers targeted curriculum areas to work on that addressed students' needs.
3. Faculty members developed a supportive climate for students.
4. Regular grade-level meetings among teachers were held to talk about teaching and focus on teacher efficacy.

sonal beliefs, planning, and decision making. It is particularly helpful when colleagues who disagree with each other about methodology work to prove what is appropriate or optimal. Personal experience some years ago with several colleagues emphasized how much fun and interest in the teaching process is generated when you discuss (argue!) with good friends about when to introduce a particular concept, what should come first, appropriate activities and materials, and motivation. Discussions such as these are good medicine for instructional improvement in the classroom.

PEER COACHING

The concept and purpose of peer coaching is often misunderstood. It is not intended as a means to remediate poor instructional practices, nor is it intended as a mentoring strategy.

Characteristics of Coaching

Colleague teachers choose to coach each other because they want to master a new instructional strategy (new to them); they want to master the use of new instructional materials/resources; or they are experimenting with new ideas, grouping, or content. The major purpose for coaching is the implementation of an innovative method of teaching to determine its effect on various groups of students. Suppose a group of teachers are learning the group investigation model of teaching. One of the teachers demonstrates the model and introduces the theory and research about the model. Next, the teachers practice the model with each other. Then several of the teachers decide to try it out in their classrooms. By utilizing a peer-coaching process, teachers can work with a partner to observe the implementation of the model. The peer partners observe each other and verify whether the syntax of the model was utilized precisely and accurately. The observer notes how well students worked with the model. Suggestions by the observer to the partner teacher support and provide insight to supplement the teacher's self-appraisal.

Based on staff development experiences, Hillary Hertzog, Margo Pensavalle, and I recommended the following format for peer coaching:

1. Peer partners share a concern or teaching problem.
2. The concern or problem is delimited so that the consulting partner can focus specifically on the teaching behavior or problem during an observation.
3. The partner consultant observes and takes notes.
4. The notes are shared, and both teachers take part in the analysis.
5. The consulting partner provides feedback only on what was specified. If additional information about teaching is sought, the partner who was observed must ask for it. It is not volunteered.

TEACHERS AS STAFF DEVELOPERS

Staff development is one of the new role responsibilities that teachers are assuming. Collegial relationships free teachers to both acknowledge and accept personal strengths and weaknesses. Teachers should not be ashamed to acknowledge areas in which they are not, and perhaps do not want to be, expert. But many teachers do have areas of expertise, and in these areas they must assume responsibility for leadership.

Teachers are uniquely qualified to lead staff development programs because of their intimate knowledge of the classroom population, the community context, and essential skills. Many of the same skills needed for motivating children are important in staff development programs. For example, the teacher-leader needs to be enthusiastic, be clear about the staff development purposes, keep the program participants engaged in the task at hand, select activities appropriate to the goal,

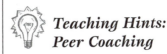

Teaching Hints:
Peer Coaching

- Coaching is situation-specific to colleague teachers.
- Colleagues are learning/practicing new skills, knowledge, and/or strategies.
- Colleagues are experimenting.
- Coaching is ongoing and continuous.
- Teachers have a collegial relationship, and coaching is a means for self-help.

and relate the program to classroom implementation. The teacher-leader should also be skillful in human relations.

Staff Development Programs

Successful staff development programs typically focus on the following:

- Improvement of specific skills
- Demonstrations and opportunities for practicing new skills and receiving feedback
- Relationship to local school problems
- Curriculum development needs and processes and new programs
- Support services

Good teaching is contagious. Successful teachers attract other teachers who want to learn new ideas and techniques. Schoolwide improvement occurs simultaneously as teachers improve. Improvement of teaching performance happens slowly and developmentally. Most teachers are motivated to improve their instructional performance because they care about their students. Research indicates that paying teachers to participate in staff development programs is not as effective as appealing to teachers' natural motivation to improve their abilities and become better at what they do.

Improvement at the school level depends on individual teachers. Concerned teachers must be involved in the planning of the improvement process. For schools to improve, teachers must meet together, be aware of the scope of the problem, and be committed to improvement. Teachers are professional experts and must make the decisions about the change process.

As teachers take on the role and responsibility for their own staff development, consideration must be given to the following questions:

- *Who* needs to learn what? (Who else, other than the teachers, need to "know"—students, parents, library personnel, principal, district personnel?)
- *How* is the new different from the old?
- *What* needs to be learned to implement the new?
- *What* support services and resources are affected by the "new"?

Teacher Leadership

There is considerable evidence that teachers are performing a variety of roles and assuming responsibilities beyond the classroom, unlike those performed in the past by traditional classroom teachers. Classroom teachers have become researchers, mentors, peer coaches, curriculum developers, and staff developers. The new teacher-leader is involved structurally in the school, participating in decision-making teams and problem-solving groups, creating standards, writing grants, and serving on personnel committees to screen new teachers.

Teachers are engaged in the study of their profession and are involved in experiences as learners, teachers, and leaders. Their activities are full-time, continuous, and interactive. Roles and responsibilities nurture inquiry processes and make teachers more thoughtful and reflective personally and professionally.

PARTNERSHIP MODELS: UNIVERSITY AND SCHOOL DISTRICT

The university–school district partnership model offers teachers another approach to continuing education and teacher leadership. There are a remarkable number of partnership models in existence. Some have informal arrangements; others have formalized the association and may call themselves *professional development schools* (PDSs).

Informal models may be "favored" schools or cooperating network schools that work with one university teacher-education program. The university assigns a cluster of student teachers and a university coordinator to the school. The close relationship and favored status evolves as teachers and university personnel become accustomed to each other and both develop expectations about the relationship, which includes relinquishing traditional controls. The teachers participate and lead school-site seminars for the student teachers and interested university faculty, and the university coordinator may help arrange staff development programs for the participating teachers.

The PDS may be a formalized partnership funded by an outside agency. The funds are often used to release teachers by paying for substitutes to enable the partner teachers to engage in staff development. PDSs are usually involved in restructuring activities. The expert teachers at the PDS and the university share responsibility for providing appropriate experiences for the student teachers.

Partnership schools are characterized by the following:

- The continuing education of teachers
- Reflective teachers engaged in site-specific inquiry
- A democratic community with shared school governance
- Collegial relationships among school faculty and between university and school faculty
- A cohort of student teachers educated jointly by the university and the expert teachers
- An environment that supports and nurtures the sharing of expertise

CHARTER SCHOOLS

A charter school provides an alternative to the traditional school system. It is an alternative for students and their parents, teachers, and administrators. Charter schools are funded with public money and may be designed by parents, teachers, or community groups. The charter must be approved by a school district or by the state government. The purpose of the charter should be:

Innovation
Freedom from school district rules
Unique means in curriculum, instruction, or
   environment

Generally the charter is set for three to five years; however, the charter may be revoked if the school's academic performance lags behind district schools with similar populations. Though publicly funded, money is not given for the use of facilities. As a consequence, charter schools beg for places within other schools or in the community to conduct classes. The charter school is a free-choice school. Teachers choose the school because they believe in the goals of the charter and because they choose to teach in a particular way. Administrators also choose the charter because of philosophic beliefs, and students attend because their parents believe that the charter is superior to the traditional school.

HOME SCHOOLING

Home schooling is for children who are unable to attend regular school classes because of illness, autism, giftedness, working responsibilities, and/or parental philosophic beliefs. There are laws that protect the parent (and the child) so that schooling can occur in the home environment. School districts are responsible for employing a credentialed teacher(s) who will supervise the home-schooling program.

The teacher's responsibilities include holding periodic classes for home-schooled children, verifying that the child is learning appropriate subject matter, testing the child, helping the parent as needed, assessing progress, and counseling both child and parent. Home-schooled children may be a very diverse group: different needs, varied ages and grades. As a consequence, the teacher has a difficult assignment, particularly when it comes to holding classes for the students.

PROFESSIONAL ASSOCIATIONS CONTRIBUTE TO PROFESSIONAL DEVELOPMENT

Teachers have a wide range of professional-group choices available to them for membership. There are professional associations related to almost every subject field. The following organizations provide services to elementary and middle school teachers; most have web sites, which can be found in Appendix A.

- American Alliance for Health, Physical Education, Recreation, and Dance
- Council for Exceptional Children
- International Reading Association
- National Art Education Association
- National Association for Bilingual Education
- National Association for Gifted Children
- National Association for Research in Science Teaching

- National Association of Music Educators
- National Council for Geographic Education
- National Council for History Education
- National Council for the Social Studies
- National Council of Teachers of English
- National Council of Teachers of Mathematics
- National Science Teachers Association

Professional development is enhanced by membership in these national groups. Each of the associations offers members periodic journals, newsletters, bulletins, and research information. In addition, they typically hold a national conference that meets over a long weekend. The conference location shifts each year to vary both the local perspective and the travel time. At the conferences, teachers take part in committee work, workshops, and discussion groups. Each association brings in noted scholars in the subject field who report on noteworthy curriculum development, research, and socially significant issues. The association, in cooperation with a local university, frequently manages compressed classes for teachers interested in unit credit. Publishers' exhibits at these conferences provide teachers with the opportunity to view and critique the latest instructional materials and media related to the subject field.

In recent years, professional associations have assumed the responsibility of providing their members with continuing education. The conference enhances professional life and provides teachers with an enjoyable way to engage in dialogue with other professionals.

Two other national groups need to be recognized for their contribution to the professional advancement of teachers: the National Education Association (NEA) and the American Federation of Teachers (AFT). Both provide members with ethical, legal, and political leadership and services. The NEA primarily serves members who live in suburban and rural areas; AFT members typically live in the large urban areas. The NEA publishes *Today's Education* and the *NEA Reporter*. The AFT publishes *Changing Education* and *The American Teacher*. Both groups furnish members with congressional and political information important for the profession, as well as curriculum and instruction articles, through their journals and newsletters.

Local and State Associations

Many of the national professional associations have local and state chapters. These smaller groups often have their own newsletter or journal and regional conferences. The local meetings focus on classroom and community problems and function as a collegial support system. Committee and task force participation is encouraged by these groups. Frequently state legislative information on problems is handled by these state associations, and state departments of education turn to the local chapters for assistance and information about educational problems and priorities.

PERSONAL DEVELOPMENT THROUGH EXTRACURRICULAR ACTIVITIES

It is as important to grow as a mature and cultured adult as it is to develop as a professional person. It is commonly recognized that "all work and no play" can truly make one a very dull person. The all-work syndrome also contributes to the phenomenon known as teacher burnout. Outside interests, activities, and friendships, distinct from professional associations and activities, help the professional person achieve balance.

Teachers join drama groups, political party groups, book clubs, and recreational organizations in order to get away from school and gain a different perspective about community life. Involvement in community affairs and in the cultural life of the community helps teachers develop vital intellectual, social, and emotional capacities. Continuing education encompasses all aspects of human development. Adult growth depends on positive relationships with others as well as interaction with one's life work.

TEAM TEACHING: CONTRIBUTION TO PROFESSIONALISM

Team teaching is a way of combining the instructional efforts of two or more teachers to use their abilities to the best advantage. Teacher aides or assistants may also be included in the teaming arrangement. Teaming can be particularly advantageous at the elementary school level because of the diversity of subjects that are taught. For example, if several fourth-grade teachers at a school teamed, each might be a team leader for a different subject of the curriculum. The team leader would accept greater responsibility for planning and teaching in the area of his or her expertise. The other members of the team would serve as assistants during instruction and would help with reinforcement.

Group planning time is critical when working in a team situation. Members of the team need to share plans and objectives and receive feedback about whether a lesson accomplished its purpose. Team teaching provides a system whereby new and inexperienced teachers can learn teaching methodologies from more experienced colleagues and receive feedback about their own teaching performance.

Implementation of teaming is different in each situation. In some schools, an experienced teacher is called the *lead teacher* and is responsible for most of the planning. However, the professional reason for teaming should be to refine instructional techniques and provide students with instruction from teachers who are motivated and superior in each subject field. Teaming provides a built-in system for staff development.

Because teachers pool their respective classes in team teaching, this organizational system allows students to be grouped by need rather than by grade. Students move from one group to another depending on the subject and the student's ability. Nongraded teaching teams from primary grades, middle grades, or upper grades are popular in many schools.

In Karen Adazzio's middle school, the students are clustered in what have been called *houses*. Teachers do team teaching in this arrangement for integrating the core subjects. At Adazzio's school, the teachers bank time in order to have extra planning time together. Banking time is a means to teach longer several days a week so that school can be dismissed earlier on another day to accommodate teachers' planning needs.

LEGAL ISSUES AFFECTING TEACHERS

Teacher Tenure

Most states have tenure laws to protect teachers from irresponsible and arbitrary dismissal. Tenure laws specify how teachers gain tenure and under what conditions or circumstances tenured teachers can be dismissed. The purpose of tenure is to provide capable teachers with security so that changes in school boards or public reaction to educational issues will not result in teacher dismissal without just cause. Generally, grounds for dismissal are described in the state's tenure statute. Most states will dismiss a teacher for immorality, unprofessional conduct, insubordination, and incompetency. Teachers must be dismissed for cause.

Dismissal of tenured teachers cannot occur without specific procedures being followed. These procedures vary from state to state. In most states, the teacher needs to be informed in writing of the charges filed against him or her prior to the dismissal hearing. After written notice, the teacher is usually given a specified amount of time to prepare for a hearing before the school board. The teacher has the right to have counsel at the hearing. If a teacher is dissatisfied with the results of the hearing, he or she may take the case before the courts.

Teachers can also lose tenure status by resigning from their school district position. Unless the school board grants a leave of absence, teachers will lose tenure status if they voluntarily absent themselves from their position. Teachers moving from one school district to another within their own state can also lose tenure unless the new school board agrees to tenure status.

Teachers gain tenure by teaching in a school district for a predetermined number of years and following the requirements of the state. Teachers are typically considered probationary teachers during the nontenured period. The probationary period varies between two and four years among the states. In some school districts, teachers must be evaluated a specified number of times during the probationary period to verify satisfactory performance. In some states, the teacher applies to the state for tenure status after serving satisfactorily in a school district; in other states, the teacher must be recognized by formal action of the school board before tenure rights are granted.

Some states have **continuing contract** laws. For teachers who have not yet gained tenure, they may expect that a school board will notify them of the expiration of their contract, usually by May 1. If they are not notified of dismissal by that date, they may assume that they have a continuing contract. The continuing contract protects nontenured teachers from summer dismissal, when it would be difficult to obtain another position.

Tenured teachers have what is called an **indefinite contract.** This means that the contract is renewed automatically each year without mutual action by teacher and school board.

Salaries

Most school districts have a single salary schedule for all teachers. Salaries are differentiated by experience and education. Salaries are adjusted both vertically (for experience) and horizontally (for education). Thus, a teacher with an advanced degree and/or special training will be placed higher on the salary schedule than a teacher without special education. Currently, however, there are controversial proposals to pay some teachers more than others based on their subject expertise—for example, teachers who are able to teach bilingually or who specialize in mathematics or science.

Some states have a minimum-salary law that affects public school teachers. In such cases, the school board may pay teachers higher than the minimum salary, but not lower.

Many states have collective bargaining laws, which identify the procedures for school boards to negotiate with teacher organizations. The teacher organization with the greatest membership in the school district is typically given the right to represent the teachers of the district for salary and benefit negotiations.

The First Amendment

The Association for Supervision and Curriculum Development (ASCD) and the First Amendment Center are working to educate school leaders, teachers, and others about the meaning and significance of the First Amendment. The First Amendment guarantees expressive and religious freedom, and one of the joint project's goals is to encourage curriculum developers and teachers to educate for freedom and responsibility. Their publication *The First Amendment in Schools* (Haynes, Chaltain, Ferguson, Hudson, & Thomas, 2003) provides guidance on many issues that affect teachers, administrators, students, parents, and board members. The authors include a special section on teacher and administrator rights and responsibilities (pp. 92–103), and I will refer to several of the questions they pose in this segment.

1. *What protection do teachers have if they feel they have been treated unfairly?* Teachers are protected by (1) teacher tenure laws, (2) collective bargaining agreement contracts between the school district and the local teacher union, and (3) the U.S. Constitution (Bill of Rights and the Fourteenth Amendment).
2. *Are teachers required to salute the flag when the Pledge of Allegiance is recited?* The authors answered, "Probably not." Citing related cases, the authors believe that teachers may refuse to salute the flag.

3. *May teachers dress as they please?* Again the response was, "Probably not." Though there have been few court cases related to this question, the authors believe that teacher dress codes can be enforced.

4. *May teachers wear religious symbols when teaching?* The experts seem to agree that symbols (cross, Star of David) may be worn, but "proselytizing" messages cannot be displayed on clothing.

5. *May teachers teach whatever they believe is appropriate?* "Probably not." Subjects considered unsuitable by the school district or parents may not be taught in the classroom, and the teacher may be fired for doing so.

6. *Do students have complete artistic freedom of expression?* Teachers may set standards and requirements for assignments. However, if the student has fulfilled the requirements and the teacher just dislikes the message communicated by the student, the student should not be "marked down." The authors note that if the student's work is "vulgar, profane, or obscene, then a teacher has the authority to remove the work or restrict its presence on school grounds" (p. 103).

Immoral Behavior

A school district learns that a young female teacher is living with her boyfriend and gives her notice of dismissal. After receiving the notice, the teacher marries her boyfriend, but the school district goes ahead with the case, claiming that she is guilty of immoral behavior. The teacher challenges the charge in court. The court finds no evidence that her behavior affected her classroom behavior and upholds the rights of the teacher. Lifestyle issues are a problem only if it can be proved that they interfere with teaching effectiveness.

Other Benefits

Most school districts allow teachers 10 full days of sick leave. Some districts allow half days. Generally, unused sick days may be accumulated from year to year, and in some districts the unused time may be part of a retirement package.

Most districts provide health care benefits for teachers and their families. Other benefits include maternity leave, child care leave, personal business leave, and sabbatical leave. Districts differ in terms of benefits paid to teachers for sabbatical leave.

Professional Liability and Malpractice

Professional liability occurs as a result of **negligence**, that is, because the teacher did not exercise due care or did not foresee harm. Fischer, Schimmel, and Kelly (1987, p. 57) identify the four conditions necessary for a teacher to be held for damages when a student is injured:

1. The teacher was required to be on duty and protect the student from injury.
2. The teacher failed to exercise due care.
3. The student was injured as a result of the teacher's failure to exercise due care.
4. The student can prove injury as a consequence.

Professional liability increases if the students are young and the teacher is expected to be on duty. Negligence charges need to be proved based on lack of supervision and foresight of foreseeable danger. Close supervision is necessary during physical education and when students use special equipment that is dangerous. Whenever students can harm each other during activities and through use of equipment, teachers can be held liable for negligence.

If the injured student failed to exercise reasonable care of him- or herself, then the student may be guilty of **contributory negligence.** This can occur only if the student is old enough and has the mental maturity to exercise reasonable care.

Comparative negligence arises in situations in which both the teacher and student are at fault. This typically means that the teacher will be held accountable for some proportion of damages to the extent that the teacher contributed to the injury (McNergney & Herbert, 1995).

Teachers can protect themselves by purchasing insurance. Insurance programs are often sponsored through professional organizations; both the NEA and AFT have liability insurance programs.

Public pressure groups seek to charge school districts with educational malpractice when a student is injured intellectually or psychologically. Such cases are often based on a student's failure to learn. Cases involving student failure to learn would involve many teachers and the school district. There does not appear to be a way for parents to prove the liability of a given teacher or school district in such a case.

Copying Materials for the Classroom

Several years ago, an instructional specialist from a small school district proudly told me how she had copied a whole chapter out of one of my textbooks for the teachers in her school district. She anticipated that I would be flattered and pleased. Imagine her surprise when I countered with, "Don't you know that you violated copyright law?"

Copyright law protects materials from being copied by others either before publication or afterward. Fischer, Schimmel, and Kelly (1987) relate the case of the UCLA professor whose lecture notes were recorded by a student in class, sold to an entrepreneur, copied, and sold to other students. The professor sued the entrepreneur, claiming that his lecture notes were protected by common-law copyright. The court agreed. Common-law copyright protects an author's or artist's creative endeavor before publication; after publication, federal law protects the author or artist.

Teachers often want to use published pictures, articles, or poems in their classrooms. In general, teachers may make a single copy for use in the classroom. Copies for each student can be made under certain conditions. Conditions include tests of brevity, spontaneity, and cumulative effect (Fischer, Schimmel, & Kelly, 1987). Most school districts have guidelines available for teachers to verify what is fair use of an author's work.

In Loco Parentis

The idea of schools operating **in loco parentis** (in place of parents) means that schools have the power to act as if they were parents from the time students leave home to the time they return home. In recent years, this doctrine has been weakened, and courts often rule in favor of First Amendment rights for students versus school rights and authority. The doctrine has also been weakened in the instance of corporal punishment; in some states, parents have the right to forbid the use of corporal punishment. In general, decisions about punishment of students fall to the local school board.

In elementary schools, in loco parentis often means that teachers perform tasks that a parent would perform. For example, primary school teachers may have to tie shoes, button sweaters, or verify that students eat their lunches. The teacher listens and sympathizes.

Students' Rights

On November 20, 1989, the United Nations General Assembly adopted the Convention on the Rights of the Child. The convention deals with three kinds of rights: participation rights, provision rights, and protection rights. Edmonds (1992) defines these rights as follows:

- **Participation rights** mean that children have the right to participate in decisions that affect their lives and futures; they have freedom of expression; freedom of conscience, thought, and religion; freedom of association and assembly; and freedom from government interference in their privacy.
- **Rights of provision** deal with the economic, social, and cultural rights of the individual. For example, rights of provision include the rights to have adequate food, shelter, health care, and conditions that do not foster conflict or abuse.
- The **right of protection** means that the convention protects children from potential abuse or harm. For example, in Guatemala, a 13-year-old youth was kicked to death by the Guatemalan police in March 1990. Amnesty International pressured the director of the national police force and, ultimately, the police officers were sentenced to 15 years in prison. This was, of course, a hollow victory, but it emphasizes the nature of the covenant.

The challenge for teachers, according to Edmonds (1992, p. 205), is to do the following:

- Learn what human rights are.
- Help young people understand their rights.
- Examine the problem of universality and global multiculturalism.
- Create a classroom and school in which children's rights are achieved.

SUMMARY

Teachers' knowledge encompasses subject-field content, pedagogical strategies, and knowledge about students. To engage in appropriate lesson planning, teachers need to know what students know and do not know. Teachers make decisions about use of resources, setting standards, organization, and management of the school environment.

Teachers improve teaching and schools by participating in professional communities and teacher networks, sharing learning and expertise, and engaging in collaborative research. Teachers share in school governance by making decisions about school culture, school organization, and the school community.

Teachers are actively engaged in classroom research to change teaching practices and the classroom environment. Peer coaching helps teachers study teaching and develop shared professional language and provides a structure for the follow-up of professional learning. Teacher-leaders participate in a variety of school-based activities: faculty committees, grade-level and subject-field leadership, collaborative sharing, curriculum development, and mentoring.

A number of legal issues affect teachers' work. Tenure laws protect teachers from irresponsible and arbitrary dismissal. Most states grant tenure after a predetermined number of years and satisfactory evaluations during the probationary period. Because schools operate in loco parentis, teachers of young children often perform tasks that a parent would perform. Students are covered by the right of protection, which guards them from harm and potential abuse.

PORTFOLIO ACTIVITY

Teachers contribute to school effectiveness by collaborating with other professionals. Identify ways that you are involved in nonteaching professional activities. These activities may include curriculum development, sharing responsibility with colleagues for decisions about instructional strategies, peer coaching, improving the school culture, relationships with parents, service learning, and demonstrating new models of teaching. Describe your activity and your relationship with others. Identify the purpose (goal) of your work and your means for accomplishing it. Analyze your progress and provide some form of evidence.

DISCUSSION QUESTIONS AND APPLICATION EXERCISES

1. You are initiating the use of cooperative learning groups in your classroom. How can you model cooperative collegial development for your students to demonstrate adult cooperative learning?

2. You are teaching primary-age children, most of whom are learning to read successfully; however, some are lagging behind. The students enjoy listening to stories, drawing pictures, and writing their own stories about the pictures. Using your knowledge of growth and development, describe several lessons you would emphasize with the students and the activities in which they would participate.

3. Identify some instructional areas for improvement. What are some activities that will help you improve your performance?

4. You are teaching middle school students. The students have been discussing mad cow disease. Identify subject fields appropriate for the topic and explain how you will incorporate the students' interest and concern into your lesson plan. Describe your students, their needs, and the activities they will participate in.

5. Using the information about successful staff development programs discussed in this chapter, suggest some questions to evaluate a staff development workshop.

6. Write a content outline and suggested activities to teach your students about human rights and, in particular, children's rights.

7. Name one or more books on the current bestseller list.

8. List the cultural events you have attended in the last month. (Delete movies from your list!)

9. Identify a teaching/learning problem in your classroom. Describe how you could gather research data to provide insight concerning the problem.

10. Describe several successful means you use to grab students' interest and participation.

11. Design a self-evaluation checklist similar to Figure 14.2.

12. Design a rubric for you and your students to assess how well students work in cooperative groups.

READER RESEARCH

You have been asked to judge another teacher's portfolio. Discuss the research on teachers' portfolios and what you will be looking for when you examine the teacher's work.

Figure 14.2   Self-Evaluation Checklist

Develop your own self-evaluation checklist similar to this one.

	Yes	No
I plan my lessons before presenting them.	_____	_____
I choose instructional materials that are relevant and appropriate for my students.	_____	_____
My directions are clear and concise.	_____	_____
My follow-up materials reinforce my lessons. (They are not busy work.)	_____	_____
I edit my handouts to see that they are grammatical and legible.	_____	_____
I pace my lessons to keep students interested.	_____	_____
I encourage students to participate.	_____	_____
I try to talk to each student individually.	_____	_____
I listen when students want to talk to me.	_____	_____

The "scripted" lesson plan is closely related to painting by the numbers!

 TECHNOLOGY APPLICATIONS

Devise a rubric in table format to self-assess your skill in facilitating students' discussion. If students are mature enough (ages 8 to 12), ask them to evaluate your skills. Read about rubrics in this text and use other resources available on the Internet. Read about facilitating class discussions in this text (Chapter 4) and use other resources.

APPENDIX A

• •

Useful Web Sites

ART

The Museum of Modern Art
www.moma.org

The Art Newspaper
www.theartnewspaper.com

J. Paul Getty Museum
www.getty.edu/museum

Louvre Museum
www.louvre.fr

The Virtual Museum of Art
www.virtualology.com/virtualmuseumofart

World Wide Arts Resources
wwar.com

The Field Museum
www.fieldmuseum.org

The Metropolitan Museum of Art
www.metmuseum.org

CHILDREN

Ask Jeeves Kids
www.askkids.com

Children's Literature Web Guide
www.ucalgary.ca/~dkbrown/index.html

FunBrain.com
www.funbrain.com

J. K. Rowling Official Site
www.jkrowling.com

A Teacher's Guide to the Holocaust
fcit.usf.edu/Holocaust

Virtual Marching Tour of the American Revolution
www.ushistory.org/march/index.html

American Museum of Natural History
www.amnh.org

Natural History Museum
www.nhm.org

LANGUAGE

¡Conjuguemos!
www.conjuguemos.com

Free Translation
www.freetranslation.com

Spanish—Learn It Online
www.spaleon.com

The Virtual Diego Rivera Web Museum
www.diegorivera.com/index.php

Vocabulary Training Exercises
www.vokabel.com

Spaghetti Book Club
www.spaghettibookclub.org

The Write Site
www.writesite.org

MATH

Algebra Help
www.algebrahelp.com/index.jsp

Cool Math
www.coolmath.com

Education for Kids
  www.edu4kids.com
  www.edu4kids.com/money

Paul's Page of Pi
  www.gusmorino.com/pag3/pi/index.html

Visual Fractions
  www.visualfractions.com

PROFESSIONAL ORGANIZATIONS AND RESOURCES

American Alliance for Health, Physical Education, Recreation and Dance
  www.aahperd.org

Kathy Schrock's Guide for Educators
  school.discovery.com/schrockguide

Nancy's Teacher Resources
  www.geocities.com/Heartland/1133/2teach.html

Council for Exceptional Children
  www.cec.sped.org

Teachers Helping Teachers
  www.pacificnet.net/~mandel

International Reading Association
  www.reading.org

National Art Education Association
  www.naea-reston.org

National Association for Bilingual Education
  www.nabe.org

National Association for Gifted Children
  www.nagc.org

National Association of Music Educators
  www.name2.org.uk

National Council for Geographic Education
  www.ncge.org

National Council for History Education
  www.nche.net

National Council for the Social Studies
  www.socialstudies.org

National Council of Teachers of English
  www.ncte.org

National Council of Teachers of Mathematics
  www.nctm.org

National Science Teachers Association
  www.nsta.org

SCIENCE

Smithsonian Institution
  www.si.edu

The Nine Planets
  www.nineplanets.org

Rader's Chem4Kids.com
  www.chem4kids.com

Franklin Institute
  www.fi.edu

Lawrence Hall of Science
  www.lhs.berkeley.edu

National Air and Space Museum
  www.nasm.si.edu

National Association for Research in Science Teaching
  www.narst.org

APPENDIX B

● ●

Preparing for a Substitute Teacher

Do you remember what it was like to have a "sub"? Sometimes it was fun, and sometimes you felt guilty because you and your classmates were so unruly. You had a lot of time when you had nothing to do because the substitute was busy looking for subject schedules, trying to figure out the bell schedule, taking attendance, conducting a lunch count, hunting for materials, and yelling at George because he was always mischievous. As you already know, instructional time is extremely important, so you must do everything you can to help your substitute have a successful day. The following list includes some of the basics needed by a new teacher:

1. A seating chart with everyone's name listed
2. Daily subject field schedule and school schedule for your children (lunch, recess, special programs)
3. Classroom rules/standards (if needed)
4. Some very general lesson plans that will tell the substitute where the class is in the subject field.
5. Teaching strategy usually used in each subject field and liked by the students
6. Location of equipment that might be needed

The substitute teacher folder needs to be left in an easy-to-spot location. If you know you are going to be absent, place it in a very obvious place. Remember that the substitute teacher is probably a very creative professional who would like some free time to teach a special lesson of his or her own design for the students. The substitute provides the opportunity for students to be challenged and motivated by a different teacher.

You are also responsible for preparing students to receive substitute teachers in a courteous manner. Students should learn that every teacher is different and that the day will progress somewhat differently than usual. No matter how good your plans that you left for the substitute, routines will vary and communication will be different.

PLANNING TO BE A SUBSTITUTE TEACHER

Planning is the secret to success as a substitute teacher. If you are planning to sub in an elementary classroom, be sure that you have informed the school district what grade levels you are willing to teach. If you are planning to teach in a middle school, then you need to inform the district what subjects you specialize in.

Anticipate the needs of the students you may be teaching. Think about the time of the school year because that may affect your plans. Create lessons that will challenge the students rather than just keeping them busy. Plan lessons in fields where you consider yourself expert. Try to provide depth and enrichment instead of robotic exercises.

With luck, you will be notified of the assignment early enough to arrive at school on time. Your first task is to find the sub folder. Check the time schedule for your class and the subject(s) to be taught. Locate the seating chart and have it handy. Find any teaching materials you will need. Be prepared so that there will be little or no time for students to be disorderly while they wait for you.

When the students arrive, introduce yourself and, if you feel it is a good idea, tell them something about yourself and how it may influence your lessons. Let them know that you will try to adhere to their normal schedule, but sometimes adjustments need to be made and you are counting on them to be courteous, respectful, and understanding.

If possible, equip yourself with several lessons in case the classroom teacher did not leave you anything. Try to find out if there are any special events going on at school that day. And hopefully the classroom teacher has let you know if any of the students will need to leave the room for a special class or event that they need to attend.

If students ask to leave the room, speak to them quietly and verify their purpose. If a student claims to be ill, send a note to the nurse and ask for a written response. This will usually flush out anyone who is faking an illness.

At the end of the school day, leave a note for the regular teacher. Leave students' work papers for the day corrected, if possible. Tidy the classroom and be sure to lock the door when you depart. Finally, remember to check out in the school office before leaving school grounds.

Bibliography

Adams, D. M., & Hamm, M. E. (1992). Portfolio assessment and social studies: Collecting, selecting, and reflecting on what is significant. *Social Education, 56,* 103–105.

Allen, R. (2007). Green schools: Thinking outside the schoolroom box. *Education Update.* Association for Supervision and Curriculum Development, 49(11), November 2007.

Ameis, J. A. (2000). *Mathematics on the Internet: A resource for K-12 teachers.* Upper Saddle River, NJ: Prentice Hall/Merrill.

American Association for the Advancement of Science (AAAS). (1993). *Benchmarks for science literacy.* New York: Oxford University Press.

American Association for the Advancement of Science (AAAS). (1990). *Science for all Americans.* Washington, DC: Author.

AAUW Report *How schools shortchange girls.* (1992). Washington, DC: AAUW Educational Foundation, Wellesley College Center for Research on Women.

Ames, C. (1992). *Achievement goals and the classroom motivational climate.* U.S. Office of Education: Research Grant DEH023T80023, Office of Special Education and Rehabilitative Services.

Archer, J. (2005). Connecticut files court challenge to NCLB. *Education Week, 25*(1), August 31, 27, 37.

Arlin, M. (1979). Teacher transition can disrupt time flow in classrooms. *American Education Research Journal, 16,* 42–56.

Astor, R. A., Benbenishty, R., & J. N. Estrada. (2007). School violence: An overview. *Urban Education,* Spring/Summer, 16–21.

Ausubel, D. P. (1963). *The psychology of meaningful verbal learning.* New York: Grune & Stratton.

Ausubel, D. P., & Robinson, F. G. (1969). *School learning.* New York: Holt, Rinehart & Winston.

Baumann, J. F., Edwards, E. C., Boland, E. M., Olejnik, S., & Kame'enui, E. J. (2003). Vocabulary tricks: Effects of instruction in morphology and context on fifth-grade students' ability to derive and infer word meanings. *American Educational Research Journal, 40*(2), 447–494.

Beck, T. A. (2008). Behind the mask: Social studies concepts and English Language Learners. *Social Education, 72*(4), 181–184.

Berliner, D. C., & Nichols, S. L. (2007). High-stakes testing is putting the nation at risk. *Education Week, 25*(27) 47, 36.

Billig, S. H. (2000). Research on K-12 school-based service learning: The evidence builds. *Phi Delta Kappan, 81*(May), 658–664.

Biological Sciences Curriculum Study. (1989). *New designs for elementary school science and health: A cooperative project of Biological Sciences Curriculum Study (BSCS) and International Business Machine (IBM).* Dubuque, IA: Kendal/Hunt.

Bowers, C. K., & Croley, C. B. (2007). Teaching content through the arts: The art detectives. *Educational Leadership, 64*(8), 51-52.

Bradley, A. (1999). Science group finds middle school textbooks inadequate. *Education Week, 19*(6) 5.

Brooks, J. G. , Libresio, A. S., & Plonczak, I. (2007) Spaces of liberty: Battling the new soft bigotry of NCLB. *Phi Delta Kappan, 88*(10), 749–756.

Bruner, J. (1966). The act of discovery. In C. E. Meyers & R. G. McIntyre (Eds.). *Readings in contemporary psychology in education* (pp. 1a-15a). New York: Selected Academic Readings.

Burns, J. (1999). *Parental perceptions of involvement in children's education.* Unpublished dissertation, University of Southern California, Los Angeles.

Caine, R., & Caine, G. (1997). *Education on the edge of possibility.* Alexandria, VA: Association for Supervision and Curriculum Development.

California Department of Education. (1997). *History-social science framework for California public schools.* Sacramento, CA. Author.

Campbell, P. B., & Clewell, B. C. (1999). Science, math, and girls—Still a long way to go. *Education Week,* September 15.

Canter, L., & Canter, M. (1992). *Positive behavior management for today's classroom.* Santa Monica, CA: Lee Canter & Associates.

Carpenter, B. S. II. (1999). Art lessons: Learning to interpret. *Educational Leadership 57,* 46–48.

Cathcart, W. G., Pothier, Y. M., Vance, J. H., & Bezuk, N. S. (2006). *Learning mathematics in elementary and middle schools* (4th ed.). Upper Saddle River, NJ: Pearson, Merrill/Prentice Hall.

Cavanagh, S. (2008). Labs at elementary level help bring science alive. *Education Week 27*(39), June 4, 1, 10.

Chaltrain, S. (2006). To make schools safe, make all children visible. *Education Week, 26*(9), October 25.

Child Abuse Prevention and Treatment Act. Pub. L. No. 93–247, 3.

Clay, M. M. (1991). *Becoming literate: The construction of inner control.* Portsmouth, NH: Heinemann.

Cohen, E. G. (1998). Making cooperative learning equitable. *Educational Leadership, 56* (1), 18-21.

Cohen, J., & Pickeral, T. (2007). How measuring school climate can improve your school. *Education Week, 26*(33) 29–30.

Coleman, J. S., Campbell, E. Q., Hobson, C. J., McPartland, J., & J. M. Mood. (1966). *Equality of Educational Opportunity.* U.S. Office of Education OE 38001.

Copeland, R. W. (1982). *Mathematics and the elementary teacher* (4th ed.) New York: Macmillan.

Cox-Petersen, A. M. (2001). Empowering science teachers as researchers and inquirers. *Journal of Science Teacher Education, 12*(2) 107–122.

Cox-Petersen, A. M. & Olson, J. K. (2007). Using drawings as an alternative assessment measure for English language learners. *Science and Children, 44*(6), 46–49.

Crawford, J. (2007) A diminished vision of civil rights. *Education Week, 26*(39), June 6.

D'Acquisto, L. (2007). Teaching content through the arts: Kids as curators. *Educational Leadership. 64*(8), 50–51.

Dargan, A., & Zeitlin, S. (2000). City play. Educational Leadership *57,* 73–75.

Darling-Hammond, L. (2007). A Marshall plan for teaching. *Education Week, 26*(18), January 10.

David, J. L. (2008). Project-based learning. *Educational Leadership, 65*(5), 80–84.

Davis, M. R. (2006). Study: NCLB leads to cuts for some subjects. *Education Week, 25*(April 30), April 5.

Dean, J., & Gross, I. K. (1992). Teaching basic skills through art and music. *Phi Delta Kappan, 73,* 613–618.

Dewey, J. (1929, 1897). *My pedagogic creed.* Washington, DC: The Progressive Education Association.

Dewey, J. (1933). *How we think.* Boston: D.C. Heath.

DiRocco, M. D. (December 1998/January 1999). How an alternating day schedule empowers teachers. *Educational Leadership, 56*(4), 82–85.

Doyle, D. P. (1999). Defacto national standards. *Education Week, 18* (42), 36, 56.

Dunn, R., & Dunn, K. (1987). Dispelling outmoded beliefs about student learning. *Educational Leadership, 44*(March), 55–62.

Duran, R. P. (2008). Assessing English language learners' achievement. *Review of Research in Education.* AERA 32, 282–327.

Edmonds, B. C. (1992). The convention on the rights of the child. *Social Education, 56,* 205–207.

Eisner, E. W. (2004) Preparing for today and tomorrow. *Educational Leadership, 61*(4), 6–11.

Emans, R. L. (1987). Abuse in the name of protecting children. *Phi Delta Kappan, 69,* 740–743.

Erickson, H. L. (2004). In H. H. Jacobs (Ed.), *Getting results with curriculum mapping,* (p. vi). Alexandria, VA: Association for Supervision and Curriculum Development.

Featherstone, L. (2005). On the Wal-Mart money trail. *The Nation magazine,* November 21.

Feller, T. R., Jr., & Gibbs-Griffith, B. (2007). Teaching content through the arts. Bulldog Beat, *Educational Leadership, 64*(8)48–49.

Fendler, L. (2003). Teacher reflection in a hall of mirrors: Historical influences and political reverberations. *Educational Researcher, 32*(3), 16–25.

Fineberg, C. (2004). *Curriculum update.* Alexandria, VA: Association for Supervision and Curriculum Development.

Fischer, L., Schimmel, D., & Kelly, C. (1987). *Teachers and the law* (2nd ed.). New York: Longman.

Flavell, J. J. (1963). *The developmental psychology of Jean Piaget.* Princeton, NJ: Van Nostrand Reinhold.

Futrell, M. H., & Gomez, J. (2008). How tracking creates a poverty of learning. *Educational Leadership, 65*(8), 74–78.

Gallahue, D. L., Werner, P. H., & Luedke, G. (1975). *A conceptual approach to moving and learning.* New York: Wiley.

Gay, G. (2004). The importance of multicultural education. *Educational Leadership, 61*(4), 30–35.

Gardner, H. (1995). Reflections on multiple intelligences: Myths and messages. *Phi Delta Kappan, 77,* (November), 200–209.

Gardner, H. (1993). *Multiple intelligences: The theory in practice.* New York: Basic Books.

Gega, P. C., & Peters, J. (1998). *Science in elementary education* (8th ed.) Upper Saddle River, NJ: Prentice Hall/Merrill.

Gewertz, C. (2006). Reactions to school climate vary by students' races. *Education Week, 25*(30), April 5, 5, 16.

Graber, K. C., Locke, L. F., Lambdin, D., & Solomon, M. A. (2008). The landscape of elementary school physical education. *The Elementary School Journal, 108*(3), 151–160.

Gray, P. (2008) The value of age-mixed play. *Education Week, 27*(33), 32.

Guskey, T. R., Smith, J. K., Smith, L. F., Crooks, T., & Flockton, L. (2006). *Educational Leadership, 64*(2), 74–79.

Hall, J. T., Sweeny, N. H., & Esser, J. H. (1980). *Physical education in the elementary schools.* Santa Monica, CA: Goodyear.

Hall, P. S., & Hall, N. D. (2003). Building relationships with challenging children. *Educational Leadership, 61*(1), 60–63.

Hanna, P. (1965). Revising the social studies: What is needed? *Social Education, 27,* (April), 190–196.

Harry, B., & Klingner, J. (2007). Discarding the deficit model. *Educational Leadership, 64*(5), 16–21.

Haynes, C. C., Chattain, S., Ferguson, J. E., Jr., Hudson, D. L., & Thomas, O. (2003). *The first amendment in schools.* Alexandria, VA: Association for Supervision and Curriculum Development.

Hertzog, H., & Lemlech, J. K. (1993). Collegial teacher preparation: Impact on the supervising teacher's role. Refereed Presentation of Association of Teacher Educators National Meeting, Los Angeles.

Hill, D. (1999). Art school. *Education Week,18*(21), 28,33.

Hoff, D. J. (2000). A teaching style that adds up. *Education Week, 19*(24) 32–37.

Honish, P. K. (2000). Assisting school nurses report and prevent child abuse. Unpublished manuscript. Los Angeles, CA: University of Southern California.

Hoven, J., & Garelick, B. (2007). Singapore math: Simple or complex? *Educational Leadership, 65*(3), 28–31.

Howard, G. R. (2007). As diversity grows, so must we. *Educational Leadership, 64,* (March), 16–22.

Jacobs, H. H. (ed.). (2004). Development of a prologue in *Getting results with curriculum mapping.* Alexandria, VA: Association for Supervision and Curriculum Development.

Jacobson, L. (2004). Schools enlist specialists to teach science lessons. *Education Week, 23*(30), 1, 15.

Joyce, B., & Weil, M. (1996). *Models of teaching* (5th ed.) Needham Heights, MA: Allyn & Bacon.

Kahlenberg, R. D. (2006). The new integration. *Educational Leadership, 63*(8), 22–26.

Khourey-Bowers, C., & Croley, C. B. Teaching content through the arts: Art detectives. *Educational Leadership, 64*(8), 51–52.

Kilpatrick, W. H. (1951). *Philosophy of education.* New York: Macmillan.

Kohn, A. (2007). Against competitiveness. *Education Week, 27*(4), 26.

Kohn, A. (2003). Almost there, but not quite. *Educational Leadership, 60*(6), 26–30.

Konstantopoulos, S. (2008). Do small classes reduce the achievement gap between low and high achievers? Evidence from Project Star. *Elementary School Journal 108*(4) 275–201.

Kounin, J. S. (1970). *Discipline and group management in classrooms.* New York: Holt, Rinehart & Winston.

Kounin, J. S., & Doyle, P. H. (1975). Degree of continuity of a lesson's signal system and the task involvement of children. *Journal of Educational Psychology, 67,* 150-164.

Kounin, J. S., & Sherman, L. W. (1979). School environments as behavior settings. *Theory Into Practice, 18,* 145-151.

Krashen, S. D. (1996). *Every person a reader.* Culver City, CA: Language Education Associates.

Krashen, S. D. (1985). *Inquiries & insights.* Englewood Cliffs, NJ: Alemany Press.

Krashen, S. D., & Terrell, T. D. (1983). *The natural approach.* Englewood Cliffs, NJ: Alemay Press.

Kretchmar, R. S. (2008). The increasing utility of elementary school physical education: A mixed blessing and unique challenge. *Elementary School Journal, 108*(3), 161–170.

Kucer, S. B., & Rhodes, L. K. (1986). Counterpart strategies: Fine tuning language with language. *The Reading Teacher, 40,* (November), 186–193.

Lapkoff, S., & Li, R. M. (2007). Five trends for schools. *Educational Leadership, 64*(March), 8–15.

Lee, C. D. (2003). Why we need to rethink race and ethnicity in educational research. *Education Researcher, 32*(5), 3–5.

Lee, J. O. (2003). Implementing high standards in urban schools: Problems and solutions. *Phi Delta Kappan, 84*(6), 449–455.

Leinwand, S., & Ginsburg, A. L. (2007). Learning from Singapore math. *Educational Leadership 65*(3), 32–36.

Lemlech, J. K. (2004). *Teaching in elementary and secondary classrooms: Building a learning community.* Upper Saddle River, NJ: Prentice Hall/Merrill.

Lemlech, J. K. (1999). *Classroom management: Methods and techniques for elementary and secondary teachers* (3rd ed.). Prospect Heights, IL: Waveland Press.

Lemlech, J. K. (Ed.). (1995). *Becoming a professional leader.* New York: Scholastic.

Lemlech, J. K. (1977). *Handbook for successful urban teaching.* New York: Harper & Row.

Lemlech, J. K., & Hertzog, H. (1999). *Reciprocal teaching and learning: What master teachers and student teachers learn from each other.* Paper presented at the annual meeting of the American Education Research Association, Montreal, Canada.

Lemlech, J. K., & Hertzog, H. (1995). *Science methodologies: Constructivist distance learning.* Los Angeles: Los Angeles County Office of Education—Teams. Funded by the Connections 2000 Star Schools Project.

Lemlech, J. K., & Kaplan, S. N. (1991, November). *Collegial preparation, reflective practice, and social studies teaching.* Paper presented at the annual meeting of the College and University Faculty Association of the National Council for the Social Studies, Washington, DC.

Lemlech, J. K., & Kaplan, S. N. (1990). Learning to talk about teaching: Collegiality in clinical teacher education. *Action in Teacher Education, 12*(Fall), 13–19.

Lemlech, J. K., & Marks, M. B. (1976). *The American teacher, 1776–1976*. Bloomington, IN: Phi Delta Kappan Educational Foundation.

Lemlech, J. K., Hertzog, H., & Hackl, A. (1994). The Los Angeles professional practice school: A study of mutual impact. In Darling-Hammond (Ed.), *Professional development schools*. New York: Teachers College Press.

Lowenfeld, V., & Brittain, W. L. (1987). *Creative and mental growth* (8th ed.). New York: Macmillan.

Lyon, G. R. (1998). Why learning to read is not a natural process. *Educational Leadership, 55*, 14–18.

Manzo, K. K. (2004). Troubled school narrows courses. *Education Week, 23*(40), 1, 24.

Manzo, K. K. (1998). NAEP paints poor picture of arts savvy. *Education Week, 18*(12), 1, 9.

Marland, S. P. (1972). *Education of the gifted and talented*. Report to Congress. Washington, DC: U.S. Government Printing Office.

Martin, L. A. (2007). What middle school students have to say about strategy use in social studies. *Theory and Research in Social Studies, 35*(4), 631–645.

McBride, R., Jr. (1999). Culture shock using art and art controversy to teach history. *Social Education, 63*, 410–414.

McCormick, R. (1995). *Instructing students who have literacy problems*. Upper Saddle River, NJ: Prentice Hall/Merrill.

McKenzie, T. L., & Kahan, D. (2008). Physical activity, public health, and elementary schools. *The Elementary School Journal, 108*(3), 171–180.

McNergney, R. F., & Herbert, J. M. (1995). *Foundations of education: The challenge of professional practice*. Boston: Allyn & Bacon.

Meier, D. (2006). As though they owned the place: Small schools as membership communities. *Phi Delta Kappan, 87*(May), 657–662.

Meier, D., & Ravitch, D. (2006). Bridging differences. *Education Week, 25*(38), May 24.

Mercer, J. (1971). Sociocultural factors in labeling mental retardates. *Peabody Journal of Education, 48*(April), 19.

Miller, P.C., & Endo, H. (2004). Understanding and meeting needs of ESL students. *Phi Delta Kappan, 85*(10), 786–791.

Mulder-Slater, A. (2001). What should we teach? *Classroom Leadership, 5*(2).

Myers, M. (1983). The shared structure of oral and written language and the implications for teaching reading, and literature. In J. R. Squire (Ed.), *The dynamics of language learning* (pp. 121–146). Urbana, IL: ERIC Clearinghouse on Reading and Communication Skills.

National Arts Education Association. (1994). *National standards for arts education*. Reston, VA: Music Educators National Conference.

National Commission on Excellence in Education. (1983). *A nation at risk*. Washington, DC: U.S. Department of Education.

National Council for the Social Studies (NCSS). (1994). *Expectations of excellence: Curriculum standards for social studies*. Washington, DC: Author.

National Council of Teachers of Mathematics (NCTM). (2000). *Principles and standards for school mathematics*. Reston, VA: Author.

National Goals Report. (1994). Washington, DC: U.S. Government Printing Office.

Noddings, N. (2004). War, critical thinking, and self-understanding. *Phi Delta Kappan, 85*(7), 489–495.

O'Brien, T C., & Barnett, J. A. (2003). Fasten your seat belts. *Phi Delta Kappan, 85*(3) 201–206.

Olshansky, B. (1995). Picture this: An arts-based literacy program. *Educational Leadership, 53*, 44–47.

Otten, M., Stigler, J. W., Woodward, J. A., & Staley, L. (2004). Performing history: The effects of a dramatic art-based history program on student achievement and enjoyment. *Theory and Research in Social Education, 32*(20), 187–212.

Paez, M. (2003). Gimme that school where everything's scripted! One teacher's journey toward effective literacy instruction. *Phi Delta Kappan, 84*(10),757–763.

Patchen, T., & Cox-Petersen, A. M. (2008). Constructing culturally relevant science: A case study of two elementary science teachers. *Science Education, 92*, 994–1014.

Pateman, B. (2004). Healthier students, better learners. *Educational Leadership, 61*(4), 70–74.

Paxton, R. J. (1999). A deafening silence: History textbooks and the students who read them. *Review of Educational Research, 69*(Fall), 315–339.

Pearl, R., Leung, Man-C., Acker, R. V., Farmer, T. W., & Rodkin, P. C. (2007). Fourth-and fifth-grade teachers' awareness of their classrooms' social networks. *The Elementary School Journal, 108*(September), 25–40.

Perkins-Gough, D. (2007). Focus on adolescent English language learners. *Educational Leadership, 64*(6), 90–91.

Perkins-Gough, D. (2004). Creating a timely curriculum: A conversation with Heidi Hayes-Jacobs. *Educational Leadership, 61*(4), 12–17.

Peters, J. M., & Stout, D. L. (2006). *Science in elementary education: Methods, concepts, and inquiries* (10th ed). Upper Saddle River, NJ: Merrill/Prentice Hall.

Peterson, P. L. (1979). Direct instruction reconsidered. In P. L. Peterson & H. J. Walberg (Eds.), *Research on teaching*. Berkeley, CA: McCutchan.

Peterson, P. L., & Janicki, T. C. (1979). Individual characteristics and children's learning in large group and small group approaches. *Journal of Educational Psychology, 71*(October), 677–687.

Phillips, C. (1998). *Comprehensive arts program: Curriculum and instructional methods for the elementary and middle school* (6th ed.). Upper Saddle River, NJ: Pearson.

Piaget, J. (1969). How children form mathematical concepts. In N. J. Vigalante (Ed.), *Mathematics in elementary education* (pp. 135–141). New York: Macmillan.

Pinnell, G. S., & Fountas, I. C. (1998). *Word matters.* Portsmouth, NH: Heinemann.

Plitt, B. (2004). Teacher dilemmas in a time of standards and testing. *Phi Delta Kappan, 85*(10),745–748.

Popham, W. J. (2008a). Timed tests for tykes? *Educational Leadership, 65*(8) 86–87.

Popham, W. J. (2008b). What's valid? What's reliable? *Educational Leadership, 65*(5), 78–79. ASCD.

Popham, W. J. (2003). The seductive allure of data. *Educational Leadership, 60*(5), 48–51.

Posner, D. (2004). What's wrong with teaching to the test? *Phi Delta Kappan, 85*(10), 749–751.

Quezada, M. S., Wiley, T. G., & Ramirez, J. D. (2000). How the reform agenda shortchanges English learners. *Educational Leadership, 57,* 57–60.

Qin, Z., Johnson, D. W., Johnson, R. T. (1995). Cooperative versus competitive efforts and problem solving. Review of Educational Research, 65, 129–144.

Rasmussen, K. (December 1999/January 2000). The changing sports scene. *Educational Leadership, 57*(4), 26–29.

Raywid, M. A. (2006). Themes that serve schools well. *Phi Delta Kappan, 87*(May) 654–656.

Renzulli, J. S. (2002). Expanding the conception of giftedness to include co-cognitive traits and to promote social capital. *Phi Delta Kappan, 84*(1), 33–40.

Resnick, L. B. (1999). Making Americans smarter. *Education Week* (June 16), 104–105.

Rink, J. E., & Hall, T. J. (2008). Research on effective teaching in elementary school physical education. *Elementary School Journal, 108*(3) 207–218.

Robelen, E. W. (2007). KIPP Student-attrition patterns eyed. *Education Week, 26* (41), 15–17.

Rosenthal, R., & Jacobson, L. (1968). *Preparation in the classroom.* New York: Holt, Rinehart and Winston.

Rotter, J. (1966). Generalized experiences for informal versus external control of reinforcement. *Psychological Monograph, 80,* 609.

Rowe, M. B. (1974). Wait-time and rewards as instructional variables: Their influence on language, logic and fate control, Part one, wait-time. *Journal of Research in Science Teaching, 11,* 81–94.

Rowe, M. B. (1969). Science, silence, and sanctions. *Science and Children, 6,* 11–13.

Rubin, J., & Blume, H. (2007). Los Angeles charter schools learn it's hard to find a place to call home. *Los Angeles Times,* April 23.

Salomone, R. C. (2003), Single-sex programs for at-risk students. *Education Week, 23*(2), 34–35.

Shaftel, F., & Fair, J. (Eds.). (1967). *Effective thinking in the Social Studies* (pp. 22–50). Washington, DC: National Council for the Social Studies.

Smith, F. (2003). *Unspeakable acts, unnatural practices.* Portsmouth, NH: Heinemann.

Smith, P., Molnar, A., & Zahorik, J. (2003). Class-size reduction: A fresh look at the data. *Educational Leadership, 61*(1), 72–74.

Sprenger, M. (1999). *Learning and memory: The brain at work.* Alexandria, VA: Association for Supervision and Curriculum Development.

Sternberg, R. J. (2007). Recognizing neglected strengths. *Education Leadership, 64*(1), 30–35.

Stevenson, H. W. (1998). Guarding teachers' time. *Education Week, 18*(2), 52.

Strahan, D. (2003). Promoting a collaborative professional culture in three elementary schools that have beaten the odds. *Elementary School Journal, 104*(2), 127–146.

Streitmatter, J. (1994). *Toward gender equity in the classroom: Everyday teachers' beliefs and practices.* New York: State University of New York.

Taba, H. (1967a). Implementing thinking as an objective in social studies. In J. Fair & F. Shaftel (eds.). *Effective thinking in the social studies* (pp. 22–50). Washington, DC: National Council for the Social Studies.

Taba, H. (1967b). *Teacher's handbook for elementary social studies.* Palo Alto, CA: Addison-Wesley.

Taylor, B.M., Pearson, P. D., Peterson, D. S., & Rodriguez, M. C. (2003). Reading growth in high-poverty classrooms: The influence of teacher practices that encourage cognitive engagement in literacy learning. *Elementary School Journal, 101*(1), 3–28.

Thomas, K. T., & Thomas, J. R. (2008). Principles of motor development for elementary school physical education. *Elementary School Journal,108*(3), 181–185.

TIMMS Video Mathematics Research Group. (2003). Understanding and improving mathematics teaching: Highlights from the TIMSS 1999 video study. *Phi Delta Kappan, 84*(10), 768–775.

Tomlinson, C. A. (2004). Deciding to teach them all. *Educational Leadership, 61*(2), 6–11.

Tompkins, G. E. (2006). *Literacy for the 21ˢᵗ century: A balanced approach* (4th ed.). Columbus, OH: Merrill/ Prentice Hall.

Tompkins, G. E. (2002). *Language arts content and teaching strategies* (5th ed.). Columbus, OH: Merrill /Prentice Hall.

Tyack, D. (1967). Turning points in American educational history. Waltham, MA: Blaisdell.

U.S. Department of Education. (1998). *Trying to beat the clock.* Washington, DC: *Author.*

Viadero, D. (2008a). Exercise seen as priming pump for students' academic strides. *Education Week, 27*(23), 14–15.

Viadero, D. (2008b). Insights gained into arts and smarts. *Education Week, 27*(27), 1,10.

Viadero, D. (2004). Pupils of licensed teachers found to score higher in math. *Education Week. 23*(3), 10.

Viadero, D., & Honawar, V. (2008). Credential of NBPT has impact. *Education Week, 27*(42), 1, 16.

Victor, E., & Kellough, R. D. (2004). *Science K-9: An integrated approach* (10th ed). Upper Saddle River, NJ: Prentice Hall/Merrill.

Villegas, A. M., & Lucas, R. (2007). The culturally responsive teacher. *Educational Leadership, 28*, 33.

Vygotsky, L. (1962). *Thought and language.* Cambridge, MA: Massachusetts Institute of Technology Press.

Wahlstrom, K. L. (1999). The prickly politics of school starting time. *Phi Delta Kappan, 80*, 344–347.

Weiner, B. (Ed.). (1974). *Cognitive views of human motivation.* New York: Academic Press.

Weinfeld, F. D. et al. (1966). *Equality of educational opportunity.* Washington, DC: U.S. Department of Health, Education, and Welfare. Office of Education/ National Center for Education Statistics.

Wolfe, P. (2001). *Brain matters: Translating research into classroom practice.* Alexandria, VA: Association for Supervision and Curriculum Development.

Yando, R. M., & Kagan, J. (1968). The effect of teacher tempo on the child. *Child Development, 39*, 27.

Name Index

Subject Index